ENERGY

Volume II: Non-nuclear Energy Technologies

ENERGY

Volume I
by S. S. Penner and L. Icerman

Demands, Resources, Impact, Technology, and Policy, 1974 (2nd printing, corrected, 1976)

Volume II
by S. S. Penner and L. Icerman

Non-nuclear Energy Technologies, 1975 (2nd printing, revised and updated, 1977)

Volume III
by S. S. Penner et al.

Nuclear Energy and Energy Policies, 1976

ENERGY

Volume II
Non-nuclear Energy
Technologies

One of a Three-Volume Set of Lecture Notes

S. S. Penner and **L. Icerman**

Energy Center and
Department of Applied Mechanics and Engineering Sciences
University of California, San Diego
La Jolla, California

1975
Addison-Wesley Publishing Company, Inc.
Advanced Book Program
Reading, Massachusetts

London · Amsterdam · Don Mills, Ontario · Sydney · Tokyo

First printing, 1975

Second printing, revised and updated, 1977
(ISBN 0-201-05568-6, 0-201-05569-4 [pbk.])

Library of Congress Cataloging in Publication Data

Penner, S   S
    Non-nuclear energy technologies.

    (Energy ; v. 2)
    Includes index.
    1. Power (Mechanics) 2. Power resources.
I. Icerman, L., joint author. II. Title.
HD9502.A2P46 vol. 2 [TJ153] 333.7s [621]   75-6934
ISBN 0-201-05562-7
ISBN 0-201-05563-5 pbk.

ABCDEFGHIJ-HA-7987

Reproduced by Addison-Wesley Publishing Company, Inc., Advanced Book Program, Reading, Massachusetts, from camera-ready copy prepared by the authors.

Manufactured in the United States of America

CONTENTS

Page

PREFACE   xxi

GLOSSARY OF SYMBOLS   xxiii

UNITS, CONVERSION FACTORS, ENERGY   xxv
   CONSUMPTION

REVIEW PROBLEMS ON ENERGY RESOURCES   xxvii

CHAPTER 9 - OIL RECOVERY FROM TAR SANDS
            AND OIL SHALE   1

  9.1   The Alberta Tar Sands   1

  9.2   The GCOS Recovery and Upgrading Procedure
       of Oil from Tar Sands   5

  9.3   The "Syncrude" Recovery and Upgrading
       Procedure of Oil from Tar Sands   9

  9.4   Economic Analysis of Oil Recovery from
       Tar Sands   9

  9.5   Oil Recovery from Oil Shale.   10

  9.6   Summary Remarks on Recovery Processes of
       Oil from Oil Shale   15

  9.7   Mining Procedures for the Recovery of Shale
       Oil   18

  9.8   Oil and Gas Recovery from Oil Shale   21

  9.9   Upgrading of Shale Oil in the U.S. Bureau of
       Mines Gas-Combustion Process   25

  9.10 Environmental Effects of Shale-Oil
       Production   27

  9.11 Economic Considerations of Shale-Oil
       Production Using Mining and Aboveground
       Retorting   30

  9.12 In Situ Recovery of Shale Oil from Oil Shale. .   35

v

Page

A. Current Studies on Non-Nuclear Fracturing
and Shale-Oil Recovery 39

B. Nuclear Fracturing and Shale-Oil
Recovery 42

C. Oil Recovery from the Leach Zone. . . . 48

D. Other Procedures for In Situ Recovery
of Shale Oil 50

9.13 Mixed-Mining-and-In-Situ Recovery
Procedures 50

9.14 Net Energy in Shale-Oil Production 53

A. Definitions of Net Energy (Ratios) 55

B. Methodologies in Evaluating $R_{1,i,j}$ and
$R_{2,i,j}$ 60

C. Some Results Obtained in the Evaluation
of Net Energy Ratios for Shale-Oil
Recovery 62

9-A Appendix - The Discounted Cash Flow (DCF)
Method for Estimating Rate of Return (ROR)
on an Investment. 65

9-B Appendix - Dependence of Costs on Time and
Production Rate 68

CHAPTER 10 - COAL: AVAILABILITY, PRODUCTION
AND TRANSPORTATION; COAL
GASIFICATION; COAL LIQUEFACTION;
IN SITU RECOVERY OF COAL 70

10.1 Coal Availability. 70

10.2 Coal Resources, Production, Costs, and
Transportation 73

A. Coal Resources 74

B. Coal Production 75

C. The Costs of Coal and Required Investments for Increased Production 78

Page

D. Transportation of Coal 81

E. Coal-Slurry Pipelines. 82

F. Development of Improved Mining
Procedures 84

10.3 Coal Gasification 86

A. Overall Description of Gasification
Processes. 86

B. Temperature- and Pressure-Control of
Reaction Vessels in Coal Gasification. . . 90

C. The Hygas-Electrothermal Process . . . 95

D. The Lurgi Reactor 102

E. Other Coal-Gasification Reactors 104

F. Long-Range Production Schedules 107

10.4 Syncrude from Coal 110

10.5 In Situ Coal Gasification 116

A. Exploratory Studies on Underground
Coal Gasification. 116

B. Recent Field Experience 119

C. A Conceptual Design for an In Situ Coal
Gasification Process 123

CHAPTER 11 - THE HYDROGEN ECONOMY; ALTER-
NATIVE FUELS 126

11.1 Hydrogen Requirements. 127

11.2 Hydrogen Production from Water 138

A. Water Electrolysis 140

B. Thermochemical Production of Hydrogen . 152

C. Direct Water Photolysis Using an
Electrochemical Cell 160

D. Biological Systems for the Direct
Photolysis of Water. 166

  Page

11.3 Hydrogen-Transmission and Distribution
       Networks.   167

       A. Hydrogen Transmission by Pipeline . . .   168

       B. Pipeline Technology for Hydrogen. . . .   173

       C. The Distribution of Hydrogen   176

       D. Transmission and Distribution of Liquid
            Hydrogen.   177

11.4 Storage of Hydrogen.   179

11.5 Applications of Hydrogen for Energy
       Production; Alternative Fuels   182

       A. Thermochemical Data   186

       B. Combustion Parameters   189

       C. Practical Applications   199

11.6 Safety Problems Connected with Hydrogen
       Use   202

       A. Hazard and Safety Aspects of Gaseous
            Hydrogen Use.   202

       B. Hazards and Safety in the Use of Liquid
            Hydrogen.   206

11.7 Climatic Impact-Assessment of a
       Hydrogen Economy   210

11.8 Alternative Energy Sources, Especially
       Methanol.   211

CHAPTER 12 - ENERGY-STORAGE SYSTEMS   217

12.1 Thermal-Energy Storage.   219

12.2 Mechanical-Energy Storage   223

       A. The Physical Properties of Flywheels . .   224

       B. Flywheel-System Technology   231

       C. Flywheel Use in Transportation Systems.   237

       D. Flywheel Use in Peak-Power Systems . .   241

Page

12.3 Electrical-Energy Storage 242

    A. Capacitive Storage. 243

    B. Inductive Storage 244

    C. Electric and Storage Batteries 246

12.4 Large-Scale Energy Storage 253

    A. Pumped-Hydraulic Storage 253

    B. Compressed-Air Storage. 259

12.5 Storage of Liquid Petroleum Products 262

    A. Aboveground Storage. 262

    B. Underground Storage. 264

12.6 Storage of Natural Gas. 271

    A. Pressurized Storage. 272

    B. Liquefied Natural-Gas Storage 275

12.7 Storage of Synthetic Fuels 278

CHAPTER 13 - TECHNIQUES FOR DIRECT ENERGY
                CONVERSION 283

13.1 Introduction 283

13.2 Magnetohydrodynamic Power Conversion
     (MHD) 285

    A. Production of Ionized Gases 287

    B. Design Problems 290

    C. MHD System Configurations 292

13.3 Fuel Cells 295

    A. An Example of Ideal Fuel-Cell Operation:
       The Hydrogen-Oxygen Fuel Cell. 297

    B. Ideal Fuel-Cell Performance 299

    C. Actual Fuel-Cell Performance 302

    D. Current Fuel-Cell Developments 302

Page

13.4 Photovoltaic Power Conversion. 310

   A. Construction of an n-Type Semi-
      conductor 311

   B. Construction of a p-Type Semi-
      conductor 311

   C. Construction of a p-n Junction 312

   D. Potentials in a p-n Junction 314

   E. Absorption of Photons and Hole-Electron-
      Pair Creation. 315

   F. A Commercial Solar Cell 317

   G. Physical Factors Determining Solar-
      Cell Performance and Materials of
      Construction 319

   H. Solar-Cell Output Power per Unit Area . 320

   I. Solar-Cell Power Output per Unit
      Weight. 321

   J. Solar-Cell Reliability 323

   K. Current Photovoltaic-Cell Developments. 327

13.5 Thermoelectric Power Generation 328

   A. The Seebeck Effect 328

   B. The Peltier Effect. 330

   C. The Thomson Effect. 330

   D. Practical Applications. 332

13.6 Thermionic Power Conversion 333

CHAPTER 14 - SOLAR-ENERGY UTILIZATION . . . 336

14.1 Introduction 336

   A. Past Applications of Solar Energy. . . . 336

   B. Solar-Energy Costs and Development
      Projections. 337

Page

C. Impact of Solar-Energy Utilization. . . . 345

D. Summary Remarks on Solar-Energy
Economics 347

E. Environmental-Impact Assessment of
Solar-Energy Utilization 349

F. "Novel" Ideas for Solar-Energy
Applications. 352

14.2 Availability of Solar Energy in the U.S. and
Land-Use Requirements 353

A. Solar Radiation Incident on the Earth for a
Completely Transparent Atmosphere. . . 357

B. Solar Radiation Incident on the Surface of
the Earth for the Real Atmosphere. . . . 363

14.3 Qualitative Description of Proposed Systems
for Solar-Energy Utilization Involving Radiant
Heating 365

A. A Solar Space- and Water-Heating System
for a House. 366

B. Solar Heating and Cooling of Homes and
Commercial Buildings 368

C. Central Stations for Electricity Generation. 368

D. Fuel Production Using Solar Energy. . . 374

14.4 Solar-Energy Collectors for Solar-Thermal
Power Conversion. 374

A. Types of Solar Collectors 374

B. Desirable Physical Properties of Solar
Collectors 378

C. Solar Collectors for Achieving Temperatures up to the Boiling Point of Water . . 383

14.5 Quantitative Description of Selected Solar-
Energy Conversion Systems 383

  Page

        A. An Optimistic View of Photosynthetic
            Production of Fuels; Animal-Waste
            Utilization   387

        B. Large-Scale, Land-Based
            Solar-Thermal Farms   390

        C. Solar-Power Cooling Units for Applica-
            tion in Tropical Areas.   390

        D. Solar Distillation and Drying.   392

        E. Some General Considerations Relating
            to Solar-Energy Utilization   393

        F. Metal Hydrides for Energy Storage in
            Solar-Energy Utilization.   396

14.6 Solar Ponds   397

14.7 Satellites for Solar-Power Collection   399

14.8 The Solar-Sea Power Plant (SSPP)   405

        A. Historical Background.   405

        B. A Proposed Installation to Generate
            100,000 kw$_e$ 407

        C. The Required Warm Water Flow Rate
            per Mw$_e$ Delivered   410

        D. A Rankine-Cycle Engine for Converting
            Thermal to Electrical Energy in the
            SSPP   413

        E. The Rankine Cycle Applied to the Use of
            Ammonia in a Solar-Sea Generator . . .   418

        F. The Rankine Cycle Used by the
            Andersons   422

        G. Economic Considerations for the
            Andersons' SSPP   423

        H. Current Developments   427

Page

   I. Cost Estimates Available for OTEC
      in 1976 428

   J. Environmental-Impact Assessments
      of OTEC Development 431

14.9 Low-Temperature Thermal Cycles Serving
      the Dual Purpose of Prototype Experiment for
      the SSPP and Bottoming Cycles for Coastally-
      Based Generation Stations 434

   A. Sitings of Prototype Experiments in the
      San Diego Region 435

   B. Bottoming Cycles for Coastally-Based
      Power Stations 438

14.10 Integration of Solar Electric Technologies
      into Utility Networks 439

CHAPTER 15 - ENERGY FROM WINDMILLS 441

15.1 General Characteristics of the Wind 442

15.2 Methods Used in the Past for Extracting
      Power from the Wind. 444

15.3 Theoretical and Actual Efficiencies of
      Windmills. 453

15.4 The Smith-Putnam Wind-Turbine Project. . . 462

15.5 Large-Scale Utilization of Wind Power. . . . 465

15.6 Economical Design of Wind-Power Systems. . 468

15.7 Recent Developments. 472

CHAPTER 16 - TIDAL- AND WAVE-ENERGY
             UTILIZATION. 475

16.1 Origins of Tides 476

   A. Description of Tide-Generating Forces. . 477

   B. Amplitudes of Tidal Oscillations 483

Page

16.2 Tidal-Power Resources and Site Selection . . 484

16.3 Tidal-Power Utilization Techniques 486

     A. One-Way, Single-Basin Generation. . . . 488

     B. Two-Way, Single-Basin Generation . . . 488

     C. Multiple-Basin Schemes 490

     D. Pumped-Storage Schemes. 493

16.4 Tidal-Power Plant Design 496

     A. Hydraulic Turbines and Generators . . . 496

     B. Water-Flow Control Equipment 498

     C. Corrosion in Tidal-Power Plants 500

16.5 The Rance Tidal-Power Development 501

16.6 The Cost of Tidal Power 503

16.7 Environmental Effects of Tidal-Power
     Stations. 505

16.8 Utilization of Wave Energy 507

CHAPTER 17 - HYDROELECTRIC-POWER
              GENERATION. 514

17.1 Physical Principles Involved in Water-Power
     Use 516

17.2 Hydroelectric Power-Plant Technology. . . . 520

     A. Water-Flow Devices 520

     B. Hydraulic Turbines. 522

17.3 The Use of Hydroelectric Power in the
     United States 534

     A. Hydroelectric Resources of the United
         States. 534

     B. Historical Development of Hydroelectric
         Power Applications in the United States. . 536

Page

    C.   Examples of Hydroelectric Power Plants
in the United States. 538

17.4 Economic Considerations of Hydroelectric-
Power Applications 542

17.5 Environmental Effects of Hydroelectric-
Power Developments. 544

CHAPTER 18 - HYDROTHERMAL-ENERGY SOURCES
              AND UTILIZATION 549

18.1 Introduction. 549

18.2 Characteristics of Hydrothermal-Energy
Resources 552

    A.   Vapor-Dominated Systems 556

    B.   Water-Dominated Systems 557

    C.   Geopressured Deposits. 558

18.3 Hydrothermal-Resource Exploration and
Assessment. 561

    A.   Geological Exploration Techniques. . . 564

    B.   Geophysical Techniques 565

    C.   Geochemical Techniques 567

    D.   Thermal Techniques 569

    E.   Exploratory Drilling 571

    F.   Known Geothermal-Resource Areas . . . 574

18.4 Utilization of Hydrothermal Energy for Electrical-Power Generation 575

    A.   Utilization of Vapor-Dominated
Reservoirs 575

    B.   Utilization of Water-Dominated
Reservoirs 578

    C.   Power from Geopressured Zones 584

Page

D.   Stimulation of Hydrothermal Reservoirs . 586

E.   Problems in the Utilization of Hydro-
     thermal Resources. 589

18.5 Hydrothermal Energy-Recovery Technology. . 591

A.   Steam Production and Handling at
     The Geysers 591

B.   Thermodynamic Analysis of Hydrother-
     mal Reservoirs in the Imperial Valley
     of California 598

18.6 Scale Formation and Corrosion in Energy
      Recovery from Hydrothermal Deposits. . . 601

18.7 Economic Aspects of Hydrothermal Energy-
      Resource Development. 603

18.8 An Environmental-Impact Assessment of
      Hydrothermal Energy-Resource
      Development. 609

A.   Vapor-Dominated Systems. 610

B.   Hot-Water Systems. 613

C.   Nuclear-Stimulated Systems 615

CHAPTER 19 - GEOTHERMAL ENERGY FROM DRY
             WELLS. 618

19.1 Assessment of Dry Geothermal Resources . . 618

19.2 Characteristics of Geothermal Energy
      Resources. 619

19.3 Utilization of Dry Geothermal Wells 620

19.4 Cost Estimates 625

19.5 Preliminary Results 626

A.   The Los Alamos Program. 627

B.   The Marysville Geothermal Project . . . 630

Page

CHAPTER 20 - ELECTRICAL POWER PRODUCTION,
                TRANSMISSION, AND DISTRIBUTION . 632

20.1 World Elecricity Production During Recent
      Years. 635

20.2 Electricity Demand and Growth in the U.S. . . 637

20.3 Service Territories of Representative Elec-
      tricity Distribution Systems in the U.S. . . . 642

20.4 Electric Utility Rate Design and Peak Load
      Fluctuations. 652

20.5 Some Long-Term Objectives in the Distribu-
      tion of Electricity to Consumers 657

20.6 Some Important Characteristics of Power
      Lines for Transmitting Electricity; Under-
      ground Transmission Lines 660

      A. HPOF Cables for Underground Trans-
          mission Lines. 660

      B. CGI Cables 669

      C. Cryoresistive Cables 669

      D. Superconducting Cables 670

20.7 Overhead Transmission Lines 670

20.8 Superconducting AC Power Lines 673

20.9 Conventional and Superconducting DC Power
      Lines 684

20.10 Electric-Equipment Development Using
      Superconductivity 687

PROBLEMS 689

Problems for Chapter 9 690

Problems for Chapter 10 692

Problems for Chapter 11 693

Page

Problems for Chapter 12 694

Problems for Chapter 13 696

Problems for Chapter 14 697

Problems for Chapter 15 699

Problems for Chapter 16 701

Problems for Chapter 17 702

Problems for Chapter 18 704

Problems for Chapter 19 706

Problems for Chapter 20 707

INDEX 711

Contents of Volume I, 1974

Chapter 1 - Energy Demands

Chapter 2 - Energy Resources

Chapter 3 - Energy Consumption by Sector

Chapter 4 - The Economic Value of Energy Utilization;
Prices for Energy Resources; Investment
Costs; Electricity Costs

Chapter 5 - Energy-Utilization Efficiencies, Waste Recovery,
and Related Topics

Chapter 6 - Geophysical Implications of Energy Consumption

Chapter 7 - The Past Societal Costs of Coal Use in Electricity
Generation

Chapter 8 - A Commentary on U.S. Energy Policy and
Resource Development

Problems

Index

Contents of Volume III, 1976

Chapter 21 - Nuclear Fission Energy

Chapter 22 - Nuclear Fission Energy: Breeder Reactors

Chapter 23 - Controlled Thermonuclear Fusion

Chapter 24 - Environmental Aspects of Nuclear Power
Applications

Chapter 25 - Nuclear Strategies

Chapter 26 - Energy Policies

Problems

Index

PREFACE

Volume II of this series of lecture notes is generally restricted to those aspects of non-nuclear energy technologies dealing with <u>new</u> developments, which promise to bring important modifications to our energy-supply base. Well-developed technologies are not reviewed. Thus, deep understanding of the engineering aspects of coal mining or petroleum recovery by conventional means is not assumed and will not be gained from study of the material contained in this volume. However, it is the authors' expectation that the patient reader will achieve considerable understanding and insight into the nature of developing technologies and will learn to appreciate the enormity of the scientific, technical, economic, and social problems that form a part of any scenario leading to greater U.S. independence from foreign energy supplies.

The authors' personal involvement in some of the newly developing technologies (e.g., <u>in situ</u> recovery of fossil fuels, the solar-sea power plant, the hydrogen economy, geothermal energy generation) is hopefully reflected by comprehensive current coverage of these topics.

We are indebted to the UCSD graduate and undergraduate students who have helped us with the development of these lecture notes by participating in early courses dealing with non-nuclear energy technologies.

We are happy to acknowledge the contributions of Laurie Smith and Kay Hutcheson who have typed the book.

Fred Boatright and Elisa LoBue have greatly contributed to the preparation of the figures.

In order to assist the reader in the use of this volume, we have reproduced Table 1.2-2 of Volume I on units, conversion factors, and energy consumption. We have also included a set of review problems dealing with energy resources.

The reader should note that reference numbers refer to individual <u>Sections</u>.

S. S. Penner
L. Icerman

GLOSSARY OF SYMBOLS

A = ampere

a.c. = alternating current

atm = atmosphere

bbl = barrel

Btu = British thermal unit

$^{\circ}$C = degrees Centigrade

cal = calorie

cm = centimeter

d = day

d.c. = direct current

ev = electron volt

(e) or subscript e = equivalent energy or electrical energy,
depending on the context

$^{\circ}$F = degrees Fahrenheit

ft = foot

g = gram

gal = gallon

h = hour

hp = horsepower

Hz = Hertz

in. = inch

$^{\circ}$K = degrees Kelvin

kcal = kilocalorie = 10^3 calories

kg = kilogram = 10^3 grams

km = kilometer = 10^3 meters

kt = kiloton = 10^3 tons

kV = kilovolt = 10^3 volts

kVA = kilovolt-ampere = 10^3 volt-amperes

kw = kilowatt = 10^3 watts

lb = pound

lbm = pound mass

m = meter

MCM = 10^3 circular mils

mi = mile

min = minute

mph = mile(s) per hour

MVA = megavolt-ampere = 10^6 volt-amperes

Mw = megawatt = 10^6 watts

n = newton

ppm = parts per million

psi = pounds per square inch

psia = pounds per square inch (absolute)

psig = pounds per square inch (gauge)

Q = 10^{18} Btu

rad = radian

rpm = revolutions per minute

sd = standard day or stream day

sec = second

SCF = standard cubic foot

t = ton = 2,000 pounds

(th) or subscript t = thermal energy

V = volt

w = watt

y = year

1 joule = 10^7 erg (= 10^7 dyne-cm) = 6.24×10^{12} Mev = 6.24×10^9 Bev = 1.0 newton-m = 0.736 ft-lb = 0.24 cal = 0.949×10^{-3} Btu = 2.78×10^{-4} wh = 3.73×10^{-7} hph = 2.78×10^{-7} kwh = 2.38×10^{-10} ton of TNT equivalent = 1.22×10^{-13} of the fusion energy from the deuterium in 1 m^3 of seawater = 1.11×10^{-14} g of matter equivalent = 1.22×10^{-14} of the fission energy of 1 kg of U-235 equivalent = 6.7×10^{-23} of the average daily input of solar energy at the outside of the atmosphere of the earth = 5.8×10^{-32} of the daily energy output from the sun.

1 metric ton of coal $\simeq 27.8 \times 10^6$ Btu (1 metric ton = 1 mt $\simeq$ 2,200 lb)

1 bbl of petroleum $\simeq$ (5.60 to) 5.82 (or more) $\times 10^6$ Btu (1 bbl = 42 gallons)

1 SCF of natural gas $\simeq 10^3$ Btu

1 cord of wood $\simeq 1.95 \times 10^7$ Btu (1 cord = 128 ft^3)

9,500 Btu (th)/kwh_e at 36% conversion efficiency.

1 Q = 10^{18} Btu = 1.05×10^{21} joule = 2.93×10^{14} kwh(th) = = 1.22×10^{10} Mwd(th) = 3.35×10^7 Mwy(th) = 1.7×10^{11} bbl of petroleum equivalent; 1 y = 8.76×10^3 h

Coal conversion to oil: $\geqslant$ 2 bbl/mt ($\geqslant$ 42% energy-conversion efficiency)

Note: See footnotes to this table on the following page.

UNITS, CONVERSION FACTORS, ENERGY CONSUMPTION[*]

Energy consumption estimates:[**]
USA (1970) -- 0.07 Q/y [2×10^8 people, 11.7 kw(th)/p].
(2000) -- 0.16 Q/y [3×10^8 people, 17.8 kw(th)/p].
(2020) -- 0.3   Q/y [4×10^8 people, 25   kw(th)/p].
WORLD (1970) -- 0.24 Q/y [4×10^9 people, 2   kw(th)/p].
(2000) -- 2.1   Q/y [7×10^9 people, 10   kw(th)/p].
(2050) -- 6   Q/y [10×10^9 people, 20   kw(th)/p].

[*] Table abbreviations used: bbl = barrel; Btu = British thermal unit; cal = calorie; d = day; g = gram; h = hour; hp = horsepower; kg = kilogram; kw = kilowatt = 10^3 watt; m = meter; Mw = megawatt = 10^6 watt = 10^3 kw; p = person; SCF = standard cubic foot, corresponding to the gas volume at a pressure of 14.73 psi (= 1 atmosphere) and a temperature of $60°$F; w = watt; y = year; the symbol (e) or the subscript e identify electrical energy; the symbol (th) or the subscript t identify thermal energy. The subscript e is also used occasionally in place of the phrase "equivalent energy"; the particular meaning attached to e should generally be clear from the context.

[**] Representative estimates from various sources; forecasts to the year 2000 and beyond are uncertain by factors of 2 or more.

REVIEW PROBLEMS ON ENERGY RESOURCES

Verify each of the following statements by using the appropriate conversion factors.

1. The 1970 U.S. electrical power-generating capacity was 3.40×10^5 Mw$_e$.

   (a) Show that the electrical energy generated during 1970, at a 90% average operating capacity, was 3.06×10^5 Mwy$_e$.

   (b) Assuming a 33.33% average conversion efficiency, show that the primary (total) energy required for electric-power generation was 9.18×10^5 Mwy$_t$ during 1970. Show that this total energy corresponds to 4.70×10^9 (bbl)$_e$ for 1970 or 1.28×10^7 (bbl/d)$_e$ of petroleum.

2. The estimated year 2000 U.S. electrical-power generating capacity is 2×10^6 Mw$_e$, corresponding to an electrical energy of 1.8×10^6 Mwy$_e$ at an average use rate of 90%, and a primary energy requirement of 5.4×10^6 Mwy$_t$ for the year 2000 or 7.59×10^7 (bbl/d)$_e$.

   (a) The total average continuous input of solar power to the surface of the earth is 18% of the continuous solar power at the outer atmospheric boundary of 5.2×10^{21} Btu/y. Show that the total average yearly input of solar power at the surface of the earth is 9.36×10^{20} Btu/y or 1.61×10^{14} (bbl)$_e$/y. Show that this input solar power corresponds to an average power of 4.41×10^{11} (bbl/d)$_e$.

Show that a utilization efficiency of 0.0172% of the solar-power input to the surface of the earth would be sufficient to supply the primary power requirements for the U.S. electrical industry in the year 2000.

(b) White has estimated that 8×10^{21} joules $= 2.5 \times 10^8$ Mwy of hydrothermal energy are available world-wide to a depth of 3 km; 4×10^{22} joules $= 1.25 \times 10^9$ Mwy are available to a depth of 10 km. The U.S. is believed to have between 5 and 10% of the world's hydrothermal resources.

Assuming that 1% of the world's hydrothermal resources to a depth of 10 km can be exploited at a 25% overall conversion efficiency, show that
$$1.25 \times 10^9 \times 10^{-2} \times 0.25 = 3.13 \times 10^6 \text{ Mwy}_e$$
are available world-wide from this energy reserve.

If we exhaust this hydrothermal reserve at a uniform rate in 50 years, show that the corresponding world-wide electrical power capacity from hydrothermal energy becomes 6.25×10^4 Mw$_e$. Show that this capacity corresponds to 3.13% of the estimated U.S. electrical-power capacity for the year 2000 or to 2.64×10^6 (bbl/d)$_e$ of primary energy.

(c) The average outward rate of heat flow of geothermal

energy from the interior of the earth is 1.25×10^{-6} cal/sec-cm^2 = 39.4 cal/cm^2-y. If the surface area of the earth is 5.1×10^{18} cm^2, show that this average geothermal power corresponds to 2.01×10^{20} cal/y = 7.94×10^{17} Btu/y = 2.66×10^{7} Mw. If 1% of this geothermal power could be converted to electrical power with a 25% conversion efficiency, show that

$$2.66 \times 10^{7} \times 10^{-2} \times 0.25 = 6.65 \times 10^{4} \text{ Mw}_e$$

would be generated. Show that this corresponds to 3.32% of the estimated U.S. year 2000 electrical power-capacity requirement.

(d) The ultimate world capacity for hydroelectric power generation has been estimated to be 2.857×10^{6} Mw$_e$. If the U.S. fraction of this total is 0.0563, show that the ultimate U.S. hydroelectric capacity is 0.161×10^{6} Mw$_e$ or 8.05% of the estimated year 2000 U.S. capacity.

(e) The world-wide tidal power dissipated in shallow basins has been estimated to be 1×10^{6} Mw. Assuming a U.S. share of 10% of the total and a 25% conversion efficiency to electrical power, show that the ultimate tidal capacity is

$$1 \times 10^{6} \times 10^{-1} \times 0.25 = 2.5 \times 10^{4} \text{ Mw}_e$$

for the U.S. or 1.25% of the total estimated requirement for the year 2000.

(f) The total power associated with winds in the Northern

hemisphere has been estimated to be 10^{11} Mw during the winter season and 0.4×10^{11} Mw during the summer season. Assume an average value of 0.7×10^{11} Mw for the year.

Assuming that 0.1% of the total is available to the U.S. and could be converted to electricity with a conversion efficiency of 25%, show that the corresponding U.S. electrical capacity is

$$0.7 \times 10^{11} \times 10^{-3} \times 0.25 = 1.75 \times 10^{7} \text{ Mw}_e.$$

Show that this wind-generated electrical power capacity corresponds to 875% of the estimated year 2000 U.S. requirement.

ENERGY

Volume II: Non-nuclear Energy Technologies

CHAPTER 9

OIL RECOVERY FROM TAR SANDS AND OIL SHALE

In this chapter, we shall consider technological and economic aspects of oil recovery from tar sands and oil shale.

9.1   The Alberta Tar Sands

Spragins[1] has given the following estimates for the Athabasca deposits: 625×10^9 bbl with 285×10^9 bbl recoverable with "current" (1967) technology.

A Sun Oil Company subsidiary, The Great Canadian Oil Sands, Ltd., (GCOS), has been exploiting this area for some years at an investment cost of $\$300 \times 10^6$ and with a cumulative deficit to 1973 estimated at $\$90 \times 10^{6}$.[*] The

---

[1] F. K. Spragins, "Mining at Athabasca--A New Approach to Oil Production," Journal of Petroleum Technology 19, 1337-1343 (1967).

[*] Various newspaper reports, December 1973.

1

1973 GCOS production in an open pit mine amounted to 0.055×10^6 bbl/d and involved the use of 140,000 tons of tar sands and removal of 130,000 tons of overburden per day. Production has been accomplished in a region where the ratio of overburden-to-tar-sands-thickness is less than unity. The overburden is scraped away to allow exposure of the bitumen-rich sands, which are then dug out with giant bucket-wheel excavators before removal on conveyor belts[2] to the bitumen recovery and upgrading plant.[2, 3] Up to 4.5 tons of Canadian tar sands must be handled for each bbl of oil produced. The producing area is covered by muskeg swamp, which is a semifloating mass of decaying vegetation with scraggly growth of tamarack and black spruce. Drainage networks are required for water removal and should ideally be installed two years before excavation begins. The low temperatures (to -50° F) encountered in the region produce extremely cohesive quartz-bitumen matrices, which are very difficult to penetrate and produce rapid deterioration of the excavator alloy cutting teeth. During the summers, temperatures may rise to 90° F and the smelly tar sands now become so sticky that the mobile equipment tends to bog down.

---

[2] E. D. Innes and J. V. D. Fear, "Canada's First Commercial Tar Sand Development" in Proceedings of the Seventh World Petroleum Congress, Volume 3, pp. 633-650, Elsevier Publishing Co., New York, 1967.

[3] W. A. Bachman and D. H. Stormont, "Plant Starts, Athabasca Now Yielding Its Hydrocarbons," Oil and Gas Journal 65, 69-88, October 23, 1967.

A $\$1 \times 10^9$ project by Syncrude of Canada (30% owned by Atlantic Richfield, Cities Service, and Exxon's Imperial Oil, with 10% ownership by Gulf Oil) is scheduled to deliver 0.125×10^6 bbl/d beginning in 1978. Syncrude uses motorized scrapers for both overburden and tar sands removal[4] on property adjoining the GCOS field.

Tar sands containing less than a critical amount of bitumen (6 to 8 weight percent) are rejected. The mean bitumen content for oil recovery in the GCOS operation[2] is 12.4 weight percent.

Shell Canada Ltd. filed (in 1973) an application with the Alberta Energy Resources Conservation Board for bitumen recovery with the objective of 0.10×10^6 bbl/d recovery by 1980.

In situ recovery operations for deeper-lying bitumen are being developed by the Shell Oil Co. on 160,000 acres of leased land at Peace River (see Fig. 9.1-1), where 38 test wells to a depth of 1,800 feet had been drilled by the end of 1973. A prototype development plan called for a $\$30 \times 10^6$ program on 50 closely-spaced injection and production wells in 1974, with injection involving either steam, hot water, or light petroleum. This type of injection-recovery scheme should be contrasted with partial-burning procedures mentioned by an earlier writer.[5] Hopefully, the porosity of

---

[4] Application of Atlantic Richfield Co. et al to the Alberta Gas Conservation Board, 1968.

[5] F. W. Camp, "The Tar Sands of Alberta, Canada," Cameron Engineers, Denver, Colorado, 1970.

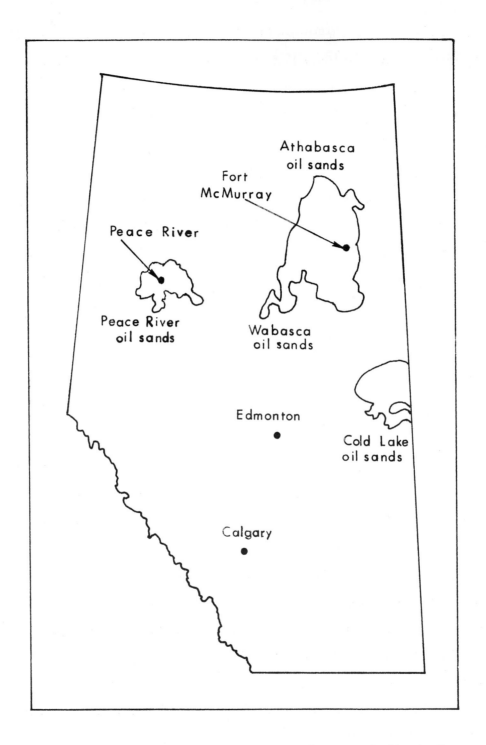

Fig. 9.1-1 Tar-sand sites. Enclosed areas indicate location of oil sands in the Alberta province of Canada.

the tar sands is sufficient to allow successful development of in situ recovery procedures. A number of other oil companies (Amoco, a Japanese group, Mobil, and Texaco) are experimenting with in situ recovery schemes.

The Committee for an Independent Canada and the Canadian environmentalist group Pollution Probe have raised objections to these developments and have questioned the desirability of a crash program for tar-sands development. A GCOS spokesman has expressed the view that "technical, environmental and legal problems are so great that it is unlikely that the rate of development will meet even the most pessimistic predictions".[6]

9.2   The GCOS Recovery and Upgrading Procedure of Oil from Tar Sands

The GCOS recovery process begins with excavation of feed consisting, for example, of a mixture of 11,700 t/sd (t = short ton = 2,000 lb; sd = standard or stream day with 350 sd/y) of bitumen-containing sands and 81,000 t/sd of minerals [① in Fig. 9.2-1]. This mixture is introduced into a conditioning drum [② in Fig. 9.2-1], together with caustic soda, water, and steam for reduction of sand-lump size. The smaller particles pass a vibrating screen [③ in Fig. 9.2-1], while oversize particles are returned to the conditioning drum for further treatment. More water is added to the particles

[6] A. R. Allen, as quoted in Chemical and Engineering News 52, 16, April 15, 1974.

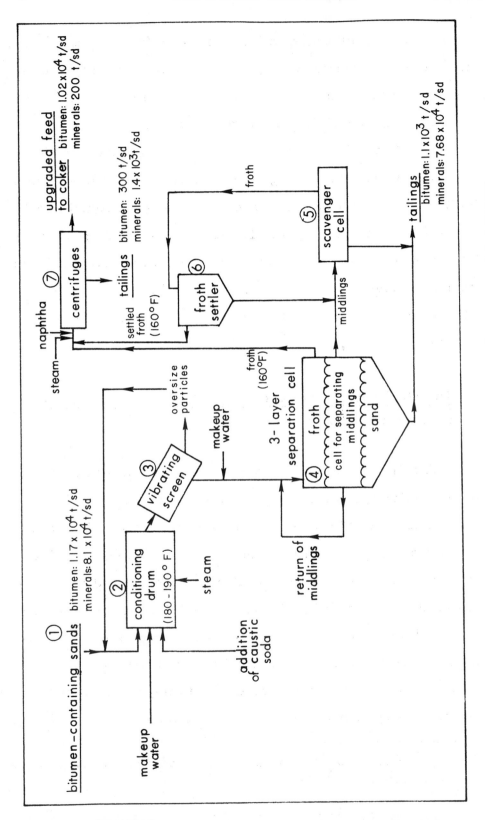

Fig. 9.2-1 The bitumen recovery scheme used by GCOS.

passing the screen prior to introduction into a three-layer separation cell [④ in Fig. 9.2-1]. The bitumen floats to the top of the separation cell and is largely recovered in this top-layer froth [④ in Fig. 9.2-1], while sand is discarded at the bottom and the middlings of intermediate density are partly returned to the separator for recycling and partly forwarded to a scavenger separation cell [⑤ in Fig. 9.2-1] for separate treatment in a froth settler [⑥ in Fig. 9.2-1]. The top-froth layers from the separation cell [④ in Fig. 9.2-1] and the froth settler [⑥ in Fig. 9.2-1] are mixed with naphtha before introduction for upgrading in centrifuges [⑦ in Fig. 9.2-1], from which tailings (bitumen-to-minerals weight ratio $\simeq$ 0.21) and upgraded feed (bitumen-to-minerals weight ratio $\simeq$ 51) for the coker are supplied; about 87% of the feed bitumen enters the coker. This feed bitumen is an 8° API oil containing 4% of sulfur.

The GCOS upgrading process for the tar sands is shown schematically in Fig. 9.2-2 and is reproduced from Roberts.[1] The total mined tar sand input of 0.105×10^6 t/sd corresponds to 0.065×10^6 bbl/sd and produces 0.050×10^6 bbl/sd of syncrude (77% conversion), as well as 2.58×10^3 t/sd of coke and 350 t/sd of sulfur. The flow diagram shown in Fig. 9.2-2 is self-explanatory. The overall hydrogen consumption is[2] 126 SCF/bbl of high-quality syncrude

[1] R. V. Roberts, "Comparative Economics of Tar Sands Conversion Processes," Stanford Research Institute, Menlo Park, California, 1970.

[2] Ref. [3] in Section 9.1.

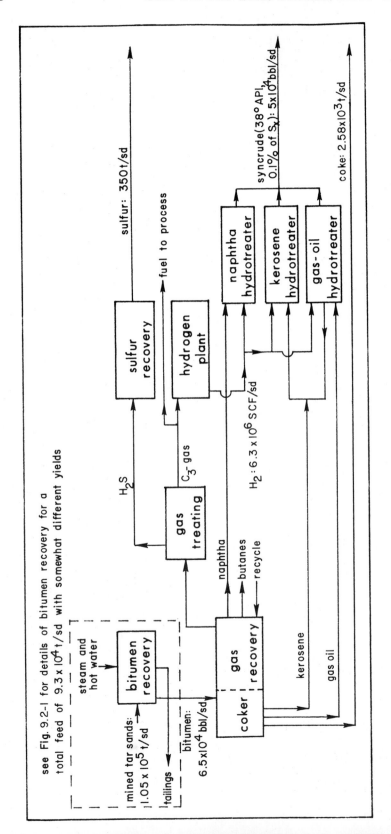

Fig. 9.2-2 The GCOS upgrading process for bitumen recovered from tar sands; reproduced with modifications from Ref. [1].

containing less than 0.1% of S_x.

9.3 The "Syncrude" Recovery and Upgrading Procedure of Oil from Tar Sands

The Syncrude upgrading procedure involves hydrovis-breaking of bitumen in such a manner that the released gases consist mostly of H_2S. The resulting liquid product is a mixture of butanes, oil residue, and intermediate fractions containing naphtha and light and heavy gases, which are further hydrotreated catalytically. The syncrude-to-bitumen recovery ratio is raised to 87% but with somewhat higher sulfur content than the GCOS syncrude.

9.4 Economic Analysis of Oil Recovery from Tar Sands

Roberts[1] performed an economic analysis in 1970 for oil recovery from the tar sands. Although this costing study requires drastic revisions in 1974, his results are useful for showing the relation between ROR and plant capacity, product value, % of operating capacity, % of bitumen in the sands, % of bitumen recovery, and % of bitumen conversion to syncrude. Roberts' 1970 analysis refers to the GCOS process on a scale of 0.05×10^6 bbl/d. He estimated a 5.8% rate of return (ROR) using the discounted cash flow (DCF)

[1] Ref. [1] in Section 9.2.

method with syncrude delivered at \$2.90/bbl.[*]   At late 1973 interest costs of 10% or more and prices of more than \$10.00/bbl, a much higher DCF ROR would be required (12 to 20%) and yet would still be competitive with prevailing oil prices.

Roberts used a project life of 15 years with a double-declining balance rate of depreciation during the first seven and one-half years of assumed plant life.   A profit tax of 50% was used with a two-and-one-half year construction period, a one-half year start-up period, the zero of time corresponding to plant completion, and a lump-sum discounting procedure for end-of-year payments.   Cost distribution was found to be about 40% each for mining and bitumen upgrading and 20% for bitumen recovery.   Other salient conclusions of Roberts' cost analysis are summarized in Figs. 9.4-1 to 9.4-6.

9.5   Oil Recovery from Oil Shale

Oil shale is the colloquial term for a sedimentary rock which contains the solid hydrocarbon wax <u>kerogen</u> in tightly-packed clay, mud, and silt.   Kerogen is decomposed at elevated temperatures with the formation of oil that is suitable for refinery processing.   However, removal of objectionable nitrogen compounds and other impurities is required.   About 1.5×10^5 t/d of oil shale (corresponding to

---

[*] The ROR DCF method for estimating the economic value of a venture is described in the Appendix of this chapter.

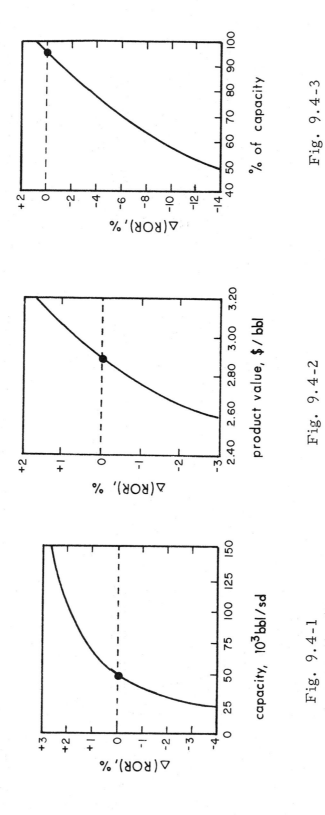

Fig. 9.4-3

Effect of operating rate on profitability in 1970; reproduced from Ref. [1].

Fig. 9.4-2

Effect of syncrude value on profitability in 1970; reproduced from Ref. [1].

Fig. 9.4-1

Effect of plant capacity on profitability in 1970; reproduced from Ref. [1]

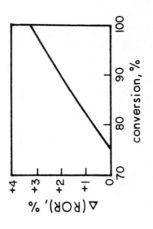

Fig. 9.4-6

Effect on profitability in 1970 of bitumen-conversion efficiency to syncrude in the upgrading step; reproduced from Ref. [1].

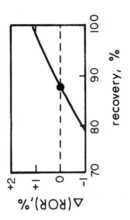

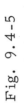

Fig. 9.4-5

Effect of bitumen-recovery efficiency on profitability in 1970; reproduced from Ref. [1].

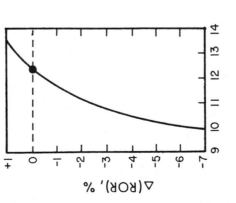

Fig. 9.4-4

Effect of tar sands quality on profitability in 1970; reproduced from Ref. [1].

more than double of the material currently handled in the
largest underground mines) will be required for retorting
in a 10^5 bbl/d operation.

The Colorado-Utah-Wyoming deposits (see Fig.
9.5-1) have been estimated[1] to contain 1.43×10^{12} bbl with
yields of 10 to 25 gallons of oil per ton of shale (about 3.5 to
8.6 weight percent); about 0.80×10^{12} bbl are in the Piceance
Basin in Colorado, 0.23×10^{12} bbl in the Utah Uinta Basin,
0.40×10^{12} bbl in Wyoming (the Green River and Washakie
Basins). In 1965, it was suggested that only 80×10^9 bbl
were "recoverable under present conditions." There are
also large deposits of carbonaceous shales in the eastern and
central areas of the United States with such low oil contents
that they have been classified[1] as marginal or sub-margin-
al for production. In fact, Hubbert[2] concluded that "the organic contents of the carbonaceous shales appear to be more
promising as a resource of raw materials for the chemical
industry than as a major source of industrial energy." The
usually-quoted (1965) resource assessment of Duncan and
Swanson,[1] as summarized by Hubbert,[2] is the following:
the total world-wide <u>recoverable</u> oil from oil shale is about

---

[1] D. C. Duncan and V. E. Swanson, <u>Organic-Rich Shales of
the United States and World Land Areas</u>, U.S. Geological
Circular No. 523, Washington, D.C., 1965.

[2] M. King Hubbert, "Energy Resources," p. 199 in Chapter
8 of <u>Resources and Man,</u> W. H. Freeman and Company,
San Francisco, California, 1969.

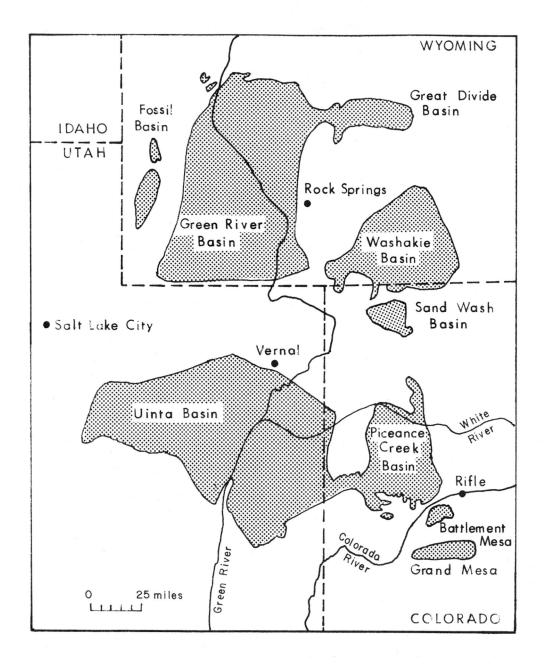

Fig. 9.5-1 Oil-shale deposits of the Green River formation
in Colorado, Utah, and Wyoming.

190×10^9 bbl while the total world-wide resource amounts
to about 2×10^{15} bbl. Duncan and Swanson's[1] Table 3 is
reproduced here as Table 9.5-1. Reference to these data
shows that the total North American deposits with 25 to 100
gallons per ton of shale (about 8.6 to 34.5 weight percent of
oil) amount to about 3×10^{12} tons of shale oil. Probably
more than 75% of these resources are located on currently
(1973) unleased federal lands.

An extensive evaluation of oil-shale availability has
been prepared by the National Petroleum Council.[3]

9.6 Summary Remarks on Recovery Processes of Oil from Oil Shale

Oil recovery from oil shale is more difficult to accomplish than from tar sands. Because the shale is not porous, the development of *in situ* recovery techniques requires
fracturing (or leaching in the particular formations associated with the leach zone) of the shale before oil removal. *In
situ* recovery of shale oil from oil shale is discussed in
Section 9.12. Conventional aboveground retorting can, of
course, also be used. Neither of these procedures has been
well developed thus far. The largest 1973-1974 development
involved a 50,000 bbl/sd plant.

Extensive environmental-impact-assessment studies

---

[3] U.S. Energy Outlook: Oil Shale Availability, National
Petroleum Council, Washington, D.C., 1973.

Table 9.5-1 Estimates of shale-oil resources of world land area (in 10^9 bbl); reproduced from Duncan and Swanson, Ref. [1], (g/t stands for gallons of shale oil recoverable per ton of shale).

Continent	Known Resources (1965)				Possible extensions of known resources			Undiscovered and unappraised resources			Total resources		
	10-100 g/t*	25-100 g/t	10-25 g/t	5-10 g/t	25-100 g/t	10-25 g/t	5-10 g/t	25-100 g/t	10-25 g/t	5-10 g/t	25-100 g/t	10-25 g/t	5-10 g/t
Africa	10	90	small	small	ne[a]	ne	ne	4,000	80,000	450,000	4,000	80,000	450,000
Asia	20	70	14	ne	2	3,700	ne	5,400	106,000	586,000	5,500	110,000	590,000
Australia and New Zealand	small	small	1	ne	ne	ne	ne	1,000	20,000	100,000	1,000	20,000	100,000
Europe	30	40	6	ne	100	200	ne	1,200	26,000	150,000	1,400	26,000	140,000
North America	80	520	1,600	2,200	900	2,500	4,000	1,500	45,000	254,000	3,000	50,000	260,000
South America	50	small	750	ne	ne	3,200	4,000	2,000	36,000	206,000	2,000	40,000	210,000
Total	190[b]	720	2,400	2,200	1,000	9,600	8,000	15,100	313,000	1,746,000	16,900	326,000	1,750,000

* Recoverable under 1965 conditions.

a ne = no estimate.

b Of the approximately 2×10^{15} bbl here indicated, 190×10^9 bbl were considered recoverable under 1965 conditions, corresponding to the sum of the resource estimates given in the first column.

for conventional mining and retorting procedures have been performed. Nevertheless, many questions remain. These relate to (a) the fact that water availability will limit regional industrial development and (b) the possibility that small concentrations of kerogen-derived hydrocarbons may prove to be carcinogenic; (c) also, water-table contamination may be produced as the result of leaching of minerals from the spent oil shale. Reconstruction and replanting of spent shale is a costly procedure. The replacement of spent shale by slurry flows has been considered.

An important limiting factor in the development of a mature oil-shale industry relates to the availability of run-off water. It has been estimated that from 1.4×10^5 to 2.0×10^5 acre-feet of water per year are required for the production of 0.1×10^6 bbl/sd of oil from shale. A 14-year development schedule (1973 to 1987) leading to a 0.5×10^6 bbl/sd industry thus implies the consumptive use of 7×10^5 to 1×10^6 acre-ft/y of run-off water by 1987. In view of existing treaties on the allowable salinity levels of Colorado River water delivered to Mexico and of limitations set by agricultural use in California's Imperial Valley, the long-term availability of such large amounts of run-off water is currently in question. Enormous underground water deposits (sufficient to support the 0.5×10^6 bbl/sd industry for as long as 50 years) have been found in the oil-shale regions. The extent to which this stored water (which is a non-renewable source) can be used is currently unclear because the long-term effects of increased ground-water salinity are not well understood.

There are significant social stresses anticipated in
the Colorado region if a regional oil-shale development boom
is coupled with a regional coal-development boom.   Furthermore, cost estimates of oil from oil shale have recently been
increased significantly (see Section 9.11 for details).   As the
result, it is not inconceivable that the entire oil-shale development plan will fail again, as it has repeatedly in the past.
It is possible that the development of innovative, low-cost,
in situ procedures will be required to make oil from shale
competitive with other petroleum sources over the intermediate term.   One should not overlook the fact that Mideastern
oil has an intrinsic production cost of perhaps 8 to 20 cents
per bbl and that large unexplored regions (e.g., off the U.S.
Atlantic Coast and on the West Coast of Alaska) may contain
petroleum reserves of sufficient magnitude to obviate the
necessity of oil recovery from shale between the present day
and the introduction of superior technologies (e.g., nuclear
breeder reactors, fusion energy) during the next 20 to 50 years.

9.7   Mining Procedures for the Recovery of Shale Oil

Among the mining procedures considered for oil recovery from oil shales are the following:

a.   Room-and-pillar mining, which leaves one-half
of the rock in place while exploiting the other half.   This procedure is an inefficient method of resource development but
is nevertheless suitable for shallow seams, particularly if
the seams are narrow.   It has been used by the U.S. Bureau

of Mines and by the oil consortium known as The Oil Shale
Corporation (TOSCO).

   b.   Open-pit mining is suitable for application to
shallow deposits and can probably also be used profitably for
thick seams, provided the deposits are sufficiently extensive.

   c.   Cut-and-fill mining is preferable to open-pit or
room-and-pillar mining for deep and extensive seams.   In this
procedure, shale is removed continuously in layers, spent
shale being employed as a floor for subsequent operation.

   d.   Block caving is a procedure in which the ore is
undercut, supporting pillars are removed, and the ore is
subsequently extracted.[1]   As ore is drawn out, overlying
blocks fall and spall.   The ore is removed through raises and
drifts.[1]   This procedure has been used successfully for
copper (65,000 t/d) and molybdenum (60,000 t/d) mines.

   e.   In sublevel caving, a drill-blast-haul sequence
is used in which overlying material "caves" as ore is extracted.   This procedure has been judged to be well adapted
for mining of homogeneous oil-shale deposits.[1]

   f.   Simultaneous recovery of oil, nahcolite ($NaHCO_3$),
and alumina from oil shale has been proposed[2] by the devel-

---

[1]W. J. Reynolds, "Mining Considerations for In Situ Oil
    Shale Development," Report UCRL-51867, Lawrence
    Livermore Laboratory, Livermore, Calif., July 1975.

[2]B. Weichman, "The Superior Process for Development
    of Oil Shale and Associated Minerals," Proceedings of
    the 7th Oil Shale Symposium, Quarterly of the Colorado
    School of Mines 69, No. 2, 25-43 (1974).

opment of conventional mining procedures. Nahcolite is useful for sulfur removal with the production of Na_2SO_4.

g. In situ recovery requires fracturing of deposits and hydrocarbon removal in the manner suggested for in situ oil recovery from the tar sands. Fracturing of the shale must produce sufficient voids to allow retorting in place and oil recovery in wells. It may be accomplished by mechanical means or by chemical or nuclear detonations (see Section 9.12 for details). The broken shale will generally be distributed in size over a very wide range. Heating to remove gas and oil may be accomplished by hot steam injection, as well as by partial combustion, or by extraction with light hydrocarbon-solvent vapors. Techniques for fracturing and subsequent in situ recovery have not been developed commercially on a large scale, although some prototype studies are currently in progress, especially for mixed-mining-and-in situ recovery procedures (see Sections 9.12 and 9.13 for details). Procedures for calculating the pressure distribution in fractured shale beds have been developed.[3]

It should be noted that even relatively rich oil shale (e.g., 30 gal/t) at an oil cost of $10/bbl is an ore of relatively low value per ton ($\sim$ $7/t) compared with such ores as silver ($\sim$ $119/t), nickel ($\sim$ $80/t), gold ($\sim$ $44/t), iron and copper ($\sim$ $11/t), and even coal ($8-12/t) at 1975 prices.

---

[3] J. F. Carley, "Pressure Distribution in Beds of Oil-Shale Rubble," Report UCRL-51957 Rev. 1, Lawrence Livermore Laboratory, Livermore, Calif., March 1976.

9.8   Oil and Gas Recovery from Oil Shale

The complete cycle for oil recovery is shown in Fig. 9.8-1, which has been reproduced from a 1968 U.S. Bureau of Mines report. The alternative paths involving either in situ or conventional recovery are clearly indicated.

A summary of development procedures for above-ground oil recovery from oil shale, corresponding to 1973 technological developments, is given in Table 9.8-1. Further details concerning recovery may be found in a summary paper by Hendrickson.[1] The TOSCO II process is shown schematically in Fig. 9.8-2.

Retorting or recovery efficiencies are expressed in terms of a Fischer assay. This is a retorting technique in which a 100-gram sample of oil shale is heated at a specified rate in an air-tight aluminum retort, attaining a temperature of $932°$F after 40 minutes. This temperature is then maintained for 20 minutes. As the kerogen decomposes, the pyrolysis products (shale oil, water, and noncondensable gases) are cooled to $32°$F and collected. The shale oil is separated from the water by centrifuging in order to determine the shale-oil yield. Actual oil recovery is generally less than that obtained in a Fischer assay. However, favorable temperature-time cycles exist which lead to oil yields in excess

---

[1] T. A. Hendrickson, "Oil Shale Processing Methods," Proceedings of the 7th Oil Shale Symposium, Quarterly of the Colorado School of Mines 69, No. 2, 45-69 (1974).

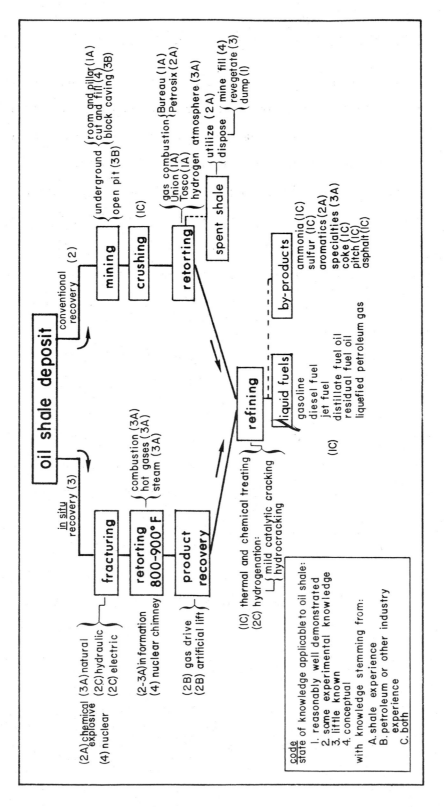

Fig. 9.8-1 Processes involved in oil-shale exploitation; reproduced from *Prospects for Oil Shale Development in Colorado, Utah, and Wyoming*, U.S. Department of the Interior, U.S. Government Printing Office, Washington, D.C., 1968.

Table 9.8-1 Late 1973 description of process development relating to oil recovery from oil shale.

Process	Technical features	Status
a. Bureau of Mines combustion process	Crushed shale (1/4"-2" rock) is preheated, retorted, partially burned, and cooled with 90% retorting efficiency. See Section 9.9 for a more complete description of this process.	260 t/sd demonstration in 1970 at the Colorado School of Mines Research Institute
b. Union Oil Co.	Shale is extracted by counter-flowing process gas with 25% of the retorts using partial combustion of the carbon residue in shale to produce peak temperatures to 2,200°F. The retorting efficiency is 91%.	10^3 t/sd in 1958
c. TOSCO II	Shale is crushed and processed through a surge hopper [①in Fig. 9.8-2] before introduction to a preheater ②, where it is exposed to hot flue gases. It then passes to a separator ③, where flue gases are removed, and then to a pyrolysis drum ④ for mixing with ceramic balls from a ball heater ⑤. The hot-shale-ceramic-ball mixture enters a drum for efficient retorting in the accumulator ⑥, with the hydrocarbon vapors exhausting to the fractionator ⑦ for gas, naphtha, and gas-oil recovery. Flue gases ⑧ passing through the ball heater are used to preheat the shale. The ceramic balls, which have moved from the ball heater ⑤ through the pyrolysis drum ④ and the accumulator ⑥, are raised back up to the level of the ball heater ⑤ during passage through the ball elevator ⑨. The overall retort efficiency is over 100% according to a Fischer assay.	10^3 t/sd in 1967

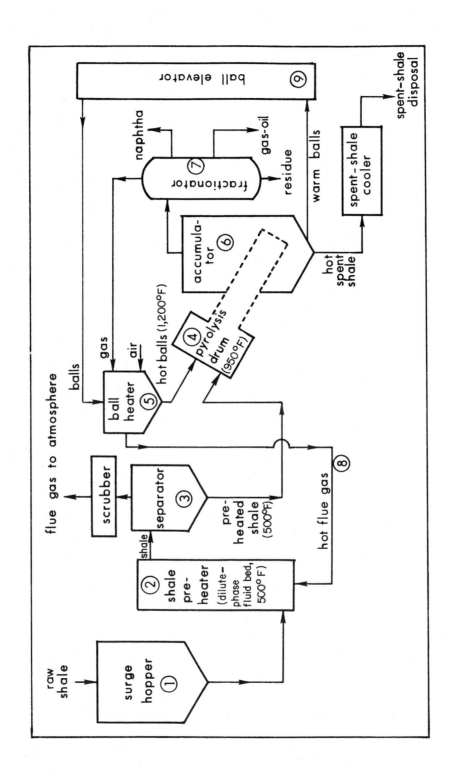

Fig. 9.8-2 Schematic diagram illustrating the TOSCO II process for oil recovery from oil shale. Approximately two tons of 0.5-inch ceramic hot balls are mixed with each ton of preheated shale in the pyrolysis drum.

of the Fischer assay. The effect of thermal history on oil yield has been measured for selected shales.[2, 3]

9.9   Upgrading of Shale Oil in the U.S. Bureau of Mines Gas-Combustion Process

The raw crude from the retorts [① in Fig. 9.9-1] is too viscous for piping and application and requires upgrading and purification (nitrogen-compound and sulfur removal) before use as feedstock at the refinery. The first step [② in Fig. 9.9-1] in upgrading involves fractionation to $650°F$ (40% of the total input) and coking (60% of the total input) to $900°F$. Naphtha streams ③ and gas oil ④ are hydrofined using hydrogen (97% pure) from a separate hydrogen plant for syncrude production. Reference to Fig. 9.9-1 shows that 7.63×10^4 t/sd of oil shale are converted to 5.93×10^4 t/sd of burned shale in addition to 3.8×10^3 t/sd of shale fines, 3.8×10^8 SCF/sd of low-Btu gas, 5.29×10^4 bbl/sd of raw crude; the ultimate products are 162 t/sd of NH_3, 74 t/sd of S_x, 5.0×10^4 bbl/sd of $43°$ API syncrude, and 820 t/sd of coke, while 2.4×10^7 SCF/sd of natural gas are consumed.

---

[2]N. D. Stout, G. H. Koskinas, J. H. Raley, S. D. Santor, R. J. Opila, and A. J. Rothman, "Pyrolysis of Oil Shale: The Effects of Thermal History on Oil Yield," Proceedings of the 9th Oil Shale Symposium, Quarterly of the Colorado School of Mines 71, 153-172 (1976).

[3]J. H. Raley and R. L. Braun, "Oil Degradation during Oil Shale Retorting," paper presented at a Symposium on Oil Shale, Tar Sands, and Related Materials, Division of Fuel Chemistry, American Chemical Society, San Francisco, Calif., August 29-September 2, 1976.

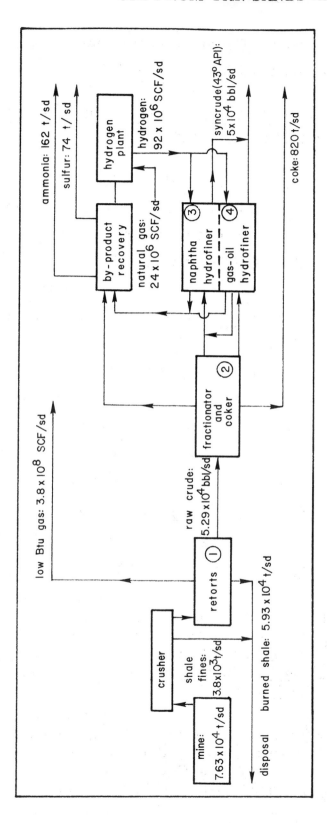

Fig. 9.9-1 Upgrading of oil from oil shale to syncrude using a gas combustion process; reproduced from R. G. Murray, "Economic Factors in the Production of Shale Oil," paper presented at the 74th National Western Mining Conference, Denver, Colorado, February, 1971.

Physical properties of oil obtained from Colorado oil shale and Fischer assay products and calorific values are summarized in Tables 9.9-1 and 9.9-2, respectively. We note that the final product is of high quality, independently of the grade of ore from which it is recovered.

9.10 Environmental Effects of Shale-Oil Production

According to Hubbard,[1] 20% to 40% of the raw crude weight, or 2% to 4% of the rock weight, are produced as water, containing organic and inorganic contaminants. For example, after in situ gas-combustion processing, the following typical inorganic substances were found: 1.04 or 3.10 g/ℓ of sodium, 1.68 or 4.45 g/ℓ of sulfates, 8.91 or 4.80 g/ℓ of ammonium salts, 14.44 or 19.22 g/ℓ of carbonates, 5.43 or 13.41 g/ℓ of chlorides, at a pH of 8.61 or 8.69. The water may be reclaimed in arid regions or it may be disposed of. Costs and environmental-effect implications have not been properly assessed as yet.

The spent shale amounts to 85% to 90% of the rock processed. Water run-off from this spent shale (except possibly in the case of in situ recovery) has a high level of mineral contamination, amounting to as much as 45 g/ℓ. Thus,

---

[1] A. B. Hubbard, "Method for Reclaiming Water from Oil-Shale Processing," American Chemical Society, Division of Fuel Chemistry Preprints 15, No. 1, 21-25, March-April 1971.

Table 9.9-1 Physical properties of shale oil derived from a Fischer assay of Colorado oil-shale samples; reprinted from T. A. Hendrickson, "Oil Shale Processing Methods," *Proceedings of the 7th Oil Shale Symposium*, Quarterly of the Colorado School of Mines 69, No. 2, 45-69 (1974); by permission of the Colorado School of Mines. Copyright © 1974 by the Colorado School of Mines.

	Low-grade shale	Medium-grade shale	High-grade shale	Very high-grade shale	Ultra high-grade shale
oil shale grade, g/t Fischer-assay oil	10.5	26.7	36.3	61.8	75.0
weight % of raw shale	4.0	10.4	13.8	23.6	28.7
specific gravity at 60°F	0.925	0.930	0.911	0.919	0.918
kinematic viscosity at 100°F, centistokes	20.71	23.72	18.19	17.12	17.28
gross heating value, 10^3 Btu/lb	18.51	18.33	18.68	18.51	18.44
pour point, °F	80	75	85	80	75

Table 9.9-2 Physical properties and heating values of shale oil; reprinted from T. A. Hendrickson, "Oil Shale Processing Methods," Proceedings of the 7th Oil Shale Symposium, Quarterly of the Colorado School of Mines 69, No. 2, 45-69 (1974); by permission of the Colorado School of Mines. Copyright © 1974 by the Colorado School of Mines.

Raw shale						
grade, gal/ton	10.5	26.7	36.3	57.1	61.8	75.0
gross heating value, Btu/lb	1,020	2,340	3,080	5,510	6,010	7,000
Assay products						
oil, weight %	4.0	10.4	13.8	21.9	23.6	28.7
water, weight %	0.5	1.4	1.5	1.2	1.1	1.5
spent shale, weight %	94.4	85.7	82.1	72.3	70.4	63.6
gas, weight %	1.1	2.0	2.2	3.9	4.2	4.6
gas, ft^3/t of shale	66	337	445	1,051	1,073	1,207
weight loss, %	------	0.5	0.4	0.7	0.7	1.6
Gross heating values of assay products						
oil, Btu/lb	18,510	18,330	18,680	18,580	18,510	18,440
water	------	------	------	------	------	------
spent shale, Btu/lb	80	250	330	1,160	1,090	1,250
gas, 10^3 Btu/t of shale	49	255	453	973	562	1,214
gas, Btu/ft^3	739	758	1,018	926	897	1,006

run-off diversion and containment may be required. Probably complete reconstitution, including planting, of the spent shale will ultimately be required.

9.11   Economic Considerations of Shale-Oil Production Using Mining and Aboveground Retorting

In 1971, Murray[1] evaluated economic factors in shale-oil recovery for the U.S. Bureau of Mines Gas Combustion Retort Process and made comparisons with both the Union Oil Co. and the TOSCO II processes. Although these cost estimates require drastic revisions (see below), they are instructive to review because they show the dominant factors which determine product cost. Shale reserves sufficient for 15 years of operation cost about $2,000/acre (in 1971). Assuming 75% recovery from a 60-ft bench test, the initial ground shale cost is about 1.6¢/t. Royalty payments on public lands may actually be 10 times larger now.

Murray[1] used a Fischer assay of 34 gal/t for the shale and production of 50,000 bbl/sd with a DCF rate of return method, and otherwise the same assumptions that were employed by Roberts in evaluating oil recovery from the tar sands (see Section 9.2 for details).

The process block-flow diagram is that shown in Fig. 9.9-1. The shale is crushed to a maximum dimension of 10

---

[1] R. G. Murray, "Economic Factors in the Production of Shale Oil," paper presented at the 74th National Western Mining Conference, Denver, Colorado, February 1971.

inches before conveyer-belt transportation to the crushing
plant, where further reduction to two inches maximum size
is effected; about 5% of the shale has dimensions less than
one-quarter inch and is discarded. The crushed shale is fed
through a star feeder to a retort, where it flows continuously
to a preheating zone, a retorting zone, a burning zone, a
cooling zone, and distribution pipes to the spent-shale disposal area. Recycle-gas flow in the retort is counter-cur-
rent and product crude leaves at the top of the retort. Burning of residual hydrocarbons and of carbon at 1,600 to 1,800°F
in the educted shale with injected air produces the heat required for retorting. About 25 to 30% of the shale carbonates
are decomposed in the combustion zone. The temperature in
the retorting zone is 800 to 900°F. The hydrocarbon gases
are finally cooled by heat exchange with raw shale, condensed
as a fine mist, and carried out by recycle gas. Subsequent
upgrading of the 20°API crude (pour point = 80°F) has been
discussed in Section 9.9. The final crude is high quality with
0.09 weight percent of nitrogen, 0.006 weight percent of sulfur, a 0.03 weight percent of carbon residue, 43° API gravity, 33 SUS viscosity at 120°F; 10, 50, and 90% are distilled
at 200, 448, and 730°F, respectively. Investment and operating costs (1971) for 50,000 bbl/sd syncrude production
amounted to $122.3 $\times$ 10^6 for depreciable items (mining,
plant), noncapitalized investment of $17.4 $\times$ 10^6 (land, mine
and plant working capital), mine-replacement expenses of
$15.2 $\times$ 10^6, and total start-up expenses of $10.3 $\times$ 10^6. Annual operating costs for the mine were estimated at $13.05

$\times 10^6$ and for the plant at $16.21 $\times 10^6$. For $3.20/bbl of syncrude, $4/t of coke, $20/t of sulfur, and $25/t of ammonia, annual income was $8.57 $\times 10^6$ with a DCF rate of return of 9.9%. Cost estimates for the Union Oil (gas combustion) and TOSCO II plants were similar, although cost distributions are different and range from 38% for mining and 29% for retorting with gas combustion to 30% and 38%, respectively, for TOSCO II, while upgrading is changed from 33% to 32% of total cost.

The effect of parameter variations on the DCF rate of return is shown in Figs. 9.11-1 to 9.11-5.

The cost estimates for oil recovery from oil shale have recently been revised upward drastically,[2] in large part because of greatly increased expenses associated with environmental control. Allowing for front-end federal land lease costs, a 20% DCF rate of return will probably correspond to oil costs of $9.00/bbl or more; even at a 12% DCF rate of return, which is reasonable for a mature industry, the per barrel cost will probably exceed $8.00.

During October 1974, an indefinite postponement for construction of a 50×10^3 bbl/d shale-oil production plant was announced by the Colony Development Operation (a joint venture of the Ashland Oil Co., Atlantic Richfield Corp., The

---

[2] S. Katell, R. Stone, and P. Wellman, "Oil Shale - A Clean Energy Source," Proceedings of the 7th Oil Shale Symposium, Quarterly of the Colorado School of Mines 69, No. 2, 1-19 (1974).

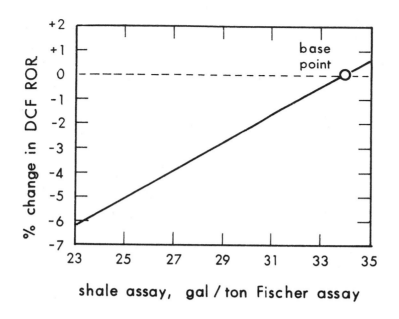

Fig. 9.11-1 A 1971 evaluation of the sensitivity of DCF ROR to shale assay; reproduced from Ref. [1].

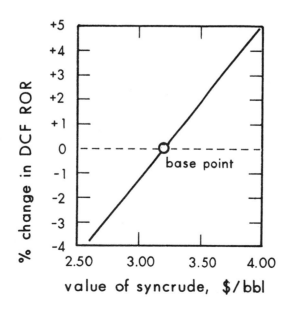

Fig. 9.11-2 A 1971 evaluation of the sensitivity of DCF ROR to syncrude value; reproduced from Ref. [1].

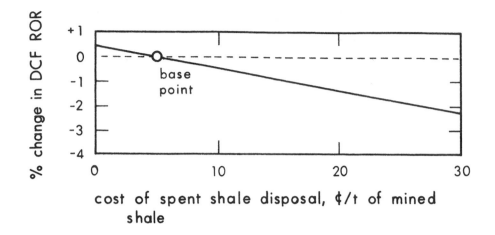

Fig. 9.11-3 A 1971 evaluation of the sensitivity of DCF ROR
          to the cost of shale disposal; reproduced from
          Ref. [1].

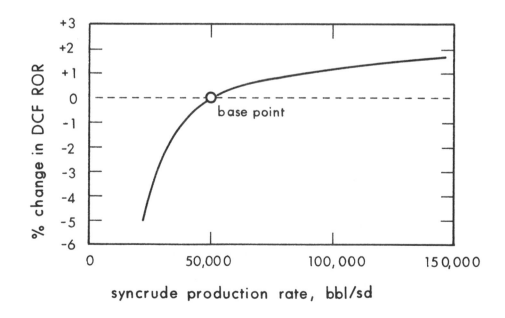

Fig. 9.11-4 A 1971 evaluation of the sensitivity of DCF ROR
          to plant size; reproduced from Ref. [1].

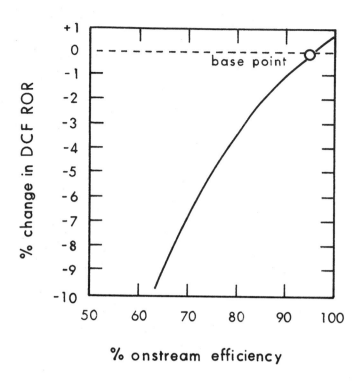

Fig. 9.11-5 A 1971 evaluation of the effect of operating rate
            on DCF ROR; reproduced from Ref. [1].

Oil Shale Corp., and Shell Oil Co.) because capital-costs (in
current dollars) had escalated from about 450×10^6 to nearly
800×10^6.[3] Three other industry groups were still study-
ing possible development of their shale-oil resources.[3]

9.12 In Situ Recovery of Shale Oil from Oil Shale

    The attractive features of in situ (in place) recovery

[3]"Colony Move Clouds Shale Oil Prospects," Chemical and
Engineering News 52, 4-5, October 14, 1974.

have been well recognized for a long time. Thus, B. F. Grant[1] described at the <u>First Symposium on Oil Shale</u> in 1964 some tests performed by the Sinclair Oil Company in 1953 and 1954 to determine the feasibility of <u>in situ</u> recovery. The experiments were performed at a narrow promontory mountain in shallow beds. A schematic diagram of the experimental configuration indicating planned performance is shown in Fig. 9.12-1. Although some of the initially drilled wells became plugged up during ignition after fracturing or ignition failed altogether, the following important facts were established in these early tests: communication between wells was established by fracturing, ignition could be accomplished, high pressures were required for air injection after ignition, underground combustion was maintained, and some oil with desirable properties was retorted and recovered at the producing wells.

The nature of the retorting process achieved and the underground temperature profile are illustrated qualitatively in Fig. 9.12-2. We note that the kerogen is decomposed and the resulting lower molecular weight decomposition fragments are distilled (retorted) in the region ahead of the combustion zone, between the injection and production wells. Great care must be taken to inject the proper amount of oxygen to achieve desirable temperature conditions for good

[1] B. F. Grant, "Retorting Oil Shale Underground - Problems and Possibilities," <u>First Symposium on Oil Shale</u>, Quarterly of the Colorado School of Mines, No. 3, 39-46 (1964).

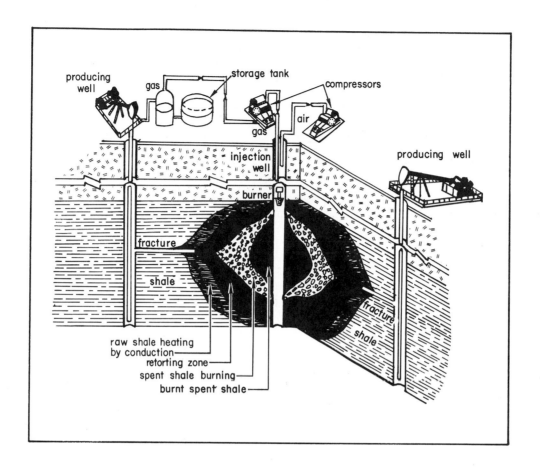

Fig. 9.12-1 Schematic diagram showing the 1953 configuration for in situ recovery used by the Sinclair Oil Co.; reprinted from B. F. Grant, "Retorting Oil Shale Underground - Problems and Possibilities," First Symposium on Oil Shale, Quarterly of the Colorado School of Mines, No. 3, 39-46 (1964); by permission of the Colorado School of Mines. Copyright © 1964 by the Colorado School of Mines.

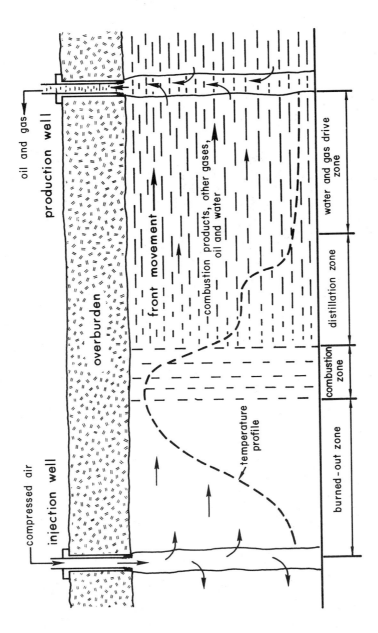

Fig. 9.12-2 Schematic diagram showing shale-oil recovery by cocurrent air and product flow between the injection and production wells; reprinted from V. D. Allred, "Some Characteristic Properties of Colorado Oil Shale Which May Influence In Situ Processing," First Symposium on Oil Shale, Quarterly of the Colorado School of Mines, No. 3, 47-75 (1964); by permission of the Colorado School of Mines. Copyright © 1964 by the Colorado School of Mines.

oil recovery ($\sim$ 30 to 50%) ahead of the combustion front (700 to 900°F).   During underground combustion, carbonaceous residues are formed which react with O_2 and CO_2;[2] the CO_2 itself is produced by the thermal decomposition of dolomite $[CaMg(CO_3)_2]$ and calcium carbonate.

Kerogen has a very large molecular weight ($\sim$ 30,000 g/mole) and is believed to decompose by at least three concurrent steps into (a) lighter bitumen, gas and carbon residue; (b) liquid oil and gas; and (c) a vaporized oil and gas mixture.   The decomposition rates and reaction paths are sensitive functions of the combustion-front conditions: temperature, pressure, gas composition (see Fig. 9.12-3).

     A.   Current Studies on Non-Nuclear Fracturing and Shale-Oil Recovery

Current studies on non-nuclear fracturing and subsequent shale-oil recovery are similar in concept and design to the Sinclair work.   A suitable site is selected and the lithology and oil content are determined by core drilling, leading to the definition of a stratigraphic column (see Fig. 9.12-4). After coring to suitable depths, a steel casing is inserted and fracturing is induced by the use of chemical-explosive charges, application of hydraulic pressure, or the use of strong electric fields (electrolinking).   Arrays of injection and production wells are made and then direct underground

[2] R. G. Mallon and R. L. Braun, "Reactivity of Oil Shale Carbonaceous Residue with Oxygen and Carbon Dioxide," Proceedings of the 9th Oil Shale Symposium, Quarterly of the Colorado School of Mines 71, 309-333 (1976).

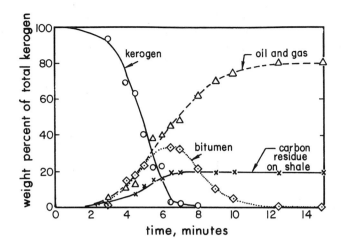

Fig. 9.12-3 Data showing the rates of change with time of kerogen, bitumen, oil and gas, and of the carbon residue on shale, for typical retorting conditions; reproduced from A. B. Hubbard and W. E. Robinson, "A Thermal Decomposition Study of Colorado Oil Shale," U.S. Bureau of Mines Report of Investigations 4744, Washington, D.C., November 1950.

retorting and oil recovery are attempted.[3,4] To date, it has been demonstrated that some oil and gas are recoverable but the methodology is still more properly classified as a concept rather than as an existing technology. In particular,

[3] G. G. Campbell, W. G. Scott, and J. S. Miller, "Evaluation of Oil-Shale Fracturing Tests Near Rock Springs, Wyoming," U.S. Bureau of Mines Report of Investigations 7397, Washington, D.C., 1970.

[4] H. C. Carpenter and H. W. Sohns, "Development of Technology for In Situ Oil Shale Processing," Proceedings of the 7th Oil Shale Symposium, Quarterly of the Colorado School of Mines 69, No. 2, 143-169 (1974).

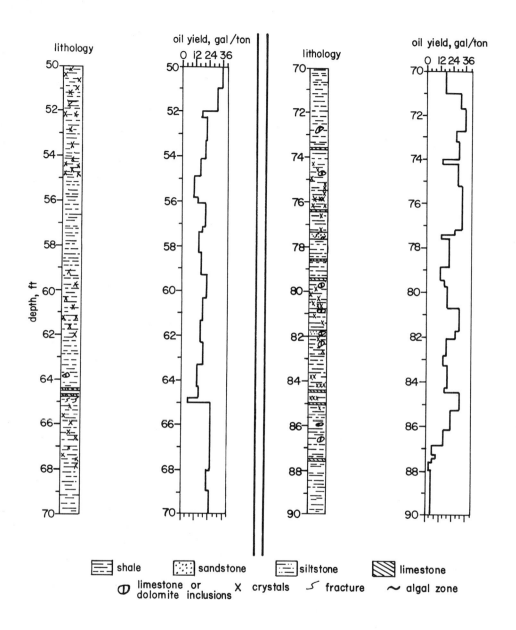

Fig. 9.12-4 Stratigraphic column and Fischer assay of oil
            yields for a typical core that is to be used as an
            injection or production well; reproduced from
            E. L. Burwell, T. E. Sterner, and H. C.
            Carpenter, "In Situ Retorting of Oil Shale,"
            Report 7783, U.S. Bureau of Mines, Washing-
            ton, D. C., 1973.

the troublesome questions associated with the feasibility of reasonable resource exploitation (say 30 to 50%), and with concurrent coring, fracturing, and retorting in confined regions, remain unanswered and are currently the subject of active field investigations. The conceptual design for an operating field installation with sequential recovery from rubblized (fractured) blocks is shown in Fig. 9.12-5.

B. Nuclear Fracturing and Shale-Oil Recovery

Underground nuclear explosions have been carried out by U.S., French, and Russian investigators.[5] Following explosions in oil shale, it is important to recover shale oil from both the chimney and fractured regions.[5] Tests in granite of in situ permeability have indicated that the fracture distance extends for about 2.7 to 3.65 cavity radii in granite. In granite and salt deposits, the exposed rock vaporizes and produces a cavity by pushing the adjacent rock strata apart. In oil shale, the cavity temperature is expected to be 200 to 400°F with 10 to 30% of bulk void space.

A schematic diagram of the expected physical states[5,6] after a nuclear explosion in oil shale is shown in

---

[5] G. C. Werth, "Effect of Nuclear Explosive in Oil Shale," Lawrence Radiation Laboratory, University of California; paper prepared for an Oil Shale Meeting at Laramie, Wyoming, February 17, 1971.

[6] A. E. Lewis, "Nuclear In Situ Recovery of Oil from Oil Shale," Report UCRL-51453, Lawrence Livermore Laboratory, University of California, Livermore, California, September 14, 1973.

Fig. 9.12-5 Conceptual design of an operating field installation for in situ recovery of shale oil; reproduced from J. S. Kain, "AEC In Situ Oil Shale Program," Report UCID-16520, Lawrence Livermore Laboratory, University of California, Livermore, California, June 1974. Photograph courtesy of Lawrence Livermore Laboratory.

Fig. 9.12-6 for a 100-kt explosion; chimney height and radial dimension of the rubblized zone, as well as extended fissure and fracture systems, are indicated. It should be noted that no actual U.S. nuclear explosions have as yet been performed in oil shale. For this reason, even the formation of a confined chimney cannot be considered to have been established. Chimneys are known to form in granite and dolomite; they are not produced in the softer and less refractory formations of which salt domes are made. Experts on nuclear explosions have emphasized the importance of preliminary experimentation at the Nevada test site of the AEC on rock formations that are similar to Western shale, before engaging in a field-development program for shale-oil exploration. At the present time, authorization for these preliminary tests has not been received and it is entirely possible that the shale-oil stimulation activities of the Plowshare Program[*] may be deferred temporarily or indefinitely for political reasons.

The radioactivity levels in the gaseous products are expected to decay rapidly with time (see Fig. 9.12-7). It is not known with certainty that the oil and gas products produced in shale after nuclear explosions will not contain long-lived radioactive materials. It is generally believed that the rubblized strata formed as the result of nuclear explosion will be structurally stable and that retorting may therefore

---

[*] The Plowshare Program is the U.S. program for peaceful applications of nuclear explosives.

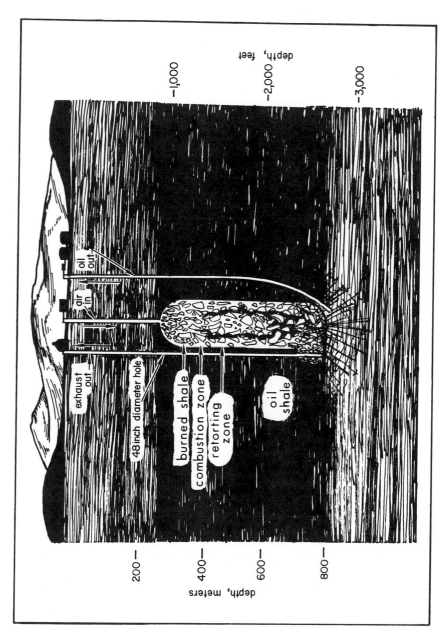

Fig. 9.12-6 Schematic diagram of in situ oil recovery from oil shale, following a 100-kt underground nuclear explosion. The chimney radius is 162 ft, the chimney height is 1,700 ft, and the chimney contains 8.4 × 10⁶ mt of rubble with 4.4 × 10⁶ bbl of oil; reproduced from Ref. [6].

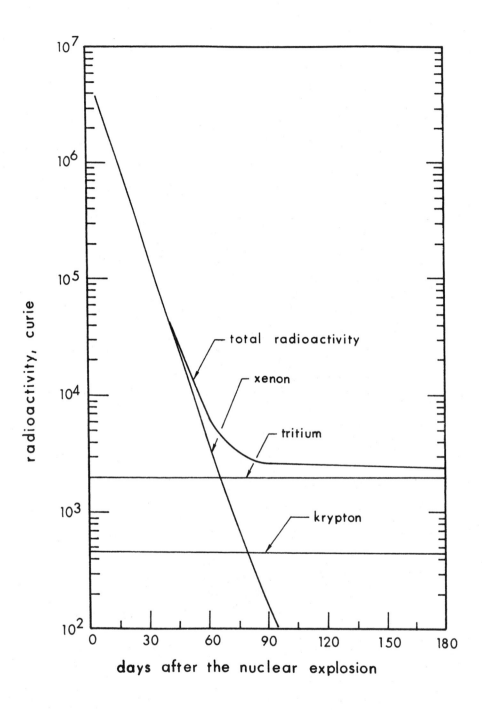

Fig. 9.12-7 The expected decay of radioactivity following a 20-kt gas-stimulation nuclear explosion; reproduced from Ref. [5].

be deferred to a convenient time.

The principal advantage of nuclear explosions is the anticipated low cost of fracturing shale. This low cost is, in large measure, the result of the fact that the costs of nuclear explosions increase very slowly with yield (see Table 9.12-1,[7] whereas expenses for chemical explosives scale roughly linearly with explosive charge and hence with yield.

The conceptual design of a commercial-scale nuclear in situ retorting plant is similar to that described in Fig. 9.12-5. A version of this type of concept is sketched in Fig. 9.12-8. Combustion retorting according to the model of Fig. 9.12-2 can hopefully be accomplished in the larger underground retorts produced by the use of nuclear fracturing procedures.

Early cost evaluations for oil recovery with nuclear fracturing indicated a 20% DCF ROR at wellhead prices of $2.00 to $3.00/bbl.[8] With 32 nuclear chimneys per year in oil shale, with thicknesses between 1,000 and 2,000 ft, production was estimated to vary from 28×10^6 bbl/y at $3.30/bbl to 121×10^6 bbl/y at $2.00/bbl.[8] Capital requirements for nuclear in situ recovery were expected to

---

[7] M. A. Lekas and H. C. Carpenter, "Fracturing Oil Shale with Nuclear Explosives for In Situ Retorting," Second Symposium on Oil Shale, Quarterly of the Colorado School of Mines 60, No. 3, 191-214 (1965).

[8] E. L. Burwell, T. E. Sterner, and H. C. Carpenter, "In Situ Retorting of Oil Shale: Results of Two Field Experiments," U.S. Bureau of Mines Report of Investigations 7783, Washington, D.C., 1973.

Table 9.12-1 Projected charges for nuclear explosives; reproduced from Ref. [7] by permission of the Colorado School of Mines. Copyright © 1965 by the Colorado School of Mines.

Yield, 10^3 tons	Approximate cost
10	$350,000
50	400,000
100	460,000
500	535,000
1,000	570,000
2,000	600,000

be much less than for aboveground retorting.[8] Problems of seismic underground motion and contamination were described[8] as "manageable". More recent economic assessments[9] are much less optimistic and have pegged the cost of shale oil for a 10% DCF ROR at $6.50 to $11.00/bbl for non-nuclear in situ recovery with an overall saving of about $2.00/bbl if nuclear fracturing is employed.

C.   Oil Recovery from the Leach Zone

The Shell Oil Company has proposed utilization of a patented procedure in which advantage is taken of the limited porosity of shale in the "leach zone". In this process, it is hoped to exploit the presence of pre-existing channels containing mineral salts by removing these through application of

[9]UCSD/NSF(RANN) "Workshop on In Situ Recovery of Shale Oil," S. S. Penner, editor, La Jolla, California, September 1974; U.S. Government Printing Office, Washington, D.C., 1975.

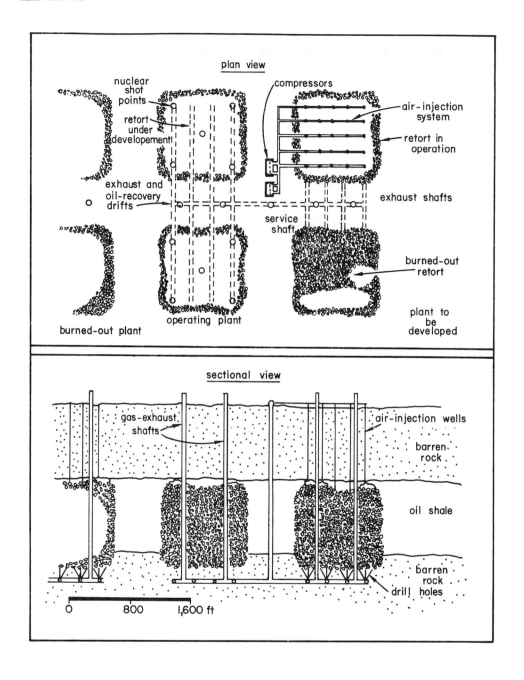

Fig. 9.12-8 Conceptual design of a commercial-scale nuclear in situ retorting plant for a 1,000-ft thick shale bed; reproduced from Ref. [7] by permission of the Colorado School of Mines. Copyright © 1965 by the Colorado School of Mines.

solvent leaching (e. g. , with an acidic water carrier).   After leaching, the shale bed may be sufficiently porous to allow direct retorting of oil from the now adequately permeable strata in this leach zone.

     D.   Other Procedures for In Situ Recovery of Shale Oil

The use of bacterial cultures for decomposing the large kerogen molecules in situ has been studied but has thus far proved to be unsuccessful.   In a practical system, the bacteria must not only decompose kerogen into smaller, easily recoverable fragments, but must also advance through the deposits at a sufficiently fast rate to make economical oil recovery possible.

The utilization of such techniques as ultrasonic or microwave heating for in situ oil recovery has not been shown to lead economically to products with higher energy content than is required for the input sources.

9.13 Mixed-Mining-and-In-Situ Recovery Procedures

At the present time, the best developed in situ recovery procedures are mixed-mining-and-in-situ recovery techniques.   The mined shale is used in a process such as TOSCO II for aboveground oil recovery.

An active development for oil recovery from oil shale by workers at the Garrett Research and Development Company involves the creation of void space in shale by conventional room-and-pillar mining, followed by fracturing of controlled volumes of adjacent shale deposits.[1] Successful prototype operation has been achieved for void volumes between 25 and 30%, although it has been claimed that a void volume as small as 15% may be sufficient. Neither cost estimates nor detailed environmental-impact assessments have been presented.[1] Among the important unanswered questions are the following:

a. Is simultaneous recovery (by combustion techniques) possible in fractured columns while mining is carried out in adjacent chambers?

b. What is the minimum void space for successful operation?

c. What is the impact of the porous, fractured columns on ground water contamination?

Application of mixed-mining-and-in-situ fracturing techniques is limited to rock strata where deep underground tunnels can be dug by conventional procedures. A detailed analysis of a mixed-mining-and-in-situ recovery process has been prepared by Snyder, Timmins and Johnson of the Mobil Oil Company.[2] Their proposed operational layout is shown in Fig. 9.13-1. Oil recovery of the underground material is to be achieved by in situ combustion. The cor-

---

[1]R. D. Ridley, "In Situ Processing of Oil Shale," Proceedings of the 7th Oil Shale Symposium, Quarterly of the Colorado School of Mines 69, No. 2, 21-24 (1974).

[2]Ref. [9] in Section 9.12.

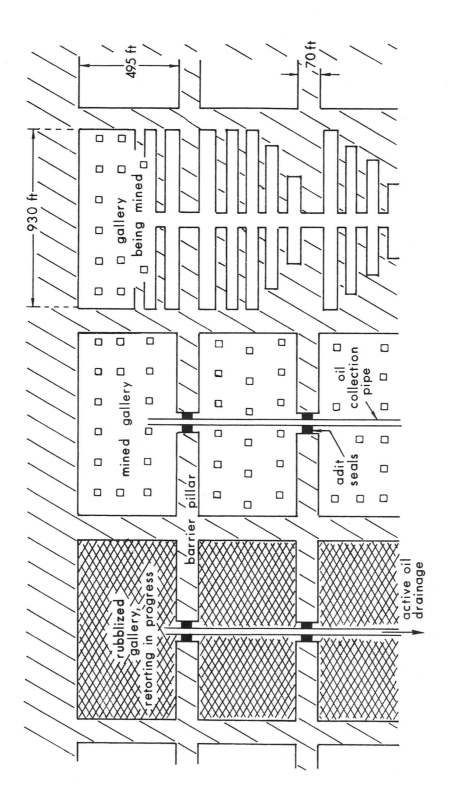

Fig. 9.13-1 Mine layout for in situ retorting of shale oil; reproduced from a paper by P. W. Snyder, Jr., T. H. Timmins, and W. F. Johnson in Ref. [2]. An adit is a nearly horizontal passage from the surface in a mine.

responding underground unit processes are shown in Fig.
9.13-2. Snyder et al[2] have presented a combustion and
economic analysis which led these authors to the conclusion
that oil should be recoverable at a cost of $10 to $12/bbl at
a 10% DCF ROR.

9.14   Net Energy in Shale-Oil Production[1]

The importance of obtaining a greater energy value
in product output than is required for product recovery in
equivalent energy sources has been emphasized in the popular literature,[2] where the term "net energy" has been used.
In particular, H. T. Odum has been quoted[2] as stating that
shale-oil recovery does not meet the essential requirement
of producing a "positive energy balance"; unnamed investigators at the Texaco Corporation were also quoted as con-
tending that shale-oil recovery barely produced as many Btus
as were consumed, a statement which was promptly denied
by Company spokesmen.[2] Unfortunately, the required complex analyses to verify statements published in the popular
press are not generally available for scrutiny.

---

[1] The material contained in this Section is based, in large
part, on a discussion of Net Energy in Shale-Oil Production held at the UCSD Energy Center, La Jolla, California,
on January 21, 1975. A conference report was prepared
by one of us (S.S.P.) and contains additional papers fur-
nished by participants at the Workshop.

[2] "The New Math for Figuring Energy Costs," Business
Week, pp. 88-89, June 8, 1974.

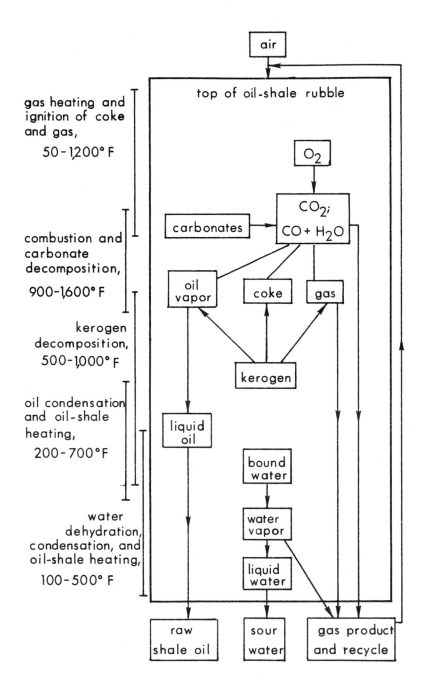

Fig. 9.13-2 Schematic diagram showing important process
changes and locations in the retort during in situ
recovery of shale oil; reproduced from a paper
by P. W. Snyder, Jr., T. A. Timmins, and
W. F. Johnson in Ref. [2].

It appears <u>a priori</u> likely that a free economy will be characterized by the simultaneous occurrence of low product prices and large net energies. Gross distortions will occur in a partially controlled economy. Thus, it is possible, at the present time, to earn money by engaging in the following energy-wasteful "energy-recovery scheme": secondary petroleum recovery using primary yields of oil or natural gas, at artificially low prices, as energy sources for the production of fuels with higher allowed product prices. We shall not be concerned with net energy evaluations under distorted conditions of this type.

A.   Definitions of Net Energy (Ratios)

Depending on the application involved, there are at least three different classes of definitions for "net energy ratios" or, more simply, "net energy" that may profitably be used. Furthermore, the detailed numbers entering into the definitions have such latitude that the resulting range of values for the net energy may lie anywhere between zero and infinity. We shall now define three net energy ratios, namely, the net energies R_1, R_2, and R_3, and shall then comment briefly on the context in which the numerical values may be advantageously employed as a guide in oil-shale development.

C. E. Clark, Jr., and D. C. Varisco of ARCO[3] have examined a hypothetical prototype plant producing

_____

[3]Contributions to Ref. [1].

10^5 bbl/sd of refined shale oil. The energy flows for this plant (in 10^9 Btu/sd) are shown in Figs. 9.14-1 and 9.14-2 with "external consumption" and "total consumption boundaries", respectively.

   i. Definitions of R_1

The flow chart with the external consumption boundary (see Fig. 9.14-1) is supposed to indicate a process absorbing only energies from external sources and not from the shale-oil recovery process itself. For this shale-oil recovery scheme, it is convenient to define the net energy

$$R_1 = \frac{\text{total energy out (as oil, coke, other fuel)}}{\text{external energy in (as fossil fuel energy required to produce electrical energy and as fossil fuel directly)}} . \qquad (9.14-1)$$

The ratio R_1 is evidently a useful parameter when the normal resource value prior to energy recovery is considered to be zero. In this case, the only operative consideration is the extent to which resource processing provides increased energy "externally". In order to reduce energies to substantially equivalent form, it is customary to convert the required electrical energy into equivalent fuel (thermal) energy by dividing the electrical energy by about 0.33, which represents the approximate value of the fraction of fossil-fuel energy that is converted to electricity in a conventional generating station. It should be noted that, in the definition given for R_1, internal energy consumption (as represented by the

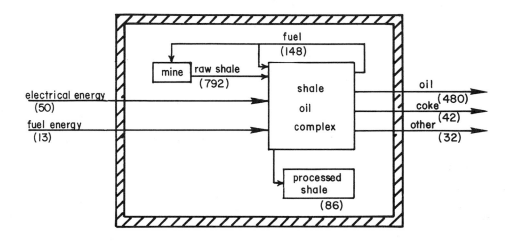

Fig. 9.14-1 ARCO's hypothetical 10^5 bbl/sd shale-oil plant
with an "external consumption boundary", show-
ing energy flows in 10^9 Btu/sd; reproduced from
a report by C. E. Clark, Jr., and D. C. Varisco
of ARCO.

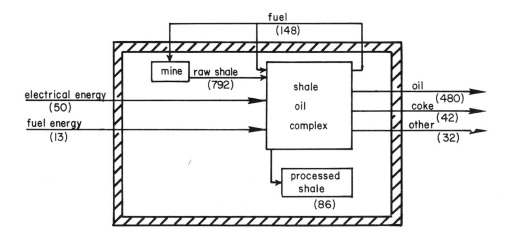

Fig. 9.14-2 ARCO's hypothetical 10^5 bbl/sd shale-oil plant
with a "total consumption boundary", showing
energy flows in 10^9 Btu/sd; reproduced from
a report by C. E. Clark, Jr., and D. C. Varisco
of ARCO.

fuel energy flow of 148×10^9 Btu/sd) is not explicitly considered in the defining relation although the magnitude of this flow clearly affects the net outflow of energy. We note that R_1 can, in principle, be made arbitrarily large by using product fuel energy within the process enclosure to produce all of the electrical- and fuel-energy requirements. Needless to say, this scheme (which yields $R_1 \to \infty$) is not generally economically advantageous. The extent to which energy requirements are profitably generated internally is both site-specific and company-specific. Thus, there is a set of values R_1 subject to such constraints as location of the site, availability of electrical energy at advantageous prices, preferred distribution systems for the operating company, etc. These factors will determine the preferred value (on economic grounds) of the net energy ratio $R_{1,i,j}$ for the ith industrial concern engaged in shale-oil recovery at the jth site. Thus, for the ith company, the development of its jth site will be heavily influenced by the applicable value of $R_{1,i,j}$ and, in a free market, the larger $R_{1,i,j}$ is, the lower and more competitive will the final product cost be for the ith concern operating at its jth site. Society at large will generally support this methodology for determining site-development strategy provided the decision has been made that the particular program for resource recovery is in the public interest.

   ii.   Definitions of R_2
   The definition of R_2[3] follows from the diagram with total consumption boundary shown in Fig. 9.14-2, viz.

$$R_2 = \frac{\text{total energy out (as oil, coke, other fuel)}}{\substack{\text{external energy in + fuel-energy derived} \\ \text{from shale oil used in processing}}} .$$

$$(9.14\text{-}2)$$

The preceding definition is again company- and site-specific and thus represents a set of values $R_{2,i,j}$ for the optimized recovery development performed at its jth site by the ith company.

If we regard the total available resource as a national asset and introduce the hypothesis that partial recovery of the resource is permissible, on the grounds that future technological developments will ultimately allow complete resource recovery, then the maximum value of $R_{2,i,j}$ attains a special significance in absolute terms in the sense that resource development is in the public interest for the largest possible value of $R_{2,i,j}$.

iii. Definitions of R_3

We may argue that the national interest requires complete resource development at every site and that any fuel not immediately recovered by an optimized process is effectively lost because secondary shale-oil recovery will be so costly that the unrecovered energy is effectively lost to society. The definition of R_3 is then

$$R_3 = \frac{\text{total energy out (as oil, coke, other fuel)}}{\substack{\text{external energy in + internal energy used} \\ \text{as processing fuel + internal energy not} \\ \text{recovered by the primary recovery} \\ \text{process}}} .$$

$$(9.14\text{-}3)$$

The ratios R_3 are again company- and site-specific. They
will almost always be less than unity (e. g. , because of retorting losses in _in situ_ processing or because of mining
loses in room-and-pillar underground mining). The use of
definitions such as $R_{3, i, j}$ is inconsistent with procedures
previously employed in the energy industries. In view of the
example set by the possibilities of using secondary and tertiary recovery schemes in conventional petroleum exploitation, the use of a term such as R_3 does not appear to be
logically defensible.

B.   Methodologies in Evaluating $R_{1, i, j}$ and $R_{2, i, j}$

It is reasonable to include all energy charges that are
directly associated with resource development. Examples
of these energy charges are the following: costs of exploration, research and development, extraction, mining, crushing and briquetting, processing following mining, transportation of materials and products to and from the development
site, prerefining and refining, product distribution, energy
charges associated with capital investments and with maintenance and operations, complete environmental impact ame-
lioration or environmental improvements, etc. All of these
specified energy costs have been included in the few published
serious efforts on shale-oil recovery.

Some divergence of views exists about the proper
handling of energy costs associated with personal energy
charges of employees and their families, who are directly

supported by the shale-oil operations. It would appear to be reasonable to include all those costs that result from product development (e.g., transportation to and from work; incremental capital costs for building new towns, schools, hospitals, etc. in remote areas); however, the average normal energy consumption by people should not be charged to a new resource development. To do so, is substantially equivalent to the assertion that the new resource development is directly responsible for population growth.

The personal energy charges which we consider to be legitimate allowances in net energy-ratio calculations have generally not been included in the results which we shall quote. However, they appear to be relatively small and their inclusion will thus not affect the final assessment substantially.

There is considerable latitude with respect to the technological components in the evaluation of net energy ratios because large-scale processing of shale-oil research does not represent developed technologies. These technological uncertainties will be reflected in divergent assessments by different groups. Some of the numerical variations may represent legitimate differences resulting from the site- and company-specific aspects of energy charges. Others may represent errors in judgement by some or differences in opinion before a definitive assessment is possible.

C.   Some Results Obtained in the Evaluation of Net
Energy Ratios for Shale-Oil Recovery

We list in Table 9.14-1 some examples of estimates
that have been made for $R_{1,i,j}$ and $R_{2,i,j}$ and give also some
indication of our assessment of the significance of the listed
data. We note that meaningful evaluation of an energy ratio
requires intimate familiarity with all aspects of the technological development.

Reference to the data listed in Table 9.14-1 shows
that the estimated values for the meaningful ratios $R_{1,i,j}$ and
$R_{2,i,j}$ are substantially larger than unity. For comparison,
we list in Table 9.14-2 applicable values for other technologies with equivalent product output. The data listed in Tables
9.14-1 and 9.14-2 indicate that shale-oil recovery meets the
requirements for economically and socially acceptable development, i.e., the applicable net energy ratios $R_{1,i,j}$ and
$R_{2,i,j}$ are substantially larger than unity.

Although a careful assessment of net energy ratios
does not exist for in situ recovery techniques, we expect
these values to be somewhat larger than those given for room-
and-pillar mining and aboveground retorting. Mining and
retorting capital charges and energy costs should be lower
for in situ processing than for the technologies used in de-
riving the data listed in Table 9.14-1.

Table 9.14-1 Some examples of net energy-ratio calculations for shale-oil recovery in plants processing 10^5 bbl/sd. All entries refer to recovery by room-and-pillar mining and aboveground retorting.

Parameter	Numerical value	Remarks
$R_{1,i,j}$	8.79[a]	Numerical estimates are based on ARCO experience in small-scale prototype studies.
	2.07[b]	This evaluation is based on data inputs from many sources. Research and exploration costs have been grossly overestimated.
	4.50[c]	Presumably based on operating experience in prototype experiments.
$R_{2,i,j}$	2.63[d]	Numerical estimates are based on ARCO experience in small-scale, prototype studies.
	4.30[c]	Presumably based on operating experience in prototype experiments.
$R_{3,i,j}$	0.58[b]	This evaluation is based on data from many sources. Research and exploration costs have been grossly overestimated.

[a]Calculated from the data in Fig. 9.14-1.

[b]Calculated from data given in an interim report prepared by the Energy Research and Planning Office, Office of the Governor, State of Oregon, Salem, Oregon 97310, July 26, 1974.

[c]Based on data analysis by M. Prats at the Workshop described in Ref. [1].

[d]Calculated from the data in Fig. 9.14-2.

Table 9.14-2 Comparisons by Clark and Varisco of values
for $R_{1,i,j}$ and $R_{2,i,j}$ in different fossil-fuel
recovery processing; reproduced from Ref. [3].
The assumed thermal efficiency at the refinery
is 89%.

Refined products from the listed resources	$R_{1,i,j}$	$R_{2,i,j}$
stripper well, upper limit	1.9	1.7
offshore well, upper limit	14.9	7.4
shale-oil recovery	8.8	2.6

9-A Appendix - <u>The Discounted Cash Flow (DCF) Method for</u>
<u>Estimating Rate of Return (ROR) on an Invest-</u>
<u>ment</u>

In the text, we refer repeatedly to the percentage of discounted-cash-flow rate-of-return, or the DCF ROR, associated with a venture in the energy industries. This term is briefly defined below, after introduction of the notion of present value (PV).

An investment I earning an annual interest i (expressed as a fraction) increases in value to $I(1 + i)$ after one year and to $I(1 + i)^N$ after N years. If an amount A is to be received (positive values of A) or invested (negative values of A) in N years and the interest remains constant, the present value of A is then

$$PV = A/(1 + i)^N \qquad (9A\text{-}1)$$

because the amount $A/(1 + i)^N$ invested now will reach a value of A after N years if the annual interest remains constant at i.

If a contractual agreement requires payment of an amount (or net cash flow) equal to A_t in t years from the present (with t = 0, 1, 2, ..., T), then the present value of the contract is

$$PV = \sum_{t=0}^{T} A_t/(1 + i)^t \qquad (9A\text{-}2)$$

for a constant interest i.   Similarly, if the net cash flow is a continuous function of time, A(t), then the present value of the contract is

$$PV = \int_{t=0}^{T} [A(t)/\exp(it)]dt. \qquad (9A\text{-}3)$$

The DCF ROR, or rate-of-return of a discounted-cash-flow, is that particular value of the interest rate i = r which discounts a cash flow to a present value of zero.   Thus, for a net cash flow equal to A_t in t years from the present (with t = 0, 1, 2, ..., T), the DCF ROR, r, is determined by the relation

$$\sum_{t=0}^{T} A_t/(1 + r)^t = 0 . \qquad (9A\text{-}4)$$

The DCF ROR is a widely used measure of profitability for investment in the petroleum industry.   It is well defined for typical ventures with initially negative and subsequently positive net cash flows.   Ventures yielding DCF RORs of 0.08 to 0.20, or 8 to 20% DCF ROR, generally cover the ranges of returns expected from investments in the energy industries. The larger the DCF ROR, the more rapidly is the return of initial investment achieved and the more rapidly profitability is assured.   The physical meaning of the DCF ROR will be apparent by reference to Fig. 9A.1.

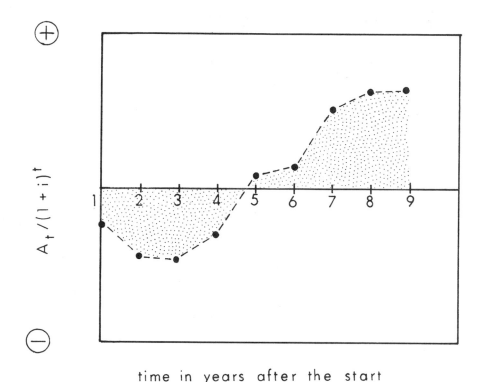

time in years after the start

Fig. 9A.1 Schematic diagram showing the discrete terms
$A_t/(1 + i)^t$ as a function of t for a typical venture.
During the construction phase of the venture,
funds are invested and the terms $A_t/(1 + i)^t$ are
negative; this situation applies in the hypothetical
example plotted for t = 1, 2, 3, and 4 years. Thereafter, a positive investment return accrues until,
at t = 9 y, the total present value of the investments (made for t = 1, 2, 3, 4 y) equals the total
present value of the returns (for t = 5, 6, 7, 8, and
9 y). For T = t = 9 years, the corresponding sum
in Eq. (9A-4) vanishes and the associated value of
i = r is the DCF ROR. The shaded areas under
the hypothetical continuous curves have also been
made equal. The time T is then equal to the pay-
back period.

9-B Appendix - <u>Dependence of Costs
on Time and Production Rate</u>[1]

The costs (C) of products and raw materials generally depend on time and production rate according to a relation of the form

$$C = f(t) \, S^b,$$ (9B-1)

where f(t) is a decreasing function of time which reflects the
development of improved technology in production while S is
the scale or total manufacture of a product.   The parameter
b ≤ 1 measures the economies of scale per unit of product.
It follows from Eq. (9B-1) that the cost ratio (R) per unit of
product when 10S is manufactured to that when S is manufactured is

$$R = \frac{f(t)(10S)^b/10S}{f(t)(S)^b/S} = 10^{b-1}$$ (9B-2)

for a constant value of f(t).   We list in Table 9B-1 the values
of R for different values of b that correspond to scale-up in
manufacturing of a factor 10.   We note from Table 9B-1 that
the unit cost on ten-fold scale-up is reduced by about 21%
for b = 0.9, 50% for b = 0.7, and 68% for b = 0.5.

Representative values of b for different types of manufacture are listed in Table 9B-2.   The value of b is itself

---

[1]C. Marchetti, "Transport and Storage of Energy," IIASA
   Report RR-75-38, Schloss Laxenburg, Austria, 1975.

Table 9B-1 The ratio R and the percentage decrease in unit
product costs for a scale-up of a factor of 10
and selected values of b; calculated from Eq.
(9B-2).

b	R	Percentage cost decrease per unit of product
0.90	0.794	20.6
0.80	0.631	36.9
0.70	0.501	49.9
0.667	0.464	53.6
0.6	0.398	60.2
0.5	0.316	68.4
0.4	0.251	74.9

Table 9B-2 Selected values of b for different types of manufacturing processes; based on data of Ref. [1].

Process	b
chemical manufacture	0.67
pipeline construction	0.67
supertanker construction	0.7
nuclear power-station complex	0.5

dependent on size. For sufficiently large manufacturing
processes, b will generally approach unity and thus limit
the scale of commercial operations above which economies
can be effected.

CHAPTER 10

COAL: AVAILABILITY, PRODUCTION AND
TRANSPORTATION; COAL GASIFICATION; COAL LIQUE-
FACTION; IN SITU RECOVERY OF COAL

Coal-resource estimates have been given in Section
2.11. A recently published, authoritative evaluation of coal
availability has been prepared by the National Petroleum
Council.[1] We summarize in Sections 10.1 and 10.2 the
salient conclusions reached in this study, before proceeding
with a discussion of technological problems associated with
the conversion of coal to syngas and syncrude. In the con-
cluding Section 10.5, we consider the possibility of in situ
recovery of coal.

10.1   Coal Availability[1]

Coal production in 1970 was 5.19×10^8 tons.
In late 1973, domestic demand was expected to grow

---

[1] National Petroleum Council, U.S. Energy Outlook:
Coal Availability, 1625 K Street, N.W., Washington,
D.C., 1973.

at an annual rate between 3.5% (to 7.32×10^8 tons in 1980,
8.70×10^8 tons in 1985) and 4.0% (to 7.68×10^8 tons in
1980, 9.35×10^8 tons in 1985). Coke production and electric-power generation used 23% and 60%, respectively, of
the coal marketed in 1970; by 1985, electricity production
was expected to account for 78% of the coal consumed.
Even at the maximum growth rate in output considered
feasible in 1973, coal production was expected to use, by
1985, less than 10% of those portions of the known 1973 resources in underground deposits (105×10^9 tons) and near
the surface (45×10^9 tons), which were located in formations of the type actively mined during 1973. These combined resources of 150×10^9 tons, in turn, constitute less
than 5% of the known U.S. resources (compare Section 2.11).

Surface layers of coal are strip-mined by using the
techniques of area or contour mining. Underground layers
in the U.S. have been recovered by conventional (55% of
total in 1965, 40% in 1970) and continuous (60% in 1970)
mining, both of which involve a room-and-pillar technique.
In longwall mining (a favorite European procedure, which
is currently being developed in the U.S.), production occurs
in a small, easily ventilated volume. Mine productivity
grew at a rate of 2.7% between 1965 and 1969. It then declined by 15 to 30% with enactment of the Coal Mine Health
and Safety Act of 1969. Improved mining technology is
being developed to compensate for this loss in productivity.

The average stripping ratio (defined as the ratio
of cubic yards of overburden removed per ton of coal pro-

duced) for surface mining in the West is 6:1. Ratios up to 30:1 have been mined, and considerable deposits of low-grade coal are available at ratios from 1.5:1 to 18:1. Surface strip-mining accounted for about 50% of total production in 1972.

Among the limiting factors in coal production are availability of competent manpower (engineers, workers), adequate transportation systems (railroad hopper cars, river locks, surface ships), and new technology for better producibility. Application of coal requires development of acceptable sulfur-control systems, as was discussed in Chapter 7.

Coal gasification procedures were expected (in 1972) to yield syngas (mostly methane, CH_4) at from $0.85 to $1.15 per 10^6 Btu; cost reductions of 10 to 15% were believed to be possible with production development. The 1985 utilization rate of syngas has been estimated[1] to lie between 0.54×10^{12} and 2.48×10^{12} SCF (with the larger value requiring 2.32×10^8 tons of coal, corresponding to a Btu-conversion efficiency for the raw materials, not counting required energy inputs to effect conversion, of about 38%). Coal-based gas has a Btu-value of 900 to 925/SCF, as compared with 1,025 to 1,050 Btu/SCF for natural gas.

Low-sulfur syncrude had not been made from coal commercially by 1973. On the assumption of an active and effective development program, the year 1985 production was estimated[1] to be perhaps as high as 0.68×10^6 bbl/d, corresponding to a supplementary coal requirement of

1.07×10^8 tons at an overall Btu-conversion efficiency of about 53%. Initial costs were expected to lie between \$6 and \$7/bbl, with ultimate production at \$4.50 to \$5.50/bbl.[1]

The combined requirements of coal for manufacture of syngas and syncrude are thus seen to be as high as 3.39×10^8 tons, corresponding to about 37% of total 1985 domestic demand, if the annual growth rate for coal demand is as high as 4.0% between 1972 and 1985.

Coal exports have traditionally contributed about 12% to the U.S. energy demand and to U.S. production. The export of U.S. metallurgical (coking) coal of 71×10^6 tons in 1970 contributed nearly $\$1 \times 10^9$ to the foreign-trade balance. The estimated 1985 export is 138×10^6 tons ($\sim$ 16% of the lower projected U.S. demand for this time period).

The estimates of coal demand depend on projections of manufacturing growth, especially in the steel industry, and also on growth in demand of electricity-generation by coal (and, therefore, on the development of nuclear reactors and their average operating characteristics).

10.2 Coal Resources, Production, Costs, and Transportation[1]

We summarize in this Section 10.2 data that will serve to amplify some of the resource estimates given in Section 2.11.

---

[1] Ref. [1] of Section 10.1.

A. Coal Resources

Averitt's[2] 1967 estimate of U.S. coal resources of 3.21×10^{12} tons is distributed as shown in Table 10.2-1.

Table 10.2-1 Averitt's 1967 estimate of U.S. coal resources (in 10^{12} tons); reproduced from Ref. [2].

Resource description	Quantity, 10^{12} tons
mapped and explored with 0 to 3,000 ft overburden	1.56
probable additional resources in unmapped and unexplored areas with 0 to 3,000 ft depth	1.31
coal in layers 3,000 to 6,000 ft deep	0.34
total	3.21

Coal tonnage located in beds more than 28 inches thick but located under overburden less than 1,000 ft deep is listed in Table 10.2-2. These entries correspond to the second bar graph of Fig. 10.2-1.

Further details concerning the distribution of over-burden are shown in Fig. 10.2-1 for 1.56×10^{12} tons of coal at depths not exceeding 3,000 ft. The designations (a) measured, (b) indicated, and (c) inferred in Fig. 10.2-1 refer, respectively, to (a) coal tonnage computed from phys-ical dimensions (as shown [1] in "outcrops, trenches, mine workings, and drill holes"), (b) coal tonnage computed

[2] P. Averitt, Coal Resources of the United States, U.S. Geological Survey Bulletin 1275, Washington, D.C., 1967.

Table 10.2-2 Coal resources in 10^6 tons in layers more
            than 28 in. thick and less than 1,000 ft deep;
            reproduced from Ref. [2].

Coal grade	Quantity, 10^6 tons
bituminous coal	261,510
subbituminous coal and lignite	119,861
anthracite	12,735
total	394,106

partly from direct measurements and partly from reasonable
extrapolations of visible data, and (c) coal tonnage based on
the nature of geological formations for which only a few
measurements are available.

Low-sulfur coal is in relatively limited supply in the
U.S. Using a sample of 1.5762×10^9 tons, only 46% was
found to have a sulfur content less than 0.7% by weight, 19%
of the total had a sulfur content between 0.7 and 1.0%, 20%
of the coal contained more than 3.0% sulfur. [1] The use of
U.S. coal for any purpose generally requires installation of
emission-control devices for removal of sulfur dioxide.

B. Coal Production

The history of U.S. coal production from 1935 to
1970 is shown in Fig. 10.2-2. We note rapid growth in output from 1938 to 1944, reasonably constant production from
1952 to 1962, and a renewed rise in output since 1962, which
is primarily attributable to increased surface mining.

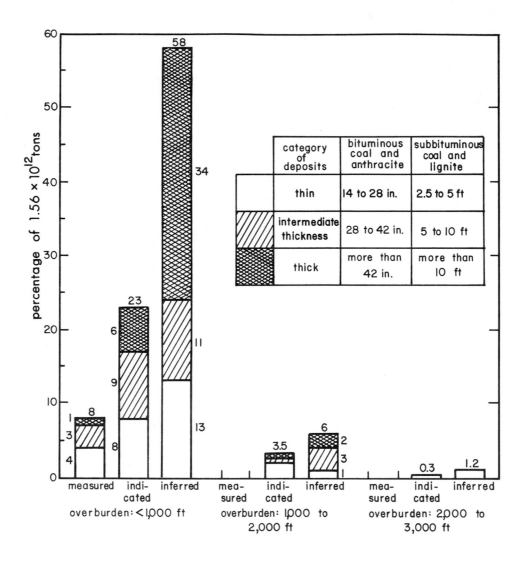

Fig. 10.2-1 Overburden for 1.56×10^{12} tons of mapped and explored coal resources in the U.S. The numbers adjacent to the vertical bars indicate the approximate percentage of coal contained in the specified deposit category. The coal resources that have been either measured or indicated in shallow or moderately thick deposits with less than 1,000 ft of overburden total 3.94×10^{11} tons. Reproduced from Ref. [2].

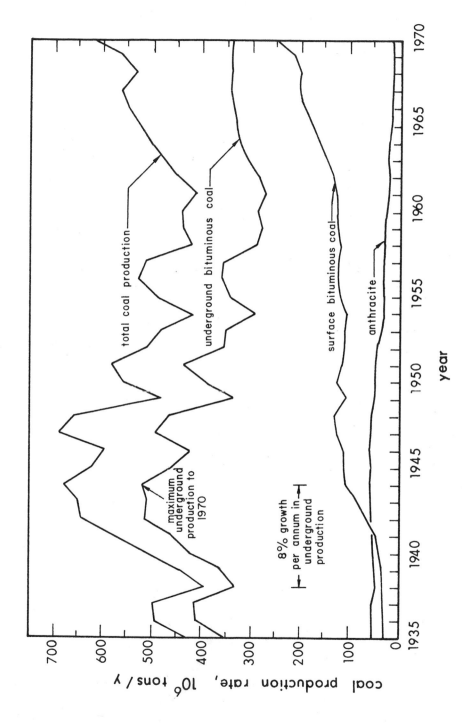

Fig. 10.2-2 U.S. production of bituminous coal (including lignite) and anthracite for the period 1935 to 1970; reproduced from Ref. [1].

C.   The Costs of Coal and Required Investments for
      Increased Production

From 1947 to 1969, the percentage of the total U.S.
work force engaged in coal production (see Fig. 10.2-3)
declined from about 0.7 to 0.15%. More recently, there
has been a slight rise in employment. While the cost of
coal was relatively constant from 1950 to 1969, a considerable cost rise has occurred in recent years and is projected
to accelerate to 1975, when it will presumably be followed
by reduced cost increases to 1985 for both underground
(see Fig. 10.2-4) and surface mining. Underground-mining
costs exceed surface-mining costs by 30 to 50%.

A summary of required investment per ton per year
of production is given in Table 10.2-3 for both underground
and surface mining.[1] It is apparent (see Table 10.2-3)
that the required total capital investment over the life of
the mine for underground mining is 1.8 to 1.9 times that
involved for surface mining. Using the per ton capital-in-
vestment estimates of Table 10.2-3, and previously defined
future coal requirements for various growth rates, we may
determine [1] the total required investment for coal production in 1985 (see Table 10.2-4). Depending on the
assumed growth rate, anticipated investment costs are seen
to lie between 9.83×10^9 (3% growth) and 14.76×10^9
(5% growth). As the result of recent rapid cost escalations,
the capital requirements shown in Tables 10.2-3 and 10.2-4
now appear to be far too low.

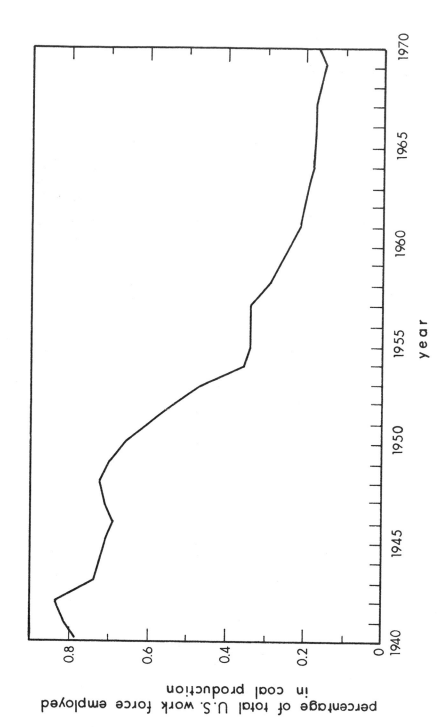

Fig. 10.2-3 Coal employees as a percentage of the total U.S. work force. The data were derived by dividing the number of bituminous coal employees by the U.S. civilian work force. Reproduced from Ref. [1].

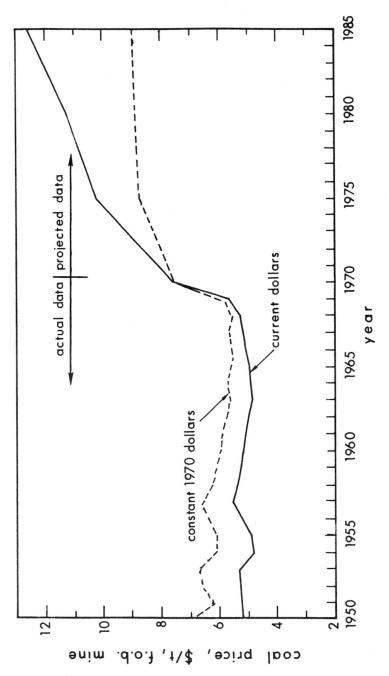

Fig. 10.2-4 Average value of bituminous coal from underground mining in current and in 1970 dollars for a 10% rate of return and a 3% growth rate. Current dollar amounts assume an average annual increase in the wholesale price index of approximately 2.5%. In the post-1970 years, costs in the coal industry have been rising more rapidly than the wholesale price index, which has also been rising much more rapidly than 2.5%/y. Reproduced from Ref. [1].

Table 10.2-3 Estimated capital investment per ton per year
of coal production, in 1970 dollars, for a
30-year mine life; reproduced from Ref. [1].

	Operating year			
	1970	1975	1980	1985
underground mines				
original capital investment	7.15	8.46	9.20	9.84
total capital investment over the life of the mine*	19.66	23.17	25.03	26.64
surface mines				
original capital investment	6.39	7.33	8.07	8.78
total capital investment over the life of the mine*	10.59	12.15	13.79	14.44

*Less salvage value of the mine.

D. Transportation of Coal

Coal transportation contributed about 25% of the total freight carried by the railroads in recent years, thereby accounting for about 11 to 12% of the total freight revenue ($\sim\$1.77 \times 10^9$ in 1969). The aggregate carrying capacity in 1969 was 27.95×10^6 tons in 388,609 cars, with an average capacity of 71.9 tons per car. The total amount of coal moved through rivers and canals was 156×10^6 tons in 1968; this type of shipment is expected to grow to 205 to 225×10^6 tons by 1980.

Water-transport costs ranged from 2.5 to 3 mills per ton-mile. Rail-revenue costs of the pit-head coal value declined from 122% in 1928 to 62% in 1969 when the f.o.b. mine

Table 10.2-4 Total capital requirements for coal mining to
1985, in 10^6; based on data in Ref. [1].

Year	McGraw-Hill capital spending survey*	Case I (5% growth)	Case IV (3% growth)
1963	124		
1965	153		
1967	325		
1969	382		
1971	457	595	459
1973	588	687	511
1975	525	776	554
1980		1,037	670
1985		1,371	807
total for the period 1970-1985		14,762	9,831

*McGraw-Hill Economics Department, "Capital Spending
Survey," Spring and Fall surveys (1964 through 1972);
figures for 1963 through 1971 are in actual dollars; figures for 1973 through 1975 are estimated; the Case I and
Case IV figures are in constant 1970 dollars.

coal cost per ton was $4.99 while the average rail freight-
revenue charge was $3.11.

With manageable growth in rail- and ship-handling
capability, transportation and distribution of coal is not expected to become a limiting factor impeding growth of coal
application.

E. Coal-Slurry Pipelines[1]

A patent was granted in 1891 for transporting coal

slurried with water through a pipe. An 8-inch line of this
type became operational in London in 1914. Today, coal-
slurry pipelines carry finely ground coal in water (about
equal amounts of coal and water by weight) from the Western
coal fields to utility stations. This underground system requires auxiliary pumping stations at intervals of 60 to 80
miles.

The Black Mesa Coal-Slurry Pipeline, owned by the
Southern Pacific Railroad, is a 273-mile system capable of
transporting over 5.5×10^6 tons of coal per year through an
18-inch pipeline. The coal transported annually by this pipeline could be handled in about 160 rail cars of coal per day.
The Black Mesa Pipeline supplies all of the energy requirements for two 750-Mw_e generating stations.

Construction of 1,000-mile pipelines with capacities
up to 30×10^6 tons of coal per year is considered feasible
with current technology. These pipelines could supply coal
markets as far east as Chicago with western coal. However,
one key factor to consider prior to the construction of a network of coal-slurry pipelines is water availability. Water
is important for both the slurry preparation and the restora-
tion of strip-mined lands. A special panel of the National
Academy of Sciences[3] has concluded that water availability
may be the limiting factor in the development of the Western
coal fields.

---

[3]"NAS: Water Scarcity May Limit Use of Western Coal, "
    Science 181, 525 (1973).

The energy throughput of coal-slurry pipelines could be increased by using oil rather than water for slurry preparation. However, coal and oil are usually not found in the same region and the cost of transporting the oil to the coal field makes this process economically unattractive. In addition, it is more difficult to utilize an oil-coal slurry than a water-coal slurry.

The transportation cost of coal by slurry pipeline is a function of the throughput, distance, physical characteristics of the coal, conditions of the terrain, and the annual capital charges of the pipeline. The two most important variables are annual throughput and distance transported. Figure 10.2-5 shows the annual transportation costs, including slurry preparation costs, of coal-slurry pipelines as a function of these two variables in 1972.

F.   Development of Improved Mining Procedures

In view of the increasing needs for coal recovery, some effort is being expended on the development of improved mining procedures. Among interesting current approaches are attempts at chemical comminution of coal.[4, 5] In this process, concentric cylinders are drilled into the coal seams. Then comminuting agents such as liquid ammonia,

---

[4] "Chemical Comminution Shows Promise for Coal," Chemical and Engineering News 52, 16-17, September 2, 1974.

[5] R. G. Aldrich, D. V. Keller and R. G. Sawyer, U.S. Patent 3,815,826, 1973.

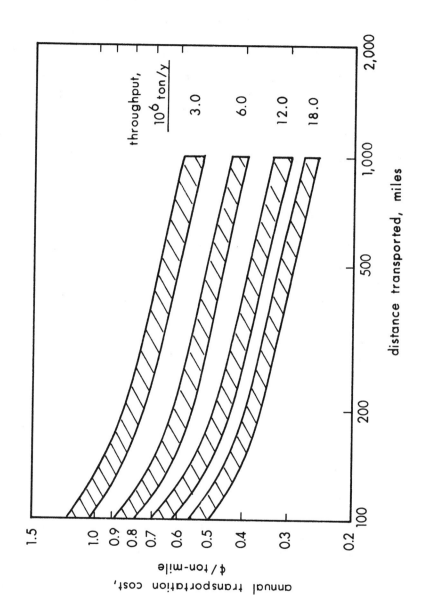

Fig. 10.2-5 Coal-slurry pipeline transportation costs. The indicated costs include charges for slurry preparation. Reproduced from Ref. [1] and based on 1972 data.

methanol, sodium hydroxide solutions, ethylamine, etc. are forced into the drilled holes. The comminuting agents enter into the naturally-occurring fault system of the coal bed and dissolve minerals within these faults, thereby causing break-up of the coal. Coal disintegration was found to occur very rapidly and required about 100 lb of comminuting agent per ton of coal; however, about 99% of the comminuting agent was recoverable. Anthracite was found to fracture more slowly than bituminous coal, presumably because of the presence of a less extensive internal faulting system. It is hoped that comminution will lead to a decrease in direct mining costs or else will facilitate in situ processing to syngas or syncrude.

10.3 Coal Gasification

A. Overall Description of Gasification Processes

A number of prototype-tested coal-gasification processes is available. A composite diagram showing the essential features that are common to all of these reaction schemes is given in Fig. 10.3-1.[1]

In the first sequence of reactions, bituminous coal or lignite is fed into a heated vessel with steam. The reac-

---

[1] J. P. Henry, Jr., and P. M. Louks, "An Economic Comparison of Processes for Producing Pipeline Gas (Methane) from Coal," Stanford Research Institute (SRI) report presented at the September 1970 meeting of the American Chemical Society in Chicago, Illinois.

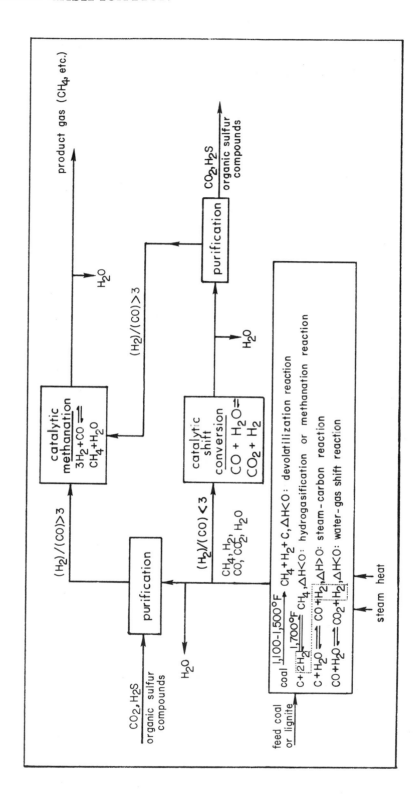

Fig. 10.3-1 General process scheme for producing methane from coal; reproduced with modifications from Ref. [1].

tion vessel is not isothermal, but rather contains sequential sections in which the temperature rises from about $1,000^\circ F$ to as high as $2,000^\circ F$.

The coal is devolatilized in the lowest-temperature section according to the reaction

$$coal \xrightarrow{\quad 1,100 - 1,500^\circ F \quad} CH_4 + C + H_2. \qquad (10.3-1)$$

This devolatilization is exothermic, i.e., heat is evolved and, using conventional thermochemical nomenclature, the reaction-enthalpy change ΔH is negative ($\Delta H < 0$). Depending on coal composition, the feed serves as a highly variable source of combustible gases and energy during devolatilization.

The carbon reacts with H_2 at somewhat higher temperatures according to the exothermic hydrogasification (sometimes also called methanation) process

$$C + 2H_2 \rightleftharpoons CH_4, \quad \Delta H < 0. \qquad (10.3-2)$$

Subsequently or concurrently, carbon and steam undergo the endothermic steam-carbon reaction

$$C + H_2O \rightleftharpoons CO + H_2, \quad \Delta H > 0. \qquad (10.3-3)$$

The relative concentrations of CO, H_2O, CO_2, and H_2 are nearly maintained in chemical equilibrium by the very rapid <u>water-gas shift reaction</u>

$$CO + H_2O \rightleftarrows CO_2 + H_2. \qquad\qquad (10.3-4)$$

A mixture of CH_4, H_2, H_2O, CO, and CO_2 leaves the reactor after occurrence of the devolatilization, hydro-gasification, steam-carbon, and water-gas shift reactions. Depending on the magnitude of the H_2/CO mole ratio, the gas mixture is then subjected to <u>catalytic shift-conversion</u> [for* $(H_2)/(CO) < 3$] or, after purification, to catalytic methanation [for $(H_2) / (CO) > 3$]. Catalytic shift-conversion increases the H_2-concentration and involves the chemical change

$$CO + H_2O \rightleftarrows CO_2 + H_2, \qquad\qquad (10.3-5)$$

while catalytic methanation increases the methane concentration as the result of the process

$$3H_2 + CO \rightleftarrows CH_4 + H_2O. \qquad\qquad (10.3-6)$$

---

*A chemical symbol enclosed by parentheses denotes molar concentrations.

Catalytic methanation cannot be accomplished effectively in the presence of sulfur compounds or of large water concentrations. For this reason, water is first removed from the gas mixture by condensation and then H_2S, organic sulfur compounds, any other sulfur-containing substances, as well as most of the CO_2, are abstracted during a suitable purification step.

Catalytic shift-conversion increases the $(H_2)/(CO)$ ratio to values larger than three. Therefore, after catalytic shift-conversion, gas purification (involving water condensation, removal of H_2S and other sulfur-containing compounds, abstraction of most of the CO_2) may be implemented, as is done immediately for the richer $(H_2)/(CO)$ ratios before further processing by catalytic methanation (see Fig. 10.3-1).

The reaction products formed after catalytic methanation are treated by water removal and then constitute methane-rich product gas of pipeline quality.

B.   Temperature- and Pressure-Control of Reaction
     Vessels in Coal Gasification

We first note that the specified reaction steps in Eqs. (10.3-2) to (10.3-6) involve the following six chemical species: C, H_2, CH_4, H_2O, CO, CO_2. Inclusion of the change

$$C + (1/2)O_2 \rightleftarrows CO \qquad\qquad (10.3-7)$$

introduces the seventh chemical species O_2. Since there are three elements (C, H, O) participating, we have three mass-conservation equations and require for a complete description of the equilibrium composition only four of the six steps specified in Eqs. (10.3-2) to (10.3-7). It is convenient to choose the hydrogasification reaction [Eq. (10.3-2)], the steam-carbon reaction [Eq. (10.3-3)], the water-gas shift reaction [Eq. (10.3-4)], and the carbon-oxidation step given in Eq. (10.3-7). These four steps contain all of the seven participating chemical species and, therefore, constitute a complete system of equations, together with the species (or mass) conservation equations, for the determination of the equilibrium gas compositions.

The sequential chemical reaction steps occurring during coal gasification are determined by the interplay of chemical rate processes, i.e., they are kinetically controlled. Nevertheless, it is useful to examine the results derived from equilibrium calculations for the specified complete system of equations in order to define desirable temperature and pressure regimes for accomplishing coal conversion. A development program then deals with implementation of requirements on the state variables to achieve the desired reactions. We list below the set of equations that

is required for determination of the equilibrium gas compositions:[2]

for $C + 2H_2 \rightleftarrows CH_4$,

(10.3-8)

$$K_{p,11} = p_{CH_4}/p^2_{H_2},$$

where p_M denotes the partial pressure of species M, carbon
has been assumed to be present as a solid substance, and
$K_{p,11}$ is listed as a function of temperature, for example,
on p. 80 of Ref. [2];

for $C + H_2O \rightleftarrows CO + H_2$,

(10.3-9)

$$K_{p,9}/K_{p,4} = p_{CO}p_{H_2}/p_{H_2O}$$

with $K_{p,4}$ and $K_{p,9}$ listed on pp. 78 and 79, respectively, of
Ref. [2];

------

[2]In the following discussion, we employ standard methodology for the determination of equilibrium gas compositions. For a detailed description of procedure, see, for
example, S. S. Penner, Thermodynamics, Chapters 6 and
12, Addison-Wesley Publishing Co., Reading, Mass.,
1968.

$$\text{for } CO + H_2O \rightleftarrows CO_2 + H_2, \qquad\qquad (10.3\text{-}10)$$

$$K_p = K_{p,10}/K_{p,4}K_{p,9} = P_{CO_2}P_{H_2}/P_{CO}P_{H_2O}$$

with $K_{p,10}$ listed on p. 79 of Ref. [2];

$$\text{for } C + (1/2)O_2 \rightleftarrows CO, \qquad\qquad (10.3\text{-}11)$$

$$K_{p,9} = P_{CO}/(P_{O_2})^{\frac{1}{2}} \; ;$$

$$2P_{H_2O} + P_{OH} + 2P_{H_2} = (RT/V)N_H, \qquad (10.3\text{-}12)$$

where R is the molar gas constant, T the temperature, V the volume of the reaction vessel, and N_H represents the total number of equivalent moles of hydrogen atoms introduced into the reaction vessel;

$$P_{H_2O} + 2P_{O_2} = (RT/V)N_O, \qquad\qquad (10.3\text{-}13)$$

where N_O is the total number of equivalent moles of oxygen atoms introduced into the reaction vessel;

$$P_{CH_4} + P_{CO} + P_{CO_2} = (RT/V) \qquad (10.3\text{-}14)$$
$$\times [N_C - N_{C(c)}] ,$$

where N_C is the total number of equivalent moles of carbon atoms introduced into the reaction vessel and $N_{C(c)}$ is the number of equivalent moles remaining in the solid (crystalline) phase. The solution of the set of relations given in Eqs. (10.3-8) to (10.3-14) is easily obtained by using appropriate numerical procedures.[2]

The equilibrium compositions are not reached in coal-gasification units because composition changes are kinetically controlled. The rate of formation of CO according to the endothermic forward step in reaction (10.3-3) becomes rapid above about $1,700^{\circ}$F. Initiation of this process requires availability of a heat source. This heat source is, in part, supplied by the exothermic coal devolatilization and, depending on the process involved, by preheating of the reactants using either electrical, nuclear, or combustion energy. Combustion energy is released by partial combustion of coal but has the undesirable side effect of decreasing the $(H_2)/(CO)$ ratio. Although steam serves as an essential source of hydrogen, its injection must be carefully controlled. The methanation reaction [Eq. (10.3-2)] proceeds incompletely at the intermediate temperatures selected for its accomplishment. If the temperatures become too high, CH_4 decomposes according to the reverse step in Eq. (10.3-2).

There are interesting fundamental aspects to coal gasification that are not understood completely and hence are not utilized optimally in the conversion scheme. For example, it is known that newly-formed carbon has a somewhat higher (positive) heat formation than aged graphite and, accordingly, freshly-formed coke is chemically more active than stored coke. The decay time for this active version of carbon is only a few seconds. In general, empirical knowledge of conversion processes is not adequately supported by basic understanding of chemical-reaction mechanisms and rates. Coal gasification may be performed in reactors using concurrent streams of coal and gas, in reactors using countercurrent flows of coal and gas, and in reactors using mixed flows and injection schemes.

Rather than attempting further summary comments on commercial designs, which actually differ markedly in detailed configuration, it is preferable to examine one of the coal-gasification systems in some detail and then comment more briefly on other developments that have been tested in pilot plants.

C.   The Hygas-Electrothermal Process

The Hygas-Electrothermal Process (see Fig. 10.3-2) has been developed by the Institute of Gas Technology (IGT).[3]

A diagram of the sequentially-arranged electro-thermal gasifier and hydrogasifier sections is shown in Fig. 10.3-3. Coal and steam are seen to be injected in countercurrent directions. Steam is preheated near the bottom of the reactor by using an independent electrical energy source.

---

[3]Office of Coal Research, Annual Report 1973-1974, U.S. Government Printing Office, Washington, D.C., 1974.

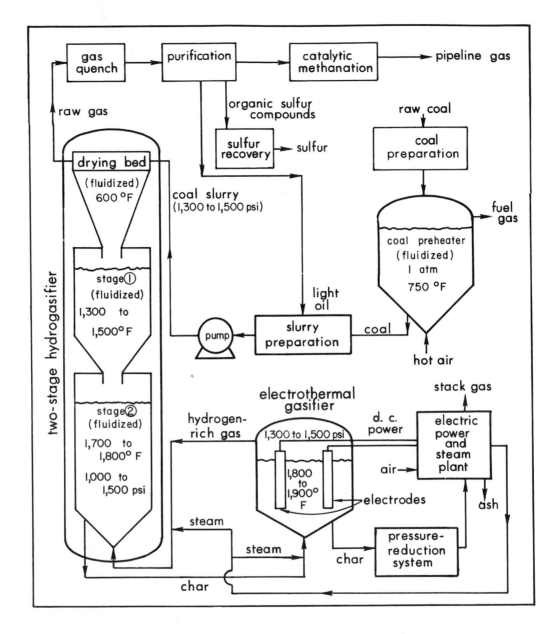

Fig. 10.3-2 Component diagram of the Institute of Gas Technology countercurrent-flow process for methane
production using the Hygas-Electrothermal System. Coal-processing sequence: caking coal is
ground to less than 1/8 in., made non-agglom-
erating by partial devolatilization with hot air
(1 atm, 750°F), mixed with light oil to make a

slurry, pumped into the hydrogasifier at 1,300 to 1,500 psi, where it is dried and fluidized at 600°F and then undergoes two successive stages of reaction: at 1,300-1,500°F, devolatilization and partial non-catalytic methanation occur with the countercurrent H_2-rich gas in stage ① while, at 1,700-1,800°F, the water-gas shift reaction, hydrogasification and the steam-carbon reaction occur with countercurrent H_2O-H_2 (stage ②). Steam is made in an electrothermal gasifier. Details concerning these processes are shown schematically in the following Figs. 10.3-3 to 10.3-6. The extent of methanation in stage ② must be sufficient to supply heat required for the endothermic steam-carbon reaction to reduce the required, costly electrical heat. The light oil used in slurry preparation evaporates in the fluidizing drying bed of the hydrogasifier and is recycled for repeated slurry preparation. The use of this unique system avoids introduction of expensive lock-hoppers employed in other gasification systems. The raw gases, with $(H_2)/(CO)$ mole ratios greater than 3, undergo catalytic methanation and, after purification (e.g., for sulfur removal in a Claus converter[*]), are used as pipeline gas. The endothermic steam-carbon reaction occurs in the electrothermal gasifier and produces a hydrogen-rich gas for introduction at the base of the hydrogasifier. The electrothermal gasifier is also maintained at a pressure of 1,000 to 1,500 psi. The residual char from this unit is mixed with air and used in a steam generator for the production of d.c. power.

---

[*]About 90% of elemental S_x is recovered in a Claus converter, where one-third of the H_2S is burned to SO_2. This effluent gas is then cooled and reacted with H_2S to form S over bauxite (Al_2O_3) catalysts. Any remaining S-compounds are incinerated to SO_2 (hopefully, less than 400 ppm remain).

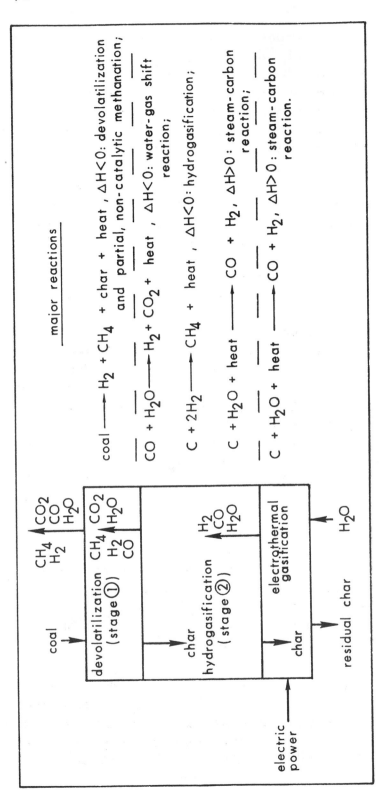

Fig. 10.3-3 Schematic diagram of the hydrogasifier and electro-thermal gasifier for the Hygas-Electrothermal System; reproduced with modifications from J. P. Henry, Jr., B. M. Louks, and S. B. Alpert, "Gasification of Bituminous Coal -- Status and Prospects," Stanford Research Institute (SRI) report presented at the Joint Power Generation Conference in Boston, Mass., September 13, 1972.

Coal is devolatilized near the top of the reactor where gas-eous products are removed, leaving the devolatilized char to react with preheated steam in the hydrogasification section. The major reactions occurring at each stage of the reaction vessel are seen to be consistent with the general discussion of reaction schemes given in Section 10.3B. Four separate temperature regimes, corresponding to the various reactor stages shown in Fig. 10.3-3, are displayed in detail in Fig. 10.3-4. The pressure is uniform throughout the system at 1,200 psia (see Fig. 10.3-4). A slurry vaporizer is seen to precede the devolatilization stage (see Fig. 10.3-4).

A detailed cost-distribution study of a representative coal gasification process was performed by Henry and Louks[4] in 1970. Their results are reproduced in Fig. 10.3-5. The principal cost items are seen to be heat (30.9% of the total), process coal (16.8%), steam supply (9.6%), catalytic methanation (6.5%), CO_2 removel (6.0%), and devola-tilization (5.7%). The sulfur credit at $5/ton may be opti-mistic for a fully-developed coal-gasification industry, unless new and large-scale sulfur uses are developed.

Final cost estimates for the product gases vary greatly for different evaluations. A reasonable range of val-ues (during 1970) fell between $0.50 and $1.25 per 10^6

---

[4] J. P. Henry, Jr., and B. M. Louks, "An Economic Com-parison of Processes for Producing Pipeline Gas (Meth-ane) from Coal," Stanford Research Institute (SRI), report presented at the September 1970 meeting of the American Chemical Society in Chicago, Illinois.

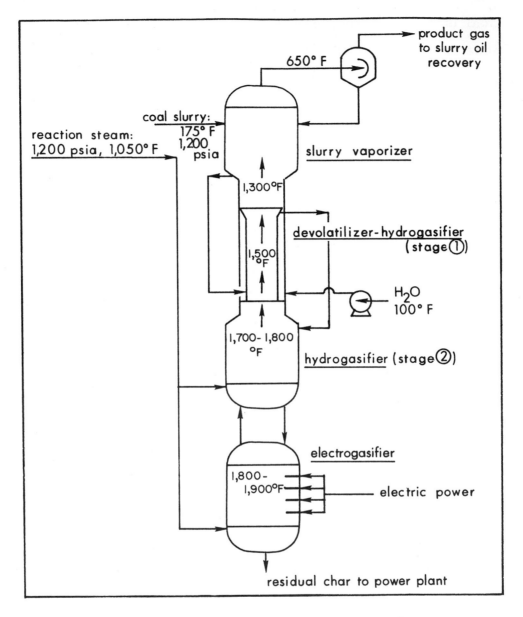

Fig. 10.3-4 The Hygas-Electrothermal gasifier showing
four operating temperature regimes; reproduced with modifications from J.P. Henry, Jr.,
B.M. Louks and S.B. Alpert, "Gasification
of Bituminous Coal--Status and Prospects,"
Stanford Research Institute (SRI), report presented at the Joint Power Generation Conference
in Boston, Mass., September 13, 1972.

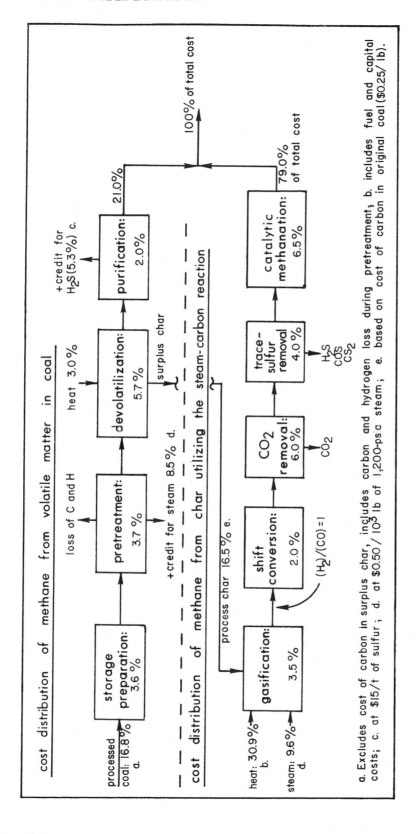

Fig. 10.3-5 Cost distribution (in percent) for producing methane from Illinois No. 6 coal. Note that the cost of producing CH_4 from devolatilized char is 79/21 of the cost of producing CH_4 by coal from devolatilization; the cost of heat for the steam-carbon reaction is 30.9% of the total cost. Reproduced with modifications from a 1970 evaluation given in Ref. [4].

Btu or per 10^3 SCF. Thus, the syngas prices ranged from as low as two to as high as six times the price paid for naturally-occurring NG sources during the early sixties. In the absence of large-scale development, it is not possible to define the most advantageous choice among competing commercial processes.

A flow diagram for a Hygas-Electrothermal reactor producing 250×10^6 SCF/sd is shown in Fig. 10.3-6.[*] This plant uses 1.6265×10^4 t/sd of coal. The overall Btu-conversion efficiency from coal to product gas is seen to be $100 \times (250 \times 10^6 \times 925)/(1.6265 \times 10^4 \times 2.53 \times 10^7)\% = 46.4\%$, not counting electrothermal energy supply, pretreatment, plant fuel, etc. At 33% conversion efficiency to electrical energy, the electrothermal source requires a total of 7.82×10^{10} Btu/d, corresponding to about 33% of the product-energy value.

D.   The Lurgi Reactor

The Lurgi Process was developed about thirty years ago. It is described in Fig. 10.3-7 with appropriate explanatory remarks. The overall gasification efficiency (measured in terms of energy availability of fuel) with this type of unit is about 95%; 1 to 2% of the unburned carbon escape with the ash and heat losses account for 3 to 4% of the available ener-

---

[*]1 sd = one standard day or one stream day = (1/350) year.

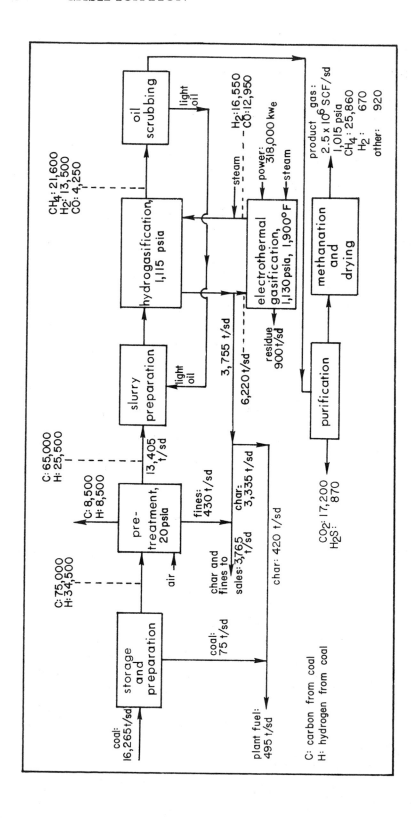

Fig. 10.3-6 Schematic diagram of the gasifier train for the Hygas-Electrothermal Process (Illinois No. 6 coal). Stream flows are given in lb-mole/h unless indicated as t/sd (= tons/standard day). Only major chemical components are shown. Reproduced with modifications from Ref. [4].

gy.   The overall Btu-conversion efficiency for gas production is about 77%.

E.   Other Coal-Gasification Reactors[5]

Among other promising schemes for coal gasification, we note the following prototype procedures: the
IGT-Hygas-Oxygen System (a process in which the electrothermal energy source of the Hygas-Electrothermal unit
is replaced by a partial-combustion heat source); the
IGT-Hygas-Iron System (in this process, the electrothermal energy source of the Hygas-Electrothermal unit is
replaced by a steam-iron reaction); the Texaco-Partial-Oxi-
dation Gasifier (this gasifier is characterized by a moving
pebble-bed heat-recovery system and sulfur removal by
a hot-carbonate scrubbing process);   Consolidated Coal Co.-
CO_2-Acceptor Process (a heat-carrier process in which
heat is supplied to the reacting coal by a circulating bed
of dolomite, MgO-CaO, that is reheated in a separate vessel by burning char with air); M. W. Kellogg Co.-Molten-
Carbonate Reactor (in this process, the coal is ground and

---

[5] For a recent progress report, see, for example,
"Further Progress in Coal Gasification, "Chemical and
Engineering News 52, 17-18, August 12, 1974. In this
discussion, special reference is made to the M. W.
Kellogg Low-Btu Process (135 to 300 Btu/SCF at an
energy cost equivalent to that of petroleum at $10/bbl
for bituminous coal costing $20/t) and to the Lurgi
Process (~950 Btu/SCF).

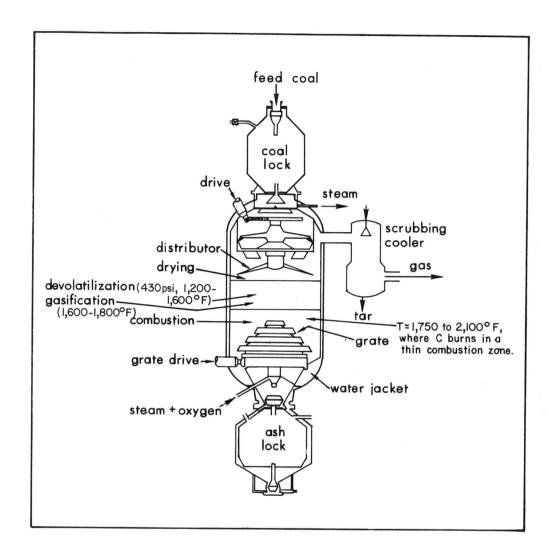

Fig. 10.3-7 The Lurgi gasifier as described by the company.
A 250×10^6 SCF/d plant requires 28 gasifiers
plus 3 standby units. This is a packed bed unit
which requires feed coal about (1/8) in. in diameter. Briquetted or pelletized coal enters
through a lock hopper. The endothermic steam-
carbon reaction above the combustion zone
maintains the temperature below the ash-fusion
point. Coal tar is formed in the devolatilization
region; this tar is quenched and removed. The
devolatilized coal is gasified with steam while

heat is supplied from the exothermic carbon combustion. About one hour of residence time is required for gasification. Exothermic hydro-gasification does not occur extensively at the low operating pressure and the required heat must, therefore, be generated by injecting O_2. The overall gasification efficiency is ~95%; about 1 to 2% of C is lost as ash; the heat losses amount to 3 to 4% of the available energy. The big unknown with application of the Lurgi process involves the use of U.S. coking coals. However, this process can clearly use non-coking Western coals. In one experiment, the feed consists of 9.8 lb of steam for 2.7 lb of air and for 1 lb of coal. A high-Btu (980 Btu/SCF) Lurgi-type gasifier gas plant, with a capacity of 2.5×10^6 SCF/d (this is about 1% of a full-scale commercial unit), went on-stream at Westfield, Scotland, during 1973. The gas cost was estimated to be $0.70 to $0.90/$10^6$ Btu. Many U.S. and European companies were co-operating in this venture. The principal purpose of these tests was verification that methanation can be carried out in a continuous operation using H_2 and CO gases generated from commercial coal, including coking U.S. coals.

---

introduced into a reactor containing molten sodium carbonate, which facilitates handling of the coal particles so that nearly any grade of coal may be used); Bituminous Coal Research Institute-Bigas System (a two-stage gasification system with coal and steam is introduced into the upper stage and, following partial gasification, the unreacted char is more completely gasified in an oxygen and steam atmosphere in the lower stage); U.S. Bureau of Mines-Synthane Process (this process is an oxygen-addition method in which gasification occurs in three stages inside the gasifier).   There are also a number of other promising experimental developments, which we shall not describe.   Table 10.3-1 shows preferred operating-chamber pressures for four of the systems mentioned.

Table 10.3-1   Representative operating-pressure levels for coal-gasification processes used in the manufacture of SNG.

Company	Process description or name	Gasification-chamber pressure, psia
Lurgi Mineralöltechnik	fixed bed, concurrent flow	~ 400
Bituminous Coal Research (BCR)	Bigas	> 1,000
Institute of Gas Technology (IGT)	Hygas	> 1,000
U.S. Bureau of Mines	Synthane	600 to > 1,000

F.   Long-Range Production Schedules

We have noted in Section 10.1 that the 1985 annual rate of production of SNG may be as large as 2.48×10^{12} SCF, corresponding to 30 plants with a capacity of 250×10^6 SCF/d at a 90% operating factor.   The corresponding investment costs for plant capacity were estimated (in 1973) as about $\$7.5 \times 10^9$ (in 1970 dollars).

A technical improvement leading to a cost saving of 1 cent per 10^3 SCF is seen to have a 1985 annual value of

24.8×10^6. This fact indicates the enormous economic importance of optimal technological accomplishment. In the absence of demonstrated superiority of a particular one of the gasification schemes on a full-scale basis, concurrent development and field implementation of four or more promising processes appear to be indicated in view of the potential cost savings on coal-gas, the enormity of projected requirements, and the magnitude of the anticipated investment costs.

An initial projection to 1985 of potential SNG production from coal is reproduced in Table 10.3-2 and includes the applicable investment capital required in both plant construction and strip mining. The data given in Table 10.3-2 do not include proper allowance for economic considerations. Another projection is shown in Table 10.3-3 for maximum buildup, with special policies to implement the buildup (Case I), rapid but practical growth rates (Cases II and III), and a minimal buildup determined by mid-1973 economic considerations (Case IV). During the post-1985 period, investments of 1.5×10^9 (in 1970 dollars) will be required to produce 6 plants per year. The initial NPC[3] appraisal for the cost of SNG (in 1970 dollars) was $0.889/10^6$ Btu with coal cost contributing $0.222/10^6$ Btu, an operating cost of $0.20/10^6$ Btu, and a capital charge of $0.467/10^6$ Btu computed at an 18% rate base.

Table 10.3-2 Initial appraisal* of potential capacity growth for SNG production from coal; reproduced from Ref. [1] of Section 10.1.

Year	Capacity added, 10^{12} SCF/y	Cumulative capacity, 10^{12} SCF/y	Investment, $\$10^6$			
			plant	strip mines†	total in year(s)	total cumulative
1975	0.08	0.08	210	40	250	250
1976	0.16	0.24	420	80	500	750
1977	0.16	0.40	420	80	500	1,250
1978	0.25	0.65	600	120	720	1,970
1979-1985	0.33	3.00	800/y	160/y	960/y	8,690

* Assumes existing technology and immediate accelerated rate of buildup, without regard for economic necessity of this development.

† Total incremental capacity (strip) in 1985: 225 to 250 $\times 10^6$ t/y using 8 to 9 $\times 10^9$ tons of identified reserves (compare Fig. 10.2-2, p. 77).

Table 10.3-3 Installed capacity in 10^{12} SCF/y (90% operating factor) of SNG plants through 1985 for Cases I to IV (see the text for definitions of these cases); reproduced from U.S. Energy Outlook: Coal Availability, National Petroleum Council, Washington, D.C., 1973.

Year	Case		
	I	II or III	IV[*]
1976	0.08	0.08	- - - -
1977	0.16	0.12	- - - -
1978	0.28	0.16	- - - -
1979	0.40	0.24	- - - -
1980	0.56	0.36	0.18
1981	0.80	0.52	- - - -
1982	1.12	0.68	- - - -
1983	1.52	0.84	- - - -
1984	2.00	1.08	- - - -
1985	2.48	1.31	0.54

[*]This case is the same shown in the Initial Appraisal. See: National Petroleum Council, U.S. Energy Outlook: An Initial Appraisal 1971-1985, Vol. II (November 1971), Table LV, p. 81. The total SNG amounted to 0.91×10^{12} SCF per year in 1985; 0.37×10^{12} SCF per year are to be produced from naphtha and 0.54×10^{12} SCF per year are to be produced from coal.

10.4 Syncrude from Coal

Economical manufacture of syncrude from coal requires more efficient production of hydrogen and improvements in existing coal-hydrogenation procedures.

The South African Coal, Oil, and Gas Corporation began operation in 1955 and has recently been producing about 3,660 bbl/d of expensive gasoline, 85 to 90 bbl/d of expensive diesel fuel, as well as some waxes, from coal at Sasol, South Africa. The SASOL production procedure involves coal gasification in a Lurgi reactor with oxygen and steam, followed by washing with CH_3OH for conventional removal of H_2S, organic sulfur compounds, and CO_2. The reformed gas is next preheated and mixed with recycle gas and powdered iron catalyst. Hydrocarbons are first condensed from the reacted mixture and subsequently distilled to yield the desired products.

Generally speaking, syncrude may be produced from coal by a variety of procedures. For example, the mixture of H_2 and CO, which is formed as the result of gasification, may be subjected to a catalyzed synthesis for hydrocarbon production (as in the SASOL process); this production method was used during the Second World War. Coal ash may be removed by treatment with a suitable hydrogen-donor solvent (e.g., tetralin) before catalytic hydrogenation at elevated pressures (200 to 1,000 psia) to yield a heavy ash and sulfur-free hydrocarbons with very large molecular weights (Pott-Broche process). Coal may also be directly hydrogenated under pressure to yield compounds with hydrogen-to-carbon ratios varying from 0.75 to 1.25 (Pott-Broche or Bergius processes). Finally, sequential pyrolysis above 800°F may be used to make gaseous products and a limited amount (<0.8 bbl/ton of coal) of liquid products.

Theoretically, useful conversion of coal to syncrude should require about 5×10^3 SCF of H_2/bbl for the removal of sulfur, oxygen, and nitrogen compounds and for the production of a hydrocarbon containing 13% by weight of hydrogen.[1] In practice, 6×10^3 to 10×10^3 SCF are required because of production of light hydrocarbons and H_2-removal by the solid residues.[1]

By the end of 1973, the following bench-tests for syncrude production were in progress, among others:

(a) A Food Machinery Corporation (FMC) pyrolysis program yielding up to 25 t/d. This process is also known as the COED (for Char Oil Energy Development) program.

(b) A Consolidated Coal Co. (CONSOL) program using solvent extraction followed by hydrogenation, with an output up to 75 bbl/d. Solvent extraction techniques are currently under active development.[2]

(c) A Universal Oil Products process in which pulverized coal is treated with a solvent and hydrogenated at high temperatures and pressures.[3] The ash is removed prior to hydrotreating the stream catalytically. Bench and pilot testing have indicated that a low-sulfur syncrude (0.15%

---

[1]Ref. [1] of Section 10.1.

[2]See, for example, "Background Information on Solvent Extraction of Coal," prepared by Hydrocarbon Research, Inc., Electric Power Research Institute, Report 123-1-0, 3412 Hillview Ave., Palo Alto, California, 1974.

[3]"UOP Set to Scale Up Oil-from-Coal Process," Chemical and Engineering News 52, 7, September 23, 1974.

sulfur by weight) can be produced from coal with a sulfur content of 3. 8% by weight at a conversion efficiency of more than 4 bbl/t of coal, with a Btu-conversion efficiency for coal of ~ 90% (but not counting H_2 and other costs).

(d) A Hydrocarbon Research, Inc. , (HRI) program involving slurry production from coal and heavy oil, followed by catalytic hydrogenation at about $850°F$ and 3, 000 psia. An economic evaluation has been published for this process.[4]

(e) The production of heavy, low-sulfur fuel oils from coal has also been described (see Ref. [1], p. 256).

The NPC[1] capacity and investment projections are reproduced in Tables 10. 4-1 and 10. 4-2 and suggest a relatively modest growth of syncrude production to the year 1985, corresponding to less than 1×10^6 bbl/d. The estimated required investment in plant development is seen to be (see Table 10. 4-2) about five times larger than the cost requirement for expanded strip-mining capacity.

Two major oil-liquefaction programs to process 250 t/d of coal to produce synthetic distillate crude oil will reach pilot-plant stages in 1978 and 1980.[5] The H-coal process has been tested at the 3 t/d scale, is planned for

---

[4]Hydrocarbon Research, Inc. , "Commercial Process Evaluation of the H-Coal Hydrogenation Process," PB-174696, U. S. Government Printing Office, Washington, D. C. , 1967; American Oil Company, "Evaluation of Project H-Coal," PB-177068, U. S. Government Printing Office, Washington, D. C. , 1967.

[5]EPRI Journal 2, 44-48 (1977).

Table 10.4-1 Commercial coal liquefaction plant buildup for
NPC Cases II/III; reproduced from Ref. [1].

Years elapsed from start of R&D	Plant addition, 10^3 bbl/d	Total capacity in operation, 10^3 bbl/d
15	50	80
16	100	180
17	100	280
18	200	480
19	200	680

operation in 1978, and is funded by ERDA, EPRI, the Commonwealth of Kentucky, Ashland Oil Co., Conoco Coal Development Co., Mobil Oil Co., and Standard Oil Co. of Indiana. Coal is first slurried with oil that is recovered during downstream distillation, mixed with H_2, preheated, and catalytically converted to the distillate from which the slurry oil is recycled. The distillate yields both light liquid products and gaseous products for hydrogen generation. In the final step, the coal is fed to a direct catalytic reactor in the liquid phase suitable for processing in a fluidized bed. The major product is heavy liquid boiler fuel. The process may also be modified to use 600 t/d of coal to produce heavy boiler fuel.

The EDS (Exxon Donor Solvent) process has been tested at the 1 t/d scale, is planned for operation in 1980, and is funded by ERDA, EPRI, and Exxon. The EDS process uses indirect catalysis. Coal is slurried and the slurry mixed with catalytically hydrogenated recycle slurry oil recovered downstream by distillation. This slurry is mixed with

Table 10.4-2 Initial appraisal of production of synthetic liquids from coal; reproduced from Ref. [1]. The listed capital requirements should be compared with those needed for expansion of power-generation capacity. The total capacity is expected to grow from about 3.4×10^5 Mw$_e$ in 1970 to about 9.77×10^5 Mw$_e$ in 1985. At \$200 per kw$_e$ installed cost, the capital requirements would grow from about \$6 $\times 10^9$ at the beginning of the period to \$12 $\times 10^9$ in 1985.

	Capacity added, 10^3 bbl/d	Cumulative capacity, 10^3 bbl/d	Investment, \$$10^6$			
			plant	strip mines†	total in year	total cumulative
New technology is assumed to be available in 1978 and a conservative rate of buildup occurs:						
1981	30	30	200	20	220	220
1985	50	80	320	35	355	575
New technology is assumed to be available in 1977 and an accelerated rate of buildup occurs:						
1980	50	50	320	50	370	370
1981	100	150	600	100	700	1,070
1982	100	250	600	100	700	1,770
1983	200	450	1,100	200	1,300	2,070
1984	200	650	1,100	200	1,300	3,370
1985	200	850	1,100	200	1,300	4,670

† Total incremental mining capacity (strip-accelerated buildup) in 1985: 140 to 150 $\times 10^6$ tons per year (using 5 to 6 $\times 10^9$ tons of identified reserves).

additional hydrogen and preheated before undergoing non-catalytic reaction in the liquid phase at such high pressures that the coal dissolves. Subsequent distillation yields gaseous products for hydrogen generation and synthetic distillate, in addition to the recycle slurry oil. The final step is a coking process which produces additional gaseous products and distillate together with hydrogen, coke, and ash.

While pyrolysis processes yield 1 to 1.5 bbl of syncrude per ton of coal, hydrogenation in the H-coal and EDS procedures increases yields to 3 to 4 bbl of syncrude per ton. Pilot-plants using 250 to 600 t/d of coal should define actual costs for syncrude production on commercial scales.

10.5   In Situ Coal Gasification

An ideal process for coal gasification would involve in situ conversion, with air or another oxidizer introduced through an injection well, followed by recovery of partially burned combustible materials through a production well.

A.   Exploratory Studies on Underground Coal Gasification

In situ coal gasification was suggested in 1868 by William Siemens and the first process patent was issued to an American, Anson Betts, in 1909. In the U.S.S.R., large-scale work on in situ coal gasification began in 1933 and continued until about 1965. Between 1945 and 1960, active experimental underground gasification projects were carried out in England, France, Belgium, Italy, and the U.S.

Underground gasification of coal has been attempted by "shaft methods" involving the driving of shafts or large diameter openings that require underground labor, by shaftless methods using boreholes for providing access to the coal deposits and requiring no underground labor, and by combination methods. The shaft methods include chamber or warehouse methods, borehole-producer methods, and stream methods; the shaftless methods include blind-borehole methods and percolation or filtration methods. The major problems that have been encountered in past in situ coal-gasification procedures are combustion control, roof control, lack of permeability, uncontrolled linking or fracturing, leakage, and inadequate control of ground-water contamination.[1]

A summary of representative heating values of the raw product gases from in situ coal gasification is given in Table 10.5-1. The expected compositions of the syngas produced by in situ coal gasification with air and oxygen injections are listed in Table 10.5-2.

Cost calculations[1] performed in 1972 for producing syngas by an oxygen-steam underground gasification process, aboveground upgrading of the raw gas, and transmission of

[1]R. M. Nadkarni, C. Bliss, and W. I. Watson, "Underground Gasification of Coal," Chemtech, 230-237, April 1974. See, also, A Current Appraisal of Underground Coal Gasification, report prepared for the U.S. Bureau of Mines by Arthur D. Little, Inc., PB-209274, December 1974.

Table 10.5-1 Heating values of product gas obtained by
              underground coal gasification; reproduced
              from Ref. [1].

Gasification agent	Heating value of product gas, Btu/SCF
air	50 to 140
oxygen	180 to 250
steam cycle using an intermittent air-steam sequence	250 to 280
hydrogen-gas production by using the steam method with air flow for short periods of time	200 to 235

Table 10.5-2 Gas compositions expected from underground
              gasification of coal; reproduced from Ref. [1]

Percentage composition of dry product gas	Gasification agent	
	air[a]	oxygen[b]
carbon dioxide	9.1	23.3
carbon monoxide	13.7	29.0
hydrogen	10.9	45.0
illuminants	0.2	0.2
methane	1.7	2.0
nitrogen	63.9	0.3
oxygen	0.5	0.2
heating value, Btu/SCF	100	235

[a] Data from S. Katell and J. H. Faber, Coal Age, pp. 40-44, September 14, 1961.

[b] Data adapted from the U.S. Bureau of Mines, RI5367 (1957), and W. Gumz, Gas Producers and Blast Furnaces, John Wiley and Sons, Inc., New York, New York, 1950.

the resulting pipeline-quality gas over a distance of 1,000 miles, yielded a range from \$0.83 to \$1.07/10^6 Btu. This cost range was competitive with other alternative sources of natural gas such as aboveground coal gasification or importation of LNG.

B. Recent Field Experience

The methodology used and the results obtained in recent tests[2] performed by workers of the U.S. Bureau of Mines at Hanna, Wyoming, will now be described briefly.

The coal-gasification site arrangement is depicted in Fig. 10.5-1. A view through the site is indicated in Fig. 10.5-2, which also shows the location of three of the test wells. The gasification of thick seams (∼ 30 ft) located deep (∼ 400 ft) underground is the practical goal. Subsurface hydraulic fracturing was accomplished by injecting, at a rate of 1,300 gallons per minute, a total of 32,000 gallons of gelled water holding 16,000 lb of sand. Major fracture lines with widths of 1.3 inches are shown in Fig. 10.5-1; minor fractures (not shown) with channel widths of less than 0.6 in. were also created. Underground ignition was implemented with a propane burner. Both forward burning (i.e., combustion in the direction of flow of injected air) and backward

---

[2]L. A. Schrider and J. W. Jennings, "An Underground Coal Gasification Experiment, Hanna, Wyoming," Paper No. 4993, Society of Petroleum Engineers of AIME, 6200 North Central Expressway, Dallas, Texas, 1974.

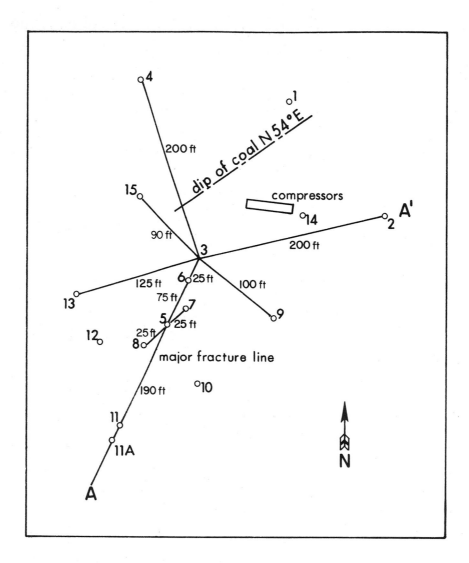

Fig. 10.5-1 Site arrangement of the in situ coal-gasification
experiment near Hanna, Wyoming. The numbers
represent well designations. Reproduced from
Ref. [2].

burning were subsequently studied using air injection. During
forward burning, about 90% of the air bypassed the coal bed
and this method of recovery was therefore abandoned.

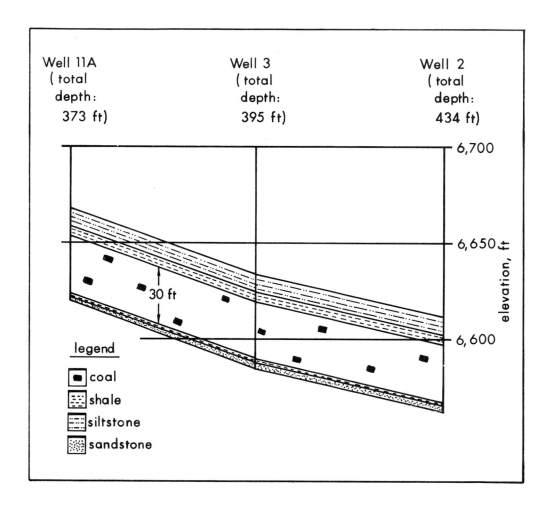

Fig. 10.5-2 A view of the southwest-northeast cross section
A-A′ (compare Fig. 10.5-1) of the in situ coal-
gasification site near Hanna, Wyoming; reproduced from Ref. [2].

An example of product-gas composition is given in
Table 10.5-3. The variations with time in gas-heating values
are indicated in Table 10.5-4. Material and energy balances
were performed. In terms of energy conversion to volatile
gases, overall efficiencies of at least 23%, and possibly as

Table 10.5-3 Typical product-gas composition obtained in an in situ coal-gasification experiment near Hanna, Wyoming. The data refer to dry gas with a heating value of 124 Btu/SCF. Reproduced from Ref. [2].

Constituent	Mole percent
H_2	15.96
Argon	0.76
N_2	53.18
CH_4	3.91
CO	6.33
C_2H_6	0.39
CO_2	19.22
C_3H_8	0.13
C_3H_6	0.04
$i-C_4H_{10}$	0.01
H_2S	0.07

high as 65%, were obtained in a number of tests. The higher efficiency corresponded to a model utilizing an estimated gasification efficiency of 80% and an overall carbonization efficiency of 20%. The preceding efficiency values do not allow for portions of the coalbed which were not swept during the recovery operation.

In situ coal gasification, just as in situ energy recovery from the tar sands and oil shale, will require considerable development before it can be considered for commercial exploitation. The definition of optimal utilization schemes

Table 10.5-4 Air-injection rates, gas-production rates, and product-gas heating values obtained in an in situ coal-gasification experiment near Hanna, Wyoming; reproduced from Ref. [2].

Dates	Air-injection rate, 10^3 CF/d	Gas-production rate,[*] 10^3 CF/d	Product gas heating values,[*] Btu/SCF
September 16, 1973, to February 28, 1974	871 to 1,394	1,010 to 2,224	65 to 165
average value	1,076	1,602	126

[*]The data refer to dry gas.

for the low Btu gas ($\sim$ 125 Btu/SCF) constitutes an essential component of this type of process development.

C. A Conceptual Design for an In Situ Coal Gasification Process

In situ recovery of coal from deep mines using the conceptual scheme illustrated in Fig. 10.5-3 has been discussed by G. H. Higgins.[3] In this scheme, coal is to be shattered by the use of chemical explosives and will then be reacted with an oxygen-water mixture at pressures between 500 and 1,000 psia and temperatures between 700 and 1,300°K.

[3]G. H. Higgins, "A New Concept for In Situ Coal Gasification," Report UCRL-51217, Lawrence Livermore Laboratory, Livermore, California, September 27, 1972.

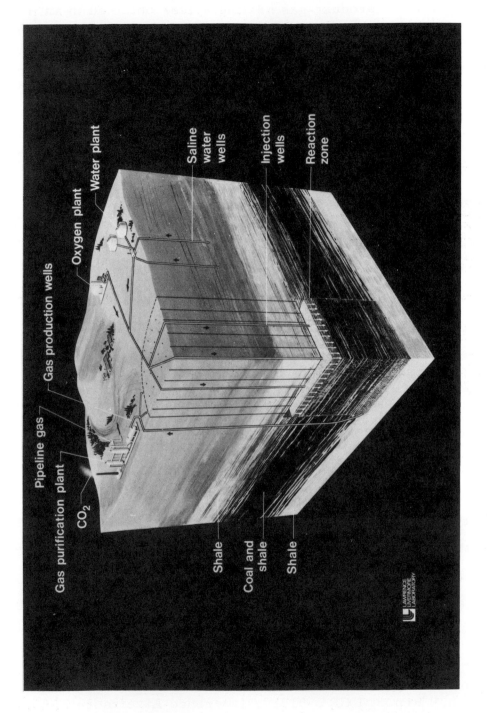

Fig. 10.5-3 Conceptual scheme proposed for in situ coal gasification; reproduced from Ref. [3]. Photograph courtesy of Lawrence Livermore Laboratory.

Reference to Fig. 10.5-3 shows that chemical reactions are expected to proceed from the top of the region downward in concurrent flow. Syngas is to be recovered from gas production wells connected to the bottom of the reacting region.

A pattern of 24-in. drill holes, spaced about 60 ft apart, is to be filled with chemical explosives (e. g., an ammonium nitrate, aluminum, and diesel-oil mixture). About 600 tons of coal will probably be fractured per ton of explosive. Access holes for the injection and recovery wells will be drilled after shattering of the coal bed. Adaptation of the in situ gasification technique may conceivably be combined with in situ recovery of shale oil (compare Section 9.12) in rock strata containing sequential layers of shale and coal.

A 1973 economic analysis of the in situ coal-gasification scheme has yielded promising results.[4] The syngas selling price is very sensitive to the required aboveground gas-upgrading system. Depending on whether in situ syngas production qualifies for a gas or coal royalty and depletion allowance and the extent of surface processing, Stephens[4] estimated that pipeline-quality syngas could be produced by in situ coal gasification for \$0.43 to \$0.62/10^3 SCF in 1971-1972 dollars at a DCF ROR of 20%.

---

[4] D. R. Stephens, "Economic Estimates of the Lawrence Livermore Laboratory Concept of In Situ Coal Gasification," Report UCRL-51340, Lawrence Livermore Laboratory, Livermore, California, February 7, 1973.

CHAPTER 11

THE HYDROGEN ECONOMY; ALTERNATIVE FUELS

Hydrogen is an excellent candidate in the search for acceptable, permanent energy sources that meet most of the obvious requirements for universal application in the energy-consumption industries. Since it can be produced from water, it is everywhere available. Hydrogen is an exceptionally clean fuel: when it burns in air, with very high energy release per unit mass, the only major reaction product formed under suitable conditions is water. Hydrogen is an easily manageable fuel and is superior to natural gas and oil in many engine-combustion applications, probably including automotive[*] and aircraft use. With proper management, it should not be more hazardous to use than conventionally-applied fossil fuels. The single important drawback is concerned with storage because the energy content per unit vol-

---

[*] The use of hydrogen was proposed for two of the winning entries of the National Urban Vehicle Design Competition, General Motors Proving Grounds, August 1972.

126

ume for hydrogen gas is very low and because the handling costs for highly-compressed gases or for cryogenic-storage facilities may turn out to be prohibitively high. Storage systems of hydrogen compounds with low decomposition temperatures may, however, provide acceptable long-term solutions (compare Section 11.4). Finally, the possibility of converting hydrogen for specialty applications into more easily manageable compounds (such as ammonia, methane, and methyl alcohol) merits consideration, although some of these conversions cannot be accomplished without losing the considerable advantage of burning pure hydrogen or relieving the pressure on carbonaceous deposits for energy applications. It is apparent that these valuable resources will last far longer if they are employed exclusively in the chemical-synthesis industries.

We shall discuss the following topics in order to gain some appreciation of the implications of the idea to develop hydrogen as a primary energy source: hydrogen requirements (Section 11.1), production of hydrogen (Section 11.2), distribution of hydrogen (Section 11.3), hydrogen storage (Section 11.4), applications of hydrogen (Section 11.5), safety problems connected with hydrogen use (Section 11.6), hydrogen-based chemicals as alternative energy sources (Section 11.7).

11.1 Hydrogen Requirements

We shall first determine the energy available for hydrogen combustion by considering the thermochemical changes for complete conversion to gaseous or liquid water. Under standard conditions (298.16°K, zero pressure[*]), we know[1] that

$$H_2(g) + (1/2)O_2(g) \rightarrow H_2O(g) - 57.796 \text{ kcal} \quad (11.1-1)$$

and

$$H_2(g) + (1/2)O_2(g) \rightarrow H_2O(\ell) - 68.315 \text{ kcal}, \quad (11.1-2)$$

where the negative heat terms represent the energy <u>evolved</u> per mole of hydrogen used when the chemical changes go to completion as indicated in Eqs. (11.1-1) and (11.1-2). Here the symbols (g) and (ℓ) identify the presence of gaseous or liquid compounds, respectively. The pressure dependence of the energy release is small,[1] while its variation with temperature is easily calculated.[1] The energy-evolution value given in Eq. (11.1-2) is indicative of the total heat release that is obtainable when the reactants are initially near room temperature and the reaction product is finally returned

---

[*] The zero-pressure specification does not constitute a serious limitation since the heat release is not a sensitive function of pressure.

[1] See, for example, S. S. Penner, <u>Thermodynamics</u>, especially pp. 14-17 and Chapters 5 and 12, Addison-Wesley Publishing Co., Reading, Mass., 1968.

to room temperature. We shall use this estimate in the following analysis, with the understanding that appropriate modifications must be made when the specified standard conditions are not satisfied in a practical application.

For comparison with NG (natural gas), it is useful to estimate the energy content per SCF of $H_2(g)$. We have noted in Table 1.2-2 that the SCF refers to 1 atmosphere and $60^\circ F$. Using the ideal gas law, we find that 1 ft^3 contains[*] 1.20 moles of ideal gas under these conditions so that the heat release per SCF, according to the process shown in Eq. (11.1-2), becomes 82 kcal/SCF or 325 Btu/SCF. This heat value is appreciably smaller than the 1,025 to 1,050 Btu/SCF derived from burning NG and indicates the low volume density of energy storage in gaseous hydrogen. Approximately 3.2 SCF of $H_2(g)$ are required to replace the energy content of 1 SCF of $CH_4(g)$.[**] On the other hand, the energy storage per unit mass is relatively high in hydrogen; thus, it is seen to be 68.315 kcal/(2g of H_2) = 135 Btu/g, while the energy

---

[*] The temperature in $^\circ K$ is 273.16 + $(^\circ F - 32) \times (5/9) = 289^\circ K$ for $60^\circ F$; since the number of moles of an ideal gas = (pressure × volume)/(molar gas constant × temperature),
$$n_{H_2(g)} = \{(1 \text{ atm} \times 1 \text{ ft}^3)/[82.06 \text{ (cm}^3\text{-atm/mole-}^\circ K) \times}$$
$$289^\circ K]\} \times (2.832 \times 10^4 \text{cm}^3/\text{ft}^3) \simeq 1.20 \text{ moles}.$$

[**] At higher pressures, the heating value per ft^3 becomes relatively larger for NG because of real-gas interactions, which have the effect of increasing the heating value for NG per unit volume more rapidly than for H_2. Some representative values are listed in Section 11.4.

stored in NG (if we approximate NG by CH_4 and use a molecular weight of 16 with 10^3 Btu/SCF) is seen to be only 52 Btu/g. Hydrogen storage in the condensed phase will be examined further in Section 11.4.

The U.S. natural-gas demands have been reviewed in Section 1.6. According to the data compiled in Table 1.6-3, the year 1990 residential and commercial demands for NG have been estimated to be 15.9×10^{12} SCF, primarily for space and water heating. If NG were to be replaced by H_2 in the year 1990 for these applications, the total requirement would amount to 4.93×10^{13} SCF. Furthermore, in order to be competitive with the estimated cost of syngas, the hydrogen would have to be available at a cost of about $1/10^6$ Btu or $0.325/10^3$ SCF of hydrogen.

In the unlikely event that the year 2020 energy-consumption estimate of 0.3×10^{18} Btu/y for the U.S. (see Table 1.2-2) were to be supplied entirely from $H_2(g)$, hydrogen production at competitive prices would have to reach 9.2×10^{14} SCF/y at this date.

By comparison, the year 1960 U.S. production of H_2 was 7.22×10^{11} SCF/y and increased to 2.28×10^{12} SCF/y by 1968 (see Ref. [2], p. III-1). Most of the hydrogen was produced from natural gas. Manufacture by electrolysis was

---

[2] A Hydrogen-Energy System, by D. P. Gregory with contributions by P. J. Anderson, R. J. Dufour, R. H. Elkins, W. J. D. Escher, R. B. Foster, G. M. Long, J. Wurm, and G. G. Yie, American Gas Association, Arlington, Virginia, 1973.

employed only in regions where electricity was available at
exceptionally low prices. We note that the actual hydrogen-
production rate in 1968 was somewhat less than 5.0% of the
estimated year 1990 hydrogen consumption rate in the residential and commercial sectors if hydrogen were used to
replace NG completely for these applications. It is thus apparent that the required growth rate in hydrogen production
can surely be accomplished over a 17-year period if economic considerations justify this growth rate. In the past, hydrogen has been produced for the following purposes: as
refinery feedstock in the petrochemical industry for the production of plastics, foodstuffs, rubbers, and pharmaceuti-
cals; as a reducing agent in metallurgical processing and in
scrap-metal recovery. There has also been an assortment
of specialty applications, such as the use of liquid hydrogen
in space-booster rockets. The year 1970 world consumption
of hydrogen for various applications is summarized in Table
11.1-1.

The extent and the time-scale on which hydrogen will
ultimately become a primary fuel is largely dependent on
price developments for hydrogen production, distribution,
and application, in relation to price developments for competing fuels and energy sources. Secondary considerations
may involve revised use-hazard assessment and relative
environmental-impact analysis. A 1973 evaluation of prices
(see Ref. [2], p. 7) is reproduced in Table 11.1-2 and is
based on 1970 data supplied by the FPC (Federal Power Commission) and AGA (American Gas Association). It is

Table 11.1-1   The year 1970 world consumption of hydrogen;
reproduced from G. Marchetti, "Hydrogen and
Energy," Chemical Economy and Engineering
Review (Japan) 5, 7-25 (1973).

Application	Consumption, $10^9 m^3$
NH_3 synthesis	100
CH_3OH synthesis	25
synthesis of other chemicals	10
hydrotreating/desulfurization	30
hydrocracking	30
refinery fuel (off-grade hydrogen)	10
total	205

Table 11.1-2   Relative prices in $/$10^6$ Btu of delivered en-
ergy; reproduced from Ref. [2] and based on
1970 FPC and AGA data. Note: the late 1973
costs for NG production from new sources are
substantially greater than $0.17/$10^6$ Btu.

Cost component	Electricity	NG	Electrolytically-produced hydrogen
production	2.67*	0.17	2.95 to 3.23*
transmission	0.61	0.20	0.52**
distribution	1.61	0.27	0.34
total cost	4.89	0.64	3.81 to 4.09

* The value $2.67/$10^6$ Btu refers to an electrical-energy cost
of 9.1 mills/kwh$_e$; this same estimate was used in arriving
at a hydrogen-production cost of $3.23/$10^6$ Btu.

** This value refers to a hydrogen cost of $3.00/$10^6$ Btu as
compressor fuel, as compared with $0.25/$10^6$ Btu for NG
as compressor fuel.

apparent that electrical-energy costs were far higher than
natural-gas costs and higher than hydrogen costs in 1970,
even using 1970 estimates for hydrogen-electrolysis costs.
As we have noted repeatedly (see Section 1.6), the natural-
gas appraisal in Table 11.1-2 is unduly optimistic. Even
allowing for the higher transmission and distribution costs
of hydrogen, about a three-fold reduction in the production-
cost component is all that is required in order to make hydrogen an economically attractive alternate fuel for energy
generation.

In practice, hydrogen would, of course, be introduced
gradually, possibly first mixed with NG, and then in pure
form in well-defined local regions during prototype evaluation. Major applications of a hydrogen-based economy are
at least 20 years away and complete conversion appears unlikely before the middle of the next century.

We shall discuss in Section 11.2 a number of reaction schemes that has been proposed for the economical
manufacture of hydrogen. All of these require an independent energy source, with nuclear reactors or the sun being
the preferred primary sources of energy. Figure 11.1-1
shows a conceptual total design of a nuclear-reactor-based
hydrogen economy.

Energy flow diagrams normalized to 10^6 Btu (by

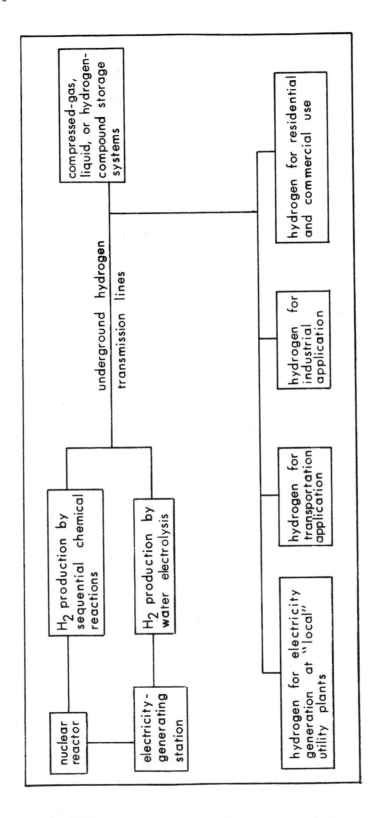

Fig. 11.1-1 Conceptual design of a nuclear-reactor-based hydrogen economy.

Winsche, Hoffman and Salzano[3]) are reproduced in Fig. 11.1-2 for nuclear-gasoline (A), nuclear-coal (B), and nuclear-hydrogen (C) economies. These three economies are seen to have about equal costs for the 1973 cost estimates employed in the analysis (including, for example, the optimistic value of a total cost of $2.10/$10^6$ Btu for hydrogen manufacture from nuclear energy by electrolysis). In order to understand the meaning of the entries in Fig. 11.1-2, we describe in detail the sequential numbers appearing in the nuclear-hydrogen-based economy (system C in Fig. 11.1-2). The nuclear reactor produced 810×10^6 Btu of nuclear energy at a unit cost of $0.05/$10^6$ Btu and requires a total investment of $41/y in nuclear-power generation. With a conversion efficiency of 0.4 and a load factor of 0.75, the 810×10^6 Btu are converted to 324×10^6 Btu_e of electrical energy at a unit cost of $1.87/$10^6$ Btu_e for a total investment of $606/y. With a conversion efficiency of 0.8 at a load factor of 0.85, the 324×10^6 Btu_e of electrical energy are used to generate hydrogen with a heating value of 259×10^6 Btu for transmission, at a unit cost of $0.28/$10^6$ Btu and a total cost of $73/y. The hydrogen with an energy-use content of 259×10^6 Btu is then transmitted at a unit cost of $0.10/$10^6$ Btu

[3] W. E. Winsche, K. C. Hoffman and F. J. Salzano, "Economics of Hydrogen Fuel for Transportation and Other Residential Applications," Proceedings of the 7th Intersociety Energy Conversion and Engineering Conference, Paper 729215, San Diego, California, 1972; published by the American Chemical Society, Washington, D.C., 1972.

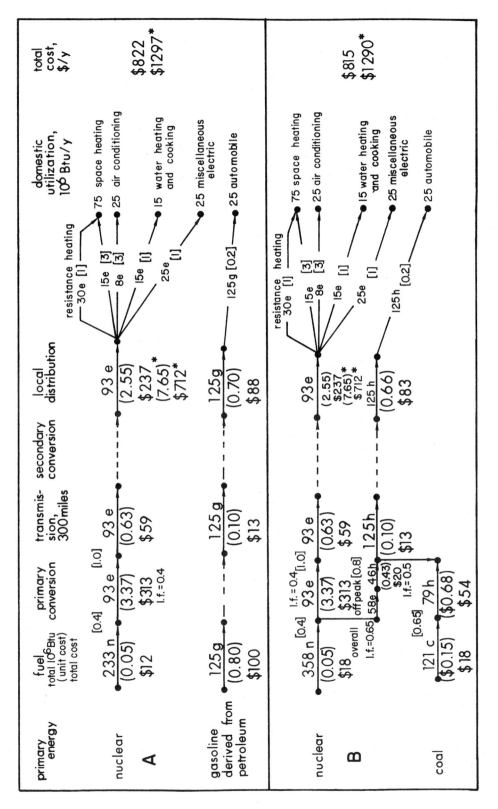

Fig. 11.1-2 Energy-flow diagrams. See the following page for explanations.

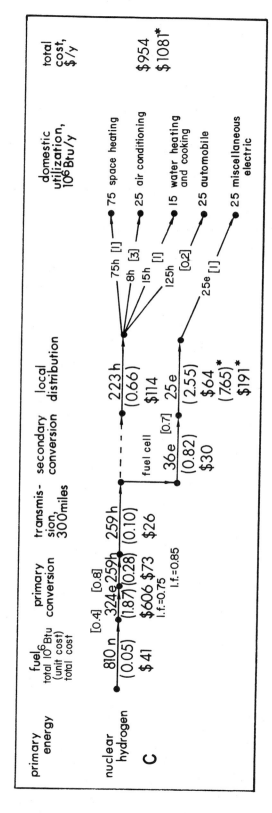

Fig. 11.1-2 Energy-flow diagram of a reference system, system A, in which the primary sources of energy are nuclear power and gasoline derived from petroleum. The number above each arrow is the total amount of energy used annually, expressed as 10^6 Btu, the cost per 10^6 Btu is shown in parentheses below each arrow. The total annual cost of each operation in the energy system is shown below the unit cost and is expressed as dollars per year. Numbers in square brackets are efficiency factors; costs marked with an asterisk are for underground distribution. Abbreviations: n, nuclear; e, electrical; g, gasoline, c, coal; h, hydrogen; m, methane, l.f., load factor. System B: hydrogen derived from nuclear energy and coal are used only for automotive propulsion. System C: hydrogen derived from nuclear energy is used to supply all domestic energy needs, except the electricity required for small appliances. Reproduced from Ref. [3]. Copyright © 1972 by the American Chemical Society.

and a total cost of \$26/y. Of the hydrogen with an energy-use content of 259×10^6 Btu, 223×10^6 Btu are employed directly for local distribution and application in space heating (75×10^6 Btu at unit efficiency), air conditioning (8×10^6 Btu at an efficiency factor of 3), water heating and cooking (15×10^6 Btu at unit efficiency), and automotive applications (125×10^6 Btu with an efficiency of 0.2). The remaining 36×10^6 Btu of hydrogen energy are converted to electricity in a fuel cell at a unit cost of $\$0.82/10^6$ Btu with a total cost of \$30/y; the 36×10^6 Btu_e are then distributed locally at an efficiency of 0.7 with a unit cost of $\$2.55/10^6$ Btu_e and a total cost of \$64/y (or they are transmitted underground at a unit cost of $\$7.65/10^6$ Btu_e with a total cost of \$191/y). The 25×10^6 Btu_e are then employed for miscellaneous electrical applications with unit efficiency. The total costs for processing the 810×10^6 Btu initially generated by nuclear reaction are \$954/y or \$1,081/y for terminal aboveground and underground electrical transmission, respectively.

11.2 Hydrogen Production from Water

Although most of the hydrogen currently used is made from natural gas by reaction with steam and oxygen or air, we shall not be concerned with a review of this technology because its large-scale implementation does not imply the complete substitution for fossil-fuel utilization which is our primary objective. Accordingly, the following remarks will be restricted to the production of hydrogen from water, using energy sources such as the sun or nuclear reactors.

Nuclear reactors may be used to generate electricity, which may then be employed in the electrolysis of water. Alternatively, nuclear energy may be used to support a sequence of reactions at temperatures below about $1,000^{\circ}K$, to which we shall refer as "thermochemical" manufacture of hydrogen.

Solar energy may be used directly to generate electricity in photovoltaic devices. Effective conversion of solar energy to electricity may also be accomplished by employing a suitable Rankine-cycle engine, in conjunction with a turbine generator, and using existing thermal gradients in the oceans. Hydrogen may then again be manufactured by electrolysis. Photovoltaic devices will be discussed in Chapter 13. The solar-sea generator will be considered in Chapter 14. Solar energy is utilized by some biological systems for the direct production of hydrogen, although the energy-conversion efficiencies achieved in these processes are very low. Finally, the direct electrochemical photolysis of water at semiconductor electrodes has been studied to some extent and may conceivably be developed to a commercially-useful procedure.

The specified list of hydrogen-production techniques suggests that hydrogen production from water is appropriately considered for the following processes:

a. Electrolysis of water, which will be discussed in Section 11.2A.

b. Thermochemical production of hydrogen from water, which will be reviewed in Section 11.2B.

c.   Direct water photolysis for water decomposition, which will be evaluated in Section 11.2C.

d.   Direct solar-energy utilization by biological systems in the production of hydrogen from water. This topic will be considered briefly in Section 11.2D.

A.   Water Electrolysis[1]

The purpose of water electrolysis is efficient implementation of the decomposition

$$H_2O(\ell) \rightarrow H_2(g) + (1/2)O_2(g) + 68.315 \text{ kcal.} \quad (11.2-1)$$

This reaction is the inverse to the process described by Eq. (11.1-2) and absorbs 68.315 kcal per mole of water electrolyzed (or per mole of hydrogen produced) under standard isothermal conditions. Currently-existing plants consume 90 to 100 Mw_e and operate at overall efficiencies of 60 to 100% (Ref. [1], Chapter III). These existing plants are only about a factor of ten smaller than the commercial electrolysis units which will be required for large-scale implementation of hydrogen manufacture in a hydrogen economy.

It should be possible to improve the efficiency achieved in practical electrolysis to about 100% because, under optimal operating conditions, the theoretically-attainable energy conversion by electrolysis is about 120% of the

_____

[1]Ref. [2] of Section 11.1.

electrical-energy input.   The physical basis for this last
statement will now be considered.

A useful definition for energy efficiency in electrolysis is the following: the energy efficiency is the ratio of the
energy released from the electrolysis products formed (when
they are subsequently used) to the energy required to effect
electrolysis.   The energy released by the process

$$H_2(g) + (1/2)O_2(g) \rightarrow H_2O(\ell) \qquad\qquad (11.2\text{-}2)$$

under standard conditions is 68.315 kcal and is numerically
equal to the enthalpy change (ΔH) for the indicated process.
On the other hand, the <u>minimum</u> energy (or useful work input) required at constant temperature and pressure for electrolysis[2] equals the Gibbs free energy change (ΔF).   There
is a basic relation derivable[2] from the first and second laws
of thermodynamics for isothermal changes, which shows that

$$\Delta F = \Delta H - T\Delta S, \qquad\qquad (11.2\text{-}3)$$

where ΔS represents the entropy change for the chemical reaction.   The Gibbs free energy change (ΔF) is also related[2]
to the voltage (ϵ) required to implement electrolysis by

[2] See, for example, S. S. Penner, <u>Thermodynamics</u>, Chapter 11, Addison-Wesley Publishing Co., Reading, Mass.,
1968.

Faraday's equation, viz.

$$\epsilon = (\Delta F/23.06\, n) \text{ volts}, \qquad\qquad (11.2\text{-}4)$$

where ΔF is in kcal/mole and n is the number of electrons
(or equivalents) per mole of water electrolyzed and has the
numerical value 2 for Eq. (11.2-1).

At atmospheric pressure and 300°K, $\Delta H = 68.30$ kcal/
mole of $H_2O(\ell)$ and $\Delta F = 56.62$ kcal/mole of $H_2O(\ell)$ for the
electrolysis of liquid water (see Table 11.2-1 on p. 142 in Ref.
[2]). Hence, the energy efficiency of electrolysis at 300°K
is about 120%. The ideal (reversible) voltage for electrolysis at 300°K and a pressure of one atmosphere is found to be
1.23 volts from Eq. (11.2-4).

The results of calculations similar to those described
in the preceding paragraphs are reproduced in Fig. 11.2-1
for a range of temperatures. In Fig. 11.2-1, the reversible
voltage line has been computed from Eq. (11.2-4) while the
thermoneutral voltage line corresponds to the relation $\epsilon =$
$\Delta H/23.06n$ and is seen to have the value 1.48 volts at 300°K.
Along the thermoneutral voltage line, $H_2(g)$ and $O_2(g)$ are
generated by electrolysis but the electrolysis cell must absorb heat from the surroundings in order to remain at constant temperature. It is this ability to produce gaseous
electrolysis products with heat absorption from the surroundings that is ultimately responsible for energy-conversion
efficiencies during electrolysis greater than unity. Figure

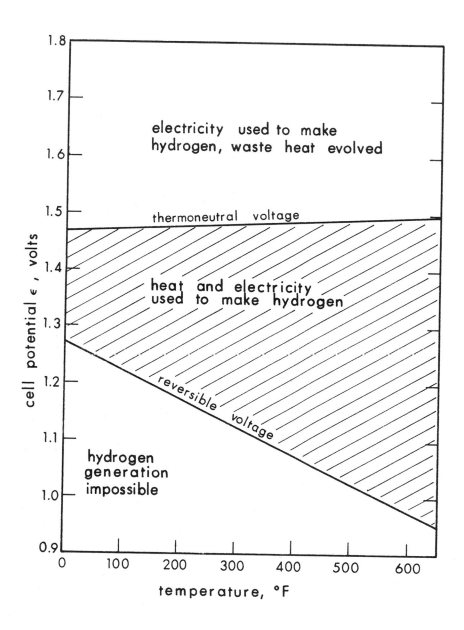

Fig. 11.2-1 Idealized operating conditions for water electrolysis; reproduced from Ref. [1].

11.2-1 contains a clear description of accessible operating regimes during water electrolysis.

A 100%-efficient water-electrolysis cell will release 6.95 cm^3 of H$_2$/minute-ampere = 14.7 CF/10^3 ampere-h at 1 atmosphere and 32°F. The preceding numerical values are easily seen to follow from the ideal gas law and the fact that the Faraday or electrochemical equivalent of current is 23.06 kcal/volt-equivalent = 96,500 coulombs/equivalent = 96,500 ampere-sec/equivalent.

1.   Commercial Water Electrolysis[3]

Industrial water electrolyzers range in output from 500 ft^3/d (at a continuous power input of about 3 kw$_e$) to more than 40 $\times$ 10^6 ft^3/d (at a continuous power input of 240 Mw$_e$), with the largest units located near hydroelectric installations where H$_2$ is produced for the manufacture of synthetic nitrogen fertilizers.

Operating temperatures range from 60 to 90°C; solutions containing from 25 to 28% by weight of KOH serve as electrolytes; the current efficiencies range from 96 to 99.9% with 15.9 SCF of H$_2$ and 7.95 SCF of O$_2$ produced at 100% current efficiency per 10^3 amperes; 200 to 300 U.S. gallons of 30°C cooling water are used per 10^3 SCF of H$_2$ produced. The actually-required cell voltages are the sums of the reversible cell voltages, of over-voltages at the anodes and

---

[3]Ref. [1], pp. III-71 to III-82, by A. K. Stuart.

cathodes, and of voltages associated with resistive losses
in the electrolytes and cell parts. The actual minimization
of the loss voltages requires deep understanding of electrochemical technology.

Commercial cells are either unipolar (with each electrode serving as either an anode or a cathode) or bipolar
(with each side of a flat electrode serving as either an anode
or a cathode). Schematic diagrams of unipolar and bipolar
cells are shown in Figs. 11.2-2A and 11.2-2B, respectively.
The voltage in unipolar cells equals twice the number of
cells, while the required voltage input for bipolar cells
equals twice the number of electrode pairs. Unipolar cells
have tank-type electrolyzers, are maintenance-free for 10
years (at which time the electrolyte is replaced), have a life
of more than 25 years, and are nearly 100% efficient. A large
iron vat holds the electrolyte into which flat, mild-steel electrodes with alternating polarities are suspended. These
heavy-duty electrodes, carrying thousands of amperes at 1 to
2 volts, are nickel-plated and welded to steel bus bars.

Bipolar cells have filter-press electrolyzers using
alternating layers of electrodes and diaphragms. Tearing
of an individual asbestos diaphragm may require significant
cell reconstruction. The overall efficiencies for these cells
are 95%. They are suitable for operation at very high current densities.

Typical performance data for unipolar and bipolar
cells are shown in Fig. 11.2-3 and indicate both the relatively higher current-carrying capacities of bipolar cells

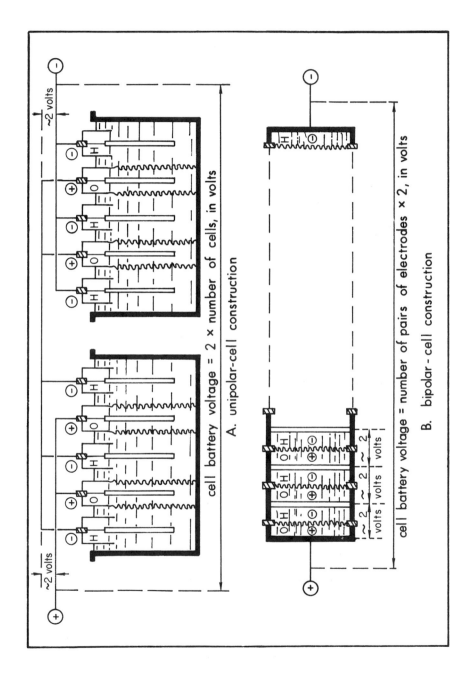

Fig. 11.2-2 Schematic diagrams showing unipolar (A) and bipolar (B) cell construction. The symbols O and H stand for oxygen- and hydrogen-evolution, respectively. Reproduced from Ref. [3].

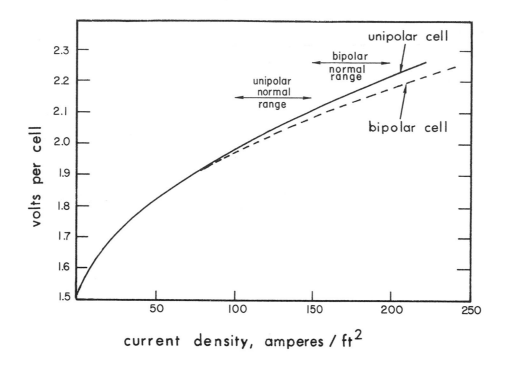

Fig. 11.2-3 Performance regions at 80°C with uncatalyzed
             electrodes for unipolar and bipolar cells; re-
             produced from Ref. [3].

and their lower voltages.

Operating performance characteristics of commercially-available and developmental electrolyzers are summarized in Fig. 11.2-4. Generally speaking, voltage-cur-
rent-density curves, below the curve for the device developed
by the Teledyne Corporation, refer to research devices.[1]

An economic evaluation has been performed for a
1,000-volt module prototype cell, with an effective cell diameter of 30 inches, as proposed by workers at the Allis-
Chalmers Corporation.[1] Two electrode current densities
(800 and 1,600 amperes/ft^2) were considered with hydrogen

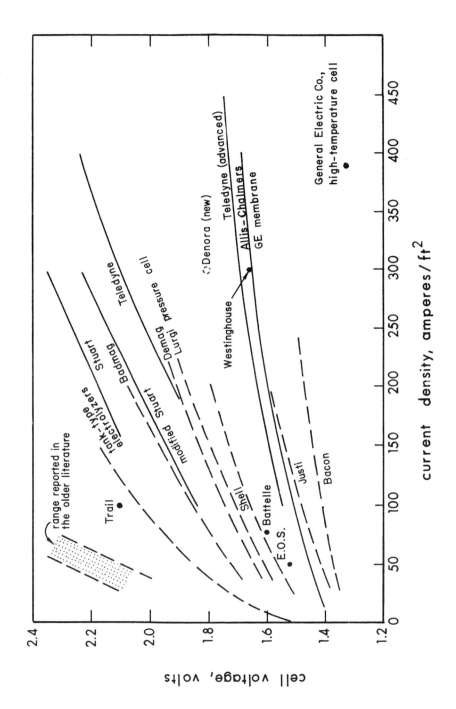

Fig. 11.2-4 Cell operating performances of various advanced electrolyzers; reproduced from Ref. [1], 1973.

outputs of 183 or 314 lb/h, respectively, at electrical power inputs of 4.03 and 7.75 Mw_e. The results of this evaluation are summarized in Fig. 11.2-5 as a function of bus-bar electricity cost for various cell efficiencies.[1] The limiting performance (see the heavy line in Fig. 11.2-5) corresponds to the heat equivalent of electricity and indicates hydrogen costs of about $1.20/$10^6$ Btu at an electricity price of 4 $mills/kwh_e$, scaling linearly up and down as the cost of electricity is increased or decreased. Practically-achievable costs currently exceed those of this limiting line by more than a factor of two.

The results of a study to determine capital-cost requirements for hydrogen electrolysis are summarized in Fig. 11.2-6. Minimum investment costs are seen to correspond to about $2 \times 10^6/(10^6$ SCF/h). A 44,000 lb/h plant using about 1,000 Mw_e costs 40×10^6, corresponding to about 10% of the investment required in the construction of the electricity-generating station.

The cost of electrolytically-produced H_2 is, of course, a linear function of the cost of electricity. Thus, for a given cost of gasoline, one may develop a relation of the form

$$\frac{\text{energy cost for } H_2 \text{ use}}{\text{energy cost for gasoline use}} = \alpha + \beta C_e \, ,$$

where α is a constant that is determined by the relative transportation and distribution costs, β is a constant, and

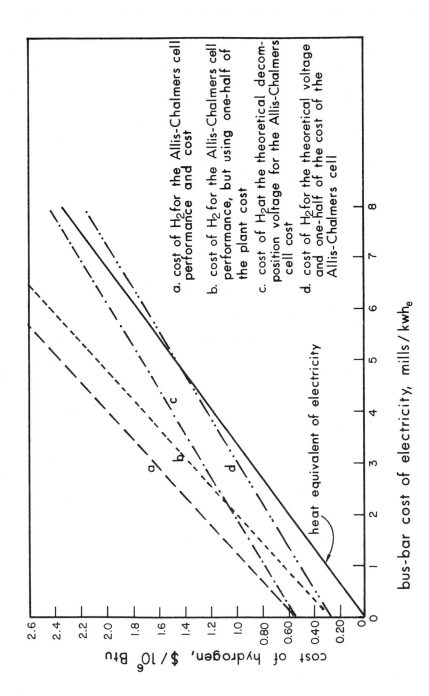

a. cost of H$_2$ for the Allis-Chalmers cell performance and cost

b. cost of H$_2$ for the Allis-Chalmers cell performance, but using one-half of the plant cost

c. cost of H$_2$ at the theoretical decom-position voltage for the Allis-Chalmers cell cost

d. cost of H$_2$ for the theoretical voltage and one-half of the cost of the Allis-Chalmers cell

heat equivalent of electricity

bus-bar cost of electricity, mills/kwh$_e$

cost of hydrogen, $/10$^6 Btu

Fig. 11.2-5 Cost of hydrogen as a function of electricity price, showing the effect of vari-ous cell efficiencies and costs; reproduced from Ref. [1], 1973.

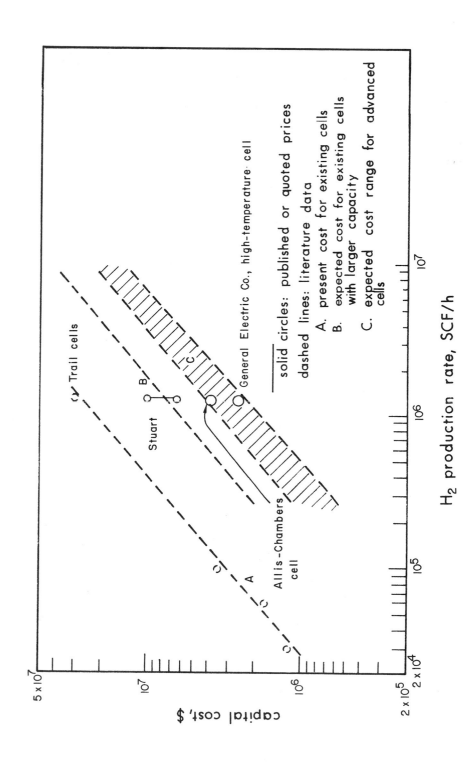

Fig. 11.2-6 Capital cost requirements for electrolytic-hydrogen installations; reproduced from Ref. [1], 1973.

C_e equals the electricity cost in mills/kwh$_e$. Winsche et al[4] have used an expression of this type. For an assumed gasoline cost of $0.19/gallon at the pump and no allowance for possible value of by-product O_2, $\alpha = 0.65$ and $\beta = 0.23$, these authors find that the energy cost for H_2 is equal to that for gasoline at $C_e = 1.5$ mills/kwh$_e$.

A hydrogen-electric utility system using fusion energy has been described recently.[5]

B. Thermochemical Production of Hydrogen

It is not difficult to define a very large number of sequential chemical reactions, which have the net effect of producing hydrogen and oxygen from water. These processes may be implemented at temperatures that are very much lower than the normal decomposition temperature ($\geq 2,500^\circ C$ at 1 atmosphere) of water. The following system of reactions has been designated[6, 7] as the Mark-1 cycle and is indicative of the processes involved:

---

[4]Ref. [3] in Section 11.1.

[5]E. C. Tanner and R. A. Huse, "A Hydrogen-Electric Utility System with Particular Reference to Fusion as the Energy Source," Proceedings of the 7th Intersociety Energy Conversion and Engineering Conference, Paper 729207, published by the American Chemical Society, Washington, D.C., 1972.

[6]G. DeBeni and C. Marchetti, "Hydrogen, Key to the Energy Market," Eurospectra 9, 46-50 (1970).

[7]G. Marchetti, "Hydrogen and Energy," Chemical Economy and Engineering Review (Japan) 5, 7-25 (1973).

$$CaBr_2 + 2H_2O \xrightarrow{730^{\circ}C} Ca(OH)_2 + 2HBr$$
(water-splitting reaction),   (11.2-5)

$$Hg + 2HBr \xrightarrow{250^{\circ}C} HgBr_2 + H_2$$
(hydrogen-switching reaction),   (11.2-6)

$$HgBr_2 + Ca(OH)_2 \xrightarrow{200^{\circ}C} CaBr_2 + HgO + H_2O$$
(oxygen-shifting reaction),   (11.2-7)

$$HgO \xrightarrow{600^{\circ}C} Hg + (1/2)O_2$$
(oxygen-switching reaction).   (11.2-8)

The overall process is evidently the decomposition reaction

$$H_2O \rightarrow H_2 + (1/2)O_2.$$

The maximum temperature required to effect decomposition is seen to be only 730°C (which is lower than the readily-accessible nuclear-reactor-coolant temperature of about 850°C). The sequential reactions are easily performed in separate reaction steps and there are theoretically no chemical losses. However, the use of mercury and of corrosive HBr constitute significant potential hazard and control problems. Furthermore, for each pound of water processed, more than 110 lb of other materials are required in the combined reaction sequence.

Among many other possible sequential-decomposition schemes, the following have been listed by Marchetti:[7]

$$H_2O + Cl_2 \xrightarrow{900^\circ C} 2HCl + (1/2)O_2,$$

$$2HCl + 2CrCl_2 \xrightarrow{200^\circ C} 2CrCl_3 + H_2,$$

$$2CrCl_3 \xrightarrow{1,000^\circ C} 2CrCl_2 + Cl_2;$$

$$\left.\begin{array}{c}\\\\\\\end{array}\right\} (11.2-9)^*$$

$$Cl_2 + H_2O \xrightarrow{700 \text{ or } 800^\circ C} 2HCl + (1/2)O_2,$$

$$2HCl + 2VCl_2 \xrightarrow{100^\circ C} 2VCl_3 + H_2,$$

$$4VCl_3 \xrightarrow{700^\circ C} 2VCl_2 + 2VCl_4,$$

$$2VCl_4 \xrightarrow{100^\circ C} 2VCl_3 + Cl_2;$$

$$\left.\begin{array}{c}\\\\\\\\\end{array}\right\} (11.2-10)$$

the manganese or Mark-2 cycle:[6, 7]

---

*This cycle was proposed by K. F. Knoche at the Technische Hochschule in Aachen, F. R. G.

$$Mn_2O_3 + 8NaOH \xrightarrow{600^\circ C} 2(MnO_2 \cdot 2Na_2O)$$

$$+ 3 H_2O + H_2,$$

$$2(MnO_2 \cdot 2Na_2O) + water \xrightarrow{100^\circ C} 8NaOH \text{ in}$$

$$water$$

$$+ 2Mn(OH)_4,$$

$$8NaOH \text{ in water} \xrightarrow{400^\circ C} 8NaOH + water \, ,$$

$$2Mn(OH)_4 \xrightarrow{700^\circ C} Mn_2O_3 + 4H_2O + (1/2)O_2.$$

(11.2-11)

Several cycles have been explored by R. H. Wentorf and his colleagues at the General Electric Company.[8] Among these are the three sequential processes listed below.

Agnes (limiting Carnot energy-conversion efficiency = 58%, achievable energy-conversion efficiency = 41%):

$$3FeCl_2 + 4H_2O \xrightarrow{450-750^\circ C} Fe_3O_4 + 6HCl + H_2 \, ,^*$$

---

[8]"Hydrogen Sought via Thermochemical Methods," Chemical and Engineering News 51, 32-33, September 3, 1973; see, also, R. H. Wentorf, Jr., and R. E. Hanneman, "Thermochemical Hydrogen Generation," Science 185, 311-319 (1974).

*See the following page for the completion of this decomposition scheme.

$$Fe_3O_4 + 8HCl \xrightarrow{100-110^\circ C} FeCl_2 + 2FeCl_3$$

$$+ 4H_2O,$$

$$2FeCl_3 \xrightarrow{300^\circ C} 2FeCl_2 + Cl_2 ,$$

$$Cl_2 + Mg(OH)_2 \xrightarrow{50-90^\circ C} MgCl_2 + (1/2)O_2$$

$$+ H_2O,$$

$$MgCl_2 + 2H_2O \xrightarrow{350^\circ C} Mg(OH)_2 + 2HCl ;$$

$$(11.2\text{-}12)$$

Beulah (theoretical and practical energy-conversion efficiencies of 63% and 53%, respectively):

$$2Cu + 2HCl \xrightarrow{100^\circ C} 2CuCl + H_2 ,$$

$$4CuCl \xrightarrow{30-100^\circ C} 2CuCl_2 + 2Cu ,$$

$$2CuCl_2 \xrightarrow{500-600^\circ C} 2CuCl + Cl_2 ,$$

$$Cl_2 + Mg(OH)_2 \xrightarrow{80^\circ C} MgCl_2 + H_2O$$

$$+ (1/2)O_2,$$

$$MgCl_2 + 2H_2O \xrightarrow{350^\circ C} Mg(OH)_2 + 2HCl;$$

$$(11.2\text{-}13)$$

Catherine (theoretical and practical energy-conversion efficiencies of 83% and 64%, respectively):

$$3I_2 + 6LiOH \xrightarrow{100-190^\circ C} 5LiI + LiIO_3 + 3H_2O,$$

$$LiIO_3 + KI \xrightarrow{0^\circ C} KIO_3 + LiI,$$

$$KIO_3 \xrightarrow{650^\circ C} KI + (3/2)O_2,$$

$$6LiI + 6H_2O \xrightarrow{450-600^\circ C} 6HI + 6LiOH,$$

$$6HI + 3Ni \xrightarrow{150^\circ C} 3NiI_2 + 3H_2,$$

$$3NiI_2 \xrightarrow{700^\circ C} 3Ni + 3I_2.$$

(11.2-14)

The preceding sets of reaction schemes should suffice to define the underlying principles. It is not difficult to invent thousands of alternative water-decomposition cycles. Since actual evaluation requires detailed knowledge of chemical kinetics, a subject in which good experimental information is especially difficult to obtain and in which reliable theoretical estimates cannot be performed, it will require years of difficult experimental work to determine a number of preferred thermochemical cycles. In the meantime, one may proceed on the assumption that desirable thermochemical processes can be implemented in practice and confine preliminary screening to those reaction sets that yield the

highest potential energy values for the hydrogen produced
relative to the energy supplied to effect water decomposition.

Generally speaking, the optimization of individual
reaction rates and conversion steps remains to be determined
empirically for each of the elementary processes defined in
the water-decomposition cycles.   The overall theoretical
energy-conversion efficiency for the formation of $H_2O(g)$
from hydrogen combustion may be shown to be 85% by evaluating the sequential energy-absorption steps in the Mark-1
cycle.   In other words, it is theoretically possible to recover
85% of the nuclear energy used for water decomposition in
the Mark-1 cycle as thermal energy by burning the resulting
$H_2(g)$ to $H_2O(g)$.   If the combustion process is arranged in
such a manner as to allow final water condensation, the recovered energy is correspondingly increased.   Actually-
achieved energy-conversion efficiencies in the Mark-1 cycle
were stated to be[7] 55% during January 1973.   A reaction
flow chart is reproduced in Fig. 11.2-7.

Commercial procedures for thermochemical water
decomposition are not yet available and a definitive cost
assessment for hydrogen production by application of these
techniques can therefore not yet be made.   Assuming that
the temperatures and pressures have been selected to accomplish the individual reaction steps as efficiently as possible, the cost of hydrogen by water decomposition is seen
to be the cost of water, plus the energy cost from a nuclear
reactor or other heat source, plus a capital investment
charge for the facilities, amortization, depreciation,

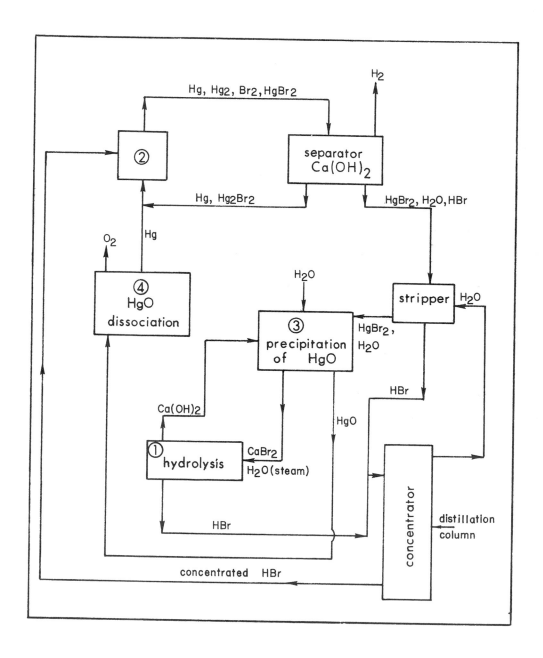

Fig. 11.2-7 The Mark-1 block diagram for thermochemical hydrogen production from water; reproduced from G. DeBeni and G. Marchetti, "Mark-1, A Chemical Process to Decompose Water Using Nuclear Heat," Progress Report for December 1972, Euratom, Ispra, Italy.

interest, and return. It is possible that the best thermo-
chemical cycles will yield hydrogen at less than $2.00/$10^6$ Btu. For a nuclear-heat cost of $0.60/10^6$ Btu and an
investment in a hydrogen plant between $70/kw and $1.50/kw,
hydrogen costs have recently been estimated to be as low as
$1.60 to $2.20/10^6$ Btu. [9]

The following estimates are indicative of commercial
costs that have been assigned for hydrogen production by
various other procedures:

$0.80 to $1.35/10^6$ Btu for open-cycle reforming
of petroleum-based naphtha compounds and partial
oxidation of hydrocarbons; [8]

$1.00 to $1.40/10^6$ Btu for open-cycle hydrogen
production from coal with externalized cost for
sulfur removal; [8]

$1.50 to $2.50/10^6$ Btu for hydrogen production by
electrolysis if electricity costs 4 to 7 mills/
kwh_e. [10]

C. Direct Water Photolysis Using an Electrochemical Cell

When a static potentiometer is used to measure the

[9] H. Barnet and R. Schulten, quoted in "Hydrogen Economy
Concept Gains Credence," Chemical and Engineering
News 52, 15, April 1, 1974.

[10] T. H. Maugh, II, "Hydrogen: Synthetic Fuel of the
Future," Science 178, 849-852 (1973).

current-voltage curves on a single-crystal wafer of an n-type semiconducting TiO_2 (rutile) electrode, notably differ-ent data are observed in the dark and on exposure[11] to light. The results obtained in measurements by Fujishima and Honda are reproduced in Fig. 11.2-8 and show that the current density tends to increase with potential but levels out at moderate positive potential levels (determined rela-tive to a saturated calumel electrode). The anodic current rise (see Fig. 11.2-8) was found to be proportional to the intensity of the light used for irradiation provided the wave-length of the incident light was shorter than 4, 150A (= 415 nm, 1 nm = 10^{-9} m). This threshold wavelength corresponds to an energy of 3 ev, which equals the band gap between the valence and conduction bands in TiO_2. The incident photons with sufficient energy formed pairs of electrons (e^-) and holes (p^+) in the semiconductor TiO_2. Since electrochemical decomposition of water can be accomplished at 1.25 ev, cor-responding to a light wavelength of 10,000A (= 1,000 nm), the band gap in TiO_2 is needlessly large and this material is not an optimal choice for the photolysis of water. A semi-conducting material with a band gap of 1.25 ev rather than 3.0 ev would utilize a much larger fraction of the incident solar energy, namely, the ratio of the number of photons in sunlight with wavelengths shorter than 10,000A to the

[11]A. Fujishima and K. Honda, "Electrochemical Photolysis of Water at a Semiconductor Electrode," Nature 238, 37-38 (1972).

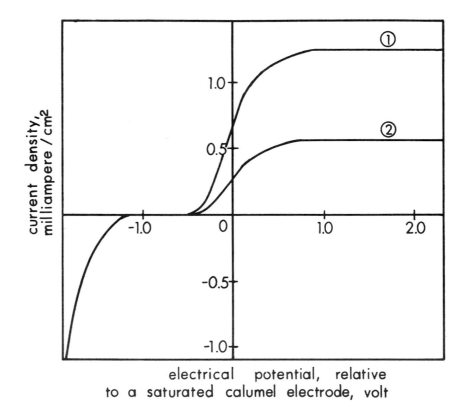

Fig. 11.2-8 Current-voltage curves for a TiO_2 n-type semiconductor. A single crystal wafer of n-type
TiO_2 (rutile) was used after treatment at $700°C$
and 10^4 to 10^5 torr for roughly 4 hours in order
to increase the conductivity of the crystal. This
wafer was approximately 1.5 mm thick and the
exposed (001) surface area was approximately
$1.0 \ cm^2$. Indium was evaporated on to one side
of the surface to insure ohmic contact and a
copper lead-wire was connected on the indium
layer with silver paste. All other surfaces
were sealed by epoxy resin. The symbols ①
and ② identify constant current densities observed at different pH (see p. 165). Reproduced
from Ref. [11].

number of photons with wavelengths shorter than 4,150A. This ratio is 4.55 for a 6,000°K blackbody (which approximates the radiation characteristics of incident sunlight) and shows that the solar-energy conversion efficiency in water photolysis for the production of H_2 would also be increased by this same factor of 4.55 if the proper type of semiconducting electrode could be found.

The manner in which semiconducting material may be used to effect water photolysis is illustrated in the schematic diagram of the experimental arrangement used by Fujishima and Honda, which is reproduced in Fig. 11.2-9.

The following process is believed[11] to occur at the TiO_2 electrode (see Fig. 11.2-9):

$$TiO_2 + 2h\nu \rightarrow TiO_2 + 2e^- + 2p^+ . \qquad (11.2\text{-}15)$$

The holes (p^+) may then be considered to react with water near the TiO_2 electrode to produce hydronium ions and gaseous oxygen, as follows:

$$\left. \begin{array}{l} 2p^+ + H_2O(\ell) \rightarrow (1/2)O_2(g)\uparrow + 2H^+, \\[2em] 2H^+ + 2H_2O(\ell) \rightarrow 2H_3O^+(\ell). \end{array} \right\} \qquad (11.2\text{-}16)$$

The electrons pass through the external circuit (in the direction opposite to the current direction) and then serve to produce hydrogen at the platinum-black electrode to which the

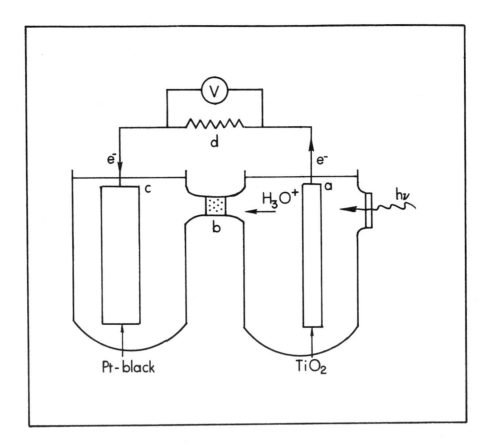

Fig. 11.2-9 Electrochemical cell in which a TiO_2 electrode
is connected with a platinum electrode. The
surface area of the platinum-black electrode
used was approximately 30 cm^2. The symbol
a refers to a TiO_2 semiconductor mounted on
an indium plate, which serves as an electrode
contact material. The TiO_2 is exposed to light
(hν). The symbol d describes an external load
across which the voltage was measured with a
voltmeter Ⓥ. The symbol c refers to a platinum-black electrode, while b describes a suitable electrolyte. The elementary processes
occurring in the cell are described in the text.
Reproduced from Ref. [11].

hydronium ions have moved:

$$2e^- + 2H_3O^+(\ell) \rightarrow H_2(g)\uparrow + 2H_2O(\ell). \qquad (11.2\text{-}17)$$

The net effect of the processes occurring in Eqs. (11.2-15) to (11.2-17) is the photolysis of water:

$$H_2O(\ell) \xrightarrow{h\nu} H_2(g) + (1/2)O_2(g).$$

The starting potential for oxygen release at the TiO_2 electrode was observed to correspond almost exactly to the potentials at which the current densities were observed to become constant for different values of the pH (see curves ① and ② in Fig. 11.2-8). Increased efficiency in photolysis was observed when Fe^{+++} ions or dissolved oxygen were added to the electrolyte in the compartment of the Pt-black electrode. For irradiation with a 500-w xenon lamp, Fujishima and Honda[11] estimated the efficiency of light utilization (i.e., the quantum efficiency) as about 0.1, with an observed cell e.m.f. of 0.5 volt.

The exploratory work of Fujishima and Honda[11] is of considerable potential practical importance since it suggests that, with proper development, semiconducting materials can be found which will allow water photolysis with that portion of the solar spectrum having wavelengths shorter than about 10^4A. Fujishima and Honda[11] speculate that direct H_2 evolution will be induced at more positive potentials when the Pt-black electrode is replaced by an irradiated p-type semiconductor.

Although it is too early to assess the long-term potential of direct water photolysis for industrial hydrogen production, it is clear that we are dealing with a subject that merits serious developmental effort.

D. Biological Systems for the Direct Photolysis of Water

It is known[12] that some biological systems facilitate the direct photolysis of water. In some green plants, the conditions for photosynthesis can be altered such that the photosynthetic process will generate molecular hydrogen instead of reducing carbon. This process can be induced[12] by limiting the carbon dioxide available to the plant, in addition to maintaining a very low oxygen level. The sensitivity of the enzyme system, which produces the molecular hydrogen, to the oxygen concentration appears to be[13] a serious problem.

Recently, a blue-green alga has been described which can simultaneously produce molecular hydrogen and oxygen from water and light.[14] However, the conversion efficiencies

[12]H. Gaffron and J. Rubin, "Fermentative and Photochemical Production of Hydrogen in Algae," Journal of General Physiology 26, 219-267 (1942).

[13]M. Calvin, "Solar Energy by Photosynthesis," Science 184, 375-381 (1974).

[14]J. R. Benemann and N. M. Weare, "Hydrogen Evolution by Nitrogen-Fixing Anabaena Cylindrica Cultures," Science 184, 174-175 (1974).

demonstrated thus far for this and other systems capable of direct water photolysis are very low.

11.3 Hydrogen-Transmission and Distribution Networks

The experience in pipeline transmission of hydrogen in the U.S. is limited to a 50-mile network in the Houston, Texas, area. Short hydrogen pipelines with operating pressures up to 1,200 psig are in use at many refinery and chemical-plant locations. The longest and oldest hydrogen pipeline network is located in the Ruhr area of Germany, where most of a 130-mile network has been in continuous operation since 1940. This network interconnects 18 industrial plants with 6- to 12-inch pipelines operating at a supply pressure of 150 psig.[1] The pipeline network has no in-line compressor stations and is constructed from seamless steel pipe.

Hydrogen distribution in low-pressure pipelines is a common industrial process. Manufactured gas, town gas, and coal gas are hydrogen-rich gases that were widely distributed in the U.S. until the middle of the twentieth century. In 1945, nearly 70,000 miles of gas main were in use for distributing manufactured gas.[2] The manufactured gases used in the U.S. typically had a hydrogen content of about 50%. Although natural-gas use has almost completely

---

[1]Ref. [2] of Section 11.1.

[2]Gas Facts, American Gas Association, Arlington, Virginia, 1947.

replaced manufactured-gas use in the U.S., manufactured gas is still commonly distributed in Europe. The town of Basilea, Germany, distributes a gas free of carbon monoxide which contains about 80% hydrogen.[3]

A. Hydrogen Transmission by Pipeline

Efficient conversion to a hydrogen economy depends, in part, upon the suitability of the existing natural-gas pipeline network for transporting hydrogen. In 1970, the U.S. natural-gas transmission network consisted of more than 250,000 miles of trunklines.[4] Trunk pipelines are usually constructed of welded steel pipe with diameters up to 48 inches. The lines are 600 to 1,000 miles long and operate at line pressures from 600 to 800 psia. Natural gas is transported through the pipeline by the use of in-line compressor stations, which are located at 100-mile intervals and use a portion of the natural gas in the pipeline for fuel. The energy transmission efficiency of these pipelines is approximately 95%, with line losses and compressor fuel accounting for the loss of 5%. Many of the existing natural-gas trunklines, after compressor station upgrading, are suitable for the transport of hydrogen gas; some may require renovation to reduce gas leakage.

---

[3]C. Marchetti, "Hydrogen, Master-Key to the Energy Market," Eurospectra 9, 117-129 (1970).

[4]Gas Facts, American Gas Association, Arlington, Virginia, 1971.

Because of the lower heating value (325 Btu/SCF) of hydrogen relative to that of natural gas (1,025 to 1,050 Btu/SCF), approximately 3.2 times as large a hydrogen volume must be transported for an equivalent energy content. Near atmospheric pressure, the lower viscosity and density of hydrogen lead to a nearly compensating increase in flow capacity. Thus, the energy-flow capacity of a natural-gas pipeline, operating near atmospheric pressure, is reduced[1] by only about 6% if it is used without modification for hydrogen transmission.

At the typical operating pressures of trunk pipelines (~750 psia), the different compressibility factors for hydrogen and natural gas lead[1] to a natural-gas to hydrogen volumetric-heating-value ratio of about 3.8. The pipeline compressor capacity is determined by the volume of compressed gas which is being transported. For the same energy-transmission capability, the compressor horsepower must actually be increased[1] by a factor of 5.5 in order to compress the greater volume of hydrogen through the same pressure ratio.

The hydrogen energy-transmission capacity of an unmodified 750-psia natural-gas pipeline is[1] the reciprocal of 3.8 or about 26% of the natural-gas energy-transmission capacity. The relative energy-transmission capacities of hydrogen and natural-gas pipelines operating at 750-psia are shown in Table 11.3-1;[*] also included are the relative required compressor capacities and horsepowers.

Investigators at the Institute of Gas Technology[1] have calculated the cost of hydrogen transmission through pipelines. The cost analysis was based on pipelines that were specifically designed for hydrogen transmission. The compressor-station spacing was assumed to be 65 miles with an average pressure drop of about 3 psig/mile. Since the major contributors to gas-transmission costs are the pipeline and compressor-station capital costs, the hydrogen transmission costs for a 65-mile compression section, corresponding to the distance between compressor stations, may be linearly extrapolated to a pipeline with 100-mile compression sections.[1] The resulting costs for hydrogen transmission as a function of annual energy throughput and operating pressure are compared with natural-gas transmission costs in Fig. 11.3-1.

The data of Fig. 11.3-1 indicate that the transmission cost of hydrogen at 750 psia ranges from about \$0.034 to \$0.048/(10^6 Btu-100 miles). This cost is reduced to about \$0.023 to \$0.033/(10^6 Btu-100 miles) for hydrogen transmission at 2,000 psia. Comparison of the hydrogen and the estimated 1972 natural-gas transmission costs at 750 psia

---

[*]A detailed derivation of these and other comparisons of the operating characteristics of hydrogen and natural-gas pipelines is given in Ref. [1], Appendix IV-A.

Table 11.3-1 The relative energy-transmission capacities
of hydrogen and natural-gas pipelines operating at 750 psia; reproduced from Ref. [1].

Pipeline	Relative compressor capacity	Relative compressor horsepower	Relative energy-transmission capacity
natural gas	1.0	1.0	1.0
hydrogen[a]	1.0	0.1	0.26
hydrogen[b]	2.1	1.0	0.56
hydrogen[c]	3.8	5.5	1.0

a. An unmodified natural-gas pipeline is assumed.

b. A natural-gas pipeline with modified compressor
capacity is assumed.

c. A natural-gas pipeline with modified compressor
capacity and horsepower is assumed.

---

indicates that the cost of hydrogen transmission is about 2.3
to 2.7 times that of natural gas.

The increased requirements for compressor capacity
and compressor horsepower of a hydrogen pipeline make the
transmission cost of hydrogen sensitive to its production
cost. The increased compressor horsepower leads to increased compressor capital costs and fuel consumption. For
a 750-psia pipeline, the ratio of the hydrogen to natural-gas
fuel costs is 5.5 times the gas-production-cost ratio. Hence,
hydrogen-fuel costs account for a significant percentage (30
to 40%) of the energy-transmission cost of a hydrogen pipe-

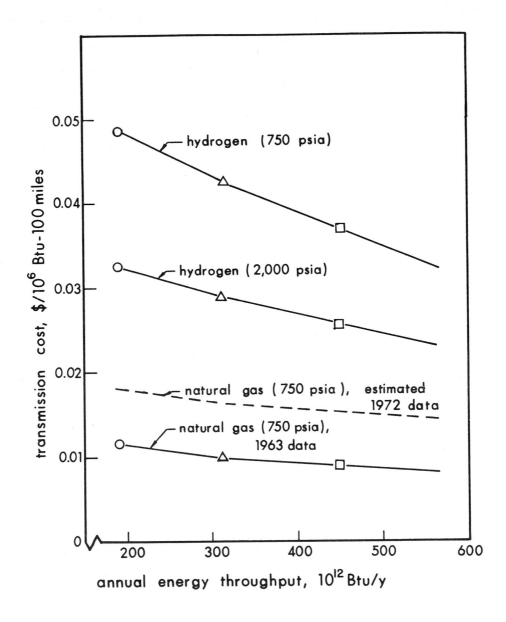

Fig. 11.3-1 Hydrogen and natural-gas transmission costs as
functions of annual energy throughput. A hydrogen compressor-fuel cost of \$3.00/10^6 Btu is
assumed. Data for 30-, 36-, and 42-inch pipelines are identified, respectively, by the symbols O, Δ, and □. Reproduced with modifications from Ref. [1].

line.[5] The impact of fuel cost on the transmission cost of
natural gas is significantly less (see Fig. 11.3-2). The
transmission costs of hydrogen and natural gas at 750 psia,
as functions of annual energy throughput for several compressor-fuel costs, are shown in Fig. 11.3-2. The hydrogen
transmission cost for a hydrogen cost of $3.00/10^6 Btu
ranges from 1.3 to 1.5 times that for a hydrogen cost of
$1.00/10^6 Btu. If both hydrogen and natural gas cost $1.00/
10^6 Btu, then the hydrogen transmission cost ranges from
1.6 to 1.7 times the natural-gas transmission cost.

B. Pipeline Technology for Hydrogen

Pipeline material compatibility with a hydrogen environment may be an obstacle to future hydrogen transmission. Although the existing mild-steel hydrogen pipelines
have not been adversely affected by hydrogen, the materials
used in conventional natural-gas pipelines may well be cor-
roded by hydrogen. Molecular hydrogen is dissociated at the
surfaces and atomic hydrogen then penetrates into the lattice
structure of steels. This phenomenon is called hydrogen
embrittlement and leads to a loss of ductility and to stress
cracking, blistering, or flaking. Another type of embrittlement (hydrogen-environment embrittlement) may have been

---

[5]L. Icerman, "Relative Costs of Energy Transmission for
   Hydrogen, Natural Gas, and Electricity," Energy Center
   Report EC-R.2, University of California, San Diego, La
   Jolla, California, 1973.

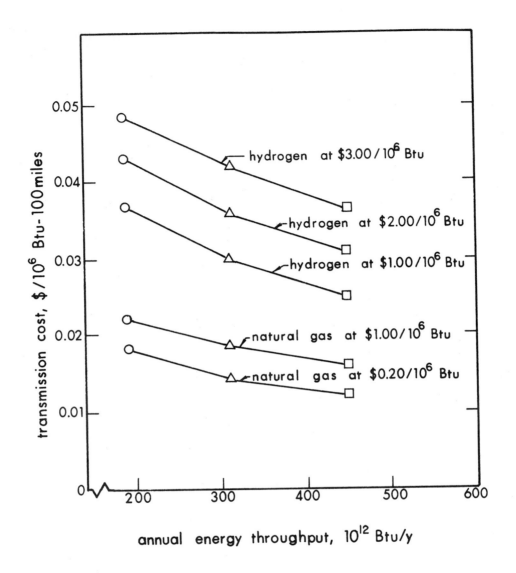

Fig. 11.3-2 Hydrogen and natural-gas transmission costs at
            750 psia as functions of annual energy through-
            put and compressor-fuel costs. Data for 30-,
            36-, and 42-inch pipelines are identified, re-
            spectively, by the symbols O, △, and □. Based
            on data of Ref. [1] and of J. Wurm and R. F.
            Pasteris, "The Transmission of Gaseous Hydro-
            gen," paper prepared for the 48th Annual Fall
            Meeting of the Society of Petroleum Engineers
            of the American Institute of Mechanical Engi-
            neers, Las Vegas, Nevada, 1973.

observed in hydrogen-fuel operations at the National Aeronautics and Space Administration (NASA). Workers at NASA have categorized materials as resistant, moderately attacked, severely attacked, and extremely susceptible to attack according to their susceptibility to hydrogen-environment embrittlement. Conventional pipeline steels are expected to fall in the severely attacked category. Nevertheless, investigators at the Institute of Gas Technology have concluded[1] that, even though the materials currently used in pipelines and auxiliary equipment may have been shown to be susceptible to hydrogen-environment embrittlement, it is not clear that this phenomenon will create a significant operational problem if natural gas is replaced by hydrogen.

Compressors are important components of hydrogen pipelines. Piston or reciprocating, radial or centrifugal, and screw compressors are suitable for use with hydrogen pipelines.[1] Conversion from natural gas to hydrogen does not require significant design changes of these compressors. Reciprocating compressors may be subject to size limitations because they are positive-displacement machines. As has already been noted, a hydrogen reciprocating compressor must have 3.8 times the capacity of a natural-gas compressor to deliver the same energy content at 750 psia.

The use of radial turbocompressors for hydrogen pipelines may be limited by the pressure ratio achievable in one stage. The rotor tip speed of a radial turbocompressor designed to pump hydrogen would have to be prohibitively high to achieve the typical pressure ratios used in natural-gas pipelines.[1] For a given pressure ratio, rotor tip speeds may be reduced by using multi-stage compressors. The volume capacity of a turbocompressor is the same for hydrogen and natural gas. Thus, to transmit the same energy at 750 psia, a hydrogen turbocompressor must also be 3.8 times larger than the corresponding natural-gas design.

The use of screw compressors may be limited by high pipeline operating pressures. Screw compressors have not been developed for applications requiring pressures above about 600 psia.[1] If higher-pressure models are developed, these compressors may prove to be useful for hydrogen pipelines.

C. The Distribution of Hydrogen

The energy-delivery capacity of existing natural-gas (terminal) distribution systems is reduced by only 6% when they are converted to hydrogen use because the lower volumetric heating value of hydrogen is nearly compensated for by its lower density and viscosity. The difference in the compressibility factors of hydrogen and natural gas is not important at typical (below 100 psia) distribution pressures.

Gas-distribution networks ordinarily do not include in-line compressor stations. Distribution networks typically contain city-gate regulator stations at the transmission-line connections and district regulator stations throughout the network. The existing natural-gas regulator stations are expected to be compatible with hydrogen use. Hydrogen

expansion at regulator stations will cause a slight temperature rise. This effect, known as the reverse Joule-Thompson
effect, is a rather unique property of hydrogen. Natural gas
and most other gases are cooled on expansion.

Many natural-gas networks utilize large-diameter
cast-iron mains originally designed for low-pressure manufactured-gas distribution in downtown areas. Suburban-area
networks are usually constructed of welded steel pipe or,
more recently, plastic pipe. Cast-iron and steel pipes are
compatible with hydrogen use. The permeability of some
plastic pipe compounds is significantly higher to hydrogen
than to natural gas and may thus limit the use of plastic distribution lines. The reverse Joule-Thompson effect may also
limit the use of plastic pipe at locations immediately following large pressure reductions at regulator stations. It is
likely that major portions of the existing terminal distribution lines will have to be replaced when pure hydrogen is
used. This problem could be avoided at minimal cost by
regulations requiring that all newly-installed distribution
lines be compatible with both NG and H_2.

D. Transmission and Distribution of Liquid Hydrogen

Liquid hydrogen is transported and distributed in
cryogenic truck trailers and rail cars. The truck trailers
typically carry 7,000 gallons ($\sim 2.1 \times 10^8$ Btu) of liquid
hydrogen. The rail cars carry up to 34,000 gallons of liquid
hydrogen. Most of the transported liquid hydrogen is used

in industrial or research facilities.

Liquid-hydrogen pipelines have been studied by workers at the Linde Company. According to Linde engineers,[6] a 2-inch liquid-hydrogen pipeline inside a liquid-nitrogen jacket could deliver 60 t/d ($\sim 2.3 \times 10^{12}$ Btu/y) of liquid hydrogen. A pipeline of this design is estimated[6] to cost from $100,000 to $200,000/mile. Compressor stations are required at 100-mile intervals. Amortization of the capital cost, not including liquefaction, operation, or compressor-fuel costs, corresponds to approximately $1.00/$10^6$ Btu-100 miles. This portion of the total costs alone is about 25 times larger than the corresponding total cost for transmission of gaseous hydrogen. Construction of larger diameter cryogenic pipelines will, however, reduce the transmission costs substantially.

Transmission of liquid hydrogen may be preferable to gaseous transmission under some conditions. Liquid-hydrogen storage facilities are more easily sited than gas-storage facilities. Liquid hydrogen is directly suitable for such end uses as transportation applications.[7] Perhaps transmission of liquid hydrogen can be coupled effectively with cryoresistive or superconducting power lines for electrical-energy transmission in an "energy pipe." Liquid

---

[6]J. E. Johnson, Linde Company, quoted in Ref. [5] of Section 11.2.

[7]L. O. Williams, "Hydrogen Powered Automobiles Must Use Liquid Hydrogen," Cryogenics 13, 693-698 (1973).

hydrogen at -423°F will provide a suitable temperature environment for cryoresistive cables. Development of superconductors with higher critical temperatures may allow replacement of liquid helium by liquid hydrogen as the refrigerant for superconducting cables (see Chapter 20 for a discussion of cryoresistive and superconducting cables). The concept of combining electrical-energy and liquid-hydrogen transmission is an intriguing one. The engineering and economic benefits of a combined system could prove to be substantial.

11.4 Storage of Hydrogen[1]

A conventional, spherical liquid-hydrogen container is shown in Fig. 11.4-1. This type of cryogenic storage system, as well as storage in compressed-gas cylinders, is too expensive for large-scale applications. Because of the low boiling point of liquid hydrogen (-423°F = -252.8°K), particular care must be taken to construct an effective insulation system. An evacuated jacket containing perlite is a suitable design for minimization of heat losses, while steels or aluminum must be used as liners because of their compatibility with liquid H_2 (see Fig. 11.4-1). The cost of liquefaction and storage for LH_2 (= liquid hydrogen) is $1.05 for sufficient hydrogen to yield an energy output during use

---

[1]Ref. [2] in Section 11.1.

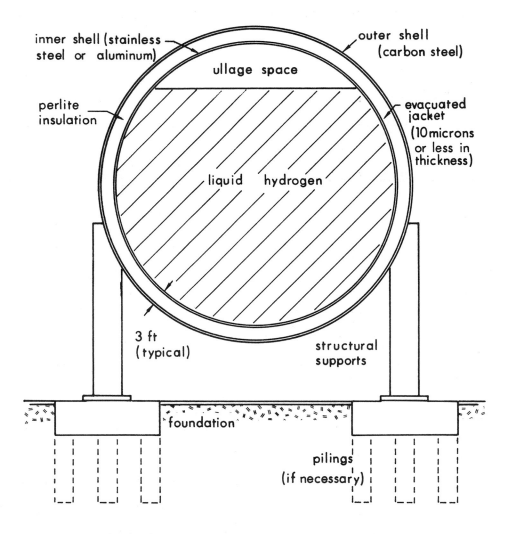

Fig. 11.4-1 Spherical liquid-hydrogen storage container of
the type used at the NASA Kennedy Space Center
Launch Complex 39 (Apollo) facility; reproduced
from Ref. [1].

of 1,000 Btu (HHV)/day;[*] the corresponding cost for LNG
(= liquid natural gas) is \$0.275. Up to 28×10^9 Btu (9×10^5
gallons of LH_2) have been stored at Cape Kennedy. This
capacity may be compared with 2×10^{12} Btu for a typical
LNG tank used for peakshaving and 56×10^9 Btu for a large
pumped hydroelectric storage facility (Ludington, Michigan).
A more direct comparison of some aspects of LH_2 and LNG
storage is shown in Table 11.4-1.

Table 11.4-1   Relative costs for LH_2 and LNG production
          and storage; reproduced from Ref. [1].

Production or storage component	Cost ratios for LH_2/LNG storage for the same Btu values
liquefaction plant	2.8
energy cost for liquefaction	2.0
storage tank (for a capacity of 0.4×10^{12} Btu)	4.8

Large-scale storage of H_2 gas appears to be economically and technically feasible in depleted gas or oil fields,
especially as aquifer storage. Fields which are tight for NG
are expected to be tight for H_2. As much as 12×10^9 SCF
of coke-oven-produced gas containing H_2 have been kept in
aquifer storage near Paris, France. Underground storage

---

[*] HHV stands for "high heating value" and refers to hydrogen
combustion with the production of liquid water.

of H_2 at 700 psia will hold only about one-quarter of the Btu-capacity of an equivalent volume of NG. The depth-pressure relation for underground storage in petroleum reservoirs is indicated in Fig. 11.4-2. The applicable pressure is seen to be generally above that corresponding to the pure-water gradient of 0.433 psi/ft, but well below the limiting line for an overburden pressure of 1 psi/ft (see Fig. 11.4-2).

Storage costs for H_2 and NG have been evaluated in Ref. [1]. They are compared per 10^6 Btu (HHV) in Table 11.4-2. Costs for gaseous and cryogenic storage are seen to be substantially higher for H_2 than for NG.

11.5 Applications of Hydrogen for Energy Production; Alternative Fuels

In order to assess the suitability of hydrogen as a universal energy source, we are interested in its total heat content, as well as in those combustion parameters that determine ease of application in boilers, transportation systems, space heating units, etc. These are non-conventional applications, different from those involving large-scale current hydrogen use for industrial processing, as listed[1] in Table 11.5-1.

---

[1]Hydrogen and Other Synthetic Fuels, Synthetic Fuels Panel, U.S. Atomic Energy Commission, Report TID-26136, U.S. Government Printing Office, Washington D.C., 1972.

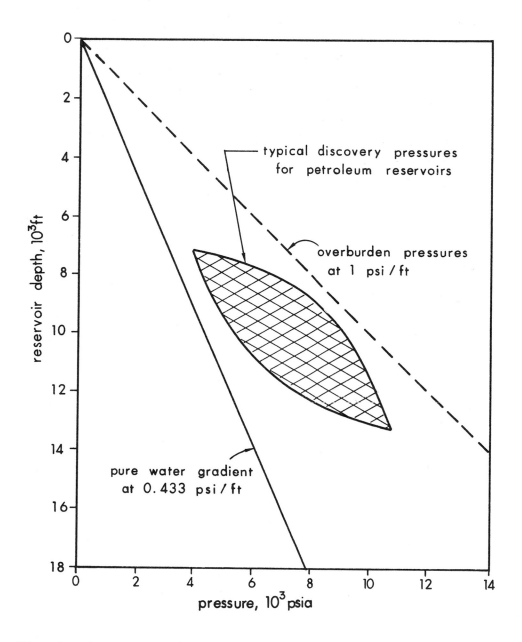

Fig. 11.4-2 Depth-pressure relation for underground reservoirs. Reproduced from M. R. Tek et al, New Concepts in Underground Storage of Natural Gas, Monograph on Project P0-50 at the University of Michigan, American Gas Association, Arlington, Va., 1966; this figure appears as Fig. V-2 in Ref. [1].

Table 11.4-2 Some comparisons of capital costs for storage of 10^6 Btu (HHV) of NG and H_2; reproduced from Ref. [1].

Gaseous storage	Natural gas	Hydrogen
underground storage (depleted field or aquifer, 10^3 psi)	$ 0.79[1]	$ 3.04*
dissolved-salt cavern, 10^3 psi	$ 2.25[2]	$ 8.65*
mined cavern, 10^3 psi	$ 4.50[2]	$ 17.30*
steel pipe (local or as an auxiliary transmission system), 10^3 psi	$ 48.00[2]	$185.00*
high-pressure bottle storage, 2.4×10^3 psi	$150.00[3]	$720.00*
aboveground pressure vessel storage, 10^3 psi	$227.00[2]	$870.00*
Liquid cryogenic storage		
flat-bottom tank with perlite insulation, purged	$ 2.50[4]	no designs
spherical tank with perlite insulation, purged	$17.00 (0.20%/day boil-off loss)[5]	boil-off is considered too high for this design
spherical tank with vacuum-perlite insulation	$22.00 (0.01%/day boil-off loss)[5]	$42.00 (0.05%/day boil-off loss)[5]
liquefaction plant	$0.275/($10^3$ Btu-day)[7]	$1.05/($10^3$ Btu-day)[6]
liquefaction energy	1.1 kwh/lb[8]	4.5 kwh/lb, [6] 6.0 kwh/lb (with present systems)[3]

Footnotes to Table 11.4-2 appear on the following page.

Table 11.4-2 continued

*Hydrogen costs are derived from natural-gas costs by
multiplication by the ratio of the natural-gas to hydrogen
volumetric heating values at the operating pressures used:
3.84 for 1,000 psi and 4.76 for 2,400 psi.

Sources

1. Based on depreciated storage-plant investment of all
   fields for which reports were made to the Federal Power
   Commission in a publication prepared at the Bureau of
   Natural Gas, Underground Storage of Natural Gas by
   Interstate Pipeline Companies for A. Calendar Year 1970,
   B. Winter 1970-1971, U.S. Federal Power Commission,
   Washington, D.C., 1971.

2. Based on mid-range data in D. L. Katz et al, Handbook
   of Natural Gas Engineering, McGraw-Hill, New York,
   1959.

3. Estimate by J. E. Johnson, Linde Division, Union
   Carbide Corporation, May 1972.

4. Based on 1 billion SCF in one tank, from a report by the
   American Gas Association, LNG Information Book, p. 133,
   Arlington, Virginia, 1968.

5. Estimate by the Chicago Bridge and Iron Company, November 1971.

6. N. C. Hallett, "Study, Cost, and System Analysis of
   Liquid Hydrogen Production," Air Products and Chemi-
   cals, Inc., NASA Contractor Report CR-73226,
   Washington, D.C., 1968.

7. Based on a rate of 40×10^6 SCF/day, from a report by
   the American Gas Association, LNG Information Book,
   p. 131, Arlington, Virginia, 1968.

8. From a report by the American Gas Association, LNG
   Information Book, p. 141, Arlington, Virginia, 1968.

Table 11.5-1   Typical industrial hydrogen requirements;
             reproduced from Ref. [1].

Use	SCF of H_2/unit of product
ammonia synthesis	70,000-80,000/(t of NH_3)
methanol synthesis	36/(lb of CH_3OH)
petroleum refining	$\geq$ 610/(bbl of crude oil)

hydrotreating:
  naphtha
  coking distillates
	
	50/bbl
	750/bbl

hydrocracking	2,000-2,500/bbl

coal conversion to:
  liquid fuel
  gaseous fuel
	
	6,000-7,000/(bbl of synthetic oil)
	$\sim$ 1,560/(10^3 SCF of synthetic gas)

oil-shale conversion
  to liquid fuel
  gaseous fuel
	
	1,300/(bbl of synthetic oil)
	1,200/(10^3 SCF of synthetic gas)

iron-ore reduction	20,000/(t of iron)
process heat	3,070/10^6 Btu or 2,700/(10^3 lb of process steam)

A.   Thermochemical Data

Physical properties, as well as LHV [= lower heating value for combustion to $H_2O(g)$, see Table 11.5-2] and HHV [= higher heating value for combustion to $H_2O(\ell)$, see Table 11.5-2] data for CH_4 and H_2, are summarized in Table 11.5-2. These data serve to emphasize the fact that H_2 is superior to NG in the liquid form per unit mass (by factors of 2.4 to 2.6) and inferior per unit volume (under standard conditions, by factors of 3.1 to 3.3).

Table 11.5-2 Physical and thermochemical data for CH_4
and H_2; based on data from standard physical
and thermochemical compilations and from
D. P. Gregory et al, A <u>Hydrogen-Energy</u>
<u>System</u>, American Gas Association, Arlington,
Virginia, 1973.

	CH_4	H_2
<u>gas density at 70°F and 1 atm</u>		
lb/CF	0.0416	0.0052
g/cm^3	6.66×10^{-4}	8.33×10^{-5}
<u>liquid density at the normal boiling point</u>		
lb/CF	26.53	4.43
g/cm^3	0.425	0.071
<u>liquid heating value in Btu/lb</u>		
HHV	23,875	61,095
LHV	21,495	51,623
<u>gas heating value in Btu/SCF</u>		
HHV	1,012	325
LHV	911	275
<u>compressibility factor at</u>		
1 atm	1.00	1.00
500 psia	0.935	1.020
1,000 psia	0.873	1.065

A broader fuel comparison is shown in Table 11.5-3
and includes gasoline, fuel oil, kerosene, jet fuel, H_2(g) at
3×10^3 psia, LH_2, magnesium hydride (MgH_2) at 500°F,
vanadium hydride (VH_2) at 50°F, CH_4 at 3×10^3 psia, LNG,
butane, ethanol, methanol, and ammonia. Under equivalent

Table 11.5-3   Combustion energies per unit mass and per unit volume and approximate fuel and storage system weight and volume requirements for selected fuels; based on data from standard thermochemical compilations and from J. A. Hoess and R. C. Stahman, "Unconventional Thermal, Mechanical, and Nuclear Low-Pollution-Potential Power Sources for Urban Vehicles," SAE Transactions, Paper 690231, 1969.

Fuel	Density		Approximate energy per unit mass		Approximate energy per unit volume		Storage-system requirements for carrying the energy equivalent of 20 gallons of gasoline	
	g/cm^3	lb/ft^3	cal/g	Btu/lb	cal/cm^3	Btu/ft^3	lb	ft^3
gasoline	0.735	45.9	10,700	19,100	7,840	876,000	138	2.9
No. 2 diesel fuel	0.838	52.4	10,600	19,000	8,900	995,000	138	2.6
kerosene	0.821	51.3	10,700	19,100	8,670	970,000	129	2.6
JP-4 (jet fuel)	0.777	48.6	10,400	18,700	8,140	910,000	138	2.8
C_2H_5OH (ethanol)	0.789	49.1	6,500	11,600	5,130	570,000	221	4.4
CH_3OH (methanol)	0.795	49.7	4,900	8,700	3,860	432,000	294	5.9
$CH_4(g)^b$ (methane)	0.136	8.5	12,000	21,500	1,640	183,000	515	28.5
$CH_4(l)^c$	0.425	26.5	12,000	21,500	5,100	570,000	248	16.6
$NH_3(l)^a$ (ammonia)	0.635	39.7	4,500	8,000	2,840	317,000	469	13.8
$C_3H_8(l)^a$ (propane)	0.579	36.2	11,100	20,000	6,470	724,000	202	5.7
$C_4H_{10}(l)^a$ (butane)	0.563	35.2	11,000	19,700	6,220	695,000	193	5.9
$H_2(g)^b$ (hydrogen)	0.017	1.1	29,000	52,000	500	56,000	1,370	92.0
$H_2(l)^c$	0.071	4.4	29,000	52,000	2,060	229,000	405	40.5
MgH_2^d (magnesium hydride)	0.870	54.4	2,070	3,710	1,800	202,000	731	12.0
VH_2^e (vanadium hydride)	6.400	400.0	610	1,100	3,920	440,000	2,300	6.0

a.   Liquid at 80°F.
b.   Gas at 80°F and 3,000 psig.
c.   Liquid at cryogenic temperatures and 1 atmosphere.
d.   Magnesium hydride bed with 40% voids at 500°F.
e.   Vanadium hydride bed at 50°F.

physical conditions, hydrogen combustion is seen to deliver the largest energy per unit mass and the lowest energy per unit volume.

B. Combustion Parameters

Practical applications of fuels involve not only considerations of energy release but also of a variety of other parameters that are more properly related to the kinetic aspects of fuel use. For example, a wide range of composition limits in which a fuel-air mixture is capable of burning will allow operation under conditions when air-fuel injection is imperfectly controlled. This desirable feature for combustion applications also represents a potential hazard when accidental fuel leakage occurs because the problem of dilution to produce non-combustible mixtures may be compounded for a fuel with wide combustion limits. Reference to the data listed in Table 11.5-4 shows that hydrogen has exceptionally wide combustible limits in air-fuel mixtures. The limits of combustible-gas composition are often referred to as flammability limits. These limits are dependent on temperature. The approximate values listed for hydrogen in Table 11.5-4 for the lean limit (lower hydrogen-concentration value) and the rich limit (upper hydrogen-concentration value) refer to some experimental measurements performed near room temperature. More detailed data as a function of temperature are shown in Fig. 11.5-1. It is apparent from the plots shown in Fig. 11.5-1 that the flammability limits

become appreciably wider as the temperature is raised.[2]
For example, at 300°C, they have broadened to 7.0 to 79.0
volume percent of H_2 as compared with 9.0 to 73.5 volume
percent at 100°C.

The data listed in Table 11.5-4 and shown in Fig.
11.5-1 refer to the ability of a gas mixture to support burn-

Table 11.5-4 Stoichiometric air-fuel ratio by weight and the
volume percent of fuel in air-fuel mixtures
which will support combustion.

Fuel	Stiochiometric air-fuel ratio by weight[a]	Approximate volume percent of fuel in combustible mixtures near room temperature[b]
gasoline	15.1	1.4 to 7.3
CH_3OH (methanol)	6.5	6.7 to 36.5
CH_4 (methane)	17.3	5.0 to 15.0
NH_3 (ammonia)	6.1	15.5 to 27.0
C_3H_8 (propane)	15.7	2.1 to 9.4
C_4H_{10} (butane)	15.5	1.9 to 8.4
H_2 (hydrogen)	34.5	4.0 to 74.2

a. An "air composition" of 21% oxygen, 78% nitrogen, and
1% argon is assumed.
b. The data refer to flammability limits in air for upward
propagation.

[2] I. L. Drell and F. E. Belles, "Survey of Hydrogen Combustion Properties, "National Advisory Committee for
Aeronautics, NACA Report 1383, Washington, D.C., 1958.

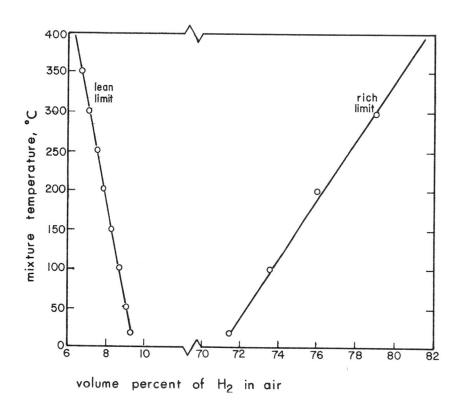

Fig. 11.5-1 Effect of temperature on flammability limits of
            hydrogen in air for downward propagation; re-
            produced from Ref. [2].

ing and not to the ease of ignition. The ease of ignition may
be indicated by the minimum energy that must be supplied
by a spark in order to initiate burning. Representative data
are reproduced in Fig. 11.5-2 for various pressures and
concentrations. For a given gas composition, the minimum
ignition energy is seen to decrease rapidly as the pressure
is increased; this change is directly associated with the fact
that chemical reaction rates accelerate with pressure as
p^n ($n \sim 2$ for many complex chemical systems). At a given

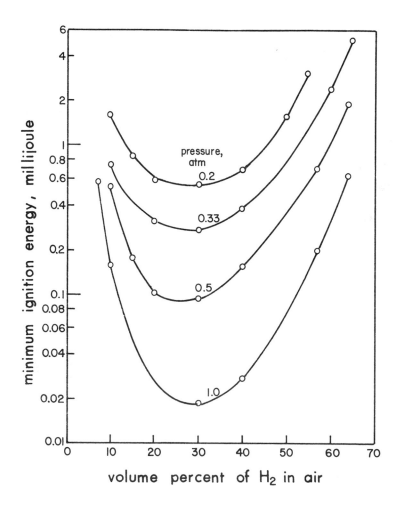

Fig. 11.5-2 Spark ignition energies for hydrogen-air mix-
           tures at various pressures; reproduced from
           Ref. [2].

pressure, the required minimum ignition energy decreases
as the stoichiometric mixture composition (at $\sim 28\%$ volume
percent of H_2) is approached from either leaner or richer
mixtures. At 1 atmosphere, the minimum ignition energy
for a stoichiometric H_2-air mixture is seen to be 0.019
millijoule; the corresponding value for a stoichiometric CH_4-

air mixture is about 0.29 millijoule.

Actually, ignition does not occur instantaneously but only after expiration of a well-defined period of time called the ignition lag. Under appropriate experimental conditions, ignition occurs spontaneously after an elapsed time which decreases as the temperature increases and which is also a sensitive function of gas composition. Some spontaneous ignition data for H_2-air and H_2-O_2 mixtures are shown in Fig. 11.5-3. These measurements may be difficult to reproduce and they are not immediately transferable to hazard assessments because they are sensitive to surface conditions in a reaction vessel. Ideally, they represent limits on ignition lags when the surfaces containing the gases are inactive and do not participate in the reactions.

At a given pressure, combustion may be suppressed by confining the gases to the immediate vicinity of surfaces. Two parallel plates may be brought together until combustion can no longer be sustained. The maximum distance between the plates when combustion is suppressed is called the quenching distance. Measured quenching distances are shown for H_2-air mixtures at various pressures in Fig. 11.5-4. At a pressure of 1 atmosphere, the minimum value is seen to be about 0.064 cm for a stoichiometric mixture of H_2 in air. The corresponding length for CH_4 is about 4 to 5 times greater. Thus, hydrogen combustion is not only easier to initiate (with lower energy) than CH_4-combustion, it is also more difficult to quench and thus easier to sustain. Flames are also more difficult to blow off a flame holder by increas-

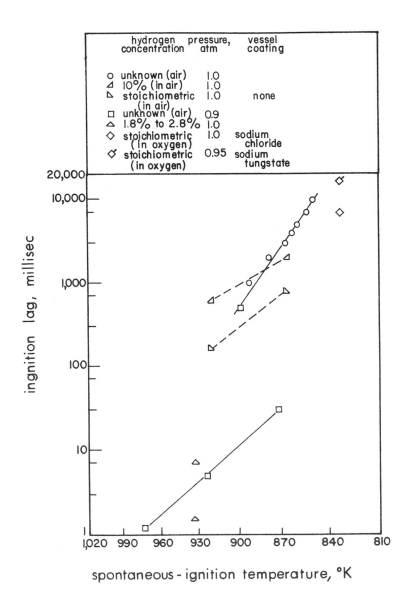

Fig. 11.5-3 Effect of spontaneous-ignition temperature on
ignition lag; reproduced from Ref. [2].

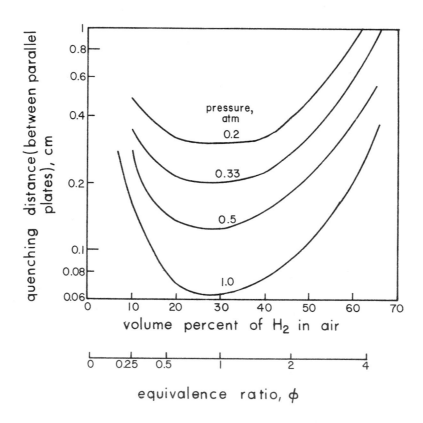

Fig. 11.5-4 Effect of hydrogen concentration on the quenching distance of hydrogen-air mixtures for
specified pressures; reproduced from Ref. [2].
The equivalence ratio, φ, is defined as the
$(H_2)/(air)$ mole ratio divided by the corresponding ratio for the stoichiometric mixture.

ing gas-flow speed in H_2-air mixtures than in more conven-
tionally-used fuel-air mixtures.

    The rate at which a flame propagates into a combusti-
ble gas mixture is called the (laminar) burning velocity or
flame speed. Hydrogen-air mixtures support exceptionally
high flame speeds. Four independent sets of measurements
on H_2-air mixtures are shown in Fig. 11.5-5 and indicate a

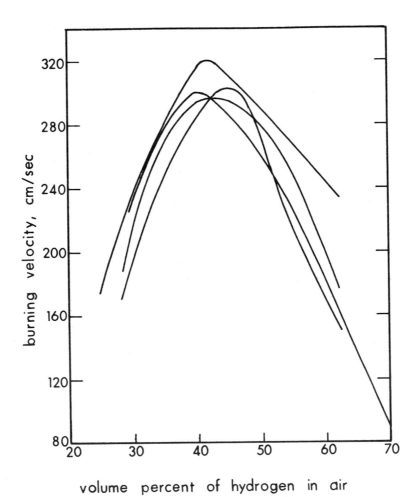

Fig. 11.5-5 Effect of hydrogen concentration on burning velo-
            cities of hydrogen-air mixtures at atmospheric
            pressure for an initial temperature of 300°K.
            The separate curves refer to independent mea-
            surements. Reproduced from D. P. Gregory
            et al, A Hydrogen Energy System, American
            Gas Association, Arlington, Virginia, 1973.

maximum flame speed of about 300 cm/sec for gases initially

at 300°K and atmospheric pressure. The corresponding

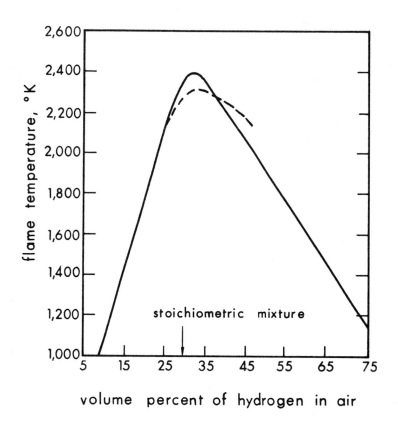

Fig. 11.5-6 Theoretical and experimental hydrogen-air flame temperatures at atmospheric pressure. The solid curve represents theoretical data while the dotted curve corresponds to experimental data. Reproduced from D. P. Gregory et al, A Hydrogen Energy System, American Gas Association, Arlington, Virginia, 1973.

values for CH_4-air, butane-air, and gasoline-air mixtures are all around 34 to 45 cm/sec. Thus, hydrogen-air mixtures tend to burn very quickly, allowing the use of exceptionally small combustion chambers.

Adiabatic flame temperatures are easily calculated for H_2-air mixtures.[3] Representative calculated and some measured data are shown in Fig. 11.5-6. The maximum value of the adiabatic flame temperature occurs for the stoichiometric mixture at about 2,400°K. The flame temperatures are about 2,200°K for stiochiometric mixtures of CH_4-air and gasoline-air. Thus, hydrogen-air flames tend to have relatively high temperatures but this disadvantage may be eliminated by operating at off-stoichiometric mixture compositions (compare Fig. 11.5-6).

Hydrogen-air mixtures produce appreciably less of the pollutant NO_x than gasoline-air mixtures at preferred mixture compositions (see Fig. 11.5-7) in single-cylinder engines. Figures 11.5-8A and 11.5-8B show, respectively, the ratio of pollutant-to-exhaust weights for hydrocarbon- and hydrogen-fueled automobiles as functions of the air-fuel ratio by weight. Fuel-rich hydrocarbon mixtures lead to increased emissions of CO and organic chemical residues, as shown in Fig. 11.5-8A. Fuel-rich hydrogen mixtures lead to decreased NO_x and increased H_2 and NH_3 emissions (see Fig. 11.5-8B) from automobile engines.

The preceding survey of fundamental combustion data shows that hydrogen is superior to gasoline and NG insofar as desirable properties for combustion of fuel-air mixtures are concerned.

---

[3]Ref. [1] in Section 11.1.

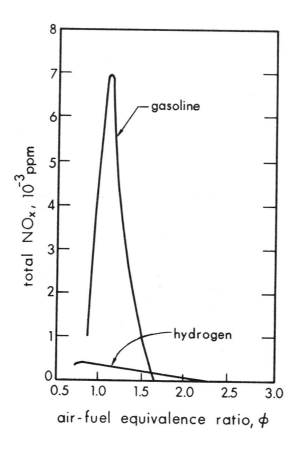

Fig. 11.5-7 Wide-open throttle emission characteristics of
single-cylinder engines; reproduced with modifications from R. G. Murray, R. J. Schoeppel,
and C. L. Gray, "The Hydrogen Engine in Per-
spective," Proceedings of the 7th Intersociety
Energy Conversion and Engineering Conference,
Paper 729216, San Diego, California, 1972; published by the American Chemical Society,
Washington, D.C., 1972. Copyright © 1972
by the American Chemical Society.

C.   Practical Applications

Hydrogen has been used as fuel in automotive vehicles,
in boilers, in aircraft-turbine and piston engines, and else-

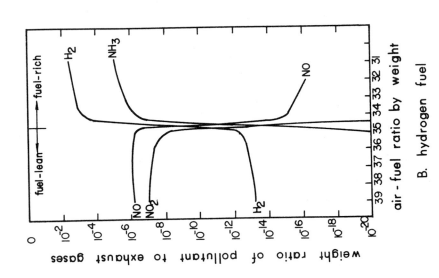

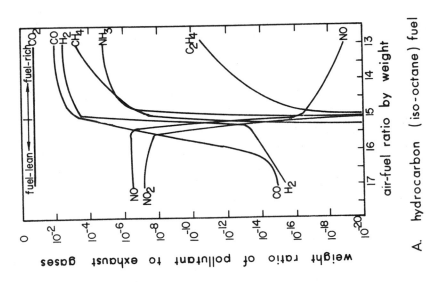

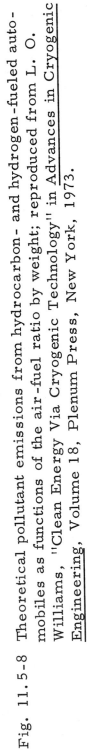

A. hydrocarbon (iso-octane) fuel

B. hydrogen fuel

Fig. 11.5-8 Theoretical pollutant emissions from hydrocarbon- and hydrogen-fueled auto-mobiles as functions of the air-fuel ratio by weight; reproduced from L. O. Williams, "Clean Energy Via Cryogenic Technology" in Advances in Cryogenic Engineering, Volume 18, Plenum Press, New York, 1973.

where where gasoline or NG are customarily applied.[4] As is expected from the higher flame speed of H_2-air mixtures, the lower ignition energy, the wider flammability limits, and the lower NO_x production, hydrogen is easier to use economically than conventional fuels, provided suitable modifications are made in the equipment used.[4,5]

In burners, smaller entrance-port sizes may be required. In automobiles, carburetors must be modified and ignition timing must be adjusted (retarded). Burning at preferred mixture ratios may require increased crankcase ventilation in conventional internal-combustion engines.

Hydrogen can probably be burned catalytically at relatively low temperatures. For space-heating applications, venting may not be essential unless the high humidity associated with water production is objectionable.

Hydrogen is a preferred fuel for direct electricity generation in fuel cells. This topic will be considered in Chapter 13.

Diesel engines should be easily adapted to hydrogen use. For long-range space missions, hydrogen is the fuel of choice because of its large energy content per unit mass.

---

[4]Ref. [2] in Section 11.1.

[5]W. J. D. Escher, "Prospects for Hydrogen as a Fuel for Transportation Systems and for Electrical Power Generation," Report ORNI-TM-4305, Oak Ridge National Laboratory, Oak Ridge, Tennessee 37830, September 1972.

Hydrogen may be distributed readily to households for use in space-heating and cooking units. This distribution problem has already been considered in Section 11.3.

11.6 Safety Problems Connected with Hydrogen Use

Hydrogen, natural gas, propane, butane, and gasoline are all hazardous materials. Hydrogen is particularly hazardous because of its wide flammability and detonability limits in air and its low ignition energy. The dangers associated with the use of natural gas, propane, butane, and gasoline have been universally accepted. Public acceptance of the hazards of hydrogen use poses a new problem. The widespread public fear of hydrogen use is explained, in part, by the spectacular hydrogen fire which destroyed the airship Hindenburg in 1937 at Lakehurst, New Jersey.

A. Hazard and Safety Aspects of Gaseous Hydrogen Use

Hydrogen is a colorless, odorless, tasteless, and non-toxic gas under normal conditions. Because of its low viscosity and molecular weight, hydrogen is prone to leakage and, when mixed with air, readily forms potentially-explosive and easily-ignited mixtures. However, a hydrogen leak disperses rapidly because of the high diffusion rate of H_2 in air. These properties make adequate ventilation, leak prevention, and elimination of ignition sources necessary requirements for the safe handling of hydrogen.

The physical and chemical properties of hydrogen, hydrogen combustion properties, and the physical properties of hydrogen fires must be understood before evaluating the safety aspects of hydrogen use. When discussing the safety aspects of a given material, a reference standard must be chosen. Since, in a hydrogen economy, hydrogen will replace our present use of natural gas, it is appropriate to adopt methane as a comparison standard. Physical, chemical, and combustion properties of hydrogen and methane are compared in Table 11.6-1.

The rates of hydrogen and methane leakage are measured by orifice capacity. On a volume basis, three times as much hydrogen as methane will escape through the same orifice. The energy content of the gases escaping from a leak of fixed size is about the same for hydrogen and methane. A hydrogen leak into a confined air space will produce a mixture at the lower flammability limit of H_2 (4% by volume) about 3.8 times faster than a methane leak will produce the corresponding mixture at the lower flammability limit of CH_4 (5% by volume). The energy contained within a confined space in hydrogen-air mixtures is about one-quarter of the energy contained in the same space for methane-air mixtures at the lower flammability limits. The time elapsed before a hydrogen leak produces an H_2-air mixture at the upper flammability limit is more than 1.6 times longer than for a methane leak.

A hydrogen leak into an unconfined space disperses much faster than a methane leak. Since the density of hydrogen is about 7% of that of air, compared to 56% for methane,

Table 11.6-1 Physical, chemical, and combustion properties of hydrogen and methane; based on data from standard physical and thermochemical compilations and from D. P. Gregory et al, A Hydrogen-Energy System, American Gas Association, Arlington, Virginia, 1973.

Fuel property	Hydrogen (H_2)	Methane (CH_4)
specific gravity, air = 1.00 (0°C and 1 atm)	0.0696	0.555
heating value, Btu/SCF	325.0	1,012.0
viscosity at 0°C and 1 atm, 10^{-6} poise	83.5	102.6
molecular speed at 0°C, m/s	1,692.0	600.0
relative volume flow rate	3.03	1.0
relative energy flow rate	0.93	1.0
air required to support combustion, SCF/10^3 Btu	7.33	9.42
total combustion products, CF/10^3 Btu	8.87	10.40
ignition energy for a stoichiometric mixture, millijoule	0.02	0.3
ignition temperature in air, °F	968-1,250	1,200-1,330
flame velocity for 20% primary air, ft/s	2.8	<0.1
flame velocity for 50% primary air, ft/s	9.2	0.1
flame velocity for 100% primary air, ft/s	6.4	0.9
maximum flame velocity, ft/s	9.4	0.9
lower flammability limit in air, volume %	4.0	5.0
upper flammability limit in air, volume %	74.0	15.0
lower detonability limit in air, volume %	18.3	6.3
upper detonability limit in air, volume %	59.0	13.5
quenching distance, cm	0.06	0.25

the hydrogen tends to rise much faster. In addition, the diffusion rate of hydrogen is about 2.8 times greater than that of methane. These buoyancy and diffusivity properties of hydrogen help decrease the hazards associated with hydrogen leakage. However, these same properties increase the difficulty of determining the precise location of a hydrogen leak.

The flammability and detonability limits of hydrogen, which are functions of pressure, temperature, and inert diluents, are much wider than those of methane. The maximum hydrogen flame velocity is more than ten times that of methane. The energy required to ignite a hydrogen mixture near the stoichiometric ratio is about 0.02 millijoule, or less than 7% of the energy required to ignite a stoichiometric methane-air mixture. The ignition temperatures of hydrogen and methane in air (see Table 11.6-1) are high compared to those of propane (870°F) and gasoline ($\sim760^\circ$F).

At atmospheric pressure, the quenching distance for hydrogen in air is about 0.06 cm; it is 0.25 cm for methane in air and 0.20 cm for propane in air. The quenching distance decreases with rising pressure and temperature.

Pure hydrogen flames are invisible and smokeless. Stationary hydrogen flames produce some acoustic noise. The sound from both premixed and diffusion flames, such as those occurring at the location of a hydrogen leak, increases as increasing gas-flow velocities become turbulent. The noise generated by a burning hydrogen mixture is greater than for a similar unignited gas flow.[1]

The flame temperature of hydrogen fires is not very different from that of most hydrocarbon fires. A hydrogen-air mixture containing 43% hydrogen by volume burns with a flame temperature of 3,680°F (see Fig. 11.5-6), as compared with 3,400°F for air with methane and 3,500°F with propane.[1] The maximum flame temperature in a hydrogen diffusion flame is approximately 3,000°F.[1] The thermal hazards associated with combustion depend also on the radiant energy emitted from the flame. Hydrocarbon fuels have effective emissivities near unity; here the emissivity is defined as the ratio of the radiant energy emitted by the flame to the radiant energy emitted from a blackbody at the same temperature. The emissivities of hydrogen flames have been reported[1] to vary from 0.01 to 0.1.

A summary of the properties of hydrogen and methane flames is given in Table 11.6-2.

B. Hazards and Safety in the Use of Liquid Hydrogen

The use of liquid hydrogen creates several additional hazard and safety problems. The low temperature of liquid hydrogen (-423°F) leads to a special type of hazard. At a temperature of -423°F, all gases except helium are liquefied.

---

[1]B. Rosen, V.H. Dayan, and R.L. Proffit, Hydrogen Leak and Fire Detection, National Aeronautics and Space Administration, Report SP-5092, Washington, D.C., 1970.

Table 11.6-2 Properties of hydrogen and methane flames;
based on data from Ref. [1] and from standard
thermochemical compilations.

Property	Hydrogen	Methane
flame color	invisible	bluish-yellow
flame temperature		
theoretical*	$4,010^{\circ}F$	$3,484^{\circ}F$
observed	$3,713^{\circ}F$	$3,416^{\circ}F$
flame emissivity	0.01 to 0.1	~1.0

*Not corrected for dissociation.

When air is liquefied, because of the difference in the boiling points of oxygen ($-297^{\circ}F$) and nitrogen ($-321^{\circ}F$), the resulting liquid becomes oxygen-enriched. Thus, improperly insulated liquid hydrogen creates local oxygen enrichment which may result in a dangerous fire hazard. Liquid hydrogen pipes and tanks, including any foam-type insulation used, must be purged with either hydrogen or helium to remove sources of air.

Additional hazards are associated with liquid-hydrogen use because of its low boiling temperature, low viscosity, and low heat of vaporization. The low boiling point and heat of vaporization of liquid hydrogen create serious boil-off problems during storage or handling. At the same time, exposure of liquid hydrogen to atmospheric conditions minimizes the duration of a possible hazard. Direct skin exposure to liquid hydrogen causes freezing and produces tissue damage similar to that resulting from severe burns. On contact with warm skin, small quantities of liquid hydrogen tend

to sputter and be exhausted (Leidenfrost effect) before tissue
damage occurs. The danger of tissue freezing by very cold
vapor is increased by the high thermal conductivity of gaseous hydrogen.[2] If a storage or handling system fails, the
very low viscosity (1.82×10^{-8} poise) of liquid hydrogen
leads to extraordinarily fast escape rates.

A comparison of the densities of saturated liquid-hydrogen vapor at $-423°$F (1.34×10^{-3} g/cm^3) and of air at
$70°$F (1.2×10^{-3} g/cm^3) indicates that the evaporated gas
will initially tend to fall. Spill and vent tests[2] on liquid
hydrogen have shown that evaporated hydrogen will persist
and is transported over considerable distances by the wind.

Investigators at the U.S. Bureau of Mines have conducted liquid-hydrogen spills to study the rate of hydrogen
cloud growth, the cloud volume, the possibility of a detonation, and the damage to the surroundings. The spills, ranging from 1 to 5,000 gallons (~ 3.1 to 15.5×10^4 Btu), were
conducted under both confined and unconfined conditions. No
detonations occurred during the unconfined tests when the
hydrogen-air mixtures were ignited by an electrical discharge. Detonations did occur with similar ignition sources
in totally confining structures when the exposed volume was

---

[2]D. B. Chelton, Chapter 10 on "Safety in the Use of Liquid
    Hydrogen," in Technology and Uses of Liquid Hydrogen,
    R. B. Scott, W. H. Denton, and C. M. Nichols, eds., The
    Macmillan Company, New York, New York, 1964.

not large in comparison with the volume of the spill.[3]

The combustion of a flammable hydrogen-air mixture over an evaporating liquid-hydrogen spill produces only a small increase in pressure.   The pressure increase is not strongly dependent on confinement.   Combustion over a partially confined 1.25-gallon spill and combustion over an unconfined 500-gallon spill produced[3] approximately the same pressure.   The power radiated from a flame above a liquid-hydrogen spill is approximately 20 kw/ft^2 of spill surface.[2]

Zabetakis and Burgess[3] concluded that the flammable zone above a liquid hydrogen spill does not necessarily coincide with the vapor cloud.   The visible cloud is, in general, below the height of the upper flammable zone.   This difference in height is affected by humidity, motion of the air, and the time interval after the spill.[3]   The flammable zones and the visible cloud height as functions of the elapsed time, after a 0.75-gallon spill of liquid hydrogen on a dry asphalt surface in ambient air at 59°F, are shown in Fig. 11.6-1.

Safe storage and handling of gaseous or liquid hydrogen require implementation of the following operating conditions: adequate ventilation in all operating areas, prevention of hydrogen leaks, purging of all storage and handling

---

[3]M. G. Zabetakis and D. S. Burgess, Research on the Hazards Associated with the Production and Handling of Liquid Hydrogen, U.S. Bureau of Mines, Report RI-5707, Washington, D.C., 1961.

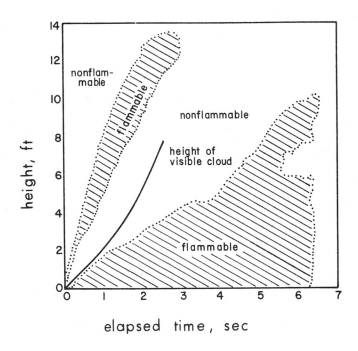

Fig. 11.6-1 Position of the flammable zones and the visible
cloud resulting from a 0.75-gallon liquid hydrogen spill; reproduced from Ref. [3]

systems before and after hydrogen use, elimination of confinement for large quantities of gaseous or liquid hydrogen,
avoidance of oxygen or air contamination, total elimination
of all possible ignition sources.

11.7 Climatic Impact-Assessment of a Hydrogen Economy

Total conversion to a hydrogen economy does not
appear likely to exert a profound effect on global climate

because the total incremental flow of water handled will
at most amount to 10^{-3} of the normal global flows. We consider, for example, the very large worldwide energy consumption of 6×10^{18} Btu$_t$/y (corresponding to 10×10^9 p
using 20 kw$_t$/p). For the overall process $H_2(g) + (1/2)O_2(g)$
$\rightarrow H_2O(g) - 57.796$ kcal, the incremental amount of water
cycled through the atmosphere is

$$\frac{6 \times 10^{18} \text{ Btu}}{y} \times \frac{0.24 \text{ kcal}}{0.949 \text{ Btu}} \times \frac{18 \text{ g}}{57.8 \text{ kcal}} \times \frac{1 \text{ kg}}{10^3 \text{ g}} \times \frac{1 \text{ mt}}{10^3 \text{ kg}}$$

$= 4.74 \times 10^{11}$ mt of water/y. Global evaporation of water
(see Volume I, p. 305) normally adds 4.48×10^{14} mt of
water/y. Thus, the man-made increment amounts to only
0.11%. While the climatic impacts of the incremental
water loads may be important locally and should be carefully studied, these loads are unlikely to be responsible for
significant global temperature or precipitation changes.

11.8   Alternative Energy Sources, Especially Methanol

Because of the acknowledged storage difficulties in
large-scale hydrogen use, as determined by the low energy
content of the gas per unit volume, and because of untried
large-scale applications for such purposes as ground transportation, considerable interest has been focused on other
synthetic hydrogen compounds, especially CH_4, CH_3OH
(methanol), C_2H_5OH (ethanol), NH_3 (ammonia), and N_2H_4

(hydrazine).[1-4] Of these, the first three are carbon-containing compounds, which may have to be supplied by cellulose derived from plants. Ammonia has a disagreeable odor and is a toxic gas under normal conditions. Hydrazine has exceptionally favorable physical properties since it is a liquid at room temperature; however, it is a highly toxic material. Large-scale introduction of unadulterated ethanol might well compound the social problems associated with alcohol use. With adulterated ethyl alcohol as primary energy source for transportation, we would expect a new type of distilling industry to develop. For the carbon compounds, the problem of CO control remains. Nearly complete removal of NO from the combustion products may be more difficult to achieve with NH_3 and N_2H_4 than with H_2.

Reed and Lerner[1] have been especially enthusiastic about the use of methanol. They noted that 1972 U.S. production of 10^9 gallons (3.2×10^9 kg) amounted to 1% of

---

[1] T. B. Reed and R. M. Lerner, "Methanol: A Versatile Fuel for Immediate Use," Science 182, 1299-1304 (1973).

[2] Ref. [1] in Section 11.5.

[3] "Report by the Committee on Motor-Vehicle Emissions," National Academy of Sciences, Washington, D.C., February 1973.

[4] D. P. Gregory and R. B. Rosenberg, "Synthetic Fuels for Transportation and National Energy Needs," paper presented at the Society of Automotive Engineers, National Meeting Symposium on Energy and the Automobile, Detroit, Michigan, May 1973.

gasoline production and the the cost was $0.183/gallon. [5]
Methanol is an easily-stored and transported liquid under
normal conditions. Up to 30% of CH_3OH may be added to
commercial gasolines without modification of the internal-
combustion engine. [1] Furthermore, addition of CH_3OH
to gasoline yields improved performance and lower emissions. Preliminary tests [1] of adding from 5 to 30% methanol to gasoline for use in unmodified automobiles have
shown fuel-economy increases from 5 to 13%, reductions
of CO emission from 14 to 72%, exhaust temperature decreases from 1 to 9%, and up to a 7% improvement in acceleration. It should, however, be noted that there have also
been claims that engine corrosion occurs with gasoline-
methanol mixtures.

We refer to the paper of Reed and Lerner [1] for further elaboration of the virtues of a partial or complete change
to a methanol economy. A less optimistic evaluation of the
benefits of methanol-gasoline blends has been given by
Wigg. [6] Here we content ourselves with a listing of heats
of combustion (Table 11.8-1), production costs (Table 11.8-2),
and storage costs (Table 11.8-3).

---

[5] Chemical Economics Handbook, Sections 674.5021 to
674.5023, Stanford Research Institute, Menlo Park,
California, 1972. The indicated cost estimate appears
to be unrealistically low for production from NG, coal
or cellulose (see Table 11.8-2).

[6] E. E. Wigg, "Methanol as a Gasoline Extender: A Cri-
tique," Science 186, 785-790 (1974).

Table 11.8-1 Heats of combustion of selected hydrogen-
based fuels; based, in part, on data in Tables
11.5-2 and 11.5-3.

Fuel	Heat of combustion[*]	
	10^3 Btu/lb	10^3 Btu/ft^3
C_8H_{18}, gasoline	19.1	876
$C_{0.28}H_{0.42}$, coal	13.9	1,123
$C_{0.32}H_{0.46}O_{0.22}$, wood	7.5	382
$CH_4(g)$, methane gas	21.5	0.911
$CH_4(\ell)$, liquid methane	21.5	570
CH_3OH, methanol	8.7	432
$H_2(g)$, hydrogen gas	51.6	0.275
$H_2(\ell)$, liquid hydrogen	51.6	229

[*]Combustion to CO_2 and $H_2O(g)$, corresponding to the
lower heating value, is assumed.

Table 11.8-2 Production costs of energy contained in selected fuels. The costs apply to large plant capacities, assuming that 15% of the plant cost is
allocated annually to profit, interest, depreciation, and maintenance. The cost bases used
for the fuels are too low by early 1974 standards. Reproduced from Ref. [2], 1972.

Fuel	Source	Cost, $/10^6$ Btu
gasoline	crude oil	1.05
methanol	natural gas[a]	1.58
	coal[b]	1.48
	lignite[c]	1.25
ethanol	petroleum feed stocks	4.60
ammonia	natural gas[d]	1.57
hydrazine		21.00
methane	well-head NG	0.15-0.40
	imported LNG	0.80-1.00
	coal	0.80-1.00
hydrogen gas	natural gas[a]	0.97
	coal[b]	1.32
	lignite[c]	0.78
liquid hydrogen	liquefaction	1.50[e]

[a] Natural gas at $0.40/10^3$ SCF.

[b] Coal at $7/ton or $0.27/10^6$ Btu.

[c] Lignite at $2/ton or $0.15/10^6$ Btu.

[d] Natural gas at $0.45/10^3$ SCF.

[e] Additional liquefaction cost.

Table 11.8-3 Capital costs for storage of selected fuels;
based on data from Ref. [2], 1972.

Fuel	Cost, $/10^6$ Btu
gasoline	
2 × 10^6 Btu	15
50 × 10^6 Btu	2
methanol	
2 × 10^6 Btu	18
50 × 10^6 Btu	3
ammonia	
2 × 10^6 Btu	85
50 × 10^6 Btu	10
LNG	
2 × 10^6 Btu	350
50 × 10^6 Btu	140
hydrogen gas[a]	
2 × 10^6 Btu	750
50 × 10^6 Btu	720
liquid hydrogen	
2 × 10^6 Btu	1,000
50 × 10^6 Btu	300

[a] Storage refers to a pressurized tank at 2,400 psig.

CHAPTER 12

ENERGY-STORAGE SYSTEMS

Energy storage involves the collection and retention of readily available energy for later use. Often sources of energy are available in abundant quantities during times of low energy demand. Energy-storage systems facilitate the efficient utilization of these energy sources. The need for adequate storage of gasoline supplies became apparent to the public during the 1973-1974 period of reduced imports. At a petroleum import rate of 9×10^6 bbl/d, a sixty-day supply is seen to require storage of 5.40×10^8 bbl. Using salt-dome storage with unit sizes of 10×10^6 bbl, the annual cost of storing a year's supply of petroleum corresponding to an import rate of 9×10^6 bbl/d is $\$1.64 \times 10^8$ since the unit storage cost is \$0.05/bbl-y. At this price, the annual storage costs for Middle-Eastern resources of 400×10^9 bbl would amount to $\$20 \times 10^9$/y.

Energy storage is of particular importance to the electric utilities and has been examined recently for appli-

cations in this sector.[1] Among the conclusions[1] reached
are the following: with an energy-storage efficiency of 75%,
energy storage can supply about 5% of U.S. electrical-energy
needs; using off-peak capacity from baseload (coal and nuclear) plants, 17% of peak demand becomes available; weekly
cycle operation would utilize about 70% of off-peak power;
in addition to pumped-water storage, hydro-pumped storage
with an underground reservoir, compressed-air storage, and
sensible-heat storage are attractive for applications in peak
and intermediate operations; advanced batteries should be
useful for peaking applications and for dispersed sitings
during the 1985-2000 time period; hydrogen-storage systems
should be considered where high capital costs and low overall efficiencies ($\sim 50\%$) are less important than large storage
capacities; thermal-storage systems may be useful when they a
are integrated with nuclear plants; flywheel-storage systems
and currently available lead-acid batteries are too expensive
for utility use. The likely long-term stability of these conclusions may profitably be assessed after careful study of
the material that is summarized in the following sections.

In this Chapter 12, we shall consider the following
topics: thermal-energy storage (Section 12.1), mechanical-
energy storage (Section 12.2), electrical-energy storage

---

[1]"An Assessment of Energy Storage Systems Suitable for
   Use by Electric Utilities," prepared by the Research and
   Development Department of the Public Service Electric and
   Gas Company, Newark, N.J., Report EPRI EM-264,
   Electric Power Research Institute, Palo Alto, California,
   July 1976.

(Section 12. 3), pumped-hydraulic and compressed-air storage systems (Section 12. 4), storage of liquid petroleum (Section 12. 5), natural-gas storage (Section 12. 6), and storage of synthetic fuels (Section 12. 7).

12.1   Thermal-Energy Storage

Energy can be stored thermally by heating, melting, or evaporating materials.   Energy storage by heating materials to elevated temperatures is known as sensible-heat storage.   The volume efficiency of sensible-heat storage is a function of the specific heat per unit mass of the material and of the density of the material, i. e., of the specific heat per unit volume.   Energy may be stored in the form of latent heat by heat transfer to materials during a phase change from solid to liquid (heat of fusion) or from liquid to gas (heat of vaporization or evaporation).

Thermal properties of several materials which may be suitable for sensible-heat storage and latent-heat storage are shown, respectively, in Tables 12. 1-1 and 12. 1-2.

The data of Tables 12. 1-1 and 12. 1-2 suggest the following general conclusions concerning the utilization of thermal-energy storage:

a.   Water is an excellent medium for sensible-heat storage below temperatures of 212°F.   A 9.4×10^2 ft^3 volume of water raised 100°F in temperature will store the energy contained in 1 bbl of petroleum.

Table 12.1-1   Properties of materials suitable for sensible-
heat storage of energy; based on data taken
from standard compilations of material
properties.

Material	Heat capacity, Btu/lb-$^\circ$F	Density, lb/ft^3	Volumetric heat capacity, Btu/ft^3-$^\circ$F
water	1.00	62	62
magnetite (Fe_3O_4)	0.17	324	55
iron	0.11	491	54
magnesium oxide (MgO)	0.23	223	51
aluminum oxide (Al_2O_3)	0.20	248	50
aluminum	0.22	168	37
granite	0.19	~175	33
asphalt	0.40	~81	32
window glass	0.20	~155	31
brick	0.24	~125	30
concrete	0.21	~140	29
dry earth	0.30	~87	26
white pine wood	0.60	~31	19

b.   Scrap iron and magnetite exhibit, over a wide
temperature range, nearly the same volumetric heat capacity
as water. A 3.1×10^2 ft^3 volume, accounting for 30% voids,
of either scrap iron or magnetite raised 500°F in temperature
will store the energy contained in 1 bbl of petroleum.

Table 12.1-2 Properties of materials suitable for latent-heat storage of energy; based on data taken from standard compilations of material properties.

Material	Melting point, $^{\circ}F$	Density, lb/ft^3	Heat of fusion, Btu/lb	Heat of fusion, Btu/ft^3
hypophosphorous acid (H_3PO_2)	79	94	63	5,900
calcium chloride hexahydrate ($CaCl_2 \cdot 6H_2O$)	86	107	73	7,800
Glauber's salt ($Na_2SO_4 \cdot 10H_2O$)	90	91	103	9,400
sodium hydroxide (NaOH)	482	133	90	12,000
lithium nitrate ($LiNO_3$)	507	148	158	23,400
ferric chloride ($FeCl_3$)	583	181	111	20,100
lithium hydroxide (LiOH)	864	91	186	17,000
lithium fluoride (LiF)	1,645	164	164	27,000
sodium fluoride (NaF)	1,818	160	300	48,000

c. Concrete, while not as efficient volumetrically as water, scrap iron, or magnetite, has obvious advantages for residential- and commercial-energy storage. Large insulated concrete storage units have been used to smooth the diurnal fluctuations in the energy requirements for space heating.

d.   A bed of crushed stone is a low-cost, sensible-heat storage medium, which is compatible with air as the energy-transport medium.   Crushed stone roofs have been in use in the U.S. for many years.

e.   The heats of fusion of the substances listed in Table 12.1-2 correspond in energy to temperature rises of 10^2 to $10^{3\circ}$ F for the substances listed in Table 12.1-1. There are no low-cost and readily available substances which are suitable for latent-heat storage at or near room temperatures.   Glauber's salt is a possibility.   However, its phase change at 90° F does not involve true melting but rather a separation into three phases of different density and composition; this decomposition is not rapidly reversible. Most organic materials have weak crystal lattices and hence low heats of fusion.   Inorganic salts generally melt at undesirably high temperatures.   Inorganic hydrates decompose at desirable temperatures but separate into an anhydrous solid residue and a dilute solution instead of actually melting.

f.   Ferric chloride and lithium nitrate are useful for high-temperature latent-heat storage.

A useful application of thermal-energy storage is involved in the utilization of waste heat for industrial processings.[1]   In a sense, these are energy-conservation measures involving waste-heat storage.   A compilation of activities of this type is given in Table 12.1-3.

---

[1]Thermal Energy Storage, Report of a NATO Science Committee Conference held at Turnberry, Scotland, March 1976; see Energy 2, 53-101 (1977).

Table 12.1-3 Industrial processes as candidates for thermal
energy storage (TES). Reproduced from Ref. [1].

Industry process	Overall merit	Process knowledge	Energy savings	New heat transfer exchange for the TES	Temperature	TES function
1. Cement						
Pre-heat by-pass	fair	good	S	no	760	s
2. Iron & Steel						
A. Coke dry cooling	good	good	L	maybe	985	s
B. Coke O_2 starvation	good	good	L	maybe	985	s
C. Electric furnace scrap preheat	fair-good	fair	M	no	485-985	s
D. Ingot casting soaking pit	fair	good	M	no	to 1315	
3. Glass						
Day tanks - annealing	fair	fair	M	no	N/A	D
4. Chemicals						
Batch processes	unknown	poor	unknown	maybe	to 220	s
5. Food, etc.						
A. Pressure cooking	fair	poor	unknown	no	~ 120	D
B. Blanching				no	< 90	D
C. Hygienics				no	~ 60	D
D. Grain drying	good	fair	unknown	no	~ 140	D
E. Tobacco curing	good	poor	unknown	no	N/A	D
6. Paper						
A. Batch digesters	poor	good	S	no	~ 145	s
B. Paper breaks	fair	good	M	no	120-150	s
7. Textiles						
Dye becks	fair	fair	M	no	~ 93	s
8. Clay/Ceramics						
Periodic kilns	good	good	L	maybe	to 980	s
9. Aluminum						
A. Bauxite drying	fair	fair	M	no	> 120	D
B. Alumina cooling	poor	fair	M	maybe	< 160	s
C. Casting/ingot cooling	poor	fair	L	maybe	< 980	s
10. Plastics & Rubber						
A. Thermosetting processes	fair	fair	unknown	unknown	200-216	D
B. Tire molding	fair	fair	M	unknown	N/A	D
11. Incineration						
Municipal solid waste	good	fair	unknown	yes	~ 815	s
12. Metals Fabrication						
Heat treating	fair	good	unknown	maybe	100-1100	s
13. Industries using Steam (Paper, Textiles, etc.)						
Steam flow variation & IPG	good	fair	L	maybe	> 535	s/D
14. Batch/Variable Equipment						
A. Crucible furnaces	fair		unknown	yes	N/A	s
B. Blast furnaces	good		S	yes	> 1480	s
C. Autoclaves	fair		unknown	yes	N/A	s

Key:
S = small
M = medium
L = large
s = variant supply
D = variant demand
N/A = not available

12.2 Mechanical-Energy Storage

Energy may be stored mechanically by a rotating
wheel, which is usually called a flywheel. The principle of

energy storage by flywheels has been known for centuries. The potter's wheel is an early example of energy storage in a flywheel. Today, all reciprocating engines rely on energy stored in flywheels to smooth the chemical-to-mechanical energy-conversion cycle.

A. The Physical Properties of Flywheels

The energy E stored in a flywheel is

$$E = (1/2)I\omega^2,$$ (12.2-1)

where I is the moment of inertia[*] about the rotational axis of the flywheel and ω is the angular frequency. The amount

---

[*]The moment of inertia is defined by

$$I = \int_O^R m(r)r\,dr,$$

where m(r) is the radial mass distribution and r is the radial distance measured from the axis of rotation. As an example, consider a thin-rim flywheel (see the fifth entry in Table 12.2-1). For this configuration, $I = MR^2$ if R is the radial distance of the mass location from the axis of rotation. If M is in grams and R in cm, then the units of I are gram-cm^2. The energy stored in the thin-rim flywheel when its angular frequency is ω(rad/sec) is given by Eq. (12.2-1). The units of E are gram-cm^2/sec^2 or erg if I is in gram-cm^2. Let ω_{max} be the minimum value of the angular frequency which the flywheel can sustain before disintegrating. Then

of energy stored in a flywheel is ultimately limited by the tensile strength of the flywheel material. The maximum tangential and radial stresses in a rotating flywheel are proportional to the product of the density of the flywheel material, the square of the radius of the flywheel, and the square of the angular frequency of the flywheel.

The maximum specific (per unit mass) energy e_{max} that can be stored in a flywheel may be written as

$$e_{max} = k_s(\sigma_{max}/\rho), \qquad (12.2-2)$$

where σ_{max} is the maximum tensile strength of the flywheel material, ρ is the flywheel-material density, and k_s is a constant, usually called the shape factor, which is a function of the rotor geometry and the flywheel-material deformation.[†] If consistent units are employed and the absence

---

$$E_{max} = (1/2)I\omega_{max}^2 = (1/2)MR^2\omega_{max}^2$$

and the specific energy becomes

$$E_{max}/M = (1/2)R^2\omega_{max}^2$$

and has the units cm^2/sec^2.

[†]In Eq. (12.2-2), we have used the symbol e_{max} for the maximum value of the specific energy, which may also be written as [see Eq. (12.2-2)]

of material deformation is assumed, the shape factor is
dimensionless and has a range from 0 to 1. A shape factor
of unity corresponds to the ideal case of a constant-stress
disc of infinite radius. Shape factors for various flywheel
geometries are given in Table 12.2-1.

For a thin-rim flywheel design without material
deformation, $k_s = 1/2$. The maximum specific energy
that can be stored in a thin-rim flywheel and the relative maximum specific energy storage, independently

_____

$$k_s \sigma_{max}/\rho,$$

where σ_{max} is expressed in $(gram/cm^2)$-cm/sec^2 [i.e.,
σ_{max} is a force in dyne, corresponding to the product of
the commonly defined maximum tensile stress (in gram/
cm^2) and the gravitational acceleration]. We see that

$$k_s \sigma_{max}/\rho = (1/2)R^2 \omega^2_{max}$$

for the thin-rim flywheel for which

$$\sigma_{max} = \rho R^2 \omega^2_{max}$$

in $(gram/cm^3) \times (cm^2/sec^2) = (g\text{-}cm/sec^2)/cm^2 = dyne/$
cm^2 if ρ is in $gram/cm^3$, R in cm, and ω_{max} in sec^{-1}; the
corresponding dimensionless value for k_s is 1/2 (compare
the fifth entry in Table 12.2-1). It is important to note
that σ_{max} is a characteristic of the material while the value
of ω_{max} depends on the particular geometric configuration
employed. The other geometric configurations listed in
Table 12.2-1 may be analyzed by using similar arguments.

Table 12.2-1 Flywheel shape factors for various flywheel geometries; reproduced from L. J. Lawson, "Design and Testing of High Energy Density Flywheels for Application to Flywheel/Heat Engine Hybrid Vehicle Drives," Proceedings of the 6th Intersociety Energy Conversion and Engineering Conference, Paper 719150, Boston, Mass., 1971; published by the American Chemical Society, Washington D.C., 1971. Copyright © 1971 by the American Chemical Society. Abbreviations used: ID = inner diameter, OD = outer diameter.

Flywheel geometry	Cross-sectional or pictorial view	Shape factor, k_s	
constant-stress disc $(OD \rightarrow \infty)$		1.000	suitable for homogeneous materials only
modified constant-stress disc (typical)		0.931	
truncated conical disc (typical)		0.806	
flat unpierced disc		0.606	
thin rim $[(ID)/(OD) \rightarrow 1.0]$		0.500	suitable for homogeneous or filamentary materials
shaped bar $(OD \rightarrow \infty)$		0.500	
rim with web (typical)		0.400	
single filament bar		0.333	
flat pierced disc		0.305	

of the flywheel design, are given in Table 12.2-2 for various flywheel materials. The data listed in the second column of Table 12.2-2 are determined by the ratios σ_{max}/ρ.

The data of Table 12.2-2, which have been calculated from Eq. (12.2-2) with $k_s = 1/2$ for the thin-rim flywheel, illustrate the desirability of using materials of high strength and low density for construction of energy-storing flywheels. Fused silica, which is currently not available on a large scale, is seen to have nearly 18 times the energy-storage capability of maraging steel.[*] By comparison, the common lead-acid automotive battery can store 10 to 15 wh/lb, which is approximately the same as the energy-storage capability of a thin-rim aluminum-alloy flywheel. The maximum storable specific-energy data given in Table 12.2-2 do not include allowances for flywheel efficiency in terms of run-down speed and the necessary auxiliary flywheel storage-system equipment. A realistic allowance[1] for these items

---

[1]
    D. W. Rabenhorst, "Potential Applications for the Super-flywheel," Proceedings of the 6th Intersociety Energy Conversion and Engineering Conference, Paper 719148, Boston, Mass., 1971; published by the American Chemical Society, Washington, D.C., 1971.

[*] A strong, tough low-carbon steel containing up to 25% Ni; hardening precipitates are formed during aging.

Table 12.2-2 Maximum specific energy storable in a thin-rim flywheel and the relative maximum specific energy storable (which is independent of flywheel design) for various flywheel materials; based on data from R. F. Post and S. F. Post, "Flywheels," Scientific American 229, 17-23, December 1973.

Material	Maximum specific energy storable in a thin-rim flywheel ($k_s = 1/2$), wh/lb	Relative maximum specific energy storable in any flywheel design
aluminum alloy	10	1
maraging steel	22	2.2
E-glass	86	8.6
carbon fiber	98	9.8
S-glass	120	12.0
polymer fiber (PRD-49)	159	15.9
fused silica	395	39.5

may be included by multiplying the rotor weight by a factor of 2.1. If an operating tensile strength of $0.7 \, \sigma_{max}$ is assumed, because of safety considerations, this factor of 2.1 should be increased to 3.0.

The available energy from flywheel energy-storage systems is a function of the operating speed ratio, which is defined to be the ratio of the highest operating speed to the lowest operating speed. We note that rotational speed and operating speed are proportional to each other. If the maximum operating angular frequency is ω_{max} and the minimum operating angular frequency is ω_{min}, then the flywheel energy remaining after slowdown is $(1/2) I \omega_{min}^2$

according to Eq. (12.2-1). The utilized energy is $(1/2)I$ $\times (\omega_{max}^2 - \omega_{min}^2)$ and the fraction of rotational energy converted to useful work is $(\omega_{max}^2 - \omega_{min}^2)/\omega_{max}^2 = 1-(\omega_{min}/\omega_{max})^2$. Thus, if the operating-speed ratio is 2, $\omega_{min}/\omega_{max}$ = 1/2 and 75% of the stored energy is used. Similarly, if the operating-speed ratio is 10, $\omega_{min}/\omega_{max}$ = 1/10 and 99% of the stored energy is used.

The term superflywheel is used for flywheels constructed from anisotropic materials such as E glass, carbon fiber, PRD-49, etc. These materials have higher maximum tensile strength per unit mass than isotropic materials such as aluminum and steel. The higher maximum tensile strength per unit mass gives superflywheel configurations superior energy-storage capabilities, even though conventional flywheels are normally constructed with geometries having higher k_s values (see Table 12.2-1).

For many applications, energy-storing superflywheels may prove to have significant advantages over other possible energy-storage systems. These applications may involve land-transportation vehicles such as golf carts, automobiles, and busses; tools such as lawnmowers and industrial elevators; power supplies ranging from emergency power supplies for hospitals to electric power peaking capability for electric-utility companies; aircraft, particularly STOL and VTOL designs; watercraft such as torpedo and mini-submarines; and spacecraft.

These applications utilize flywheels that are typically

either coupled with an electric motor-generator or a standard
heat engine. Schematic diagrams of a motor-generator flywheel system and a flywheel/heat-engine hybrid configuration are shown, respectively, in Figs. 12.2-1 and 12.2-2.
The use of flywheels for these and other energy-storage applications is discussed in Refs. [1] to [4].

B.   Flywheel-System Technology

There has been only limited operating experience
with large-scale mechanical-energy storage in flywheels.
The applications of flywheel energy-storage systems discussed in Refs. [1] to [4] will require technologies that
have not been fully developed.

Construction and testing of a conventional steel
flywheel, designed for an energy-storage capacity of 0.5
kwh, has been completed by workers at the Lockheed

[2] G. L. Dugger et al, "Flywheel and Flywheel/Heat Engine
Hybrid Propulsion Systems for Low-Emission Vehicles,"
Proceedings of the 6th Intersociety Energy Conversion
and Engineering Conference, Paper 719149, Boston,
Mass., 1971; published by the American Chemical
Society, Washington, D. C., 1971.

[3] L. J. Lawson, "Design and Testing of High Energy Den-
sity Flywheels for Application to Flywheel/Heat Engine
Hybrid Vehicle Drives," Proceedings of the 6th Inter-
society Energy Conversion and Engineering Conference,
Paper 719150, Boston, Mass., 1971; published by the
American Chemical Society, Washington, D. C., 1971.

[4] R. F. Post and S. F. Post, "Flywheels," Scientific
American 229, 17-23, December 1973.

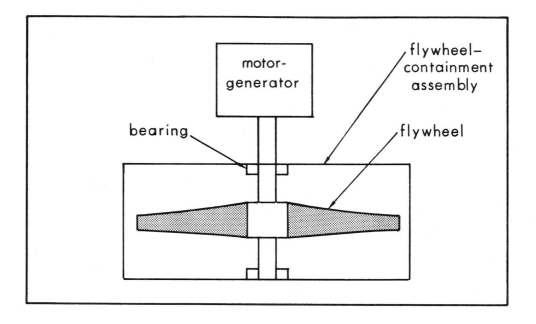

Fig. 12.2-1 Schematic diagram of an electric motor-
generator flywheel-storage system.

Missiles and Space Company.   The test flywheel weighed 46
pounds and was designed to rotate at speeds up to 24,000
revolutions per minute (rpm) in an evacuated chamber (the
pressure was equal to 0.22 mm of Hg).   Spindown tests
indicated[3] that bearing and brake drag were the major
sources of energy loss.   A disintegration test was performed to verify the design analysis.   The flywheel failed
at 35,590 rpm or a peripheral velocity of 3,170 ft/sec.
The calculated stress at the time of failure was 97% of the

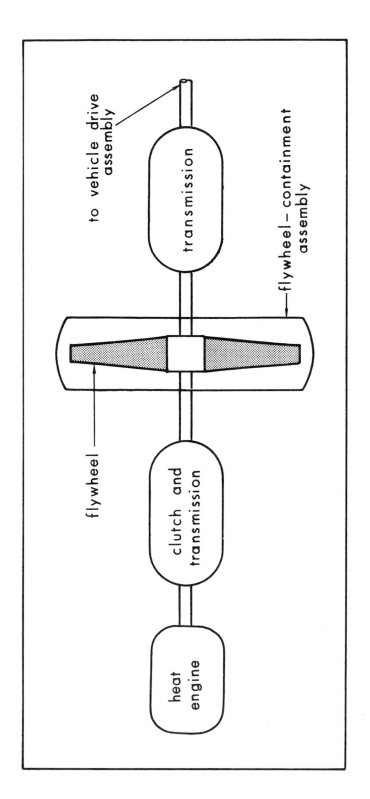

Fig. 12.2-2 Schematic diagram of a flywheel/heat engine hybrid configuration.

measured maximum tensile stress. Prior to disintegration,
the flywheel stored about 1.2 kwh for an energy density of
26 wh/lb.[3]

It has been estimated[1] that a superflywheel having
an energy-storage capability of 30 wh/lb will rotate at a
tip speed of about 3,800 ft/sec, independently of the material
from which it is constructed. For a diameter of 30 inches,
this tip speed is equivalent to approximately 30,000 rpm.
At these high rotational speeds, the superflywheel rotor
must operate in a partial vacuum. Energy may be transmitted to the vacuum-sealed rotor by using a continuously-
variable transmission with an electrical, magnetic, hydraulic, mechanical, or hydromechanical drive mechanism.[2]
Conventional high-speed bearings or, in some applications,
magnetic-fluid bearings may be required.

Most of the materials suggested for superflywheel
construction were initially developed for high-technology
aircraft and spacecraft applications. Many of these materials are now produced commercially on a large scale.
However, the fabrication of these materials into flywheel
geometries and their subsequent testing is still under
development. In addition, the seals and bearings required
for superflywheels involve the use of relatively untried
technologies.

The aerodynamic- or bearing-drag losses may
severly limit the energy storable in a superflywheel. The
aerodynamic drag may be reduced by operating the superflywheel in a partial vacuum. At constant pressure, this

drag is further reduced by a factor of six for a helium atmosphere or a factor of ten for a hydrogen atmosphere, because of reduced viscous losses at constant temperature. Operation of superflywheels in low-pressure atmospheres cannot generally be accomplished with conventional high-speed bearings. When magnetic fluids are used to seal the evacuated superflywheel container, then conventional high-speed bearings may be mounted externally to the vacuum container. Magnetic-fluid seals have essentially zero leakage and have been tested up to 50,000 rpm.[5]

Reduction of drag losses in the bearings may be accomplished by minimizing the bearing loads. The static gravity loading of the bearings can be eliminated by using magnetic levitation. The gyroscopic precession loads on the bearings may be minimized[1] by using an internal gimbal arrangement, which suspends the superflywheel in such a manner that it remains level when the support is tipped. Another method for reducing bearing losses involves use of magnetic-fluid bearings that have no solid surfaces in contact with the rotating shaft and, thus, a very long life. These bearings, which are presently under development, are expected[1] to have considerably lower frictional losses than the best currently available bearings. A schematic diagram of a superflywheel design utilizing a vacuum canister, magnetic-

---

[5]D. W. Rabenhorst, "New Concepts in Mechanical Energy Storage," Proceedings of the 5th Intersociety Energy Conversion and Engineering Conference, Paper 709035, Las Vegas, Nevada, 1970; published by the American Chemical Society, Washington, D.C., 1970.

fluid seals, internal gimbals, magnetic levitation, and magnetic-fluid bearings is shown in Fig. 12.2-3.

The remaining components of a conventional or
superflywheel energy-storage system, such as a motor-
generator, clutch and transmission, vacuum canister, and
safety containment shield have all been well developed for
other uses. These components should not be responsible
for any serious limitations in the application of flywheel
energy-storage systems.

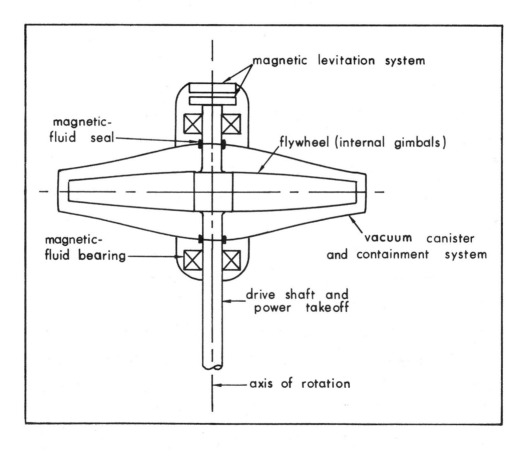

Fig. 12.2-3 Schematic diagram of a superflywheel design;
        reproduced from Ref. [5]. Copyright © 1970
        by the American Chemical Society.

C.   Flywheel Use in Transportation Systems

The use of flywheels for land-based transportation propulsion was demonstrated in the early nineteen fifties by the introduction of the Swiss Oerlikon electrogyrobus. The Oerlikon bus used a conventional 3,300-lb steel flywheel designed to store 3 wh/lb. An electric motor was used to store energy in the flywheel during bus stops. Between stops, the electric motor operated as a generator, driven by the flywheel, to run another electric motor which powered the bus.

The Ground Vehicle Systems Division of the Lockheed Aircraft Company is currently constructing an experimental bus, using the same principle as the Oerlikon bus, for the San Francisco Municipal Railway. The flywheel, operating in a vacuum canister, is manufactured from alloy steel and is designed to have a stored energy density about 10 times larger than that of the Oerlikon electrogyrobus. The Lockheed bus, which is scheduled for testing in 1975, is expected to have a range of approximately 6 miles before the flywheel must be recharged.

There has also been considerable interest in the use of flywheels and flywheel/heat-engine hybrid configurations to power automobiles. A schematic diagram of the drive-train and control system for a typical flywheel/heat-engine hybrid automobile is shown in Fig. 12.2-4. Lawson[3] concluded in 1971 that the specific energy-storage capability of present-day flywheels was not sufficient to make

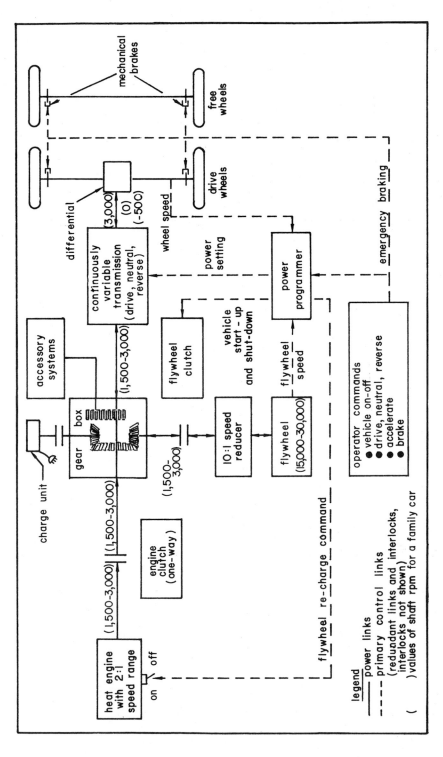

Fig. 12.2-4 Schematic diagram of the drivetrain and control system for a typical flywheel/heat-engine hybrid automobile. Numbers in parentheses identify rotational speeds in rpm for a family car. Reproduced from Ref. [2]. Copyright © 1971 by the American Chemical Society.

flywheel-only automobiles practical but flywheel/heat-engine hybrid vehicles were entirely feasible. Lawson[3] utilized a computer technique to screen 165 possible flywheel configurations with an energy-storage capacity of 500 wh to be used in a flywheel/heat-engine hybrid car. Flywheel geometries, materials and dimensionless ratios (radius to thickness) were treated as variables in the program, which yielded flywheel weight, dimensions, and maximum rotational speed, as well as the flywheel assembly weight, volume, and cost for each configuration. The eleven most practical flywheel-assembly designs[3] had a cost range of $128 to $240 at an energy level of 500 wh.

A small automobile would require[4] approximately 30 kwh of stored energy to provide a 200-mile range at 60 mph.* To store this amount of energy in lead-acid batteries requires a battery bank weighing more than a ton. A flywheel manufactured from 130 pounds of (currently unavailable) fused silica fibers, or from 280 pounds of PRD-49, could easily store 30 kwh of energy (compare the data in Table 12.2-2). In addition to the weight advantage, a flywheel system has a significantly higher rate of energy storage and energy release than a battery system. A flywheel

---

*The specified energy requirement is very optimistic, as may be seen by converting 30 kwh to gallons of gasoline equivalent, viz. 30 kwh = 1.024×10^5 Btu $\approx 1.75 \times 10^{-2}$ $bbl_e \approx 0.74$ gallon of gasoline equivalent. An automobile powered by an internal combustion engine would have to deliver 27 miles per gallon at one-tenth of the claimed efficiency for the flywheel-powered vehicle.

may also be used to take effective advantage of regenerative braking because of its extraordinarily high ($\sim 95\%$) output-to-input energy efficiency. The rundown time for a flywheel rotor contained in a vacuum canister has been estimated[4] to be from six to twelve months.

If an optimistic capital cost of \$32.50/kwh$_e$, estimated[4] for a very large flywheel system, is assumed to be valid also for smaller assemblies, then it follows that the capital cost of a flywheel power plant for a "small" flywheel-only automobile can be expected to be nearly \$1,000. This cost is more than twice the cost of a small internal-combustion engine. However, this cost comparison is not particularly meaningful since the important problem of vehicle range is not included.

Let us consider an advanced flywheel design which yields 60 wh/lb at a cost of \$C/lb. This flywheel is to provide the range of a conventional automobile on the assumption that its conversion efficiency is five times that of the fuel-conversion efficiency in a car. We consider a car with a 21-gallon tank storing approximately 3×10^6 Btu $= 8.79 \times 10^5$ wh. We note that the flywheel must weigh 2.93×10^3 lb at five times the efficiency of the car engine. Hence the flywheel will cost \$$2.93 \times 10^3$ C. Considering that the production cost for a conventional engine-gas-tank system is about \$350, we see that the equal-range flywheel must be constructed for \$0.12/lb, which seems unattainably low for the foreseeable future. Hence flywheel-only automobiles will certainly have to be built with much shorter operating ranges than conventional cars.

D.   Flywheel Use in Peak-Power Systems

As a result of recent advances in the manufacture of composite materials, the feasibility of utilizing a flywheel system as a peak-power device has increased. A peak-power system having an energy-storage capability of 1×10^5 kwh_e is envisioned[1] to have four superflywheel rotors which are approximately 60 feet in diameter, 10 to 20 feet high, and weigh 500 tons each. The superflywheel installations would be located underground for safety in case of an accident. This 1×10^5 kwh_e system would have the energy-generation capacity of an average gas-turbine peaking plant. The capital cost has been estimated[1] to be slightly less than that of an equivalent pumped-storage system which, on the average, costs about 20% more than a gas-turbine system. The operating cost of the superflywheel system has been estimated[1] to be about one-half that of a pumped-storage system and less than one-quarter that of a gas-turbine system. The lower operating costs of the superfly-wheel system reflect the greater versatility and the higher conversion efficiency that are achievable. However, the estimated costs for the superflywheel system are based on presently undeveloped technologies and, therefore, may be optimistic.

Another design suggested[4] for a peak-power fly-wheel system consists of flywheels which are 15 to 20 ft in diameter and weigh 100 to 200 tons. The flywheels would operate in a hydrogen or helium atmosphere at low pressure to reduce drag losses. Each flywheel unit would store 10,000 to 20,000 kwh$_e$ at a rotational speed of about 3,500 rpm. The flywheel would be coupled to a motor-generator that functions either as a motor during off-peak hours to spin up the flywheel and store energy or as a generator during peak hours to generate electric power by drawing on the stored energy in the flywheel. A flywheel system of this design storing 10,000 kwh$_e$ of energy and having a power rating of 3,000 kw$_e$ has been estimated[4] to cost $325,000. The corresponding capital cost per installed kilowatt is about $110, which is nearly 40% less costly than the Ludington pumped-storage plant (see Fig. 12.4-1). The flywheel system would operate at an output-to-input energy efficiency of 93 to 95%, as compared to the 50 to 70% output-to-input energy efficiency of pumped-storage systems. In addition, only 400 ft^2 of floor space are required to store 10 Mwh$_e$ in a flywheel system while 2 to 4 acres of reservoir area are typically required to store 10 Mwh$_e$ in a pumped-storage system.

12.3   Electrical-Energy Storage; Batteries

Electrical energy may be stored directly by capacitive storage, inductive storage, or in storage batteries.

A. Capacitive Storage

Capacitive-energy storage is commonly used in electric-power and electronic applications. These applications do not, in general, require the storage of large amounts of energy for long time periods. The energy density (u = energy per unit volume) that can be stored in a capacitor is given by

$$u = (1/2) K \epsilon_o E^2, \qquad (12.3-1)$$

where K is the dielectric constant, ϵ_o is the permittivity constant ($= 8.85415 \times 10^{-12}$ coulomb^2/newton-m^2), and E is the electric field strength.* It is apparent from Eq. (12.3-1) that large stored energy densities are obtained if we use dielectric materials with high dielectric constants and high electric field strengths. The maximum electric field strength is determined by the dielectric strength, which equals the maximum potential gradient that may exist in the dielectric without the occurrence of electrical breakdown. To avoid significant energy loss from leakage

---

*The field strength is defined to be the ratio of the force (e.g, in newton) produced by a test charge (in coulomb), i.e., E has the dimension of newton/coulomb. With E in these units, u is then expressed in (coulomb^2/newton-m) $\times$ (newton/coulomb)^2 = newton/m^2 = newton-m/m^3 = joule/m^3.

currents during long storage times, the dielectric material should also have a very high resistivity or, equivalently, a very low conductivity.

Because of the relatively low energy density obtainable in capacitive-storage systems, this technique is not a suitable alternative for storing significant amounts of electrical energy. It has been estimated[1] that a capacitor bank with a volume of at least 6×10^4 ft^3 would be required to store 1 Mwh$_e$. Furthermore, for most practical applications, the high-voltage d.c. output of the capacitor would have to be converted to a lower a.c. voltage. Utilization of d.c. to a.c. inverters generally result in significant energy losses because of conversion inefficiencies.

B. Inductive Storage

Inductive storage, like capacitive storage, is commonly used in electric-power and electronic applications. Inductive storage has not been used for large-scale electrical-energy storage. The energy density stored in an inductor is

$$u = (1/2)B^2/\mu_o, \qquad (12.3-2)$$

---

[1] A. B. Cambel et al, *Energy R & D and National Progress*, U.S. Government Printing Office, Washington, D.C., 1964.

where μ_o is the permeability constant (= $4\pi \times 10^{-7}$ weber/
ampere-m) and B is the magnetic induction.[*] Equation
(12.3-2) indicates that high inductive storage-energy densities may be reached by using large magnetic fields. However, the inductive-storage system must support the high
mechanical forces created by the high magnetic field.

An inductor stores electrical energy at low voltages
and high currents. The energy densities which have been
obtained in inductive-storage devices are approximately
100 times larger than those obtainable in capacitive-storage
devices. Because of the high currents used and the resistance of the inductor material, inductive-storage systems
are limited by power losses in the inductor. Also, recovery
of stored energy from an inductive storage system involves
the opening of a circuit carrying a high current, which is a
difficult electrical operation.

At the present time, large-scale inductive-energy
storage is not a feasible alternative for storing significant
amounts of electrical energy. Superconducting inductor
coils could operate without experiencing the power-loss

---

[*] In mks units, the magnetic induction may be expressed in
weber/m^2. If B is given in these units, then u has the
dimensions of $(weber/m^2)^2/(weber/ampere-m)$ = weber-
ampere/m^3; but one weber equals one volt-sec while one
volt-ampere equals one watt so that u has the dimensions
of watt-sec/m^3. However, one watt-sec is a joule; thus,
u is seen to be a volumetric energy density expressed in
joule/m^3.

limitations of conventional inductors. Long-term storage and charging times could be achieved with superconducting inductors. Large-scale superconducting inductive-energy-storage systems may become a feasible alternative for electrical-energy storage after significant technological developments in the field of superconductivity have been achieved. Other related applications of superconductors may include a.c. and d.c. electrical power transmission lines, which are discussed in Sections 20.8 and 20.9.

C. Electric and Storage Batteries

The electric battery was discovered more than 170 years ago. The simplest battery or electrochemical energy conversion device is the primary cell consisting of an anode, electrolyte, and a cathode. The open-circuit voltage of a primary cell depends on the electrochemical properties of the materials from which it is constructed. The Leclanché cell is the most commonly used dry cell and has an energy density of about 22 wh_e/lb; the source of electrical energy is the displacement of NH_4^+ by Zn. Cost estimates[1] for the Leclanché dry cell are about \$30/kwh_e, which is less than the cost for other common dry cells. Primary cells supply electrical energy by electro-chemical reactions, which are not reversible. In the Leclanché cell, NH_4^+ is decomposed into ammonia and hydrogen.

The storage battery supplies electrical energy by electrochemical reactions occurring at the anode and cathode;

it is often called a secondary cell. Electrical energy may
be stored by electrical regeneration of the reactants. This
reversible process in storage batteries extends the useful
cell life considerably. The physical principles involved in
storage-battery operation are similar to those of fuel-cell
operation (see Section 13.3).

A storage battery designed for extended commercial
use should have the following characteristics:[2] high energy
density, low internal resistance, simplicity and strength of
construction, high durability, and low production cost. An
ideal storage battery should not suffer chemical deterioration or stored-energy loss and the transformation of electrical-to-chemical-to-electrical energy should be completely
reversible. The average achievable conversion efficiency
of electrical-to-chemical-to-electrical energy of storage
batteries is approximately 75%.

The lead-acid storage battery was devised by Planté
in 1859 and has been widely adopted. It possesses nearly
all of the specified desirable characteristics except that the
energy density and the mechanical strength of the lead plates
are relatively low. The following chemical reaction occurs
during discharge at the anode: $PbO_2 + H_2SO_4 \rightleftarrows PbSO_4 +
H_2O + (1/2)O_2$; the cathode reaction is $Pb + H_2SO_4 \rightleftarrows PbSO_4
+ H_2$. The hydrogen and oxygen combine to form water (water
losses from storage batteries are produced by evaporation).
Thus, the overall process becomes

---

[2]C. L. Mantell, Batteries and Energy Systems, McGraw-
Hill, New York, 1970.

$$PbO_2 + Pb + 2H_2SO_4 \rightleftharpoons 2PbSO_4 + 2H_2O \qquad (12.3-3)$$

for discharging (in the forward direction) and charging (in the backward direction). The lead-acid batteries designed for automotive use have energy densities up to about 15 wh_e/ lb with cycle lives (i.e., the number of possible recharges) up to 300 cycles.[2]

The nickel-iron storage battery (Edison cell) was developed by Edison in 1910. It has an extremely long cycle life. The electrical-to-chemical energy transformation in a nickel-iron battery is not completely reversible. The major obstacles to the widespread use of nickel-iron batteries are high material and construction costs.

Nickel-cadmium batteries have long cycle lives (2,000 to 3,000 cycles) and energy densities of 10 to 25 wh_e/lb. The main disadvantage of nickel-cadmium batteries is high cost.

Silver has been used in several battery designs, including the silver-zinc and silver-cadmium storage batteries. Silver-zinc storage batteries have an energy-density range of 30 to 100 wh_e/lb and relatively short cycle lives of about 100 to 200 cycles. Silver-cadmium storage batteries have energy densities of 15 to 75 wh_e/lb with cycle lives up to 300 cycles. Both silver-zinc and silver-cadmium storage batteries require large amounts of silver for construction. The high material cost of silver makes both of these designs expensive.

A summary of the characteristics of several common storage-battery systems is given in Table 12.3-1. Capital-cost comparisons are shown in Table 12.3-2.

Zinc-air, nickel-zinc, organic-electrolyte, sodium-sulfur, and lithium-chlorine storage batteries are relatively new devices. The zinc-air cell was originally a primary cell but has been developed into a secondary cell by circulating the electrolyte. Zinc-air storage batteries have a high recharging rate and an energy density range of 60 to 80 wh_e/lb.[3] Preliminary cost estimates indicate that the zinc-air storage battery should be competitive with lead-acid storage batteries.

Nickel-zinc storage batteries are lighter and cheaper than nickel-cadmium storage batteries. Energy densities in the range of 25 to 30 wh_e/lb are expected.

Organic-electrolyte storage batteries use lithium or sodium as one electrode. Several promising combinations use a lithium anode, a copper or nickel chloride or fluoride cathode, and a propylene carbonate electrolyte. Energy densities are expected[3] to range from 100 to 150 wh_e/lb. The power density is relatively low and the cycle life is short.

Sodium-sulfur batteries operate at elevated temperatures (250 to 350°C) with relatively high energy and power

---

[3] The Automobile and Air Pollution: A Program for Progress, Part II: Subpanel Reports to the Panel on Electrically Powered Vehicles, U.S. Department of Commerce, U.S. Government Printing Office, Washington, D.C., 1967.

Table 12.3-1 Characteristics of common 12-volt storage systems rated at 100 ampere-h; reproduced with modifications from Ref. [2] with permission of McGraw-Hill Book Company. Copyright © 1970 by McGraw-Hill Book Company.

Material	Open circuit voltage, volts	Average closed circuit voltage, volts	Number of cells	Specific energy density, wh_e/lb	Volumetric energy density, wh_e/in^3	Charging time at constant potential, hours	Estimated life cycles	Estimated life years
lead acid								
automotive	2.1	1.9	6	15.0	1.30	5 to 10	300	3
industrial	2.1	1.9	6	13.1	1.35	5 to 10	1,600	5 to 10
nickel-cadmium								
pocket	1.3	1.2	10	11.0	0.60	7 to 8	2,000	10 to 20
sintered	1.3	1.2	10	11.5	0.88	2 to 10	3,000	10 to 20
nickel-iron (tube type)	1.5	1.2	10	10.6	9.92	6 to 7	2,000	15 to 20
silver-zinc	1.8	1.55	8	85 to 100	3.00	4 to 20	200	1
silver-cadmium	1.3	1.06	11	50 to 75	2.50	4 to 20	500	2 to 3

Table 12.3-2 Capital costs of storage-battery systems; based
              on data in Refs. [1] and [2] with permission of
              McGraw-Hill Book Company. Copyright ©
              1970 by the McGraw-Hill Book Company.

Storage-battery type and application[a]	Capital costs[b]			Relative capital costs per kwh_e stored[c]
	$	$/y	$/cycle	
lead-acid				
automotive	40	13	0.130	1.00
industrial	70	9	0.043	0.26
nickel cadmium				
pocket	150	6	0.075	0.94
sintered	300	20	0.100	0.64
nickel-iron	130	7.5	0.065	0.24
silver-zinc	800	800	4.000	25.50
silver-cadmium	1,000	400	2.000	7.60

a. 100 ampere-h, 12-volt design. b. 1972 data.
c. Based on 1962 data and including amortization over an
    average cycle life and charging current.

densities. The energy density of sodium-sulfur batteries
has been projected to exceed 100 wh_e/lb with a power density in excess of 100 w_e/lb.[4] Cost estimates[3] for sodium-
sulfur batteries range from $20 to $40/$kwh_e$. Workers at
TRW, Inc., have concluded[4] that the anticipated long life,
high performance, low cost, and low maintenance of sodium-
sulfur cells, considering the general capability of batteries

[4] Development Program for Solid Electrolyte Batteries,
    report prepared by TRW, Inc., for the Electric Power
    Research Institute, EPRI 127, Palo Alto, California,
    October 1974.

to respond rapidly to load fluctuations, make the sodium-sulfur batter an attractive candidate in load-leveling storage systems for electric utilities.

Lithium-chlorine storage batteries are examples of fused-salt electrolyte batteries. The lithium-chlorine battery operates at 600 to 700°C and uses molten lithium chloride as an electrolyte. The energy density is expected[3] to approach 200 wh_e/lb with power densities varying from 3 to 200 w_e/lb.

A 1-kwh_e zinc-chlorine battery has been developed with the expectation that batteries of this type will be applied for load-leveling in electric utility operation.[5] Tests on the 1-kwh_e unit at 27°C showed an average energy efficiency of 74.6% at a current density of 33 mA/cm^2 for 100 charge-discharge cycles in which all of the zinc was utilized at a chlorine pressure of less than 1 psig; graphite plates were used at the zinc electrode while porous, ruthenized titanium served as the chlorine electrode. The chemical processes during charging (forward reaction) and discharging (reverse reaction) are $ZnCl_2 \rightleftarrows Zn + Cl_2$. Engineering-design considerations[6] have served to

---

[5]P. C. Symons and M. J. Hammond, "Evaluation of a 1 kwh Zinc Chloride Battery System," Report EPRI EM-249, Electric Power Research Institute, Palo Alto, California, September 1976.

[6]R. F. Battey, "Engineering Design and Cost Analysis of Chlorine Storage Concepts for a Zinc-Chlorine Load-Leveling Battery," Report EPRI EM-259, Electric Power Research Institute, Palo Alto, California, November 1976.

emphasize the requirement of large storage capacity for chlorine (150 tons of chlorine are needed to operate a 40-Mw_e, 5-h battery). Chlorine storage in the form of chlorine hydrate (a solid ice consisting of water and chlorine) is more efficient and less costly[6] than storage as liquid chlorine.

A comparison of the energy densities and the power densities of several commonly-used and recently-developed storage batteries is shown in Fig. 12.3-1.

12.4   Large-Scale Energy Storage

Pumped-hydraulic storage and compressed-air storage are two feasible, large-scale, electrical-energy storage systems which may satisfy the energy-storage requirements of electric utilities.

A.   Pumped-Hydraulic Storage

Pumped-storage facilities constitute the only significant energy-storage systems that are presently used by the U.S. electric-utility industry. Pumped-storage facilities may either generate power from water which has been pumped into a reservoir or from a combination of pumped and natural runoff water. The former design is a pure pumped-storage development; the latter design is a combined pumped-storage development. A time history of the development of pumped-storage facilities in the U.S. is shown in Table 12.4-1.

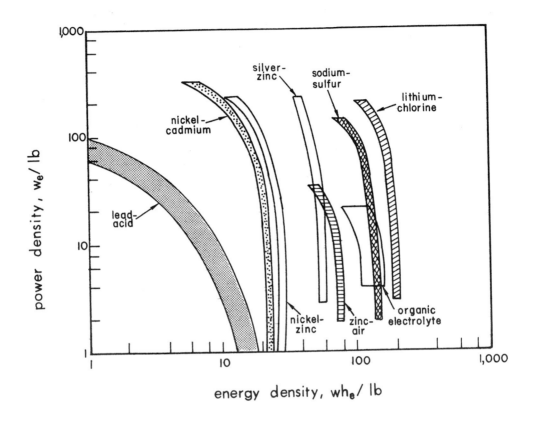

Fig. 12.3-1 Specific energies and power densities of storage
batteries; reproduced from Ref. [3].

The data of Table 12.4-1 indicate recent rapid
growth of pumped-storage facilities in the U.S. During
the four-year period ending in 1972, the U.S. capacity increased by 86%, the capacity under construction by 165%,
and the total capacity by 130%.

Table 12.4-1   Pumped-storage capacity in the United States;
reproduced from Hydroelectric Power Re-
sources of the United States, Federal Power
Commission, U.S. Government Printing
Office, Washington, D.C., 1972.

| Year | Installed reversible capacity, 10^3 Mw$_e$ | | | | |
| | developed | | under construction | | total |
	pure	combined	pure	combined	
1960	0	0.1	0	0.2	0.3
1964	0.4	0.3	0.7	0.5	1.9
1968	1.6	0.5	1.2	1.6	4.9
1972	2.6	1.3	6.0	1.4	11.3

A pumped-storage facility consists of a pumping-
generating unit and upper and lower water-storage reservoirs.
Electric power is generated by discharging water from the
upper to the lower reservoir. During off-peak hours, low-
value off-peak energy is used to pump water into the upper
reservoir, which is later discharged to supplement high-
value, peak electrical-energy generation. Pumped-storage
reservoirs often have desirable ecological impacts (flood
control, recreation) that are not immediately related to
energy storage.

The energy-storage efficiency of a pumped-storage
facility is a function of pump-turbine efficiency, motor-
generator efficiency, conduit head losses, upper reservoir
water evaporation, and plant operation policies. The maximum cycle efficiency (output-to-input energy ratio expressed

in percent) is estimated[1] to be about 80%. Some existing
plants operate with cycle efficiencies as low as 50%; however, most plants operate with cycle efficiencies ranging
from 66 to 72%.[1]

Nearly all of the operating and proposed pumped-
storage developments in the U.S. utilize reversible pump-
turbine motor-generator units. These units range in capacity from 100,000 to 382,500 kw$_e$. The operating heads are
usually 600 to 1,200 ft, although plants with heads as low
as 125 ft are in operation. A maximum head of about 1,700
ft is obtainable with present single-stage, reversible equipment. The head height has a substantial influence upon the
economic evaluation of pumped-storage projects.

There are several advantages and disadvantages to
both pure and combined pumped-storage facilities. A combined pumped-storage installation has the advantage of
having a lower pumping head than generating head. The
upper reservoirs of combined plants usually have large
water capacities which allow long power-generation times.
Small stream flows and reservoir capacities may be developed economically as combined pumped-storage installations; this fact increases siting alternatives substantially.
Pure pumped-storage installations do not necessarily require natural stream flows because the same water is re-
circulated between reservoirs. This feature reduces the

---

[1] The 1970 National Power Survey, Part IV, Federal
Power Commission, U.S. Government Printing Office,
Washington, D.C., 1971.

siting constraints and may allow site developments with higher heads than those obtainable in combination projects. Pure pumped-storage projects are compatible with nuclear or fossil-fuel generating plants, while combination projects are ordinarily included in the design of conventional hydroelectric installations. Both pure and combination projects possess the favorable operating characteristics of rapid startup and loading, low operating and maintenance costs, long life, and low outage rates.

The capital costs of a pumped-storage project are a function of the local geology. The most economical installations are high-head, large upper reservoir capacity projects. The capital costs of pumped-storage installations typically range from \$100 to \$150/kw_e.[1] The world's largest pumped-storage facility is located near Ludington, Michigan, and cost approximately \$3.5 $\times 10^8$ or \$182/kw_e.[2]

The Ludington pumped-storage facility, rated at 1,872 Mw_e, is located on a 1,900-acre site adjacent to Lake Michigan, which serves as the lower reservoir (see Fig. 12.4-1). The upper reservoir is a man-made area, 2.25 miles long and enclosed by a 108-ft dike. Six 1,300 ft long (24 to 28 feet in diameter) penstocks connect the upper and lower reservoirs. The upper reservoir discharge passes through six 312-Mw_e turbine-pump motor-generators. The head varies from a maximum of 362 ft to a minimum of

[2]D. P. Gregory, A Hydrogen-Energy System, American Gas Association, Arlington, Virginia, 1973.

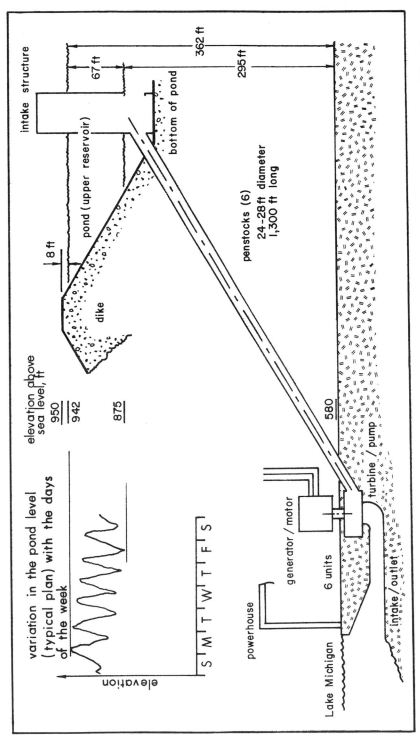

Fig. 12.4-1 Schematic diagram of the Ludington pumped-storage plant facility. Plant rating: 1,872 Mw_e (maximum); output duration at 1,872 Mw_e is 8.7 hours; energy-storage capacity: 16,300,000 kwhe (potential); plant cost: $340 million (approximately) or $182/$kw_e$; associated transmission cost: $20/$kw_e$. Reproduced from Ref. [2].

295 ft. The energy-storage capacity is 1.63×10^7 kwh$_e$ or 5.56×10^{10} Btu$_e$, which is approximately one-eighteenth of the energy-storage capacity of a 1×10^9 SCF natural-gas tank (assuming a 100% chemical-to-electrical energy conversion efficiency). The capital cost of the Ludington installation, on an energy-storage capacity basis, was more than $6,100/$10^6$ Btu$_e$. The capital cost of the storage installation and the associated electrical-energy network was $202/kw$_e$.

B. Compressed-Air Storage

Compressed-air storage systems may be either constant-volume or constant-pressure storage facilities. A compressed-air storage system consists of an air compressor, an expansion turbine, a motor-generator, and an underground cavern or aboveground storage tank. Energy is stored by compressing and storing air. Electric power is generated by venting the compressed air through an expansion turbine. During off-peak electricity-demand hours, low-value off-peak energy is used to compress air, which is later expanded to supplement high-value, peak, electrical-energy-generation capacity.

A constant-volume compressed-air storage facility may store compressed air in pressure tanks, salt domes, mined caverns, depleted oil or gas fields, or abandoned mines. These systems have the disadvantage of yielding power outputs which decrease with use because of air-pressure reductions as the compressed air is withdrawn from storage. An energy-storage capacity of 7.5×10^5 kwh$_e$ requires[3] about 3×10^6 ft^3 of air storage at 600 psi.*

A constant-pressure, compressed-air storage facility may store air in an aboveground variable-volume tank or an underground aquifer. A variable-volume tank maintains a constant pressure by the weight of the tank cover. An energy-storage capacity of 1×10^5 kwh$_e$ requires[3] about 1.5×10^6 ft^3 of air storage at 600 psi. Compressed-air storage in an aquifer maintains a constant pressure by hydrostatic pressurization. When air is pumped into the aquifer, the pressure remains approximately constant while the storage volume increases because of water displacement in the surrounding rock formations. Water displacement of the compressed air during energy generation causes a slight decrease in storage pressure, which leads to a 2 to 6% decrease in power output.

The energy-storage efficiency of a compressed-air storage facility is a function of compressor efficiency, motor-generator efficiency, heat losses, and compressed-air leakage. The overall cycle efficiency has been estimated[3] to be about 50%. Thus, two kwh$_e$ are used in air compression for every kwh$_e$ generated by air expansion.

---

*The utilization (with 100% efficiency) of 3×10^6 ft^3 at 600 psi of ideal gas produces 3×10^6 ft$^3 \times (600 - 14.7)$ psi $\times$ $(144$ in^2/ft$^2) = 2.53 \times 10^{11}$ ft-lb $= 9.6 \times 10^4$ kwh if the ambient pressure is 14.7 psi. Because of deviations from ideal-gas behavior at elevated pressures (especially during storage in caverns, salt mines, etc.), substantially larger energy outputs are achieved for the specified conditions.

[3] Power Generation Alternatives, Department of Lighting, City of Seattle, Washington, 1972.

The feasibility of a hybrid compressed-air storage, gas-turbine-peaking power plant has been studied[4] by workers at the Battelle Pacific Northwest Laboratories. In this design, air is compressed during off-peak periods and stored in a cavity made by a nuclear explosion. During peak demand, the air is withdrawn from storage and mixed with fuel. The air-fuel mixture is then burned in a combustion chamber prior to expansion through a turbine.

The capital costs of a peaking plant of the specified design were estimated[4] to be about $66/kw$_e$. This cost is about 50% of the capital cost of pumped-storage facilities. The peak-power electrical-energy cost was estimated[4] to be 9.4 mills/kwh$_e$, which is about 20 to 25% less than that of either pumped-storage or gas-turbine installations. This energy cost is based on 1973 gas-turbine technology, low (120°F) air-storage temperatures, favorable rock formations (i.e., rocks with low grain density, high water content, and high porosity in which a relatively large void volume is produced for a given nuclear explosive yield and implant depth), an off-peak power cost of 2 mills/kwh$_e$, and a load factor of 21%. Peaking units located in areas of less favorable rock formations and high (660°F) air-storage temperatures are expected[4] to supply peak electrical energy at a cost of 19.1 mills/kwh$_e$. This energy cost is about a

---

[4]B. C. Fryer, <u>Air Storage Peaking Power Plants Utilizing Modified Industrial Gas Turbines and Cavities Created with Nuclear Explosives</u>, Battelle Pacific Northwest Laboratories, Report BNWL-1748, Richland, Washington, 1973.

factor of two higher than that for competing peaking systems. The energy cost is expected[4] to decrease to 7.6 mills/kwh$_e$ for advantageous rock and storage-temperature conditions and 1980 gas-turbine technology.

12.5   Storage of Liquid Petroleum Products

Alternatives for storage of liquid petroleum products include aboveground storage in steel or concrete tanks and underground storage in salt domes, mined caverns, abandoned mines, or nuclear cavities.

A.   Aboveground Storage

Aboveground tank storage provides the most versatile storage system for liquid petroleum products. Steel-tank storage systems have been used for many years and have been shown to be highly reliable and compatible with a wide range of environments. Prestressed concrete storage tanks represent a relatively new technology. The reliability of concrete-tank storage has not been demonstrated to the extent that the reliability of steel-tank storage has.

The major considerations in the construction of steel-tank storage systems are the availability of land and steel plating. A 1×10^6 bbl steel-tank storage unit requires a minimum of 4 acres of land for the tank, associated facilities, and open space.[1] Large tank farms require[2] from 20 to 30 acres of land for each 1×10^6 bbl of stored petroleum. Approximately[2] 3×10^3 tons of steel plate per 10^6 bbl of storage capacity are used in steel-tank storage construction. The steel plate required for storage of 1×10^6 bbl amounted to more than 0.8% of the 1972 plate production for the construction of tanks, bins, and hoppers and nearly 0.6% of the entire 1972 production of the steel-plate fabrication industry.

Steel-tank storage units may be constructed for use in practically any environment and on a variety of land areas. In areas with normal soil conditions, steel tanks can be built on simple foundations. Locations with soft soil require pile foundations. The normal tankage costs are approximately $3/bbl. The tankage costs increase to about $5/bbl when pile foundations are necessary.

A 1973 estimate[1] of the capital costs for a 1×10^6 bbl steel-tank storage unit is 4.14×10^6 for the facility and and 2×10^5 for the land. The management and maintenance charges were estimated[1] to be 1.9×10^5 per year. The

---

[1]W. J. Mead, Testimony before the Committee on Interior and Insular Affairs, U.S. Senate, May 30, 1973; printed in Strategic Petroleum Reserves, U.S. Government Printing Office, Washington, D.C., 1973.

[2]National Petroleum Council, Emergency Preparedness for Interruption of Petroleum Imports into the United States: An Interim Report, Washington, D.C., 1973.

total annual storage cost is 450×10^5 or \$0.45/bbl-y
($\approx$\$0.077/10^6 Btu-y) assuming a 6% capital and deprecia-
tion charge on the facility and a 6% capital charge on the
land; another estimate was made by workers at the U.S.
Department of the Interior in 1973 and corresponds to
\$0.86/bbl-y or \$0.15/10^6 Btu-y for an annual capital charge
of 11.5%. Studies at the American Petroleum Institute,
Division of Statistics and Economics, have suggested that the
capital cost of a prestressed, concrete-tank storage facility
might be less than for a steel-tank storage facility.

B.   Underground Storage

Approximately two-thirds of the U.S. underground
petroleum-storage capacity is located in salt domes. A
salt dome is a massive column of rock salt from one-half
to six miles in diameter. These salt domes thrust upwards
from salt beds located as much as 30,000 feet below the
surface and are covered by thick caprock. Since the top of
the salt is often near the surface, the salt from these domes
may be mined for commercial use. The Gulf Coast (consisting of parts of Texas, Louisiana, and Mississippi) contains
more than 350 known salt domes within an area of 50,000
mi^2. Investigators at the Bureau of Mines[1] have identified
130 of these as offering good possibilities for storage sites.
Salt-dome formations also occur in the Great Lakes region
and are scattered throughout the Rocky Mountain states.

Construction of a salt-dome storage unit involves drilling into the salt bed, pumping fresh water into the salt formation, and withdrawing and disposing of the resulting brine. This process is repeated until a storage unit of the desired size has been produced. Approximately 10 bbl of fresh water are required for each bbl of storage capacity. Thus, the availability and cost of large volumes of fresh water will determine the storage costs of a salt-dome system. The brine may be disposed of by offshore dumping or by subsurface disposal. The development of a 2×10^8 bbl storage unit produces about 1.1×10^6 bbl/d of brine over a period of 5 years. The subsurface storage of this volume of water may be impossible in many locations and extraordinarily costly in other areas. Thus, offshore disposal may be required for the development of large-scale storage facilities. Fortunately, there are many locations of major salt-dome formations in the Gulf Coast area, where offshore disposal facilities are nearby. The long-term environmental effects of converting large volumes of fresh water to sodium chloride brine, which is subsequently dumped offshore, have not been properly assessed.

Salt-dome storage facilities have been in use for more than 20 years and have proved to be safe and reliable for petroleum products. Approximately 1×10^8 bbl of salt-dome storage capacity is in use in the U.S. The individual storage units or wells range from 1 to 2×10^6 bbl, with future units expected to grow to 5×10^6 bbl. There is some product loss in salt-dome storage because all of the petroleum that is stored cannot be recovered. The average recovery from salt-dome storage has been more than 90%.[1]

Storage cavities leached in underground salt beds may also be used for petroleum storage. This technology is well developed but application may be limited by several problems. Most of the suitable salt beds are located in regions where the availability of large supplies of fresh water is limited and the cost is high. These regions are typically inland areas which require subsurface brine disposal and thus make large-volume projects impractical. Furthermore, these salt caverns often contain layers of impurities that make construction difficult and may contaminate the stored petroleum.

A summary of a 1973 economic analysis,[1] indicating large economies of scale achievable with salt-dome storage, is shown in Table 12.5-1.

The data of Table 12.5-1 indicate that increasing the storage capacity from 1 to 10×10^6 bbl causes a decrease of nearly a factor of six in the annual storage cost per bbl. The annual storage costs are seen to range from \$0.28/bbl-y to \$0.05/bbl-y or, equivalently, from \$0.048/10^6 Btu-y to \$0.009/10^6 Btu-y.

The authors of a cost analysis[2] for large-scale storage projects (to 2×10^8 bbl) of many individual wells, with capacities of 5 to 10×10^6 bbl, concluded that the construction costs of salt-dome storage cavities range from \$0.40 to \$0.70/bbl. These estimates assume a 5-year development period, with usable storage capacity becoming

Table 12.5-1 Capital and operating costs for salt-dome
storage of petroleum; based on data from
Ref. [1], 1973.

Costs	Storage capacity, 10^6 bbl		
	1	2	10
capital costs, $\$10^6$			
facility	4.4	4.96	8.3
land	0.1	0.15	0.5
total	4.5	5.11	8.8
annual costs, $\$10^5$			
capital charges[a]	2.70	3.07	5.28
maintenance and			
management	0.10	0.12	0.15
total	2.80	3.19	5.43
annual storage cost, $/bbl-y	0.28	0.16	0.05

a. A 6% interest and depreciation charge for the facility
and a 6% interest charge on the land are assumed.

---

available at the rate of 4×10^7 bbl/y after the first year.
In this study, it is also assumed that a plentiful and inexpensive supply of fresh water is available and that offshore brine disposal may be accomplished. If the fresh
water costs increase by a factor of ten, the construction
costs rise by approximately $0.20/bbl. In 1973, workers
at the U.S. Department of the Interior estimated that the
annual salt-dome storage cost was $0.20/bbl-y or $0.034/
10^6 Btu-y, assuming an 11.5% annual capital charge rate.

There are several storage installations utilizing
caverns mined in hard rock. The storage capacities

range up to a maximum of 8×10^5 bbl for pressurized storage of light petroleum products. The construction time for
a mined-cavern project depends on the rock formation involved and varies from one to two years. The storage
costs[2] are very high and ranged from \$10 to \$20/bbl-y or
\$1.72 to 3.44/10^6 Btu-y at early 1973 prices.

    Although no abandoned-mine storage exists in the
U.S., the technology required for this technique has been
developed and demonstrated in South Africa. Abandoned
mines that are suitable for conversion to storage systems
must be structurally stable, surrounded by fracture-free
and relatively impermeable rock formations, composed of
chemically-inert materials with respect to petroleum and
petroleum products, and free of contaminant-carrying
water flows. They must also be located sufficiently far
below the local water table so that the hydrostatic pressure
will act to retard the loss of stored petroleum by seepage
into adjacent rock formations.[3]

    An analysis based on the abandoned-mine storage
experience in South Africa suggests that a mine storage
facility may be developed for approximately 15% of the cost
of steel-tank storage facilities. This estimate corresponds
to an abandoned mine-to-storage facility conversion cost of
about \$0.60/bbl. A 1973 estimate[1] of the conversion

---

[3]H. W. Brandt, "Abandoned Coal Mine Converted into Man-
Made Oil Field," Oil and Gas Journal 70, 76, December
25, 1972.

cost for a 1×10^7 bbl abandoned mine was 5.4×10^6. The purchase price of an abandoned mine is highly variable; a nominal cost of 5×10^5 was assumed. The maintenance and management costs were estimated[1] to be 3×10^4. Assuming a 6% interest and depreciation charge on the facility and a 6% interest charge on the land, the total annual storage cost becomes 3.84×10^5 or $0.038/bbl-y ($\approx$0.007/$10^6$ Btu-y). This storage cost is about 80% of the cost associated with a salt-dome storage facility of equal capacity.

Petroleum storage in deep underground cavities made by nuclear explosives is an untested technology. Because of possible surface damage, future nuclear-cavity storage projects will most likely be limited to unpopulated areas. It has been estimated[1] that a twenty-five kiloton nuclear device, exploded about 2,000 feet below the surface, would create approximately 1×10^6 bbl of storage capacity. The storage chamber would be on the order of 250 feet high and 150 feet in diameter. All of the radioactive contaminants must be flushed out, thus deferring petroleum storage to a time about six months after the nuclear detonation. The radiation danger should be less for petroleum storage than for nuclear-stimulated natural-gas production. The fissile material from the nuclear device is entrapped by the molten rock that accumulates near the bottom of the nuclear cavity. Experience with nuclear stimulation of natural-gas production has indicated that the radiation level in this case is about 1% of the natural background exposure. Evidence accumulated from many underground nuclear explosions in the past suggests that cavity production by nuclear devices will not result in long-term seismic effects.

Cost estimates for petroleum storage in nuclear cavities, based on a 1973 analysis, [1] are shown in Table 12.5-2.

The relatively high cost estimates shown in Table 12.5-2 for nuclear-cavity storage are equal to the costs for salt-dome storage units of the same capacity. The lower cost estimate for nuclear-cavity storage is more than a factor of three smaller than the cost of an aboveground tank-storage unit of the same capacity.

Table 12.5-2 Cost estimates for storage of 1×10^6 bbl of petroleum in a nuclear cavity; based on data from Ref. [1], 1973.

Costs	Cost estimates	
	optimistic	pessimistic
capital costs, 10^6		
facility	2.07	4.14
land	0.20	0.20
total	2.27	4.34
annual costs, 10^5		
capital charges[a]	1.36	2.60
maintenance and management	0.20	0.20
total	1.56	2.80
annual storage cost, $/bbl-y	0.16	0.28

a. A 6% interest and depreciation charge for the facility and a 6% interest charge on the land are assumed.

A comparison of the cost estimates for petroleum storage in aboveground steel tanks and underground salt domes, mined caverns, abandoned mines, and nuclear cavities is given in Table 12.5-3.

Table 12.5-3 Estimated storage costs for alternative petroleum-storage systems; based on data in Refs. [1] and [2], 1973.

Storage system and capacity	Range of estimated costs	
	$/bbl-y	$/10^6 Btu-y
aboveground steel tank 1 × 10^6 bbl	0.50 to 0.86	0.086 to 0.15
salt dome 1 × 10^6 bbl 2 × 10^6 bbl 10 × 10^6 bbl	0.20 to 0.28 0.16 0.05	0.035 to 0.048 0.028 0.009
mined cavern 0.8 × 10^6 bbl	10.0 to 20.0	1.73 to 3.46
abandoned mine 10 × 10^6 bbl	0.038	0.007
nuclear cavity 1 × 10^6 bbl	0.16 to 0.28	0.028 to 0.048

12.6 Storage of Natural Gas

Natural gas may be stored in pressurized tanks, depleted gas and oil wells, aquifers, salt domes and cavities, mined caverns, and a number of unconventional locations.

Natural-gas storage represents the largest energy-storage capability in the U.S. In 1970, there were 325 natural-gas storage facilities in operation in 26 states. The total underground natural-gas storage capacity in the U.S. was estimated[1] to be nearly 6×10^{12} SCF. Approximately 50% of the reservoir capacity of underground gas-storage facilities is allocated to a permanent inventory of natural gas, which is required to maintain the deliverability of the remainder of the stored gas. The capital cost required to develop new natural-gas storage facilities ranges from \$1,000 to \$1,250 per 10^6 SCF.[1]

Natural gas may also be liquefied and stored in aboveground or underground vessels, excavated pits, and mined caverns.

A.   Pressurized Storage

Natural gas may be stored at low pressure in either an inverted cylindrical bell that is sealed in water and free to move within a guide frame or in a cylinder below a piston seal. The cylindrical-bell storage system is called a water-sealed holder and the piston-storage system is called a waterless or dry holder. The pressure within these holders is essentially uniform and is produced solely by the weight of the cylindrical bell or piston. The design pressures of low-pressure holders range from 4 to 20 inches of water (1 inch

---

[1]Ref. [2] of Section 12.5.

of a water column = 0.0364 psig $\approx$ 1.0025 atmospheres absolute). The capacities of water-sealed holders range from 25×10^3 SCF to 10×10^6 SCF. Dry holder capacities range from 25×10^3 SCF to 20×10^6 SCF. The construction costs for both types of low-pressure holders are similar and are estimated[2] to be about 0.15×10^6 for a capacity of 1×10^5 SCF ($\approx$$1,500/10^6$ Btu), 0.6×10^6 for a capacity of 1×10^6 SCF ($\approx$$600/10^6$ Btu), and 2.5×10^6 for a capacity of 10×10^6 SCF ($\approx$$250/10^6$ Btu).

High-pressure natural-gas holders store natural gas at pressures from 50 to 2,240 psig. The capacities of horizontal and vertical high-pressure holders, often called bullets, range from 35 to 500×10^3 SCF for 50-psig operating pressures. Spherical-storage tanks at similar pressures have capacities up to 1×10^6 SCF. The construction cost[2] for a 1×10^5 SCF capacity storage bullet is approximately 2.5×10^4 or $250/10^6$ Btu. The construction cost[2] for a 1×10^6 SCF spherical-storage tank is about 2.25×10^5 or $225/10^6$ Btu at a gas value of $1/10^6$ Btu.

Underground high-pressure bottle holders have been used for natural-gas storage. Underground installation capacities vary from 1.5 to 120×10^6 SCF. These storage systems consist of many high-pressure bottle holders and require about 1.25 acres per 10^6 SCF of storage capacity. The construction cost[2] for a facility with

---

[2]Gas Engineers Handbook, C. G. Segeler, editor, The Industrial Press, New York, N.Y., 1965.

50×10^6 SCF capacity is about 4.5×10^6 or $90/10^6$ Btu.

The earliest underground natural-gas storage facilities were located in depleted natural gas or oil wells. The
feasibility of using this type of storage system is constrained
by regional geology. Porous permeable rock formations,
usually associated with sedimentary formations, are required for successful natural-gas storage in depleted fields.
Regions in Pennsylvania, Michigan, and Ohio are particularly well suited for this type of storage.

Aquifer-storage facilities are created by injecting
natural gas into sedimentary rock structures which are
covered by an impervious caprock. The natural gas is
under high pressure (~1,000 psi) and displaces the native
water in the porous rock to create an artificial storage volume. The caprock region is sealed to gas passage by cap-
illary water movement into the voids of the caprock layer.
The estimated capital costs[3] for storage of 1×10^3 SCF
of natural gas, in a depleted field or an aquifer operating at
an overpressure of 1,000 psi, are $0.79 or $0.79/10^6$ Btu.

Salt domes, salt cavities, and mined caverns may
also be used for natural-gas storage. These storage systems
have not been well developed; they are characterized by
large open volumes in which natural gas may be stored.
Capital-cost estimates[4] in 1959 for storing 1×10^3 SCF

---

[3]Ref. [2] of Section 12.4.

[4]D. L. Katz et al, <u>Handbook of Natural Gas Engineering</u>,
    McGraw-Hill, New York, N.Y., 1959.

at 1,000 psi in a salt cavern or a mined cavern were $2.25 ($\approx$$2.25/10^6 Btu) and $4.50 ($\approx$$4.50/10^6 Btu), respectively.

Natural-gas storage in gas-transmission pipelines is called linepack storage. Linepack storage may be used when the actual throughput of a transmission pipeline is less than the designed throughput. Many gas utilities with more than one transmission line use linepack storage regularly. The capital costs for linepack storage at 1,000 psi were estimated[4] in 1959 to be $48.00/10^6 Btu.

Unconventional methods of storing natural gas include absorption, adsorption, and reversible chemical combination. Natural gas is soluble in some liquid or easily liquefiable compounds, of which propane is the most suitable. Adsorbed layers of films are created on many solid surfaces when exposed to natural gas. Natural gas forms reversible chemical bonds with water to produce hydrates. These unconventional methods are not attractive for large-scale natural-gas storage. Two potentially-attractive, unconventional natural-gas storage systems are underwater storage in a hydrostatically-balanced and anchored vessel and storage in cavities created by underground nuclear explosions.

B. Liquefied Natural-Gas Storage

Liquefied natural gas (LNG) is a cryogenic liquid form of natural gas with a boiling point of -260°F. The volumetric energy content of liquefied natural gas at -260°F and 1 atmosphere is about 600 times that of natural gas at 60°F and 1 atmosphere. Common applications of energy storage in the form of liquefied natural gas involve gas distribution for peakshaving and transportation by ship, railcar, or truck.

Liquefied natural gas is stored aboveground in insulated, double-wall metal tanks with either a flat-bottom or a spherical configuration. The cryogenic tanks are typically constructed with an outer tank made of carbon steel, using three to five feet thick perlite (expanded volcanic lava) insulation and a 9% nickel-steel alloy inner tank. Prestressed-concrete, cryogenic storage tanks have been used to store liquefied natural gas underground. Mined caverns may be either lined or unlined, depending on the heat transfer properties of the surrounding rock. Pit storage involves excavating a pit, lining the pit walls, and installing a vapor-tight covering.

Capital-cost estimates, based on a 2.85×10^4 bbl (equivalent to 1×10^9 SCF) capacity, for various liquefied natural-gas storage schemes, are shown in Table 12.6-1.

The data of Table 12.6-1 indicate the substantial cost savings that are realizable in underground storage when liquefaction costs are not included. A more recent estimate of the capital costs required for aboveground storage of 1×10^6 Btu of liquefied natural gas is given in Table 12.6-2. An estimate of the cost for a natural-gas liquefaction plant is included in Table 12.6-2.

Table 12.6-1   Capital-cost estimates for liquefied natural-gas storage systems; reproduced from Ref. [2].

Cryogenic storage system	Capital costs,[a] $/10^6 Btu
aboveground double-wall tank	2.85 to 6.50
underground prestressed concrete tank, lined	1.25 to 1.50
mined cavern, lined	1.55 to 2.12
quarried limestone pit, lined and covered	0.71 to 0.77

a.   1960 data.

Table 12.6-2   Capital-cost estimates of aboveground liquefied natural-gas storage facilities and an associated natural-gas liquefaction plant; reproduced from Ref. [3].

Cryogenic storage system	Capital cost, $/10^6 Btu
flat-bottom tank with perlite insulation, purged	2.50[a]
spherical tank with perlite insulation, purged (0.20%/d boil-off loss)	17.00[b]
spherical tank with vacuum perlite insulation (0.01%/d boil-off loss)	22.00[b]
liquefaction plant	$275/10^6 Btu-d[c]

a. 1968 data based on a 1×10^9 SCF storage capacity.
b. 1971 data.
c. 1968 data based on a 40×10^6 SCF/d plant capacity.

12.7   Storage of Synthetic Fuels

Energy storage in the form of synthetic fuels is a well-developed technology. Synthetic fuels are stored in both large-scale systems for future transmission and distribution and in small-scale systems for future consumption. The importance of synthetic-fuel storage will increase as the world economy changes from a fossil-fuel economy to a nuclear-solar energy economy. The major candidates for future synthetic-fuel systems are hydrogen and hydrogen-derived fuels such as ammonia and methanol. Future transportation systems may be powered by hydrogen, ammonia, or methanol. Only slight engine modifications are required to operate internal-combustion engines on any of these fuels. The storage capabilities of hydrogen have a significant impact on the evaluation of the proposed hydrogen economy, as compared to an all-electric economy (see Chapter 11, especially Section 11.4, for discussions of the hydrogen economy and alternative hydrogen-storage systems).

The estimated capital costs for large-scale energy storage in the form of synthetic fuels are given in Table 12.7-1. The capital costs of liquid natural-gas and fuel-oil storage are included for comparison.

The data of Table 12.7-1 indicate that storing gaseous hydrogen in pressurized tanks on a large-scale is prohibitively expensive. The costs given for mined cavern and aquifer hydrogen storage do not refer to specific installations because they are highly dependent on the regional

Table 12.7-1   Capital costs of large-scale synthetic-fuel
               and fossil-fuel storage systems; reproduced
               from Ref. [1].

Fuel	Storage volume, gallons	Capital costs,	
		$/gallon	$/10^6 Btu
gaseous hydrogen			
steel tank (2,400 psi)	small*	5.00*	750.00
mined cavern	5×10^6 *	1.00*	350.00
aquifer	--	--	3.00 to 6.00
liquid hydrogen	1×10^6	1.00	36.00
ammonia	10×10^6	0.157	2.90
methanol	10×10^6	0.055	0.80
liquid natural gas	25×10^6	0.30	3.50
fuel oil	10×10^6	0.055	0.40

*Equivalent water volume.

---

geology.   Examination of the data of Table 12.7-1 shows
that the storage cost for methanol is less than 1/30 of that
of liquid hydrogen and about 1/3.5 of that of ammonia, on
an equivalent energy basis.

The costs given for ammonia, methanol, liquefied
natural gas, and fuel oil are based on mature technologies
and are unlikely to be reduced significantly in the future.
The hydrogen-storage costs do not include expenses associated with the liquefaction and/or compression processes.

[1] J. E. Johnson, The Storage and Transportation of Synthetic Fuels, Report ORNL-TM-4307, Oak Ridge National
Laboratory, Oak Ridge, Tennessee, 1972.

The latter costs will outweigh the actual storage costs
significantly. Since large-scale hydrogen storage is a
relatively recent technology, which was developed during
the U.S. space program, important reductions in the cost
of hydrogen-storage systems may be realizable in the
future.

The estimated[1] capital costs for small-scale synthetic-fuel storage systems are shown in Table 12.7-2.
Capital costs of liquid natural gas, gasoline, and lead-acid
batteries are included for comparison. Table 12.7-2 also
includes estimates of the specific and volumetric energy
content of the fuel and container for small-scale energy-
storage systems.

An examination of the data of Table 12.7-2 shows
the enormous economic and volumetric advantages of
storing energy in the form of gasoline. For a storage
capacity of 50×10^6 Btu, the unit capital cost for gasoline
storage is $2/10^6$ Btu, which is 0.67% of the liquid-hydrogen cost, 0.28% of the gaseous-hydrogen cost, 20% of the
ammonia cost, 67% of the methanol cost, and 1.4% of the
liquid natural-gas cost, on an equivalent stored energy
basis. The specific-energy content of a gasoline-storage
system is seen to be no less than twice that of any of the
alternative storage systems considered. The two most
likely future transportation fuels, liquid hydrogen and
methanol, have the same specific energy content, equivalent to one-half that of gasoline. Methanol is superior to

Table 12.7-2 Capital costs, specific energy content, and volumetric energy content of small-scale energy-storage systems; reproduced from Ref. [1], 1972.

| Storage system | Storage capacity | | | Fuel and container storage system | |
| | 2 × 10^6 Btu^a | | 50 × 10^6 Btu | | |
	present capital costs, $	mass-production capital costs, $^{b}	capital costs, $	specific energy content, Btu/lb	volumetric energy content, Btu/ft^3
liquid hydrogen	2,000	1,200-1,800	15,000	8,000	140,000
gaseous hydrogen^c	1,500	1,200	36,000	1,200	40,000
magnesium hy-drided	---	160	----	5,000	250,000
ammonia	170	100	500	6,000	250,000
methanol	35	35	150	8,000	510,000
liquefied natural gas	700	300-500	7,000	6,700	350,000
gasoline	30	30	100	16,000	950,000
lead-acid battery	---	15,000	----	80	10,000

a. Approximate energy-storage capacity of an automobile gasoline tank.
b. Present engineering design standards are assumed.
c. Storage in a 2,400-psi steel tank.
d. A magnesium cost of $0.50/lb, no container or heat exchanger costs, and a void content of 50% are assumed.

hydrogen in volumetric energy content.   The volumetric energy content of a gasoline-storage system is about 1.9 times that of methanol and nearly 6.8 times that of a liquid-hydrogen storage system.   This summary of the data of Table 12.7-2 explains, in part, why present transportation systems are heavily dependent on gasoline as a fuel.

CHAPTER 13

TECHNIQUES FOR DIRECT ENERGY CONVERSION

13.1   Introduction

Techniques for direct energy conversion are procedures for the production of electrical energy from other energy sources, without the intervention of steam generation
and the use of conventional steam-turbine generating plants.

Five alternative direct energy-production techniques
are described in Fig. 13.1-1. All of the procedures listed in
Fig. 13.1-1 have been employed for specialty use and have
also been considered for active development in large-scale
energy-production systems. Magnetohydrodynamic generators are under active development for use at utility power
stations. Fuel cells have found practical applications in
small stations and have been considered for a variety of purposes, including utilization in vehicles for personal transportation. Photovoltaic panels utilizing solar energy, although
still very costly, constitute standard energy sources in space

283

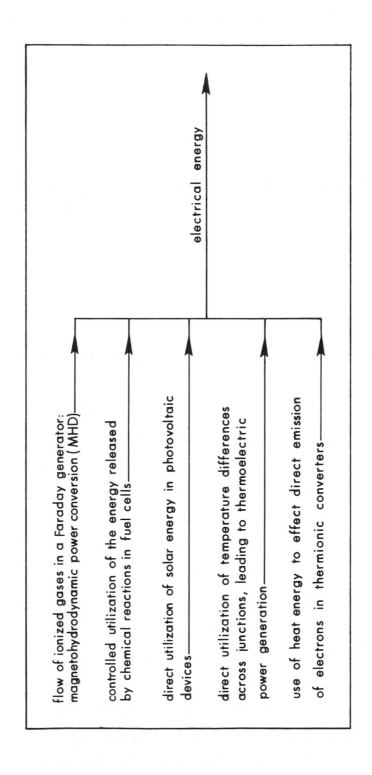

Fig. 13.1-1 Schematic diagram describing energy sources for use in direct energy conversion for electricity production.

vehicles.   Thermoelectric and thermionic generators have found wide application in instrument development.

MHD power conversion and direct electricity generation in fuel cells will serve to increase conversion efficiencies in electricity generation.   These are technical conservation measures for more efficient utilization of fossil fuels. If we succeed in implementing current program objectives, existing supply sources will be used far more efficiently, thereby alleviating the ever-increasing pressure to find new primary energy sources.

In the following sections, we shall consider the salient scientific principles involved in direct energy conversion and examine the development and economic problems relating to large-scale implementation.

13.2   Magnetohydrodynamic Power Conversion (MHD)

When an ionized gas flows in a direction perpendicular to an applied magnetic field, an electric field is induced in the direction which is perpendicular to both the gas-flow vector and the magnetic-field vector.   The electrons and ions in the flowing gases support electric-current flow under the influence of the induced electric field.   This phenomenon was discovered by Faraday and is often referred to as the Faraday effect.   Linear-flow, vortex-flow, and radial-flow in MHD generators have been considered.[1]   A linear-flow MHD

---

[1]G. W. Sutton and A. Sherman, Engineering Magnetohydrodynamics, McGraw-Hill Book Co., Inc., New York, 1965.

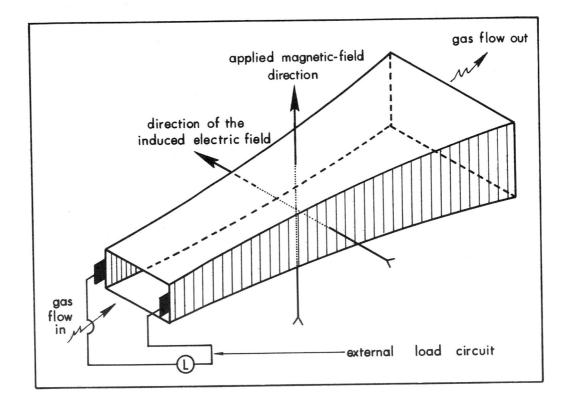

Fig. 13.2-1 Schematic diagram of a linear MHD generator.
MHD power conversion is accomplished in a
diverging channel through which partially-ionized
gases flow in a direction perpendicular to the
applied magnetic field. The Faraday effect induces an electric field that is perpendicular to
both the direction of gas flow and to the direction
of the magnetic field. The shaded channel walls
become electrodes and MHD power conversion
is accomplished by connecting the shaded channel walls through an external load L. The shaded
channel walls are made of electrically-conducting
materials.

generator is shown schematically in Fig. 13.2-1. MHD converters are generally d.c. generators; a.c. power converters are more difficult to design but have also been considered.[1]

A significant evaluation of achievable efficiencies in MHD power generation requires discussion of plasma physics, the physics of ionized gases. We shall content ourselves here with a brief description of important features governing the application of this science in MHD generators.

A.   Production of Ionized Gases

Ionized gases may be produced with direct heating by combustion products. This type of thermal ionization is facilitated by the introduction into the gas flow of easily-ionized materials, especially alkali metals.* Required seeding ratios are only a few percent. The equilibrium ionization at the temperature T, corresponding to the process

$$M \rightleftharpoons M^+ + e^-, \qquad\qquad (13.2-1)$$

may be calculated from Saha's equation, viz.,

$$(e^-)(M^+)/(M) = (2Q_{M^+}/Q_M)(2\pi m_e kT/h^2)^{3/2}$$

$$\times [\exp(-e_M/kT)]. \qquad\qquad (13.2-2)$$

---

*Alkali metals and their ionization potential (e_M, in electron volts) are: Li (5.363), Na (5.12), K (4.318), Rb (4.16), Cs (3.87), Ca (6.09), Ba (6.19).

Here (e^-), (M^+) and (M) represent, respectively, the concentrations (in mole per unit volume) of electrons, ions, and neutrals; Q_{M^+} and Q_M denote, respectively, the internal partition functions of the ions and neutrals and are easily evaluated as functions of temperature by the use of standard procedures in statistical mechanics; m_e is the mass of the electron, k stands for Boltzmann's constant, and h is Planck's constant. The values of (e^-) and (M^+) are determined by the temperature and pressure for a given M.

Adequate ionization may be achieved under non-equilibrium conditions at lower temperatures than are required for equilibrium ionization by subjecting seeded noble gases to magnetic induction.[1]

The extent of ionization determines the electrical conductivity of the gases. The electrical conductivity, which generally has different values in different directions, determines the achievable current density. The following numerical values are indicative of attainable results: equilibrium gases containing 1% of K (potassium) reach an electrical conductivity of about 5 mho/cm for T between 3,500 and 4,000°K at a pressure of 10^{-2} atm; at 2,500°K and atmospheric pressure, the electrical conductivity is only about 8×10^{-2} mho/cm.

Current densities are shown as a function of electrical conductivity, under non-equilibrium conditions, in Fig. 13.2-2 for an Ar-K mixture containing 0.4% of K at a carrier gas temperature of 2,000°K. The applicable electron temperatures T_e (which measure the translational speeds of the

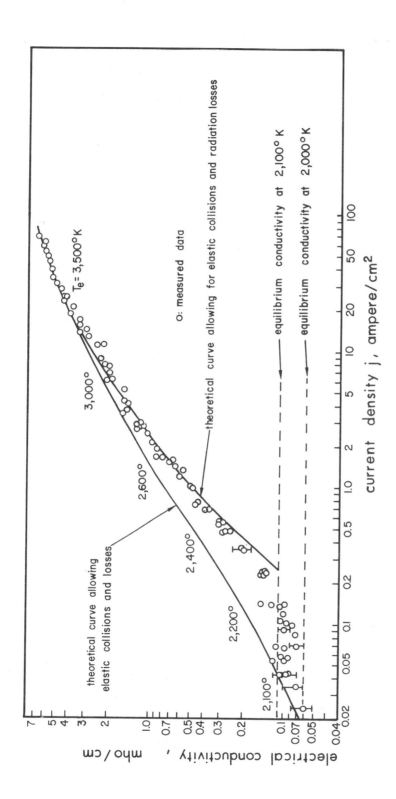

Fig. 13.2-2 Non-equilibrium ionization in Ar at 2,000°K, seeded with 0.4% of potassium. The current density is shown as a function of electrical conductivity in argon; reproduced from T. A. Cool and E. E. Zukoski, "Recombination Rates and Non-Equilibrium Electrical Conductivity in a Seeded Plasma," Sixth Symposium on Engineering Aspects of Magnetohydrodynamics, University of Pittsburgh and Carnegie Institute of Technology, Pittsburgh, Pennsylvania, 1965.

electrons) are also indicated in Fig. 13.2-2. The non-equilibrium electrical conductivities are seen to be appreciably higher than the equilibrium electrical conductivities.

B.   Design Problems

In addition to the Faraday current flowing perpendicular to the directions of fluid flow and of the magnetic field, a Hall current is produced parallel to the direction of the fluid flow. This is an undesirable phenomenon because it interferes with the efficient abstraction of electrical energy. The Hall current may be partially controlled by suitable electrode design. Thus, the use of a segmented-electrode generator with separate loads connected between opposite pairs (see Fig. 13.2-3) emphasizes current flow perpendicular to the direction of the gas flow and minimizes the Hall currents.

The state variables (temperature and pressure) must be selected in such a manner that both the radius of gyration of charged particles (Larmor radius) and the characteristic length over which space charges exist (Debye length) are small in comparison with the dimensions of the apparatus. These conditions may be satisfied in practice by maintaining the operating pressure at sufficiently large values. A detailed analysis of MHD power generation falls beyond the scope of the present discussion and requires the simultaneous solution of the governing equations (i.e., of the equations for conservation of mass for the separate constituents, of momentum, of energy, and of charge), subject to the appli-

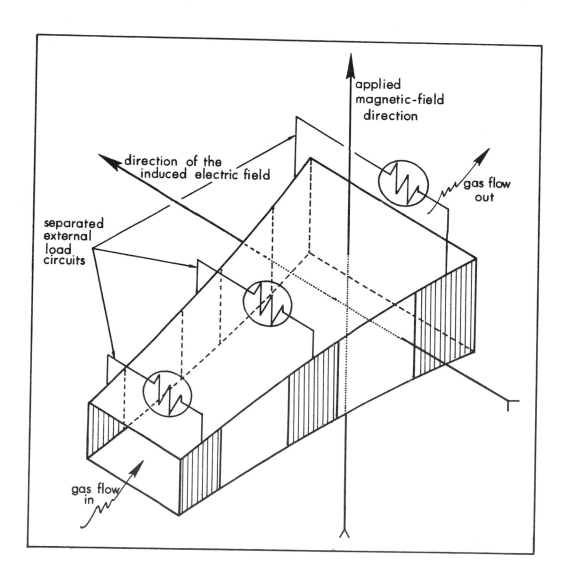

applied
magnetic-field
direction

direction of the
induced electric field

gas flow
out

separated
external
load
circuits

gas flow
in

Fig. 13.2-3 Schematic diagram showing the linear MHD generator of Fig. 13.2-1 redesigned with oppositely-
located conducting segments in order to minimize the undesirable effect of Hall currents.
The conducting electrodes are shaded as in Fig.
13.2-1.

cable boundary conditions. Conversion losses in MHD generators are produced by frictional losses associated with gas channel-flows and by inhomogeneous current flows associated with eddy currents, end losses at the generator inlet and outlet and in the vicinity of the segmented electrodes, Hall currents, and flow instabilities produced by inhomogeneous electrical forces. In diverging channels, substantial gas-flow speeds may be reached.

Because higher temperatures occur in the MHD channel than in a steam generator since combustion gases are used in the channel, the theoretically achievable thermal efficiency in MHD power conversion is about 50% in an open-cycle configuration and about 60% when the MHD unit is combined with a conventional steam-generation system (see Section 13.2C for a description of MHD power configurations). These conversion efficiencies are appreciably higher than the 33 to 45% achievable in conventional fossil-fuel utilization systems. The d.c. output obtained in an open-cycle MHD generator may be changed to a.c. by the use of rather costly converters. Current research efforts are directed toward construction of MHD converters using oil, gas, or coal. Major development problems have been encountered in connection with electrode performance and electrode life.

C.   MHD System Configurations

A schematic diagram of an open-cycle MHD generator is shown in Fig. 13.2-4. Compressed air passes through

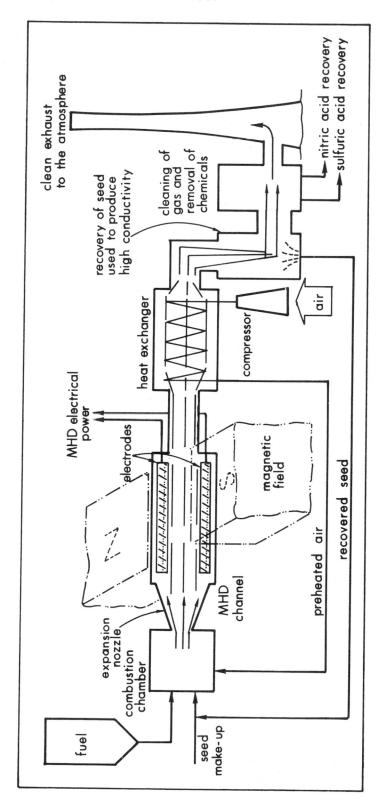

Fig. 13.2-4 Schematic diagram of an open-cycle MHD generator; reproduced with modifications from Power Generation Alternatives, City of Seattle, Department of
Lighting, Seattle, Washington, 1972.

the heat exchanger (regenerator) and cools the combustion products sufficiently to remove most of the ionized seed gas, which is then recovered for reuse and is thereby prevented from contributing to atmospheric pollution. The stack gases are cleaned before exhausting into the atmosphere. A secondary boiler loop may be added after the heat exchanger to produce process steam for application in a conventional steam-turbine generator. This type of combined steam and MHD generation plant has been used in the Russian U-25 pilot plant generating up to 25 Mw_e in the MHD channel and an additional 50 Mw_e in the steam-turbine section. The Russian plant had operated successfully by 1972 for well over 1,000 hours.

A closed-cycle, two-fluid MHD generator, using a nuclear reactor as primary heat source, has also been suggested.[2] A low vapor pressure, liquid metal circulates through the reactor loop and is mixed with another metal of still lower vapor pressure before condensation and separation by expansion through a de Laval nozzle. This separator is then followed by an MHD generator. The achievable efficiencies appear to be relatively low for this type of configuration,[3] although the development has not received adequate attention for definitive evaluation.

---

[2] D. G. Elliott, "Two-Fluid Magnetohydrodynamic Cycle for Nuclear-Electric Power Conversion," ARS J. 32, 924-928 (1962).

[3] D. G. Elliott, "D.C. Liquid-Metal Magnetohydrodynamic Power Generator," Sixth Sumposium on Engineering Aspects of Magnetodydrodynamics, University of Pittsburgh and Carnegie Institute of Technology, Pittsburgh, Pa., 1965.

It is possible that the full potential of MHD power
generation will not be realized for application in fossil-fuel
technology. Full development of MHD technology may require too long a period of time, at marginal economic savings, to justify its introduction while large-scale conversion
to nuclear-power generation and to alternative energy sources
is in progress. On the other hand, a moratorium on the construction of nuclear reactors should contribute to more rapid
commercialization of MHD power conversion for fossil-fuel
applications. MHD power conversion will probably not find
useful implementation on nuclear reactor development because
the operating temperatures are too low.

13.3 Fuel Cells

We have repeatedly noted that the overall conversion
efficiency from chemical (thermal) energy to electrical energy has been limited to 33 to 45% when conventional boiler-
steam-turbine-generator systems are employed. In this sequence, very efficient (approaching 100%) conversion of chemical to thermal energy occurs, conversion of thermal to
mechanical energy with overall efficiencies of 37 to 47% is
limited by the Carnot-cycle efficiency (which defines the ultimately achievable conversion in accord with the second law
of thermodynamics), whereas final generation of electricity
from mechanical energy in the turbine generator is again
achieved with losses amounting to only a few percent. The
Carnot efficiency in percent is one hundred times the ratio

of useful work W done for a thermal energy input Q and is given by the relation

$$\eta_C = 100\,\frac{W}{Q} = 100\,\frac{T_u - T_\ell}{T_u}, \qquad\qquad (13.3\text{-}1)$$

where T_u and T_ℓ denote, respectively, the absolute upper and lower temperature levels between which the engine operates. The Carnot-engine efficiency represents an upper achievable limit when heat is introduced into an isothermally-expanding ideal gas and is abstracted from an isothermally-compressed ideal gas.[1] The complete Carnot cycle involves sequentially isothermal expansion, adiabatic expansion, isothermal compression, and adiabatic compression returning the system to its original state. Practical engine cycles such as the Otto cycle, the Brayton or Joule cycle, and the Rankine cycle have lower efficiencies than the Carnot engine.[1]

In order to avoid the energy loss associated with efficiency limitations in thermal-to-mechanical energy conversion dictated by the second law of thermodynamics, we may convert chemical energy directly into electrical energy in a fuel cell. Theoretically-achievable efficiencies now exceed 80%, although practically-available fuel-cell systems for electricity generation have been limited to overall efficiencies of less than 60%. In the fuel cell, the heat of reac-

---

[1]S. S. Penner, Thermodynamics, Chapters 4 and 10, Addison-Wesley Publishing Co., Reading, Mass., 1968.

tion that is normally released by the combustion processes is directly converted to electrical energy at low and moderate temperatures. We shall now discuss the design of a typical fuel cell (Section 13.3A), the thermodynamic limits on ideal fuel-cell performance (Section 13.3B), actual fuel-cell performance (Section 13.3C), and current fuel-cell developments (Section 13.3D).

A. An Example of Ideal Fuel-Cell Operation: The Hydrogen-Oxygen Fuel Cell

A schematic diagram of a hydrogen-oxygen fuel cell is shown in Fig. 13.3-1. Gaseous hydrogen and oxygen are injected at the anode and cathode, respectively.[*] At the anode (the negative terminal), hydrogen is ionized with the release of two electrons per molecule of gas ionized, i.e.,

$$H_2(g) \rightarrow 2H^+ + 2e^-. \tag{13.3-2}$$

The electrons then pass through the external circuit while the H^+ ions move to the cathode through the electrolyte. The following overall reaction occurs in the vicinity of the cathode:

---

[*] It is customary to designate the negative and positive terminals as the anode and cathode, respectively, in sponta-neous cells such as fuel cells or batteries. In non-sponta-neous cells used for electrolysis, the anode and cathode denote, respectively, the positive and negative terminals. Thus the nomenclature is reversed for spontaneous and non-spontaneous cells.

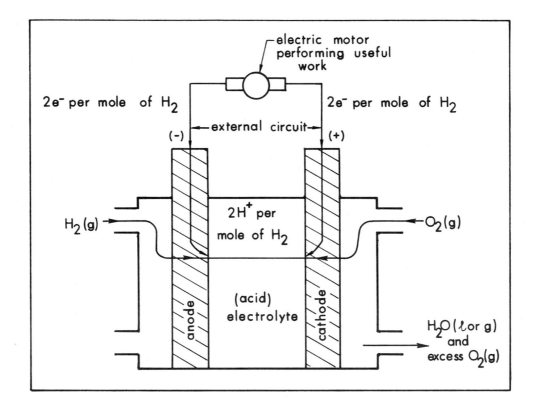

Fig. 13.3-1 Schematic diagram of the ideal hydrogen-oxygen
           fuel cell, used as a source of electrical energy;
           reproduced from Ref. [1].

$$2H^+ + 2e^- + (1/2)O_2(g) \rightarrow H_2O(\ell), \qquad (13.3\text{-}3)$$

with $(1/2)O_2(g)$ first being reduced by the electrons to oxygen
ions. Addition of Eqs. (13.3-2) and (13.3-3) defines the overall process as

$$H_2(g) + (1/2)O_2(g) \rightarrow H_2O(\ell) - 68.3 \text{ kcal,} \qquad (13.3-4)$$

where 68.3 kcal corresponds to the heat released for complete reaction when one mole of gaseous hydrogen and one-half mole of gaseous oxygen form one mole of liquid water at 300°K and atmospheric pressure. The overall heat release (enthalpy change) for the overall reaction is a function of temperature and depends also on the physical state in which the water is finally produced. Thus, per mole of gaseous water formed at 300°K, the heat released is reduced from 68.3 kcal by the molar heat of evaporation of water at 300°K (10.5 kcal) and the overall heat release becomes, therefore, 57.8 kcal per mole if $H_2O(g)$ is formed at 300°K.

Operation of the hydrogen-oxygen fuel cell is seen to correspond to the reverse of water electrolysis (compare Section 11.2A).

B. Ideal Fuel-Cell Performance

The ideal fuel-cell efficiency is defined as the ratio of the useful work ($\equiv \Delta\varphi$) done at constant temperature and pressure to the enthalpy change (ΔH = heat released) for the overall fuel-cell reaction. The useful work done, $\Delta\varphi$, equals the Gibbs free energy change, ΔF, for the fuel-cell reaction.[1] Thus, the cell efficiency is determined by the relation

$$\eta_{FC} = \Delta\varphi/\Delta H = \Delta F/\Delta H. \qquad\qquad (13.3-5)$$

Here ΔF and ΔH may be easily estimated from tabulated thermochemical data for a variety of possible fuel-cell reactions. Some representative data are listed in Table 13.3-1 for cells operating at $300^{\circ}K$ and at $1,000^{\circ}K$. Ideal fuel-cell efficiencies are seen to range from 69.1 to 105.1%, using the definition for η_{FC} given in Eq. (13.3-5). The electrode processes are generally easier to implement at high temperatures than at low temperatures.

Of the five fuel-cell types indicated in Table 13.3-1, only the first has been extensively tested and developed. The listed cell voltages, ϵ, were calculated by noting that the useful electrical work done during fuel-cell operation equals the product of the voltage (ϵ) and charge transfer (Δq), with the charge transfer (Δq), in turn, equal to the product of the negative of the number of equivalents (or electrons produced per mole), n, and of the Faraday constant, $\mathfrak{F}_a = 96,487$ coulombs/equivalent = 23.06 kcal/volt-equivalent. Thus, the ideal cell voltage may be calculated from the general relation

$$\Delta\varphi = \Delta F = \epsilon\,\Delta q = -\epsilon n \mathfrak{F}_a$$

or

$$\epsilon = -(\Delta F/23.06n) \text{ volt} \qquad\qquad (13.3-6)$$

Table 13.3-1 Summary of representative theoretical fuel-cell performance data; abstracted from F. D. Rossini, "Thermodynamic Considerations of Fossil-Fuel Cells," paper presented at the Seventh World Petroleum Congress, Mexico City, April 1967; reproduced from Ref. [1]. The values of ΔH and ΔF are given per mole of fuel.

Fuel-cell reaction	$-\Delta H$, kcal	$-\Delta F$, kcal	η_{FC}	ϵ, volt
$H_2(g) + \frac{1}{2}O_2(g) \rightarrow H_2O(\ell)$:				
at $300^\circ K$	68.30	56.62	0.829	1.228
at $1,000^\circ K$	- - - -	- - - -	- - -	- - - -
$H_2(g) + \frac{1}{2}O_2(g) \rightarrow H_2O(g)$:				
at $300^\circ K$	57.80	54.62	0.945	1.184
at $1,000^\circ K$	59.21	46.03	0.777	0.998
$CO(g) + \frac{1}{2}O_2(g) \rightarrow CO_2(g)$:				
at $300^\circ K$	67.64	61.41	0.908	1.332
at $1,000^\circ K$	67.55	46.67	0.691	1.012
$C(c, graphite) + O_2(g) \rightarrow CO_2(g)$:				
at $300^\circ K$	94.05	94.33	1.002	1.022
at $1,000^\circ K$	94.32	94.61	1.003	1.026
$C_3H_8(g) + 5O_2(g) \rightarrow 3CO_2(g) + 4H_2O(g)$:				
at $300^\circ K$	488.5	495.7	1.015	1.075
at $1,000^\circ K$	488.9	513.6	1.051	1.124

if ΔF is expressed kcal. As an example, at $300^{\circ}K$, the ideal

$H_2(g) + (1/2)O_2(g) \rightarrow H_2O(\ell)$ fuel cell has a value (see Table

13.3-1) of $\Delta F = -56.62$ kcal with $n = 2$ so that $\epsilon = 1.228$ volts.

Ideal fuel-cell efficiencies η_{FC} greater than unity

correspond to processes in which heat is transferred from

the surroundings to the fuel cell operating under conditions

of constant temperature and pressure. This type of occur-

rence is seen to be analogous to the corresponding efficiency

increases for electrolysis discussed in Section 11.2A.

C. Actual Fuel-Cell Performance

In actual fuel cells, losses occur during electron

transfer at an electrode (activation polarization), during mass

transport through concentration gradients (concentration po-

larization), and during electron transport through the elec-

trodes and ion transport through the electrolyte (resistive

or ohmic polarization). As the result, overall energy losses

during fuel-cell operation may exceed 25%. [2]

D. Current Fuel-Cell Developments [3]

Advanced fuel-cell development has been funded pri-

marily for space applications. With decreased funding from

---

[2] "Fuel Cell Systems," No. 47 in the Advances in Chemistry
Series, American Chemical Society, Washington, D.C.,
1965.

[3] T. H. Maugh II, "Fuel Cells: Dispersed Generation of
Electricity," Science 178, 1273-1276 (1972).

NASA, some proprietary programs have been continued in various industrial laboratories, especially on hydrocarbon-air fuel cells.

Fuel-cell systems require connection in series of the low-voltage devices described in Table 13.3-1. For example, using 10^4 cells with individual outputs of 1 volt and 200 milliamperes of current per cm^2 of electrode may produce a 10-kv array with a power level of 100 Mw$_e$ if the cells have a cross-sectional area of 5 m^2. The complete system generally contains a reformer for fuel processing and an inverter to convert the d.c. fuel-cell output to a.c. Fuel-cell systems are generally not significant sources of air and thermal pollution and currently have primary appeal as low-output power sources (10 to 200 kw$_e$) in remote areas and as topping cycles or supplements (25 to 100 Mw$_e$) in central utility-station operations. Practical fuel-cell systems do not show the rapid decrease in efficiency with decreasing power output that occurs for other types of electricity-generation units. This last statement is exemplified by the data summarized in Fig. 13.3-2 for hydrocarbon-air fuel cells, which are seen to have overall efficiencies for a.c. power generation between 40 and 50% at power outputs exceeding about 20 kw$_e$. The corresponding overall efficiencies are about 55% for $H_2(g)$-air and 60% for $H_2(g)$-oxygen fuel cells.

Fuel-cell development has been supported by 35 natural-gas transmission companies under the TARGET (= Team to Advance Research for Gas Energy Transformation) program. By the end of 1972, almost sixty 12.5-kw$_e$ fuel-cell

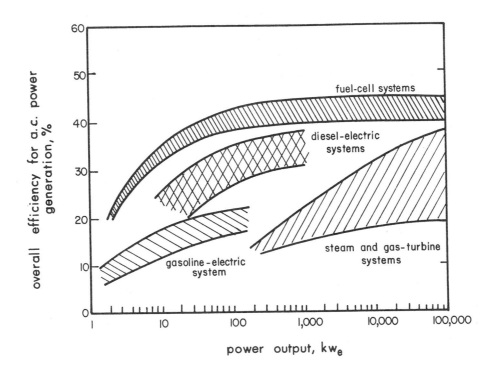

Fig. 13.3-2 Fuel-cell efficiencies for hydrocarbon-air sys-
            tems producing $H_2O(g)$; reproduced from <u>Hydro-
            gen and Other Synthetic Fuels,</u> U.S. Atomic
            Energy Commission, TID-26136, U.S. Govern-
            ment Printing Office, Washington, D.C., 1972.

stations were being tested at 37 locations in the U.S. and
Canada. It is apparent that an increase in the efficiency of
gas utilization to 50% would represent enormously-important
energy savings. Fuel cells may often be located in close
proximity to the user of electricity. Because of lower costs
of gas transmission, as compared with the transmission of
electricity over long distances (compare Section 11.3), addi-

tional energy and dollar savings may be obtained in this manner.

We have seen that fuel-cell development also constitutes a natural component of advanced energy-storage systems (compare Chapter 12). Modular construction of fuel-cell units in the design of electrical-energy sources of desired size is an appropriate long-range goal. Although fuel-cell costs in late 1972 were nearly twice as high ($350 to $450/ kw_e) as other fossil-fuel electricity-generating plants on a per kw_e basis, it is apparent that they become more attractive as fuel costs rise because higher energy-conversion efficiencies to electricity are achieved. A major development program remains, namely, to increase cell life appreciably over the 16,000-hour limits available in 1973.

Active research has been underway (e.g., at Westinghouse) for some years to develop high-temperature fuel cells operating near $1,000°C$ with overall efficiencies of about 60%. At high temperatures, the fuel reaction at the anode occurs rapidly and without a catalyst. With CO, d.c. current densities of 600 milliamperes/cm^2 have been achieved.[3] Solid electrolytes made of zirconium oxide doped with yttrium oxide have been tested. The anode consists of finely divided nickel in a zirconium oxide matrix, while the cathode is antimony-doped stannic oxide or tin-doped indium oxide. Some details of this type of fuel-cell construction are shown in Fig. 13.3-3. Practical realization of cells of this type will require considerable development and is some years away.

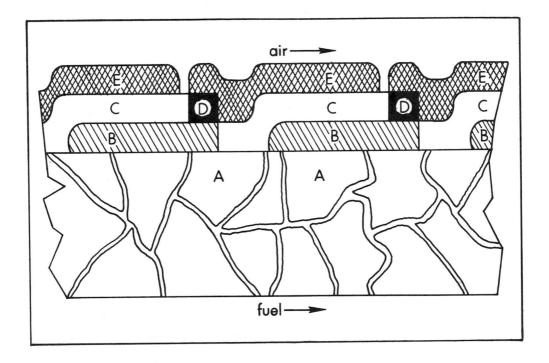

Fig. 13.3-3 Cross-section of a high-temperature fuel cell
            assembly: (A) porous carrier tube; (B) fuel
            electrode; (C) electrolyte; (D) interconnections;
            (E) air electrode. Reproduced from Westing-
            house Electric Corporation, 1970 Final Report:
            Project Fuel Cell, U.S. Government Printing
            Office, Washington, D.C., 1971.

A 1976 program[4] on advanced fuel-cell technology

has as a goal the development of a device costing no more

---

[4](a) "Advanced Technology Fuel Cell Program" by J. M.
    King, Jr., Report EPRI EM-335, October 1976, and (b)
    "Economic Assessment of the Utilization of Fuel Cells in
    Electric Utility Systems" by W. Wood, M. P. Bhavaraju
    and P. Yatcho, Report EPRI EM-336, November 1977,
    Electric Power Research Institute, Palo Alto, California.

than \$250/kw$_e$ (including costs of fuel storage and of elec-
trical connections); the heat rate during operation is to be
less than 9,300 Btu/kwh$_e$ (i.e., a conversion efficiency >
37%). These performance figures represent minimum targets for economically competitive systems that may be used
as peaking units in conjunction with coal-fired or (nuclear)
baseload capacity in electric utility operation. Integration
of the fuel cell into the electric network is shown schematically in Fig. 13.3-4. The following fuel cells are among
those that are currently under active development: the molten-carbonate cell (see Fig. 13.3-5) which is used according
to the scheme shown in Fig. 13.3-6; the solid-oxide cell in
which a non-porous ceramic oxide is used as the electrolyte
which eliminates CO_2 evolution at the anode and CO_2 addition
at the cathode; fuel cells in which phosphoric acid serves as
the electrolyte; an alkaline electrolyte fuel cell. These fuel
cells may presumably be operated with any conveniently
available mixtures of fuel and air or oxygen.

The molten-carbonate cell operates at a temperature
near 1,200°F so that the carbonates are melted and
serve as good ionic conductors. At these cell temperatures,
nickel is sufficiently active to act as a catalyst for both the
anode and cathode reactions.

At the anode, hydrogen reacts with the carbonate ion
to produce water, carbon dioxide, and electrons, i.e.,

$$H_2 + CO_3^= \rightarrow H_2O + CO_2 + 2e^-. \qquad (13.3-5)$$

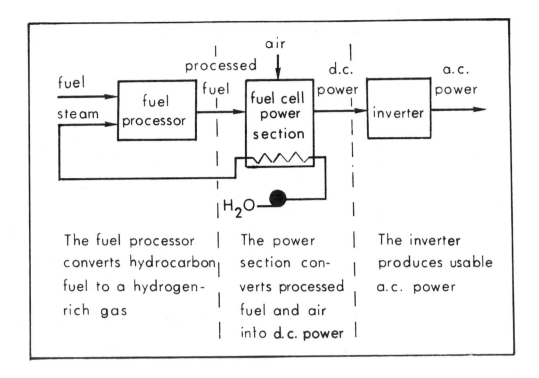

The fuel processor converts hydrocarbon fuel to a hydrogen-rich gas

The power section converts processed fuel and air into d.c. power

The inverter produces usable a.c. power

Fig. 13.3-4 Fuel cell integration into the utility network. Reproduced with modifications from Ref. [4a].

Near the cathode, oxygen from the process air and carbon dioxide react in the presence of electrons that have passed through the external circuit (see Fig. 13.3-6) to produce carbonate ions by the reaction

$$(1/2)O_2 + CO_2 + 2e^- \rightarrow CO_3^=. \qquad (13.3-6)$$

The overall cell reaction is the oxidation of hydrogen to form water, electricity, and waste heat, which is evident from Eqs. (13.3-5) and (13.3-6) and Fig. 13.3-6.

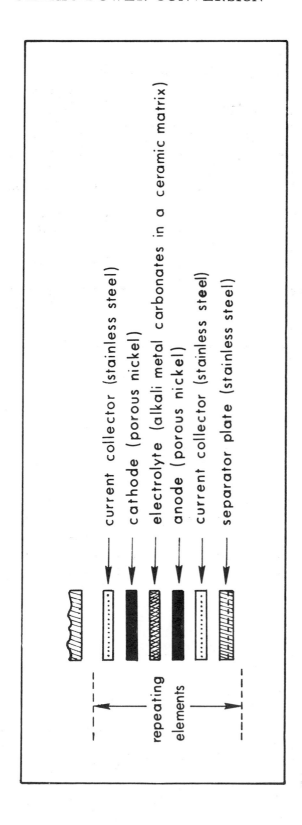

Fig. 13.3-5 Schematic diagram of a molten-carbonate fuel cell constructed from readily available materials. The electrolyte consists of alkali metal carbonates dispersed in a ceramic matrix; the anode and the cathode are made of porous nickel while the current-collector and separator plates are manufactured from stainless steel. Reproduced with modifications from Ref. [4a].

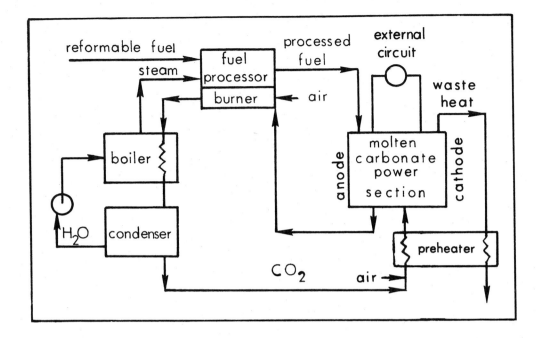

Fig. 13.3-6 Schematic diagram showing integration of the
            molten-carbonate cell into the power-plant
            system. Processed hydrocarbon fuel containing
            H_2, CO_2, and CO is fed to the anode, where most
            of the hydrogen is consumed. The remaining
            H_2 and processed gases and the anode-reaction
            products (CO_2, H_2O) are burned to supply heat
            for the reformer. Water vapor in the burner-
            exhaust gas is condensed, which leaves a stream
            of CO_2 required at the cathode.

13.4   Photovoltaic Power Conversion

Photovoltaic power conversion involves the direct
production of electricity in suitable solid-state devices
(solar cells) on absorption of solar radiation. A solar cell
is constructed from a semiconductor (such as silicon or

germanium) by doping the semiconductor material to produce n-type and p-type slices.[1]

A. Construction of an n-Type Semiconductor

If phosphorus atoms with 5 valence electrons are
introduced into a silicon block composed of atoms with 4
valence electrons, 4 of the 5 valence electrons in P become
bonded to Si while the fifth valence electron may separate
and wander through the semiconductor when its thermal
energy is sufficiently high. This type of semiconductor is
called an n-type (because negative charge carriers are released on doping the silicon matrix with phosphorus) and is
shown schematically in Fig. 13.4-1, where we have presented P with a single positive charge to identify the P-atom,
which is chemically bonded to the Si-matrix. For each P^+,
a free electron (e^-) becomes available.

B. Construction of a p-Type Semiconductor

When boron with three valence electrons is introduced
into silicon, there is a deficiency of one electron per atom
insofar as bonding to the quadrivalent silicon is concerned.
This electron deficiency may be symbolized by an excess
positive charge $\oplus$ or hole. The resulting semiconductor is
said to be of the p-type (because it is characterized by a

[1]"Photovoltaic Energy Conversion" by J. F. Elliot, Chapter 1 in Direct Energy Conversion, edited by G. W. Sutton,
McGraw-Hill Book Co., Inc., New York, 1966.

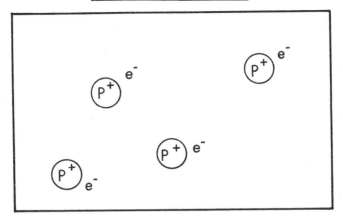

Fig. 13.4-1 Schematic diagram of an n-type semiconductor
            formed by inserting P-atoms into an Si matrix.

deficiency of electrons and, therefore, has effectively labile
positive charges) and is shown schematically in Fig. 13.4-2.

C. Construction of a p-n Junction

When the p-type and n-type semiconductors are joined,
a p-n junction is produced. Although the blocks of p-type and
n-type material are electrically neutral on a macroscopic
scale, they contain, respectively, free equivalent positive
($\oplus$) and negative (e^-) charge carriers. In the arrangement
shown schematically in Fig. 13.4-3, the holes ($\oplus$) will tend
to move to the left and the electrons (e^-) to the right. Movement of holes should be visualized as the transfer of an

p-type semiconductor

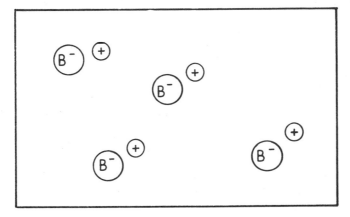

Fig. 13.4-2 Schematic diagram of a p-type semiconductor
            formed by inserting B-atoms into an Si-matrix.

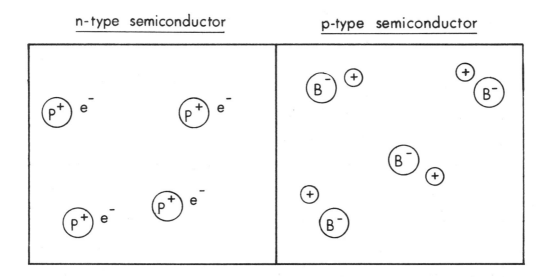

Fig. 13.4-3 Schematic diagram showing a p-n junction con-
            structed from wafers of silicon doped, respec-
            tively, with P and B. The diagram shows the
            distribution of charge carriers prior to diffu-
            sion of holes and electrons.

<u>electron deficiency between positively-charged nuclei and</u>
<u>not as the physical relocation of positive charge carriers.</u>
After some time, diffusion of holes from the p-type semiconductor to the n-type semiconductor, and of electrons from
the n-type semiconductor to the p-type semiconductor, will
lead to the production of a p-n junction with positively and
negatively charged regions, as is shown schematically in
Fig. 13.4-4.

As the result of diffusion of holes and electrons, an
electric field is established at the interface region between
the p-type and n-type semiconductors. Diffusion terminates
when the electric-field differentials become sufficiently large
to inhibit further (thermal) motion of holes and electrons.

D.   Potentials in a p-n Junction

The potential gradients seen by electrons and holes
are shown in Fig. 13.4-5. The potential energy of the electrons has been drawn in such a manner that it increases upwards while that of the holes increases downwards. The
preferred directions of motions for electrons and holes are
accordingly to the left and to the right, respectively, in the
directions of decreasing potential energies. The potential
curves are separated by the band gap. Electrons with energies exceeding the values corresponding to the electron potential-energy curve are free to move and are said to be in
the conduction band. Holes with energies exceeding those
corresponding to the hole potential-energy curve are free to

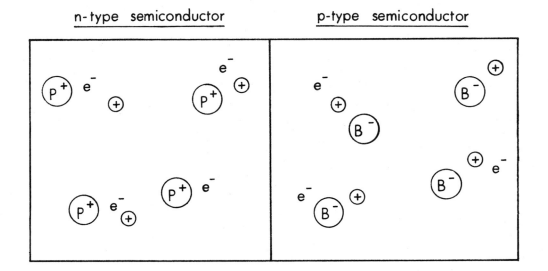

n-type semiconductor   p-type semiconductor

Fig. 13.4-4 Schematic diagram showing a p-n junction constructed from wafers of silicon doped, respectively, with P and B. The diagram suggests a
distribution of charge carriers after diffusion
of holes and electrons.

move and lie in the valence band.

The band gap measures the minimum energy required
to move a hole from the valence band to the conduction band
or an electron from the conduction band to the valence band.

E.   Absorption of Photons and Hole-Electron-Pair
Creation

When a photon with energy greater than the band-gap
energy is absorbed, it will create a hole-electron pair. The
electron will tend to move to the left (in the direction of

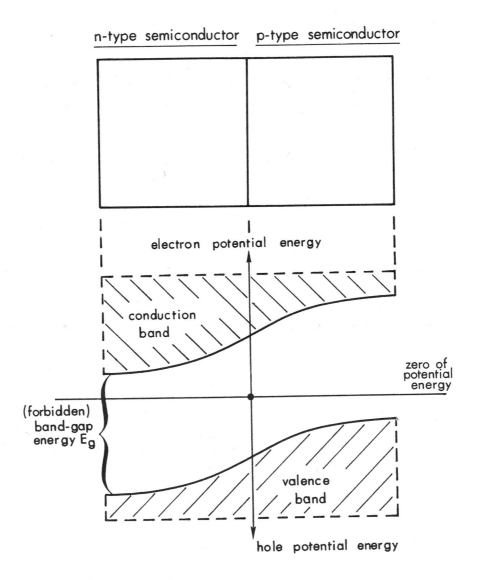

n-type semiconductor   p-type semiconductor

electron potential energy

conduction
band

zero of
potential
energy

(forbidden)
band-gap
energy E_g

valence
band

hole potential energy

Fig. 13.4-5 Schematic diagram showing the potential energy
            curves for electrons and holes across a p-n
            junction. The absolute values of the potentials
            depend on the concentrations of electrons and
            holes in the semiconductor. It should be noted
            that the electron and hole potential energies have
            positive values in the upward and downward di-
            rections, respectively, as is indicated by the
            arrows above and below the line labeled "zero
            of potential energy".

decreasing electron potential energy) while the hole tends to move to the right (in the direction of decreasing hole potential energy). If this separation of holes and electrons occurs sufficiently rapidly so that hole-electron-pair annihilation (recombination) cannot occur (i.e., the minority carrier lifetime is sufficiently long), then charge separation has been induced at the p-n junction and photovoltaic energy conversion has been accomplished.

Under the influence of many energetic photons, many hole-electron pairs are created, leading to positive-charge and negative-charge accumulation at the right and left, respectively. This charge accumulation will ultimately limit the production of further electron-hole pairs. The resulting limiting condition determines the open-circuit voltage of the device. A large band gap corresponds to a large open-circuit voltage.

F. A Commercial Solar Cell

A commercial solar cell for the conversion of photon energy to electricity is shown in Fig. 13.4-6. The maximum conversion efficiency for a photovoltaic cell is defined as follows:[1]

$$\eta_{PC} = \frac{\text{output electric power}}{\text{input radiant power}}$$

$$= \frac{kV_{oc}I_{sc}}{\text{input radiant power}},$$

(13.4-1)

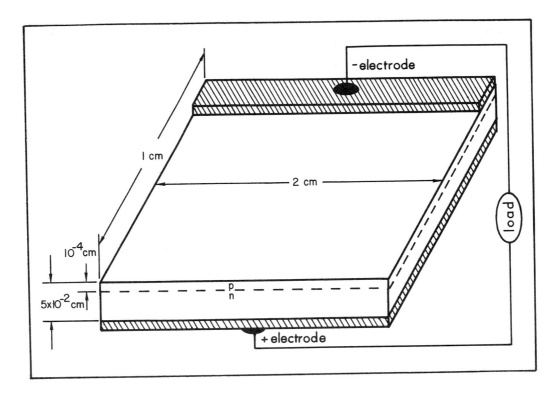

Fig. 13.4-6 Typical geometry and physical configuration of a p-on-n silicon solar cell. Characteristics: $V_{oc} \approx 0.58$ volt; $I_{sc} \approx 45 \times 10^{-3}$ ampere; actual cell voltage during operation ≈ 0.44 volt; output power density $\approx 12 \times 10^{-3}$ $w_e/2cm^2$; $\eta_{PC} \approx 12\%$. The solar-energy flux is incident on the upper portion of the cell. Reproduced with modifications from Ref. [1] with permission of McGraw-Hill Book Company. Copyright © 1966 by McGraw-Hill Book Company.

where V_{oc} = open-circuit voltage, I_{sc} = short-circuit current for the converter, and k lies generally between 0.25 and 1.00 and thus measures the efficiency with which photovoltaic power can be utilized in the converter. The magnitude of the short-circuit current is directly proportional to the number of incoming photons with energies exceeding the band-gap energy.   The band-gap energy determines the open-circuit potential.   As the band gap increases, V_{oc} increases while I_{sc} decreases for a given light source such as the sun.

G.   Physical Factors Determining Solar-Cell Performance and Materials of Construction

In order to maximize photovoltaic conversion, the semiconductor materials should have low reflectivity (which is obtained for materials with index of refraction close to unity) and should not interfere with the penetration of the incoming solar radiation to such depths that hole-electron-pair creation can be readily accomplished.   In other words, the semiconductor materials should have appropriate absorption coefficients for photons of desired energy.   This desirable physical property applies for silicon and has been responsible for its wide use in solar cells.

A well-designed solar cell has high light-collection efficiency (Q) for low optical reflection coefficients and small values of $\exp(-\bar{\alpha}l)$ with $\bar{\alpha}$ denoting the mean absorption coefficient for photons capable of hole-electron-pair creation and l representing the distance of the junction below the cell surface.   The theoretical efficiency for solar cells constructed of different materials is shown in Fig. 13.4-7 while the theoretical temperature dependence is indicated in Fig. 13.4-8.

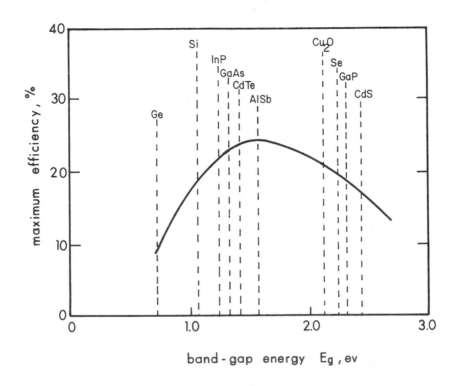

Fig. 13.4-7 The theoretical efficiency of solar cells constructed from semiconductor materials with
different band gaps. The data refer to cell
operation outside of the atmosphere of the
earth; reproduced from J. J. Loferski, "Recent Research on Photovoltaic Solar Energy
Converters," Proceedings of the IEEE 51,
667-674 (1963).

H. Solar-Cell Output Power per Unit Area

Solar-cell voltages and current densities are shown
in Fig. 13.4-9 for silicon and gallium-arsenide semiconductors at an incident energy of 100×10^{-3} w/m^2. The products
of the voltages and current densities provide an indication of

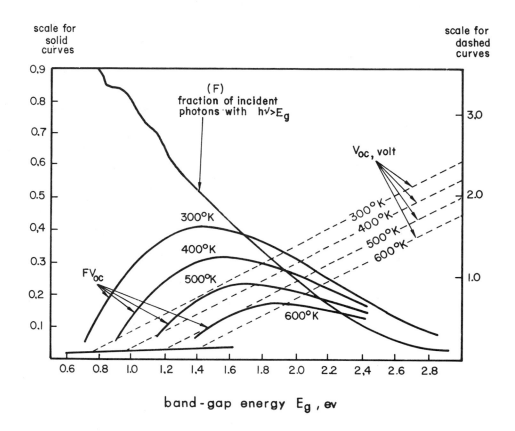

Fig. 13.4-8 Theoretical temperature dependence of the
solar-energy conversion efficiency FV_{oc} for
cells with different band-gap semiconductor materials; reproduced from R. E. Halsted, "Temperature Consideration in Solar Battery Development," J. Appl. Phys. 28, 1131 (1957).

output power per unit area. Silicon solar cells are seen to
be capable of higher current densities whereas gallium-arsenide cells show larger voltages.

I. Solar-Cell Power Output per Unit Weight

In space applications, the power output per unit
weight is of primary importance. The data reproduced in

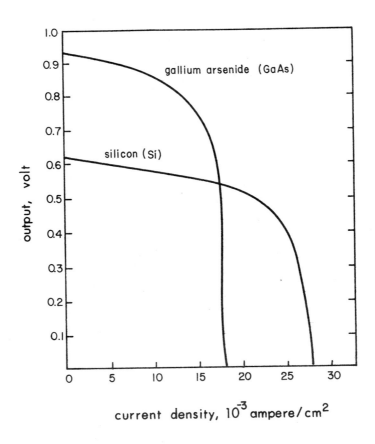

Fig. 13.4-9 Current density-voltage curves for Si and GaAs
             solar cells at an incident solar energy of $100 \times$
             10^{-3} w/cm^2; reproduced from R. D. Gold,
             "Current Status of GaAs Solar Cells," Tran-
             script of the Photovoltaic Specialists Confer-
             ence, Volume 1, Photovoltaic Materials, De-
             vices, and Radiation Damage Effects, July 1963.

Fig. 13.4-10 show the relation between cell thickness and
minority-carrier lifetime for silicon solar cells. There is
a well defined minimum thickness above which the conversion efficiency of a solar cell increases only very slowly.

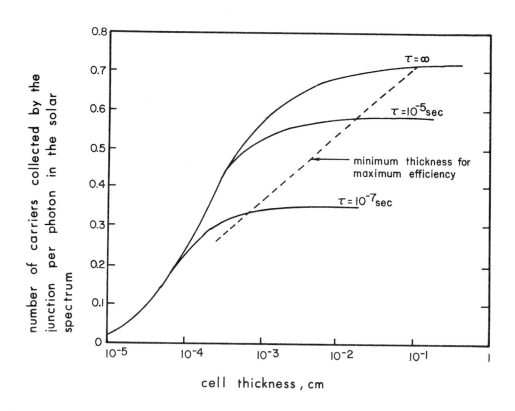

Fig. 13.4-10 Relative efficiency of silicon solar cells as a function of cell thickness. The symbol τ identifies the carrier lifetime. Reproduced from J. F. Elliott, "Home Generation of Power by Photovoltaic Conversion of Solar Energy," Electrical Engineering 79, 735-738 (1960).

J. Solar-Cell Reliability

Applications of solar cells in the space program have shown that reliable performance may be achieved for long periods of time with appropriately shielded cells. In ground-based applications, where weight considerations are unimportant, long life can clearly be achieved at a price.

K.   Current Photovoltaic-Cell Developments[2]

As photovoltaic-cell production increases in volume, costs should decrease. Projected costs for silicon solar cells for the SSPS (Satellite Solar-Power Stations) are shown in Fig. 13.4-11. The projected cost decreases are very large: from current costs for space-power stations of about $200/$w_e$ to $0.30/$w_e$ in order to achieve market penetration for central-power station applications. Implicit in these projections is an increase in cell efficiency from current values of about 11% to nearly the theoretical limit of 22%. Silicon solar cells may conceivably be replaced by gallium-arsenide cells. Important cost reductions are expected to be achieved by diminishing the cell thicknesses from current values of 500 to 1,000 $\times 10^{-4}$ cm to perhaps 50 $\times 10^{-4}$ cm. New technologies[3] such as EFG (edge-defined, film-fed growth) should lead to important savings. Generally, industry-capacity cost reductions tend to follow a 70% decreasing slope with increasing production, corresponding to a 0.3 reduction

---

[2]P. E. Glaser, O. E. Maynard, J. Mackovciak, Jr., and E. L. Ralph, "Feasibility Study of a Satellite Solar Power Station," NASA Contractor Report, NASA CR-2357, National Aeronautics and Space Administration, Washington, D.C., 1974.

[3]H. E. Bates et al, "The Edge-Defined Film-Fed Growth of Silicon Crystal Ribbon for Solar Cell Applications," 9th IEEE Photovoltaic Specialists Conference, p. 386, Silver Spring, Maryland, May 1972.

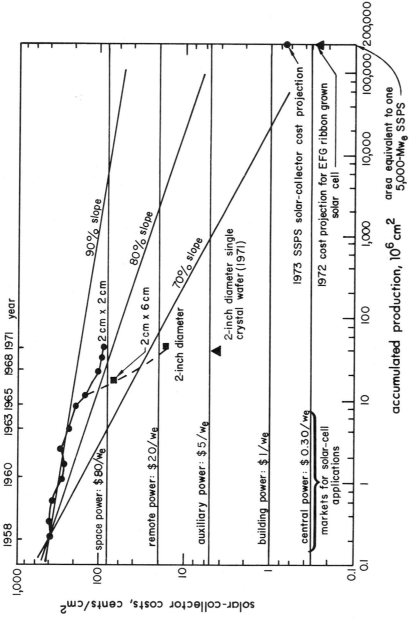

Fig. 13.4-11 Projected costs for silicon solar cells; reproduced with modifications from Ref. [2]. To arrive at a 1970 cost estimate in $/kw$_e$ for a collector cost of $1.00/cm^2, we may use the data of Fig. 13.4-6 of 12×10^{-3}w$_e$/2cm^2; the resulting capital investment is easily calculated to be $167,000/kw$_e$. During the middle of 1974, solar cells became available for about $20,000/kw$_e$.

of the cost for an increase in production by a factor of two (see the 70% curve in Fig. 13.4-11).[4]

We refer to the literature for recent developments on photovoltaic cells,[5-9] especially introduction of the edge-defined crystal-growth process.[5,8,9]

A summary report of a recent conference dealing with photovoltaic power conversion contains the following

---

[4] *Perspectives on Experience*, The Boston Consulting Group, Inc., Boston, Mass., 1968.

[5] B. Chalmers, T. Surek, A. I. Mlavsky, R. O. Bell, D. N. Jewett, and J. C. Swartz, "Continuous Silicon Solar Cells," Report NSF/RANN/SE/GI-37067X/PR/73/2, Harvard University (Cambridge, Mass. 02138) and Tyco Laboratories (16 Hickory Drive, Waltham, Mass. 02154), September 1973.

[6] W. A. Hasbach and R. G. Ross, Jr., "Summary Report on the Development, Design and Test of a 66-w/kg (30-w/lb) Roll-Up Solar Array," Jet Propulsion Laboratory, Technical Report 32-1562, California Institute of Technology, Pasadena, California, September 1972.

[7] P. A. Berman, "Photovoltaic Solar Array Technology Required for Three Wide-Scale Generation Systems for Terrestrial Applications: Rooftop, Solar Farm, and Satellite," Jet Propulsion Laboratory, Technical Report 32-1573, California Institute of Technology, Pasadena, California, October 1972.

[8] B. Chalmers, T. Surek and J. Swartz, "Continuous Silicon Solar Cells," Report NSF/RANN/SE/GI-37067X/PR/74/2, Harvard University (Cambridge, Mass. 02138) and Tyco Laboratories (16 Hickory Drive, Waltham, Mass. 02154), July 1974.

[9] A. L. Hammond, "Solar Power: Promising New Developments," Science **184**, 1359-1360 (1974).

items: 5.5% conversion efficiency has been achieved with
amorphous-silicon cells using either a p-i-n junction (in
which the p and n junctions are separated by an undoped,
inert layer) or a Schottky diode (in which the p junction is
omitted and its function is performed by a charged region
near the metal electrode); more than 22% efficiency was
achieved in gallium-arsenide photocells; single-crystal
solar cells have yielded 12% efficiency; 7.8% efficiency was
achieved in a CdS-Cu$_2$S cell; 5% efficiency was obtained in
cells produced by using a chemical spray on glass to produce
films that were only a few microns thick (at a production
level of 10^6 ft^2/y, the anticipated cost is $425/kw$_e$ in 2-ft^2
cells).[10] The ERDA goal of achieving large-scale production costs of $500/kw$_e$ by 1985 was viewed as optimistic by
some and as realistic by others.[10] Some recent inventions
in photovoltaics have substantially higher overall photoelec-
tric conversion efficiencies than 22% (e.g., up to 40% for
stacked, multiple-junction cells using different parts of the
solar spectrum and 30 to 50% for "thermophotovoltaics" in
which transmitted, unused light is absorbed and reradiated
to the cell at longer wavelengths).[11]

---

[10]Physics Today 30, 17-19, January 1977.

[11]A. L. Hammond, "Photovoltaics: The Semiconductor
    Revolution Comes to Solar," Science 197, 445-447 (1977).

13.5 Thermoelectric Power Generation

Thermoelectric power conversion[1] depends on application of the Seebeck, Peltier, and Thomson effects. From the practical point of view, the efficiency of thermoelectric power generation is of interest in connection with possible utilization of existing thermal gradients or of thermal gradients that may be created by the application of abundant energy sources (e.g., nuclear-breeder or fusion reactors, solar energy). The origin of thermoelectric phenomenon may be assessed by using the science of irreversible thermodynamics. Energy-conversion efficiencies for thermoelectric power generation generally do not exceed one-sixth of the corresponding Carnot efficiency.

A.   The Seebeck Effect

The Seebeck effect is associated with the production of a potential difference across an open loop when the junctions of dissimilar, connected metals are heated to different temperatures (see Fig. 13.5-1). The Seebeck coefficient is defined as

---

[1] "Thermoelectric Power Generation," by S. I. Freedman, Chapter 3 in Direct Energy Conversion, edited by G. W. Sutton, McGraw-Hill Book Co., Inc., New York, 1966.

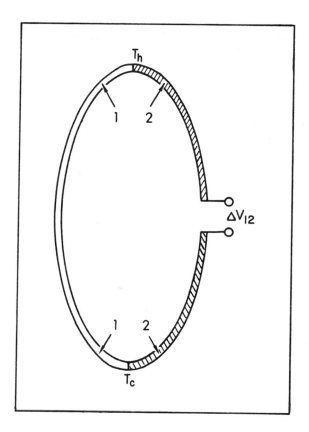

Fig. 13.5-1 An open loop constructed of dissimilar metals develops a potential difference when the metal junctions are heated to different temperatures. The ratio of the voltage difference to the temperature difference is known as the Seebeck coefficient.

$$\alpha_{S,12} = \lim_{T_h - T_c \to 0} \Delta V_{12} / (T_h - T_c)$$

$$= dV_{12}/dT,$$

(13.5-1)

where T_h and T_c represent, respectively, the hot and cold junction temperatures and ΔV_{12} is the voltage difference developed when metals 1 and 2 are connected in the manner shown in Fig. 13.5-1. Here ΔV_{12} and $\alpha_{S,12}$ are functions of T_h and T_c and depend on the properties of the connected metals 1 and 2.

B.   The Peltier Effect

When electrical current flows through a metal junction (see Fig. 13.5-2), heat is absorbed or liberated at the junction. The Peltier coefficient is defined as

$$\alpha_{P,12} = Q_{12}/i , \qquad\qquad (13.5-2)$$

where i represents the current density if Q_{12} is the heat absorbed or liberated per unit of cross-sectional area. Both Q_{12} and $\alpha_{P,12}$ depend on the junction temperature for given metals.

C.   The Thomson Effect

When current flow occurs through a wire in the presence of a temperature gradient (see Fig. 13.5-3), heat is absorbed or liberated. The Thomson coefficient is defined as

$$\alpha_{T,1} = \lim_{\Delta T \to 0} (\Delta Q_1/i)\Delta T , \qquad\qquad (13.5-3)$$

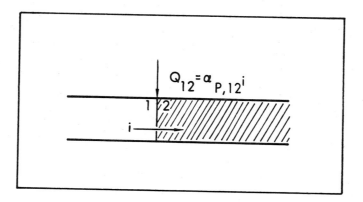

Fig. 13.5-2 Heat is absorbed or liberated at the junction between two dissimilar metals when current flow occurs through the junction. The ratio of the heat change to the current flow is defined as the Peltier coefficient.

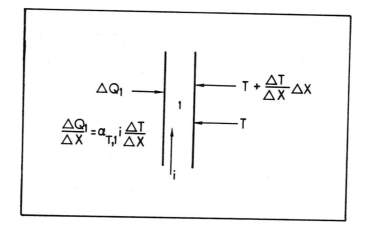

Fig. 13.5-3 Heat changes occur when current flows through a wire supporting a temperature gradient. The ratio of the heat change per unit current flow to the local temperature is defined to be the Thomson coefficient.

where ΔQ_1 is the heat change per unit area when the current density equals i.   Both ΔQ_1 and $\alpha_{T,1}$ are functions of the temperature for the given material 1.

The Seebeck, Peltier, and Thomson effects are reversible and interrelated. Their connection is best established by using the methodology of irreversible thermodynamics.

D.   Practical Applications

Exploration of practical applications of the thermoelectric effects has been carried out in connection with solar-energy utilization.[2] Fossil-fueled thermoelectric generators have been developed,[3] particularly for space[4] and oceanographic[5] applications. Isotope-and reactor-heated thermoelectric devices have been developed by the

[2]M. Telkes, "Solar Thermoelectric Generators," Journal of Applied Physics 25, 765-777 (1954).

[3]R. W. Fritts, "The Development of Thermoelectric Power Generators," Proceedings of the IEEE 51, 713-721 (1963).

[4]R. W. Fritts, "Design Parameters for Optimizing the Efficiency of Thermoelectric Generators Using p-Type and n-Type Lead Telluride," Transactions of the AIEE (Communications and Electronics) 78, 817-820 (1960).

[5]W. R. Corliss and D. L. Harvey, Radioisotope Power Generation, Prentice Hall, Inc., Englewood Cliffs, N. J., 1964.

AEC.[6, 7, 8] We refer to the literature for further elaboration of these topics.

Applications of thermoelectricity have been extensive for special devices, especially instruments. For example, the thermopile has been widely used for the quantitative determination of radiant-energy intensities. It is unlikely that the relatively high cost of these devices will allow an important early impact on central-station power generation.

13.6 Thermionic Power Conversion

Thermionic power conversion involves the liberation of electrons from an emitting surface under the influence of heat addition (see Fig. 13.6-1).[1, 2] The freed electrons migrate to a collector against retarding forces. At the col-

[6] R. T. Carpenter, "Space Isotopic Power Sources," Astronautics and Aerospace Engineering 1, 68-72, May 1963.

[7] G. M. Anderson, "Nuclear Reactor Systems," Astronautics and Aerospace Engineering 1, 27-36, May 1963.

[8] R. F. Wilson, J. E. Brunings, and G. S. Budney, "SNAP-10A-Prologue to Flight," Nucleonics 23, 44-47, June 1965.

[1] "Thermionic Energy Conversion," by E. Blue and J. H. Ingold, Chapter 5 in Direct Energy Conversion, edited by G. W. Sutton, McGraw-Hill Book Co., Inc., New York, New York, 1966.

[2] G. N. Hatsopoulos and E. P. Gyftopoulos, Thermionic Energy Conversion, The MIT Press, Cambridge, Mass., 1973.

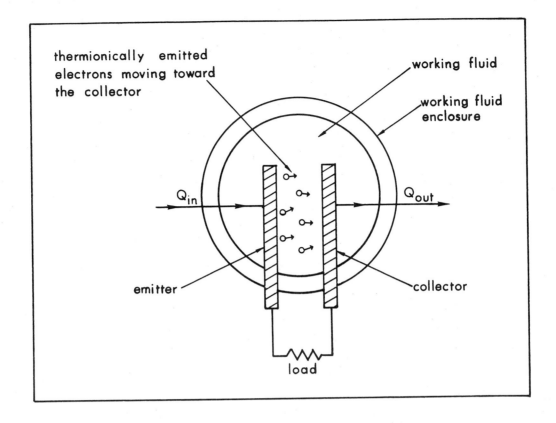

Fig. 13.6-1 Schematic diagram illustrating the principles
involved in thermionic power conversion.

lector, the electrons lose some of their energy by heating
and pass subsequently through an external load. Thermionic
devices have been widely used in laboratory studies. A
type of high-pressure converter has been developed to deliver about 40 watts$_e$/cm^2 for emitter temperatures of
2,200°K and electrode spacing of about 1×10^{-2} cm; the
overall efficiencies are near 20%.

Central-station power application of these costly de-

vices does not appear to have been considered.   However,
thermionic devices have been proposed as elements of a
power reactor for nuclear-energy sources. [3]

[3]D. T. Allen, H. C. Carney, C. R. Fisher, D. J. Heisser,
W. G. Homeyer, W. D. Leech, A. C. Marshall, M. H.
Merrill, and E. J. Steeger, "Undersea Thermionic Reac-
tors," Report Gulf-GA-A12419, Gulf General Atomic Co.,
P. O. Box 81608, San Diego, California 92138, February
1973.

CHAPTER 14

SOLAR-ENERGY UTILIZATION

14.1 Introduction

The solar-energy resource assessment presented in Section 2.17 has indicated the enormous magnitude of this renewable energy reservoir. Wide application is only limited by economic considerations.

A. Past Applications of Solar Energy

Solar heating has been utilized in various forms since ancient times, when the focusing effects of lens-like materials were first learned by man. Joseph Priestley used solar heating in 1774 to decompose HgO into Hg and oxygen. A solar distillation unit producing up to 6,000 gallons per day of fresh water was built in 1872 and was used in the North Chilean desert for 40 years to provide fresh water for min-

ers recovering nitrate deposits.[1] Solar-heated steam
boilers were demonstrated as early as the 1878 Paris exhi-
bition.[1] Daniels[1] has emphasized the importance of this
energy source in remote regions where other, more concentrated energy sources are not available but notes that serious
modern technological development on solar-energy utilization
was not initiated until the early nineteen fifties.

B. Solar-Energy Costs and Development Projections

A 1972 assessment[2] of various energy costs for
space heating is reproduced in Fig. 14.1-1 and shows that
solar heating was judged to be competitive with electrical
heating. This economic assessment has been made significantly more favorable by the escalation of gas and oil prices
which occurred during 1973 and 1974. Installation costs in
$/kw$_e$ for different types of electricity-generating plants are
compared in Chapter 4, Fig. 4.5-1.

Of course, all of the estimates for solar-energy costs
and for electricity-generation using solar energy are highly
tentative and will remain doubtful until large-scale installations are completed. Implicit in cost estimates are com-

---

[1]Farrington Daniels, Direct Use of the Sun's Energy, Yale
University Press, New Haven, Connecticut, 1964, Chapter 2.

[2]"An Assessment of Solar Energy as a National Energy Re-
source," prepared by the NSF/NASA Solar Energy Panel,
Department of Mechanical Engineering, University of
Maryland, College Park, Maryland, December 1972.

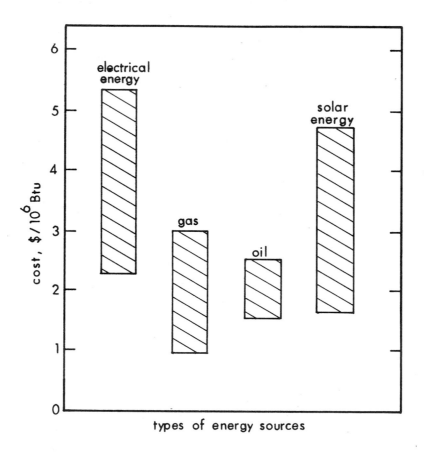

Fig. 14.1-1 A 1972 assessment of relative energy costs for
space heating using electrical energy, gas, oil,
or solar energy; reproduced from Ref. [2].

ponent-performance figures such as those shown for solar-collector costs per ft^2 in Table 14.1-1 for space heating of a residence with solar energy using thermal-energy transfer in various metropolitan areas: at \$4/ft^2 (corresponding to optimistic estimated minimal costs for 1973), solar energy was not competitive with gas or oil; at \$2/ft^2 for a solar col-

Table 14.1-1 A 1970 estimate of space-heating costs, in $/10^6$ Btu delivered to the consumer; reproduced from Ref. [2].

Location	Optimized solar-heating cost in $/10^6$ Btu in a 25,000 Btu/degree-day house, with capital charges at 6% for 20 years		Electric heating costs in $/10^6$ Btu when using 30,000 kwh$_e$/y	Fuel cost for fuel heating, $/10^6$ Btu	
	collector at $2/ft^2	collector at $4/ft^2		gas	oil
Santa Maria, CA	1.10	1.59	4.28[1]	1.52	1.91
Albuquerque, NM	1.60	2.32	4.63	0.95	2.44
Phoenix, AZ	2.05	3.09	5.07	0.85	1.89
Omaha, NB	2.45	2.98	3.25[3]	1.12	1.56
Boston, MA	2.50	3.02	5.25	1.85	2.08
Charleston, SC	2.55	3.56	4.22	1.03	1.83
Seattle-Tacoma, WA	2.60	3.82	2.29[2,3]	1.96	2.36
Miami, FL	4.05	4.64	4.87	3.01	2.04

Notes: 1. Electric-power costs refer to Santa Barbara; electric-power data for Santa Maria were not available.

2. Electric-power costs are those for Seattle.

3. These costs refer to a publicly-owned utility.

Footnotes to Table 14.1-1 are continued on page 323.

Additional footnotes to Table 14.1-1:

Solar-heat costs refer to optimally-designed systems yielding lowest cost for heat.   Electric-energy costs were obtained from the U.S. Federal Power Commission, All
Electric Homes, Table 2 (1970).   Conventional fuel costs
are derived from prices per million Btu reported in P.
Batestra, The Demand for Natural Gas in the Unites States,
Tables 1.2 and 1.3 (North Holland Publishing Co., 1967).
The 1962 costs were updated to 1970 by use of national price
indices on gas (121.1 in 1970, 112.8 in 1962) and on fuel oil
(119.22 in 1970, 101.2 in 1962) as adjustment factors on
each fuel price in each state.   Bureau of Labor Statistics
fuel-price indices were obtained from Gas Facts, American
Gas Association, Arlington, Virginia.   Fuel prices were
converted to fuel costs by dividing by the following national
average heat (combustion) efficiencies: gas, 75%; oil, 75%.
Heat efficiencies were obtained from the American Society
of Heating, Refrigerating and Air Conditioning Engineers,
Guide and Data Book, pp. 692-694, 1963 edition.   All solar-
heat costs are based on amortizing the solar-system capital
costs in 20 years at 6% interest.   The capital charges have
been computed for a 1970 price of solar water heaters at
$4/ft^2 plus applicable costs of other components, and for an
anticipated lower solar-collector price of $2/ft^2.

---

lector (which may become applicable during the mid-eighties),
solar energy will probably be competitive with oil but not with
gas if this commodity is still sold at controlled low prices.
Near-term energy contributions[3] for solar-energy utilization are indicated in Fig. 14.1-2, together with a summary

---

[3] W. E. Morrow, Jr., "Solar Energy Utilization," a report
    prepared for the Federal Power Commission National Pow-
    er Survey, Lincoln Laboratory, Massachusetts Institute of
    Technology, Lexington, Massachusetts, June 1973.

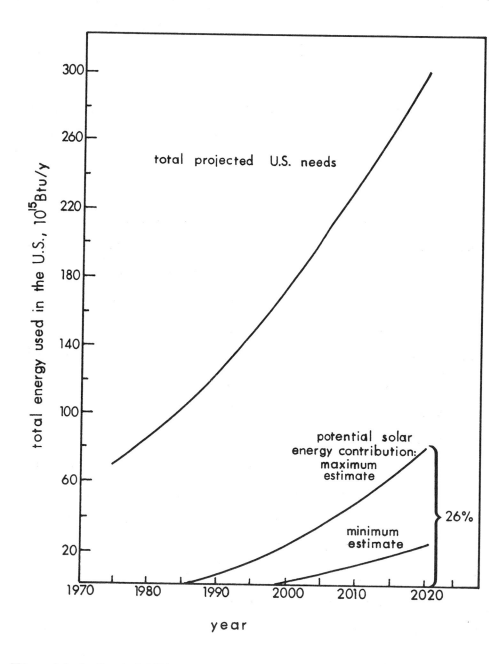

Fig. 14.1-2 A 1973 estimate of the developing contribution
that may be made by solar-energy utilization
to the total U.S. energy needs; reproduced from
Ref. [3].

curve showing total projected U.S. energy needs.   According
to this assessment, solar energy was expected to provide between 8 and 26% of the total required energy by the year 2020,
with contributions over the 1% of total use level phased in between 1985 and 1998.   As the result of fossil-fuel price escalation and increasing research support during the early
seventies, the same schedule for introduction of solar-energy
applications may well be reduced by 5 to 10 years.

According to a late-1976 study prepared for ERDA[4]
by researchers at the MITRE Corporation, solar water and
space heating systems in 1976 are economically competitive
with electric space (baseboard) and water heating for well-
insulated new homes in major population centers throughout
most of the United States.   Solar-energy use was evaluated
for new homes (but not for old homes which require retro-
fitting) that are constructed with brick veneer, an asphalt
roof, storm windows, and 12 inches of attic insulation.   Conventional heating systems were assumed to provide backup
capability for the primary solar space and water heating
systems.   The analysis refers specifically to a 1,500 ft^2,
four-person residence, with brick veneer, asphalt roof, 12-
inches of attic insulation, a 15-mph wind factor, a 30-year
mortgage at 8.5% interest, homeowners in the 30%
incremental tax bracket, zero additional property tax for

---

[4]"An Economic Analysis of Solar Water and Space Heating,"
     ERDA Division of Solar Energy, Report DSE-2322-1,
     U.S. Government Printing Office, Washington, D.C.,
     November 1976.

the solar unit, an annual inflation rate of 6%, fuel-price escalation of 10% per year, and operating and maintenance costs of 2% of the solar system capital costs for the first year with an escalation rate of 6%/y thereafter.

Solar systems were defined to be economically competitive if annual fuel savings exceed annual expenditures for principal and interest on the solar system within five years or if the solar installation pays for itself as the result of reduced fuel costs within 15 years. According to these criteria, solar space and water heating systems which cost $20/ft^2 of collector area were judged to be economically attractive as a principal replacement for electric space (baseboard) and water heating in each of the 13 cities studied, except in Seattle where electricity prices are among the lowest in the U.S. because of the availability of inexpensive hydroelectric power (see Table 14.1-2). Depending on local conditions, desirable collector areas range from 10 to 40% of the house floor area, which leads to a $3,000 to $12,000 additional solar water and space heating system investment for a well-insulated 1,500-ft^2 residence. *

---

*For the case of solar systems at $20/ft^2 compared to electric space (baseboard) and water heating, the economically-optimal collector areas are: Atlanta, 195 ft^2; Bismarck, 488 ft^2; Boston, 493 ft^2; Charleston, 211 ft^2; Columbia, 354 ft^2; Dallas/Fort Worth, 150 ft^2; Grand Junction, 414 ft^2; Los Angeles, 235 ft^2; Madison, 540 ft^2; Miami, 123 ft^2; New York, 605 ft^2; Washington, D.C., 291 ft^2. An economically-optimal collector area was not obtained for Seattle because an arbitrary minimum solar load of 40% was not achieved.

Table 14. 1-2 Time required for fuel savings to exceed annual
payments of principal and interest on solar
systems (t_s) and for the net cumulative savings
to equal the balance due for the solar system
(t_p). Solar loads insufficient for accurate economic estimates (i.e., less than 40%) are indicated by the absence of an entry in the table.
Based on the data of Ref. [4].

	Solar systems at $20/ft^2 compared to electric space (baseboard) and water heating		Solar systems at $10/ft^2 compared to natural gas space and water heating	
	t_s, years	t_p, years	t_s, years	t_p, years
Atlanta, Georgia	3	14	5	16
Bismarck, North Dakota	4	14	-	-
Boston, Massachusetts	3	14	4	14
Charleston, South Carolina	1	11	-	-
Columbia, Missouri	3	14	-	-
Dallas/Fort Worth Texas	3	13	3	13
Grand Junction, Colorado	1	12	5	16
Los Angeles, California	1	10	4	15
Madison, Wisconsin	3	14	-	-
Miami, Florida	1	9	4	15
New York City, New York	1	12	2	13
Seattle, Washington	-	-	-	-
Washington, D.C.	4	14	5	15

Solar systems at $15/ft^2$ are economically competitive with electric heat pumps in Bismarck, Grand Junction, Los Angeles, Madison, and New York City; they are competitive with oil in Atlanta, Bismarck, Charleston, Grand Junction, Los Angeles, and Miami. Solar-system prices of $\$10/ft^2$ would make solar energy competitive with oil heating in all cities studied and with natural-gas furnaces in all cities except Bismarck, Charleston, Columbia, Madison, and Seattle (see Table 14.1-2). The definitions used for economic acceptability (see Table 14.1-2) are optimistic.

C.   Impact of Solar-Energy Utilization

A 1972 estimate of the impact on other resources of possible[2] staged introduction of solar energy for water heating, space heating, cooling, and combined thermal systems is shown in Table 14.1-3. We note (see Table 14.1-3) that this 1972 estimate[2] involves about a 50% increase in energy costs for water and space heating over actual costs associated with the use of conventional methods, while the required initial capital investments are two to four times larger for home-heating units and perhaps 10 times larger for home-cooling units than the corresponding costs for conventional systems; also, the combined thermal-system costs are larger by a factor of about four. As has already been stated, these cost estimates will remain highly doubtful until large-scale field implementation has been accomplished.

Table 14.1-3   An impact assessment of solar-energy utilization at the 1% and 10% levels for water heating, space heating, cooling, and in combined thermal systems; reproduced from Ref. [2].

	Water heating	Space heating	Cooling	Combined thermal systems
introduction of solar units				
in new buildings	1975: 1% 1980: 10%	1980: 1% 1985: 10%	1980: 1% 1985: 10%	1980: 1% 1985: 10%
in total buildings	1980: 1% 1985: 10%	1985: 1% 1990: 10%	1990: 1% 2000: 10%	1990: 1% 2000: 10%
resource effects				
on fuels	1 to 2% will supply the total U.S. energy budget with 100% installation	Ultimately,(a) 30 to 80% of the fuels and electricity normally used for space heating and cooling can be saved.		
on materials	10%/house increase in glazing	Use of an average additional 1,000 ft^2 of glass/house plus other materials. No shortage of materials.		
environmental impact				
on land use	3D zoning; sun rights	3D zoning	3D zoning	3D zoning
on noise	none	No increase over present systems.		
on visual aspects	minimal	Significant element in total design.		
economic impact				
on capital requirements	$200-$400(b) for the unit cost	$1,500-$2,500(c)	$3,000-$4,000(c)	$3,000-$4,000(d)
$/10^6 Btu for solar energy	$3-$6(e)	$2-$3		$1.50-$2.50(d)
$/10^6 Btu for conventional energy	$2-$4, present $3-$5, estimated for 1990	$1.50-$2.50, present $2.50-$4.50, estimated for 1990		$1.50-$2.50(f), present $2.50-$4.50, estimated for 1990
$/ton-hour(g) of solar cooling			$0.08-$0.20	
$/ton-hour of conventional cooling			$0.05-$0.15(h)	

NOTES: (a)

Year	Percent of energy use replaced by solar energy for space heating and cooling	Percent of total U.S. energy
1990	7	1
2000	30-80	10

(b) 50-ft^2 collector; 100-200 gallon hot-water tank; thermal transfer, controls.
(c) 500-ft^2 collector, $2-$4/ft^2, plus controls and storage cost.
(d) Including a $1,500 cost for the cooling unit.
(e) $200-$400 unit cost; 15%/year discount, corresponding to a charge of $30-$60/year; 1,200 Btu/ft^2 day insolation level; utilization efficiency = 50%; 3,000 kwh$_t$ delivered/year.
(f) Including cost of heat supply to cooling unit.
(g) One ton-hour is a unit of energy absorbed by a refrigerant which equals 12,000 Btu.
(h) Electrically-operated compression systems and heat-operated systems using natural gas.

D.   Summary Remarks on Solar-Energy Economics

The present cost for photovoltaic converters is more than a few hundred dollars per watt$_e$, which is too high by at least two orders of magnitude for competitive solar-power utilization in central power stations. [5]

The direct use of solar energy for heating has been judged to be most attractive for development at the present time.   Thermal-energy conversion in steam engines is limited by the Carnot efficiency, which equals a fraction of a percent for temperature differences up to about 10 degrees. Hence, thermal-energy conversion should preferably be accomplished at elevated operating temperatures ($\sim$500°C), as is further discussed in Sections 14.4B and 14.5B.

The dry weight of crops (including algae) has a heating value of about 16×10^6 Btu/t = 8×10^3 Btu/lb; at an energy cost of $\$1/10^6$ Btu, the allowable dry crop cost is seen to be about 0.8 cent/lb.   The use of crops with high carbon content for NG-production by bacterial digestion has been pro-

---

[5]In a recently-published article, K. W. Boer ["Direct Solar Energy Conversion for Terrestrial Use," The Journal of Environmental Sciences 17, 8-14, January/February 1974] has proposed the residential use of low-priced CdS/ Cu$_2$S solar cells, in conjunction with power-processing units.   Solar harvesting is treated as a peak-shaving power source interconnected with the available utility grid. Boer's final cost estimate for the supplementary solar array corresponds to $\$0.74/10^6$ Btu at a solar-panel cost of $\$1.86/\text{ft}^2$.

posed recently by D. L. Klass[6] of the Institute of Gas
Technology. Although the "energy plantation" is not favored
for current development by most planners, this technology
does have its enthusiastic supporters.[7] According to Szego
and Kemp,[7] at an easily-achievable solar-energy conversion efficiency to fuel of 0.4%, fuel costs are of the order of
$1.00 to $2.00/$10^6$ Btu. S. Katell in a comment to Ref. [7]
states that, for plant yields of about 5 tons per acre-year,
land-purchase costs of $50/acre, harvesting costs of $9/ton,
and charges for interest and taxes equal to 8.6% of the land
costs, the fuel cost is about $1.00/$10^6$ Btu. In these analy-
ses, the power transmission costs have not been adequately
included. We note that a 1,000-Mw$_e$ steam-electric plant
operating at 35% efficiency with a 75% load factor requires
about 1,000 square miles of land area at 0.4% solar-to-fuel-
energy conversion efficiency for a mean insolation level of
1,600 Btu/ft^2-day.[7] This land area is comparable to that
required in the management of a large pulp mill. Actually
achieved solar-energy conversion efficiencies in plants range
from 0.29% for alfalfa (with three cuttings per season), to
0.41 to 0.69% for corn, to 1.2% for mature sugar cane.[7]
The corresponding oven-dried yields for these crops are 4.6,
7 to 11, and 20 tons per acre-year.[7] The fuel value of all

---

[6]D. L. Klass, "A Perpetual Methane Economy - Is It Pos-
    sible?," Chemtech, 161-168, March 1974.

[7]G. C. Szego and C. C. Kemp, "Energy Forests and Fuel
    Plantations," Chemtech, 275-284, May 1973.

three dried crops is 6.5×10^3 Btu/lb. Fuel derived from pulpwood and chips had a value of \$1.16 to \$1.36/10^6 Btu at 1971 prices.[7] Thus the energy plantation designed for production of the nearly sulfur-free (less than 0.1% of sulfur) "Btu-bush" (or of "erg-growth") must be considered to be a serious contender for solar-energy application. Its overall environmental impact may be beneficial. This approach for growing our energy supplies is further examined in Section 14.5A by using more optimistic production estimates than have been specified in the preceding discussion.

E.   Environmental-Impact Assessment of Solar-
     Energy Utilization

At first thought, one might be tempted to concur with Landsberg[8] that solar-energy utilization would eliminate the environmental thermal load associated with the use of fossil-fuel and nuclear energy sources and would thus remove energy use as an essential restriction on attainable growth limits for a long time to come (namely, until all available solar energy is put to some "desirable" use). However, as has been noted by Damon,[9] this view cannot be valid for an economically-competitive solar-power system because of necessary redistribution of energy inputs and thermal-energy

---

[8]H. H. Landsberg, "Low-Cost, Abundant Energy: Paradise Lost?," Science 185, 247 (1974).

[9]P. E. Damon, "Solar Power," Science 185, 478-480 (1974).

outputs that must be associated with solar-energy utilization.
An adequate assessment is very difficult to make. Consider,
for example, a photovoltaic power-conversion system of high
efficiency built in the Arizona or California deserts. The
presence of this system must change the desert-surface albedo. In the desert, about 35% of the incident solar energy
is normally reflected. This reflected energy is partially
absorbed in the atmosphere above the desert surface and
partially transmitted and ultimately lost from the earth.
With an efficient photovoltaic-conversion device, the desert-
surface reflectivity will be reduced. For useful application,
the electrical energy generated in the desert will be transmitted (with some thermal losses and a corresponding added
environmental heat load) to metropolitan areas where additional energy (in the form of "useful" electrical energy and
as thermal losses) appears. The net effects are (a) redistribution of thermal loads between the desert and metropolitan locations and (b) a net reduction of reflected solar energy
from the desert location, which generally will not be totally
compensated by additional emitted radiant energy in metropolitan locations. Thus, somewhere, additional thermal
energy will appear as a heat load on the earth when solar
energy is utilized efficiently. The complex effects of this
application scheme on climate remain to be calculated.

A very important aspect of biomass production for
energy utilization relates to the fact that biomass is not a
producer of CO_2 to the atmosphere. The buildup of CO_2
associated with fossil-fuel combustion is such that doubling

of atmospheric CO_2 concentrations from a current level of about 330 ppm (parts per million) to 660 ppm may be anticipated within a period of about 50 years. About 40% of the CO_2 produced by fossil-fuel burning remains in the atmosphere, while the remaining 60% are removed especially to the oceans. Uptake by the top 70 m to 100 m of ocean waters occurs fairly quickly. A major mechanism for CO_2 uptake in the ocean involves the reaction

$$CaCO_3(s) + CO_2(g) + H_2O \rightarrow Ca^{++} + 2HCO_3^{=};$$

removal of $CaCO_3$ from the continents is often referred to as weathering. As fossil-fuel utilization proceeds, very much larger atmospheric concentrations of CO_2 (up to $\sim 1,500$ ppm) are likely to be produced unless remedial measures (e.g., major expansion of permanent plant reservoirs) are taken on an unprecedented scale. The climatic impacts that are anticipated as the result of CO_2 buildup may be assessed on the basis of existing climate models. Unprecedented and possibly irreversible changes cannot be ruled out. Mean surface-temperature rises of 2 to $3°C$ have been calculated for doubling of the atmospheric CO_2 concentration, but these estimates may be too large or too small in view of uncertainties in the existing climate models. Furthermore, atmospheric circulation patterns, evaporation and rain distribution, and crop growths are likely to be profoundly influenced, with wide variations in different regions of the world. In the past, mean temperature rises of 2 to $3°C$

have been associated with appreciable rises in sea level
($\sim$ 5 meters).   Although our present assessment of climate
changes that are likely to be produced as the result of CO_2
buildup cannot be considered to be definitive, it is clearly
important to develop (a) a variety of energy-supply options
other than fossil fuels and (b) remedial measures among
which a very large temporary expansion of plant growth
(with or without biomass production for energy use) appears
to be of unique importance.

F.   "Novel" Ideas for Solar-Energy Applications

Among the more obvious and only recently advocated
applications of solar energy is its use for auxiliary <u>interior</u>
lighting during the day.[10]   This may be accomplished by
using a sun-tracking mirror on the roof of a building and an
appropriate mirror system to "pipe" the light to rooms with
insufficient windows.   Since the net overall conversion efficiency of sunlight to electricity is unlikely to exceed 10% in
the foreseeable future, while the electricity-to-light conversion efficiency is also only 10% (for incandescent bulbs) to
20% (for fluorescent bulbs), this application of sunlight has
a ten- to five-fold economic advantage over conversion to
electricity prior to interior electric lighting.   Infrared
filters may be used to reduce room heating.

---

[10]The idea was proposed and tested by M. Duguay and
    R. Edgar of Sandia Laboratories in Albuquerque, New
    Mexico; see Science 194, 1404 (1976).

14.2 Availability of Solar Energy in the U.S. and Land-Use Requirements

We have seen in Section 6.3 that the solar-power input per unit area on the earth varies from less than 20 to over 100 w/m^2 in representative cities of the Northern hemisphere.* It is a simple matter to consider in greater detail the solar flux at various locations, with proper allowance for the angle of latitude, attenuation by cloud cover, etc. The results[1] of calculations of this type are summarized in Figs. 14.2-1 and 14.2-2, respectively, for yearly averages in the U.S. and for December averages in the U.S. We note that the yearly averages increase from about 150 w/m^2 in Northern New England to about 245 w/m^2 in the Southwestern States, while the corresponding December means lie between 50 and 150 w/m^2.

For a mean U.S. insolation level of 1,500 Btu/ft^2-d (corresponding to about 200 w/m^2), we may easily calculate the required land area, and hence the percentage of the land

---

*A frequently used measure for the energy of radiation per unit area is the langley (Ly) corresponding to 1 cal/cm^2. The number of langleys of solar radiation received in a specified time interval is easily converted into an equivalent average radiant-flux density over the specified time interval.

[1]F. Bennett, "Monthly Mass of Mean Daily Insolation for the United States," Solar Energy 9, 145-158 (1969); see, also, Ref. [3] in Section 14.1.

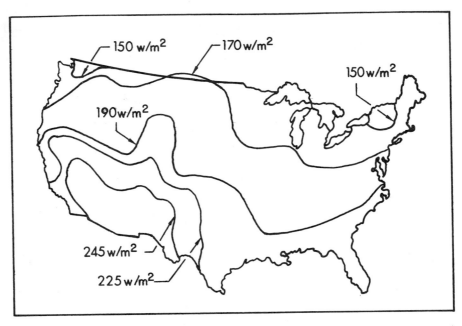

Fig. 14.2-1　Yearly average of solar flux densities in w/m². The numbers represent applicable 24-hour average values reaching the surface of the earth. Reproduced from Ref. [1].

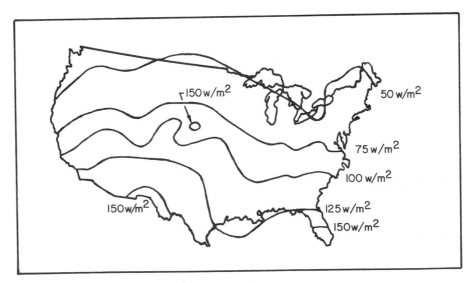

Fig. 14.2-2　December average of solar flux densities in w/m². The numbers represent applicable 24-hour average values reaching the surface of the earth. Reproduced from Ref. [1].

area in the 48 contiguous states, which must be employed
in the collection of solar energy at various levels of conversion efficiency in order to supply the estimated U.S. electrical and total energy needs during the period 1970 to 2020.
The results obtained in these calculations are shown in Fig.
14.2-3. We note, for example, that at a conversion efficiency of 10%, about 1.1% of the U.S. land area was sufficient
for collection of all of the energy used during 1970, whereas
about 4.5% of the land area will be required by the year 2020.
As we shall see, practically-achievable conversion efficiencies for solar-energy utilization are currently far lower than
10%. The portion of the total energy budget corresponding
to electrical-power generation can be supplied by a smaller
area, which equals about 2.3% of the U.S. land area by the
year 2020 for 10% conversion efficiency (see Fig. 14.2-3).

It is of interest to note the data listed in Table 14.2-1
on the distribution of world land use during 1966. We note
that a little more than 10% of the world land area was tilled,
more than 20% was used for pasture, and nearly 30% remained as forests. These data suggest that considerable
room remains for growing energy-producing farms. For a
good discussion of the environmental effects of expanded land
use and related topics, reference should be made to a recent
paper by Holdren and Ehrlich.[2]

---

[2] John P. Holdren and Paul R. Ehrlich, "Human Population
and the Global Environment," American Scientist 62,
282-292 (1974).

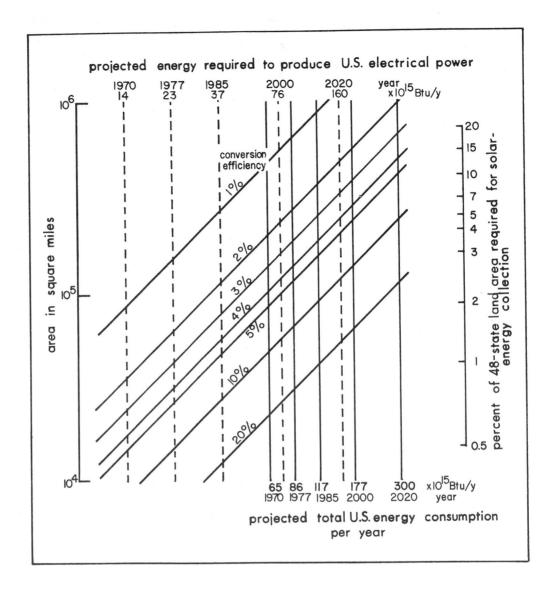

Fig. 14.2-3 Land-area requirements as a function of solar-
             energy conversion efficiency to supply U.S.
             electrical and total energy needs by solar-ener-
             gy utilization for the period 1970 to 2020. The
             plotted data refer to an average insolation of
             1,500 Btu/ft^2-d ($\simeq$200 w/m^2). The land area of
             the 48 contiguous states is 2.97 $\times$ 10^6 mi^2. Re-
             produced from Ref. [2] in Section 14.1.

Table 14.2-1 World land areas by use category during 1966, in 10^6 km^2; reproduced from G. Borgstrom, Too Many, MacMillan and Co., New York 1969.

Region	Total area	Tilled	Pasture	Forest	Other*
Europe	4.9	1.5	0.9	1.4	1.1
U.S.S.R.	22.4	2.3	3.7	9.1	7.3
Asia (exclusive of the U.S.S.R.)	27.9	4.5	4.5	5.2	13.7
Africa	30.3	2.3	7.0	6.0	15.0
North America	22.4	2.6	3.7	8.2	7.9
South America	17.8	0.8	4.1	9.4	3.5
Oceania	8.5	0.4	4.6	0.8	2.7
total**	134.2	14.4	28.5	40.1	51.2
percentage	100%	10.7%	21.2%	29.9%	38.2%

*Deserts, wasteland, built-up area, glaciers, wetlands.
**Exclusive of Antarctica.

A. Solar Radiation Incident on the Earth for a Completely Transparent Atmosphere

The solar constant, S_o, is defined as the flux of solar energy incident on unit area perpendicular to the rays of the sun and located at a mean distance R_m between the earth and the sun. The earth-sun distance lies between the early January minimum of 1.47×10^8 km and the early July maximum of 1.52×10^8 km. Since the solar-energy density varies inversely with the square of the distance, the solar energy received by unit area of the earth perpendicular to the rays of the sun at the mean distance R is $S_0(R_m/R)^2 = S_0/f^2$ where $f = R/R_m$. If we consider the sun to move on the surface of a unit sphere with the earth located at the center, unit area of the horizontal plane has the fraction $\cos z_\odot$ perpendicular to the rays of the sun (see Fig. 14.2-4), where $z_\odot$ is the zenith angle. Hence, the radiant power received by unit area on the surface of the earth located in the horizontal plane is equal to

$$Q_s = (S_0/f^2) \cos z_\odot. \qquad\qquad (14.2-1)$$

The value of the zenith angle $z_\odot$ depends on latitude, time of the year, and time of the day. On a celestial sphere (see Fig. 14.2-5), the latitude is measured by the latitudinal angle φ while $\delta_\odot$ defines the angle of declination of the sun (see Fig. 14.2-5). The relative inclination between the planes HH′ and AA′ is determined by the time of year (season).

The following relation holds for the spherical triangle NZS:

$$\cos z_\odot = (\cos NZ)(\cos NS)$$

$$= (\sin NZ)(\sin NS)(\cos \omega),$$

from which it follows (see Fig. 14.2-5) that

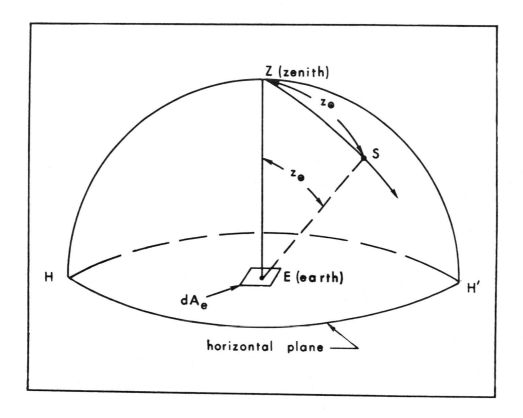

Fig. 14.2-4 As the sun moves on the surface of a unit sphere from the location of the zenith (which is perpendicular to the horizon) in the direction of the arrow, the zenith angle $z_\odot$ increases from 0 to $\pi/2$ while the projection of the area dA_e on the surface of the earth, which is perpendicular to the rays of the sun, decreases according to the relation $dA_e \cos z_\odot$. On the unit sphere, the length of the arc ZS is numerically equal to $z_\odot$ measured in radian.

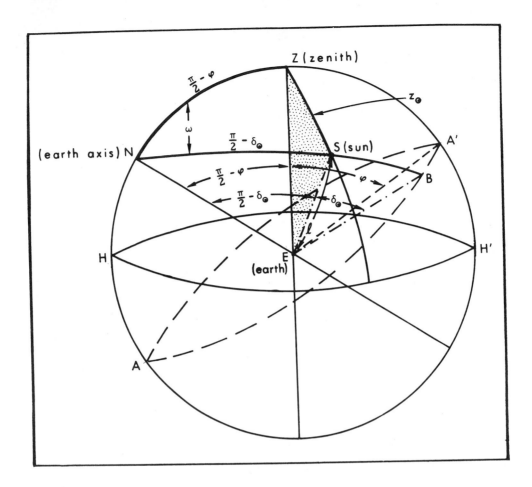

Fig. 14.2-5   A unit sphere showing the horizontal plane
              HH' (with the center coinciding with the earth
              E), the celestial equator AA', the zenith angle
              $z_\odot$, the latitudinal angle φ of the plane con-
              taining the sun with respect to the celestial
              equator, and the angle of declination $\delta_\odot$ mea-
              sured between vector radii from E to S and E
              to B, where B is located at the intersection of
              the great circle NS with the celestial equator
              AA'.   The angle ω is the hour angle of the sun,
              which passes through a complete period every
              24 hours and is therefore conveniently repre-
              sented by $\omega = (2\pi/\tau)t$ with $\tau = 24$ h.   The angle
              between the planes AA' and HH' changes with
              the time of year (season).

$$\cos z_\odot = (\sin \varphi)(\sin \delta_\odot)$$

$$+ (\cos \varphi)(\cos \delta_\odot)(\cos \omega). \qquad (14.2-2)$$

Combination of Eqs. (14.2-1) and (14.2-2) leads to the result

$$Q_s = (S_o/f^2)[(\sin \varphi)(\sin \delta_\odot)$$

$$+ (\cos \varphi)(\cos \delta_\odot)(\cos \omega)]. \qquad (14.2-3)$$

The hour angle ω_o for which sunlight disappears in the interval $-\omega_o \leq \omega \leq \omega_o$ is thus given by

$$\cos \omega_o = - (\tan \varphi)(\tan \delta_\odot). \qquad (14.2-4)$$

The incident radiant power on the entire surface of the earth is readily evaluated for $z_\odot = 0$ and found to be $(S_o/f^2)\pi r_e^2$ where r_e is the radius of the earth. The corresponding mean flux for the entire surface area of the earth is $(S_o/f^2)\pi r_e^2/4\pi r_e^2 = S_o/4f^2$.

It is convenient to calculate the incoming solar energy for different latitudinal zones in terms of the hours of daylight with $-\omega_o \leq \omega \leq \omega_o$. This objective may be accomplished by writing Eq. (14.2-3) for the incident solar power in differential form as

$$d\mathcal{E}_s \equiv Q_s\,dt = (S_o/f^2)[(\sin \varphi)(\sin \delta_{\odot})$$

$$+ (\cos \varphi)(\cos \delta_{\odot})(\cos \omega)]dt$$

and then setting

$$\omega = (2\pi/\tau)t \text{ or } dt = (\tau/2\pi)d\omega \text{ (with } \tau = 24 \text{ h)}$$

so that

$$d\mathcal{E}_s = (S_o/f^2)[(\sin \varphi)(\sin \delta_{\odot}) + (\cos \varphi)(\cos \delta_{\odot})(\cos \omega)]$$

$$\times (\tau/2\pi)d\omega. \qquad\qquad (14.2\text{-}5)$$

The diurnal input or radiant energy for a transparent atmosphere then becomes

$$\mathcal{E}_s = \frac{\tau S_o}{2\pi f^2} \int_{-\omega_o}^{+\omega_o} [(\sin \varphi)(\sin \delta_{\odot})$$

$$+ (\cos \varphi)(\cos \delta_{\odot})(\cos \omega)]d\omega$$

or

$$\mathcal{E}_s = \frac{\tau S_o}{\pi f^2} [\omega_o (\sin \varphi)(\sin \delta_\odot)$$

$$+ (\sin \omega_o)(\cos \varphi)(\cos \delta_\odot)], \qquad (14.2-6)$$

where ω_o is given by Eq. (14.2-4). A special case of Eq. (14.2-6) holds near $\varphi = 90°$ and $\omega_o = \pi$. The result is

$$\mathcal{E}_s = \frac{\tau S_o}{f^2} (\sin \varphi) (\sin \delta_\odot). \qquad (14.2-7)$$

Long-term averages of Eqs. (14.2-6) and (14.2-7) may be found by summing over the desired number of days.

Results calculated from Eqs. (14.2-6) and (14.2-4) are summarized in Tables 14.2-2 and 14.2-3 for $S_o = 2$ cal/cm^2-min.

B. Solar Radiation Incident on the Surface of the
     Earth for the Real Atmosphere

The evaluation of solar radiation incident on the surface of the earth for the real atmosphere is considered in specialty treatises and falls beyond the scope of this discussion.[3, 4]

[3]K. Ya. Kondratyev, Radiation in the Atmosphere, Academic Press, New York, 1969.
[4]K. L. Coulson, Solar and Terrestrial Radiation: Methods and Measurements, Academic Press, New York, 1975.

Table 14.2-2 Diurnal totals of solar radiation incident upon the surface of the earth under a completely transparent atmosphere in kcal/cm^2.

Latitude	Mar. 21	June 22	Sept. 23	Dec. 22
90°N	--	1.11	--	--
80°	0.16	1.09	0.16	--
70°	0.32	1.04	0.31	--
60°	0.49	1.01	0.46	0.05
50°	0.59	1.02	0.59	0.18
40°	0.71	1.02	0.70	0.33
30°	0.80	1.00	0.79	0.48
20°	0.87	0.96	0.86	0.62
10°	0.91	0.90	0.90	0.76
0°	0.92	0.81	0.91	0.87
10°	0.91	0.71	0.90	0.96
20°	0.87	0.58	0.86	1.03
30°	0.80	0.45	0.79	1.07
40°	0.71	0.31	0.70	1.09
50°	0.59	0.17	0.59	1.09
60°	0.46	0.05	0.46	1.08
70°	0.32	--	0.31	1.11
80°	0.16	--	0.16	1.17
90°S	--	--	--	1.18

Table 14.2-3 Sums of solar radiation incident upon the surface of the earth under a completly transparent atmosphere in kcal/cm^2.

Latitude	Summer half-year	Winter half-year	Full year
0°	160.5	160.5	321
10°	170	147	317
20°	175	129	304
30°	174	108	282
40°	170	84	254
50°	161	59	220
60°	149	34	183
70°	139	13	152
80°	135	3	138
90°	133	0	133

14.3 Qualitative Description of Proposed Systems for Solar-Energy Utilization Involving Radiant Heating[*]

In this Section 14.3, we present qualitative descriptions of systems that have been proposed for solar-energy

[*] The late Th. von Kármán labeled discussions of the type presented in this Section as examples of "picture-book engineering". The designs bear no significant relation to real engineering constructions but the pictures are informative since they portray concepts thay may form the basis for hard engineering designs.

utilization, including water- and space-heating units, integrated heating and cooling systems, electricity-generating stations, complete solar systems for all types of home-energy use, fuel production using solar energy, and anaerobic fermentation for the conversion of organic material (especially algae) to methane. The critically-important design of solar collectors will be discussed in Section 14.5.

A.   A Solar Space- and Water-Heating System for a House

A schematic diagram of a solar space- and water-heating system for a house is shown in Fig. 14.3-1. A solar collector (see Fig. 14.4-3 in Section 14.4 for a schematic diagram of a solar collector) of appropriate size faces in the southward direction and heats an entering cold-water flow from about 25°C to about 65°C in a suitably-designed heat exchanger. The hot water is stored in a 5,000-gallon tank, which serves as a heat-storage system for the hot-water home-heating unit and hot-water supply. The water supply is introduced from the water main and is heated on passage through the storage tank before use. Water is pumped through the heat-exchanger-solar-collector only when the sun shines. The primary water-heating, storage, and solar-energy collection unit is seen to be completely enclosed. Space heating is accomplished by means of hot-water coils embedded in the building structure.

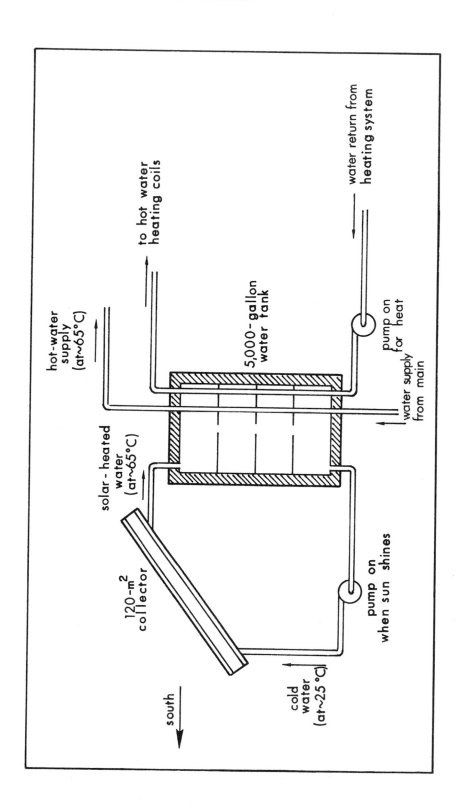

Fig. 14.3-1 Solar space- and water-heating system for a typical house; reproduced from Ref. [3] of Section 14.1.

B. Solar Heating and Cooling of Homes and Commercial Buildings

Two concepts for residential or commercial heating and cooling systems are shown in Figs. 14.3-2 and 14.3-3.

The system described in Fig. 14.3-2 employs an auxiliary air-heating unit and conventional warm-air circulation for space heating during the cold months (winter operation). During the summer months, the auxiliary heater is turned off and the air is cooled by exposure to an absorption air or a humidifier cooling unit. The auxiliary heating unit is available for supplementary heating as needed.

The commercial system of Fig. 14.3-3 is provided with an auxiliary loop carrying a steam-turbine generator for the production of electricity. Both hot-water and high-temperature (at $\sim 750^{\circ}$ C) heat-storage units are required.

A detailed schematic diagram of a solar-powered total-energy system for residential use is shown in Fig. 14.3-4. The principal added components are seen to be supplementary electricity-producing units connected to the utility line. A fuel cell for peak shaving or supplementary energy storage has also been introduced into the loop.

C. Central Station for Electricity Generation

A two-axis steerable array for a central solar-power electricity-generating and water-electrolysis system is shown in Fig. 14.3-5. The complementary design, consisting of stationary light collectors and a movable light-collection

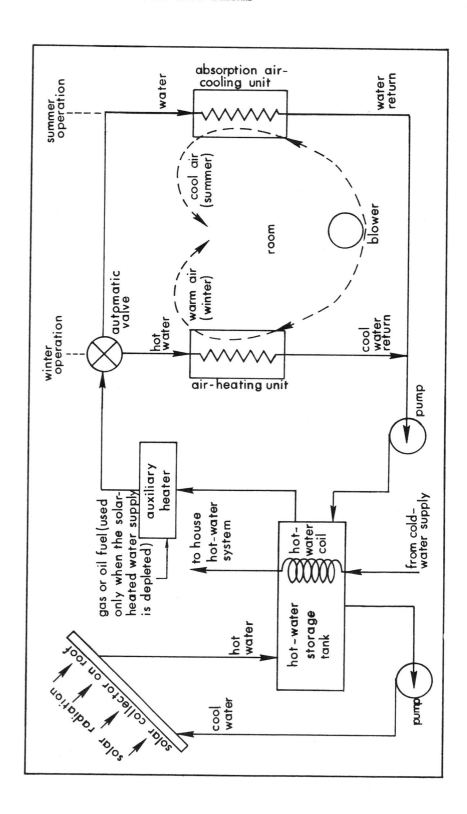

Fig. 14.3-2 Schematic diagram of a residential-heating and cooling system; reproduced from Ref. [2] of Section 14.1. The cold water inlet and exit at the absorption air-cooling unit are not shown.

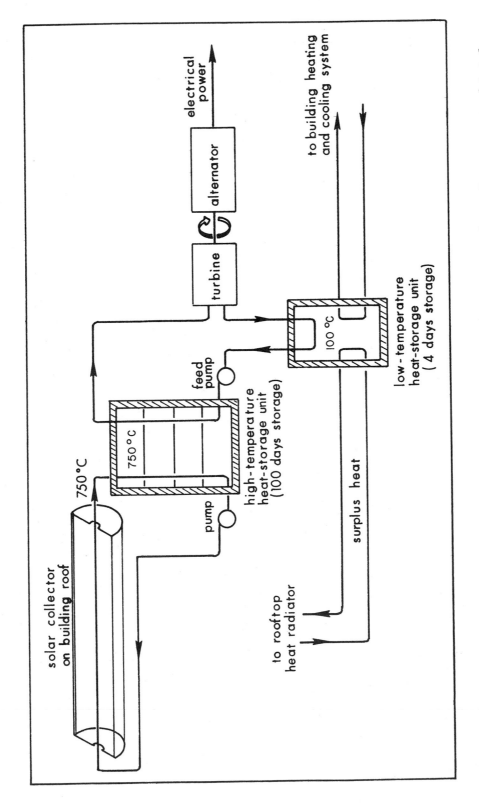

Fig. 14.3-3 Schematic diagram showing some of the components of a solar-powered total-energy system for commercial installations; reproduced from Ref. [3] of Section 14.1.

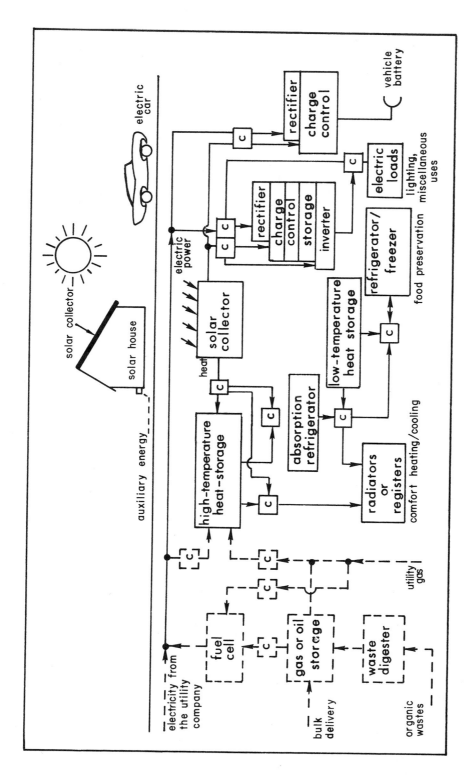

Fig. 14.3-4 Schematic diagram of a complete solar-energy system for residential use. The symbol C identifies an appropriate control unit. Reproduced from Ref. [2] of Section 14.1.

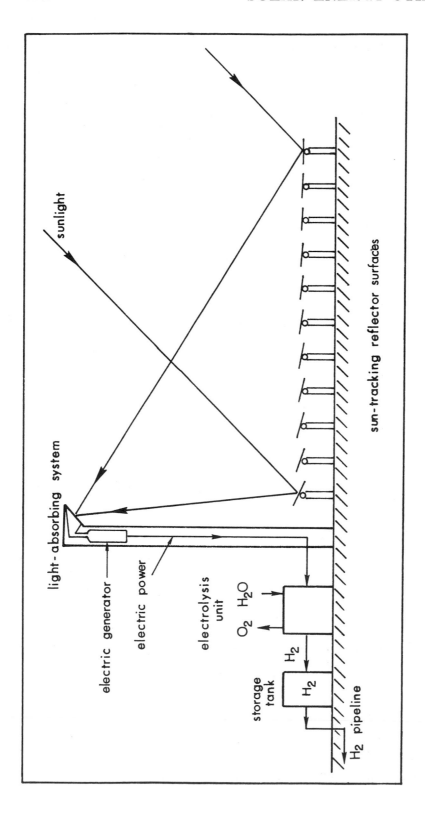

Fig. 14.3-5 A solar generating plant (power tower) using steerable light-collectors and a stationary light-absorbing system. An electrolysis unit is shown for the production of hydrogen. Reproduced with modifications from Ref. [3] of Section 14.1.

unit, has also been proposed.

The conceptual design shown in Fig. 14.3-5 is commonly referred to as a power tower and represents the major research and development effort in the U.S. to produce electricity from solar energy.[1] These systems employ large numbers of steerable light collectors (heliostats) to focus sunlight on a stationary tower, which supports a power receiver or boiler designed to reach temperatures up to about 500°C. Typical overall conversion efficiencies of sunlight to electricity are expected to be about 16%.

Development of the power tower concept is scheduled to proceed from a small testing facility to the first commercial plant in four stages. During 1978, a 5-Mw_t test facility is scheduled for completion and construction will begin on a 10-Mw_e pilot plant. These designs will be followed by a 100-Mw_e demonstration plant and, finally, by a 100-Mw_e prototype commercial plant to be completed sometime beyond 1990.

Current heliostat costs range from $500 to $1,000/m^2 as compared to the ERDA cost goal of $70/m^2. Reduction of heliostat costs is crucial to the successful development of the power tower concept because the heliostat field may represent 60% or more of the total capital cost of the facility. Manufacturing techniques that meet exacting tolerances will be required for heliostat production and materials must be developed for receiver construction that will withstand both

---

[1] W. D. Metz, "Solar Thermal Electricity: Power Tower Dominates Research," Science 197, 353-356 (1977).

high and variable power densities (e.g., nearly instantaneous changes in power densities from 0 to 5 Mw_t/m^2).

Preliminary capital cost estimates made by workers at the Jet Propulsion Laboratory and the Electric Power Research Institute range from \$1,250 to \$2,000/kw_e, depending on eventual heliostat costs. [1] Both studies, however, assumed significant reductions in heliostat costs as compared to 1977 values.

D.   Fuel Production Using Solar Energy

Alternative techniques of fuel production from solar energy, without the intervention of electricity-generating and hydrolysis plants, are shown in Fig. 14.3-6. An example of anaerobic fermentation for methane production is illustrated in Fig. 14.3-7 and refers specifically to conversion of algae to fuel.

14.4   Solar-Energy Collectors for Solar-Thermal Power Conversion

A.   Types of Solar Collectors

A solar collector focusing the radiant-energy input onto an axis is shown schematically in Fig. 14.4-1. Water flowing through the pipe along the focal axis of the collector is heated. The critical parameters determining the efficiency with which solar heating is accomplished are the area-concentration ratio R (which equals the ratio of the solar-

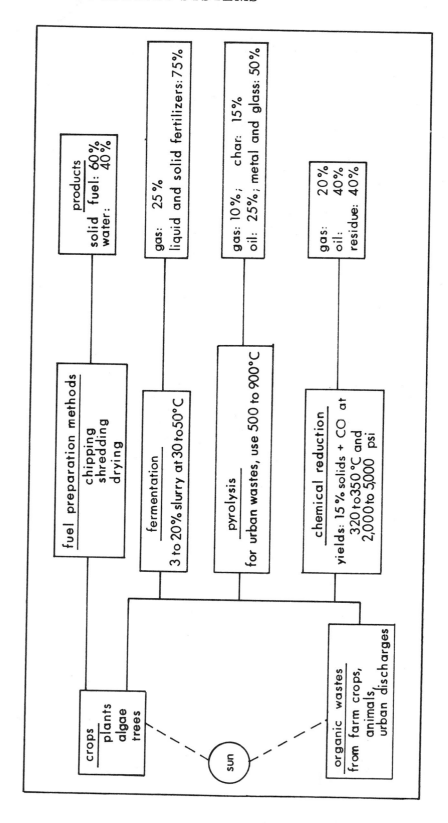

Fig. 14.3-6 Schematic diagram illustrating methods of fuel production by the use of solar energy; reproduced from Ref. [2] of Section 14.1.

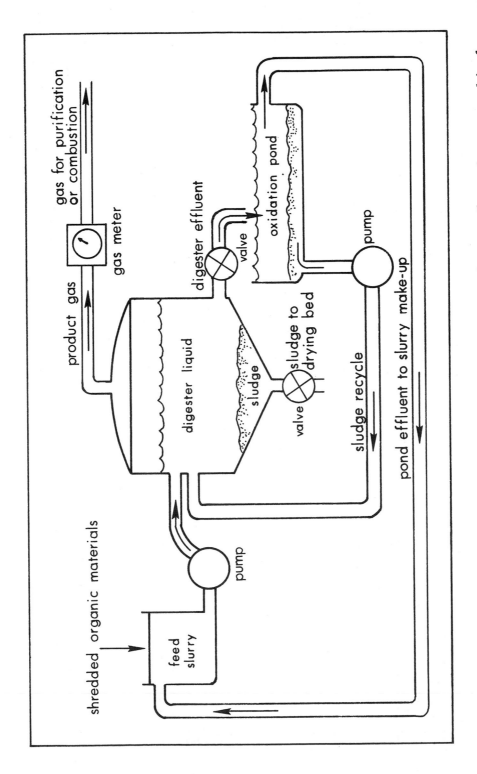

Fig. 14.3-7 Continuous unit for converting organic material to methane by anaerobic fermen-tation; reproduced from Ref. [2] of Section 14.1.

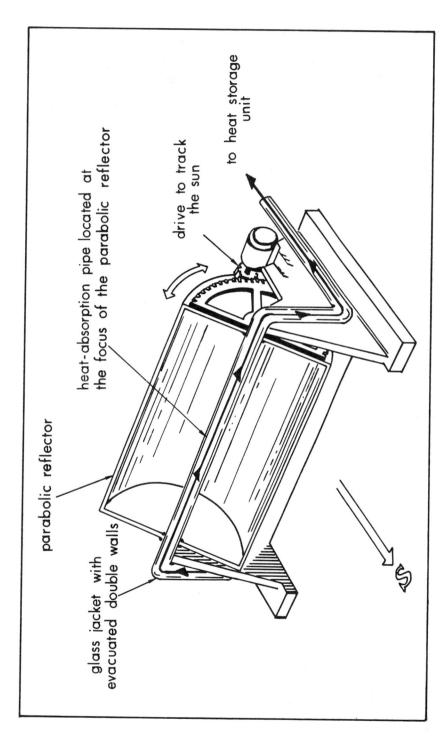

Fig. 14.4-1 Schematic diagram of a solar-energy collector which focuses the incident radiant energy on one axis. Evacuated double walls are used to minimize convective and conductive heat transfer. Reproduced from Ref. [3] of Section 14.1.

collector area to the insolated area of the heat-absorption pipe), the collector absorptivity A (which equals the fraction of the incident radiant energy that is absorbed), and the emissivity E of the heat-absorption pipe (which equals the fraction of the blackbody radiancy at the temperature of the pipe which is actually emitted from the pipe). Large ratios of RA/E are evidently desirable. Achievable outlet temperatures for various "absorber qualities" RA/E, at different utilization efficiencies, are shown in Fig. 14.4-2 and are seen to reach values of $1,000°$ C with about 27% efficiency for RA/E equal to 300, which is a readily-achievable value for one-axis concentrators; flat-plate collectors may be constructed with RA/E values of 10 while two-axis collectors have been made with ratios as high as 10^4.

A typical solar collector for residential use is shown in Fig. 14.4-3. The solar-energy collection efficiency is strongly dependent on orientation (see Table 14.4-1).

B.   Desirable Physical Properties of Solar Collectors[1]

Solar collectors for achieving high temperatures must have high absorptivity (A) at wavelengths below about 1.3μ and low emissivity (E) in the infrared beyond 1.3μ. This statement may be understood by reference to Fig. 14.4-4a: a good collector should absorb the incident solar radiation

[1]A. D. Meinel and M. P. Meinel, "Physics Looks at Solar Energy," Physics Today 25, 44-50, February 1972.

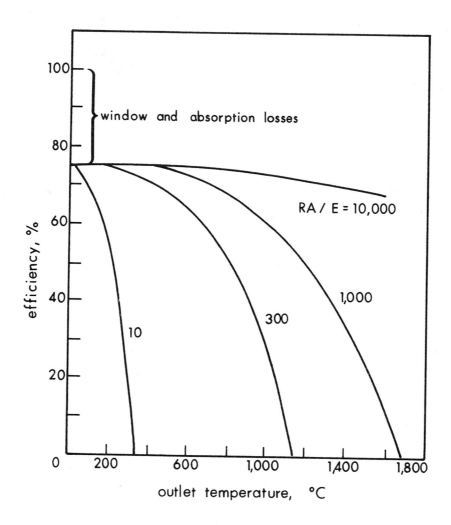

Fig. 14.4-2 Achievable water outlet temperatures for various ratios of RA/E; reproduced from Ref. [3] of Section 14.1.

and reemit only a small fraction of the absorbed radiant energy.

The radiancy is the radiant energy emitted from a unit area of an isothermal source <u>at equilibrium</u> per unit

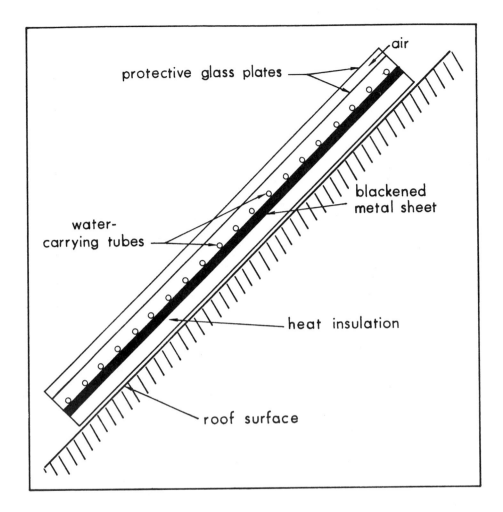

Fig. 14.4-3 A solar collector for residential use. One to three protective glass covers are generally placed over a blackened, light-absorbing surface; two glass covers are shown in the diagram. The light-absorbing surface consists of black sheet metal to which (1/2)- to 1-inch diameter tubes are bonded. These water-carrying tubes are connected together through a manifold. The black sheet metal is backed up by 2 to 4 inches of heat insulation and placed on the roof. A typical collection unit may be 3 to 6 inches thick, 3 to 25 feet long, and 8 to 60 feet wide. The desirable roof slope depends on geographic location and on seasonal solar-flux variations.

Table 14.4-1 An example showing the effect of collector
             orientation on collection efficiency at a par-
             ticular location; reproduced from Ref. [3] of
             Section 14.1.

Collector orientation	Estimated relative flux density	
	annual average	December average
fixed, horizontal	1.00	1.00
fixed, facing south at 45° above the horizontal	1.30	1.90
one-axis, steerable in elevation	1.33	1.98
two-axis, steerable in elevation	1.86	2.70

time into a solid angle of 2π steradians; it cannot exceed the
limiting value corresponding to the blackbody radiancy at the
temperature of the source. The blackbody radiancy is giv-
en by the Stefan-Boltzmann equation and is proportional to
the fourth power of the temperature; the proportionality constant is the Stefan-Boltzmann constant and has the value
5.670×10^{-5} erg/cm^2-sec-(°K)^4. The radiant-energy distribution as a function of wavelength is determined by
Planck's equation for a blackbody. This equation gives maximum relative radiancy at the wavelength determined from
Wien's displacement law, viz., $\lambda T = 0.2898$ cm-°K. Relative values of radiant intensities (radiant intensities are ra-
diancies divided by 2π and thus represent radiant energies

emitted from unit area in unit time per unit of solid angle)
for blackbody emitters at 700, 900 and 6,000°K (corresponding to the apparent temperature of the sun) are shown in
Fig. 14.4-4a. The absolute values of the radiant intensities
increase at all wavelengths when the temperature is raised
in accord with Planck's law. At a given temperature, the
actual value of the radiancy equals the product of the emissivity (which is less than or equal to unity) and of the radiancy. The emissivities vary with wavelength and temperature for real light sources. For "grey" bodies, the emissivities are defined to be independent of wavelength. The
spectral emissivities and absorptivities (i.e., the emissivities and absorptivities at a given wavelength) for all substances are equal in accord with Kirchhoff's law.

A good solar-energy collector must have high
absorptivity in the visible region of the spectrum from about
0.3 to 1.1 microns (1 micron = 10^{-4} cm = 10^4 Angstrom
units), where most of the solar energy is concentrated (see
Fig. 14.4-4a). At the same time, a good solar collector
should have a small value of the emissivity in the near-infra-
red region of the spectrum from about 2 to 15 microns,
where the collectors, at temperatures between room temperature and about 900°K, tend to emit radiant energy
relatively strongly (compare Fig. 14.4-4a).

The interference stacks (made from metal-dielectric
multilayers) and bulk-absorber stacks (made by vapor deposition on semiconductors) shown in Figs. 14.4-4b and
14.4-4d approach the desired spectral performance for a light

absorber (see Figs. 14.4-4c and 14.4-4e, respectively).
The lifetimes and costs for large-scale production of these
stacks are not known at the present time.

For 70% energy extraction, RA/E must be about 120
to reach a surface temperature of 50°C (compare Fig. 14.4-
2). The geometric design shown in Fig. 14.4-5, with liquid
sodium (or organic fluids or salt eutectics) flowing through
the inner pipe has been claimed to yield RA/E = 100 with
R = 10.[1] Sunlight concentration is accomplished by means
of a cylindrical glass Fresnel lens (or, alternatively, by
using a paraboloid reflector).

   C. Solar Collectors for Achieving Temperatures up
       to the Boiling Point of Water

In unpressurized systems, the collector consists typically of a copper heat exchanger on which sunlight is concentrated by using a suitable optical system. The copper
surface is painted black (or is blackened by sputtering) to
absorb the incident radiant energy. This relatively inexpensive type of system is preferred for the uses suggested
by the schematic diagrams shown in Figs. 14.3-1 and
14.3-2.

14.5 Quantitative Description of Selected Solar-Energy
      Conversion Systems

In order to assess the economic value of some of the
qualitative conceptions presented in Section 14.3, we must

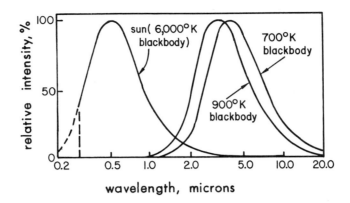

a. The intensity distributions as functions of
    wavelength for blackbody light sources at
    6,000°K ($\simeq$ the surface temperature of the
    sun), 900°K, and 700°K.

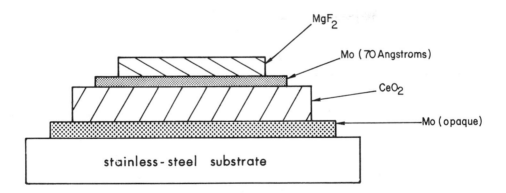

b. Schematic diagram of interference stacks.

Fig. 14.4-4 Composite diagrams showing how desirable
             physical properties may be obtained for solar
             collectors; reproduced with modifications from
             Meinel and Meinel, Ref. [1]. Figs. 14.4-4 c,
             d, and e are on page 385.

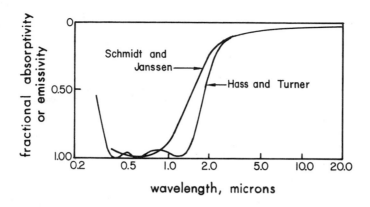

c.   The optical properties of the interference
     stacks shown in Fig. 14.4-4b.

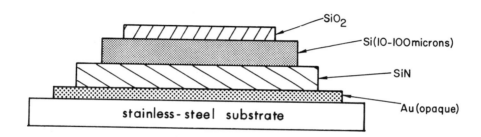

d.   Schematic diagram of bulk-absorber stacks.

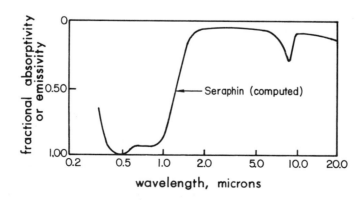

e.   The optical properties of the bulk-absorber
     stacks shown in Fig. 14.4-4d.

Fig. 14.4-4, continued.

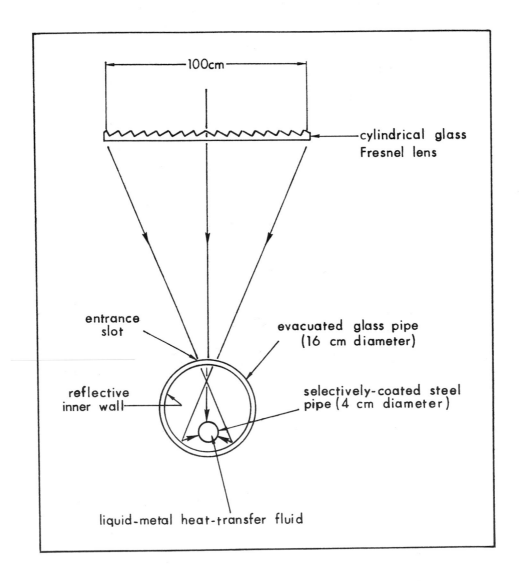

Fig. 14.4-5 A "linear energy-collection element" described
by Meinel and Meinel.[1] A "solar module" for
a large-scale structure would contain 6 to 8 of
these units supported on a single shaft. The optical concentration ratio R for this design is
about 10.

perform careful quantitative evaluations of feasibility and costs. Some examples of evaluations of this type will now be presented.

A. An Optimistic View of Photosynthetic Production of Fuels; Animal-Waste Utilization

Some current crop-production data have been given in Section 14.1D. With intensive cultivation in the U.S., the best crop growth that can be achieved has been estimated to be as high as 40 tons of dry material per acre.[1] This value may be contrasted with a productivity of 4 to 26 tons of dry material per acre normally achieved with trees and grasses (compare Section 14.1D). Allowing a heating value of 16×10^6 Btu/ton (corresponding to about 63% of the heating value per ton of coal), we find an optimal heat-energy production with single crops of 6.4×10^8 Btu/acre-y or (since 1 acre = 43,560 ft^2 = 4,047 m^2 = 1.56×10^{-3} mi^2) of 4.1×10^{11} Btu/mi^2-y. Thus, the 1970 thermal-energy requirements for electrical-energy production of 17×10^{15} Btu/y could have been grown in single crops, under optimal conditions and allowing for a 33% conversion efficiency from thermal to electrical energy, on 4.15×10^4 mi^2 or about 1.4% of the total land area in the lower 48 states. This value for the required land area might conceivably be further reduced by a factor of 2 or even 3 if rapid crop rotation could be accom-

----

[1]Ref. [2] of Section 14.1.

plished. It follows, therefore, that the growing of crops as a primary energy source appears to represent a feasible solution to our energy needs.

We note that, with a mean insolation of $1,500$ Btu/ft^2-d ($\simeq 200$ w/m^2), the production of 6.4×10^8 Btu/acre-y of dry organic crop represents an overall energy-conversion efficiency of 2.7%.

A population of 1.18×10^8 head of cattle in the U.S.[2, 3] has been estimated to produce 1.3×10^8 tons of dry waste per year or, at a heating value of 16×10^6 Btu/ton, a thermal energy equivalent of 2.08×10^{15} Btu. To supply the electrical energy used in 1970, a thermal energy of 17×10^{15} Btu/y was required. With 10% waste recovery, the required cattle population to produce the dry waste for this thermal-energy production is seen to be about 9.6×10^9 head of cattle. Thus, the idea of feeding cattle and using cattle waste to supply all of our fuel needs is seen to be infeasible.

Biophotolysis of water to produce hydrogen is among the intriguing solar-energy-utilization techniques that has been proposed.[1] Although the photosynthetic step has an efficiency of 10%, the overall energy-conversion efficiencies that are currently achievable are far smaller and much too

[2] C. E. Knapp, "Agriculture Poses Waste Problems," Environmental Science and Technology 4, 1098-1100 (1970).

[3] "Cattle, Sheep and Goat Inventory," Statistical Reporting Service of the U.S. Department of Agriculture, Publication No. LV-GN-1(72), Washington, D.C., January 1972.

low to make biophotolysis a practically attractive procedure at the present time. However, further research in this area is clearly indicated.[4]

The use of anaerobic fermentation for methane production has been mentioned in Section 14.3D. Between 4.5 and 6.5 SCF of CH_4 are produced per pound of dry organic material. At a heating value of 10^3 Btu/SCF, the thermal energy of the product is seen to lie between 9 and 13×10^6 Btu/t and to correspond to 56 to 81% of the heating value of the original organic material. The development and utilization of anaerobic fermentation has been considered in connection with the production of algae. It has been estimated that 100% of U.S. gas needs could be supplied by the year 2020 on 5% of the U.S. land area with 2% overall solar-energy-conversion efficiency.[1] The economic assessment, which may well have been highly optimistic for this method of waste utilization, was stated to be consistent with a credit of $0.88/$10^6$ Btu for the methane produced in a plant processing 1,000 tons of waste per day[1] and is thus seen to be competitive with other gas-production techniques; as was stated in Section 14.1D, the corresponding crop value after drying must be less than about 0.8 cent/lb.

[4]W. D. McElroy, UCSD/NSF (RANN) Conference on Enzyme Engineering as Related to Food and Energy Production, La Jolla, California, July 22-25, 1974.

B. Large-Scale, Land-Based Solar-Thermal Farms[5]

Using the high-temperature thermal technology described in Section 14.4B, we may postulate overall conversion efficiencies in excess of 10%. To produce 10^6 Mw$_e$ at 30% conversion efficiency will require[1] solar-power collection over an area of about 5,000 mi^2 (compare Fig. 14.2-3). Meinel and Meinel[5] have expressed the belief that a budget of \$60/m^2 might be sufficient for implementation of a solar-energy farm, which would then generate electricity at 5.3 mills/kwh$_e$.[5]

More generally speaking, we may use the curves shown in Fig. 14.2-3 to estimate required land areas at various conversion efficiencies, define the size of the power plant, estimate a depreciation and amortization schedule, and then determine the number of dollars available per ft^2 for light collection in an economically-competitive plant. Application of this procedure shows that solar-energy collectors will have to be built at costs of about \$0.50 to \$1.50/ ft^2 for currently achievable thermal-energy-conversion efficiencies.

C. Solar-Power Cooling Units for Application in Tropical Areas

The use of solar energy for residential and commercial cooling in tropical areas represents an especially attrac-

---

[5]Ref. [1] from Section 14.4.

tive application of solar energy since it refers to locations where sunlight is normally abundant. An example of an experimental installation is provided by the Brisbane Solar House.[6]

This box-like house[6] is 58 ft long, 24 ft wide, and 8 ft high. The house is covered by a free-standing roof with a length of 79.5 ft and a width of 40 ft; the roof is arranged in such a way as to shade the house completely during the summer. A 58-ft side faces in the Northern direction. The living space in the house is 1,318 ft^2 while 74 ft^2 are allocated to the solar plant. The house is well insulated, with 3-inch plywood-faced-polystyrene-foam panels used for the walls and ceiling; the floor consists of a 6-inch concrete slab. The windows are constructed from insulating double-glass and cover only 23.5% of the wall area.

The roof is designed to hold 16 solar collectors, which are made of 4 ft × 4 ft overlapped glass covers and are 16 ft × 4 ft in size. Results have been obtained after installation of one of the required sixteen collector units. The collector plate was made of blackened (i.e., oxidized) copper and held 0.5-inch diameter tubes at 6-inch centers. The collector plate was thermally insulated at the back with 3-inch urethane foam and was shielded with double-glass covers.[6] The collector-hot-water output was appropriately augmented with electrically-heated water. A modified

---

[6] N. R. Sheridan, "Performance of the Brisbane Solar House," Solar Energy 13, 395-401 (1972).

commercial LiBr-H_2O absorption air conditioner, with a capacity of 3 tons, gave an average coefficient of performance of 0.68 with water temperatures up to 200°F and produced an output of 100 to 600 Btu/min.[6]

Study of the data output indicates[6] that the solar collector, with a redesigned refrigerator, will provide acceptable performance on clear days (the interior temperature can be cooled to 70°F) and also on days with intermittent cloud cover and, with adequate (about 5 ft^3) refrigerant storage, will allow cooling for 1 to 2 hours on cloudy days with moderate outside temperatures. On clear days, about 20% of the incident thermal energy was ultimately abstracted during cooling.[6]

Sheridan concluded:[6] "...as a new development should show substantial savings over its more conventional competition to warrant adoption, it cannot be confidently stated that solar air-conditioning has immediate potential." In this instance, the more conventional competition bore the following energy costs:[7] for distillate fuel, 11 to 23 Australian cents per therm (1 therm = 10^5 Btu) or, using 1972 currency rates, U.S. $1.32 to $2.76/10^6 Btu; for electricity, an average of U.S. $7.20/10^6 Btu.

D. Solar Distillation and Drying

Among the economically acceptable specialty uses of

[7]N. R. Sheridan, "Criteria for Justification of Solar Energy Systems," Solar Energy 13, 425-429 (1972).

solar energy are water distillation and industrial drying, especially in areas of the world where conventional energy sources are not readily available.

In solar stills applied to stationary ponds, light-reflecting layers build up on the surface and interfere with efficient operation. [8] Water distillation, as well as agricultural and industrial drying, have been discussed by Daniels. [9]

E. Some General Considerations Relating to Solar-
    Energy Utilization

It is reasonable to assess the economic promise of solar-energy development on the basis of the following assumptions:

i. Solar-energy sources must ultimately be competitive with other energy sources.

ii. Solar-energy converters should be constructed in such a manner as to involve a capital cost equivalent to the sum of the fuel and capital costs for fossil-fuel generators. Since fossil-fuel and plant-capital costs are roughly comparable, solar-energy sources should be allowed about double the capital costs of coal, oil, or gas plants, i.e., about $400/kw$_e$ to $500/kw$_e$ at 1973 prices. Using the higher

---

[8] P. I. Cooper, "Some Factors Affecting the Absorption of Solar Radiation in Solar Stills," Solar Energy 13, 373-381 (1972).

[9] Ref. [1] of Section 14.1, Chapters 10 and 7.

estimate, the solar-collection system alone could then cost
about $750/kw$_e$ with the remaining $750/kw$_e$ allocated to a
conventional turbine-generator for a high-temperature solar-
collection unit and to a suitable energy-storage system.

      iii. Nuclear fuel accounts for about 10 to 15% of the
cost of electricity produced by nuclear power plants. Hence,
solar-energy plants should be introduced at capital investments about 1.15 times those allocated for nuclear plants,
i.e., $1,000 to $1,200/kw$_e$ at 1976 price levels. Using the
higher estimate and assuming a doubling of nuclear-fuel costs,
as well as making a 50% allowance for energy storage and
auxiliary facilities, the solar collector should cost about
$700/kw$_e$.

      For an average insolation level of 200 w_t/m^2 and a
conversion efficiency of 20%, the allowable cost for the solar-
collector system, when considering the long-term competition
with nuclear-power generators, may be as high as $28/m^2$ or
about $2.60 ft^2.

      Solar-thermal collection systems are not likely to
become available at this cost and a utilization efficiency of
20% in the foreseeable future. Hence the development of
large-scale solar-energy installations for central-station
applications does not now appear to be economically competitive with nuclear power plants, unless nuclear-plant costs
escalate significantly above 1976 levels while solar-thermal
cost estimates remain constant.

      Cost comparisons of solar-thermal electric plants
with either fossil-fuel or nuclear plants require many

assumptions and may therefore lead to widely different results. The following factors are of crucial importance:
current fuel costs and anticipated fuel-cost escalations,
capital investment costs, replacement charges for capital
costs, interest rates, etc. An elementary view,[10] which
leads to pessimistic conclusions for the solar-electric
installation, will now be described.

A high capital cost for a coal-fired plant is 1×10^9
to generate 5×10^9 kwh$_e$/y, which corresponds to [1×10^9/
$(5 \times 10^9$ kwh$_e$/y$)] \times (8.76 \times 10^3$ h/y$) = \$1,750$/kw$_e$; the capi-
tal investment per unit of energy output is seen to be $0.20/
(kwh$_e$/y) or, at a fixed charge of 0.15/y, $0.03/kwh$_e$. If
coal energy is converted to electricity with an efficiency of
34% and costs $25/t, then the fuel cost is (1 Btu/0.34 Btu$_e$)
$\times (1$ mt/27.8 $\times 10^6$ Btu$) \times (0.949 \times 10^{-3}$ Btu$_e$/2.78 $\times 10^{-7}$ kwh$_e$)
$\times (1.1$ t/mt$) \times (\$25$/t$) = \$0.01$/kwh$_e$. Thus, the total cost of
electricity generated in this manner from coal is $0.04/kwh$_e$.

For the solar-electric plant, we have capital charges
associated with the collector, the storage system, and other
costs such as land, structures, the steam-electric system,
cooling towers, etc. If the collector costs $10/ft^2, the fixed
charge is 0.21/y and the collector output (at 17% average
conversion efficiency) is 30 kwh$_e$/ft^2-y, the collector cost
becomes (\$10/ft^2) $\times (0.21$/y$)/(30$ kwh$_e$/ft^2-y$) = \$0.07$/kwh$_e$.
If the storage unit costs $25/kwh$_e$ for 5 days of storage

[10]G. Pollard, "The Long-Range Prospects of Solar
    Energy," American Scientist 64, 424-429 (1976); dis-
    cussions of this paper appear in 64, 606-609 (1976).

capacity and the fixed charge is 0.21/y, then the storage unit

costs $[(5 \text{ days})/(365 \text{ days/y})] \times (\$25/kwh_e) \times (0.21/y) = \$0.072/$

kwh_e. If the auxiliary costs are $\$100/kw_e$ for a peak solar

power of 300 Btu/ft^2-h, the total solar insolation is 175 $kwh_e/$

ft^2-y or 6×10^5 Btu/ft^2-y, and the fixed charges are 0.15/y,

then the auxiliary costs are (300 Btu/ft^2-h) $\times$ (0.15/y) $\times$ ($\$100/$

$kw_e)/(6 \times 10^5$ Btu/ft^2-y) = $\$0.0075/kwh_e$. The total cost of

solar thermal-electric energy is thus seen to be $\$0.15/kwh_e$.

The coal-fired plant will become as costly as the

solar-thermal-electric plant when coal costs have escalated

eleven-fold above the assumed high value of $25/t.

F.   Metal Hydrides for Energy Storage in Solar-Energy Utilization

The use of decomposing metal hydrides for energy

storage is being investigated. The hydrides decompose on

(solar) heating, the released H_2 is stored, and the energy

absorbed by dissociation is regenerated during exothermic

reaction as needed by allowing the hydrogen and metal to

recombine. It has been estimated[11] that 200,000 Btu of

thermal energy (corresponding to the daily requirements in

an average household) may be stored by decomposing 2,700

lb of a hydrided lanthanum-nickel alloy, 1,230 lb of a

vanadium hydride, or 1,650 lb of iron-titanium hydride with

the stoichiometric formula FeTiH. The ability to control

---

[11]"Solar Energy Work Advancing Rapidly," Chemical and
Engineering News 52, 17-18, September 16, 1974.

recombination rates and hence heat-release rates adds
greatly to the convenience of using metal-hydride storage
systems. On the other hand, the large weights of active
material required, as well as the necessity to store H_2,
may turn out to have serious disadvantages.

14.6   Solar Ponds

An interesting concept for solar-energy utilization
involves direct radiant-heat transfer to a shallow pond.[1,2]
A schematic diagram of this design is shown in Fig. 14.6-1.
A representative 1 km^2 pond area would deliver about 8.5
Mw_e ($\simeq$ 360 bbl of oil per day equivalent) with a mean efficiency of 2.8%.[2]   The unit cost of the collector is now so
low that the design may become competitive with other energy-production techniques (compare Section 14.5E). However,
this system seems to be characterized by serious operational
difficulties arising from uncontrolled convection currents.
Also, the technology for efficient generation of electricity in
low-temperature thermal cycles requires development.

---

[1] A. F. Clark, "Solar Ponds Extended," Report UCID-16317, Lawrence Livermore Laboratory, University of California, Livermore, California, October 1973.

[2] L. F. Wouters, "The Shallow Solar Pond Scheme: Performance Assessment of a Model System," Report UCID-16437, Lawrence Livermore Laboratory, University of California, Livermore, California, October 1973.

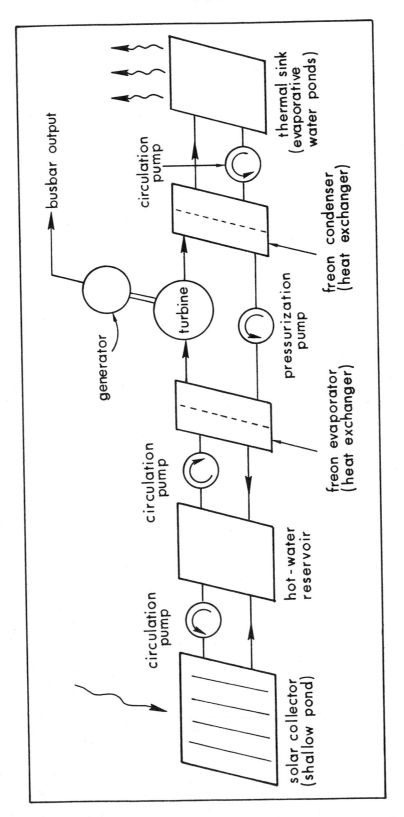

Fig. 14.6-1 Schematic diagram of a solar-pond collector, heat-exchanger, and turbine-generator system; reproduced from Ref. [2].

14.7 Satellites for Solar-Power Collection[1]

A space station in a synchronous orbit is continuously illuminated by unattenuated solar radiation, except for the losses associated with the divergence of beams and increasing irradiated area, which vary as the square of the distance from the sun. The establishment of Satellite Solar-Power Stations (SSPS) in synchronous orbit (22,300 miles from earth) and final energy-conversion on earth was apparently first suggested as a serious engineering development in 1968.[2] This concept has been studied[3] in some detail in a series of NASA-supported investigations. An operating system is shown schematically in Figs. 14.7-1 and 14.7-2. This system is seen to involve photovoltaic power conversion in space, microwave power generation in space, microwave transmission to the earth, and conversion of microwave radiation to electricity. Theoretical calculations show that optimal space-station power-to-weight ratios correspond to large power outputs, between 3×10^3 and 15×10^3 Mw$_e$.

---

[1] P. E. Glaser, "Solar Power via Satellites," Astronautics and Aeronautics 11, 60-68, August 1973.

[2] P. E. Glaser, "Power from the Sun: Its Future," Science 162, 857-861 (1968).

[3] P. E. Glaser, O. E. Maynard, J. Mackovciak, Jr., and E. L. Ralph, "Feasibility Study of a Satellite Solar Power Station," NASA Contractor Report, NASA CR-2357, National Aeronautics and Space Administration, Washington, D.C., 1974; see, also, the references cited in Ref. [3].

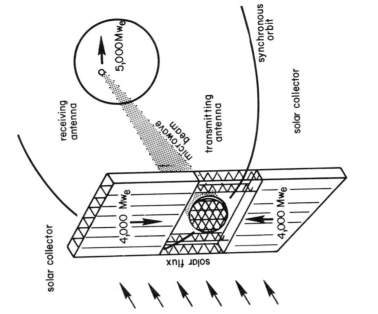

Fig. 14.7-1 Schematic diagram illustrating the SSPS concept with photovoltaic power conversion in a synchronous orbit, microwave transmission to earth, and conversion to electricity of the received microwave radiation; reproduced from Ref. [3]. Photograph courtesy of Arthur D. Little, Inc.

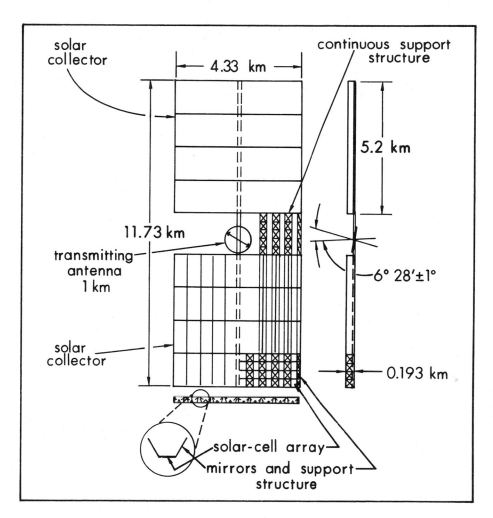

Fig. 14.7-2 Suggested dimensions for the conceptual design of an SSPS; reproduced from Ref. [3].

The microwave radiation can be transmitted to any desired location on earth by using (steerable) antennas.

It has been estimated that terrestrial solar-energy conversion at reasonable efficiency becomes competitive with other energy sources at a cost of about $28.00/m^2 ($\sim$ $2.60/ft^2 for the solar collectors). In view of perhaps 15 times higher overall energy conversion efficiency in space, [4] the cost of solar converters for orbital use may be as high as $39.00/ft^2. For space applications, photovoltaic rather than solar-thermal power conversion will generally be preferred because of the essential requirement that payloads must be minimized in satellite launchings.

The performance of photovoltaic cells has been discussed in Section 13.5. Early design targets for the SSPS are summarized in Table 14.7-1; the solar-cell cost goal is seen to be about $3.50/ft^2, i.e., well below current costs but too high for a ground-based competitive system.

The microwave generation, transmission, attenuation, and collection system does not appear to pose intrinsically insurmountable problems, although the concentrated microwave beam will represent a significant environmental hazard over the limited area which it covers.

Environmental problems that have been considered include waste-heat release at the receiving station, land despoilment (an estimated 270 km^2 will be used per station), atmospheric pollution, ionospheric interactions (which are expected to occur for power densities above about 20 mw/cm^2 and at frequencies greater than 2.45 GHz), microwave exposure, and radiofrequency interference. [5]

---

[4] M. Wolf, "Cost Goals for Silicon Solar Arrays for Large-Scale Terrestrial Applications," 9th IEEE Photovoltaic Specialists Conference, pp. 342-350, Silver Spring, Maryland, May 1972.

[5] The SSPS concept has been reviewed recently by P. E. Glaser, "Solar Power from Satellites," Physics Today 30, 30-38, February 1977.

Table 14.7-1 Early design goals in SSPS development; reproduced from Ref. [3].

Key issue	Performance goal
solar-cell performance cost	18% efficiency, 2-mil thick cell 0.38 cent/cm^2 (~$3.50/ft^2)
blanket weight cost	950 w$_e$/kg (430 w$_e$/lb) 0.68 cents/cm^2
solar-collector cost and weight	$310/kw$_e$, 3 lb/kw$_e$
operational life	30-year life, 6% degradation in 5 y
energy input to process	1 to 3 year payback
high-voltage circuit control	40 kV; 5% loss

Current and expected efficiencies for the microwave system are shown in Table 14.7-2 and are seen to yield an overall performance between 26.5 and 77.0%.

A large-scale SSPS has been proposed with the following design objectives:[5] 5,000 Mw$_e$ of power are to be delivered to the earth with a 2.5×10^7-lb payload in orbit and a 3×10^4 lb/y supply of propellant for station keeping.[1] A 20-year SSPS will then require a total payload of 2.56×10^7 lb and, if placed in orbit at a cost of 7.8×10^4/lb, would require a total initial investment of $2,000 \times 10^9$. This design corresponds to an initial charge for power of 4×10^5/kw$_e$, which is far too high for a competitive system,

Table 14.7-2 Microwave generation, transmission, collection, and rectification efficiencies; reproduced from Ref. [3].

Microwave system characteristics	Efficiency		
	Presently demonstrated[a]	Expected with present technology[a]	Expected with additional development[a]
microwave power generation efficiency	76.7[b]	85.0	90.0
transmission efficiency from output of generator to collector aperture	94.0	94.0	95.0
collection and rectification efficiency (rectenna)	64.0	75.0	90.0
transmission, collection, and rectification efficiency	60.2	70.5	85.0
system performance	26.5[c]	60.0	77.0

a. The entries refer to a frequency of 2,450 MHz (12.2-cm wavelength).

b. This efficiency was demonstrated at 3,000 MHz and a power level of 300-kw cw (cw = coherent wave).

c. This value could be increased immediately to 45% if an efficient generator were available at the same power level at which the efficiency of 60.2% was obtained.

even allowing for zero fuel cost over a twenty-year period. Cost estimates become more optimistic as launching costs are reduced.[*] A 1977 development-cost estimate is $20 $\times 10^9$ for power-station technology and $24 $\times 10^9$ for transportation systems.[5]

An optimistic integrated projection for solar-collector costs is reproduced in Table 14.7-3; the final cost of about $350/kw$_e$ is clearly competitive with other projected power sources. A 1977 busbar-cost estimate for electricity is 27 mills/kwh$_e$ for a 5,000-Mw$_e$ power station.[5]

14.8 The Solar-Sea Power Plant (SSPP)[**]

A. Historical Background

Among the large unused energy sources is solar-sea power. D'Arsonval[1] proposed in 1881 that power be generated by operating a heat engine with the warm surface tem-

---

[*]Development of a modified space shuttle with 80,000 kg payload capability is expected to reduce lifting costs to low-earth orbits to $200 to $400/kg, which will greatly reduce the launching costs into synchronous orbits and thus make SSPS far more attractive.[5]

[**]This system is often referred to as OTEC (ocean thermal energy conversion).

[1]J. d'Arsonval, Revue Scientifique, September 17, 1881.

Table 14.7-3 Cost projections for the SSPS solar collector (with a channel-type concentrating mirror design); reproduced from Ref. [3].

System	Area, cm^2/w_e	Weight, $gram/w_e$	Cost, $\$/w_e$
blanket	26.3	0.742	0.179
reflector	55.7	0.111	0.036
bus and support	----	0.030	0.005
subtotals (power generated in orbit)		0.883	0.220
orbit-to-earth factor (equivalent power generated on earth)		(1.6X)	(1.6X)
total		1.413	0.352

perature of the ocean as a source of heat and the colder water at lower layers as a heat sink. Unsuccessful early attempts to develop the power cycle were made by the American engineer Campbell and by the Italian engineers Dornig and Boggia. Georges Claude[2] made an unsuccessful attempt in 1926 at economical power generation by using water as working fluid in a Caribbean pilot plant; in this installation, he generated 25 kw_e at the expenditure of 80 kw_e. Claude's poor performance results reflect design deficiencies rather than intrinsic problems, as has been discussed

[2]G. Claude, "Power from the Tropical Seas," Mechanical Engineering 52, 1039-1044 (1930).

by the Andersons.[3] A highly optimistic theoretical study
of a Rankine-cycle engine using propane as working fluid has
been described by the Andersons.[4] This optimism is echoed
in a recent semi-popular survey by Zener,[5] who favors the
use of ammonia in a Rankine-cycle engine, together with direct utilization of electrical energy for water electrolysis
and transmission of gaseous H_2 and O_2 to users.

The enormous potential of thermal-sea power plants
using solar energy as primary source may be appreciated in
view of the following estimate:[3] existing thermal gradients
in the Gulf Stream are sufficient to generate 1.82×10^{14} $kwh_e/$
y, compared with an estimated 1980 __total__ U.S. thermal energy requirement of 2.8×10^{13} kwh/y = 9.6×10^{16} Btu/y.

B. A Proposed Installation[4] to Generate 100,000
    kw_e

A schematic diagram of the Andersons' proposed installation is shown in Fig. 14.8-1. A 360 ft long, 40 ft wide,
and 10 ft deep sea-surface-water skimmer admits the warm
surface water at a linear flow speed of a few feet per second.

---

[3] J. H. Anderson and J. H. Anderson, Jr., "Power from
the Sun, Via the Sea," paper presented at the Susquehanna
Section of the ASME, November 1964, and quoted in Ref.[4].

[4] J. H. Anderson and J. H. Anderson, Jr., "Thermal Power from Sea Water: 100,000 kw at 3 mills/kwh," Mechanical Engineering __88__, 41-46, April 1966.

[5] C. Zener, "Solar Sea Power," Physics Today __26__, 48-53,
January 1973.

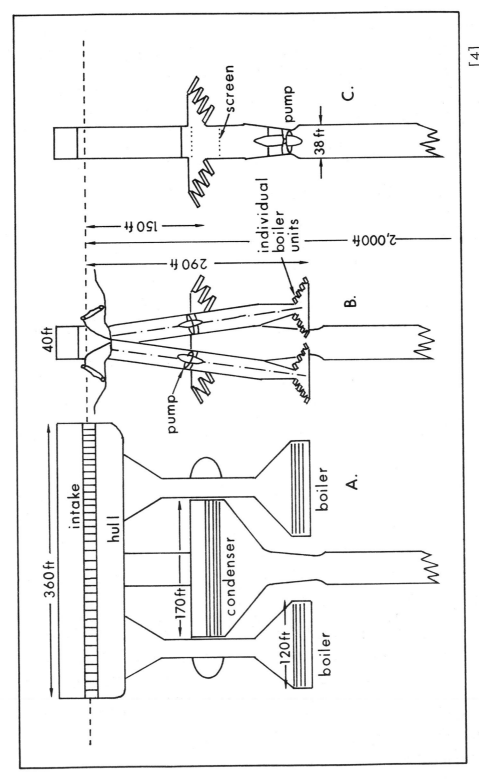

Fig. 14.8-1 Schematic diagram of the Andersons' proposed solar-sea power system. [4]
Footnotes to Fig. 14.8-1 are continued on page 376.

Footnotes to Fig. 14.8-1:

A. The floating power plant of 100 Mw$_e$ capacity requires
    efficient collecting, pumping, and distributing systems
    for large quantities of seawater. Water, which has been
    heated by the sun, is skimmed from the surface. Water
    which is 39°F colder enters through an inlet at a depth
    of 2,000 ft. The hull dimensions are determined by the
    required surface-water intake.

B. The boiler section shows the proposed warm-water path
    to the boilers. Individual boiler units measure 4 ft × 8 ft
    and are shown as small rectangles; they are cross-flow
    heat exchangers. Each of the four boilers consists of
    many heat-exchanger units placed side by side in four
    tiers. The boilers are at a depth of 290 ft. The pumps
    are located at such depths as to avoid cavitation during
    pumping.

C. The condenser design is similar to that of the boilers.
    Because less water is needed, only one inlet and pump
    are required. All pumps are driven by propane turbines
    located within the pump hub diameter. The condenser
    requires 8,500 hp to drive the pump for a flow of 10,000
    cfps at a head of 6.35 ft-lbt/lbm (the symbols lbt and lbm
    stand for lb-torque and lb-mass, respectively).

A condenser is located 150 ft below the surface and is cooled
by sea water pumped up from a depth of 2,000 ft. The boiler
is floated at a distance of 290 ft from the surface; individual
boiler units are cross-flow heat exchangers and have cross-
sectional areas of 4 ft × 8 ft. All pumps are driven by propane
turbines located within the pump hub diameters. The entire
system is buoyant with internal- and ambient-pressure differentials of about 1 atm. We note that the pressure rise
with depth is roughly

$$64 \ (lb/ft^3) \times (1 \ ft^2/144 \ in^2) \ = \ 0.444 \ psi/ft;$$

thus, the ambient pressures at 150 and 290 ft are 67 and 129 psi, respectively. With a pressure drop of one atmosphere, the internal pressures in the working fluid are about 82 and 144 psi, respectively. The boiler must be located below the condenser because the internal pressure in the boiler is higher than in the condenser (see Figs. 14.8-1 and 14.8-2).

C.   The Required Warm Water Flow Rate per Mw_e Delivered

The energy driving the SSPP is provided by the warm-water flow rate and the extent to which the warm water is cooled during the operating cycle. The required warm water flow rate is easily estimated from the relation

$$\text{power output} = \text{(thermal-energy input by warm-water flow)} \times \text{(conversion efficiency to electricity).} \quad (14.8-1)$$

We assume a sea water density of 64 lb/ft^3 and a heat capacity of 1 Btu/lb-$^{\circ}$F, a temperature drop of 3°F for the warm water during passage through the boiler section, and a Rankine-cycle efficiency of η_R for electricity generation in the low-temperature propane-turbine system (see Fig. 14.8-2). The required warm-water flow rate Q (in ft^3/sec) for a

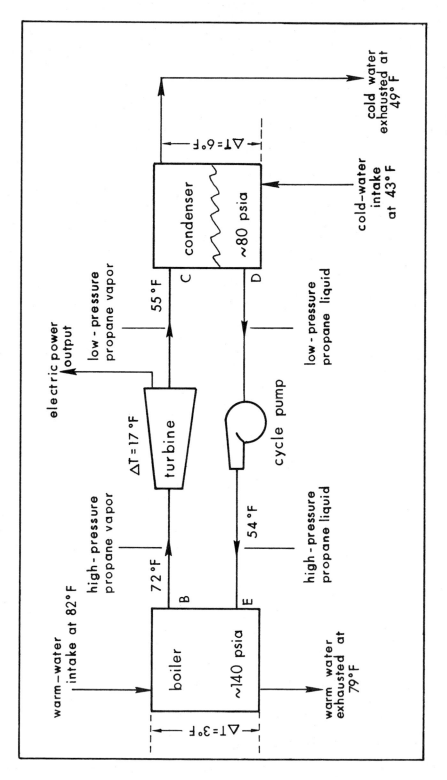

Fig. 14.8-2 Schematic diagram of a solar-sea power plant using propane as the working fluid. The indicated temperature and pressure levels refer to the design proposed by the Andersons in Ref. [4]. Points B, C, D, and E correspond to working fluid states shown in Fig. 14.8-4.

100-Mw$_e$ plant is then determined by using the appropriate terms in Eq. (14.8-1), viz.

$$\underbrace{100 \times 10^3 \ \text{kw}_e}_{\text{power output in kw}_e} = 64 \overbrace{\left(\frac{\text{lb}}{\text{ft}^3}\right) \times 1 \left(\frac{\text{Btu}}{\text{lb-}^\circ\text{F}}\right) \times 3(^\circ\text{F}) \times Q\left(\frac{\text{ft}^3}{\text{sec}}\right)}^{\text{thermal-energy input in Btu/sec}}$$

$$\times \underbrace{\frac{2.78 \times 10^{-7} \ \text{kwh}}{0.949 \times 10^{-3} \ \text{Btu}} \times \frac{3,600 \ \text{sec}}{\text{h}}}_{\text{conversion factors equal to unity}}$$

$$\times \underbrace{\eta_R \left(\frac{\text{kw}_e}{\text{kw}}\right)}_{\substack{\text{Rankine-cycle conversion} \\ \text{efficiency from thermal to} \\ \text{electrical energy}}}$$

or

$$Q = (4.94 \times 10^2/\eta_R) \ \text{ft}^3/\text{sec-100 Mw}_e.$$

As we shall see, a hoped-for approximation to η_R is 90% of the Carnot-cycle efficiency for the propane-Rankine-cycle system. For a secondary cycle operating between a boiler temperature of 72°F and a condenser temperature of 55°F, the estimated Rankine-cycle efficiency then becomes

$$\eta_R = 0.90 \times \frac{(460 + 72) - (460 + 55)}{(460 + 72)} = 2.88 \times 10^{-2}.$$

Hence, the required warm-water flow rate becomes 1.72×10^4 ft^3/sec or 7.72×10^6 gallons of sea water per minute (since 1 gallon = 0.13368 ft^3) for a 100-Mw$_e$ plant. Thus, the water-flow rate is 7.72×10^4 gallons per minute per Mw$_e$ of capacity, which is very much larger than the volumetric water flow rates (4×10^2 to 1.6×10^3 gallons per minute per Mw$_e$ capacity) for cooling land-based fossil-fuel power plants; it is also appreciably larger than the water flow rates handled in hydroelectric plants of equivalent power output. For locations in the Gulf Stream, approximately 40% of the required warm-water flow rate may not have to be pumped. Nevertheless, supplying the warm-water flow rates may represent an important design challenge for the SSPP.

D. A Rankine-Cycle Engine for Converting Thermal to Electrical Energy in the SSPP

A schematic diagram of a Rankine-engine cycle with propane as working fluid is sketched in Fig. 14.8-2. Representative temperature and pressure levels within the working fluid, at "near-optimal" conditions for a Caribbean installation, are also shown in Fig. 14.8-2.

Following the Rankine cycle clockwise from the boiler, we note that the working fluid (propane in the present instance) is evaporated on exposure to the warm intake water. Heat is abstracted from this water, which is thereby cooled from a value of 82°F at the heat-exchanger intake to 79°F at the heat-exchanger outlet. The pressure level in the boiler is maintained at 140 psia. The evaporated propane is heated to 72°F. Temperature gradients across the heat-exchanger walls account for the specified temperature differences.

The working fluid next expands through a turbine while driving the turbine shaft and thereby generating electricity. The propane is cooled 17°F as the result of expansion through the turbine. At the same time, the operating pressure decreases from the initial value of about 140 psia to nearly 80 psia.

At C (see Fig. 14.8-2), propane at about 55°F enters the condenser. This unit is also a heat exchanger. The cold intake water enters at 43°F and exits at 49°F. The energy abstracted from the propane cools this working fluid sufficiently to produce liquefaction at the operating pressure of 80 psia.

Liquid propane at about 80 psia leaves the condenser at D (see Fig. 14.8-2) as the result of application of a cycle pump, which has the function of increasing the pressure level to 140 psia at the boiler intake E (see Fig. 14.8-2). The working fluid has now passed through a complete cycle and returned to its original state.

The net result of cycling propane through the loop shown in Fig. 14.8-2 is the following: thermal energy abstracted from the warm-water flow is used to drive the

turbine and to heat the cold water at the condenser heat exchanger. In a well-designed unit, the thermal-to-mechanical
energy transfer, which is responsible for rotation of the turbine components, is accomplished with an efficiency approaching the Carnot efficiency for an ideal cycle between
the specified high-temperature (boiler) and low-temperature
(condenser) reservoirs. Mechanical-to-electrical energy
conversion is implemented with high efficiency (see below for
details) by using conventional procedures.

The details of the operating cycle will now be described more quantitatively, with a numerical example worked
out for an ammonia Rankine cycle that is analogous to the cycle shown in Fig. 14.8-2.

1. Rankine-Cycle Efficiency[*]

In Figs. 14.8-3a, 14.8-3b, and 14.8-3c, we show the
ideal Rankine cycle in the (temperature-entropy) T-S, (pres-
sure-volume) p-V, and (enthalpy-entropy) H-S planes, respectively. In each diagram, the boiler is located between
stations E and B, the turbine between stations B and C, the
condenser between stations C and D, and the liquid pump between D and E. The intrinsic efficiency, η_R, of the ideal
Rankine cycle is lower than the intrinsic efficiency, η_C, of

---

[*] In this subsection and the following subsection 14.8e, we
assume familiarity with thermodynamics. These subsec-
tions may be deleted by readers who are not interested in
the details of numerical evaluation of SSPP performance.

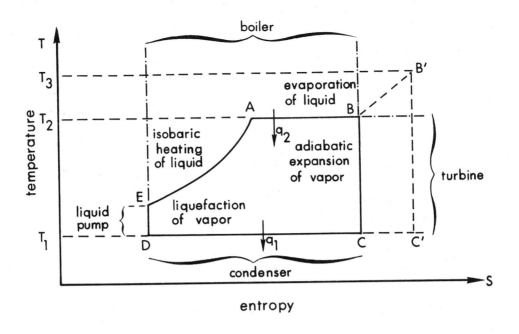

Fig. 14.8-3a The Rankine cycle in the T-S plane; the branch BB'C'C corresponds to the addition of a super-heater.

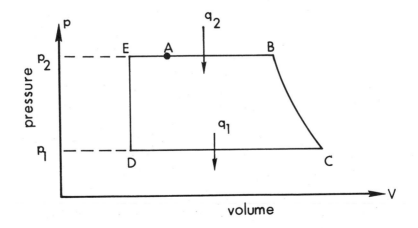

Fig. 14.8-3b The Rankine cycle in the p-V plane.

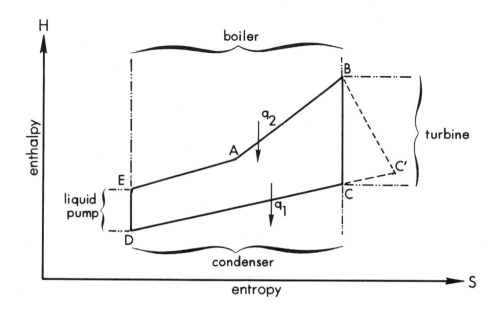

Fig. 14.8-3c The Rankine cycle in the H-S plane (Mollier
diagram); the slopes of constant-pressure
lines equal the temperature according to the
relation $(\partial H/\partial S)_p = T$.

the ideal Carnot cycle, because some of the total heat input
q_2 is added in the boiler below the peak operating temperature (corresponding to the section EA of the working cycle).
The diagram shown in Fig. 14.8-3c is the Mollier diagram,
in which vertical lines represent enthalpy changes and measure the work done while the slopes of lines at constant pressure define the temperature in accord with the thermodynamic relation $(\partial H/\partial S)_p = T$. The Rankine cycle with super-

heater is shown by the branch $BB'C'C$ in Fig. 14.8-3a but is probably not useful for a solar-sea power generating plant.

The ideal Rankine-cycle efficiency is given by the relation

$$\eta_R = (q_2 - q_1)/q_2 < \eta_C = (T_2 - T_1)/T_2, \quad (14.8\text{-}2)$$

where the Carnot-cycle efficiency is determined by the operating temperature levels; with superheater, the ideal cycle efficiency becomes

$$\eta'_R \simeq 1 - [q_1 + T_1(S_{B'} - S_B)]$$
$$(14.8\text{-}3)$$
$$\times [q_2 + (T_3 + T_2)(S_{B'} - S_B)/2]^{-1}.$$

E. The Rankine Cycle Applied to the Use of Ammonia in a Solar-Sea Generator

Zener[5] has proposed the use of an ammonia cycle in the solar-sea generator and has emphasized the fact that the Rankine-cycle efficiency approaches the Carnot-cycle efficiency when relatively little energy is required to heat the liquid to the boiling point (along EA in Figs. 14.8-3a to 14.8-3c) and most of the energy input into the boiler is used for evaporation (AB in Figs. 14.8-3a to 14.8-3c). This novel feature of low-temperature thermal cycles will now be verified in a cycle with ammonia as working fluid operating between achievable temperature limits. In high-temperature cycles, the Rankine engine generally yields about one-half of the Carnot efficiency.

We refer to the Rankine-cycle diagram shown in Fig. 14.8-3b and use the design limits specified below. In the boiler: $T = 75^{\circ}F$, $p = 140$ psia; the boiler is assumed to be located 300 ft below the surface of the ocean. In the condenser: $T = 40^{\circ}F$, $p = 73.3$ psia; the condenser is assumed to be located 175 ft below the surface of the ocean. The liquid-ammonia volume per lbm (= pound of mass) equals 0.0253 ft^3/ lbm along DE, corresponding to 73.3 psia and $40^{\circ}F$.

The work done by the pump (along DE in Figs. 14.8-3a to 14.8-3c) is

$$w_p = (h_E - h_D) + (300 - 175) \text{ ft} \qquad (14.8\text{-}4)$$

$$\times \frac{32.2 \text{ ft/sec}^2}{32.2 \text{ lbm-ft/lbt-sec}^2} \times \frac{1}{778 \text{ ft-lbt/Btu}},$$

where $h_E - h_D$ and w_p are expressed in Btu/lbm with lbt standing for pound-torque. But, for constant volume (and isentropic) pump compression along DE,

$$h_E - h_D = \int_D^E vdp = 0.0253 \frac{\text{ft}^3}{\text{lbm}} \times (140 - 73.3) \frac{\text{lbt}}{\text{in}^2}$$

$$(14.8\text{-}5)$$

$$\times \frac{144 \text{ in}^2}{\text{ft}^2} \times \frac{1}{788 \text{ ft-lbt/Btu}} = 0.308 \frac{\text{Btu}}{\text{lbm}}.$$

It follows from Eq. (14.8-4) that w_p = 0.469 Btu/lbm; also, in view of Eq. (14.8-5), after noting that h_D = 86.8 Btu/lbm,

$$h_E = 87.11 \text{ Btu/lbm.}$$

The heat input required along EB may now be evaluated by noting that

$$q_2 = (h_B - h_A) + (h_A - h_E),$$

where $h_A - h_E$ = 0.161 Btu/lbm represents the enthalpy change required to heat the ammonia to the boiling point. Furthermore, h_B = 629.9 Btu/lbm so that q_2 = (629.9 - 87.11) Btu/lbm = 542.8 Btu/lbm.

If we assume isentropic expansion through the turbine, then the turbine work, w_t, equals $h_B - h_C$. We use the isentropic relation

$$S_B = S_C = 1.2065 \text{ Btu/lbm-}^\circ F$$

to determine the quality (i.e., the mass fraction of vapor-phase material), x, at C. Since all of the ammonia is in gaseous form at B, $S_B = S_{g,B}$ and

$$S_{g,B} = 1.2065 = x_C S_{g,C} + (1 - x)_C S_{\ell,C}$$

$$= S_{g,C} + (1 - x)_C (S_{\ell,C} - S_{g,C}),$$

where the subscripts g and ℓ identify the gaseous and liquid states. Since $S_{g,C}$ = 1.2618 Btu/lbm-°F and $S_{g,C} - S_{\ell,C}$ = 1.0733 Btu/lbm-°F, $(1 - x)_C$ = 0.0515 and, therefore,

$$h_C = h_{g,C} - (1 - x)_C (h_{g,C} - h_{\ell,C})$$

$$= 623.0 - (0.0515) \times 536.2 = 595.4 \text{ Btu/lbm.}$$

The turbine work is thus found to be $w_t = h_B - h_C$ = 629.9 - 595.4 = 34.5 Btu/lbm.

The condenser heat output is $q_1 = h_C - h_D$ = 595.4 - 86.8 = 508.6 Btu/lbm.

The applicable Rankine-cycle efficiency is finally obtained from Eq. (14.8-2). It is found to be

$$\eta_R = (542.8 - 508.6)/542/8 = 0.0630$$

while the Carnot efficiency is seen to be

$$\eta_C = (535 - 500)/535 = 0.0654.$$

Thus, the low-temperature Rankine cycle with ammonia as working fluid, as proposed for use with the solar-sea generator (SSPP), has an efficiency equal to 97.5% of the Carnot efficiency.* Since the plant has been estimated[3] to use

---

* The result $\eta_R \simeq \eta_C$ is obtained because only a small portion of the energy required for evaporation of the working fluid is used to heat the working fluid to the boiling point.

about 14% of its output for operation, the overall efficiency
(including pump and turbine losses) is reduced to about 86%
of the Carnot efficiency; pump and turbine losses are briefly
considered in the following subsection.

F.   The Rankine Cycle Used by the Andersons[3]

In the T-S plane, the real working cycle of the
Andersons[3] with propane as the working fluid assumes the
non-ideal form sketched in Fig. 14.8-4, where we also show
the applicable temperature values; the Mollier diagram of
Fig. 14.8-3c must be similarly modified for the real cycle
with a non-vertical leg B-C replacing the line B-C (see Fig.
14.8-3c).

Let η_{cp} = cycle pump efficiency (~ 0.90), η_t = turbine efficiency (~ 0.85), η_g = electrical-generator efficiency
(~ 0.98); we note that, for the lower operating temperature
limits indicated in Fig. 14.8-4, the Carnot efficiency becomes

$$\eta_C = [(72 + 460) - (54 + 460)]/(72 + 460) = 3.38 \times 10^{-2}.$$

For the specified cycle-pump, turbine and electrical-generator efficiencies, the overall cycle efficiency is expected to be
about $0.75 \, \eta_C$. Actually, the Andersons[4] and Zener[5] have
used a value for η_R close to that of η_C. The total energy
available from the system under discussion is $(9.05 \times 10^8$
cal/sec) $\times (4.187$ joule/cal$) = 3.8 \times 10^9$ watt. Of this energy,

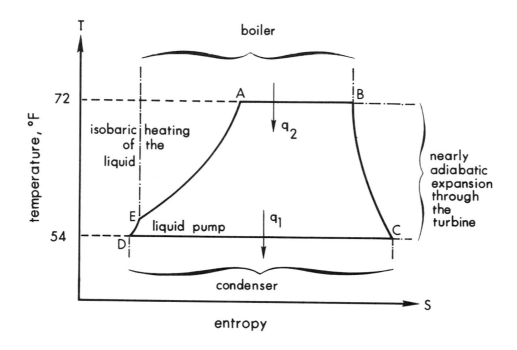

Fig. 14.8-4 Schematic diagram of the approximate Rankine-
cycle used in the solar-sea energy source.

the SSPP converts to electricity about $(3.8 \times 10^9$ watt$) \times (\eta_{cp}$
$= 0.90) \times (\eta_t = 0.85) \times (\eta_g = 0.98) \times \eta_R \simeq 10^8$ watt$_e$ or 100,000
kw$_e$ for $\eta_R \approx \eta_C = 3.38 \times 10^{-2}$.

G. Economic Considerations for the Andersons' SSPP

The Andersons[4] concluded that, although Claude's
attempt at economical power generation failed, it was possible to succeed for the following reasons: propane (like ammonia, which is favored by Zener[5] for a Rankine cycle

operating between somewhat higher temperature limits) is a nearly ideal, non-corrosive working fluid; the development of a floating power plant allows the use of relatively short water lines, thereby eliminating a major cost item; the use of a buoyant system, with nearly equal internal and external pressures, allows construction of low-cost, flat-plate heat exchangers; undersea transmission of power is a demonstrated technology at \$30 to \$50/kw$_e$ installation cost for a transmission line-length of a few miles; alternatively, the generated power could be used[5] to electrolyze water so that the power-transmission problem becomes modified to a gas-transmission problem; stable floating platforms can be built without difficulty; construction and maintenance of undersea structures, as well as suspension of long pipes in sea water, represent developed technologies for some applications.

The Andersons' summary of estimated systems costs for the propane cycle is given in Table 14.8-1. We note that the main-plant cost ($\$9.56 \times 10^6$) corresponds to about 57% of the total estimated investment cost. The major separate cost components in the main plant are the condenser (\$2.45 $\times 10^6$) and the boiler ($\$2.4 \times 10^6$), the generator at about \$12/kw$_e$ ($\$1.235 \times 10^6$), and water pumps for the boiler and condenser ($\$1.46 \times 10^6$). The structure and assembly cost is $\$4.21 \times 10^6$ (about 25% of the total). These cost estimates agree with the rough guideline that the total cost $\simeq 1.6 \times$ (component costs).

Since the estimated total plant cost was about \$16.6 $\times 10^6$ for a design power output of 10^5 kw$_e$, the Andersons

Table 14.8-1 Cost summary for the Andersons' 1966 design: cost per kw_e = \$166; yearly owning and operating cost = \$1,873,000; rated yearly capacity = 8.76×10^8 kwh_e; estimated yearly output = 6.57 $\times 10^8$ kwh_e; cost per kwh_e = \$0.00285. Reproduced from Ref. [4].

Components	Cost, $
main plant	\$ 9,560,000
auxiliaries	443,200
structure and assembly	4,210,000
assembly of cold pipe	262,000
engineering and supervision	724,000
contingency	1,448,000
total	\$16,647,200

arrived at a cost of \$166/kw_e for the installation. The yearly energy output capacity becomes 10^5 kw_e $\times 8.76 \times 10^3$ h/y or 8.76×10^8 kwh_e/y. Assuming 75% output of rated capacity, the actual yearly energy output is 6.57×10^8 kwh_e/y. The yearly owning and operating cost was estimated at 11.25% of the total plant cost and equals \$$1.87 \times 10^6$ so that the actual generating cost becomes \$$1.87 \times 10^6/6.57 \times 10^8$ kwh_e = \$2.85 $\times 10^{-3}$ per kwh_e = 2.85 mills/kwh_e. If the plant-to-shore transmission cost is as low as \$50/kw_e and is similarly capitalized, we should increase the energy-cost production estimate to $2.85 \times (21.6/16.6)$ mills/kwh_e = 3.7 mills/kwh_e.

The Andersons' analysis of costs is probably optimistic for the following reasons:

(a) The incremental plant-to-shore costs for electrical-energy transmission have not been included explicitly.

Inclusion of these costs raises the energy-production estimate to 3.7 mills/kwh$_e$ for short transmission lines and to much larger values for long transmission lines.

(b) The overall Rankine-cycle efficiencies will approximate only $(3/4)\eta_C$ so that the final energy-production cost estimate becomes at least 4.9 mills/kwh$_e$.

(c) The Andersons used yearly owning and operating costs equal to 11.25% of the total plant cost. This estimate is based on experience with conventional land-based utility stations. It may be highly optimistic for a buoyant salt-water installation. If we define the yearly owning and operating cost for the solar-sea energy source to be X%, then the generating cost in mills/kwh$_e$ must be multiplied by the factor (X/11.25).

In summary, it appears that a more conservative 1966 estimate for the cost of producing solar-sea power in the Andersons' 100,000-kw$_e$ installation using propane as the working fluid would have been

$$C = (2.85 \text{ mills/kwh}_e) \left[\frac{(\$16.6 + Tr) \times 10^6}{\$16.6 \times 10^6} \right]$$

$$\times \left(\frac{4}{3} \right) \times \left(\frac{X}{11.25} \right),$$

where Tr = incremental sea-to-shore transmission cost for 100,000 kw$_e$ and X = an as yet unknown percentage of capital investment required for yearly owning and operating expenses in a solar-sea power plant.

Representative distances from shore for favorable SSPP locations are the following:[6] 1 km off the Florida coast; 2 km off the coasts of Cuba, Jamaica, Haiti, and some other Caribbean locations; 3 km off Venezuela; 32 km off the coasts of Iran and Pakistan; 65 km off the east coast of India, the northeast corner of Australia, and Cameroun; 100 km or more off the northern coasts of Brazil, Surinam and most of Australia.

H.   Current Developments

Since the solar-sea power plant at 3 to 8 mills/kwh$_e$ is clearly competitive with energy derived from other sources, whereas theoretical estimates greater than about 20 mills/kwh$_e$ are less interesting, it is imperative to perform careful systems-optimization studies for a variety of working fluids (e.g., C_3H_8, NH_3, freon, isobutane, etc.), before additional large-scale field tests are instituted. A serious theoretical evaluation, with careful consideration for optimized component design, was begun in 1973 by C. Zener and his colleagues[7] at the Carnegie-Mellon University and by W. E. Heronemus and his collaborators at the University of Massachusetts. Definition of two complete systems de-

---

[6]A. Lavi and C. Zener, "Energy," IEEE Spectrum 10, 22-27, October 1973.

[7]C. Zener, A. Lavi, R. Rothfus, F. McMichael, and C. C. Wu, "Solar Sea Power," NSF/RANN project reports, 1973-1974, Carnegie-Mellon University, Pittsburgh, Pa.

signs, under grants from the National Science Foundation, was initiated in mid-1974 by industrial teams headed by the Lockheed Corporation and by TRW. The mid-1974 plan called for tests at the 25-Mw_e level by 1980 and subsequent construction of a demonstration plant. Configurations other than that shown in Fig. 14.8-1 were being considered. In these, the condenser and the boiler may be at the same ocean level or the condenser may even be placed below the boiler. Both moored and freely floating designs may be possible.

It is apparent that no real progress in SSPP development can be expected until after implementation of significant field tests.

I. Cost Estimates Available for OTEC in 1976

Both J. H. Anderson, Sr., and Zener have noted that costs for the SSPP vary roughly inversely as the cube of the available temperature difference between the warm and cold water that is available for application. Zener has emphasized that the gross power output for an optimized system with fixed area available for heat transfer is proportional to (a) the Carnot efficiency (which is a linear function of ΔT), (b) the mass flow rate of fluid through the boundary layer over the heat-transfer surface (which may be shown to be proportional to ΔT), and (c) the rate of heat transfer by conduction per unit area per unit time across the boiler and condenser heat-exchanger surfaces (which also varies linearly with ΔT). Thus, the gross power is approximately proportional to ΔT^3 and, therefore, the cost of generating electricity varies roughly as $(\Delta T)^{-3}$.

Systems analyses and preliminary designs performed in three independent studies have yielded significantly different configurations, capital-cost estimates and busbar costs for electrical energy. The results (see Table 14.8-2) have been included in a paper presented at a Conference on "Sharing the Sun! Solar Technology in the Seventies," A Joint Conference 1976 of the American Section, International Solar Energy Society, and the Solar Energy Society of Canada, Inc. [8] In their classical design study performed in 1965, the Andersons had arrived at capital costs of $166/kw$_e$ and electricity costs of 3 mills/kwh$_e$; at a 7% average annual inflation rate between 1965 and 1976, the corresponding 1976 estimates are $350/kw$_e$ and 6.3 mills/kwh$_e$, i.e., well within a factor of two of the entries appearing in the third column of Table 14.8-2.

The following critical studies had not yet been performed by 1976: biofouling of low-temperature heat exchangers in tropical ocean waters, long-term operation of of low-temperature secondary cycles, long-term collection of cold, deep-ocean waters.

---

[8]The Conference was held at Winnipeg, Manitoba, Canada, August 15-20, 1976. The data summarized in Table 14.8-2 have been abstracted from a paper by G. L. Dugger, E. J. Francis, and W. H. Avery on "Technical and Economic Feasibility of Ocean Thermal Energy Conversion."

Table 14.8-2 OTEC cost estimates in 1976.

	Lockheed Ocean Systems, Bechtel Corporation, T. Y. Lin International	TRW Ocean and Energy Systems, Global Marine Development, United Engineers and Constructors	Applied Physics Laboratory, Sun Shipbuilding and Dry Dock Co., Hydronautics, Inc., Woods Hole Oceanographic Institution, Avondale Shipyards, Inc., Kaiser Aluminum and Chemical Co.
Study team			
Design features	Anchored configuration, made primarily of reinforced concrete; $\Delta T = 33.5°F$; Ti-tubes used in heat exchangers; net power output 160 Mw$_e$; 38-y systems life with survival in hurricane belts.	Floating, cylindrical surface vessel with shrouded-pipe water jets; 100 Mw$_e$; $\Delta T = 40°F$; Ti-tubes used in heat exchangers; 40-y life.	Symmetric floating platform located around a central, reinforced-concrete water pipe; Al-tubes; $\Delta T = 43°F$; 100 Mw$_e$.
Capital costs and modifications	$2,660/kw$_e$ for the first 25 plants; for $\Delta T = 38°F$, power output rises to 250 Mw$_e$.	$2,100/kw$_e$ for the first plant with possible reduction to $1,100/kw$_e$ by the fifth or sixth plant.	$1,130/kw$_e$ initially and $566/kw$_e$ later on.
Busbar cost of electrical energy	20 mills/kwh$_e$ for $\Delta T = 38°F$ with Al-coil heat exchangers and 10% interest rate.	35 mills/kwh$_e$ initially with reduction to 20 mills/kwh$_e$ with municipal funding by the fifth or sixth plant.	10 mills/kwh$_e$ for mature designs.

J.   Environmental-Impact Assessments of OTEC
      Development

A major worldwide development of OTEC will have
a profound effect on atmospheric cooling and perhaps also
on the atmospheric CO_2 concentration because the amounts of
ocean water pumped per year from depths of 2,000 to 4,000
ft (depending on location) will be very large. The OTEC
condensers, which will normally be located above the boilers,
may be brought close to the surface, thereby assuring not
only significant ocean upwelling but also introduction of relatively cold water into the surface layers of tropical oceans.

Preliminary designs of OTEC systems indicate that
about 10^2 ft^3/sec of cold water will be pumped per Mw_e of
power output. A worldwide estimate of electrical power requirements for the year 2025 is about 6×10^6 Mw_e. If one-
half of this power were produced by using OTEC, 3×10^8
ft^3/sec or 9.46×10^{15} ft^3/y $\simeq 2.7 \times 10^{14}$ m^3/y of cold
water would be incidentally pumped to service the conden-
sers of the secondary (Rankine) power-cycle systems used
in electricity generation. Since the surface area of the
oceans is about 3.6×10^{14} m^2, we find that the defined
large-scale use of OTEC would contribute a layer of cold
water about one meter in depth to the ocean surface. This
value may be compared with an estimate of about 4 m/y
corresponding to normal upwelling.

i.   Atmospheric cooling

The thermal capacity of the ocean water pumped per

year is about $(2.7 \times 10^{14} \text{ m}^3/\text{y}) \times (1 \text{ cal/g-}^\circ\text{C}) \times (1 \text{ g/cm}^3)$ $\times (10^6 \text{ cm}^3/\text{m}^3) = 2.7 \times 10^{20} \text{ cal/}^\circ\text{C-y}$. Heating the cold water to the normal ocean surface temperature requires a temperature rise of about $30^\circ\text{F} = 16.7^\circ\text{C}$ and the corresponding thermal capacity of the pumped cold water for complete accommodation is thus $4.5 \times 10^{21} \text{ cal/y}$. At a worldwide energy utilization rate from fossil and nuclear fuels of $1.2 \times 10^{18} \text{ Btu/y} \simeq 3 \times 10^{20} \text{ cal/y}$, the thermal capacity of the pumped water associated with $3 \times 10^6 \text{ Mw}_e$ exceeds the total thermal energy released by about a factor of 15 and, if a mixed technology involving 50% OTEC ($\sim 2 \times 10^7 \text{ Mw}_e$) and 50% nuclear or fossil fuels were used, by about a factor of 100 while upwelling would amount to $\sim 2.5 \text{ m/y}$.

While the details of the thermal exchanges and cooling mechanisms are unclear, it does appear likely that large-scale OTEC development will offer an effective technology for transferring man-made heat addition from the atmosphere to the oceans.

ii. Influence on CO_2 concentration

The effect of man-made upwelling corresponding to 1 m/y or more on atmosphere-ocean CO_2-exchange requires careful study. The forced upwelling of deep ocean waters with 15% more dissolved carbon dioxide at depth than in the ocean surface layers is a potential source of CO_2. At the same time, the induced convective mixing of ocean waters to a depth of about 1,000 m with the atmosphere may transfer atmospheric CO_2 to the ocean.

Depending on their origin, the cold waters that are pumped upward to serve as heat-exchange medium for the condensers of the secondary power cycle used in OTEC may be rich in nutrients such as phosphorus and nitrogen and deficient in oxygen. Thus, there is the possibility of using the pumped ocean water in large-scale mariculture. The associated plant growth will remove CO_2 from the atmosphere.

iii. Conclusions

Large-scale OTEC development may afford important means (a) for ameliorating the influence of man-made heat addition on atmospheric temperature changes by using the oceans as a heat sink, (b) for reducing atmospheric CO_2 concentrations both by accelerating transfer of CO_2 from the atmosphere to deeper ocean layers and by facilitating mariculture in relatively barren oceans and (c) for increasing atmospheric CO_2 concentrations by bringing supersaturated ocean waters from considerable depths to the ocean surface.

The quantitative long-term impacts of large-scale OTEC development are unclear and require careful study. Climatic impacts may well turn out to be of major magnitude.

14.9   Low-Temperature Thermal Cycles Serving the Dual
        Purpose of Prototype Experiment for the SSPP and
        Bottoming Cycles for Coastally-Based Generating
        Stations[*]

The investment costs of prototype experiments for
low-temperature thermal cycles may be greatly reduced by
making use of warm-water effluents that are a by-product of
the cooling systems of existing base-load electrical power
generating stations in coastal regions. We present estimates
on the possible scale of these development studies for the
San Diego coastal region.

A minimal scale for a useful sea-based study corresponds to about the 10-Mw_e level, i.e., a level equal to about
one percent of a modern, full-size generating station. It is
our purpose in this discussion to emphasize that important
savings (amounting to about 25% of total cost for capital investment and additional substantial savings associated with
a favorable logistic arrangement) may be accomplished in
these studies by utilizing the warm-water effluents in conveniently accessible U.S. coastal regions. The only component
of the sea-based solar-sea power plant which is not required

---

[*]The material presented in this Section has been reproduced
from a note "A Solar-Sea Generator Prototype Experiment
Using the Warm-Water Effluents from Power Stations in the
San Diego Region" by S. S. Penner and D. Hogan, Energy
Center, University of California, San Diego, La Jolla,
California, May 1974.

is the warm surface-water collection system. The construction of this feature of the SSPP probably does not constitute
a critical problem. By eliminating the necessity for construction of the warm-water collection system, the prototype
experiment can be performed in conveniently-accessible
Pacific Coast or Atlantic Coast waters, while the available
funds are fully allocated to the cold-water collection system
and to a study of the critical heat transfer units in the boiler
and condenser for the required low-temperature Rankine cycles; these represent the principal new engineering-design
features of the SSPP.

A. Sitings of Prototype Experiments in the San Diego Region

The power-plant capacity is determined by the hot-
water flow rate (Q in ft^3/sec), the temperature drop across
the boiler (ΔT in $^\circ$F), and the efficiency η_R of the Rankine
cycle used for the low-temperature working fluid. We as-
sume (compare Section 14.8E) that the Rankine-cycle efficiency η_R should approximate about 90% of the Carnot-cycle
efficiency. From the condition of energy conservation, it
is easily shown [compare Eq. (14.8-1)] that the required
water-flow rate per Mw$_e$ of capacity is

$$Q = 14.8/\eta_R \, \Delta T = 16.4/\eta_C \Delta T \ \ \text{ft}^3/\text{sec-Mw}_e.$$

We list in Table 14.9-1 three power plants in the San Diego region, each of which provides output water about $20^\circ F$ above the intake water. Surface water temperatures vary between winter lows of about $53^\circ F$ and summer highs of about $69^\circ F$, thus suggesting maximum available water temperatures of 73 to $89^\circ F$, depending on the season. At a depth of about 1,800 ft, the summer and winter water temperatures converge to about $42^\circ F$. For a temperature drop of $6^\circ F$ across the condenser, a minimum operating temperature difference of $25^\circ F$ remains available throughout the year, while temperature differences of more than $35^\circ F$ may be employed for well over 6 months of the year. For an upper water temperature of $82^\circ F$, a $4^\circ F$ temperature drop across the boiler, and a lower working-fluid temperature of $48^\circ F$, $\eta_C = 5.58 \times 10^{-2}$; for a maximum water temperature of $73^\circ F$ under otherwise the same conditions, $\eta_C = 3.96 \times 10^{-2}$. The corresponding values of Q range from 73.5 to 103.5 $ft^3/sec\text{-}Mw_e$. The SSPP prototype power rating for these water-flow limits is listed in Table 14.9-1 for three power stations. Reference to the data of Table 14.9-1 shows that a prototype experiment at the 7.3- to 7.8-Mw_e power-level is currently feasible at a number of locations during the winter months while power levels of 11.4 to 12.2 Mw_e are accessible during the warmer periods.

The available upper (69 to $85^\circ F$) and lower ($\sim 48^\circ F$) temperature levels determine the choice of working fluid. In the California coastal region, one of the following fluids may well find application in the prototype Rankine-cycle

Table 14.9-1 Effluent warm-water flows from electric power stations in the San Diego region; reproduced from Penner and Hogan, Ref. [1].

Plant	Temperature rise of water above the intake value, °F	Warm-water flow rate, ft³/sec	SSPP prototype power rating in Mw$_e$ for Q =	
			73.5 ft³/sec-Mwe	103.5 ft³/sec-Mwe
San Onofre nuclear generating station (current)	20	778	10.6	7.5
San Onofre nuclear generating station (projected)	20	>1,900	>25.9	>18.4
Encina power plant (current)	~20	750	10.2	7.3
Encina power plant (projected)	~20	1,180	16.1	11.4
South Bay power plant (current)	~23	802	10.9	7.8

experiment: ammonia, propane, butane, freon-12, methyl chloride, sulfur dioxide, or isobutane.

B. Bottoming Cycles for Coastally-Based Power Stations

In addition to serving as a 1% scale prototype experiment for the SSPP, implementation of the low-temperature Rankine-cycle design should yield useful information concerning the following two subjects: (a) the desirability of planning construction of future large-scale power stations in coastal regions in conjunction with one or more cycles using low-temperature working fluids and (b) the environmental impact (especially on fish productivity) associated with uplifting of cold water from considerable depths.

We note that the temperature drop per pass through a low-temperature cycle is relatively small and that it is, therefore, possible to utilize multiple-pass systems with a small loss in efficiency. By adopting this procedure, it should be possible to obtain a 10% or greater increase in generating capacity for coastally-based power stations through the addition of sequential, low-temperature working cycles. The development of low-temperature thermal cycles as additions to utility generating stations is not under active current development.

14.10 Integration of Solar Electric Technologies into
       Utility Networks[1]

Thermal-energy storage to utilize off-peak utility
generation-capacity leads to savings that exceed capital costs
by factors of 2 to 4.[2] Magnesite bricks or other materials
that may be heated to 1,200°F are desirable storage materials because of the importance of the high temperatures required for thermal storage for off-peak electrical generation. It may be easily seen that the intermittent solar-electric systems are not competitive with off-peak energy-storage
systems because the allowable annual capital cost per unit
area of solar collector area, C, must be less than the product of collected and converted solar energy per unit area
and the cost of supplying off-peak electricity, viz.

$$C(\$/m^2\text{-}y) < (300 \text{ kwh}_e/m^2\text{-}y)$$

$$\times (\$10 \times 10^{-3}/\text{kwh}_e) \qquad (14.10\text{-}1)$$

or $C < \$3/m^2$-y. In Eq. (14.10-1), a high value of 300

[1] J. G. Asbury and R. O. Mueller, "Solar Energy and
    Electric Utilities: Should They Be Interfaced?," Science
    195, 445-456 (1977).

[2] J. G. Asbury et al, "Assessment of Energy Storage Tech-
    nologies and Systems (Phase 1): Electric Storage Heating,
    Storage Air Conditioning and Storage Hot Water Heaters,"
    Argonne National Laboratory, Publication No. ANL/ES-54,
    Argonne, Illinois, October 1976.

kwh_e/m^2-y has been used for the collected solar energy per year that is converted to electricity while the cost of supplying off-peak electricity (10 mills/kwh_e) has been set equal to the sum of base-load fuel cost of $1/$10^6$ Btu ($\simeq$ \$8.5 $\times 10^{-3}$/kwh_e at 40% conversion efficiency to electricity) and base-load operating and maintenance costs.[1] At a capital recovery rate of 10% per year, the allowable capital cost for collectors is seen to be only \$30/m^2 or about \$3/ft^2.

If pricing and scheduling sequences are implemented which eliminate off-peak electricity entirely, solar-electric systems at substantially higher costs will, of course, be allowable. Thus, if the cost of electricity is \$70 $\times 10^{-3}$/kwh_e, an analysis similar to that given above suggests an allowable cost of about \$21/ft^2 for both the solar collector and the corresponding required energy-storage system.

Using analogous arguments, it has been shown that heat-pump-assisted solar-collection systems will always require lower solar-collector costs per unit area than systems without heat pumps for break-even.[1]

CHAPTER 15

ENERGY FROM WINDMILLS

The utilization of wind energy in the United States began with the introduction of the American windmill in 1854 by Daniel Halladay. Shortly thereafter, the water-pump windmill became a familiar site in Midwestern rural areas. A mature technology for the production of electricity by wind power existed in Europe by the early part of the twentieth century. Because the U.S. had abundant fossil-fuel resources suitable for inexpensive production of electrical energy, interest in the generation of electricity from wind power did not grow as it had in Europe. The development of the airplane propeller led to renewed interest in the utilization of wind power in the nineteen forties. The production of large-scale wind-power systems in the U.S. peaked during World War II and died shortly after termination of the Smith-Putnam Wind-Turbine Experiment in 1945. Today, nearly three decades later, active work on the generation of electrical power from the wind has been reborn.

15.1   General Characteristics of the Wind

The availability of natural winds is a highly variable function of location and time. In general, both flatplains regions and coastal regions experience winds which are characterized by positive velocity gradients with height, which typically lead to wind velocities at altitudes near five hundred feet that are about 1.35 to 1.45 times the wind velocities observed at heights near fifty feet.[1] Mountainous regions and especially mountain crests experience, on the average, stronger surface winds than flat and coastal regions. According to an extensive wind-power feasibility study,[2] mountain-top areas often show negative wind-velocity gradients, leading to lower wind velocities at altitudes of several hundred feet than at one hundred feet.

The daily wind pattern is highly variable. The wind speed and direction may change over wide ranges during a given day and from day to day. Daily periodic wind patterns recur in some areas. For example, some coastal regions regularly experience higher wind velocities during the day than at night.

The monthly average speed and direction of the wind for a given area are surprisingly predictable. In marked

---

[1] P. H. Thomas, Electric Power from the Wind, Federal Power Commission, Washington, D.C., 1945.

[2] Final Report on the Wind Turbine, Office of Production Research and Development, War Production Board, Washington, D.C., 1946.

contrast with the daily wind patterns, monthly average wind patterns vary only slightly throughout the year and from year to year. This predictability on a monthly basis may be explained, in part, by the fact that most wind variations can be accounted for by meteorological conditions which have relatively short durations. Because of these short persistence times, daily fluctuations tend to cancel when monthly averages are computed.

In any given location, the monthly average wind velocity is only rarely less than one-half of the annual average. Most of the monthly average wind velocities fall within 15% of the annual average.[1] The average wind velocity for the year is, as would be expected, even more stable than the monthly averages. The annual average wind velocity for any given location seldom fluctuates by more than 10 to 15% from the long-time annual average wind velocity.[1]

The stability of the monthly average wind patterns and of the annual average wind patterns is of great importance in the utilization of wind power. The output reliability of a wind-power system is directly dependent on the stability of the average wind patterns. The economics of wind-power systems are significantly influenced by the consistency of the average wind patterns. Capital costs of a wind-power system are strongly affected by the costs of energy-storage systems that may be required because of variations in wind velocities. Accordingly, the unit cost of energy generated from a given wind-power system depends on the consistency of the average wind patterns (see Section 15.6 for a more detailed discussion of this topic).

15.2   Methods Used in the Past for Extracting Power from the Wind

Many different windmill designs have been constructed to extract power from the wind. The earliest known references to windmills relate to a Persian millwright in 644 A.D. and to windmills in Seistan, Persia, in 915 A.D.

These early windmills, which were used for moving water, consisted of several sails that rotated on a vertical axis. A windmill with sails or vanes mounted on a vertical axis is called a vertical windmill. The earliest horizontal windmills (windmills with a horizontal axis of rotation) appeared during the twelfth century. By the end of the fifteenth century, many horizontal windmills had been constructed in Europe for grinding of grain and raising of water.

During the eighteenth century, important design variations were developed for horizontal windmills. The earliest designs were again used for grinding grain and raising water. Later designs were built for sawing timber, pressing oil from seeds, and paper making. An example of an early eighteenth century windmill is the Dutch plane-vane design (see Fig. 15.2-1). This design had 8 to 12 sails mounted on an axle which was inclined upward from the horizontal at angles of 5 to 15 degrees. The sails were typically constructed from sailcloth stretched over a wooden frame. The individual

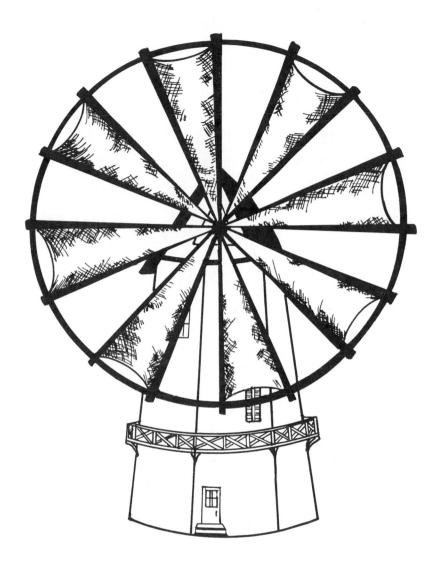

Fig. 15.2-1 Schematic diagram of an early eighteenth century Dutch plane-vane windmill.

sails were flat planes and inclined at a constant angle to the
direction of rotation.   Late eighteenth century windmills were
characterized by 4 to 6 whips or arms that supported long
rectangular sails constructed from either sailcloth or nar-

row wood slats. The whips were often 30 to 40 feet in length.
The sails were typically 5 to 6 feet in width and 80 to 85% of
the whip length.

Many windmills were built and operated in Denmark,
England, Germany, and the Netherlands during the eighteenth
century. In 1750, the Netherlands alone had between 6,000
and 8,000 windmills in operation.[1] Windmills were used
in Northern Germany for centuries. It has been estimated[1]
that the number of windmills in use in Germany was about
18,000 in 1895, 17,000 in 1907, 11,400 in 1914, and between
4,000 and 5,000 in 1933.

The classical 4-vaned windmill employed for electric-
power generation was developed in Denmark by LaCour in
1890. LaCour's experimental mill (see Fig. 15.2-2) involved
the first application of momentum extraction from the wind
to generate electric power. The LaCour windmill used patent sails (i.e., sails constructed of hinged wood shutters
which could be controlled remotely) that were oriented by
twin fantails and mounted on a steel tower. The sails were
constructed with a continuously changing angle of twist of
the type used in an airplane propeller. LaCour's original
mill had a 75-foot rotor diameter, an 8.25-foot sail width,
and powered two 9-kw_e generators.[1]

The multi-bladed (16 to 32 vanes) American windmill,
once commonly used for pumping water in rural areas, was

---

[1] E. W. Golding, The Generation of Electricity by Wind
Power, Philosophical Library, New York, 1956.

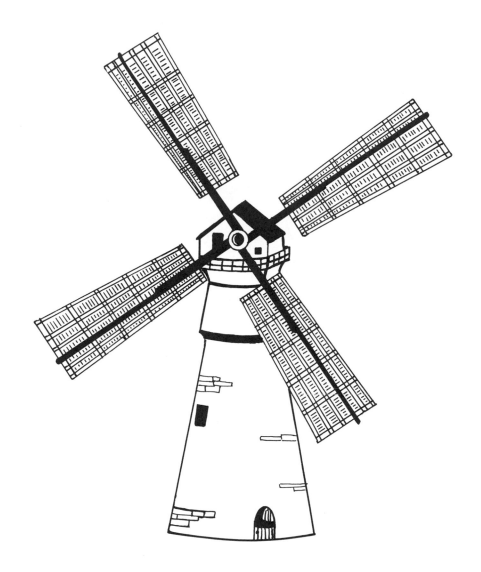

Fig. 15.2-2 Schematic diagram of a LaCour windmill.

introduced into the United States during 1854. This design
(see Fig. 15.2-3) was made of many small steel vanes or
blades set radially to produce a wheel-like configuration.
These windmills incorporated automatic governers for the
control of yaw by a tail vane. The torque output of the wind-

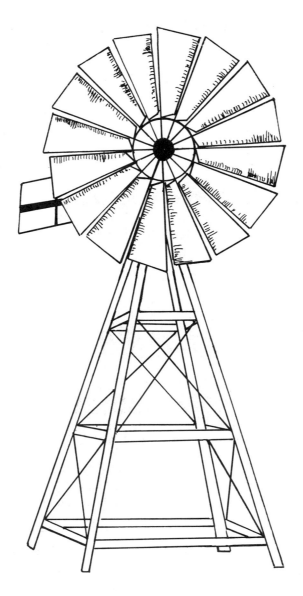

Fig. 15.2-3 Schematic diagram of an early American windmill.

mill was, to some extent, determined by mounting the multi-
vaned, wheel-like configuration off-center with respect to
the vertical yaw axis. In this special arrangement, increases
in wind velocity will rotate the windmill on a vertical axis,

thereby reducing the effective frontal area and, therefore, the rotational speed and torque.

During the early part of the twentieth century, two quite different vertical windmill designs were developed. One of the designs, known as the Savonius[2] rotor (see Fig. 15.2-4), was formed by cutting a cylinder into two semicylindrical surfaces, moving these surfaces sideways along the cutting plane to form a rotor with cross-section in the form of the letter "S", placing a shaft in the center of the rotor, and closing the end surfaces with circular end plates. The other vertical windmill design, patented in 1927 by Darrieus (see Fig. 15.2-5), consisted of two thin airfoils with one end mounted on the lower end of a vertical shaft and the other end mounted on the upper end of the same shaft. The resulting configuration is nearly circular in shape, with the airfoils describing the circumference and the shaft describing a vertical diameter. The feasibility of this design for single-family electric-power generation is currently under study at the NASA Langley Research Center. Operation of both Savonius and Darrieus windmills is independent of the wind direction.

Another design for extracting power from the wind became popular toward the end of World War I. This design, called a wind turbine, was basically a propeller with slender, tapered blades (see Fig. 15.2-6). Various designs of wind turbines were developed at nearly the same time in Germany,

[2]S. J. Savonius, "The S-Rotor and Its Applications," Mechanical Engineering 53, 333-338 (1931).

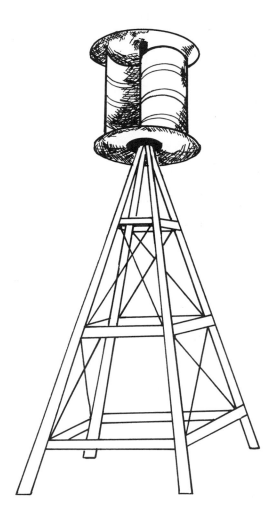

Fig. 15.2-4 Schematic diagram of a Savonius rotor windmill
            design.

France, the U.S.S.R., and the United States. Many different designs of wind turbines using two or more blades have
since been considered. The two- and, possibly, the three-
bladed designs appear to be the most suitable for electric-

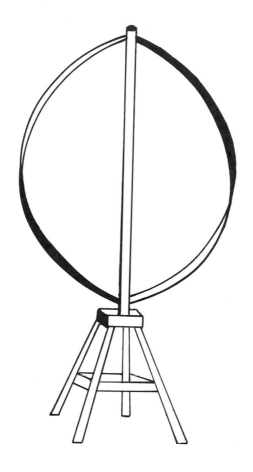

Fig. 15.2-5 Schematic diagram of a Darrieus vertical-axis
windmill.

power generation. In general, higher rotational speeds may
be obtained with a two-bladed design. However, the addition
of more blades may increase the starting torque, reduce the
tip losses, and improve the smoothness of operation. The
largest presently operating wind turbine is a three-bladed
200-kw$_e$ design that operated successfully near Gedser,
Denmark, from 1957 to 1967 (see Fig. 15.2-6). This design

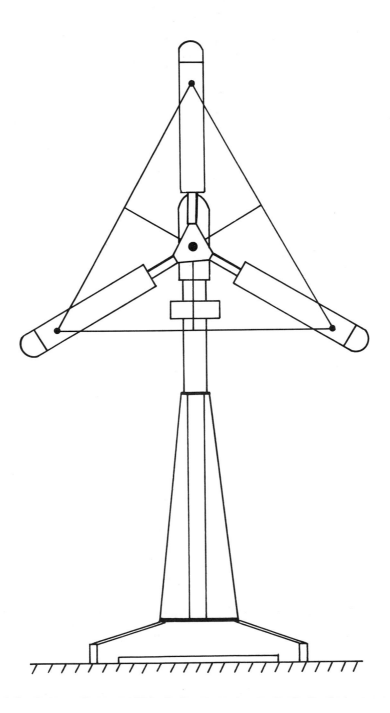

Fig. 15.2-6 Schematic diagram of the three-bladed wind
turbine which is located near Gedser, Denmark.

has 12-meter blades mounted on a 25-meter tower.[3] The largest wind turbine that has been constructed and operated was a two-bladed 1,250-kw$_e$ experimental design which was in use intermittently near Rutland, Vermont, during the period from 1941 to 1945. This turbine had 65-ft blades and was mounted on a 107-ft tower (see Section 15.4 for a more detailed discussion of this experiment).

15.3 Theoretical and Actual Efficiencies of Windmills

The efficiency of a windmill is defined to be the ratio of the power extracted from the wind to the power contained in the wind that passes through the swept area of the windmill. A theoretical maximum efficiency for wind-power extraction devices may be calculated from one-dimensional aerodynamic flow theory. A. Betz of Göttingen first obtained a theoretical expression for the maximum windmill efficiency in 1927.

The aerodynamic theory that describes the action of a windmill rotor on the airflow is called the simple Rankine-Froude momentum theory. In this theory, it is assumed that the rotor may be physically replaced by an actuator disk having an infinite number of blades and producing a uniform change in the velocity of the airflow passing through the disk.

---

[3]J. Juul, "Design of Wind Power Plants in Denmark," Proceedings of the United Nations Conference on New Sources of Energy 7, 229-240 (1961).

In the following development of this momentum theory, it is assumed that the flow is incompressible and the flow in front of and behind the disk is potential (irrotational) flow. However, the flow through the disk cannot be described by irrotational flow theory. Figure 15.3-1 shows the airflow through a windmill rotor removing energy from the air stream.

For steady flow (i.e., flow in which the velocity is constant in time at any point occupied by the fluid), Bernoulli's equation for energy conservation per unit volume of fluid is

$$p + (1/2)\rho v^2 = \text{constant}, \qquad (15.3\text{-}1)$$

where p = the fluid pressure, ρ = the density of the fluid, and v = the fluid velocity. As already noted, Bernoulli's equation may be used to describe flow in front of and behind the disk.

Let v_f = free-stream wind velocity, v_r = wind velocity acting on the rotor, v_w = wake wind velocity; then, using Eq. (15.3-1), the pressure head in front of the disk (h_f) and the pressure head behind the disk (h_w) may be written, respectively, as

$$h_f = p + (1/2)\rho v_f^2 = p_r + (1/2)\rho v_r^2, \qquad (15.3\text{-}2)$$

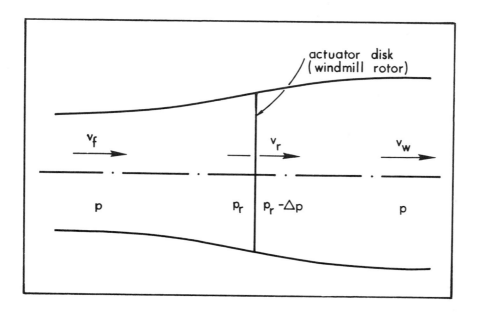

Fig. 15.3-1 Schematic diagram of a windmill removing en-
        ergy from the wind.

and

$$h_w = p + (1/2)\rho v_w^{\,2} = p_r - \Delta p + (1/2)\rho v_r^{\,2} , \quad (15.3-3)$$

where p_r is the air pressure acting on the rotor and Δp is
the average change in pressure across the disk or rotor.

Subtraction of the second evaluation of h_w in Eq.
(15.3-3) from the second evaluation of h_f in Eq. (15.3-2)

gives

$$\Delta p = h_f - h_w .\qquad(15.3\text{-}4)$$

Substitution of the first evaluation of h_f in Eq. (15.3-2) and of the first evaluation of h_w in Eq. (15.3-3) into Eq. (15.3-4) shows that

$$\Delta p = p + (1/2)\rho v_f^2 - [p + (1/2)\rho v_w^2]$$

$$= (1/2)\rho(v_f^2 - v_w^2).\qquad(15.3\text{-}5)$$

According to Newton's second law of motion, the force D exerted by the actuator disk on the column of air which it intercepts is the product of the change of momentum per unit volume and the volume of air passing through the disk per unit time; thus,

$$D = [\rho(v_f - v_w)](\pi r^2 v_r).\qquad(15.3\text{-}6)$$

Here, D, the force exerted by the actuator disk on the wind, is called the aerodynamic drag and r is the radius of the actuator disk, which is equal to the radius of the windmill rotor. The drag may also be expressed as

$$D = \pi r^2 \Delta p .\qquad(15.3\text{-}7)$$

Substituting Eq. (15.3-5) into Eq. (15.3-7) and

equating the resulting relation with Eq. (15.3-6) yield

$$(1/2)\rho \pi r^2 (v_f^2 - v_w^2) = \rho \pi r^2 v_r (v_f - v_w)$$

or

$$v_r = (1/2)(v_f + v_w) . \qquad (15.3-8)$$

In order for the windmill to extract power from the wind, the wind velocity acting on the rotor must be less than the free-stream velocity. We define the parameter $\underline{a}$ by the relation

$$v_r = v_f(1 - a) , \qquad (15.3-9)$$

where $\underline{a}$ is called the axial-interference factor. Substitution of Eq. (15.3-9) into Eq. (15.3-8) yields

$$v_w = v_f(1 - 2a) . \qquad (15.3-10)$$

Comparison of Eqs. (15.3-9) and (15.3-10) indicates that one-half of the wind-velocity decrease occurs in front of the rotor and one-half behind the rotor.

Substitution of Eqs. (15.3-9) and (15.3-10) into Eq. (15.3-6) yields

$$D = (2\rho a v_f)[\pi r^2 v_f(1 - a)] . \qquad (15.3-11)$$

In this calculation, it has been assumed that the axial-interference factor $\underline{a}$ is constant over the entire radius of the rotor. This is a reasonable assumption for the present investigation since it can be shown from the theory of propeller aerodynamics that the highest propeller efficiency is obtained when the axial-interference factor is a constant.

The power P that is extracted from the wind by the rotor is the product of the drag and the air velocity v_r acting on the rotor. Thus,

$$P = [2\pi r^2 \rho v_f^2 a(1 - a)][v_f(1 - a)]$$

$$= 2\pi r^2 \rho v_f^3 a(1 - a)^2 . \tag{15.3-12}$$

By equating the derivatives of D and P with respect to $\underline{a}$, at constant v_f, to zero, it is easily seen that the maximum drag is developed when $\underline{a} = 1/2$ and the maximum power is developed when $\underline{a} = 1/3$. Substitution of $\underline{a} = 1/3$ into Eq. (15.3-12) yields

$$P_{max} = (8/27)\pi r^2 \rho v_f^3 . \tag{15.3-13}$$

It follows from Eq. (15.3-10) that, when the maximum power is extracted from the wind, the wake wind velocity is reduced to one-third of the free-stream wind velocity.

If the windmill created no disturbance of the airflow, the kinetic energy $\dot{E}$ of the air passing through the swept area of the rotor per unit time would be

$$\dot{E} = (1/2)\pi r^2 \rho v_f^3 . \qquad (15.3\text{-}14)$$

Hence, from Eqs. (15.3-13) and (15.3-14), the theoretical maximum efficiency η_{max} of a windmill is seen to be

$$\eta_{max} = P_{max}/\dot{E} = 16/27 = 0.593 . \qquad (15.3\text{-}15)$$

The theoretical efficiency η of a windmill is often called the theoretical power coefficient.

The ability of a windmill to start under load is a function of the design tip-to-wind speed ratio. This ratio is

$$\mu = \omega r/v_f , \qquad (15.3\text{-}16)$$

where ω is the angular frequency of the rotor. As the design tip-to-wind speed increases, the ability of the windmill to start under load decreases. The tip-to-wind speed ratios and the actual efficiencies of several types of windmills are given in Table 15.3-1. The data in Table 15.3-1 indicate that there have been significant increases in practical windmill efficiencies with time. However, the highest actual windmill efficiency is still only about two-thirds of the maximum theoretical efficiency.

The maximum possible power theoretically obtainable from the wind is given by Eq. (15.3-13). Table 15.3-2 indicates the maximum power available from the wind as a func-

Table 15.3-1   Actual windmill efficiencies and typical tip-to-
                wind speed ratios.

Type of windmill	Efficiency range, %	Typical tip-to-wind speed ratio
Dutch (plane-vane)	5 - 10	0.5 - 1.0
LaCour (4-vane)	20 - 22	2.3 - 2.5
steel (multi-vane)	15 - 30	1.0 - 2.0
S-rotor (Savonius)	30 - 35	0.7 - 1.7
wind turbine	35 - 40	5.0 -10.0

Table 15.3-2   Maximum possible power theoretically obtain-
                able from the wind as a function of the rotor
                radius and the free-stream wind speed.

Wind speed, mph	Approximate extractable power,[a] kw			
	r = 10 ft	r = 25 ft	r = 50 ft	r = 100 ft
10	1	6	25	100
20	8	50	200	800
30	27	169	675	2,700
40	64	400	1,600	6,400
50	125	781	3,125	12,500
60	216	1,350	5,400	21,600

[a]An air density of 2.5×10^{-3} slug/ft^3 (8.04×10^{-2} lbm/ft^3) is assumed.

tion of the rotor radius and the free-steam wind speed.

The actual power coefficient of a given windmill design is a highly variable function of the tip-to-wind speed
ratio. Very small fluctuations from the design tip-to-wind
speed ratio result in large decreases in the actual power

coefficient.[1] Because of this phenomenon, the average pow-

er coefficient of a windmill will often be substantially less

than the power coefficient corresponding to the optimal tip-

to-wind speed ratio.

According to Putnam,[2] an economical windmill will

show a maximum overall efficiency of about 35%, usually at

some low value of the wind velocity ($\sim$18 mph), and will con-

vert approximately 6% of the energy in the wind passing

through the rotor swept area to electrical energy. The use

of this conversion-efficiency estimate and of the data of Table

15.3-2 implies that fifty windmills, each with a rotor radius

of 50 ft operating in a 20-mph average wind, would be re-

quired to generate 1 Mw$_e$ of electrical power. The total

swept area of these fifty windmills would be more than 3.9

$\times 10^5$ ft^2. Production of 1% of the 1.6×10^9 Mwh$_e$ of elec-

trical energy generated in the U.S. in 1971, by windmills

with a rotor radius of 50 ft operating continuously in a 20-mph

average wind, would have required more than 90,000 wind-

mill installations. The total swept area occupied by windmill

rotors would have been more than about 25 mi^2.

The wind-to-electrical energy conversion efficiency

given by Putnam[2] implies that, because of losses associated

with both windmill operation off the design tip-to-wind speed

ratio and with mechanical-to-electrical energy conversion,

---

[1]Ref. [1] in Section 15.2.

[2]P. C. Putnam, <u>Power from the Wind</u>, D. Van Nostrand
   Company, New York, New York, 1948.

the average performance coefficient of a windmill may only be 17% of the maximum power coefficient. These losses appear to be unrealistically high. A more optimistic estimate is an average wind-to-electrical energy conversion efficiency of 25%. Approximately 22,000 windmills with a rotor radius of 50 ft, operating continuously with this efficiency in a 20-mph average wind, would have generated 1% of the electrical energy used in the U.S. in 1971.

15.4   The Smith-Putnam Wind-Turbine Project[1]

The results of the Smith-Putnam Wind-Turbine Project provide the only available data relating to the feasibility of large-scale utilization of wind power for the generation of electric power suitable for a synchronous connection with an electric-utility system. This project involved six years of design and testing of a 175-ft, 1,250-kw$_e$ experimental wind turbine on Grandpa's Knob near Rutland, Vermont (see Fig. 15.4-1). The project was sponsored by the S. Morgan Smith Company, manufacturers of hydraulic turbines. P.C. Putnam organized the project and designed the wind turbine.

The wind-turbine rotor was a two-bladed propeller. The blades, each weighing eight tons and constructed from stainless-steel skin supported by stainless-steel ribs, had an airfoil cross-section with constant chord. The blades had pitch control to regulate rotational speed and had freedom to

---

[1]Ref. [2] in Section 15.3.

Fig. 15.4-1 The Smith-Putnam wind turbine. The lower
            blade is shown during the process of being po-
            sitioned prior to mounting on the hub. Photo-
            graph courtesy of the Central Vermont Public
            Service Corporation.

move independently through a coning angle (i. e., the angle parallel to the wind direction) to reduce the bending moments in the root sections of the blades. The wind turbine was designed for a maximum rotational speed of nearly 29 revolutions/minute. The rotor turned a 24-inch mainshaft coupled to a gearbox, which increased the rotational speed to 600 revolutions/minute for the purpose of driving a General Electric synchronous generator rated at 1,250 kilovolt-amperes and 2,400 volts. The rotor, generator, and accessory equipment were all mounted on a 40-ft rotatable carriage at the top of a 107-ft steel tower.

Between 1941 and 1945, the wind turbine operated intermittently for a total of about 1,100 testing hours. Following a main bearing repair in 1945, the turbine was operated as a generating station, without interruptions for routine testing, for three weeks before the project was terminated by a blade failure.

The Smith-Putnam Wind-Turbine Project allowed an analysis of the economics of wind-power generation of electricity. The study referred to the construction of a 1,500-kw_e production model incorporating refinements to the original experimental design. In 1973, Hewson[2] produced a first-order update of Putnam's economic analysis. The results of these economic analyses are given in Table 15.4-1.

---

[2]E. W. Hewson, Wind Power Potential in Selected Areas of Oregon, Oregon State University, Report No. PUD 73-1, Corvallis, Oregon, 1973.

Table 15.4-1   A 1973 cost summary of the 1945, 1,500-kw$_e$
              Putnam design; based on data from Refs.
              [1] and [2].

Item	Cost in dollars	
	1945	1971
engineering	10,500	20,000
manufacturing	210,100	756,100
installation	39,500	134,600
connection	18,600	45,200
subtotal	278,700	955,900
contingency, 10%	27,900	95,600
total	306,600	1,051,500

The data in Table 15.4-1 lead to a cost per installed kw$_e$ of \$205 in 1945 and \$701 in 1971. The 1945 cost per installed kw$_e$ was considered nearly 40% too high to be economically competitive with existing systems in 1945. The 1971 cost per installed kw$_e$ was about a factor of two higher than the corresponding cost for nuclear power-generating stations. Future extrapolations of wind-power costs are only marginally competitive with established technologies, as is discussed in the following sections.

15.5   Large-Scale Utilization of Wind Power

There are several reasons why the large-scale adoption of wind power appears attractive. Wind power is a renewable resource, most of the required technology has already been developed, and there is no air, water, or thermal pollution associated with wind-power systems. Weather modification because of wind utilization is probably not an important consideration. However, wind-power utilization has a low efficiency compared to other energy-conversion processes, the capital costs are high, and noise and aesthetic pollution will be associated with wind-power systems.

Wind power is not a reliable energy source.[*] The output of a wind-power system is a function of the wind velocity. Since wind-velocity variations do not, in general, coincide with power-requirement variations, it is mandatory that any large-scale wind-power system includes energy-storage facilities. There are three storage systems that are compatible with wind-power systems: pumped-hydraulic storage, compressed-air storage, and synthetic-fuel storage. However, Heronemus[1] has noted that neither pumped-hydraulic storage nor compressed-air storage is feasible for large-scale wind-power systems. The production of hydrogen by electrolysis and the subsequent collection and storage of hydrogen

---

[*] A wind-energy system with storage capacity sufficient to deliver the yearly average output power for 10 hours may make wind-energy generators comparable in dependability with that of an average nuclear reactor; see B. Sørensen, "Dependability of Wind Energy Generators with Short-Term Energy Storage," Science 194, 935-937 (1976).

[1] W. E. Heronemus, "The United States Energy Crisis: Some Proposed Gentle Solutions," paper presented to local sections of the ASME and the IEEE; reprinted in the Congressional Record 118, 3587-3592, February 9, 1972.

gas may be combined with wind-power systems. A storage system of this type is particularly useful for wind-power systems because the hydrogen may be used directly or transported from the site to a nearby community and reconverted into electricity in fuel cells. The transportation cost of the energy produced by wind-power systems is an important factor because the high (20- to 30-mph) average wind velocities required for economical wind-power utilization are not, in general, found near heavily-populated areas.

Heronemus[1] has analyzed the wind-power potential of six locations in the Great Plains Region of the U.S. Two wind-power systems are suggested: a 210-ft diameter, 2-bladed turbine atop a 1,000-ft tower and twenty 50-ft diameter, 2-bladed turbines arranged on a 600-ft tower. The estimated capital costs for the array-type wind-power system are \$350/kw$_e$ for 1 to 100 units per year, \$250/kw$_e$ for 100 to 1,000 units per year, and \$100/kw$_e$ for 1,000 to 20,000 units per year.[1]

A wind-power system located at the least desirable of the six locations (20-mph average wind velocity) and producing electrolytic hydrogen, 25% of which goes into storage as liquid hydrogen and is then transported to regional fuel-cell stations for conversion to electricity, is estimated[1] to cost \$720 per equivalent installed nuclear generating station kilowatt. This cost assumes a wind-turbine capital cost of \$100/kw$_e$. Heronemus[1] concluded that this system is competitive for a produced electricity price of 20 mills/kwh$_e$.

15.6   Economical Design of Wind-Power Systems

      The costs of wind-power systems are very difficult
to analyze because of the many variables that must be assessed. Given a wind-power system design with a known investment cost, the cost per unit of output is a function of the
mean annual wind speed at the site and of the fluctuation of the
actual wind speed from the annual mean. The results of a
1957 study[1] by investigators at the United Nations indicate
the average effects of these variables. The total wind-power
system cost, the system power capacity, and the cost per
unit of capacity as functions of the design wind speed are
shown in Table 15.6-1.

      The data of Table 15.6-1 indicate the economic im-
portance of designing a wind-power system for the proper
wind speed. The cost per unit of output of a wind-power system designed for 15-mph winds is 5.37 times the corresponding cost of the system designed for 35-mph winds. However,
this cost rise is not the only important criterion for the economy of energy generation by a wind-power system. Reductions in the design wind speed affect the achievable annual
energy output per unit of installed capacity, which is called
the specific output and is measured in kwh_e generated per
kw_e installed. The specific output is an important perfor-

---

[1] New Sources of Energy and Economic Development, Department of Economic and Social Affairs, United Nations,
New York, New York, 1957.

Table 15.6-1 Relative wind-power system costs, power capacities, and costs per unit of capacity as functions of the design wind speed;[a] reproduced from Ref. [1].

Design wind speed, mph	Relative total system cost	Relative system-power capacity	Relative cost per unit of capacity
35	1.00	1.00	1.00
30	0.86	0.63	1.36
25	0.71	0.36	1.97
20	0.57	0.19	3.00
15	0.43	0.08	5.37

[a] Calculated for a fixed rotor radius.

mance parameter for a wind-power system. Table 15.6-2 shows the relative specific output as a function of the design wind speed for sites with different annual mean wind speeds. We note that the specific output increases with wind speed for all design wind speeds and that it is larger for smaller design wind speeds.

Reference to Tables 15.6-1 and 15.6-2 shows that, although a reduction in the design wind speed from 35 to 15 mph increases the cost per kw_e more than five-fold, the specific output is simultaneously increased more than 24 times if the annual mean wind speed at the site is actually 10 mph.

The data of Tables 15.6-1 and 15.6-2 may be used to calculate the relative costs of energy produced by wind-power systems with various design wind speeds located at sites with different annual mean wind speeds. The relative costs per unit of electrical energy generated by a wind-power system

Table 15.6-2 Relative specific output of wind-power systems as a function of the design wind speed for sites with different annual mean wind speeds; based on data from Ref. [1].

Design wind speed, mph	Relative specific outputs for given annual mean wind speeds (annual kwh_e generated per installed kw_e)		
	10 mph	15 mph	20 mph
35	1.0	8.0	16.1
30	2.9	12.4	22.2
25	6.3	19.1	30.1
20	12.4	27.2	39.3
15	24.2	37.8	48.1

as functions of the design wind speed and the annual capital charges for sites with different annual mean wind speeds are given in Table 15.6-3.

Several conclusions may be drawn from an examination of the data of Table 15.6-3. When an installation site experiences a mean wind speed of 15 mph, the optimum value for the design speed is about 25 mph. If the mean wind speed at the installation site is around 20 mph, the design wind speed for the most economical energy production should be 30 to 35 mph. For installation sites with low annual mean wind speeds of about 10 mph, the design wind speed should be 15 to 20 mph. The variation of the unit energy cost with the design wind speed, near the minimum cost design, is sufficiently small so that the precise value chosen for the design wind speed is probably not of critical importance.

Table 15.6-3 Relative costs per unit of electrical-energy output for wind-power systems as functions of the design wind speed and the annual capital charges for sites with different annual mean wind speeds; computed from the data of Tables 15.6-1 and 15.6-2.

Design wind speed, mph	Relative annual capital charges[a]	Relative costs per unit of electrical-energy output for given annual mean wind speeds[b]		
		10 mph	15 mph	20 mph
35	1.00	1.000	0.125	0.062
30	1.36	0.469	0.110	0.061
25	1.97	0.313	0.103	0.065
20	3.00	0.242	0.110	0.076
15	5.37	0.222	0.142	0.112

[a] The same percentage of annual capital charges is assumed in all cases.
[b] These figures are obtained by dividing the relative annual capital charges by the value of the relative specific output for each wind speed, as given in Table 15.6-2.

Finally, if a single design wind speed must be chosen for a system that is expected to operate under highly variable wind conditions, the most suitable values of the design wind speeds appear to be near 25 mph.

15.7   Recent Developments

A shrouded aerogenerator has been studied experimentally and has been shown to increase achievable wind-power efficiencies by as much as a factor of about two.[1] In the shrouded aerogenerator, the turbine is located at the throat of a shroud (see Fig. 15.7-1). The effect of the shroud is essentially that of increasing the full-stream cross-sectional area from which fluid is collected to pass through the turbine because of induced "suction" at the turbine.

The shroud has the effect of producing a suction at the turbine and thus increases the effective cross-sectional area A_∞ from which air flows into the turbine, thereby augmenting wind-power utilization. In representative tests, the following results were obtained. At a yaw angle of 0° (the yaw angle is the angle between the axis of the shrouded aerogenerator and the wind direction), the measured augmentation above the theoretical limit of Eq. (15.3-13) for an axial turbine without shroud was found to be 68% while it increased to 118% at a yaw angle of 30°.[1] The shroud minimizes

---

[1] O. Igra, "The Shrouded Aerogenerator," Energy (in press, 1977).

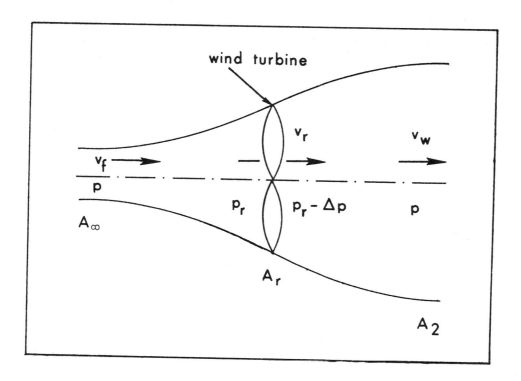

Fig. 15.7-1 Schematic diagram of the shrouded aerogenerator; reproduced with modifications from Ref. [1].

rotor-tip losses, eliminates the necessity of rotating the turbine for moderate changes in wind direction, and facilitates the use of axial flow turbines with fixed stator and rotor blades in providing fairly stable output at varying wind velocities.

The power, P, generated by the turbine is the product of pressure drop across the turbine, cross-sectional area $A_r = \pi r^2$ of the turbine, and the linear flow speed v_r at the turbine, viz.

$$P = A_r \Delta p v_r. \qquad (15.7\text{-}1)$$

It is easily verified that Eq. (15.7-1) is equivalent to Eq. (15.3-12) by using Eq. (15.3-5) for Δp, Eq. (15.3-9) for v_r, and Eq. (15.3-10) for v_w. For an axial-flow turbine, $A_r = A_2$ where the index 2 identifies downstream conditions. A turbine-load factor C_D may be defined by the relation

$$C_D = \Delta p / (1/2) \rho v_r^2. \qquad (15.7\text{-}2)$$

In terms of C_D, Eq. (15.7-1) becomes

$$P = (1/2) \rho v_r^2 C_D (\pi r^2) v_r. \qquad (15.7\text{-}3)$$

As C_D goes to zero, P also decreases to zero; an increase in C_D may be accompanied by a decrease in the cross-sectional area A_∞ from which air is sucked in; as $C_D \to \infty$, the flow through the shroud must vanish and $P \to 0$. Thus, there is an optimum value for C_D at which P is maximized. The performance ratio, ℛ, of the shrouded aerogenerator with respect to the maximum power that can be extracted from the ideal windmill is the ratio of P as given by Eq. (15.7-3) to the value of P specified in Eq. (15.3-13), viz.

$$ℛ = (27/16) C_D (v_r/v_f)^3 = (27/16) C_D (A_\infty/A_r)^3. \quad (15.7\text{-}4)$$

The ratio ℛ has been determined empirically in Ref. [1] for various operating conditions.

CHAPTER 16

TIDAL- AND WAVE-ENERGY UTILIZATION

During the eleventh century, tidal energy was utilized in tide mills located on the Atlantic Coast of France, Great Britain, and Spain. (The practice of utilizing tidal energy in coastal regions which experience large tidal ranges continued throughout the early part of the nineteenth century.) Tidal-power installations are reported to have operated in Great Britain, Germany, Italy, the U.S.S.R., and the United States during this period. As late as 1824, part of the water supply for London was pumped by 20-ft waterwheels, which had been installed in 1580 under the arches of London Bridge. Tidal power was still used in 1880 in Hamburg, Germany, for sewage pumping. One of the largest tide-mill installations was constructed in Rhode Island during the eighteenth century and used waterwheels which were 11 ft in diameter, 26 ft in width, and weighed 20 tons.

The early tide mills typically extracted only a small part of the total available tidal energy to produce mechanical energy. The mechanical power of these mills ranged from 30 to 100 kw and was used at the installation sites. The use of tidal power disappeared during the late nineteenth century when large electrical-power networks were introduced and the price of industrial energy began to decline.

The use of large tidal power plants for electrical-energy production has been investigated in more recent times. Preliminary design studies have been carried out for the estuary of the Severn River in England, the Carlingford and Strangford estuaries in Northern Ireland, the Bay of Fundy and the Passamaquoddy Bay in North America, the Gulf of San Jose in Argentina, and various sites in France, Western Australia, and the U.S.S.R. Examples of plants producing electrical power from tidal power are a 240-Mw$_e$ installation at the Rance River in France and a 400-kw$_e$ experimental installation at Kislaya Bay in the U.S.S.R.

Recent technological and engineering advances in water-barrier construction and low-head turbine-generator design, together with rapidly rising costs of energy produced from more conventional sources, have led to increased interest in tidal-power development.

16.1 Origins of Tides

Tides correspond to periodic increases and decreases in the surface levels of the oceans. These are primarily generated by gravitational- and kinematic-force interactions of the earth-moon-sun system. The influences of the sun and

the moon on the earth define the equilibrium theory of the
tides. Other celestial bodies have a negligible effect on tidal
forces because relatively large distances or small masses
are involved.

A. Description of Tide-Generating Forces

Gravitational forces are determined by Newton's law
of gravitation, which states that the force of attraction (F)
between two bodies is

$$F = Gm_1 m_2 / r^2 , \qquad (16.1-1)$$

where m_1 and m_2 are the masses of the bodies, r is the distance between the centers of mass of the bodies, and G is the
universal gravitational constant (= 6.67×10^{-11} n-m^2/kg^2).

Motion of the earth and moon around the center of
gravity of the earth-moon system produces centrifugal forces
which must be equal and opposite to the gravitational forces
at the centers of the bodies. If the diurnal rotation of the
earth is neglected, each point on the surface of the earth experiences a centrifugal force equal in magnitude and direction
to the centrifugal force acting on the center of the earth.
This result applies because every point on the surface of the
earth describes the same motion about the center of gravity
of the earth-moon system as does the center of the earth.
The gravitational force exerted on the surface of the earth by
the moon varies with position because it depends on the dis-

tance between locations on the surface of the earth and moon.
The vector sum of the gravitational and centrifugal forces at
any location on the surface of the earth is the tide-generating
force. The tide-generating force at a point on the surface of
the earth is shown in Fig. 16.1-1. The distribution of the
tide-generating forces along a complete meridional plane is
shown in Fig. 16.1-2.

i. Semidiurnal tides

The tide-generating forces shown in Fig. 16.1-2 may
be divided into tangential and vertical components. The tangential component is often called the tractive force and is
responsible for the semidiurnal tides on the earth. The vertical component alters the local force of gravity but only to
a negligibly small extent. Semidiurnal tides are produced by
earth-sun interactions, as well as by earth-moon interactions.
The earth-sun interaction has a smaller impact on the tides
than the earth-moon interaction because the resultant tide-
generating forces (see Fig. 16.1-2) are smaller. It may be
shown that the tide-generating forces are directly proportional to the mass of the tide-producing body (i.e., the sun
or the moon) and inversely proportional to the cube of the
distance between the earth and the tide-producing body.[1]
The sun is 2.7×10^7 times as massive as the moon and

---

[1]See, for example, G. B. Pillsbury, <u>Tidal Hydraulics</u>,
Corps of Engineers, U.S. Army, Vicksburg, Mississippi,
1956.

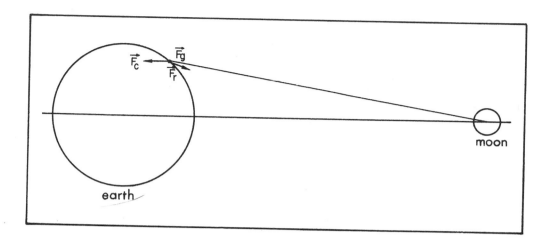

Fig. 16.1-1 The gravitational ($\vec{F}_g$), centrifugal ($\vec{F}_c$), and
resultant tide-generating ($\vec{F}_r$) forces at a point
on the surface of the earth, produced by interactions between the earth and the moon.

3.9×10^2 times farther from the earth. Thus, the tide-
generating force of the sun is approximately $2.7 \times 10^7/$
$(3.9 \times 10^2)^3 \simeq 0.46$ as large as that of the moon.

To an observer on the earth, both the moon and the
sun appear to rotate around the earth. The periods of the
apparent motions of the moon and the sun are 24 hours and
50 minutes and 24 hours, respectively. Accordingly, a
semidiurnal tide resulting from the earth-moon interaction
occurs every 12 hours and 25 minutes and a semidiurnal
tide resulting from the earth-sun interaction occurs every
12 hours.

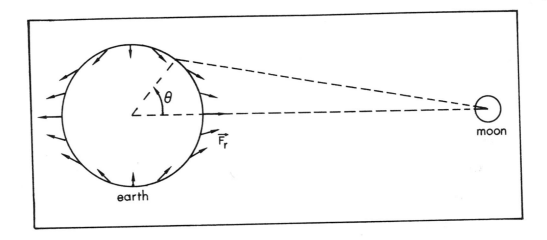

Fig. 16.1-2 Distribution of tide-generating forces produced
            in a meridional plane (great circle plane passing
            through the poles of the earth) on the surface
            of the earth. The maximum tangential compo-
            nents of the tide-generating force occur at θ
            equal to $45°$, $135°$, $225°$, and $315°$. Semi-
            diurnal lunar tides arise because maximum
            tangential forces occur twice daily in a given
            direction at each point of the rotating earth
            during each 24 h and 50 min period.

        ii.   Diurnal tides

    Diurnal tides are created by variations in the angle
of incidence (see Fig. 16.1-3) of attractive forces produced
by the moon and the sun during the lunar and solar days.
These variations occur because, in general, the axis of
rotation of the earth is not perpendicular to the plane of the
apparent lunar and solar orbits around the earth. The
variation of the attractive force of the sun, which has a

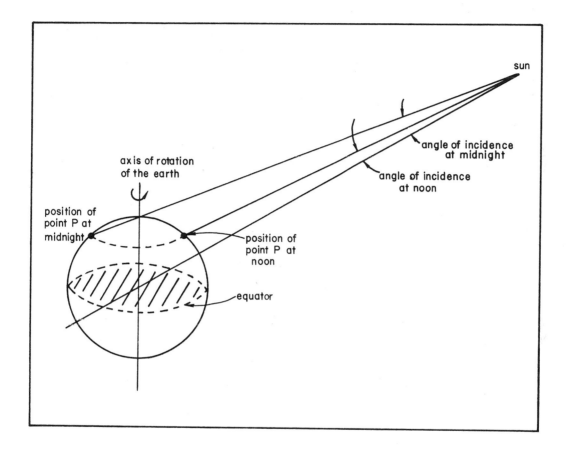

Fig. 16.1-3 Diurnal variation of the angle of incidence of
the gravitational force produced by the sun.
Because the rotation of the earth during a
24-h period brings each point on the earth
relatively closest to the sun once per day,
diurnal tidal forces are produced by the sun
with a 24-h period. The angle of incidence
is defined as the angle subtended at the sun by
the local position and a line through the equator.

maximum and minimum at a given point on the earth once during the solar day, is shown in Fig. 16.1-3.

iii. Semiannual and fortnightly tides

The tides are also affected by the elliptical shape of the apparent lunar and solar orbits around the earth; these tidal effects occur semiannually for the sun and fortnightly for the moon.

iv. Biweekly tides

The differences in the lengths of the lunar and solar days give rise to spring and neap tides. When the sun and the moon are nearly in line with the earth (during periods of the new and full moon, i.e., during the second and fourth quarters of the moon each month), the resultant tidal forces reach a maximum and lead to the spring tides. When the gravitational forces of the moon and the sun are $90°$ out of phase (during the first and third quarters of the moon each month) with respect to the earth, the resultant tidal forces reach a minimum and give rise to the neap tides. The resulting oscillation in tidal amplitude has a period of approximately two weeks.

The total tide-generating forces are small. The largest single contributor to the total tidal forces is the principal (semidiurnal) lunar-tide-generating force. The maximum value of the tangential component (tractive force) of this force is about 1×10^{-7} times the force of gravity. Tidal forces are so small that negligible effects are produced on bodies of water as large as the Great Lakes. However, the variations in the tidal forces acting over areas of the size of the oceans produce the observed tidal fluctuations.

B. Amplitudes of Tidal Oscillations

The tidal range (R) is the difference in height between high tide and low tide at a given station. The tidal range in the open ocean is about two feet. The open-ocean range is amplified by shoaling effects because of interactions with continental shelves. This amplification produces tidal ranges in coastal regions that are typically three or four times larger than in the open ocean.[2] In estuaries or bays with a basin length that is approximately one-half or one-fourth of the wave length of the tides, the tidal range may be further amplified two to four times by resonance effects. For example, the tides at the mouth of the Bay of Fundy, which is located between Nova Scotia and New Brunswick, are amplified by a factor of nearly 2.7 at the head of the bay.[3] The funneling

---

[2]E. M. Wilson, Section 42 on "Tidal-Energy Development" in the Handbook of Applied Hydraulics, C. V. Davis and K. E. Sorenson, editors, McGraw-Hill, New York, New York, 1969.

[3]B. P. Pelletier and R. M. McMullen, "Sedimentation Patterns in the Bay of Fundy and Minas Basin" in Tidal Power, T. J. Gray and O. K. Gashus, editors, Plenum Press, New York, New York, 1972.

effect of a converging tidal basin may also amplify the tidal range.[2]

The influence of rotation of the earth on the tides may be described by a fictitious Coriolis force (compare Section 6.2C). When the ebb and flow of the tides are locally in a north or south direction, the tidal range is affected by the Coriolis force. In the Northern Hemisphere, the Coriolis force deflects tidal flow in a rightward direction. In the Irish sea, which is located between Great Britain and Ireland, the flow tides move northward and the ebb tides move southward. The Coriolis force acting on these tides causes the tidal range on the eastern (British) coast to be about 8 ft greater than on the western coast.[2]

Tidal oscillations may be altered by construction of a barrier or dam if the artificial barrier affects the resonance properties of the basin. The tidal range outside of the barrier may either increase or decrease. If a barrage is constructed to utilize tidal power, it is important that construction of the barrier does not decrease the tidal range and thus make the project less productive than was anticipated.

16.2   Tidal-Power Resources and Site Selection

The total rate of tidal-energy dissipation on the earth

is about 3×10^6 Mw.[1,2] Munk and MacDonald[2] have estimated the tidal-power dissipated in bays and estuaries as about 1×10^6 Mw.

The most important parameters in evaluating tidal-power sites are the tidal range and the surface area of the tidal basin. The maximum electrical energy which can be produced during a tidal cycle is

$$E_{max} = \eta \rho g R^2 S , \qquad (16.2-1)$$

where ρ is the sea density, g is the gravitational acceleration, R is the tidal range, S is the surface area of the tidal basin, and η is the tidal-to-electrical energy-conversion efficiency. If R is expressed in meters, S in square kilometers, and η is assumed to be 15%, then, using Eq. (16.2-1), the annual electrical-energy production from a tidal basin becomes, with two tides per day during 365 days per year,

$$E \approx (0.3 \times 10^6) R^2 S \; kwh_e/y . \qquad (16.2-2)$$

A third important parameter in the determination of the suitability of a tidal basin for a tidal-power installation

[1]H. Jeffreys, "Tidal Friction," Nature 246, 346 (1973).

[2]W. H. Munk and G. J. F. MacDonald, The Rotation of the Earth, A Geophysical Discussion, Cambridge Monographs on Mechanics and Applied Mathematics, Cambridge University Press, Cambridge, England, 1960.

is the length of the barrage (L) necessary to enclose the basin.   The ratio of L/S is a measure of the geographical suitability for enclosure of a basin.   A small ratio is, of course,
desirable.   The suitability of a site for power production may
be measured by the ratio L/E, which provides a first-order
classification of sites in terms of potential economic value.
Sites with relatively large potential economic values are
characterized by relatively small ratios of L/E.   The tidal
range, basin area, potential electrical-energy production,
barrage length, L/S ratio, and L/E ratio are given in Table
16.2-1 for various proposed tidal-power sites.

The data of Table 16.2-1 indicate relatively high geographical suitability for the sites at Brest, Rance and Chausey
in France and at Passamaquoddy in the United States.   The
Rance and Chausey sites appear to be most attractive.   The
Passamaquoddy and Severn sites are less attractive because
the required L/E ratios are approximately 2.5 times larger
than for the French sites.   The data included in Table 16.2-1
provide first-order measures of site suitability for tidal-power generation.

16.3 Tidal-Power Utilization Techniques

Several different tidal-power utilization schemes have
been developed.   The energy-output pattern of a tidal-power
plant determines the contribution which the plant can make
to the base-load and peaking requirements of an electric-
utility network.   Utilization schemes have been developed to

Table 16.2-1 Site-selection criteria for tidal-power developments; based on data published in <u>New Sources of Energy and Economic Development</u>, United Nations Department of Economics and Social Affairs, New York, New York, 1957.

Country and site	Tidal range, m	Basin area, km^2	Potential annual electrical-energy production,[a] 10^6 kwh$_e$/y	Barrage length, m	L/S, m/km^2	L/E, m/(10^6 kwh$_e$/y)
France:						
Lorient	4.5	16.0	97	750	47	7.7
Brest	6.4	92.0	1,130	3,640	40	3.2
Alber-Benoit	7.4	2.9	48	200	69	4.2
Alber-Vrach	7.4	1.1	18	190	173	10.6
Arguenon and Lancieux	11.4	28.0	1,090	6,275	224	5.8
La Fresnaye	11.4	12.0	470	2,760	230	5.9
Rance	11.4	22.0	860	725	33	0.8
Rotheneuf	12.0	1.1	48	330	300	6.9
Chausey	12.4	610.0	28,140	23,500	39	0.8
Somme	9.3	49.0	1,270	5,100	104	4.0
United Kingdom:						
Severn	11.5	44.0	1,750	3,500	80	2.0
United States:						
Passamaquoddy	7.5	120.0	2,025	4,270	36	2.1

a. Calculated from Eq. (16.2-2).

overcome the basic weakness in tidal-power utilization,
namely, variable energy production which is not generally
consistent with energy-demand patterns.

A.   One-Way, Single-Basin Generation

The one-way, single-basin scheme is the simplest
and the oldest form of tidal power utilization. This technique
uses a single basin formed by closing off the estuary or bay
by a barrage (see Fig. 16.3-1). During periods of rising
tides, water fills the basin through the sluiceways. When the
water level in the basin is higher than the level of the sea,
the potential energy of the impounded water is converted into
electrical power by emptying the basin through turbine generators located in the power house (see Fig. 16.3-1). This
scheme is characterized by about 5 hours of generation, followed by 6 to 7 hours of basin refilling and standstill. The
energy output of a one-way, single-basin technique is improved by installing turbine generators that can be used as
motor pumps to assist during the refilling operation.

B.   Two-Way, Single-Basin Generation

The two-way, single-basin scheme permits power
generation with water moving either from the basin to the
sea or from the sea to the basin (see Fig. 16.3-2). More
energy is generated by use of the two-way scheme than by
a one-way scheme at the same location. However, the average available head is lower in a two-way method than in the

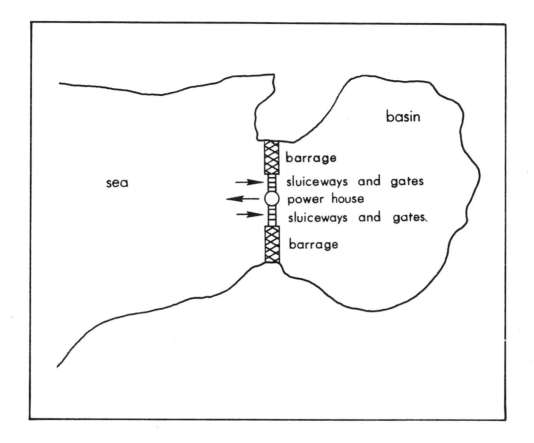

Fig. 16.3-1 Schematic diagram of a one-way, single-basin tidal-power installation. The directions of water flows are indicated by arrows.

one-way method. As the result, the turbines in a two-way scheme must be larger and are, therefore, more expensive. The energy output of a two-way generation technique may also be slightly improved by pumping. The Rance tidal-power development is designed for two-way, single-basin operation with pumping. Both one-way and two-way, single-basin

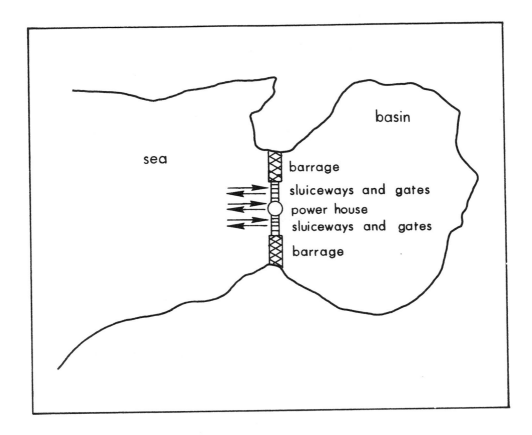

Fig. 16.3-2 Schematic diagram of a two-way, single-basin
tidal-power installation. The directions of water flows are indicated by arrows.

schemes produce time-dependent power outputs.

C.   Multiple-Basin Schemes

The simplest multiple-basin scheme consists of two
one-way, single-basin installations that are interconnected
electrically. Operating advantages are realized in cases

where the installations experience tidal cycles of different
phase.

The linked-basin scheme (see Fig. 16.3-3) permits
continuous power generation and, thereby, overcomes, in
part, the intermittent and out-of-phase-with-demand power
generation that usually characterizes tidal-power developments. In this technique, the high-level basin is filled
through sluiceways as the tide rises. When the falling sea
level is equal to the water level in the high-level basin, the
sluiceway gates to this basin are closed to prevent outflow
to the sea. Subsequently, water flows continuously from
the high-level basin through turbine generators to the low-
level basin. When the falling seawater level becomes lower
than the rising water level in the low-level basin, sluiceway
gates in the low-level basin are opened to allow water to flow
from the low-level basin to the sea. This process continues
until the water level in the low-level basin equals the now
rising tides of the sea. At this time, the sluiceway gates of
the low-level basin are closed to prevent filling from the sea.
After the low-level basin sluiceway gates are closed, the low-
level basin starts filling while the water level in the high-
level basin continues to fall because of continued flow from
the high-level to the low-level basin through turbine generators. The cycle is completed when the rising level of the
tides surpasses the falling water level in the high-level basin
and the high-level basin sluiceway gates are again opened to
refill the high-level basin. The period of the cycle is approx-

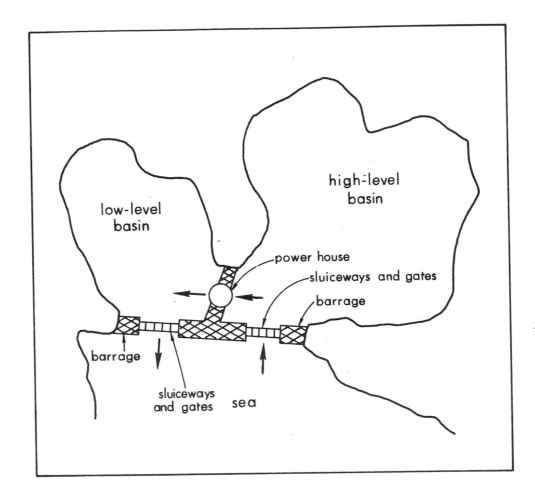

Fig. 16.3-3 Schematic diagram of a linked-basin tidal-power
            installation. The directions of water flows are
            indicated by arrows.

imately equal to the period of the semidiurnal tides or about
12.5 hours.

||The linked-basin scheme provides continuous power
output. However, the magnitude of the continuous power output fluctuates because of the continuously varying head available to the turbines. The magnitude of the fluctuations is

determined by the relative basin size and the installed generation capacity. In general, the power output will fluctu-
ate[1] by about a factor of two during a single operating cycle
and by approximately a factor of five during the lunar month.
Because of these large variations, the firm energy output of
a linked-basin tidal power station is low compared to the total installed generating capacity. Although the linked-basin
technique provides continuous power output, the total energy
supply in a linked-basin scheme is only about one-half that
of a one-way, single-basin scheme for the same basin.[1]

D.   Pumped-Storage Schemes

The combination of tidal power with both high-head[1]
and low-head[2, 3] pumped storage has been proposed. By
combining tidal-power and pumped-storage facilities, the
operating characteristics of tidal power are altered in such
a manner that on-peak power is supplied with only slight variations in total generation capacity. For this reason, the
tidal-power component of an integrated-power system will
be economically more attractive than a pure tidal-power in-

---

[1]Ref. [2] in Section 16.1.

[2]K. E. Sorenson, "Pumped-Storage Tidal Power" in _Tidal
Power_, T. J. Gray and O. K. Gashus, editors, Plenum
Press, New York, New York, 1972.

[3]C. K. Haswell et al, "Pumped Storage and Tidal Power in
Energy Systems," Journal of the Power Division, Proceedings of the American Society of Civil Engineers _98_, 201-
220 (1972).

stallation. The proposed high-head, pumped-storage tidal-power combinations consist of a high-head pumped-storage plant which is electrically connected to the output of the tidal-power plant and other thermal-electric power plants in the utility network. The low-head pumped storage units are physically and electrically connected to the tidal-power plant in a linked-basin scheme. Existing thermal-electric plants in the utility network may also be electrically connected to the pumped-storage tidal-power installation in order to provide some of the required pumping energy.

The use of high-head pumped storage is advantageous because the turbine generators operate at relatively high hydraulic efficiency and are comparatively inexpensive. The difficulty in using this combination scheme is associated with lack of availability of high head pumped-storage facilities near either the energy-load center or the tidal-power installation.

The low-head pumped-storage scheme is similar to the linked-basin scheme because both require a high-level and low-level basin. The relative sizes of the basins are determined by the energy-storage requirements and the achievable basin-level ranges. The turbine generators may be installed between the sea and the basins in three different configurations (see Fig. 16.3-4). The three designs shown in Fig. 16.3-4 have similar operational characteristics. In general, pumping occurs when the tide is high, with one basin being filled by the tides and by pumping; when the tide is low, the other basin may be lowered by outflow and by pump-

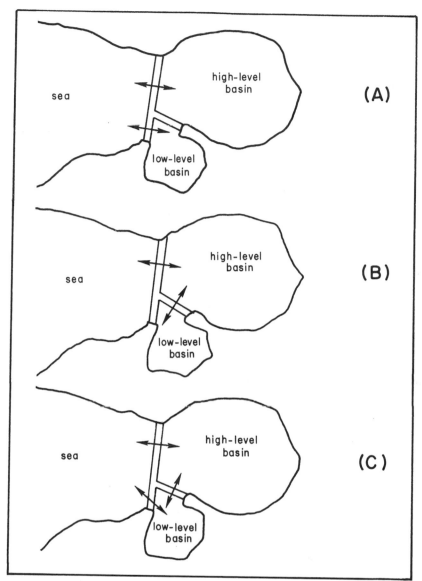

Fig. 16.3-4 Schematic diagrams of low-head pumped storage
and tidal-power configurations. The double arrows indicate the locations of pump turbines.
The pump-turbine layouts (A) and (B) have been
studied in detail by Haswell et al,[3] with layout
(A) estimated to be the more efficient and layout (B) more easily constructed. Layout (C)
may be preferred because of the operational
flexibility of the design but it may be prohibitively expensive.

ing. The installation generates electrical power continuously by water discharge through turbine generators. During periods of high tides, the discharge occurs either between the high and low basins or between the sea and the low basin. The high-level basin is discharged through turbine generators into the sea when the tide is low. The timing and the extent of the pumping and generating phases are determined by station output required for proper integration into the utility network.

16.4 Tidal Power Plant Design

The design of tidal power plants includes three major structures. The power house contains the hydraulic turbines and the associated generating units. The filling and emptying of the tidal basin are regulated by sluiceways and control gates. The barrage or dam creates the controlled tidal basin.

A. Hydraulic Turbines and Generators

Tidal power plants typically operate under very low energy heads. Suitable low-head turbine designs include bulb-type, tube-type, and straight-flow turbines. Diagrams of low-head turbine installations are shown in Fig. 16.4-1. The bulb-type turbine (see Fig. 16.4-1A) is used in the Rance tidal development in France. The generator, which is enclosed in the bulb-shaped housing, is driven by the horizontal turbine shaft. These units are characterized by improved

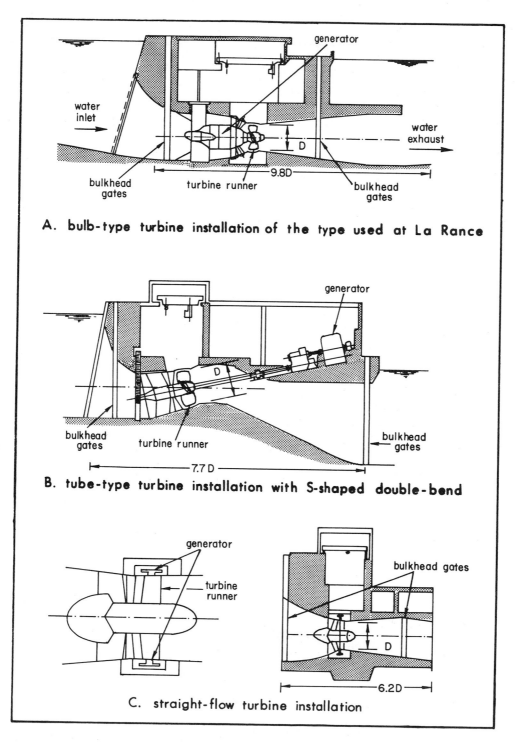

A. bulb-type turbine installation of the type used at La Rance

B. tube-type turbine installation with S-shaped double-bend

C. straight-flow turbine installation

Fig. 16.4-1 Schematic diagrams of low-head turbine installations. The difference in length requirements
for the three designs should be noted.

hydraulic efficiency, greater discharge capacity, and higher power output for a given turbine size than hydraulic turbines of other design.[1] The bulb-type turbine may be operated as a turbine and as a pump in either direction and can also be used as an orifice for up to about 50% of the design-discharge capacity.

The tube-type turbine operates in a water passageway with a gentle S-shaped double-bend (see Fig. 16.4-1B). The hydraulic efficiency of tube-type turbines is slightly lower than that of the other low-head turbine designs. However, this disadvantage is offset, in part, by the relative simplicity of the design.

Straight-flow turbines operate in relatively short horizontal waterways (see Fig. 16.4-1C). The hydraulic efficiency of straight-flow turbines is similar to that of tube-type turbines but this design is only suitable for operation in one direction. The generator design consists of a rotor which is mounted on the ends of the turbine blades and turns in a sealed annular recess in the water passageway. The stator surrounds the rotor recess and is not exposed to the water flow.

B. Water-Flow Control Equipment

A number of possible barrage designs has been con-

---

[1]F. L. Lawton, "Tidal Power in the Bay of Fundy" in Tidal Power, T. J. Gray and O. K. Gashus, editors, Plenum Press, New York, New York, 1972.

sidered for use in tidal power plants. A conventional dry-land mode of dam construction was used behind cofferdams during building of the Rance installation. Construction of cofferdams in estuaries or bays is difficult because of interference by tidal currents and wave action. This technique may become extremely difficult to apply, as well as prohibitively expensive, for large-scale tidal development. An alternative construction method, which is called the caisson concept, has been used in construction of the Kislaya Bay tidal-power station in the U.S.S.R. This method involves prefabricating the power station, sluiceways, and gates in sections or caissons on drydocks or on slipways. These caissons are floated to the barrage site and then sunk at low tide onto a dredged level-rock foundation. The feasibility of implementing this construction technique has been demonstrated for simple barrages and subway tunnels. However, experience in building tidal-power stations by use of this technique is very limited. We refer to Refs. [2] and [3] for summaries of the development of this construction technique.

[2] J. D. Gwynn, F. Spaargaren, and A. J. Woestenenk, "Modern Techniques for Barrage Construction" in Tidal Power, T. J. Gray and O. K. Gashus, editors, Plenum Press, New York, New York, 1972.

[3] P. R. Tozer and T. J. Sluymer, "Precast Floated In Construction as Applied to Tidal Power Developments" in Tidal Power, T. J. Gray and O. K. Gashus, editors, Plenum Press, New York, New York, 1972.

Since tidal power plants depend on continuously-varying differences between water levels in the basin and the ocean, sluiceways must be equipped with gates which can be operated rapidly and reliably. The gates must open and close during each tidal cycle, dissipate dynamic loads from wave action, and withstand the extremely corrosive sea environment. Because of these requirements, the design of sluiceways and gates will be important in the construction of an economical tidal power plant.

C. Corrosion in Tidal Power Plants

Since tidal power plants are located in a marine environment, corrosion prevention is of much greater importance than in conventional hydroelectric power plants. The barrage, sluiceways, gates, turbines, generator units, embedded parts, control and relay equipment, and all other structural elements of a tidal-power station are subject to corrosive attack. Experience with sea-water corrosion has been gained during ship building, especially in connection with propeller construction. The pumping of large volumes of sea-water for thermal-electric power-plant cooling has also provided valuable experience with sea-water corrosion. Sea-water corrosion can be controlled, or at least reduced, by use of appropriate materials, protective coatings of paints or metals, and cathodic protection. Nevertheless, corrosion will significantly influence the design, construction, operation, and cost of tidal power plants. We refer to the literature for more detailed discussions of the corrosion behavior of non-ferrous metals,[4] ferrous metals,[5] and concrete[6] in marine environments.

16.5   The Rance Tidal-Power Development

The Rance tidal power plant, which is located across the estuary of the Rance River between Saint-Malo and Dinard, France, is the only large-scale tidal-power development in operation.   This plant was officially inaugurated in November 1966.   A 750-meter barrage is located about 4 kilometers inland from the mouth in the river estuary.   The water impounded by the barrage extends upstream about 19 kilometers, and has a surface area of about 22 km^2 and a water-storage volume of about 180×10^6 m^3.   The tidal range varies between 3.5 and 14.5 m and has a mean value of 9.2 m.

The power station is a 330-m hollow concrete structure, which supports a two-lane highway.   The powerhouse

---

[4] M. J. Pryor and R. V. L. Hall, "Corrosion Characteristics of Non-Ferrous Metals in Marine Applications" in Tidal Power, T. J. Gray and O. K. Gashus, editors, Plenum Press, New York, New York, 1972.

[5] J. F. McGurn, "Corrosion Behavior of Ferrous Alloys in Marine Environments" in Tidal Power, T. J. Gray and O. K. Gashus, editors, Plenum Press, New York, New York, 1972.

[6] C. R. Wilder, "Performance of Concrete in a Marine Environment" in Tidal Power, T. J. Gray and O. K. Gashus, editors, Plenum Press, New York, New York, 1972.

contains 24 bulb-type turbines which have four 5.35-m variable-pitch blades. Twelve of the turbines have stainless-steel blades and the remaining twelve have blades constructed from an aluminum-bronze alloy. Each turbine drives a generator which is mounted in the bulb-shaped housing and is rated at 10 Mw$_e$ and 3.5 kV. A man-access shaft is connected to the interior of each bulb. The total installed capacity is 240 Mw$_e$. The turbine blades are designed so that the station can utilize flow from the basin to the sea or from the sea to the basin. The station may also be operated in a pumping mode or serve as a flow orifice. Each turbine installation is equipped with gates on both the sea and estuary sides to permit external maintenance in a dry environment.

The sluiceway section of the barrage is 115 m long and contains six gates. The gates are of a vertical fixed-roller design and are 15 m wide and 10 m high. The remaining parts of the barrage are rock-filled sections; a lock is included for navigational purposes.

The gross annual output of the Rance tidal-power station is estimated[1] to be 537×10^6 kwh$_e$ for basin-to-sea generation and 71.5×10^6 kwh$_e$ for sea-to-basin generation. The energy used in pumping is estimated to be 64.5×10^6 kwh$_e$. Thus, the estimated net annual energy output is 544×10^6 kwh$_e$. This output corresponds to an average plant factor of approximately 26%. For this plant, a tidal-to-elec-

---

[1] Ref. [2] in Section 16.1.

trical energy-conversion efficiency of approximately 25% has been achieved. Representative estimated efficiencies for tidal power plants fall between 8 and 20%. The economic aspects of the Rance tidal-power development are discussed briefly in Section 16.6.

16.6   The Cost of Tidal Power

The cost of the Rance Project has been reported[1] to be between \$85.5 and \$102 $\times 10^6$ in 1966 dollars. Thus, the capital cost per installed kilowatt of the Rance tidal-power station was approximately \$360 to \$430/kw$_e$. The corresponding unit energy cost, based only on the capital costs and a 15% annual capital charge, is 23.6 to 28.2 mills/kwh$_e$ based on the estimated annual energy output of 544 $\times 10^6$ kwh$_e$/y. This cost is about a factor of 2.5 times greater than the energy costs of alternative power-generation techniques.

In 1968, Lawton[2] investigated the economics of several proposed tidal-power stations for possible location in the Bay of Fundy. The capital-cost estimates ranged from \$210 to \$240/kw$_e$. These cost figures correspond to installed capacities of two-way stations with about 2.3 times the dependable peak-power capacities. Based on estimated

---

[1]Ref. [2] in Section 16.1.

[2]F. L. Lawton, "Economics of Tidal Power" in Tidal Power, T. J. Gray and O. K. Gashus, editors, Plenum Press, New York, New York, 1972.

dependable peak-power capacities, the capital-cost figures ranged from \$480 to \$550/kw$_e$. These costs correspond to more than twice the capital costs of fossil-fuel plants in 1968. If an annual capital charge of 15% is assumed, the unit energy costs, based on capital costs only, range from 14.3 to 19.5 mills/kwh$_e$ for the specified annual energy outputs.

The economic assessment of tidal power and pumped-storage combinations depends on the utility network characteristics, the demand pattern, and the projected energy-demand growth rate. Cost comparisons for these systems and for alternative systems must be made by considering overall network economies. Wilson[1] and others have pointed out that no other method of comparison provides useful data.[3, 4]

The two factors that have determined the slow development of tidal-power projects are high capital cost and unavailability of firm generating capacity. The capital cost may be reduced[1] by eliminating cofferdam construction methods, shortening the required construction time, and simplifying the hydraulic machinery. These three cost-saving opportunities are presently under active investigation. Tidal-power installations have the following multipurpose benefits:[1] the barrages may be used as bridges while pre-

---

[3] Ref. [3] in Section 16.3.

[4] T. L. Shaw, "Some Considerations of a Possible New Role for Tidal Power," in *Tidal Power*, T. J. Gray and O. K. Gashus, editors, Plenum Press, New York, New York, 1972.

venting exceptionally high water levels in estuaries or bays; navigation is facilitated to ports within the tidal basin; recreational opportunities may be enhanced within the basin.

Although the capital and unit energy costs suggest that tidal-power developments are not generally economically viable at the present time, a number of factors may make tidal power more attractive in the future. These include increases in fuel costs for alternative power-generation techniques, increased costs of environmental-pollution control, technological advances in low-head hydraulic turbines, and reductions in dam-construction costs.

16.7 Environmental Effects of Tidal-Power Stations

The construction of a tidal-power station causes physical and oceanographic changes in the area surrounding the development. The barrage or dam alters the mean tide level and tidal range in the impoundment. The tidal-current patterns may be changed and the flow velocities and tidal exchange or flushing will be reduced. As the result, less vertical mixing, lower oxygen exchange rates, larger stratification, higher summer water temperatures, lower winter temperatures or icing, reduced salinity in surface layers, reduced oxygen concentration in lower layers, and erosion and siltation effects may be observed.[1] These physical

[1]D. H. Waller, "Environmental Effects of Tidal Power Development" in Tidal Power, T. J. Gray and O. K. Gashus, editors, Plenum Press, New York, New York, 1972.

effects may alter the local ecology, navigational routes, and land transportation.

The ecological changes and especially the effects on fisheries of a tidal-power station are difficult to assess. Altered oceanographic conditions near a tidal-power installation may have beneficial influences on some fish species and detrimental effects on others. The net result on fisheries is not easily evaluated.[2] Navigational routes may be influenced by tidal-power developments because of the presence of an aritificial barrier, reduced water levels, or production of silt. The restrictions on navigation may be reduced if locks are incorporated into the design of the tidal-power station. A tidal-power development may produce increased use of existing transportation systems by tourists. Tidal-power stations may be designed to incorporate a highway on top of the tidal barrier and thereby reduce travel distances between metropolitan centers.

The costs for adequate environmental controls associated with construction of a tidal power plant have been estimated[3] to be about 1% of the plant capital costs. This esti-

---

[2] A detailed discussion of the effects on individual fish species is included in Ref. [1]; see, also, "Report of the International Passamaquoddy Tidal Power Project," October 1959.

[3] J. G. Warnock and J. A. M. Wilson, "The Total Contribution of Tidal Energy to the System" in Tidal Power, T. J. Gray and O. K. Gashus, editors, Plenum Press, New York, New York, 1972.

mate includes provisions for fish passages, siltation control, and shoreline development. The costs of environmental controls for thermal-electric plants have been estimated[3] to be about 8% of the plant capital cost in 1968; they are expected to rise as high as 33% of the plant capital cost by 1990. These control costs include the costs of cooling towers, precipitators, scrubbers, underground power-transmission lines, and public safety programs.

Tidal power plants do not deplete nonrenewable resources, produce waste products, or contribute to air pollution. A carefully designed installation should not cause significant thermal or other water-pollution problems. The creation of an impoundment could, however, aggravate an existing pollution problem by altering the physical and ecological systems which served to dissipate and control the existing pollutant before construction.[1] The overall environmental effects of tidal-power developments appear to be relatively small. Nevertheless, possible environmental effects should be carefully considered for each individual installation because of the large-scale, capital-intensive, and essentially irreversible nature of tidal-power developments.

16.8 Utilization of Wave Energy

The waves in the open ocean are determined by wind acting on the ocean surface. The total rate of wave-energy dissipation on the earth has been estimated to be about

2.5×10^6 Mw, which is comparable in magnitude to the total rate of tidal-energy dissipation.[1] Wave energy is a renewable resource and is generally more reproducible than wind energy. Energy that is extracted from the waves is rapidly replenished by wind and ocean-surface interaction.

The power developed per cycle by a sinusoidal wave train of width w in the deep ocean may be estimated from the average change in potential energy as the water level rises above and falls below the ambient sea level (see Fig. 16.8-1). The mass of water, m, in half of the sinusoid lies above sea level and may be shown to be

$$m = w\rho \, (\lambda/2)(h_{tc}/2\sqrt{2}), \tag{16.8-1}$$

where ρ is the density of sea water, λ is the wavelength, and h_{tc} is the wave height from trough to crest (see Fig. 16.8-1). The center of gravity of the wave crest is located a distance $h_{tc}/4\sqrt{2}$ above sea level while the center of gravity of the wave trough lies at an equal distance below sea level. During a complete wave cycle, the change in potential energy, ΔPE, is

$$\Delta PE = gw\rho(\lambda/2)(h_{tc}/2\sqrt{2})^2$$

$$= w\rho g \lambda \, h_{tc}^2/16, \tag{16.8-2}$$

[1]J. D. Isaacs and D. J. Seymour, "The Ocean as a Power Source," International Journal of Environmental Studies 4, 201-205 (1973).

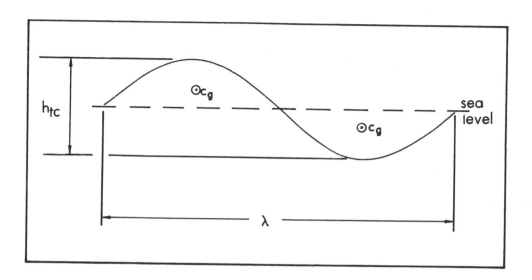

Fig. 16.8-1 Schematic diagram of a sinusoidal gravity wave
in the deep ocean; λ is the wavelength, h_{tc} is
the trough-to-crest wave height and c_g denotes
the position of the center of gravity.

where g is the gravitation acceleration. The frequency f, of
gravity waves in the deep ocean is[2]

$$f = (g/2\pi\lambda)^{\frac{1}{2}} .$$
(16.8-3)

The rate of change of potential energy or the power developed

[2]See, for example, H. U. Sverdrup, M. W. Johnson, and
R. H. Fleming, The Oceans: Their Physics, Chemistry
and General Biology, Prentice-Hall, Inc., Englewood
Cliffs, New Jersey, 1942; see, also, J. J. Myers, C. H.
Holm, and R. F. McAllister, Handbook of Ocean and Un-
derwater Engineering, McGraw-Hill, New York, New
York, 1969.

during a wave cycle, P, is the product of ΔPE and f, viz.

$$P = w\rho g \lambda h_{tc}^2 (g/2\pi\lambda)^{\frac{1}{2}}/16$$

or

$$P = w\rho g^2 h_{tc}^2 \, T/32\pi \tag{16.8-4}$$

since the wave period $T = 1/f$ is

$$T = (2\pi\lambda/g)^{\frac{1}{2}} \; . \tag{16.8-5}$$

Consider a wave train of width w = 50 miles with waves of height 20 ft and wave length 200 ft. The total wave power per 200-ft wavelength associated with this configuration relative to the flat ocean is found to be 1.77×10^4 Mw from Eq. (16.8-4).

The extraction of energy from waves breaking or rolling in the open ocean has not been widely developed because of engineering difficulties. Wave motion has been used, to a limited extent, for air-column excitation and bell-clapping in navigational aids. Several patents have been filed in the U.S. and Britain for devices to convert wave motion into electrical energy; a number of unpatented ideas has also been described.[3,4] The Japanese have designed navigational buoys that generate the required electrical power from wave motion at the installation site.

The energy heads available for wave-energy utilization are limited by the relatively low (6 to 10 ft) wave heights usually encountered. Implementation of wave-energy utilization techniques is complicated by the wide range of amplitudes and frequencies that characterize wave motion. The variable characteristics of wave motion require development of wave-energy extraction devices with energy-storage systems, if constant power output is desired.

Workers at the Scripps Institution of Oceanography[3] have designed and tested a small (1 kw) prototype wave-energy extraction device. The design is a pump consisting of a vertical riser tube, a flapper check valve, and a buoyant float, which is slack-tethered, thus allowing it to respond directly to wave motions (see Fig. 16.8-2). During approximately one-half of the wave cycle, the check valve is closed and the water in the riser follows the motion of the float. When the float begins downward motion, the check valve opens and the inertial forces pump water to a height greater than

---

[3] J. D. Isaacs and D. Castel, "Wave-Powered Generator System," University of California Sea Grant Annual Report, Scripps Institution of Oceanography, La Jolla, California, 1971-1972.

[4] P. L. Whitehead, Sr., and H. A. Cazel, "Sea Wave Electric Power System," IEEE 1971 Engineering in the Ocean Environment Conference 2, 159-160 (1971).

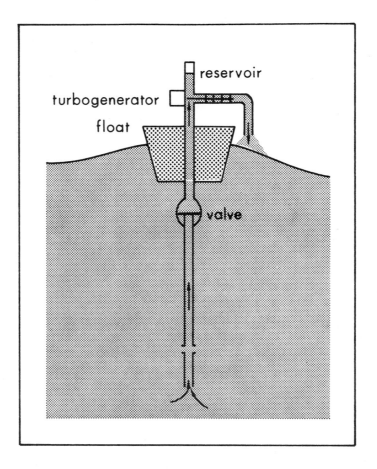

Fig. 16.8-2 Schematic diagram of a small wave-power gen-
            erator; reproduced from D. Castel, "Wave-
            Powered Generator," unpublished report,
            Scripps Institution of Oceanography, La Jolla,
            California, 1973.

the wave height. Subsequent wave cycles raise the reservoir
water level successively higher until an energy head suitable
for power generation is attained. The water may then be
discharged through a turbine generator to produce electrical
power. The attainable energy head is only limited by the
length of the vertical riser tube.

Isaacs and Castel[3] have suggested that wave-power generators of this type could be used as independent power sources for remotely moored buoys and, possibly, in non-polluting, commercial electrical-power generation.

S. H. Salter[5] is enthusiastic about the potential of wave-powered generators. Salter[5] has proposed conversion of the to and fro movement of waves into electrical energy rather than utilization of the vertical motion favored by Isaacs and Castel.[3] Salter has claimed[6] that his design could capture 80% of the mechanical energy of a wave and that a single unit, located at a favorable site and about the size of a supertanker, could generate an annual energy of 50 Mwy$_e$.

[5]S. H. Salter, "Wave Power," Nature 249, 720-724 (1974).
[6]Chemical and Engineering News 52, 16, October 14, 1974.

CHAPTER 17

<u>HYDROELECTRIC-POWER GENERATION</u>

The utilization of water power in water mills began perhaps 3,000 years ago. The earliest water mills had horizontal wheels mounted on a vertical shaft. The Romans improved the water mill by mounting the wheel vertically and gearing the horizontal shaft to a vertical shaft to turn a millstone. The use of water mills spread rapidly throughout Western Europe. By the sixteenth century, water power had been adapted to many industrial processes requiring stationary power sources. Technological advances during the late nineteenth century preceded the large-scale application of water power for the production of electrical energy.

Hydroelectric power is a renewable resource associated with solar-energy input and the resulting evaporation, rainfall, and runoff cycles. Hydroelectric plants generally do not have as many adverse effects on the environment as thermal-electric plants (see Section 17.5 for a discussion of the environmental effects of hydroelectric projects).

514

Because of rapid startup and loading capabilities and facility
for altering the power output quickly, hydroelectric plants
are particularly suitable for satisfying peak electrical-
energy demands. Hydroelectric plants are characterized
by low operating and maintenance costs (see Section 17.4),
long life times, and low outage rates. Unscheduled outages
in hydroelectric plants are less frequent than in thermal-
electric plants because hydroelectric machinery operates at
relatively low temperatures and speeds. Overhaul down-
times are less because of the relative simplicity of hydroelectric equipment. Hydroelectric plants are normally out
of service about two days per year because of forced outages
and about one week per year for scheduled maintenance. [1]
This total outage time of about 3% per year is approximately
one-fourth of the average outage rate for modern steam-
electric power plants.

Hydroelectric plants do have some disadvantages as
compared with steam-electric plants. These disadvantages
include high capital costs (see Section 17.4), remote locations and hence long-distance energy transmission requirements, dependence on variable stream and river flows, and
alteration of water quantity and quality. However, the favorable characteristics and frequent multiple-use benefits of

---

[1] The 1970 National Power Survey, Part I, U.S. Federal
Power Commission, U.S. Government Printing Office,
Washington, D.C., 1971.

hydroelectric projects provide strong incentives for developing the remaining, economically-viable hydroelectric potential in the United States and the world.

17.1   Physical Principles Involved in Water-Power Use

The energy abstracted from water in conventional hydroelectric-power applications is the sum of the potential energy (which is determined by position or elevation) and of the kinetic energy (which is determined by the water-flow speed). The potential energy of stationary water is easily converted into kinetic energy in the form of flowing or falling water to drive a hydraulic turbine.

The energy head is a useful measure of the energy contained in a water stream of constant discharge at any point. The energy head per unit mass h_e is defined as

$$h_e = z + v^2/2g, \qquad (17.1-1)$$

where z is the elevation of a free water surface above a reference level (datum), v is the mean speed of the water stream, and g is the acceleration of gravity. For flow in an open channel, z is the elevation of the center of gravity of the flow above the datum. For flow in a conduit, z is equal to the sum of the elevation of the center of gravity of the flow and the pressure head which would be shown in a riser or piezometer tube. In an ideal system without losses,

the principle of conservation of energy requires a constant
energy head. The friction and heat losses of constant-dis-
charge systems are accounted for by Bernoulli's equation

$$z_u + v_u^2/2g = h_e + z_d + v_d^2/2g, \qquad (17.1-2)$$

where the subscripts u and d refer, respectively, to upstream and downstream flow cross sections and h_e is the energy head loss between cross sections. A diagram illustrating the energy transformations in a typical hydroelectric
generating plant is shown in Fig. 17.1-1.

The energy line (see Fig. 17.1-1) is a line connecting
the values of the remaining energy head at all points throughout the plant. The potential energy head of the reservoir
water, without inflow or outflow, is represented by the center
of gravity of the water in Fig. 17.1-1. During steady-state
conditions of equal water inflow and outflow, the potential
energy head is larger than z and equals h. When water flows
out of the reservoir, a drop in the potential energy head equal
to the velocity head $v_1^2/2g$ occurs. At any location in the
penstock (see Fig. 17.1-1), the remaining energy head consists of the elevation of the flow z_2, the pressure head h_p,
and the velocity head $v_2^2/2g$. The energy-head losses in
a typical hydroelectric plant are shown in Fig. 17.1-1 by
decreases in the energy line. The total energy head, which
is converted to heat and hence lost, is the sum of losses
associated with friction at the entrance, bends, and else-

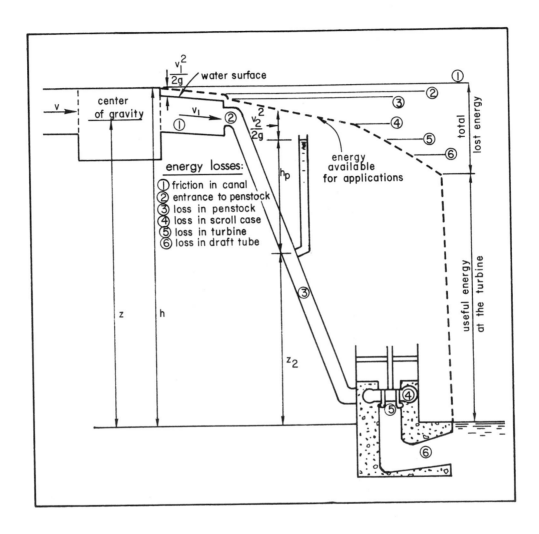

Fig. 17.1-1   Energy transformations in a typical hydroelectric plant; reproduced from the <u>Handbook of Applied Hydraulics</u>, C. V. Davis and K. E. Sorenson, editors, McGraw-Hill, New York, 1969; with permission of the McGraw-Hill Book Company.   Copyright © 1969 by the McGraw-Hill Book Company.

where in the canal, as well as losses in the penstock, scroll case, turbine, and draft tube. According to Bernoulli's theorem, Eq. (17.1-2), the sum of the energy head available to the turbine and the energy-head losses must be equal to the original energy head (see Fig. 17.1-1).

The theoretical power P_t available from flowing or falling water depends on the mass flow rate Q and on the height of the fall or the ideal energy head h_e. Thus,

$$P_t = gQh_e .\qquad (17.1-3)$$

If Q is expressed in units of 10^3 kg/sec or, approximately, in m^3/sec, h_e is given in m, and g is given as 10 m/sec^2, then Eq. (17.1-3) gives the theoretical power in tens of kw; it follows from Eqs. (17.1-1), (17.1-2), and (17.1-3) that the actual power P available from the water is

$$P = gQh_e [1 - (h_\ell / h_e)],\qquad (17.1-4)$$

where h_ℓ represents the total energy-head losses in the plant (see Fig. 17.1-1). The value of $[1 - (h_\ell / h_e)] \equiv \eta$ is the hydraulic efficiency of a hydroelectric plant and ranges typically from 0.75 to 0.80. Thus, a 1,000-Mw_e hydroelectric installation with an energy head of 50 m requires a water flow rate of 2,500 m^3/sec or, equivalently, 2.5×10^6 kg/sec $= 3.3 \times 10^8$ lb/min for $\eta = 0.80$.

17.2   Hydroelectric Power-Plant Technology

In this Section 17.2, we depart from our general expository procedure by reviewing briefly the mature technology involved in a developed industry.

Hydroelectric power plants contain four structures that are unique to power plants of this type. These structures are the forebay, penstocks, hydraulic turbines, and draft tubes (see Fig. 17.2-1). The generators and the auxiliary electrical equipment such as transformers, switching gear, and transmission lines are not significantly different from those installed in fossil-fuel or nuclear-powered generating facilities.

A.   Water-Flow Devices[1]

If the hydroelectric plant is located at the base of a dam, the water reservoir acts as the forebay. For plants located at the end of a canal, the canal may be enlarged to provide a forebay. Some installations have neither an enlarged canal nor a reservoir; in these cases, the canal itself is used as the forebay. In installations where a pipeline supplies the water, a surge tank constitutes the forebay. The forebay serves as a water-storage system during times of reduced plant loads and as a water-supply system during periods of load increases.

---

[1] Handbook of Applied Hydraulics, C.V. Davis and K.E. Sorenson, editors, McGraw-Hill, New York, New York, 1969.

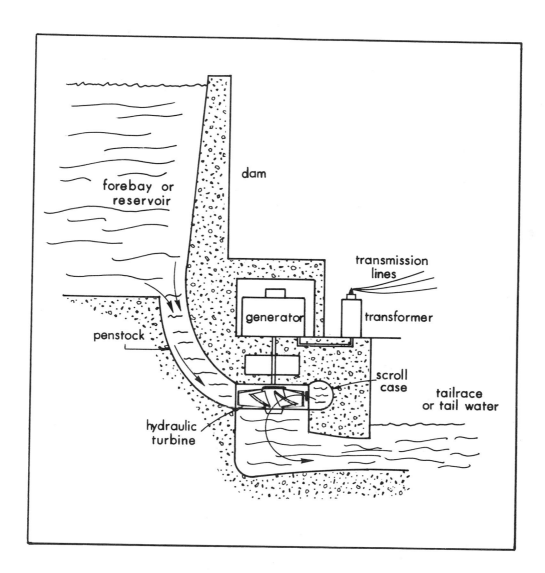

Fig. 17.2-1 Design of a typical hydroelectric power plant;
reproduced from Power Generation Alternatives,
City of Seattle, Department of Lighting, Seattle,
Washington, 1972.

The connection between the forebay and the turbine inlet or scroll case is called a penstock (see Fig. 17.1-1). Penstocks may be constructed from steel, wood, or reinforced concrete. The flow in the penstocks is controlled by forebay-penstock gates, turbine-penstock gates, or a combination of the two. When the distance from the forebay to the turbine is short or when the plant operates with a high head, a separate penstock is ordinarily installed for each turbine. In plants with moderate heads or long penstock distances, several turbines are often supplied by a single penstock. In some installations, a header penstock is used with branches supplying each of the turbines.

The draft tube connects the turbine outlet with the tailrace (water exhaust channel) or the tail water (free water to which the plant water is exhausted). Because the draft tubes play an integral part in determining the performance characteristics of hydraulic turbines, the turbine-draft-tube combination is ordinarily designed as a unit. The draft tube functions to decelerate the water at the turbine exit with a minimum of energy loss. This deceleration permits the removal of more energy from the water by the turbine than if the turbine-exhaust water is dumped directly into the tailrace or tail water.

B. Hydraulic Turbines[1]

Hydraulic turbines perform a continuous transformation of the potential and kinetic energy of a fluid into useful

work. Hydraulic turbines are classified as either impulse
or reaction turbines, depending on the type of hydraulic
action involved. In an impulse turbine, the total available
energy head is converted into a kinetic-energy head by a
contracting nozzle. The resulting water jet then imparts
kinetic energy to the revolving turbine structure or runner
by filling bucket-like structures connected to the turbine
runner hub. This hydraulic action takes place at nearly atmospheric pressure in a housing designed to prevent splashing
and to guide the discharge water. The discharge water flows
freely through the discharge passage into the tailrace or
tail water. Early water wheels were of the impulse type.
The only modern turbine of the impulse type is the Pelton waterwheel or turbine. A Pelton impulse-type turbine installation and a Pelton turbine runner are shown in Figs. 17.2-2
and 17.2-3, respectively.

In a reaction turbine, only part of the total available
energy head is converted into a kinetic-energy head. The
remainder of the head must be maintained as a pressure head,
which then decreases through the turbine passage. This pressure head is required because water flow through the penstock,
turbine, and draft tube occurs in a closed conduit system.
The water flow entering a reaction turbine exerts an impulse
on the turbine runner in the direction of the flow; the discharged water exerts a reaction on the runner in the direction
opposite to the flow. Reaction turbines have been designed
to operate with radial, axial, or mixed flow through the runner.

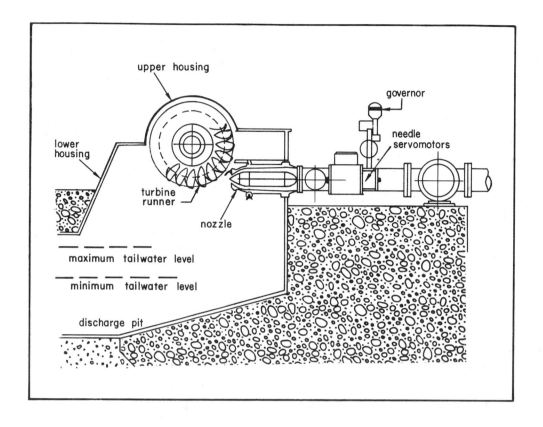

Fig. 17.2-2 Typical Pelton impulse-type turbine installation.

The Francis turbine and the propeller turbine are two types
of reaction turbines that are in wide use for hydroelectric-
power generation.

     Francis turbines are usually designed in either an
axial- or mixed-flow configuration. An axial-flow Francis
turbine typically has a runner constructed of 12 to 16 blades
or vanes set in a wheel-like configuration. The vanes are
mounted between the hub and an outer rim. The mixed-flow

Fig. 17.2-3 Pelton turbine runners. Photograph courtesy of the Allis-Chalmers Corporation.

design also has 12 to 16 blades or vanes which are either free at the outer end or mounted on a partial outer band. In the mixed-flow design, the water flow enters the runner after passing through a circular series of wicket gates, which increases the velocity head and imparts both radial and tangential velocity components to the flow. The resulting

whirling water is deflected into an axial flow by the turbine
vanes until the discharge water has only a small whirl component remaining.   The cross sections of a hydroelectric
plant using a Francis turbine and a Francis turbine runner
are shown, respectively, in Figs. 17.2-4 and 17.2-5.

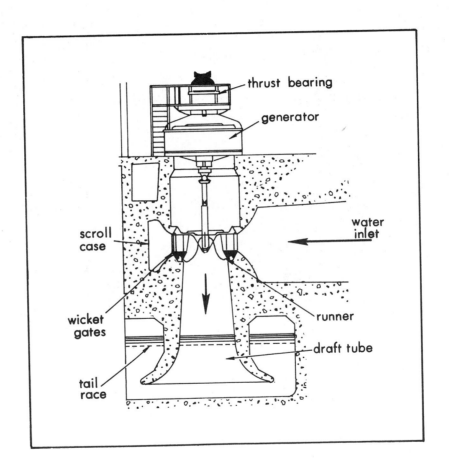

Fig. 17.2-4 Cross section of a Francis reaction-type turbine
             installation; reproduced from the McGraw-Hill
             Encyclopedia of Science and Technology,
             McGraw-Hill, New York, 1971; with permission
             of McGraw-Hill Book Company. Copyright ©
             1971 by the McGraw-Hill Book Company.

DACW-62-70-C-0012
OCTOBER 7, 1974
ALLIS CHALMERS COPR.

Fig. 17.2-5 Francis mixed-flow turbine runner and shaft
             assembly. Photograph courtesy of the Allis-
             Chalmers Corporation.

Propeller turbines have either fixed blades or adjust-
able blades and are usually designed for use in axial flow.
The fixed-blade design typically has from 3 to 10 blades
mounted on a hub with free outer ends and is similar in construction to a marine propeller (see Fig. 17.2-6). The

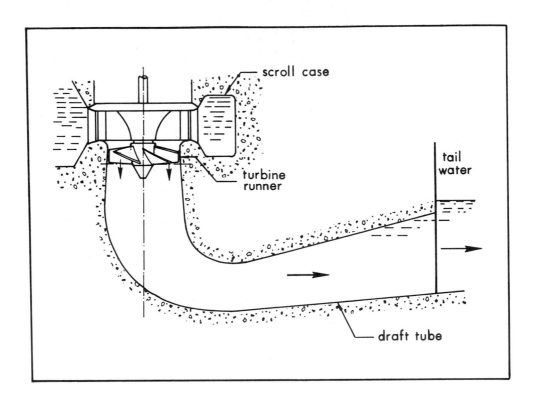

Fig. 17.2-6 Fixed-blade propeller turbine installation;
             reproduced from Ref. [1]; with permission of
             McGraw-Hill Book Company. Copyright ©
             1969 by the McGraw-Hill Book Company.

blades have little curvature and are pitched in a direction
that is more nearly tangential than axial. The adjustable-
blade design, which is known as a Kaplan turbine, has individual blades that can be pivoted at the hub mounting. The
blades may be adjusted during operation to compensate for
fluctuations in power demands and operating head. A photo-

graph of a Kaplan turbine, including the blade control mechanism, is shown in Fig. 17.2-7.

Preferential selection of a Pelton, Francis, or Kaplan turbine depends almost entirely on the available energy head. Pelton impulse-type turbines are ordinarily installed at sites with heads over 1,000 ft. A hydroelectric plant in Austria uses Pelton turbines operating under a 5,800-ft head. The Francis reaction-type turbine is commonly used at sites with heads ranging from 100 to 1,000 ft. A Francis turbine operating under a 2,205-ft head represents the highest head installation of this type. Fixed-blade propeller turbines or Kaplan turbines are normally preferred for heads up to 100 ft. The highest head installation using a Kaplan turbine has a 290-ft head and is located in Italy. Horizontal axial-flow bulb and tubular turbines have been developed recently for use at sites with energy heads between 15 and 50 ft.

The bulb-type turbine and the associated generator placed in a bulb-shaped housing are positioned in the center of the water passageway (see Fig. 17.2-8). The tubular turbine design (see Fig. 17.2-9) uses an axial-flow turbine mounted in the center of the water passageway. The turbine is connected by a shaft to a conventional horizontal-type generator located outside of the water passageway. The bulb-type and tubular turbines have economic advantages in low-head installations because the spiral or semi-spiral scroll cases and the elbow-type draft tubes necessary for Francis and Kaplan reaction turbines are eliminated.

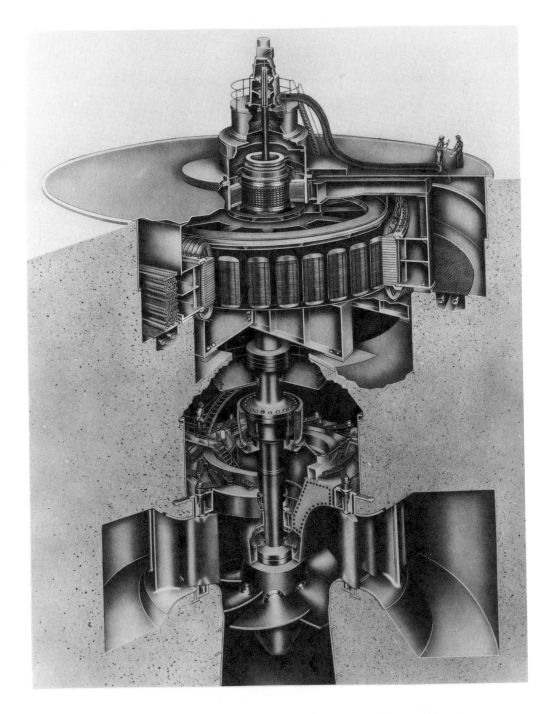

Fig. 17.2-7 Kaplan turbine installation. Photograph courtesy of the Allis-Chalmers Corporation.

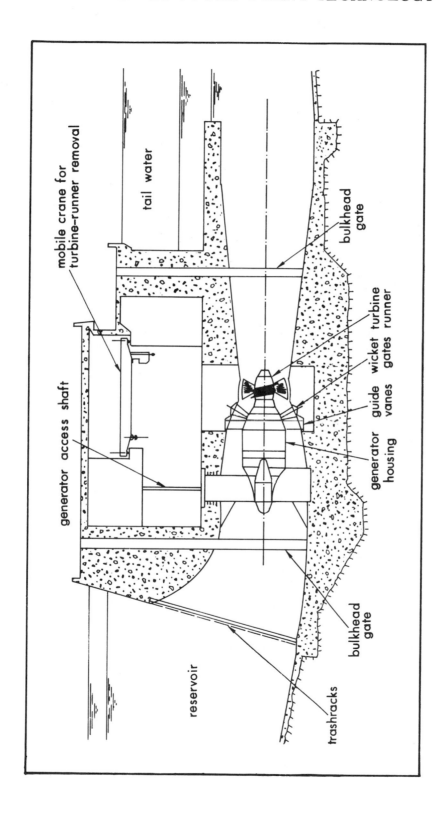

Fig. 17.2-8   Diagram of a bulb-type axial-flow turbine installation.

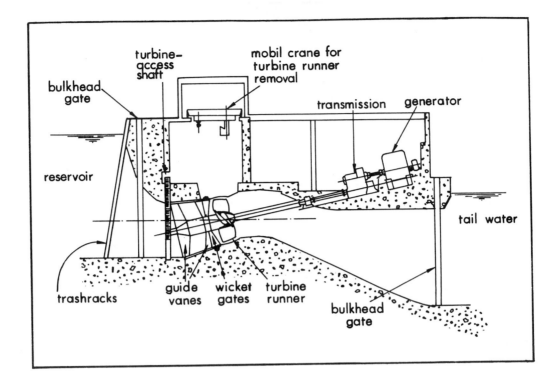

Fig. 17.2-9 Tubular turbine installation.

The efficiency of hydraulic turbines is defined as the ratio of the energy extracted from the flowing water to the energy contained in the water entering the turbine. Efficiencies of 0.90 or more have been obtained with Pelton, Francis, and Kaplan turbines under optimal conditions. Typical efficiencies of Pelton, Francis, and Kaplan turbines as functions of the operating capacity, expressed as a percent of the design capacity, are shown in Fig. 17.2-10. Efficiencies are seen to decrease rapidly for operations below about the 40% capacity level. The curves shown in

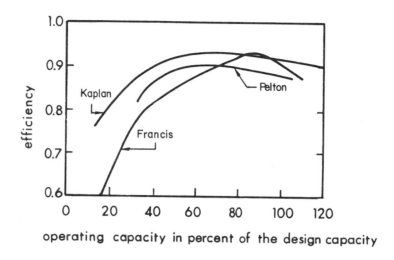

Fig. 17.2-10 Typical efficiencies of Pelton, Francis, and Kaplan hydraulic turbines as functions of the operating capacity; reprinted from B. M. Weedy, Electric Power Systems, John Wiley & Sons Inc., London, 1967; by permission of John Wiley & Sons, Inc. Copyright © 1967 by John Wiley & Sons, Inc.

Fig. 17.2-10 indicate that Kaplan turbines have an efficiency of 0.90 or more in an operating range from about 40 to 110% of the design capacity. To obtain an efficiency of 0.90, Francis turbines must operate in a smaller range of about 70 to 100% of the design capacity. The Pelton turbine must operate at about 60% of the design capacity in order to reach an efficiency of 0.90. The maximum efficiencies of Pelton and Kaplan turbines occur at about 60% of the design capacity, while the maximum efficiency of a Francis turbine occurs at about 90% of the design capacity (see Fig. 17.2-10).

17.3   <u>The Use of Hydroelectric Power in the United States</u>

In 1972, the installed electrical generating capacity in the U.S. was 418×10^3 Mw$_e$ of which 57×10^3 Mw$_e$ or 13.6% was hydroelectric. During 1972, there were 1.853×10^{12} kwh$_e$ of electrical energy generated in the U.S. of which 0.273×10^{12} kwh$_e$ or 14.7% were generated by hydroelectric installations. The 1972 average plant-use factor for U.S. hydroelectric power plants was about 55%.

A. Hydroelectric Resources of the United States

The ultimate U.S. hydroelectric capacity has been estimated[1] to be 186.8×10^3 Mw$_e$ (compare Section 2.20). The installed capacity in 1972 was only about 30.5% of the total potentially available. An estimate for the ultimate U.S. capacity is developed from stream-flow records of the major drainage systems in the U.S. These records have been collected for many years by the U.S. Geological Survey. The major drainages and the corresponding developed and undeveloped hydroelectric capacities are shown in Fig. 17.3-1.

---

[1] U.S. Geological Survey estimate prepared for the World Energy Conference, Detroit, Michigan, 1974; compiled by R.F. Meyer, Deputy Chief, Office of Energy Resources, U.S. Geological Survey, Reston, Virginia.

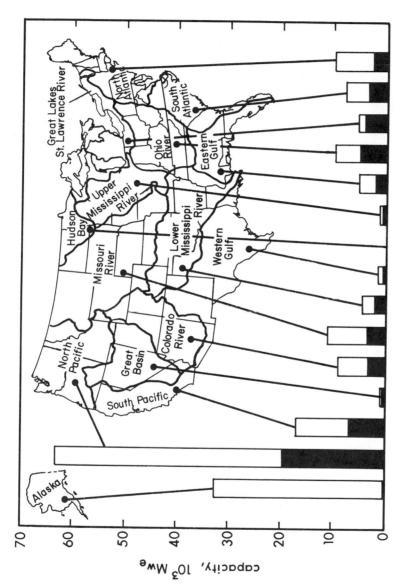

Fig. 17.3-1 The major drainages of the United States and the corresponding developed (darkened portions of the bargraphs) and undeveloped (remaining undarkened portions of the bargraphs) hydroelectric capacities. The hydroelectric potential of Hawaii, amounting to 54 Mw_e of which 19 Mw_e are developed, is not shown. Reproduced from Hydroelectric Power Resources of the United States, U.S. Government Printing Office, Washington, D.C., 1972.

The North Pacific drainage is seen to have the largest developed and undeveloped capacities in the U.S. (see Fig. 17.3-1). The North Pacific developed capacity is about 37% of the total U.S. developed capacity while the undeveloped capacity is about 34% of the total U.S. undeveloped capacity. The state of Washington has the largest developed capacity (12.4×10^3 Mw$_e$) and the largest total potential capacity (34.7×10^3 Mw$_e$). Alaska has the largest undeveloped capacity (32.5×10^3 Mw$_e$).[2]

B. Historical Development of Hydroelectric Power
    Applications in the United States

On September 30, 1882, only 26 days after the Pearl Street steam-electric plant began operation in New York City, a hydroelectric station was placed in operation on the Fox River in Appleton, Wisconsin. This plant was also the first hydroelectric power plant in the world. The Appleton plant had a 42-inch waterwheel which operated under a 10-ft head. The waterwheel drove two Edison type-K direct-current generators with a total output of about 25 kw$_e$. The electrical-energy output was sold to two paper mills and one residential consumer for lighting with incandescent lamps.

In 1890, the first alternating-current hydroelectric power plant was placed in operation on the Willamette River

---

[2] Hydroelectric Power Resources of the United States, U.S. Federal Power Commission, U.S. Government Printing Office, Washington, D.C., 1972.

near Oregon City, Oregon. This plant provided power for the first "long-distance" transmission of a. c. power in the U.S., namely, a 13-mile 4,000-volt power line to Portland, Oregon. The first dam constructed exclusively for electric-power generation in the U.S. was built on the Willamette River site in 1894. In 1895, the first large hydraulic turbines were installed in a hydroelectric plant located at Niagara Falls, New York. These hydraulic turbines drove 3,750-kw$_e$ generators which produced electricity for Buffalo, New York.

Since 1930, there has been a five-fold increase in the installed hydroelectric generating capacity of the U.S. This rapid growth in capacity has, however, been overshadowed by the phenomenal expansion of steam-electric plant capacity during the same period. During the early years of this century, hydroelectric plants provided about one-third of generating capacity; by 1972, hydroelectric plants contributed only about 14% of the electrical energy. According to workers at the Federal Power Commission, [2] this trend is expected to continue because of the advent of nuclear power, continued economic superiority for the use of fossil fuels, and the growing difficulty in developing additional hydroelectric plant sites. Perhaps a partial reversal will occur because of increased fossil-fuel prices, environmental problems involved in the use of both nuclear and fossil-fuel power plants, and technological advances in hydroelectric power-generation equipment.

In 1972, there were 1,511 hydroelectric plants in the U.S. This total included 1,492 conventional plants, 10 combined pumped-storage plants, and 9 pure pumped-storage plants (see Section 12.3 for a discussion of pure and combined pumped-storage installations). Since 1960, the number of large hydroelectric plants (over 100 Mw_e) has increased from 85 to 129 (i.e., by about 52%). The average capacity of these installations is nearly 300 Mw_e and they represent 72.3% of the 1972 total developed hydroelectric capacity in the U.S. During this same period, the number of plants with capacities less than 100 Mw_e has decreased[2] by 221, a 14% reduction. At the beginning of 1972, about 7.8×10^3 Mw_e of hydroelectric capacity were under construction, which correspond to nearly 15% of the 1972 installed capacity. At the same time, 17 hydroelectric plants, each with a potential capacity of 100 Mw_e or more, were either under construction or authorized.

C.   Examples of Hydroelectric Power Plants in the United States

Notable examples of hydroelectric power-generation stations are located at the Grand Coulee Dam of the Columbia River in Washington and at the Hoover Dam of the Colorado River on the Nevada-Arizona border. Both of these dams were designated by the American Society of Civil Engineers in 1955 as being among the seven engineering wonders in the United States.

The Grand Coulee Dam installation will be the largest hydroelectric facility in the world when its ultimate capacity of 9,780 Mw_e is reached.

Hoover Dam was built after Congress passed in 1928 the Boulder Canyon Project Act authorizing construction of both the dam and the All-American Canal System. Its primary purpose was flood and drought control. The Hoover Dam reservoir is Lake Mead, which has the capacity to store two years of average Colorado River flow. The lake is used to control irrigation of 0.75×10^6 acres in the U.S. and of 0.5×10^6 acres in Mexico. The cumulative gross value of crops grown on project land was estimated[3] as $\$32 \times 10^9$ in 1972. The water supplements the needs of 10 million residents. The dam itself (see Fig. 17.3-2) is 726.4 ft high with a crest length of 1,244 ft; it is 660 ft thick at the bottom and 45 ft thick at the top, where it accommodates a major two-lane highway. The dam contains 3.25×10^6 yd^3 of concrete. Lake Mead is 110 miles long when it is full, holds 26.2×10^6 acre-ft of available water, has a maximum depth of 500 ft, and covers 157,900 acres when the water reaches the top of the spillway at an elevation of 1,221.4 ft above sea level.

The hydroelectric plant of Hoover Dam has a generating capacity of 1,344.8 Mw_e. Electricity is generated by 17 large generators rated at 40,000 kw_e (one), 50,000 kw_e

---

[3]Hoover Dam, U.S. Department of the Interior, Bureau of Reclamation, U.S. Government Printing Office, 1972 O-461-72, Washington, D.C., 1972.

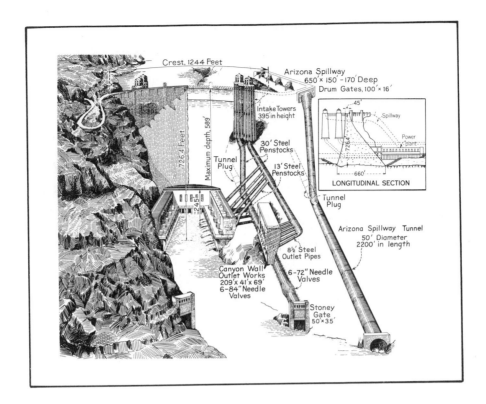

Fig. 17.3-2 Hoover Dam hydroelectric power plant. The
              Nevada wall of Black Canyon is shown as solid,
              whereas the Arizona wall is cut away to reveal
              the intake towers, spillway, penstock pipes, and
              outlet works. Inside the Nevada wall, there is
              a similar set of diversion works. The principal
              dimensions of the facility are shown. Repro-
              duced from Ref. [3].

(one), 82,500 kw$_e$ (14), and 95,000 kw$_e$ (one); there are two
station service generators rated at 2,400 kw$_e$ each. The
corresponding turbine capacities are 55,000 hp (one), 70,000
hp (one), and 115,000 hp (15); the station service turbines
are rated at 3,500 hp each. The 115,000-hp turbines are

Francis turbines designed to be operated under heads from 420 to 590 ft at 180 rpm. The station service turbines are Pelton turbines designed to operate at 300 rpm.

Hoover Dam cost 175×10^6 to build (i. e. , $130/kw$_e$ or approximately one-third of the 1971 capital cost of nuclear power stations). The construction contract was let in 1931. The dam began to impound water on February 1, 1935. The last concrete was laid on May 29, 1935 -- two years ahead of schedule. The power plant structures were completed in 1936 and commercial power generation began on October 26, 1936. The final generator unit began operation on December 1, 1961. The electrical energy output is sold to public and private agencies at variable costs, with some as low as 2 mills/kwh$_e$. Customers include the States of Arizona and Nevada (17.6259% of the total capacity); the Metropolitan Water District of Southern California (35.2517%) and the cities of Burbank (0.5773%), Glendale (1.8475%), Pasadena (1.584%), and Los Angeles (17.5554%); the Southern California Edison Company (7.9316%).[4] The equipment of Hoover Dam is operated by the Los Angeles Department of Water and Power and by the Southern California Edison Company under federal license. In 1971, annual electric operating income was[4] nearly 11×10^6, with cumulative revenue from power operations exceeding 280×10^6.

---

[4] The Story of Hoover Dam, U.S. Department of the Interior, Bureau of Reclamation, U.S. Government Printing Office, Washington, D.C., 1972.

17.4   Economic Considerations of Hydroelectric-Power
        Applications

The capital investment required for a new hydroelectric project varies widely according to the type of project, the size and location of the plant, the cost of the land,
and the cost of relocation of highways, railroads, buildings,
or other improvements. The average investment cost per
installed kw for conventional hydroelectric plants is higher
than for thermal-electric plants. However, the annual operating expenses of hydroelectric plants are normally significantly lower than those of thermal-electric plants, largely
because a hydroelectric plant requires no fuel and operating
and maintenance expenses are usually lower. The most
economical hydroelectric plants provide the lowest cost
sources of electrical energy available in the United States.

The 1970 capital costs for hydroelectric power plants
were between \$200 and \$400/kw$_e$.[1] The corresponding investment costs for five non-federal hydroelectric plants
ranged[2] from \$93 to \$726/kw$_e$ in 1971. During the same
period, investment costs for five federal hydroelectric plants

[1] The 1970 National Power Survey, Part IV, U.S. Federal
Power Commission, U.S. Government Printing Office,
Washington, D.C., 1971.

[2] Hydroelectric Plant Construction Cost and Annual Production Expenses, U.S. Federal Power Commission,
U.S. Government Printing Office, Washington, D.C.,
1973.

ranged[2] from $275 to $509/kw$_e$. The federal cost figures
include a portion of the cost for joint-use facilities. The
unit investment cost and the annual operating expenses for
hydroelectric plants can, in general, be reduced by operating
under high energy heads and by installing large units. For
example, the estimated[1] investment cost of the powerhouse and electrical generation equipment for a 100-Mw$_e$
installation decreases from $130/kw$_e$ for a plant operating
under a 100-ft head to $90/kw$_e$ for a plant operating under
a 400-ft head. In some applications, operating costs may
be reduced by installing automatic or remote control operating systems.

The annual operating expenses of hydroelectric
plants are normally divided into production expenses, including operating and maintenance costs, and administra-
tive and general expenses including depreciation, taxes,
interest, dividends, and other return charges. The weighted-
average production expenses for twenty non-federal systems
consisting of 398 plants were[2] 0.56 mill/kwh$_e$ in 1971.
Operating and maintenance expenses accounted, respectively,
for 0.35 mill/kwh$_e$ (63%) and 0.21 mill/kwh$_e$ (37%) of the
total production expenses. The average plant factor was
63%. These 20 non-federal systems account for 58% of the
installed capacity and 71% of the annual energy generation
of all non-federally owned hydroelectric plants. The Tennessee Valley Authority (TVA) system consisted of 29 plants
and involved weighted-average production expenses[2] of

0.78 mill/kwh$_e$ in 1971. The 20 multi-purpose plants in the TVA system had[2] weighted-average production expenses of 0.71 mill/kwh$_e$.

In 1971, the weighted-average production expenses for steam-electric plants were[2] 4.71 mills/kwh$_e$. Fuel accounted for 3.77 mills/kwh$_e$ or 80% of the total production expenses, while operating expenses contributed 0.42 mill/kwh$_e$ and maintenance expenses contributed 0.52 mill/kwh$_e$. During the period from 1967 to 1971, the weighted-average production expenses for steam-electric plants increased by 38%, while the weighted-average production expenses for hydroelectric plants increased by only 12%. The increase in production expenses for steam-electric plants was principally caused by a 42% increase in fuel costs. Thus, as fossil-fuel prices have risen, the competitive advantages of hydroelectric plants in terms of production expenses have become greater.

17.5 Environmental Effects of Hydroelectric-Power Developments

The environmental effects of hydroelectric power facilities are quite complex and must be evaluated on an individual project basis. Hydroelectric projects often have desirable ecological impacts such as flood and drought control, improved wildlife habitats or food supply, and recreational opportunities. Undesirable environmental effects may include upstream flooding of river valleys, downstream water shortages, reduced wildlife mobility, and required clearing of energy transmission corridors. The ecological impacts of a hydroelectric installation are irreversible (at least until the project is removed or abandoned), complex with both strong positive and negative aspects, and require a systematic analysis for thorough understanding. Unfortunately, past developments of hydroelectric installations have not generally been preceded by adequate environmental-impact analyses.

The environmental effects of hydroelectric projects have been studied[1] in detail by Lagler. The analysis by Lagler divides the impact of a hydroelectric dam into its effects on physical, biological, and human systems. The effects on physical systems include changes in microclimate, water quantity, and water quality. The known effects on water quality include nitrogen addition as a result of spill-way operation, oxygen concentration reduction in deep reservoirs, and temperature increases in shallow reservoirs.[2] The aquatic and terrestrial ecosystems near the project are also affected. Land is ordinarily drowned by the reservoir, which may result in aesthetically displeasing effects such

---

[1]K. F. Lagler, Chapter 10 on "Ecological Effects of Hydro-electric Dams" in Power Generation and Environmental Change, D. A. Berkowitz and A. M. Squires, editors, The M. I. T. Press, Cambridge, Mass., 1971.

[2]Ref. [1] in Section 17.4.

as partially submerged trees. The aquatic ecosystem is affected because the local watershed is disturbed. A summary of the possible ecological and social effects of a hydroelectric dam is shown in Fig. 17.5-1.

A less optimistic analysis of environmental impacts produced by hydroelectric-power generation has been given by Nisbet.[3] The most important of the many downstream benefits, which are often claimed to result from dam construction, are flood control and the option for augmentation of low river flows (i.e., maintaining an adequate water supply for navigation, industry, power-plant cooling, diluting pollutants, etc.). However, Nisbet[3] points out that the term flood control is often used as a euphemism to encourage building in flood plains and that periodic flooding is necessary to maintain the productivity and diversity of flood-plain ecosystems, including those used for agriculture. Even if operation of the dam does not alter the average river flow, low-flow augmentation, which tends to reduce river-flow fluctuations, may have adverse effects on a river since most aquatic organisms are naturally adapted to take advantage of seasonal fluctuations in flow rates, nutrient levels, and temperatures, and do not function normally if these fluctuations are reduced or eliminated.[3]

---

[3]I. C. T. Nisbet, "Hydroelectric Power: A Non-Renewable Resource?", Technology Review 7, 5, 64, June 1974.

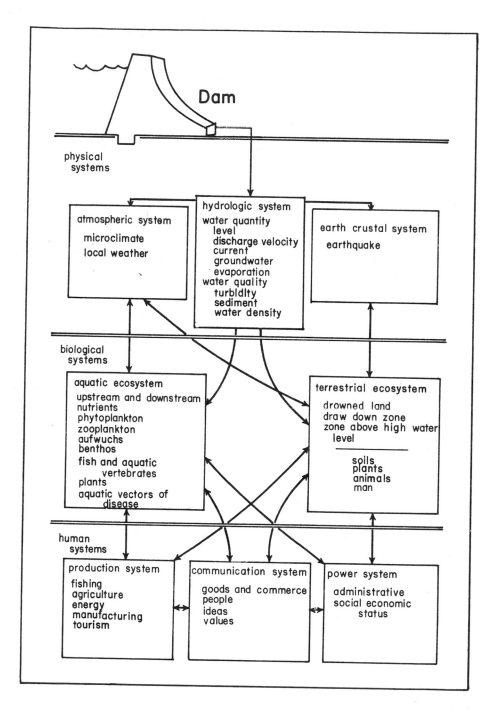

Fig. 17.5-1 Possible environmental effects of a hydroelectric-power project; reproduced from Ref. [1].

If exploitation of hydroelectric resources reduces the total flow of a river, the capacity of the river to absorb heat and pollutant loads is reduced, sediment transport is limited, and biological systems are further stressed. In some cases, diversion of river water may cause extensive intrusion of salt into the estuaries and lower reaches of the river. An example is provided by the Colorado River which, at times of low flow, is nearly dry before reaching the sea. At the same time, the rate of water withdrawal is not sufficient to prevent increases in the salinity levels of irrigated lands in the Imperial Valley of California.

Nisbet[3] concludes that perhaps the most damaging environmental consequence of dam construction is loss of the sediment load that is normally transported downstream. Substantial reduction of the natural input of silt and nutrients leads to agricultural requirements for artificial fertilizers in order to maintain farm-land productivity. An important example is provided by dams built during the past 100 years on the Nile River in Egypt. These have continually restricted the supply of silt that maintains the river delta and the nutrients that support marine life, thus causing a loss in productivity.

CHAPTER 18

HYDROTHERMAL-ENERGY SOURCES AND UTILIZATION

The term hydrothermal energy refers to naturally-occurring beds of dry or wet steam for which a resource estimate has been given in Section 2.18. Specifically excluded from the discussions in Section 2.18 and this Chapter 18 is the inadequately assessed <u>dry</u> geothermal potential (see Chapter 19 for a discussion of the utilization of these dry beds).

18.1   Introduction

Application of hydrothermal energy dates back to the use of hot springs as medicinal spas in ancient Greece, Rome, Babylonia, and Japan. Since the beginning of this century, natural hot springs in Italy, Germany, and Iceland have been augmented by man-made hot-water wells. Utilization of natural steam and hot water for heating homes and greenhouses was first developed in the Nordic and Middle European countries. In 1943, a large program to exploit natural hot

549

water for heating homes and for industrial uses was initiated
in Reykjavik, Iceland. Nearly the entire city is heated hydro-
thermally today. Several other countries, including the U.S.,
are currently utilizing hydrothermal heating on a small scale.
The cities of Boise, Idaho, and Klamath Falls, Oregon, are
partially heated by waters from nearby hydrothermal wells
and hot springs.

Hydrothermal-energy sources have also been used in
fish farming, pulp and paper processing, water desalination,
and steam cleaning. Hydrothermal heat energy may be used
as a direct heat source for refrigeration and air-conditioning
units. Naturally occurring hydrothermal waters may serve
as sources of extractable minerals and potable water. A
large potential impact of hydrothermal energy relates to the
production of electric power. Application of hydrothermal
energy for electrical-power generation began in Lardarello,
Italy, in 1904. Five light bulbs were supplied with electricity
by a small dynamo and a three-quarter horsepower generator
linked to a steam vent. Construction of a 250-kw$_e$ plant was
initiated during the following year.

Commercial operation at the Lardarello plant began
in 1912 and remained as the only example of hydrothermal
production of electrical power until 1958, when a small plant
located in the Wairakei area of New Zealand was converted
to commercial operation. Two years later, The Geysers
field in California was placed into commercial use and presently supplies the lowest cost electrical energy in the

San Francisco area. By 1973, eight countries were utilizing hydrothermal energy (for electrical-power production)
with a cumulative capacity of about 1.06×10^3 Mw$_e$, which
is approximately 0.1% of the electrical-power generation
capacity in the world.[1] An additional 0.82×10^3 Mw$_e$ is
scheduled for installation by 1977. It should be noted that
the development of additional electrical generating capacity
from hydrothermal resources in New Zealand was terminated
following recent discoveries of natural gas: the NG was
easily identified as a more economical energy source for the
region. The hydrothermal development program has, however, recently been reactivated in New Zealand.

The 1973 hydrothermal generating capacity in the
U.S. was 396 Mw$_e$ which corresponded to about 0.1% of the
U.S. installed electrical generating capacity. The U.S.
hydrothermal power capacity is expected[1] to reach 923 Mw$_e$
by 1977. Evaluations of the long-term potential for this resource differ significantly. It has been estimated[2] that
4×10^3 Mw$_e$ of hydrothermal electrical-power capacity
will be installed in the U.S. by 1985 and 4×10^4 Mw$_e$ by the
year 2000, assuming only minimal federal support for research or development. With federal subsidies, the

---

[1] R. L. Fuchs and W. H. Westphal, "Energy Shortage Stim-
ulates Geothermal Exploration," World Oil 177, 37-41,
December 1973.

[2] Final Environmental Statement for the Geothermal Leasing Program, Volume 1, U.S. Department of the Interior,
U.S. Government Printing Office, Washington, D.C., 1973.

projections[3] of installed U.S. capacities are 1.9×10^4 Mw$_e$ in 1985 and 7.5×10^4 Mw$_e$ by 2000. If massive research and development funding leads to significant technological break-throughs, the 1985 installed geothermal electrical-power ca-pacity could reach 1.32×10^5 Mw$_e$ and could be increased to 3.95×10^5 Mw$_e$ by the year 2000.[4] In late 1974, workers at the Electric Power Research Institute (EPRI)[5] projected the 1985 U.S. installed hydrothermal electrical-power generating capacity to lie between 2.5×10^3 and 4×10^3 Mw$_e$.

18.2   Characteristics of Hydrothermal-Energy Resources

Hydrothermal-energy resources are derived from the natural heat of the earth. Radioactive decay, friction from crustal plate motion, and primeval heat are possible origins of the heat flow in the earth. In general, this heat flow is

---

[3] Assessment of Geothermal Energy Resources, Panel on Geothermal Energy Sources, U.S. Department of the In-terior, U.S. Government Printing Office, Washington, D.C., 1972.

[4] Geothermal Energy: A National Proposal for Geothermal Resources Research, University of Alaska, Fairbanks, Alaska, 1972.

[5] D. F. Spencer, "A Need for Focusing Geothermal Research and Development Efforts," paper prepared at EPRI, Palo Alto, California, for presentation to the NSF Conference on Research for the Development of Geothermal Energy Resources, California Institute of Technology, Pasadena, California, September 23-25, 1974.

too diffuse to be utilized as an energy resource with present technology. However, in some locations (e.g., the Salton Trough as shown in Fig. 18.2-1), the natural heat of the earth has been concentrated at the interface between the crust of the earth and the upper mantle (see Fig. 18.2-2) by volcanism and tectonism. Thermal energy is brought upward both by rising magma and by convection of circulating fluids through magma chambers. Surface and near-surface water serves as the heat transfer medium by percolating through fractures in rock heated by the underlying magma chamber. The hot water rises and, in some cases, appears at the surface of the earth in the form of hot springs, geysers, fumaroles, and similar surface manifestations. This concentrated storage of the natural heat of the earth, by water within pores and fissures of rock strata, defines the hydrothermal energy resources. Because of their origin, hydrothermal energy reservoirs are generally replenished by geothermal heat flows; however, the time scales for nearly complete recovery are generally unknown.

Hydrothermal resources are classified in accordance with the absence or presence of liquids and by the reservoir pressure and temperature. The three major types of hydrothermal systems are: (1) vapor-dominated or dry-steam deposits, (2) water-dominated or wet-steam deposits, and (3) geopressured deposits. Not included in this classification scheme are the hot dry rock deposits (see Chapter 19) and the magma systems which contain thermal energy in liquid

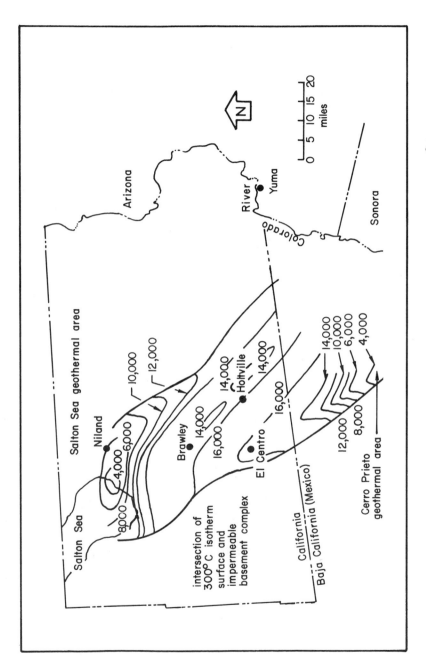

Fig. 18.2-1 The Salton Trough showing the depths in ft at which 300°C isotherms occur; reproduced from L. C. Dutcher, W. F. Hardt, and W. R. Moyle, Jr., Pre-liminary Appraisal of Ground Water in Storage with Reference to Geothermal Resources in the Imperial Valley Area, California, U. S. Geological Survey Circular 649, U. S. Government Printing Office, Washington, D. C., 1972.

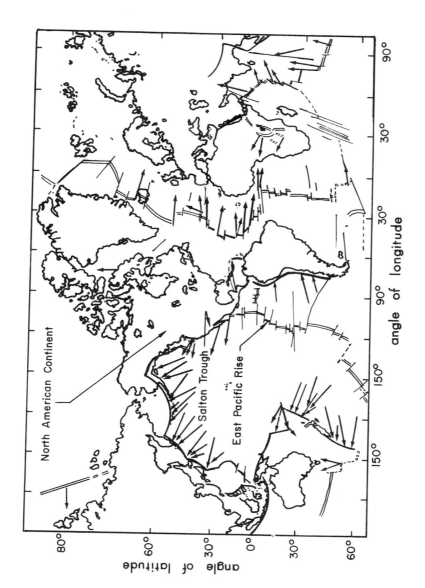

Fig. 18.2-2 World-wide ridges and trenches with which hydrothermal resources are often associated; reproduced from B. Isacks, J. Oliver, and L. R. Sykes, "Seismology and the New Global Tectonics," Journal of Geophysical Research 73, 5855-5899 (1968). Copyright © by the American Geophysical Union.

or near-liquid rock at temperatures ranging from about 1,100°F to 2,700°F.

A. Vapor-Dominated Systems

Vapor-dominated or dry-steam deposits are the least common of the three classes of hydrothermal resources. Saturated steam and water coexist in a dry-steam hydrothermal reservoir. The reservoir pressure is controlled by the steam phase. As the contained fluids rise toward the surface of the earth through either natural or man-made paths, the pressure decreases and the fluids tend to be converted first to saturated and then to superheated steam. The superheated steam may have as much as 130°F superheat at a well-head pressure range of 70 to 100 psig; it will contain minor amounts of other gases such as carbon dioxide, hydrogen sulfide, and ammonia.[1] Little or no liquid water remains with the superheated steam.

The dry-steam reservoirs often lie above hot brine deposits while serving as a cap for the upward flowing part of a convective hydrothermal system. The geological formations surrounding known dry-steam deposits have not been well defined. Dry-steam reservoirs are the most easily exploited hydrothermal resources. The hydrothermal fields in Lardarello, Italy, and The Geysers in Sonoma County, California, are examples of dry-steam deposits. Similar deposits have been identified and partially exploited in Japan.

---

[1]Ref. [4] in Section 18.1.

B. Water-Dominated Systems

Wet-steam hydrothermal deposits are found[1] to be approximately twenty times more common than dry-steam deposits. Water-dominated hydrothermal systems are often associated with thermally-driven convective cells. Hydrothermal energy is stored in the surrounding rock and in the water and/or steam occupying the rock pores and fractures. Water-dominated hydrothermal systems are most commonly found in areas of volcanism and mountain building. In some locations, the hot-water convective system penetrates the surface of the earth and may be recognized as hot springs, geysers, or other thermal surface manifestations.

For hydrothermal wet-steam deposits located at considerable depths below the surface of the earth, the reservoir pressures are so high that the equilibrium temperatures of the hot water are significantly above the normal boiling point at atmospheric pressure. Known reservoir temperatures range from 100°F to 700°F, [2] with common well-head pressures falling between 50 and 150 psig. [3] When water-dominated hydrothermal systems penetrate to the surface, either naturally or through man-made wells, they tend to flash into steam.[4]

---

[2]Ref. [3] in Section 18.1.

[3]Ref. [2] in Section 18.1.

[4]H. C. Helgeson, "Geologic and Thermodynamic Characteristics of the Salton Sea Geothermal System," American Journal of Science 266, 129-166 (1968).

The water contained in wet-steam deposits is usually contaminated by dissolved salts and minerals. Sodium, potassium, lithium, chlorides, bicarbonates, sulfates, borates, and silica are commonly found (see Table 18.2-1) in hydrothermal waters.[2] The known salinities of hydrothermal waters vary by more than two orders of magnitude, with values as high as 350,000 ppm[4] occurring in the Salton Sea area of California. The water-dominated hydrothermal fields in Wairakei, New Zealand, and Cerro Prieto, Mexico, are examples of currently exploited wet-steam deposits. The Imperial Valley of California (see Fig. 18.2-1) is known to hold many water-dominated hydrothermal deposits. Yellowstone National Park in Wyoming contains probably the most concentrated area of wet-steam deposits in the world but these resources are protected as part of a National Park.

C. Geopressured Deposits

Geopressured zones occur throughout the world in deep sedimentary basins of Tertiary Age (younger than 65 million years) and do not exhibit surface manifestations. These basins are often undercompacted below depths of 1 or 2 miles, which causes the trapped fluids in the geopressured zone to support a part of the overburden. As the result, the pressure in the formation may be substantially higher than the normal pressures at these depths. In regions where the normal heat flow of the earth is retarded by impermeable clay beds, the geopressured fluids may

Table 18.2-1 Observed mineral contents in ppm for geother-
mal wells at the Salton Sea in California, at
Cerro Prieto in Mexico, and at Yuma in Arizona.
Reproduced with modifications from L. C.
Dutcher, W. F. Hardt, and W. R. Moyle, Jr.,
<u>Preliminary Appraisal of Ground Water in</u>
<u>Storage with Reference to Geothermal Re-</u>
<u>sources in the Imperial Valley</u>, U.S. Geologi-
cal Survey Circular 649, U.S. Government
Printing Office, Washington, D.C., 1972.

Element	Niland, Salton Sea, California		Cerro Prieto, Mexico	Yuma, Arizona
	Well 39	Well 57	M 3	Musgrove 1
Sodium	50,400	10,600	5,610	141[a]
Potassium	17,500	1,250	1,040	---
Calcium	28,000	1,130	320	148
Lithium	215	40	14	---
Magnesium	54	74	b	43
Strontium	400	85	27	---
Barium	235	3	57	---
Rubidium	135	---	b	---
Cesium	14	---	b	---
Iron	2,290	0.7	b	---
Manganese	1,400	6.4	b	---
Lead	102	---	b	---
Zinc	540	---	b	---
Silver	b	---	0.05	---
Copper	8	---	0.09	---
Silica	400	120	b	18
Chloride	155,000	19,700	9,694	188
Boron	390	100	12[c]	---
Fluoride	15	1	0.88	---
Sulfur	b	---	≈10	---
Dissolved solids	258,973	34,800	≈17,000	1,000

a. Includes potassium content.
b. No data reported.
c. Calculated from the H_3BO_3 concentration.

become abnormally heated. Temperatures up to $290^{\circ}C$ ($\sim550^{\circ}F$) and pressures up to 500 atmospheres have been measured in geopressured reservoir systems.[3]

Water contained in geopressured zones generally has two unusual characteristics. Because it was originally expelled from clays as the clays were transformed into shales by increasing temperatures and pressures, the salinity of the water is lower than normal. Additional purification of the water occurs when the water migrates through the shales and into the porous sands which characterize geopressured deposits. Water from aquifers a few thousand feet below the top of a geopressured zone typically contains less than 10,000 mg/liter of dissolved solids.[1] In some locations, the water is potable and contains less than 1 mg/liter of dissolved solids.[1] The geopressured waters may occasionally be saturated with natural gas. At common reservoir pressures and temperatures, the solubility of methane in water is greater than 30 SCF/bbl. Geopressured reservoir waters typically contain 10 to 16 SCF of recoverable natural gas per bbl of water.[1]

Geopressured deposits occur in the northern basin of the Gulf of Mexico. Similar deposits have been discovered in California, Oklahoma, Colorado, Wyoming, and Utah during oil and gas exploration programs. Geopressured formations have also been identified in Mexico, South America, Europe, Africa, the Middle East, the Far East, and the U.S.S.R.

18.3   Hydrothermal-Resource Exploration and Assessment

Hydrothermal systems may be classified as showing surface manifestations or as being hidden.[1] A cross section of the first-named hydrothermal resource, which may be either vapor- or water-dominated, is shown in Fig. 18.3-1 and is characterized by permeable rock formations and significant surface manifestations. Hidden hydrothermal resources are often associated with impermeable clay and shale layers and occasionally show displaced, feeble surface manifestations (see Fig. 18.3-2). Representative temperature-depth profiles for hydrothermal systems are given in Fig. 18.3-3.

Exploration techniques for identification and assessment of resources include geological, geophysical, geochemical, and thermal methods. In isolated cases, some of these have been useful in locating and assessing hydrothermal areas. The most widely used technique for the discovery of new hydrothermal reservoirs begins with an investigation of areas with significant surface manifestations.[2]

---

[1] Testimony of G. P. Eaton, Deputy Assistant Chief Geologist, Geological Division, U.S. Geological Survey, Denver, Colorado, before the Subcommittee on Water and Power Resources, Committee on Interior and Insular Affairs, U.S. Senate, June 13, 1973. Printed in Geothermal Resources, U.S. Government Printing Office, Washington, D.C., 1973.

[2] Ref. [3] in Section 18.1.

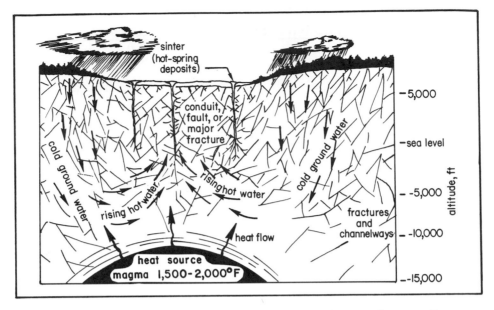

Fig. 18.3-1 Cross section of a typical hydrothermal reservoir. The Geysers field in northern California is an example of this type of system. Reproduced from Ref. [1].

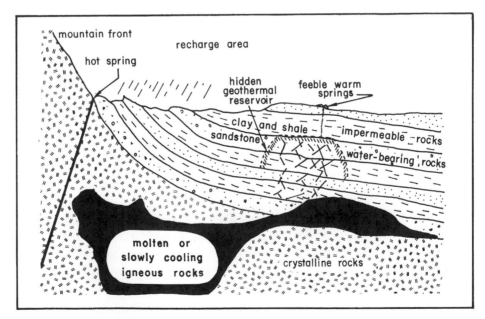

Fig. 18.3-2 Cross section of a hidden hydrothermal reservoir. Hydrothermal reservoirs in the Imperial Valley area of California are systems of this type. Reproduced from Ref. [1].

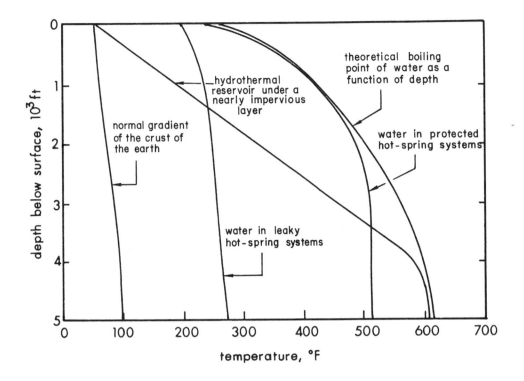

Fig. 18.3-3 Representative temperature-depth profiles for hydrothermal-energy reservoirs; reproduced from Ref. [1].

The development of hydrothermal resources has been handicapped, in part, by the relatively primitive nature of present exploration techniques, by inadequate understanding of the parameters that characterize hydrothermal systems, by lack of inexpensive techniques for drilling exploratory hydrothermal wells, and by the use of inadequate

borehole loggings and sampling techniques.[2] Adequate
characterization of the properties of hydrothermal reservoirs
requires three-dimensional temperature profiles, definition
of circulation patterns of hydrothermal fluids, and descriptions of geochemical alteration of reservoir-rock formations
and deposition of minerals.

A. Geological Exploration Techniques

Geological techniques are employed for the predic-
tion of hydrothermal conditions from studies of the local
geological environment, structure, and stratigraphy. Geological mapping provides[3] data on the types and properties
of rock formations at depth, on structures controlling the
migration of thermal fluids, and on the geological time history of the region. The greatest concentrations of thermal
springs coincide with regions of late Tertiary and Quaternary
volcanism.[4] The presence of thermal surface manifestations
in such volcanic regions indicates, in general, the existence
of high temperatures within 3,000 ft of the surface. Hydrothermal areas are also often associated with eruptions of

---

[3]D. E. White, "Preliminary Evaluation of Geothermal Areas
   by Geochemistry, Geology, and Shallow Drilling," United
   Nations Conference on New Sources of Energy, Volume 2,
   Rome, Italy, 1961.

[4]J. Healy, "Pre-Investigation Geological Appraisal of
   Geothermal Fields," United Nations Symposium on the
   Development and Utilization of Geothermal Resources,
   Pisa, Italy, 1970.

large volumes of rhyolitic (i. e., acidic lava) and dacitic
ignimbrites that suggest the occurrence of crustal melting
or intrusion. [4]

The existence of individual surface manifestations
over a large area implies that the area overlies a relatively
shallow aquifer capped by impermeable rock formations.
Low geothermal gradients are often indicated by hot springs
with large discharge volumes and temperatures below boiling. Surface manifestations with small discharge volumes
identify formations of low permeability at some depths or
the existence of impermeable cap rock with infrequent fissures or faults. [4]

B. Geophysical Techniques

Applications of geophysical exploration techniques
include measurements of electrical resistivity and magnetic
or gravity surveys. Several seismic exploration methods
(e.g., reflection or scattering) are also in current use.
Indirect resistivity measurements may prove to be valuable
exploration tools in the future.

Electrical resistivity surveys are probably the most
successfully applied physical technique for hydrothermal
exploration, especially in water-dominated systems. Exploration by electrical resistivity surveys is based on the
principle that hot fluids have significantly lower resistivities
than cold fluids. However, resistivity surveys are not good
predictors of the actual temperatures and volumes of hydro-

thermal systems because large resistivity variations are
also associated with changes in porosity, water salinity,
rock texture and clay content, and with partial boiling of
hydrothermal waters.[5]

Magnetic and gravity surveys have been useful in
determining the gross structural features of the earth, which
often indicate the location of potential hydrothermal deposits.
Gravity survey methods are based on the assumption that
densification of rocks within the area being studied is the
result of hydrothermal alteration of the rock formations.
Positive local gravity anomalies may, however, also be
caused by local structural highs, buried volcanic rocks, or
intrusive rocks. Negative magnetic anomalies often coincide with hydrothermal deposits. These anomalies may result from hydrothermal alteration of magnetic rock (e.g.,
magnetite) to non-magnetic rock (e.g., pyrite). On the other
hand, some hydrothermal deposits exhibit positive magnetic
anomalies which are associated with young intrusive and volcanic rocks. Gravity and magnetic mappings are of limited
value in estimating the boundaries of hydrothermal anomalies
because these properties are known[5] to vary significantly
from one area to another. Further research is required before a quantitative relation between either gravity or magnetic

[5] *Energy from Geothermal Resources,* Subcommittee on
Energy, Committee on Science and Astronautics, U.S.
House of Representatives, U.S. Government Printing
Office, Washington, D.C., 1974.

anomalies and the occurrence of hydrothermal reservoirs can be established.

Seismic exploration methods include reflection and refraction studies and monitoring of microearthquakes and natural ground noise. The geological structure determines the nature of seismic reflection and refraction. High attenuation and shifts to lower frequency of transmitted seismic waves tend to be associated with hydrothermal deposits and may be indicators of hydrothermal reservoir temperatures.[6] Microearthquakes are minor and frequent movements along fault lines, which often serve as paths for the propagation of hydrothermal fluids toward the surface of the earth.

C. Geochemical Techniques

Applications of geochemical exploration methods involve the collection and analysis of hydrothermal fluids from hot springs, geysers, fumaroles, ground water, and drill holes. The type of hydrothermal system, the minimum reservoir temperature, the homogeneity of the water supply, the chemical composition of the reservoir water, and the source of recharge water may be estimated by using geochemical techniques. Applicable geochemical methods involve analyses based on the distribution of gases and liquids and on the abundances or the ratios of abundances of chemical constituents and stable isotopes. Chloride analyses are

---

[6]Ref. [4] in Section 18.1.

used to discriminate between vapor- and water-dominated hydrothermal systems; chloride contents greater than about 50 ppm characterize most high-temperature, water-dominated systems while hot springs associated with vapor-dominated systems consistently have chloride contents below 20 ppm.[7]

The calibration of hydrothermal thermometers is based on the assumption that chemical equilibrium exists for the hydrothermal system and that transport to the surface occurs so rapidly that precipitation or retrograde exchange at lower temperature is prevented; furthermore, negligible contamination by other water sources is assumed. The most commonly used hydrothermal thermometers involve concentration measurements on silica,[8] on the ratios of sodium to potassium,[9] and on the ratios of sodium

---

[7] D. E. White, "Geochemistry Applied to the Discovery, Evaluation, and Exploitation of Geothermal Energy Resources," United Nations Symposium on the Development and Utilization of Geothermal Resources, Pisa, Italy, 1970.

[8] R. O. Fournier and J. J. Rowe, "Estimation of Underground Temperatures from the Silica Content of Water from Hot Springs and Wet-Steam Wells," American Journal of Science 264, 685-697 (1966).

[9] R. O. Fournier and A. H. Trusdell, "Chemical Indicators of Subsurface Temperature Applied to Hot Spring Waters of Yellowstone National Park, Wyoming, U. S. A.," United Nations Symposium on the Development and Utilization of Geothermal Resources, Pisa, Italy, 1970.

to potassium and calcium.[10] Stable isotope studies are useful in specifying the origin of hydrothermal waters.[11]

D. Thermal Techniques

Thermal exploration methods, which include measurements of temperature, heat flow, and temperature gradients, provide a direct technique for assessing the presence of hydrothermal resources. Measurements at depths require boreholes. Surface and near-surface measurements may be significantly influenced by insolation, topography, precipitation, and ground-water movement. Even a relatively small movement of ground water across a thermal anomaly may displace surface-termperature patterns significantly.[4]

The average geothermal conductive heat flow is about 1.5×10^{-6} cal/cm^2-sec. Exothermic chemical reactions, radioactive decay, friction along faults, and migration of waters of different origins into areas with nearly normal geothermal temperature gradients account for heat flows that are slightly larger than normal. Elevated heat

[10] R.O. Fournier and A.H. Trusdell, "An Empirical Na-K-Ca Geothermometer for Natural Waters," Geochim. Cosmochim. Acta 37, 1255-1276 (1973).

[11] J. Combs and J.P. Muffler, "Exploration for Geothermal Resources" in Geothermal Energy, P. Kruger and C. Otte, editors, Stanford University Press, Stanford, California, 1973.

flows associated with these phenomena are ordinarily of restricted extent and of limited duration. [11] Hydrothermal
deposits are often characterized by heat flows that are both
larger than normal and are also of longer duration. These
anomalous heat flows are attributable to nearby rocks of
near-magmatic temperatures. [12]

Temperature-gradient measurements in boreholes
of intermediate depths (50 to 450 ft) may be made with a
relatively high level of precision and reliability. These
measurements may, however, be affected by the lateral
movement of ground water. Favorable temperature gradients
at intermediate depths are greater than 7°C per 100 m, while
normal geothermal gradients are about 3°C per 100 m. [11]
Thermal gradients are directly proportional to heat flow
if the mean thermal conductivity is constant. The thermal
conductivities of rocks generally increase with depth near
hydrothermal deposits. Total heat-flow measurements are
independent of the thermal conductivity of the rock formations and are therefore preferred for assessments of potential hydrothermal deposits.

Recently, there have been attempts made to locate
thermal anomalies by infrared aerial photography. This
method has not proved to be very successful because of

[12] D. E. White, Hydrology, Activity, and Heat Flow of the
Steamboat Springs Thermal System, Washoe County,
Nevada, U.S. Geological Survey Professional Paper
458-C, U.S. Government Printing Office, Washington,
D.C., 1968.

interference resulting from slope direction, slope magnitude, soil moisture, fog or condensation, variance in rock properties, and vegetation.[11] The minimum heat flow detectable in normal aerial infrared mapping is greater than 100 to 150 times the normal heat flow.[13, 14]

E. Exploratory Drilling

Geological, geophysical, geochemical, and thermal exploration techniques serve to define the preferred sites for exploratory drilling. The actual monitoring of the flow characteristics of test wells is the only exploration technique which is capable of yielding meaningful data on the potential of a hydrothermal reservoir. Borehole data that are helpful in evaluating hydrothermal reservoirs include temperature-depth distributions, pressure-depth distributions, and measurements of permeability, porosity, lithology and stratigraphy, and fluid compositions.[11]

Application of exploratory drilling for assessment of hydrothermal deposits is limited by high costs. Because of the high temperatures encountered in hydrothermal areas,

[13] M. P. Hochstein and D. J. Dickinson, "Infra-Red Remote Sensing of Thermal Ground in the Taupo Region, New Zealand," United Nations Symposium on the Development and Utilization of Geothermal Resources, Pisa, Italy, 1970.

[14] D. E. White and L. D. Miller, "Calibration of Geothermal Infrared Anomalies of Low Intensity in Terms of Heat Flow, Yellowstone National Park," American Geophysical Union Transactions 50, 348 (1969).

the costs of drilling wells are at least a factor of two higher than the drilling costs for oil and gas wells. Representative drilling costs for exploratory hydrothermal wells are listed in Table 18.3-1. Drilling costs as a function of depth are shown in Fig. 18.3-4.

Table 18.3-1 Drilling costs in 1972 for exploratory hydrothermal wells as a function of depth; based on
data compiled by K. E. Brunot of the National
Science Foundation.

Depth range, ft	Cost range, 10^3
6,000 to 8,000	400 to 620
8,000 to 10,000	525 to 870
10,000 to 15,000	735 to 1,155
15,000 to 20,000	1,040 to 2,850

Average 1973 costs for exploratory drilling in the Imperial Valley of California to depths of 5,000 ft were about $40/ft; drilling costs in The Geysers field were about 3.5×10^5 for 7,000-ft production wells.[15]

New drilling technologies may be useful in overcoming some of the problems encountered in hydrothermal exploration. Development of rock melting drill bits may be

[15] J. Cromling, "How Geothermal Wells are Drilled and
Completed," World Oil 177, 42-45, December 1973.

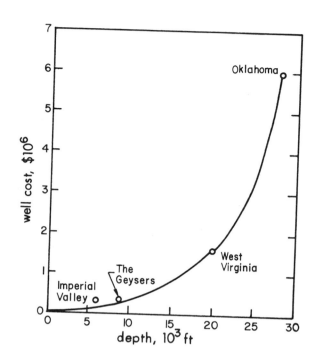

Fig. 18.3-4 Drilling costs as a function of depth; reproduced from J. H. Anderson, "Statement on Geothermal Power" to the U.S. Senate Committee on Interior and Insular Affairs, June 22, 1972, Geothermal Energy Resources and Research, U.S. Government Printing Office, Washington, D.C., 1972.

useful. [16] The most favorable characteristic of the rock-melting penetrators that are currently under development is

[16] J. C. Rowley, "Rock Melting Technology and Geothermal Drilling," paper prepared at the Los Alamos Scientific Laboratory, Los Alamos, New Mexico, for presentation to the NSF Conference on Research for the Development of Geothermal Energy Resources, California Institute of Technology, Pasadena, California, September 23-25, 1974.

their ability to operate in rocks at elevated temperatures
and to produce glass linings around the boreholes as an integral part of the drilling process. Preliminary testing [16]
of an electrically-heated, rock-melting penetrator tip indicates that a 150-kw$_e$ tip can penetrate from 6 to 10 ft/h
while consuming energy (e.g., ~ 2.5×10^5 Btu/ft for an 11.5-
inch diameter hole) in quantities comparable to that of conventional drilling machinery.

F.   Known Geothermal-Resource Areas

The Geothermal Steam Act of 1970 defines a known
geothermal resources area (KGRA) as "an area in which the
geology, nearby discoveries, competitive interests, or other
indicia would, in the opinion of the Secretary, engender a
belief in men who are experienced in the subject matter that
the prospects for extraction of geothermal steam or associated geothermal resources are good enough to warrant expenditures of money for that purpose." It is important
to note that the establishment of a KGRA does not require a
producing or producible geothermal well.

In accord with the Geothermal Steam Act of 1970,
the U.S. Geological Survey has classified about 1.8×10^6
acres of land in the western United States as being within
the boundaries of a KGRA;[2] about 56% (1×10^6 acres) of
the land is federal land. An additional 96×10^6 acres are
identified as having "prospective value" for geothermal
resources;[2] approximately 60% (58×10^6 acres) of this

land is federally controlled.

A KGRA is established after the information derived from geological, geochemical, and geophysical data, as well as evidence based on nearby discoveries, competitive interests, and other indicia, have been adequately evaluated.[17] The boundaries of a KGRA are defined[17] by regional characteristics such as the pattern of temperature gradients, geologic structure, stratigraphy, porosity, conductivity, permeability, heat source, and fluid recharge rate.

18.4 Utilization of Hydrothermal Energy for Electrical-Power Generation

The design of a suitable hydrothermal power plant depends on the resource type and reservoir production pressure and temperature. The major design concepts include direct steam utilization, flashed-steam systems, binary-cycle designs, and total-flow systems.

A. Utilization of Vapor-Dominated Reservoirs

The preferred technology for exploitation of vapor-dominated, hydrothermal resources involves direct utilization of dry steam as at The Geysers, California, and

---

[17] L. H. Godwin et al, Classification of Public Lands Valuable for Geothermal Steam and Associated Geothermal Resources, U.S. Geological Survey Circular 647, U.S. Government Printing Office, Washington, D.C., 1971.

at Lardarello, Italy. The system produces electric power by direct expansion of the dry steam through a turbine, which drives a conventional electric generator (see Fig. 18.4-1). The dry steam produced from a hydrothermal well or from wells at comparatively low pressures is filtered to remove liquid water and solid particles prior to entering the turbine. The steam discharged from the turbine is condensed to water. During condensation, thermal energy is transferred to a cooling medium, which is subsequently cooled (evaporated) in a cooling tower by rejecting heat to the atmosphere. The steam condensate may be reinjected into the hydrothermal system, discharged, or recycled to serve as the cooling medium for later production. Recycling of the condensate as a cooling medium is particularly desirable because both the external water requirements of the plant and the exit pressure of the turbine are reduced. The thermal efficiency of the plant is increased significantly by operating at lower unit pressures. The noncondensible gases produced with the steam may be either reinjected, collected and disposed of elsewhere, or directly released into the atmosphere.

The wellhead pressures and temperatures of dry hydrothermal steam are significantly lower than the corresponding values in a conventional steam-electric plant. As the result, hydrothermal plants operate at lower efficiencies. They require steam-production rates two to three times larger than conventional plants for equivalent power outputs.

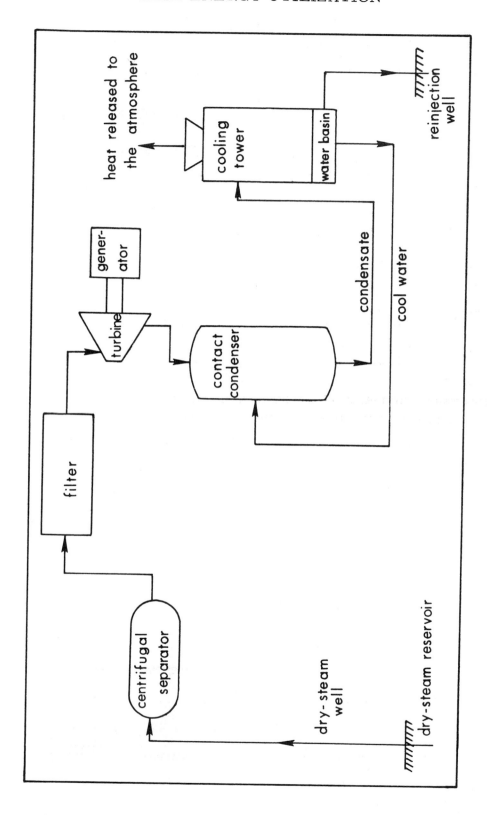

Fig. 18.4-1 Schematic diagram of a hydrothermal, dry-steam power plant.

The steam turbines and auxiliary equipment must be correspondingly larger than in conventional designs.

The steam-production rate at The Geysers is about 2×10^6 lb/h per 100 Mw$_e$ of capacity and requires the supply from 12 to 14 hydrothermal wells.[1] Units 5 and 6 at The Geysers became operational in 1971 and have a design turbine inlet temperature and pressure of 355°F and 100 psia, respectively, as compared to typical fossil-fuel power-plant values of 1,000°F and 3,500 psia. The design heat rate for Units 5 and 6 is [1] 21,690 Btu/kwh$_e$, which corresponds to a thermal-to-electrical conversion efficiency of somewhat less than 16%.

B. Utilization of Water-Dominated Reservoirs

The utilization scheme for a water-dominated system depends on many parameters, including the reservoir pressure and temperature, well depth, and fluid salinity. Three basic designs have been proposed for energy recovery from water-dominated hydrothermal deposits. The Wairakei, New Zealand, and Cerro Prieto, Mexico, power plants use flashed-steam processes. A binary-cycle design or a total-flow system may prove to be preferable for use in the Salton Sea area of California.

---

[1] P. Matthew, "Geothermal Operating Experience at The Geysers Power Plant," Journal of the Power Division, Proceedings of the American Society of Civil Engineers 99, 329-338 (1973).

Production wells that tap a water-dominated reservoir produce a mixture of wet steam and hot water. The wet steam is produced as the reservoir pressure is relieved in the well pipe. In a typical flashed-steam design, the steam and water are separated and the steam is piped to a high-pressure turbine. The remaining hot water may be flashed to steam by further pressure reduction. The steam produced and the exit steam from the high-pressure turbine are then expanded through a low-pressure turbine which drives a generator. Exhaust steam from the low-pressure turbine is condensed in a contact condenser. The condensate is typically cooled in a cooling tower and recycled to the condenser. Depending on the water quality (i. e., on the amount of liquid mass per unit mass of liquid-vapor mixture), the hot water that was not flashed to steam and any surplus condensate may be either purified and subsequently utilized or disposed of by reinjection, in evaporation ponds, or by direct surface disposal. Figure 18.4-2 shows a schematic diagram of a typical flashed-steam power-plant design. The Wairakei installation is an operating example of the flashed-steam process illustrated in Fig. 18.4-2. The Cerro Prieto station uses a modified design in which the secondary flashing unit is omitted, the cooling tower is replaced with an evaporative pond, and the surplus hydrothermal condensate is not reinjected for disposal.

Binary-cycle designs are particularly useful in utilizing moderate-temperature reservoirs, as has been emphasized

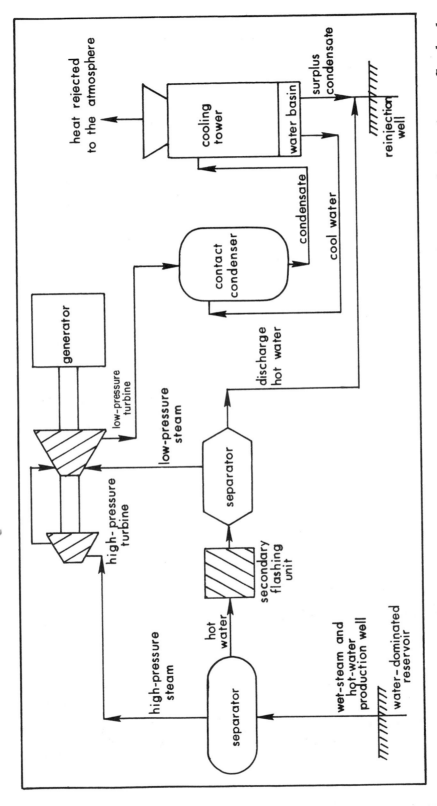

Fig. 18.4-2 Typical design of a hydrothermal, water-dominated power plant using a flashed-steam process. The terms high- and low-pressure turbine refer to the higher and lower operating components, respectively. In terms of conventional applications, the maximum pressure encountered with the high-pressure turbine is relatively low.

in Section 14.8 in another connection. In these cycles, the production well may be pumped in order to prevent flashing at the surface. Heat is transferred from the hot water to a secondary fluid (e.g., isobutane, ammonia, or freon) that has a lower boiling point. The selection of an optimal secondary fluid depends on the reservoir-production temperature. High-pressure vapor produced in the secondary-fluid boiler is expanded through a turbine which drives a generator. The turbine-exhaust vapor is then condensed in a surface-type condenser and pumped back to the heat exchanger to complete the secondary-fluid cycle (compare Section 14.8). Heat is removed from the condenser-cooling medium by circulation through a cooling tower. A schematic diagram of a hydrothermal power plant using a typical binary-cycle design is shown in Fig. 18.4-3 and is seen to be analogous to the configuration depicted in Fig. 14.8-2 for the Rankine cycle in the SSPP.

In order to optimize a binary-cycle system, many parameters must be evaluated. For a given reservoir temperature and pressure, the most critical factors are the choice of secondary fluid, design turbine-inlet temperature and pressure, condensing temperature, and type of cooling system.[2]

---

[2]J. H. Anderson, "Vapor-Turbine Cycle for Geothermal Power Generation" in Geothermal Energy, P. Kruger and C. Otte, editors, Stanford University Press, Stanford, California, 1973.

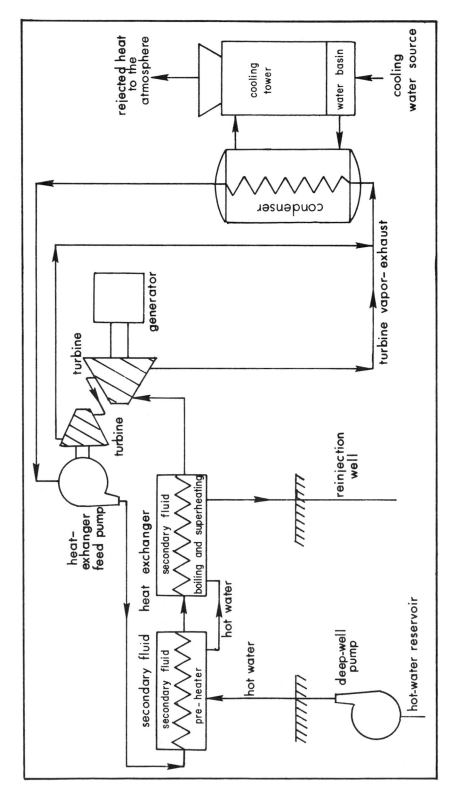

Fig. 18.4-3 Schematic diagram of a binary-cycle hydrothermal power plant. The binary cycle using isobutane is a low-temperature Rankine cycle (compare Section 14.8).

A comparison[3] of binary-cycle and flashed-steam designs for intermediate reservoir temperatures (300°F to 450°F) indicates that the binary-cycle design is more efficient than the flashed-steam design for a hot water energy content (enthalpy) of less than about 450 Btu/lbm. Anderson[4] has discussed in detail the relative advantages and disadvantages of adopting a binary-cycle or flashed-steam production scheme. Many binary-cycle designs have been suggested. Hybrid cycles incorporating both a flashed-steam and a binary-cycle process have also been considered.[5]

Investigators[6] at the Lawrence Livermore Laboratory have proposed a total-flow system for the utilization of

[3] J.M. Hollander et al, "Utilization of Intermediate-Temperature Geothermal Brines in the Production of Electric Power," LBL-2034, Lawrence Berkeley Laboratory, Berkeley, California, 1973.

[4] J.H. Anderson, "Statement on Geothermal Power to the U.S. Senate Committee on Interior and Insular Affairs," June 22, 1972, Geothermal Energy Resources and Research, U.S. Government Printing Office, Washington, D.C., 1972.

[5] D.W. Brown, "The Potential for Hot-Dry Rock Geothermal Energy in the Western United States," report presented to the Subcommittee on Energy of the Committee on Science and Astronautics, U.S. House of Representatives, Geothermal Energy, U.S. Government Printing Office, Washington, D.C., 1973.

[6] A.L. Austin, G.H. Higgins, and J.H. Howard, "The Total Flow Concept for Recovery of Energy from Geothermal Hot Brine Deposits," UCRL-51366, Lawrence Livermore Laboratory, Livermore, California, 1973.

water-dominated reservoirs (see Fig. 18.4-4). Application of the total-flow system permits[6] theoretically about a 60% increase in electrical-energy production from a given well, as compared with either the flashed-steam or binary-cycle systems. Production wells in the total-flow system are not pumped and the hot water is allowed to flash to steam as in the flashed-steam system. The steam and hot water mixture is then expanded through a nozzle to produce a low-pressure, high-velocity stream. A corrosion-resistant impulse turbine is needed to convert the kinetic energy of the total fluid stream into mechanical energy to drive a generator. The exhaust flow from the turbine is condensed in a modified barometric condenser which allows return of the cooling water without excessive contamination by the turbine-exhaust flows. A cooling tower or spray pond may be used to transfer heat from the cooling medium to the atmosphere.

The use of an impulse turbine appears to be a far more promising methodology for handling corrosive and scale-producing brines than is heat transfer in binary-cycle systems.

C. Power from Geopressured Zones

The development and utilization of geopressured zones are still in the conceptual stage. The potential energy sources from geopressured deposits include hydraulic energy from high-pressure (>2,000 psig) water at the wellhead, hydrothermal energy from the heat stored in water, and

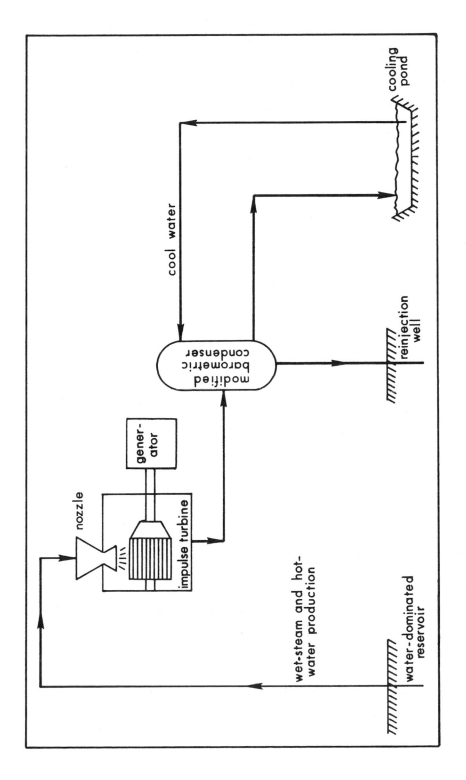

Fig. 18.4-4 Schematic diagram of a power plant utilizing the total-flow system.

natural-gas production.   Several designs[7,8] have been
proposed for the production of energy from geopressured
zones; an example is shown in Fig. 18.4-5.   In this design,
high-pressure hot water is passed through a high-pressure
separator for natural-gas extraction prior to driving a water
turbine attached to a generator.   The turbine-exhaust water
is then passed through a low-pressure separator for further
natural-gas extraction.   The low-pressure hot water is
finally used as a heat source for a binary-cycle system.
The waste water may be reinjected or transported to an offshore disposal site.

D.   Stimulation of Hydrothermal Reservoirs

Stimulation of hydrothermal reservoirs, by either
conventional or nuclear explosives, may prove to be useful for increasing hydrothermal well production rates and

[7] A. T. Maasberg and O. Osborn, statement on behalf of
the Dow Chemical Co., Midland, Michigan, to the Subcommittee on Energy of the Committee on Science and
Astronautics, U.S. House of Representatives, Geothermal Energy Research, Development and Commercial
Demonstration Acts of 1973 and 1974, U.S. Government
Printing Office, Washington, D.C., 1974.

[8] C.O. Durham, Jr., "Proposed Geothermal Energy Investigation Under Auspices of the "Geothermal Energy Research, Development, and Commercial Demonstration
Act of 1974," Geothermal Energy Research, Development,
and Commercial Demonstration Acts of 1973 and 1974,
Subcommittee on Energy of the Committee on Science and
Astronautics, U.S. House of Representatives, U.S. Government Printing Office, Washington, D.C., 1974.

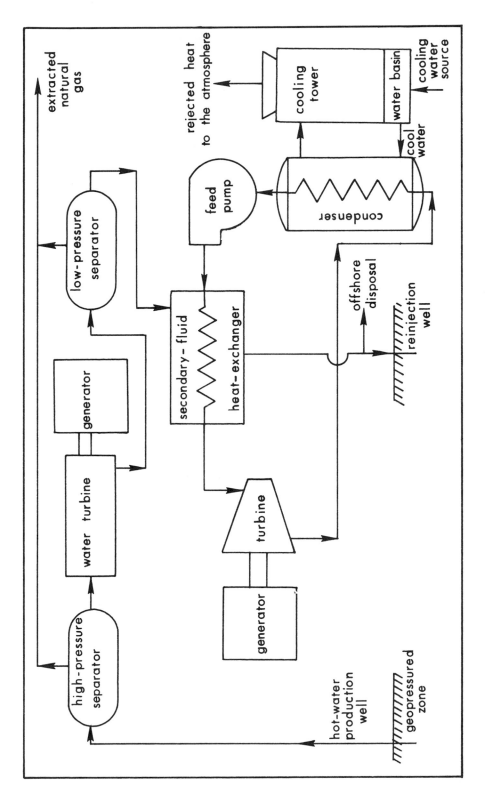

Fig. 18.4-5 Conceptual flow diagram for the utilization of geopressured zones.

lifetimes.   The absence of adequate permeability may prevent utilization of a large hydrothermal resource.   In some
cases, the required increase in permeability may be achievable by explosive stimulation.   This procedure may be beneficial for both vapor-dominated and water-dominated deposits.

Explosive stimulation may also be useful in providing
larger wellbore diameters to prevent the deposition of solids
from impeding the flow of hydrothermal fluids, creating adequate volume and permeability to allow economical reinjection of waste hydrothermal fluids, and creating voids to
encourage in situ steam separation in order to increase the
steam-to-liquid production ratio of hydrothermal wells.[9]
We refer to the literature [10, 11, 12] for further discussions

[9] A. H. Ewing, "Stimulation of Geothermal Systems" in Geothermal Energy, P. Kruger and C. Otte, editors, Stanford
University Press, Stanford, California, 1973.

[10] C. F. Austin and G. W. Leonard, "Chemical Explosive
Stimulation of Geothermal Wells" in Geothermal Energy,
P. Kruger and C. Otte, editors, Stanford University
Press, Stanford, California, 1973.

[11] H. J. Ramey, Jr., P. Kruger, and R. Raghavan, "Ex-
plosive Stimulation of Hydrothermal Reservoirs" in
Geothermal Energy, P, Kruger and C. Otte, editors,
Stanford University Press, Stanford, California, 1973.

[12] D. H. Stewart, The Status of Plowshare Geothermal
Power, BNWL-SA-4079, Battelle Pacific Northwest
Laboratories, Richland, Washington, 1971.

of the potential of explosive stimulation of hydrothermal reservoirs.

E.   Problems in the Utilization of Hydrothermal Resources

Difficult problem areas in the utilization of hydrothermal resources involve drilling technology and cost assessments.   For hydrothermal wells with an average power output of 5 Mw_e and an average drilling cost of \$2. 5 $\times 10^5$, the required drilling costs for hydrothermal utilization are \$5 $\times 10^4/Mw_e$.   Thus, incremental drilling costs of about \$9. 5 $\times 10^8$ will be required to reach the 1985 capacity goal of the U.S. Department of the Interior, which is 1. 9 $\times 10^4$ Mw_e.

A major difficulty (see Section 18. 7 for details) impeding the development of binary-cycle power plants is the development of scaling in the boiler heat exchangers.   In some applications, this problem is avoided by transferring thermal energy to a secondary fluid by using flashed steam rather than hot water.[13]   Direct contact heat exchange between the hot water and the secondary fluid is another

[13] B. Holt and J. Brugman, "Investment and Operating Costs of Binary Cycle Geothermal Power Plants," paper presented at the NSF Conference on Research for the Development of Geothermal Energy Resources, California Institute of Technology, Pasadena, California, September 23-25, 1974.

technique for eliminating scale deposition.[14] The inadequate reliability of downhole pumps may also inhibit the development of binary cycles for utilization of relatively low-temperature (<400°F), water-dominated reservoirs that ordinarily require pumping.[6]

Development of the hydrothermal hot-brine deposits in the Imperial Valley of California may be severely impeded by the highly corrosive nature of these waters, which contain significant concentrations of dissolved chloride salts. Corrosion tests with these hot brines indicate that new corrosion-resistant materials will be required before full-scale production can be implemented.

The dissolved solids in hydrothermal waters may pose significant handling and disposal problems. If highly saline hydrothermal waters are evaporated in cooling towers or spray ponds, large quantities of solids are produced. The Cerro Prieto plant requires about 100 pounds of hydrothermal water per kwh_e and operates with water containing on the average 20,000 ppm of dissolved solids. A 1,000-Mw_e plant with similar design specifications would produce 2.4×10^4 tons per day of solids. Solid production rates in the

---

[14] R. F. Boehm, H. R. Jacobs, and W. W. Coats, "Application of Direct Contact Heat Exchangers to Power Generation Systems Utilizing Geothermal Brines," paper presented at the 9th Intersociety Energy Conversion and Engineering Conference, San Francisco, California, August 26-30, 1974.

Salton Sea area of California , with a brine salinity of 250,000 ppm, could reach values as high as 6×10^5 t/d for a 1,000-Mw$_e$ plant, corresponding to a brine-production rate of 200 lb/kwh$_e$.

Noncondensable gases do not seriously affect the performance of binary-cycle designs. However, they have a major influence on the development of flashed-steam, water-dominated reservoirs and on the direct utilization of dry-steam deposits.

18.5 Hydrothermal-Energy Recovery Technology

The only significant experience in hydrothermal energy-recovery technology in the U.S. has been obtained during operations at The Geysers. This technology differs from operation at conventional steam-power plants in applications of steam-well drilling, steam-gathering systems, and condensate reinjection.

A. Steam Production and Handling at The Geysers

The steam-production rate of a dry-steam well depends on borehole and casing geometry because the flow rates are limited by frictional resistance. Steam output at The Geysers is described[1] by the production-rate equation,

---

[1] C. F. Budd, Jr., "Steam Production at The Geysers Geothermal Field" in Geothermal Energy, P. Kruger and C. Otte, editors, Stanford University Press, Stanford, California, 1973.

which is applicable for gas wells and has the form

$$w = c(p_s^2 - p_f^2)^n . \tag{18.5-1}$$

Here w is the steam flow rate; p_s is the static reservoir pressure; p_f is the wellbore pressure at steam entry and thus corresponds to the bottom-hole pressure; c is a time-varying empirical parameter which depends on the nature of the reservoir matrix, fluid properties, flow rate, and wellbore condition; n is an empirically-determined constant between 0.5 and 1.0 for the usual range of steam production. The bottom-hole pressure is the sum of the wellhead-flowing pressure, the pressure drop associated with frictional resistance, and the column weight of the fluid. The theoretical performance curves estimated from Eq. (18.5-1), for typical hydrothermal wells at The Geysers, are shown in Fig. 18.5-1. Here the dotted curve contains no allowance for frictional losses, while these have been appropriately included for the various bore-hole sizes indicated on the other curves.

The cost per foot of drilling increases rapidly with depth at The Geysers and elsewhere. Furthermore, increased depths imply longer steam-flow columns (i.e., higher bottom-hole pressures and correspondingly lower production rates). As the result, the probability of finding an economical steam-producing well decreases rapidly with depth (see Fig. 18.5-2). Attempts at maximization of production flow rate per dollar of drilling investment at The Geysers have led to the type of well completion configuration shown

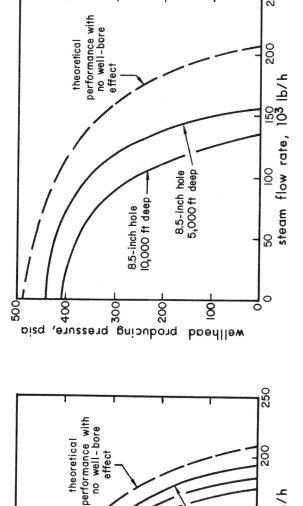

Fig. 18.5-2 Steam flow rate for a typical steam well at The Geysers as a function of wellhead pressure for two well depths; reproduced from Ref. [1]; with permission of the publisher, Stanford University Press. Copyright © 1973 by the Board of Trustees of the Leland Stanford Junior University.

Fig. 18.5-1 Steam flow rate as a function of wellhead pressure for various completion geometries of a typical 5,000-ft steam well at The Geysers, California; reproduced from Ref. [1]; with permission of the publisher, Stanford University Press. Copyright © 1973 by the Board of Trustees of the Leland Stanford Junior University.

in Fig. 18.5-3. The wellbore consists of 1,900 ft of 13.375-inch casing, 2,000 ft of 9.625-inch casing, and an 8.75-inch open hole for the remainder of the well depth.[1]

Reservoir production and pressure records have been monitored at The Geysers since mid-1967. Hydrothermal reservoir performance data over a wide region are required for realistic evaluation of production potential. With the actual flow rates used, The Geysers and Larderello fields have failed[1] to sustain constant rates of production over a period of several years (see Fig. 18.5-4). Well production may be strongly affected by well spacing (see Fig. 18.5-5) and decreases with time relatively more rapidly for closer well spacings.

The design of surface steam-handling systems is an important factor in the development of hydrothermal fields. Large-diameter steam-collecting pipelines permit high production rates, reduce frictional pressure losses, and lower wellhead production pressures. However, pipeline costs increase with size and heat losses increase because of increased surface area. Smaller pipelines show smaller heat losses but also yield decreased production rates and increased frictional losses. A steam-gathering system designed to deliver 2×10^6 lb/h of dry superheated steam at The Geysers is shown in Fig. 18.5-6. The main trunk lines are over-sized at the extremities to allow for insertion of collection lines from additional wells as the original wells decline in productivity.

A centrifugal-type horizontal separator, with 99%

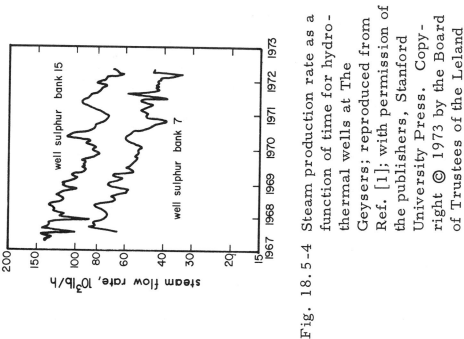

Fig. 18.5-4 Steam production rate as a function of time for hydro-thermal wells at The Geysers; reproduced from Ref. [1]; with permission of the publishers, Stanford University Press. Copyright © 1973 by the Board of Trustees of the Leland Junior University.

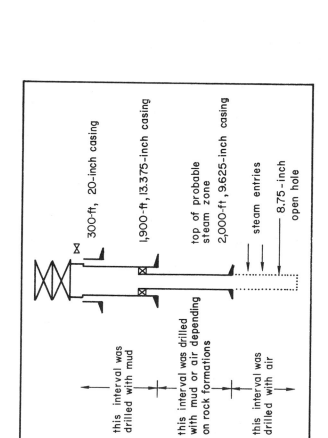

Fig. 18.5-3 Typical well-completion configuration used at The Geysers; reproduced from Ref. [1]; with permission of the publisher, Stanford University Press. Copyright © 1973 by the Board of Trustees of the Leland Stanford Junior University.

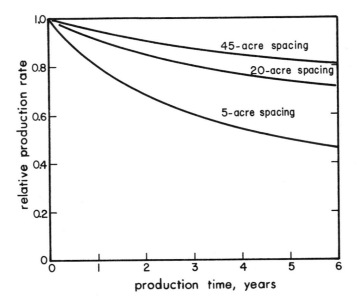

Fig. 18.5-5 Production rate as a function of time for several well densities. The data have been calculated from a reservoir simulation model. Reproduced from Ref. [1]; with permission of the publisher; Stanford University Press. Copyright © 1973 by the Board of Trustees of the Leland Stanford Junior University.

efficiency in removing particles larger than 10 microns, is located near each of the wellheads in the steam-gathering system. The separator is followed by a monitoring unit for well-production rate and pressure. Legs to collect dirt particles are introduced as tees through which the steam flows vertically, with the remaining dead-end leg of the tee serving as a receptacle for dirt collection. Control valves are included in the steam lines to relieve pressures in excess of 150 psig. For additional safety, rupture disks rated at 180 psig are installed in the gathering lines. These safety devices are required because wellhead pressures at The Geysers

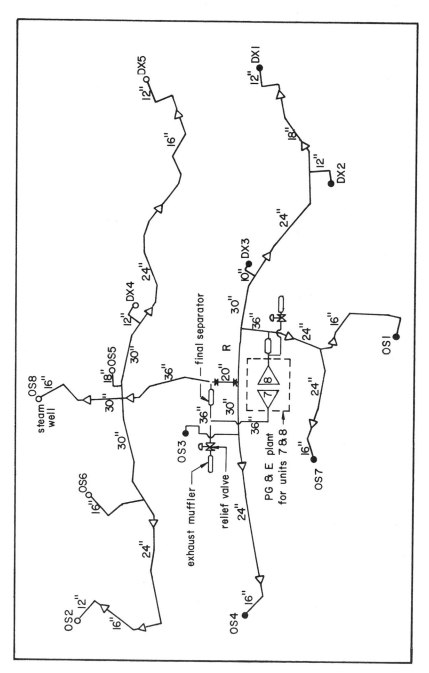

Fig. 18.5-6 Schematic diagram of a steam-gathering system designed for Units 7 and 8 at The Geysers; reproduced from Ref. [1]; with permission of the publisher, Stanford University Press. Copyright © 1973 by the Board of Trustees of the Leland Stanford Junior University.

reach 480 psig when the wells are shut-in.   Each wellhead
is equipped with a blow-down tee through which the well may
be opened to the atmosphere and blown-down to line pressure
before connection to the steam-gathering system.   A typical
wellhead and pipeline configuration in use at The Geysers is
shown in Fig. 18.5-7.

B.   Thermodynamic Analysis of Hydrothermal Reservoirs in the Imperial Valley of California

For specified hydrothermal reservoir states, the
wellhead conditions may be determined by using appropriate
force balances, momentum conservation, and mass conservation.[2]   The flow rate per unit area and well-friction factor (which is proportional to the flow resistance per unit surface area) for specified reservoir conditions determine the
wellhead pressure.   Once the wellhead pressure is known,
the other state variables of the wellhead product may be determined from steam tables.

Investigators at the Lawrence Livermore Laborato-
ry[2] have calculated the wellhead characteristics for a $300^\circ C$
brine deposit at a depth of 5,100 ft with a reservoir pressure
of 2,213 psia.   The wellhead product characteristics summarized in Table 18.5-1 apply for a flow rate of 500 lb/sec-
ft^2 and a friction factor of 0.04.

---

[2]See, for example, Ref. [6] of Section 18.4.

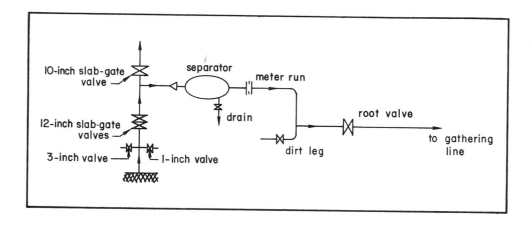

Fig. 18.5-7 Schematic diagram of a typical wellhead and
             pipeline configuration in use at The Geysers;
             reproduced from Ref. [1]; with permission of
             the publisher, Stanford University Press. Copy-
             right © 1973 by the Board of Trustees of the
             Leland Stanford Junior University.

Table 18.5-1 Calculated wellhead product characteristics;
              based on data in Ref. [2].

Variable	Numerical value
flow rate per unit area	500 lb/sec-ft^2
pressure	360 psia
volume per unit mass	0.26 ft^3/lb
temperature	434°F
enthalpy	562.5 Btu/lb
flow velocity	130 ft/sec
vapor-liquid volume ratio	16
quality (mass of vapor per unit mass of product)	0.19

The data of Table 18.5-1 allow calculation of the total (thermal) power obtained per unit of production area as follows: $(500 \text{ lb/sec-ft}^2) \times (562.5 \text{ Btu/lb}) \times (2.78 \times 10^{-7} \text{ kwh}_t / 0.949 \times 10^{-3} \text{ Btu}) \times (3,600 \text{ sec/h}) \times (10^{-3} \text{ Mw}_t/\text{kw}_t) = 296.6 \text{ Mw}_t/\text{ft}^2$. The specified wellhead product characteristics are needed to compare the flashed-steam, binary-cycle, and total-flow utilization schemes. The Carnot efficiency for a feasible condenser temperature of 120°F is found to be 35.1%.

The theoretical power per unit area available to the turbine of a flashed-steam system, utilizing an isenthalpic centrifugal separator and recovery of power from the saturated steam alone, has been calculated[2] to be 39.5 Mw_t/ft^2 for a condensing temperature of 120°F. A similar calculation,[2] assuming identical wellhead and condenser conditions, leads to a turbine-input power of 40.4 Mw_t/ft^2 for a binary-cycle system. The total-flow system has a turbine input power of 63.1 η^2 Mw_t/ft^2 where η is the nozzle-velocity coefficient.[2] The estimated[2] turbine outputs, with allowance for losses in the wet-steam turbine of a flashed-steam system, turbine and secondary-fluid pumping losses in a binary-cycle design, and nozzle (at a nozzle-velocity coefficient of 0.9) and impulse-turbine losses of a total-flow scheme, are shown in Table 18.5-2. Included in Table 18.5-2 are the overall system efficiencies, which are defined to be the percentages of wellhead power recovered by use of the specified design. The data of Table 18.5-2 indicate that the total flow system should yield about 60% more power than the other two recovery techniques.

Table 18.5-2 Estimated turbine power output per unit well
production area and overall system efficiencies
for various hydrothermal-energy recovery
techniques; based on data from Ref. [2].

Recovery technique	Turbine power output, Mw_t/ft^2	System efficiency, %
flashed steam	27.7	9.3
binary cycle	28.3	9.5
total flow	44.2	14.9

18.6 Scale Formation and Corrosion in Energy Recovery from Hydrothermal Deposits

Hydrothermal fluids generally produce severe corrosion and exhibit an extraordinary tendency for scale formation. Corrosion and scaling tests have been performed at the Cerro Prieto, Mexico,[1] and Wairakei, New Zealand,[2] wet-steam fields. Significant corrosion and scaling have been observed in the hot-water distribution system and hydrother-

[1] E. Toliva M., "Corrosion Measurements in a Geothermal Environment," United Nations Symposium on the Development and Utilization of Geothermal Resources, Pisa, Italy, 1970.

[2] P. K. Foster, T. Marshall, and A. Tombs, "Corrosion Investigations in Hydrothermal Media at Wairakei, New Zealand," United Nations Conference on New Sources of Energy, Rome, Italy, 1961.

mal space-heating units of Iceland[3] and, especially, at the Larderello dry-steam field.[4]

Because of chloride salt concentrations of several hundred thousand ppm and high acidity, the hydrothermal deposits in the Imperial Valley of California are exceedingly corrosive and also have an exaggerated tendency for scale formation. No materials with acceptable corrosion resistance have as yet been found for these brines. Magnetite (Fe_3O_4), Hausmanite (Mn_3O_4), and silica (SiO_2) scales form on surfaces exposed to the brines.[5] Austin, Higgins, and Howard[5] have suggested that scale formation may involve a series of reactions with casing materials. It is likely that efficient recovery schemes will involve the use of de Laval nozzles for condensation and fluid acceleration, followed by energy extraction through impulse turbines. Application of heat exchangers in binary cycles appears to be an especially difficult technology to develop economically for the Imperial Valley.

---

[3]S. Hermannsson, "Corrosion of Metals and the Forming of a Protective Coating on the Inside of Pipes Carrying Thermal Waters Used by the Reykjavik Municipal District Heating Service," United Nations Symposium on the Development and Utilization of Geothermal Resources, Pisa, Italy, 1970.

[4]G. Allegrini and G. Benvenuti, "Corrosion Characteristics and Geothermal Power Plant Protection," United Nations Symposium on the Development and Utilization of Geothermal Resources, Pisa, Italy, 1970.

[5]Ref. [6] in Section 18.4.

18.7 Economic Aspects of Hydrothermal Energy-Resource
Development

Cost comparisons for electrical-power generation
from various sources are difficult to make because of the
lack of standardization in accounting practices. We have
repeatedly quoted power-cost comparisons. Here we note
a 1973 compilation prepared by investigators at the U.S. Department of the Interior. This compilation, which is based
on 1970-1971 cost data, is now out of date, except for providing a reasonable relative cost scale. The listed capital
and energy production costs[1] are as follows: gas-fired
plants--$105/kw$_e$, 6.7 mills/kwh$_e$ (for artificially low gas
prices); coal-fired plants--$225/kw$_e$, 8.2 mills/kwh$_e$ (not
counting the social cost of coal use); hydroelectric plants--
$390/kw$_e$, 9.6 mills/kwh$_e$; nuclear plants--$300/kw$_e$, 9.6
mills/kwh$_e$; hydrothermal water-dominated plants--$290/
kw$_e$, 9.7 mills/kwh$_e$; oil-fired plants--$115/kw$_e$, 10 mills/
kwh$_e$ (for unrealistically low oil prices). The hydrothermal
dry-steam energy cost is 5.25 mills/kwh$_e$. These costs
were calculated on the assumption of an annual fixed charge
of 17%, an 80% load factor, and the applicable heat rate for
each specified type of power plant.

        There are many factors that affect the unit cost of
energy produced by a hydrothermal power plant. Interrela-

---

[1]Ref. [2] in Section 18.1.

tionships between these factors have been studied in detail for electrical-power production in Japan by Hayashida.[2] The 1970 capital cost for a 10-Mw$_e$ plant has been estimated[2] as $340/kw$_e$ and decreases to $251/kw$_e$ for a 70-Mw$_e$ capacity. Assuming a plant factor of 90% and an annual capital charge of 13%, Hayashida arrives at an energy-production cost of about 9 mills/kwh$_e$ for the 10-Mw$_e$ plant and about 5 mills/kwh$_e$ for the 70-Mw$_e$ installation. These energy costs, which include interest, depreciation, taxes, and operating costs, are competitive with present energy-production costs from alternative sources with substantially larger plant capacities.

In 1970, Kaufman[3] estimated the potential energy-production costs from hydrothermal developments in the Western United States as 3 mills/kwh$_e$ for a 1,500-Mw$_e$ plant operating with an average load factor of 90%. The data of Hayashida[2] and Kaufman[3] suggest that economies of scale can be achieved in hydrothermal developments. However, these cost savings are not likely to be as large as for alternative energy sources because of an intrinsic unit-size limitation for individual wells. It is not surprising to note that

[2] T. Hayashida, "Cost Analysis on the Geothermal Power," United Nations Symposium on the Development and Utilization of Geothermal Resources, Pisa, Italy, 1970.

[3] A. Kaufman, "Economics of Geothermal Power in the United States," United Nations Symposium on the Development and Utilization of Geothermal Resources, Pisa, Italy, 1970.

it appears[4] to be less costly to operate large units by col-
lecting and transporting the hydrothermal resources rather
than by interconnecting outputs of smaller units electrically.
The possibility of using hydrothermal power economically
in relatively small unit sizes (20 to 50 Mw_e) is particularly
convenient for applications in less developed countries and
rural areas where power requirements and load growth are
typically low.

In 1960, the investment cost for the first 12.5-Mw_e
unit at The Geysers field was estimated[3] to be $266/$kw_e$,
including steam-winning costs of $113/$kw_e$. By the time
The Geysers field had reached a capacity of 193 Mw_e in 1971,
the average capital cost had decreased by nearly 50% to $138/
kw_e, including steam-winning costs of $34/$kw_e$. This in-
vestment cost was roughly equivalent to that for large gas-
or oil-fired plants. When The Geysers capacity reaches
502 Mw_e, the average capital cost, excluding steam-winning
costs, will be reduced[5] to $121/$kw_e$. In 1967, the produc-
tion expenses of The Geysers field were[3] about 70% of the
production expenses for fossil-fuel plants located in the same
area. The 12-year average energy-production costs of The

---

[4]Ref. [13] in Section 18.4.

[5]Statement of J. P. Finney, Pacific Gas and Electric Company, to the Committee on Interior and Insular Affairs,
U.S. Senate, June 15 and 22, 1972. Printed in Geothermal
Energy Resources and Research, U.S. Government Printing Office, Washington, D. C., 1972.

Geysers plant are[6] 5.4 mills/kwh$_e$ with an average plant factor of 77.5%. The corresponding energy costs for fossil-fuel plants in the same utility network are 7.6 mills/kwh$_e$ for an average plant factor of 47%. When the hydrothermal energy costs are calculated on the basis of the fossil-fuel plant factor (47%), the unit cost of hydrothermal energy rises to 7.3 mills/kwh$_e$.[6]

The annual fixed charges per installed kilowatt are slightly higher for The Geysers plant than for fossil-fuel plants. Matthew[6] concluded that current construction costs for incremental fossil-fuel capacity are higher than for hydrothermal units. The maintenance costs for the hydrothermal units at The Geysers field are more than 2.5 times larger than for fossil-fuel units. This increased cost occurs[6] because of higher required overhaul frequencies (at intervals of 2 to 3 years rather than of 5 to 8 years), smaller unit sizes, more severe steam conditions, corrosion, remote siting, and more extreme weather conditions. The operating costs of The Geysers plant are approximately 1.3 times larger than for fossil-fuel units because the simplicity of the hydrothermal units is more than offset by smaller unit sizes and remote location.

Since there are no current hot-water hydrothermal energy-resource exploitations in the United States, the economic evaluation of these systems is more speculative than

---

[6]Ref. [1] in Section 18.4.

for the dry-steam applications. The total-flow concept of hydrothermal energy extraction in the Salton Trough area has been estimated[7] to cost less than \$200/kw$_e$. The corresponding electrical-energy sales price would be less than 8 mills/kwh$_e$. These cost figures are slightly higher than for The Geysers field but would be competitive with other alternative electrical-energy production facilities.

The relation between economic viability of a hydrothermal, water-dominated, binary-cycle development and reservoir temperature has been evaluated by Holt and Brugman.[4] The installed plant cost (including the cost of the cooling tower operating with a condensing temperature of 65°F) for a 50-Mw$_e$ installation is shown in Fig. 18.7-1 as a function of reservoir temperature. The early-1974 data do not include land costs, working capital, royalties, or production, transmission, and reinjection costs of hot water (which is assumed to be non-fouling). Reservoirs with temperatures less than 400°F are assumed to be pumped while those above 400°F are assumed to be self-flowing. Reference to Fig. 18.7-1 indicates that the capital cost of about \$475/kw$_e$ at a reservoir temperature of 250°F decreases to about \$250/kw$_e$ with a doubling of the reservoir temperature. Holt and Brugman[4] suggest that considerable economies of scale will be obtained by building 50-Mw$_e$ units rather than 10-Mw$_e$ units; the unit cost of a 10-Mw$_e$ development has been estimated to be 25 to 35% higher than the corresponding cost for a 50-Mw$_e$ station.

---

[7]Ref. [6] in Section 18.4.

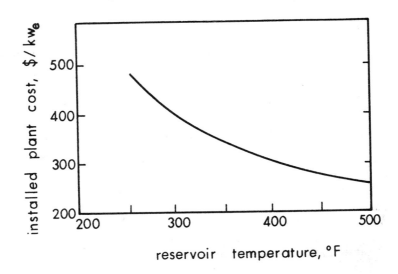

Fig. 18.7-1 Capital cost of a hydrothermal, binary-cycle
             power plant as a function of reservoir temper-
             ature; reproduced from Ref. [4].

If an annual fixed charge, including capital return and interest,
depreciation, taxes, insurance, maintenance, and general ad-
ministrative expenses of 21.5% is assumed for a 50-Mw$_e$ unit
operating 8,000 h/y with a reservoir temperature of 500°F,
the energy cost corresponding to the capital costs alone is
found to be 6.75 mills/kwh$_e$. The remaining direct operating
costs[4] are about 1.4 mills/kwh$_e$. Thus, the energy cost,
excluding the cost of the hot water, is 8.15 mills/kwh$_e$. If
the hot water costs $1.00/10^6 Btu and an overall thermal-to-
electrical conversion efficiency of 14.5% is achieved, the
resultant electrical-energy cost is about 32 mills/kwh$_e$.

18.8 An Environmental-Impact Assessment of Hydrothermal Energy-Resource Development[*]

Hydrothermal energy-resource development should have a relatively minor adverse effect on the environment, which varies with the nature of the hydrothermal system being exploited. Nuclear stimulation of hydrothermal resources may create additional environmental hazards.

Site exploration, test drilling, production testing, field development, power-plant and transmission-line construction, and full-scale plant operation contribute to the environmental impacts. These include thermal effects, land despoilment, ground and surface-water contamination, release of noxious exhaust gases, developmental and operational noise, land subsidence, seismic excitation, and cooling-water supply problems. Since all of the steps taken in the fuel cycle are localized at the plant site, the total environmental impact of electrical-power generation from hydrothermal sources is concentrated at or near the production facility.

---

[*] A detailed description of the environmental impact of the development and production of hydrothermal energy resources, including exploration, test drilling, production testing, field development, power-plant and transmission-line construction, and full-scale power generation, is given in the Final Environmental Statement for the Geothermal Leasing Program, U.S. Department of the Interior, U.S. Government Printing Office, Washington, D.C., 1973.

A.   Vapor-Dominated Systems

Land requirements for a 1,000-Mw$_e$ hydrothermal power plant are extensive.   For example, at The Geysers field the individual wells have an average production capacity of about 7 Mw$_e$, which indicates that nearly 150 wells covering 12 mi^2 will be required for a 1,000-Mw$_e$ installation.[1] However, only a small fraction of this land area will be modified by wells, pipelines, and the power plant.   The Larderello hydrothermal field has been compatible with agricultural industries during 70 years of development and production. Multiple land use practices have also been successful at The Geysers field.

High noise levels associated with the drilling operations and steam escape during production testing are significant environmental problems associated with dry-steam hydrothermal developments.   Drilling of dry-steam wells requires air, rather than the more conventionally used mud, for the circulating fluid which removes the drill cuttings from the hole.   As the result, the noise levels and dust-escape rates are sufficiently high to make the development of hydrothermal plants using a vapor-dominated production scheme incompatible with residential or recreational land use.[2]

---

[1]R. G. Bowen, "Environmental Impact of Geothermal Development" in Geothermal Energy, P. Kruger and C. Otte, editors, Stanford University Press, Stanford, California, 1973.

[2]Ref. [3] in Section 18.1.

Vapor-dominated hydrothermal developments should not produce land subsidence because of the particular geological circumstances under which dry-steam fields develop.[1] There has been almost no subsidence at The Geysers. However, some crumbling of inclined ground areas and surface slides have occurred, but it is not certain that these surface deformations were caused by hydrothermal development.[3] The absence of significant subsidence is explained by the fact that surface deformation is, in general, proportional to the total volume of liquid extracted and that only a small volume of liquid is actually extracted at The Geysers.[3] Vapor-dominated systems do not contribute to ground- or surface-water contamination since detrimental salts are not transported in the steam phase and other impurities, such as boron or ammonia which form salts during the condensation process, are normally reinjected. Water is not needed for cooling vapor-dominated systems because the dry steam provides cooling capacity, by condensation and subsequent evaporation, in excess of plant requirements. The Geysers hydrothermal plant produces about 20% more condensate (containing traces of boron compounds and ammonia) than is evaporated; the surplus condensate is disposed of by reinjection.

---

[3] B. E. Lofgren, "Monitoring Ground Movement in Geothermal Areas," paper prepared for presentation to the NSF Conference on Research for the Development of Geothermal Energy Resources, California Institute of Technology, Pasadena, California, September 23-25, 1974.

Very little noxious gas is released from vapor-dominated hydrothermal developments. The natural dry steam at The Geysers field consists, on the average, of about 99.5% water vapor and 0.5% of noncondensable gases. Carbon dioxide makes up[1] about 80% of the noncondensable gases, with the remainder consisting of methane, ammonia, hydrogen, nitrogen, and hydrogen sulfide. The hydrogen sulfide is the most damaging of these. At The Geysers field, the average hydrogen sulfide concentration in the noncondensable gases is 4.5% or about 225 ppm of the steam.[4] A 1,000-Mw_e dry-steam hydrothermal plant releases[1] about one fourth of the sulfur dioxide coming from a fossil-fuel plant of similar capacity and using coal with a 1% sulfur content. The carbon dioxide released from a 1,000-Mw_e dry-steam hydrothermal plant is estimated[1] to be less than 5% of that released by a fossil-fuel plant with the same electrical capacity. Of course, hydrothermal plants do not release NO_x, unburned hydrocarbons, or smoke.

The unstable conditions in the crust of the earth leading to the presence of hydrothermal resources are also associated with seismic disturbances. Therefore, the possibility must be considered that seismic hazards will result from hydrothermal-resource exploitation. Because of vari-

---

[4]M. Goldsmith, "Geothermal Resources in California: Potential and Problems," California Institute of Technology, Environmental Quality Laboratory, Pasadena, California, 1971.

ations in the nature of geological formations, evaluation of potential seismic hazards must be done on an individual site basis. Unfortunately, the required data are too inconsistent for a definition of the relation between hydrothermal developments and seismic activity.[1,4] No seismic hazards have developed at either Larderello or The Geysers fields.

B. Hot-water Systems

In applications where the process water is not reinjected into the hydrothermal well to maintain natural pressure levels, subsidence poses a significant environmental hazard. Subsidence has occurred[5] during exploitation of the hot-water hydrothermal resources located at Wairakei, New Zealand. Significant ground movement was observed over an area of 25 mi^2, with subsidence rates as high as 1.3 ft/y and a cumulative subsidence of 10 ft in some areas.[3] The noise levels associated with drilling and testing of water-dominated hydrothermal wells are significantly lower than those associated with dry-steam developments because conventional drilling techniques may be used. Thus, drilling of hot-water wells has, in the past, been compatible with residential or recreational land use.

---

[5] J. W. Hatton, "Ground Subsidence of a Geothermal Field During Exploitation," United Nations Symposium on the Development and Utilization of Geothermal Resources, Pisa, Italy, 1970.

Ground- and surface-water pollution hazards are a major concern in the development of hot-water hydrothermal wells. In the Imperial Valley, California, exposure of irrigation waters to saline brines would constitute a significant environmental hazard. In some other locations, hydrothermal waters have been used for agricultural, industrial, and residential use. Although hot-water hydrothermal fields have been developed successfully at Wairakei, New Zealand, and Cerro Prieto, Mexico, the potential hazards of surface- and ground-water contamination have contributed to delays in the development of hot-water hydrothermal wells in the United States. However, there are proposed hydrothermal developments in the United States which will use waste-water reinjection techniques.[2]

When hot-water hydrothermal resources are used in a binary-cycle system, large supplies of cooling water must be provided from an external source for the power-generation cycle. Thus, the lack of adequate water resources may impede hot-water hydrothermal development.

The quantities of noxious gases rejected to the atmosphere depend on the local water supply and the utilization scheme. The binary-cycle applications are expected to reject negligible amounts of noxious gases into the atmosphere. The flashed-steam and total-flow systems appear to be potentially more hazardous.

The likelihood of increased seismic activity during operation of hot-water hydrothermal power plants may be larger than for dry-steam hydrothermal plants because large volumes of water are removed and reinjected. Increased seismic activity has been reported[6, 7] near the Rocky Mountain Arsenal in Colorado as the result of injecting fluids into wells during waste-disposal operations. Similar experience has been documented[7, 8] in several oil fields.

C.   Nuclear-Stimulated Systems

The environmental effects of hydrothermal-energy exploitation stimulated by nuclear explosives must be evaluated for the entire life cycle of a hydrothermal site. The two most important environmental considerations relate to ground motion and to radiation containment following underground nuclear explosions. Theoretical and experimental data concerning these topics have been accumulated during the Plowshare Program established by the U.S. Atomic Energy Commission in 1957.

The potential environmental damage from ground motion is similar to that resulting from natural earthquakes. Although many radioactive isotopes are produced by nuclear stimulation of a hydrothermal well, the most significant ra-

[6] D. M. Evans, "Man-Made Earthquakes in Denver," Geotimes 10, 11-18, May-June 1966.

[7] J. H. Healy, W. W. Rubey, D. T. Griggs, and C. B. Raleigh, "The Denver Earthquakes," Science 161, 1301-1310 (1968).

[8] D. H. Hamilton and R. L. Meehan, "Ground Rupture in the Baldwin Hills," Science 172, 333-334 (1971).

diological hazard appears[9] to be the production of tritium. Experience has shown that a glassy material is condensed at the bottom of the cavity after an underground nuclear explosion. This material contains most of the radioactive isotopes; less than 10% of the radioactivity content is available for release by water leaching. The hot-water leaching of nuclear-stimulated hydrothermal sites may, however, pose a significant environmental hazard. Radioactivity may also be released immediately following the detonation by either direct venting into the atmosphere or by seepage of radioactive material into ground-water aquifers. Experimental evidence suggests that the probability of environmental damage by either of these means should be remote.[9] Other possible environmental hazards include surface extrusion of molten rocks and hydrothermal explosions by flashing of water to steam near the surface.

During hydrothermal plant and site construction, environmental damage occurs because of drilling, excavation, and construction. Experience has shown[9] that greater ecological damage results from these activities than from underground nuclear explosions. The greatest environmental hazard during operation of a nuclear-stimulated hydrothermal development is the transport and distribution of radioactive

[9]G. M. Sanquist and G. A. Wahn, "Environmental Aspects of Nuclear Stimulation" in Geothermal Energy, P. Kruger and C. Otte, editors, Stanford University Press, Stanford, California, 1973.

materials by either slow operational losses or by rapid releases following a containment failure. Some level of control and monitoring of a nuclear-stimulated hydrothermal site will be required, even after energy production has terminated, in order to insure public safety and continued compatability with the environment.

CHAPTER 19

GEOTHERMAL ENERGY FROM DRY WELLS

The normal geothermal heat flow of the earth has been described in Section 2.19. Here we shall try to obtain first a reasonable estimate for the total long term value of this energy resource and then discuss the potential energy recovery from anomalous heat reservoirs existing near the surface of the earth.

19.1 Assessment of Dry Geothermal Resources

According to the compilation of data given in Table 6.3-2, the total mass of the earth is 5.983×10^{27} g. If the mean heat capacity is 0.2 cal/g-$^{\circ}$C, the total heat capacity of the earth is seen to be 4.73×10^{24} Btu/$^{\circ}$C (i.e., about 10^3 times larger than the estimate for the heat capacity of the oceans of 5.4×10^{21} Btu/$^{\circ}$C given in Table 6.3-2). A 0.01°C decrease in the mean earth temperature (which is probably too small to detect) could thus supply the estimated

618

year 2000 world-energy consumption of 2.1 Q for about 2.25 $\times 10^4$ years.

The thermal energy available from a hot granite deposit with a volume of 40 cubic miles, when cooled by 350°F, is about 6.8×10^{16} Btu, which is approximately equal to the total thermal energy consumption of the United States in 1970. The total energy stored in the hot rocks of the Western United States has been estimated[1] to be as high as 180 Q for deposits located at depths less than 6 km, while 360 Q of thermal energy may be stored in deposits between 6 km and 10 km. The potential of these deposits is roughly comparable with the total U.S. coal reserves. We thus arrive at the important conclusion that geothermal energy from dry wells may represent an important energy resource in future years.

19.2 Characteristics of Geothermal Energy Resources

Geothermal reservoirs in which thermal energy is contained in impermeable rock of very low porosity are called hot dry rock deposits. Hot dry rock deposits are located throughout the crust of the earth at depths greater than those accessible with present drilling technology. However, anomalous hot spots are occasionally found near the surface of the earth in regions characterized by large-scale faulting, moun-

---

[1]Assessment of Geothermal Energy Resources, Panel on Geothermal Energy Sources, U.S. Department of the Interior, U.S. Government Printing Office, Washington, D.C., 1972.

tain building, crustal plate spreading, and other tectonic activities that may lead to volcanism and high heat flows. The energy associated with these geological transformations may lead to the intrusion of large molten masses of igneous rock (batholiths) into the crust of the earth. These magmatic intrusions are believed to be the origin of hot dry rock anomalies. Hot dry rock deposits with temperatures of about $300^{\circ}C$ ($\sim 570^{\circ}F$) are believed[1] to occur commonly in the Western United States at depths less than 5 km.

19.3 Utilization of Dry Geothermal Wells

Techniques for the recovery of energy from hot dry rock deposits have been investigated by workers at the Los Alamos Scientific Laboratory and the Battelle Pacific Northwest Laboratories. The energy-recovery scheme under investigation at the Los Alamos Scientific Laboratory (see Fig. 19.3-1) involves drilling of an injection well for the passage of water into an underground rock formation, where ambient rock temperatures are 300 to $700^{\circ}C$ or even higher. Water is pumped down the injection well with sufficient pressure to induce fractures. Hydraulic fracturing continues until the rock permeability exceeds the pumping capacity. Hydraulic fracturing of this type is widely used in the completion of

---

[1]D. W. Brown, "The Potential for Hot Dry Rock Geothermal Energy in the Western United States," Report LA-UR-73-1075, Los Alamos Scientific Laboratory, Los Alamos, New Mexico, 1973.

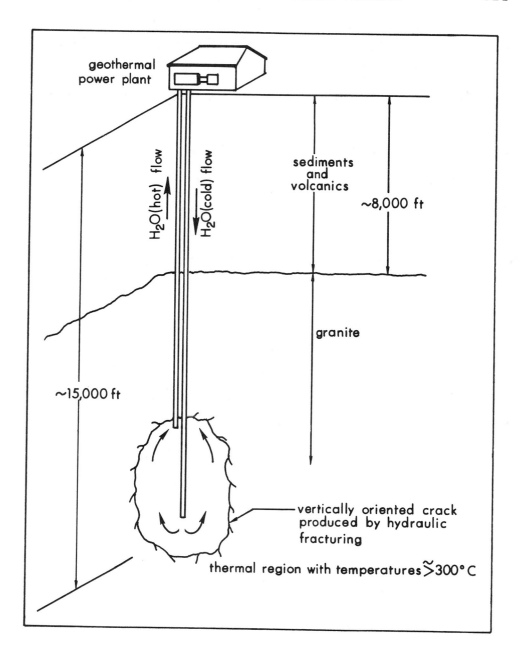

Fig. 19.3-1 Schematic diagram of a scheme for energy recovery from dry geothermal wells; reproduced
from D. W. Brown, M. C. Smith, and R. M.
Potter, "A New Method for Extracting Energy
from Dry Geothermal Reservoirs," Report LA-
DC-72-1157, Los Alamos Scientific Laboratory,
Los Alamos, New Mexico, 1972.

oil and natural-gas wells. In deep formations, vertically-oriented, pancake-shaped fractures will be formed. These are generally less than 0.5 in. wide and have a fracture radius of up to several thousand feet. Additional cracking of hot rock may occur as the result of thermal stresses created by differential shrinkage of the rock formation as it is cooled by injected water.[1]

Circulation of the water used to extract thermal energy from dry hot rock is accomplished by using a single concentric injection and production pipe or by drilling a second well for production. The water is injected into large thermal convection cells in the fractured rock formations and is subsequently allowed to exhaust through the recovery line as hot water or superheated steam. The heated fluid may be used directly or else may serve as a heat source for a secondary fluid in an appropriate power cycle. Preliminary calculations[2] indicate that approximately ten times more thermal energy may be recovered through a given system if the thermal transport fluid is liquid water rather than superheated steam. The influence on energy recovery of the choice of the fluid has been discussed by Smith et al.[2]

[1]F. Harlow and W. Pracht, "A Theoretical Study of Geothermal Energy Extraction," Journal of Geological Research 77, 7038-7048 (1972).

[2]M. C. Smith, R. M. Potter, D. W. Brown, and R. L. Aamodt, "Introduction and Growth of Fractures in Hot Rock" in Geothermal Energy, P. Kruger and C. Otte, editors, Stanford University Press, Stanford, California, 1973.

Successful long-term production of energy from dry hot rock deposits will require that the thermal stresses in the initial production zone are sufficiently severe to assure creation of self-propagating crack and fissure systems. Occurrence of this critical fissure-propagation process must be verified in practice. Of equal importance is the ability of granite walls to contain the water flows. The internal pressures created within the fracture zone will be approximately equal to the equilibrium vapor pressure of gaseous water at the ambient wall temperatures.

Burnham and Stewart[3] have described a conceptual design for utilizing nuclear explosives to create cavities in hot dry rock prior to recovery of geothermal energy. The rock is first fractured by an array of sequentially-fired nuclear explosives. Subsequently, water injection and steam production wells are drilled. Feedwater is then injected and the recovered steam or hot water is employed in an appropriate power cycle. In order to minimize potential environmental contamination, any product steam is condensed and subsequently reinjected. The design of a geothermal power plant of this type is shown schematically in Fig. 19.3-2.

---

[3] J. B. Burnham and D. H. Stewart, "Recovery of Geothermal Energy from Hot, Dry Rock with Nuclear Explosives" in Geothermal Energy, P. Kruger and C. Otte, editors, Stanford University Press, Stanford, California, 1973; see, also, "A Feasibility Study of a Geothermal Power Plant," study performed at the Battelle Pacific Northwest Laboratories for the American Oil Shale Corporation and the U.S. Atomic Energy Commission, PNE-1550, 1971.

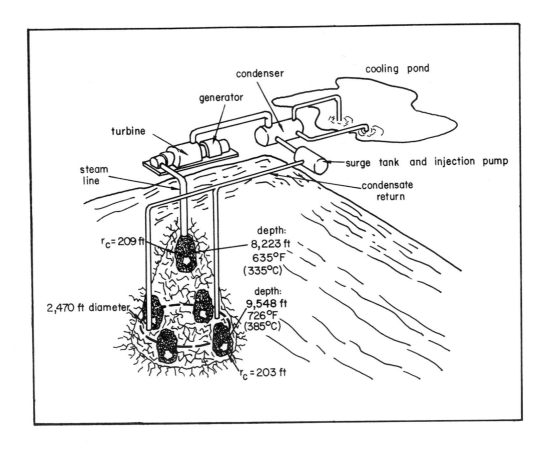

Fig. 19.3-2 Schematic diagram of a power plant utilizing the
Plowshare geothermal recovery concept. The
nuclear explosives are assumed to be 1,000-kt
devices which produce the indicated nuclear-
cavity diameters (r_c) in a granitic intrusive
formation with a thermal gradient of 125°C/km.
Reproduced from D. H. Stewart, "The Status of
Plowshare Geothermal Power," paper submitted
to the Committee on Interior and Insular Affairs,
U.S. Senate, Geothermal Energy Resources and
Research, U.S. Government Printing Office,
Washington, D.C., 1972.

19.4 Cost Estimates

A 100-Mw$_e$ geothermal power plant operating in the Western United States would require two pairs of injection and production wells drilled to a depth of about 15,000 ft ($\sim$ 4.6 km) into rock at $\sim$ 570°F ($\sim$ 300°C). A preliminary (1973) estimate of the capital cost[1] for this plant, including the development of the underground circulation system and the construction of forced-draft dry cooling towers, is $186/kw$_e$, which corresponds to an electrical-energy production cost of about 4.7 mills/kwh$_e$. The capital cost[1] for a 100-Mw$_e$ binary-cycle geothermal power plant operating in the Eastern United States is $316/kw$_e$, corresponding to an energy-generation cost of 8 mills/kwh$_e$. These cost estimates assume that five pairs of 18,000-ft injection and production wells are drilled into hot dry rock at a temperature of 340°F.

Costs of energy extraction from nuclear cavities created in hot dry rock are strongly dependent on the yield of the nuclear explosives and on the fracturing efficiency. Preliminary energy production estimates[2] for a 200-Mw$_e$ power plant, using nuclear cavities created with high fracturing efficiencies in hot rock with a temperature of 350°C ($\sim$ 660°F), range from about 10 mills/kwh$_e$ for 200-kt devices to about

---

[1]Ref. [2] in Section 19.3.
[2]Ref. [3] in Section 19.3.

6.5 mills/kwh$_e$ for yields of 1,000 kt. Lower fracturing efficiencies will increase energy-production costs to values as
high as 17 mills/kwh$_e$ for 500-kt devices and 11 mills/kwh$_e$
for 1,000-kt devices.[2]

Significant reductions in the capital costs required
for exploitation of dry geothermal energy resources may be
achieved in the future as the result of advances in drilling
technology. Among promising new technologies, we note
particularly a rock-melting penetrator that is under development at the Los Alamos Scientific Laboratory.[3]

19.5 Preliminary Results

There are two active programs in the United States
dealing with assessment and exploitation of hot dry rock geothermal resources. Workers at the Los Alamos Scientific
Laboratory are developing an energy extraction system while
scientists at the Battelle Pacific Northwest Laboratories
have investigated a possible major geothermal anomaly in
Montana, which was initially expected to be an appropriate
site for a second major demonstration.

---

[3]J. H. Alseimer, "Geothermal Well Technology and Poten-
tial Applications of Subterrene Devices - A Status Review,"
Report LA-5689-MS, Los Alamos Scientific Laboratory,
Los Alamos, New Mexico, 1974.

A. The Los Alamos Program

In early 1973, a test well was drilled to a depth of 2,575 ft on the edge of a volcanic caldera in the Jemez Mountains within the Santa Fe National Forest (see Fig. 19.5-1). This well extends about 500 ft into the hot granitic rock and has a bottom-hole temperature of 213°F, which is significantly above the boiling point of water at the local ground elevation of 8,500 ft. Successful fracturing was initiated in pre-existing rock fissures of all types. No unexpected problems were encountered in either the drilling or fracturing processes. Successful hydraulic fracturing of the rock formations occurred with wellhead pressures of 1,100 to 1,700 psia.[1] The observed fractures were thin and occurred preferentially in the vertical direction with a consistent northwest-southeast trend. In accord with theoretical predictions, the fracture direction was controlled by the natural stress field of the earth in this region. Cracks and fissures in rock formations are (cemented) closed over long periods of time by minerals leached from ground water. Probably for this reason, hydraulic fracturing is initiated with about

---

[1]M. C. Smith, "The Potential for the Production of Power from Geothermal Resources," statement prepared for the Subcommittee on Water and Power Resources of the Committee on Interior and Insular Affairs, U.S. Senate, June 13, 1973, Geothermal Resources, U.S. Government Printing Office, Washington, D.C., 1973.

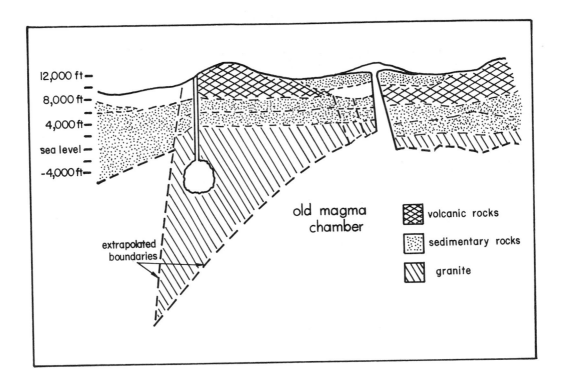

Fig. 19.5-1   The rock structure surrounding the magma chamber located at the edge of the Jemez Caldera
near Los Alamos, New Mexico, in which workers from the Los Alamos Scientific Laboratory
have drilled test wells; reproduced from D. W.
Brown, M. C. Smith, and R. M. Potter, "A
New Method for Extracting Energy from Dry
Geothermal Reservoirs," Report LA-DC-72-
1157, Los Alamos Scientific Laboratory, Los
Alamos, New Mexico, 1972.

equal difficulty in all types of strata.[2] Seismic signatures

at the surface may be used to monitor the progress of hydro-

[2]A. L. Hammond, "Dry Geothermal Wells: Promising Experimental Results," Science 182, 43-44 (1973).

fracturing.   The minimum principal stresses required to maintain open fractures in the rock formations were also estimated. [2]

After hydraulic fracturing, the test hole showed water losses of only a few gallons per day with wellhead pressures as high as 1,000 psi. [1] This low degree of permeability in hot granitic rock deposits is required for the successful utilization of dry geothermal resources.

The Los Alamos research group completed a second test well (1.5 miles from the first well) to a depth of 6,701 ft in 1974.   Hot dry rock was encountered between 3,500 ft and 6,701 at a bottom-hole temperature of 147° C. [3] This hole was drilled to verify horizontal and vertical extrapolations of measurements on rock type, structure, temperature, permeability, and fracturing.   Since favorable results were again obtained, program development calls for the drilling of deeper wells.   Within three years, the first energy extraction system is scheduled to be operational and its performance and reliability should be demonstrated by 1980.

A requirement for drilling pairs of injection and production wells is successful interception of the hydraulically-fractured zone by the production well.   Drilling at angles may be required to assure the intersection of the vertical plane

---

[3]M. C. Smith, "Progress of the LASL Dry Hot Rock Geothermal Energy Project," paper presented to the NSF Conference on Research for the Development of Geothermal Energy Resources, California Institute of Technology, Pasadena, California, September 23-25, 1974.

of the fractured zone by the production well. B. Rayleigh
(quoted in Ref. [2]) of the U.S. Geological Survey has suggested that dry geothermal wells be drilled at angles perpendicular to the expected orientation of the fractures. In this
manner, parallel and vertical fractures may perhaps be created at spacings as close as 100 ft. Slant-drilling techniques
have not yet been demonstrated successfully in crystalline
rocks and their implementation is likely to be expensive.

B.   The Marysville Geothermal Project

A region of abnormally high geothermal heat flow near
Marysville, Montana, was discovered by D. D. Blackwell in
1968. During the summer of 1973, Blackwell conducted surveys of the geology, heat flow, gravity, magnetic field, and
microseismic noise at the Marysville site. Based on the data obtained, the Marysville hot spot was expected[4] to be a
granite pluton (solidified molten magma) or magmatic intrusion associated with recent volcanism (10,000 to 80,000
years ago). Temperature-gradient measurements above the
anomaly indicated a value of 200° C/km, thus yielding expected rock temperatures between 300 and 500° C. Gravity

---

[4]W. R. McSpadden, "A Summary of the Marysville, Montana,
   Geothermal Project," statement prepared for the Subcommittee on Energy of the Committee on Science and Astronautics, U.S. House of Representatives, February 11,
   1974, Geothermal Energy Research, Development, and
   Commercial Demonstration Acts of 1973 and 1974, U.S.
   Government Printing Office, Washington, D.C., 1974.

surveys predicted an anomaly with a roughly elliptical surface projection and a volume of about 100 km^3 above a depth
of 5 km and within 2 km of the surface. The predicted location coincided with the observation that nearby trees were
about 2°F hotter than similar trees in other areas. [5]

If this hot rock formation has the average heat capacity of granite (0.54 cal/cm^3-°C) and a mean temperature
of 400°C, it will supply 4.27 $\times 10^{16}$ Btu ($\sim 7.4 \times 10^9$ bbl of
petroleum equivalent $\simeq 1.8\%$ of the readily-recoverable reserves of the Middle East) if we allow the heat source to cool
to 200°C. Thus, the Marysville anomaly may prove to be
an energy source equivalent to a very substantial oil field.

During the summer of 1974, a test drilling site was
established above the anomaly and drilling was continued for
81 days. The test well reached a total depth of 6,790 ft and
many fractured water-bearing zones were encountered below
1,800 ft. [5] Water-flow rates down the hole reached 1,000
gal/min while the recorded bottom-hole temperature was only
200°F.

Additional investigations are required for a proper
evaluation of the energy potential of the Marysville site.

[5]W. R. McSpadden and J. T. Kuwada, "A Report on the
Marysville Geothermal Project," paper presented to the
NSF Conference on Research for the Development of Geothermal Energy Resources, California Institute of Technology, Pasadena, California, September 23-25, 1974.

CHAPTER 20

ELECTRICAL POWER PRODUCTION, TRANSMISSION, AND DISTRIBUTION

The commercial production and distribution of electricity began in New York City in 1882 after development of the following facilities: the dynamo and its regulation equipment, the construction of a distribution grid to the consumer for transmission of currents at specified voltage, the design and implementation of switching gear and of protective circuit devices in case of failure along the system network, installation of meters to measure the delivered energy, and commercialization of Edison's electric light bulb (which replaced the incandescent, gas-heated mantle). The first commercial station was located at Pearl Street in New York City and had a power output of 792 kw_e (about one thousandth of that of a modern utility plant) produced by 6 generators.

By the year 1970, the total electric-generating capacity in the U.S. had grown to 3.40×10^8 $kw_e = 3.40 \times 10^5$ Mw_e, an increase by a factor of about 430,000 in 88 years. An estimate for the total U.S. electric-power production by the year 2000 is about 2×10^6 Mw$_e$.

Power stations do not generate electricity continuously at 100% of rated capacity. The total electrical energy delivered in 1920 was 4.0×10^7 Mwh$_e$; in 1970, it was 1.53×10^9 Mwh$_e$; it is estimated to reach 8.64×10^9 Mwh$_e$ in the year 2000 (see Table 20.2-1). The past U.S. average annual growth rate of electricity production has been 7.65%.

In order to grow from a capacity of 3.40×10^5 Mw$_e$ in 1970 to a capacity of 1.75×10^6 Mw$_e$ in the year 2000, the average annual required supplementary power-generating capacity that must be added is 4.7×10^4 Mw$_e$/y. At an average investment cost of $400 (in 1973 U.S. dollars)/kw$_e$ installed, the corresponding required annual investment is 18.8×10^9 for a total investment to the year 2000 of 564×10^9, which is somewhat greater than one-half of the total U.S. GNP in 1973.

Achievement of the stated growth during the remainder of this century requires significant scientific and technical accomplishments. Some of the problem areas that require attention are discussed in later sections of this chapter. Alternative non-nuclear energy sources have been considered in the preceding chapters; nuclear fission and fusion sources will be reviewed in the following Volume 3 of this series.

Electricity production has been a major consumer of energy ($\approx 25\%$ during recent years). It is currently growing more rapidly than the other components of the energy industries. For this reason, it is appropriate to consider this topic in a separate discussion of power production and electricity distribution, with emphasis on the possible development of new techniques for improved efficiency in transmission and distribution systems.

The power carried by an electrical network and the rate of consumption of electrical energy in the developed countries have doubled about every 10 years. At the same time, the service territory for each utility station has doubled in about 25 years. The capacity of generating equipment has doubled about every seven years. Since the capacity per generating station has increased more rapidly than the rate of consumption, the total number of required power stations has decreased. We may expect this trend to apply also to nuclear reactors. Reasonable distribution distances for hot water, electricity, and hydrogen produced on a nuclear farm are tens, hundreds, and thousands of miles with current technology.

Waste heat produced in electricity-generating stations is not generally used with optimal efficiency. District heating systems using waste energy rejected from utility generating stations are currently in use in many European metropolitan areas. This type of heating system serves 1.5 to 2 million Swedes, about 3 million Germans, over 30% of the Danish population, and is being introduced in Eastern Europe in such cities as Moscow, Leningrad, and Kiev.[1]

---

[1] J. Karkheck, J. Powell and E. Beardsworth, "Prospects for District Heating in the U.S.," Science 195, 948-955 (1977).

It is not widely employed in the U.S. where annual per capita heating expenditures in large cities such as Chicago, Detroit and New York are greater than in Northern European cities, even though relatively warmer climates prevail. It has been estimated[1] that about 50% of the U.S. population (103 $\times 10^6$ people) could have been served by district heating with a capital investment of $180 $\times 10^9$ ($5,000 per household) and at an annual (1972) oil saving of 1.1 $\times 10^9$ bbl_e (3 $\times 10^6$ bbl_e/d) at a reduction of about $13 $\times 10^9$ in fuel-import costs at 1976 prices; for 115 $\times 10^6$ people, the year 2000 energy savings would be 1.32 $\times 10^9$ bbl_e. The 1976 production of waste heat in steam-electric plants was about 8.4 $\times 10^{18}$ joules (8 $\times 10^{15}$ Btu or nearly 10% of total annual energy consumption). Technological implementation requires raising of outlet steam pressures to 1 atm from the present value of about 0.05 atm in order to increase condenser temperatures to 100°C from 40°C. As the result, the efficiency to electricity conversion is reduced from about 33% to about 25% while the overall energy-utilization efficiency is raised from 33% to 53% in a fossil-fuel plant and to 85% in a nuclear reactor in the hybrid electricity-district-heating system.

20.1   World Electricity Production During Recent Years

A summary of electricity production rates (in 10^9 kwh_e per y) is given in Table 20.1-1 for the major producing countries during the years 1969, 1970, and 1971. Although the U.S. was by far the heaviest producer, the growth rate of

Table 20.1-1 Electricity production, in units of 10^9 kwh$_e$, during recent years. Nations with annual production of less than 12×10^9 kwh$_e$ are not listed. Reproduced from Chemical and Engineering News **51**, 63, April 16, 1973. Copyright © 1973 by the American Chemical Society.

Nation	1969	1970	1971	Average annual growth 1966-1971, %
North America				
Canada	190	204	215	6.3
U.S.	1,553	1,638	1,718	6.6
Western Europe				
Belgium	29	31	33	7.7
France	132	141	148	6.9
F.R.G.	226	243	260	7.9
Italy	110	117	122	6.3
Netherlands	37	41	45	10.3
Austria	26	30	29	3.9
Denmark	16	18	17	14.0
Finland	20	23	23	8.1
Norway	57	58	63	5.3
Spain	52	56	60	9.7
Sweden	58	61	66	5.6
Switzerland	30	32	33	3.2
U.K.	239	248	251	4.5
Eastern Europe				
Bulgaria	17	20	21	12.3
Czechoslovakia	43	45	47	5.3
East Germany	65	68	69	4.1
Hungary	14	15	15	4.8
Poland	60	65	70	8.1
Romania	32	35	39	13.6
U.S.S.R.	689	740	800	8.0
Yugoslavia	23	26	29	11.4
Japan	316	359	379	12.0
Latin America				
Argentina	15	17	19	9.9
Brazil	42	45	48	8.1
Mexico	26	29	31	10.4
Australasia				
Australia	51	56	60	8.4
New Zealand	13	14	15	5.3
Other				
India	49	55	59	11.5
South Africa	44	49	53	8.7

electricity production for the period 1966 to 1971 in the U.S. was less than in many other countries (see Table 20.1-1). Reference to Table 20.1-1 shows that growth rates as high as 10 to 14% per year were not at all uncommon and that the following countries had average annual growth rates of 12% or more during the period 1966 to 1971: Denmark, Romania, Bulgaria, and Japan. The U.S. growth rate was 6.6% while annual growth rates of less than 5% occurred in the following countries: Switzerland, Austria, East Germany, U.K., and Hungary.

The U.S. electricity production during 1970 amounted to 1.638×10^{12} kwh$_e$ = 5.59×10^{15} (Btu)$_e$ $\simeq 1.68 \times 10^{16}$ (Btu)$_t$ or about 24% of the total energy of 7×10^{16} Btu consumed during the year.

20.2 Electricity Demand and Growth in the U.S.

Electricity production in the U.S. during 1960 and 1970, as well as predictions for 1985 and 2000, are summarized in Table 20.2-1 and compared with total equivalent energy consumption in Table 20.2-2. These predictions were grossly outdated by 1976 because deferrals and other actions already taken had reduced achievable nuclear capacities for the year 2000 to less than 15% of total. In Table 20.2-2, the column (%)$_e$ has been added and represents the percentage of total energy utilization employed in electric-power generation from an energy source. The relatively

Table 20.2-1 Electric-power generation and equivalent fuel consumption in the U.S. for selected years; reproduced from Underground Power Transmission by Super-conducting Cable, E. B. Forsyth, editor, Brookhaven National Laboratory, Report BNL 50325, Upton, New York, 1972.

Energy source	1960			1970			1985			2000		
	A*	B**	%†	A	B	%	A	B	%	A	B	%
hydroelectric	146	62	19.4	247	100	16.1	275	110	6.9	320	120	3.7
natural gas	160	69	21.2	370	155	24.2	370	148	9.2	360	135	4.2
coal	402	172	53.4	709	298	46.5	1,600	640	40.0	1,675	628	19.4
nuclear	---	---	----	22	9	1.4	1,350	540	33.8	4,150	1,537	48.0
oil	45	19	6.0	181	76	11.8	405	162	10.1	2,135	800	24.7
total	753	322	100.0	1,529	638	100.0	4,000	1,600	100.0	8,640	3,220	100.0

*The letter A stands for generation in 10^9 kwh$_e$.

**The letter B signifies equivalent bituminous coal consumption in 10^6 tons.

†The symbol % indicates percentage of total electricity generation contributed by the indicated energy source.

The entries for the years 1985 and 2000 are projected data.

Table 20.2-2 Total equivalent energy consumption in the U.S. for selected years; reproduced from Underground Power Transmission by Superconducting Cable, E. B. Forsyth, editor, Brookhaven National Laboratory, Report BNL 50325, Upton, New York, 1972.

Energy source	1960 C*	1960 %	1960 (%)e**	1970 C	1970 %	1970 (%)e	1985 C	1985 %	1985 (%)e	2000 C	2000 %	2000 (%)e
hydroelectric	67	3.9	92.5	100	3.7	100.0	110	2.4	100.0	120	2.0	100.0
natural gas	539	31.4	12.8	903	33.2	17.2	1,030	22.4	14.4	870	14.3	15.5
coal	397	23.2	43.3	490	18.0	60.8	955	20.7	67.0	1,220	20.0	51.5
nuclear	---	----	----	9	0.3	100.0	540	11.7	100.0	1,560	25.5	98.5
oil	711	41.5	2.7	1,220	44.8	6.2	1,965	42.8	8.2	2,330	38.2	34.3
total	1,714	100.0	18.8	2,722	100.0	23.4	4,600	100.0	34.8	6,100	100.0	52.8

* The letter C signifies equivalent bituminous coal consumption in 10^6 tons.

** The symbol $(\%)_e$ indicates percentage of total-energy utilization employed for electric-power generation. This column is calculated by dividing the appropriate entry in column B of Table 20.2-1 by the corresponding entry in column C of Table 20.2-2 for each specified year.

The entries for the years 1985 and 2000 are projected data.

low percentages of total gas and oil consumed for the purpose of electric-power generation are noteworthy.

More detailed long-range projections to the year
2000 are shown in Fig. 20.2-1 for extrapolated growth
(curve A), reduced economic and population growth (curve
B), and reduced growth coupled with price increases (curve
C). The curves in Fig. 20.2-1 correspond to an energy-
source distribution (see Table 20.2-3) in the year 2000
that is radically different from the energy-source distribution postulated for the year 2000 in Table 20.2-2.

The effects of assumptions made about population
growth and electricity price on the growth rate of electricity
demand are indicated by the data summarized in Table
20.2-4. We note that case F of Table 20.2-4 corresponds
roughly to curve A of Fig. 20.2-1. All of the other cases
of Table 20.2-4 lie well below curve C of Fig. 20.2-1.
The various cases of Table 20.2-4 correspond to the growth
projections plotted in Fig. 20.2-2. Comparison of Figs.
20.2-1 and 20.2-2 shows that there is considerable uncer-
tainty about where we are heading insofar as electricity
growth rates are concerned.

A regional break-down of electricity growth rates
for case E of Table 20.2-4 is reproduced in Table 20.2-5.
The reader may assess the likelihood of requiring the projected demands shown in Table 20.2-5 by referring back
to Section 1.7, and noting that the type of regional-demand
analysis for electricity growth given in Section 1.7 does not

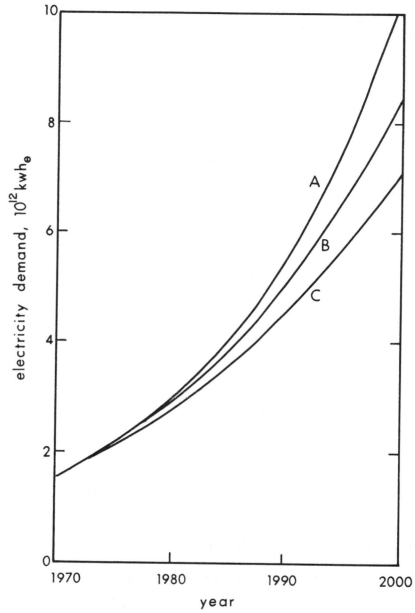

Fig. 20.2-1 Alternative estimates for electricity demands. The curves labeled A, B, and C correspond, respectively, to an extrapolated National Petroleum Council estimate, a reduced economic and population-growth scenario, and conditions of reduced growth and energy-price increases. Reproduced from the Cornell Workshop on Energy and the Environment, U.S. Government Printing Office, Washington, D.C., 1972.

Table 20.2-3 Energy source distribution used in connection with the construction of Fig. 20.2-1; reproduced from the Cornell Workshop on Energy and the Environment, U.S. Government Printing Office, Washington, D.C., 1972.

Energy source	Fuel supply, %	
	1970	2000
nuclear	1.4	52
coal	46	30
hydroelectric	16	7
gas	24	5
oil	12	5

generally form the basis for the federal growth projections; the demand estimates given in Table 20.2-5 will probably turn out to be too high.

20.3   Service Territories of Representative Electricity-Distribution Systems in the U.S.

There are hundreds of privately-owned and publicly-owned utility companies in the U.S., which operate as independent corporate or municipal units. All are subject to regulation by the Federal Power Commission (FPC), which oversees performance in assigned service territories and regulates prices charged to consumers, usually by allowing the privately-operating utilities to earn a profit that

Table 20.2-4 Electricity demand growth and alternative assumptions. BEA, Bureau of Economic Analysis; FPC, Federal Power Commission; ZPG 2035, zero population growth reached in 2035. In the constant price assumption, 1970 prices are maintained in each region. In the "double by 2000" assumption, the average price in each region increases annually by 3.33% of its 1970 value for 30 years. In case F, the FPC demand projection and the BEA population projections were used. Electricity demand here includes losses of about 9% to make the figures comparable with the assumed generation totals. A total of 1.53×10^{12} kwh of electricity was generated in 1970 (compare Table 20.2-1). Reproduced from D. Chapman, T. Tyrrell, and T. Mount, "Electricity Demand Growth: Implications for Research and Development," paper submitted to the Committee on Science and Astronautics, U.S. House of Representatives, May 1972. Printed in Energy Research and Development, U.S. Government Printing Office, Washington, D.C. 1972.

Case	Population assumption	Electricity price assumption	Electricity demand, 10^{12} kwh$_e$				
			1975	1980	1990	2000	
A	BEA	FPC	1.98	2.38	3.01	3.45	
B	BEA	double by 2000	1.88	2.07	2.11	2.01	
C	ZPG 2035	FPC	1.98	2.37	2.95	3.29	
D	ZPG 2035	double by 2000	1.88	2.05	2.07	1.91	
E	BEA	constant	2.02	2.54	3.56	4.56	
F	BEA	*	2.14	3.05	5.66	9.89	

* Average prices decline 24 percent from 1970 to 1980, and 12 percent every 10 years thereafter until 2000.

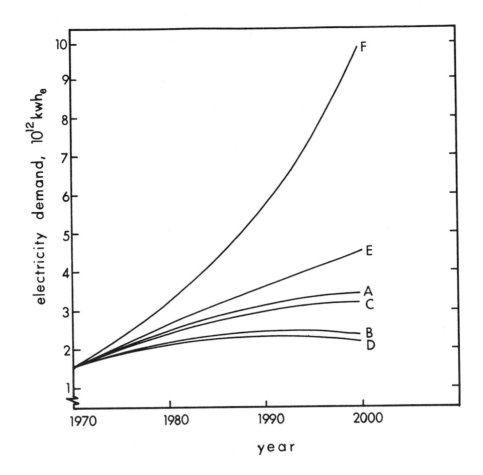

Fig. 20.2-2 Electricity-demand projections from Table
            20.2-4. The near-term agreement and far-
            term divergence should be noted.

represents a reasonable return on capital investment (around
8 to 8.5% in most cases). Performance data during 1970 for
a number of utilities are listed in Table 20.3-1. The utility
lines are interconnected in order to assure adequate and
reliable regional supply of electricity. Three representative system interties are shown in Figs. 20.3-1 to 20.3-3.

Table 20.2-5 Detailed estimates of electricity demand in 10^6 kwh$_e$ for case E of Table 20.2-4. The BEA projection and constant price assumption are used (see Table 20.2-4). Total demand includes other uses such as subways, street lighting, and so forth. The estimated transmission losses (average about 9%) are added to the demand in order to derive the generating requirements. Reproduced from D. Chapman, T. Tyrrell, and T. Mount, "Electricity Demand Growth: Implications for Research and Development," paper submitted to the Committee on Science and Astronautics, U.S. House of Representatives, May 1972. Printed in Energy Research and Development, U.S. Government Printing Office, Washington D.C., 1972.

Area of application	Electricity demand, 10^6 kwhe						
	1970	1975	1980	1985	1990	1995	2000
Residential demand							
New England	20,900.0	31,733.7	42,246.4	51,858.4	60,529.6	68,495.2	75,994.9
Mideast	69,146.0	100,351.0	129,657.1	155,928.6	179,365.1	200,764.2	220,864.0
Great Lakes	79,687.0	110,721.4	139,981.8	166,671.1	191,007.4	213,706.6	235,384.2
Plains	35,339.0	49,549.8	62,558.2	74,049.1	84,223.4	93,471.7	102,123.9
Southeast	129,124.0	202,016.5	272,694.1	336,848.4	394,286.7	446,574.9	495,391.5
Southwest	40,127.0	61,098.3	81,273.6	99,686.9	116,378.9	131,778.9	146,326.1
Rocky Mountains	9,652.0	12,842.5	15,795.9	18,572.1	21,249.3	23,866.1	26,454.3
Far West	63,820.0	81,279.3	98,599.3	115,467.0	131,860.8	147,990.2	164,024.0
United States	447,795.0	649,592.4	842,806.1	1,019,081.6	1,178,901.0	1,326,647.0	1,466,544.0

Table 20.2-5, continued.

Commercial demand							
New England	14,643.0	22,546.0	30,840.3	39,148.1	47,410.6	55,799.5	64,453.8
Mideast	57,696.0	79,827.4	103,129.0	150,476.4	150,476.4	174,782.6	199,969.4
Great Lakes	53,911.0	80,329.4	108,139.0	136,017.4	163,702.7	191,792.2	220,749.2
Plains	21,406.0	30,375.9	39,663.0	48,934.9	58,153.1	67,499.6	77,109.3
Southeast	63,556.0	96,842.8	132,157.8	157,914.3	203,815.9	240,472.1	278,392.0
Southwest	33,628.0	47,667.9	62,652.6	78,141.6	94,053.6	110,588.8	127,900.1
Rocky Mountains	10,356.0	14,273.2	18,474.5	22,925.2	27,639.5	32,644.4	37,960.4
Far West	57,554.0	78,612.2	102,300.1	127,479.1	153,682.2	181,191.9	210,218.7
United States	312,750.0	450,474.8	597,356.1	747,297.6	898,933.8	1,054,771.0	1,216,752.0
Industrial demand							
New England	18,161.0	20,136.2	22,897.8	26,100.4	29,578.1	33,285.7	37,194.1
Mideast	94,108.0	107,519.6	123,566.9	141,013.1	159,293.4	178,356.0	198,167.6
Great Lakes	123,395.0	127,440.1	139,361.6	155,343.8	173,705.3	193,840.3	215,382.5
Plains	30,703.0	38,085.8	45,549.8	52,938.6	60,241.7	67,563.8	74,978.0
Southeast	160,003.0	193,058.1	229,185.7	267,079.3	306,206.7	346,648.6	388,467.9
Southwest	50,853.0	69,864.1	88,833.6	107,463.4	125,841.4	144,249.6	162,912.2
Rocky Mountains	16,642.0	17,973.4	20,065.0	22,706.8	25,779.2	29,180.9	32,849.0
Far West	78,657.0	90,713.8	106,143.1	123,604.7	142,426.2	162,457.5	183,594.9
United States	572,522.0	664,791.1	775,603.4	896,249.8	1,023,071.9	1,155,582.0	1,293,544.0
Total demand							
New England	55,261.4	76,573.9	98,768.0	120,502.9	141,506.3	162,150.2	182,794.4
Mideast	233,765.1	304,384.5	377,021.4	448,252.3	517,504.7	586,029.1	654,884.1
Great Lakes	267,272.7	331,230.6	402,981.6	476,353.5	549,552.0	622,312.6	698,376.5
Plains	90,421.2	122,023.8	152,795.1	181,903.8	209,507.2	236,305.3	262,854.4
Southeast	365,732.3	510,118.4	657,496.9	800,400.0	937,768.7	1,071,942.0	1,205,254.0
Southwest	129,966.1	186,311.3	242,768.4	297,559.4	350,733.7	403,241.8	455,935.3
Rocky Mountains	38,262.6	47,073.0	56,726.1	67,029.1	77,953.3	89,461.8	101,543.2
Far West	210,632.6	263,887.4	323,315.8	385,978.0	450,651.4	517,696.4	587,403.0
United States	1,391,312.0	1,841,601.0	2,311,872.0	2,777,978.0	3,235,174.0	3,690,136.0	4,149,043.0

Table 20.3-1 Performance characteristics (1970) for a number of utility companies; based on data from Underground Power Transmission by Superconducting Cable, E. B. Forsyth, editor, Brookhaven National Laboratory, Report BNL 50325, Upton, New York, 1972.

System statistics	Pacific Gas and Electric Co.	TVA	American Electric Power Co.	Consolidated Edison Co. of New York
number of hydroelectric plants	65	48	17	- - - -
operating capacity, 10^6 kw$_e$	2.5	4.3	- - - -	- - - -
number of steam plants	12	11	19	- - - -
operating capacity, 10^6 kw$_e$	7.2	15.1	- - - -	8
power available from other sources, 10^6 kw$_e$	2.4	1.8	- - - -	1.5*
gross system output, 10^9 kwh$_e$	56.8	101.3	60.1	32.4
capacity under construction, 10^6 kw$_e$	5.4	10.4	5.9	4.7

*1×10^6 kw$_e$ is generated by a gas-turbine installation.

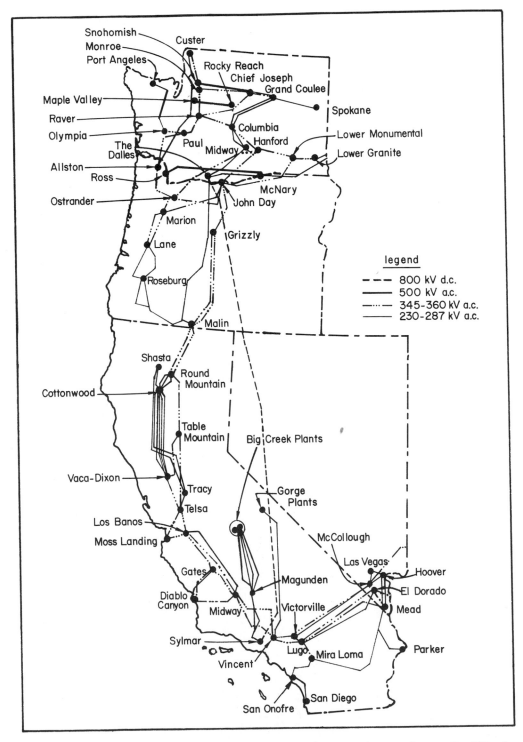

Fig. 20.3-1 Pacific Northwest-Southwest intertie and allied facilities.

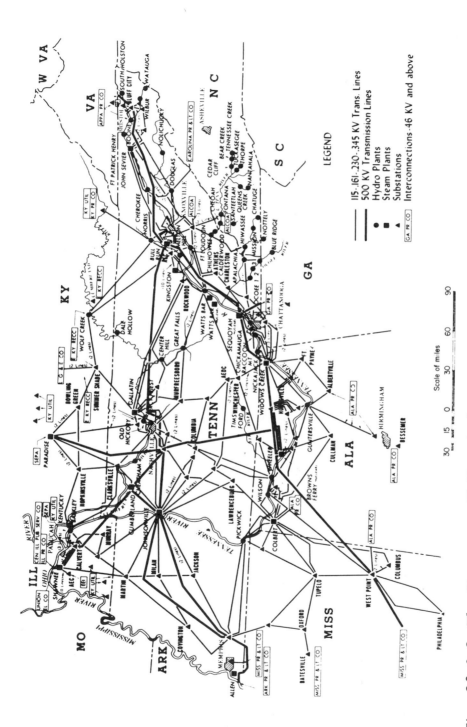

Fig. 20.3-2 The Tennessee Valley Authority power system. Transmission lines of 115 kV or higher, interconnections, and all generating facilities in operation, under construction, or authorized in July 1971 are shown. Photograph courtesy of the Tennessee Valley Authority.

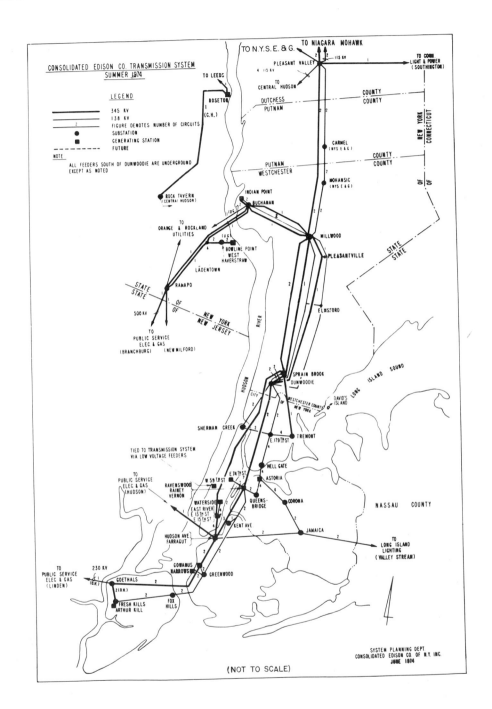

Fig. 20.3-3 The Consolidated Edison Company transmission
system serves metropolitan New York City and
surroundings. Photograph courtesy of the
Consolidated Edison Company of New York, Inc.

Figure 20.3-1 shows the Northwest to Southwest interconnections, which are dominated by one 800-kV d.c. line and two 500-kV a.c. lines. The interties connect service areas of the Bonneville Power Administration, Portland General Electric Co., Pacific Power and Light Co., The Bureau of Reclamation, Pacific Gas and Electric Co., Southern California Edison Co., Los Angeles Department of Water and Power, San Diego Gas and Electric Co., and Arizona Public Service Co. An important feature of the Southern distribution network is a 500-kV a.c. line from the Four Corners generating stations to the heavily-populated areas in Southern California.

Figure 20.3-2 shows the service area of the Tennessee Valley Authority (TVA), which is the largest (publicly-owned) power-producing company in the U.S. (the 1970 system output was 1.01×10^{11} kwh$_e$). An important aspect of the TVA system is the large number of steam plants located on the Tennessee River and interconnected by 500-kV a.c. lines.

The American Electric Power Co. (AEP) is the largest, privately-owned utility in the U.S. (the 1970 system output was 6.01×10^{10} kwh$_e$). Installation of 1,200 miles of transmission lines operating at 765 kV a.c. has been completed by AEP. These lines have nearly the highest voltage for operating transmission lines in the U.S. Other transmission lines belonging to this mid-continent system carry from 138 to 500 kV a.c. The system is interconnected with the TVA at 500 kV a.c. and with the Commonwealth Edison Co. (which serves the Chicago area) through a

765-kV a.c. line.   The total service area of the American
Electric Power Co. encompasses 41,000 square miles in
parts of Michigan, West Virginia, Virginia, Tennessee,
Kentucky, Indiana, and Ohio.

Figure 20.3-3 shows the 660 square-mile service territory of the power company for New York City, the Consolidated Edison Co.   Within the city limits, all but one major
tie-line are underground.   Interconnections are seen to exist
to the Public Service Electric and Gas Co., Orange and Rock-
land Utilities, Niagara Mohawk Power Co., Central Hudson
Gas and Electric Co., Connecticut Light and Power Co., and
Long Island Lighting Co.   Normally, less than 5% of the electrical energy distributed by the Consolidated Edison Co. is
imported.   This system was the focus of a 1965 power blackout involving many of the Northeastern states.   During the
summer of 1977, the Consolidated Edison system suffered a
lightning-induced cascade failure, which resulted in a second
major blackout in New York City.

20.4   Electric Utility Rate Design and Peak Load Fluctuations

For more than eighty years after the first electric
utility system began operation in New York City in 1882,
network expansion was accomplished at decreasing unit production costs because of technological innovation and economies of scale associated with increasing capacity.   The con-
stant-dollar (deflated) price of electricity generally decreased

(see Fig. 4.4-1) while disposable per capita income and most other prices increased.

The unit rates paid by industrial consumers have historically been lower than those paid by commercial and residential customers because of lower distribution costs. Within each customer classification, the price structure has generally followed a declining block rate, as illustrated in Fig. 20.4-1. This rate design, under which the unit price of electrical energy declines with increased consumption, has been criticized because it tends to encourage users to increase the consumption of electrical energy in order to achieve a lower unit cost. Users of large amounts of electrical energy may pay only 8 to 33% as much per kwh$_e$ as do small consumers. The declining block rate does not reflect current costs accurately.

The utilization efficiency and production costs for electrical energy are determined, in part, by the load factor (see Section 4.5), which is equal to the ratio of actually produced electrical energy to the potential annual production. The average load factor in the United States has been about 50% in recent years, [1] which is slightly higher than the world average but lower than the load factor achieved in 1972 in Japan (56%) and in Canada (53%). During the same year, a load factor of only 40% was reached in the United Kingdom.[2]

---

[1] Statistical Abstract of the United States, U.S. Government Printing Office, Washington, D.C., 1973.

[2] United Nations Statistical Yearbook 1973, United Nations, New York, New York, 1974.

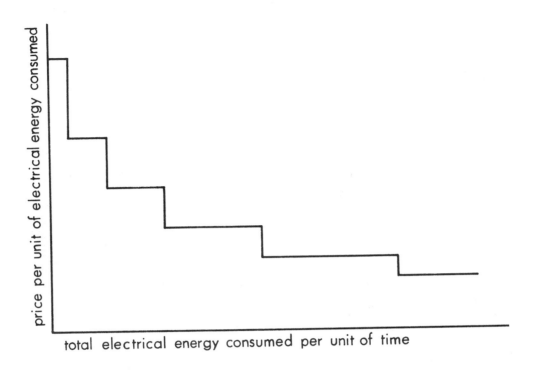

Fig. 20.4-1 Schematic diagram showing the declining block
             price rate with increased consumption, which
             has characterized the price structure for elec-
             trical-energy charges.

Electrical-energy demand in the U.S. shows diurnal,
weekly, and annual cycles. Demand fluctuations result in
cyclic peak-load curves for electric utilities (see Fig. 20.4-2).
The dependence of demand on the weather is indicated in Fig.
20.4-3. Electric utilities are designed to meet peak demands.
The plants producing electricity at the lowest cost are used
to supply base-load demands, while peak demands are met
by less economical generation facilities. Electrical-energy
prices to the consumer, financial requirements of the utili-

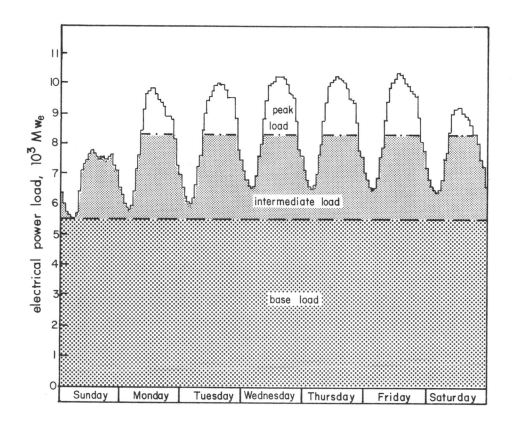

Fig. 20.4-2 A weekly peak power-demand curve for a large
utility operating with a weekly load factor of
about 80%. The average monthly and annual
load factors for this system are substantially
lower than 80%. This figure has been reproduced from The 1970 National Power Survey,
U.S. Federal Power Commission, U.S. Government Printing Office, Washington, D.C.,
1971.

ties, and environmental costs involved in electricity production would all be reduced substantially by smoothing the cy-
clic-demand fluctuations.

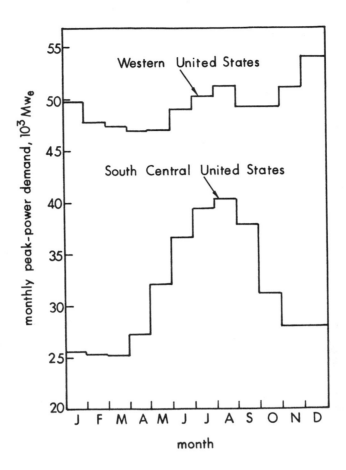

Fig. 20.4-3   Monthly peak-power demands in the South Central and Western United States. The use of air conditioning accounts for the high summer peak loads in the South Central Region. This figure has been reproduced from The 1970 National Power Survey, U.S. Federal Power Commission, U.S. Government Printing Office, Washington, D.C., 1971.

The fact that the current rate design involves cross-subsidization among and between customer classes and between users who demand peak loads at different times during

the day has been noted by E. R. Habicht. [3] Off-peak consumers are effectively subsidizing the users of electrical
power during periods of peak demand who, at the same time,
force the utilities to expand capacity and to operate less efficient generating facilities that may also consume scarce or
expensive fuels. Electrical-energy rates should reflect the
actual production costs. [3] It is likely that "time-of-day
pricing" (i. e., increasing utility rates according to demand)
would tend to defer some of the peak loads to off-peak periods. Time-of-day meters and pricing have been used in
France and have been shown to reduce peak demands. [3]
Some electric utilities in the United States and in other countries, including Great Britain and New Zealand, have been
experimenting with differential diurnal rate structures.

20.5 Some Long-Term Objectives in the Distribution of Electricity to Consumers

The 1965 Northeastern power blackout was the result
of inadequate matching between the power-transmitting capabilities of interconnected transmission lines (i. e., too
much power interconnected by too little copper). It reminded
us not only of our extreme dependence on the electrical-sup-
ply lines but also of the consistently high performance reli-

---

[3]E. R. Habicht, Jr., "The Social Origins and Economic
Basis of the Demand for Electricity," paper presented at
the New Zealand Energy Conference, University of
Auckland, Auckland, New Zealand, May 25, 1974.

ability which we tend to take for granted in our electricity-
distribution networks. Conventional lines are expected to be
down, on the average, one day for every 1,000 circuit-mile-
year; thus, the expected outage for a one-mile line is one day
every 1,000 years; for a ten-mile line, it is one day every
100 years; for a 100-mile line, the reliability objective is one
day of outage every 10 years. These reliability goals are all
the more astonishing if we consider the complexity of the
transmission-line system and of its manyfold components.
Of course, the reliability-design objectives are not met under
hazardous environmental conditions (e.g., high winds, heavy
snowfalls).

Looking at the entire complex of the electricity supply
system, the following problem areas for research have been
singled out by knowledgeable experts:[1]

a. The turboelectric units for electricity generation
in fossil-fuel plants currently produce 800 Mw_e on a single
shaft or 1,300 Mw_e on two shafts on rotating machinery operating at 3,600 rpm. Future design objectives are 1,670
Mw_e on a single shaft or 5,000 Mw_e on three-shaft units.

b. The turboelectric units for electricity generation
in nuclear plants currently produce up to 1,200 Mw_e on rotating machinery operating at 1,800 rpm. Future design objectives are 1,670 Mw_e per shaft or 5,000 Mw_e on three-shaft

---

[1]Underground Power Transmission by Superconducting
Cable, E.B. Forsyth, editor, Brookhaven National Laboratory, Report BNL 50325, Upton, New York, 1972.

units, as for fossil-fuel plants. With nuclear reactors,
these design objectives may not be attained without the use
of water-cooled rotors or superconducting cores. The development of electrical equipment using superconductivity is
briefly discussed in Section 20.9.

     c. Voltages between 345 and 760 kV have been used
on a.c. transmission lines. For efficient transmission of
the much higher powers (more than about $1,600 \text{ Mw}_e$) required for future delivery, still higher voltage lines are required. Also, more extensive use of high-voltage d.c. transmission lines may be indicated.

     d. The interconnections between power-generation
systems must be made completely reliable in order to assure
adequate regional supplies as demand-growth rates require
heavier facility utilization in increasingly large parts of the
country.

     e. There must be strict cost control on all compo-
nents of the electrical-utility networks in order to limit the
very large required future capital investments.

     f. The development of superconducting power lines
and matched generating facilities holds promise for decreasing costs and removing the principal esthetic objection to
overhead transmission lines, namely, their very existence.
Thus, it may be possible to replace overhead transmission
lines and develop an efficient and complete system for underground transmission and distribution of electricity to the
consumers. With superconducting lines, power transmission
lines will probably reach capacities in the 2 to 10×10^3

Mw$_e$ range.

It must be remembered that electrical energy is usually generated as it is consumed. Gas-turbine generators are often employed to meet peak-load requirements. Energy storage (as in displaced water levels of a hydroelectric system or in a large electrical capacitor) is used only to a limited extent (see Chapter 12 for a detailed discussion of energy storage). Voltages are stepped up and down by transformers. The transmission lines, which are protected by circuit breakers, are tapped at load centers for power transmission to consumers at 440, 220, and 110 V. The a.c. systems are preferred because of the ease with which voltage changes may be accomplished. Underground transmission lines generally cost about 10 times as much to install as equivalent overhead lines; as the result, investment in the underground lines, which constitute about 1% of the total transmission-line capacity, represents nearly 10% of the total investment cost.

20.6 Some Important Characteristics of Power Lines for Transmitting Electricity; Underground Transmission Lines

Electricity is usually generated and transmitted at constant voltage, at a frequency of 60 Hz (1 Hz = 1 Hertz = 1 cycle per sec), which equals an angular frequency ω of 377 rad/sec, with three separate balanced (i.e., equal) voltage components which are 120° out of phase relative to each other (see Fig. 20.6-1). Each voltage or single-phase circuit has a time-varying component, in an arbitrary but specified direction, of the type sketched in Fig. 20.6-2. We note that the root-mean-square or effective voltage is

$$|E_{rms}| = \{(1/T) \int_0^T |E_{pk}| (\sin \omega t) dt\}^{1/2}$$

(20.6-1)

$$= |E_{pk}|/\sqrt{2} \ ,$$

where E_{pk} is the peak voltage (see Fig. 20.6-2). It is known from elementary circuit theory that the current flow-vector $\vec{I}$, in a line described by ideal resistance, capacitance and inductance, is also a sinusoidally-varying function of time, but is generally out of phase with the electric voltage vector. If we choose the direction of the real axis to coincide with the instantaneous direction of the voltage vector and the direction of the imaginary axis to be perpendicular to the real axis, then the current will generally be represented on this diagram by a complex number with a component along the real axis (i.e., in the direction of the voltage vector) determined by the phase angle φ which the current vector makes with respect to the voltage vector (see Fig. 20.6-3). The instantaneous value of the power carried by the transmission line is then

$$P = \vec{E} \cdot \vec{I} = |\vec{E}| \, |\vec{I}| \, \cos \varphi$$

(20.6-2)

and is measured in watt (w) if the potential ($\vec{E}$) is measured

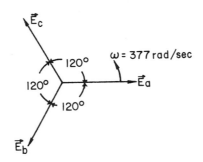

Fig. 20.6-1   Schematic diagram showing the three equal
              (balanced) voltage vectors $\vec{E}_a$, $\vec{E}_b$, and $\vec{E}_c$, at
              relative phase-angle displacements of 120°.
              The entire diagram rotates at a rate of 377 rad/
              sec for 60-Hz lines.

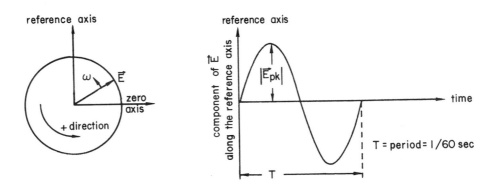

Fig. 20.6-2   Diagram showing the variation of the projection
              of $\vec{E}$ along the reference axis with time for a
              60-cycle a. c. voltage system.

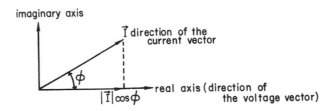

Fig. 20.6-3   Diagram showing the phase angle φ between the
              direction of the current vector $\vec{I}$ and the voltage
              vector $\vec{E}$ (along the real axis).

in volt (V) and the current ($\vec{I}$) is measured in ampere (A). Because the value of the phase angle is determined by the relative magnitudes of resistances (for a <u>pure</u> resistive circuit, $\varphi = 0$ and $\cos\varphi = 1$), capacitances (for a <u>pure</u> capacitive circuit, $\varphi = \pi/2$ and $\cos\varphi = 0$), and inductances (for a <u>pure</u> inductance, $\varphi = -\pi/2$ and $\cos\varphi = 0$), it is customary to express the transmission-line capacity in millions of volt-ampere or MVA units rather than in Mw_e (the Mw_e are known only if φ is specified). As has been noted, the value of φ depends on the load characteristics through their effects on resistance, capacitance and inductance.

Practical three-phase electrical transmission lines are arranged in Y- or Δ- connections (see Fig. 20.6-4), which may be shown to be electrically equivalent (see Fig. 20.6-5). The voltages $\vec{E}_a$, $\vec{E}_b$, and $\vec{E}_c$ correspond to the voltage vectors shown in Fig. 20.6-1. The symbols Z_y and Z_Δ stand for the (complex) circuit impedances, the numerical values of which depend on the magnitudes of the resistances, capacitances and inductances. The voltages are connected to a ground or neutral line in the Y-connection but not in the Δ-connection.

We shall first comment briefly on the underground terminal-distribution network and then turn to a somewhat more detailed discussion of long-distance <u>underground</u> electrical transmission lines, an area in which current research promises significant technological and systems improvement in the not too distant future. About 40% of the total annual

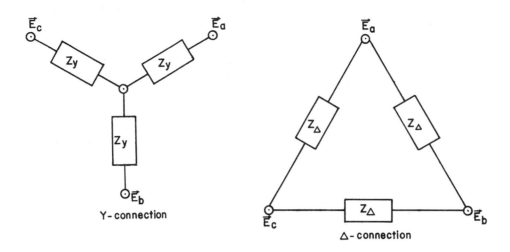

Fig. 20.6-4 Circuit arrangements in Y- and Δ-connections
of three-phase transmission lines.

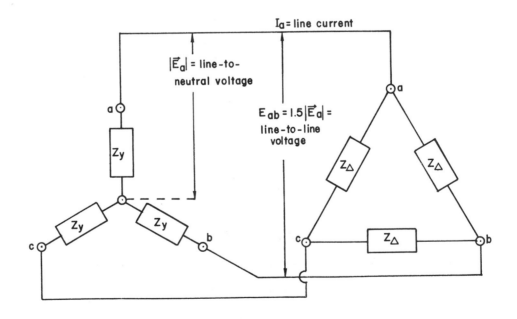

Fig. 20.6-5 Diagram showing the equivalence of the Y- and
Δ-connections. The line-to-line voltage E_{ab} is
$\sqrt{3}\,|\vec{E}_a|\cos 30^\circ = 1.5\,|\vec{E}_a|$.

utility-investment cost is associated with the distribution network.

For terminal distribution, power is taken from a 12 kV <u>backbone</u> <u>feeder</u>, which costs about $50,000 per mile (plus right-of-way charges) to install. Solid dielectric covers were introduced about 1960 and were initially made of poly-vinylchloride but are now constructed of polyethylene. Thus, a representative line consists of a conducting core covered by a conducting polyethylene-plus-carbon shield and encased in a concentric cover of polyethylene insulation. A 12-kV line has a conducting wire about 0.865×10^{-3} inch in diameter. A three-conductor cable of this size is installed in a five-inch-diameter duct. The specified cable carries up to 500A singly, while two cables in the same trench will carry about 2×400A. A 12-kV line is typically located at a depth of 4 ft and is serviced by 14-ft deep manholes. Telephone lines carry 32 volts and may be installed at a depth of 18 in.

If a subdivider digs and refills a trench for the power cable in new construction, then there is usually no differential charge made for the electrical installation. The developer is paid by the Gas Company for installing a gas line. The Telephone Company will also pay for use of the trench. Finally, cable TV may be supplied and will then serve as an additional source of revenue. Individual homeowners pay for undergrounding in existing construction. In recent years, a fixed percentage of utility-company revenues has been allocated for conversion to undergrounding in a number of municipalities. Heavy underground lines (up to 750 kV) may be two-wire systems with a ground connection.

A number of large industrial concerns (e.g., the General Cable Co., Alcoa Corp., Essex Co., Kaiser Co.) supply cables to the utilities. With adequate quality control, the rejection rate is about 80%. The smaller lines for undergrounding are laid from 1,200-ft reels which stand 8 ft in height.

A. HPOF Cables for Underground Transmission Lines

The most widely used electrical transmission cable is the high-pressure, oil-filled (HPOF) cable. The three conductors carrying the three phases of the a.c. power supply are wrapped with paper insulation (about one-half inch thick for voltages up to 138 kV, impregnated with oil at a pressure of 15 atmospheres, and contained in a steel pipe). Cables of this type have been used in power lines carrying up to 550 kV. HPOF cables are generally only useful for relatively short lengths (a few tens of miles) because of heating during current conduction: a "charging current" flows in the "shunt capacitance". Line losses and voltage drops caused by load currents are compensated for by external capacitors or inductors. Heat is conducted radially outward from the current-carrying wires to the insulation and oil and then to the steel pipe and surrounding backfill. The HPOF cables suffer from eddy-current and dielectric losses and capacitive charging currents. Because of mutual heating, two lines placed next to each other in the same trench carry only about 70% more power than a single line.

Conductor size is measured in thousands of circular mils (MCM), where a circular mil is a unit of <u>area</u> and is defined to be equal to $(\pi/4)$ times a square mil with a mil equal to 10^{-3} inch. Thus, one square mil $= 1(\text{mil})^2 = 10^{-6}(\text{inch})^2$ and one circular mil $= (\pi/4) \times 10^{-6}(\text{inch})^2$. A wire with a diameter of d mil has a cross-sectional area of $(\pi/4)d^2$ square mil or d^2 circular mil or $10^{-3}d^2$ MCM. Figure 20.6-6 shows power ratings for HPOF cables as a function of conductor size for voltages from 69 to 345 kV. Reference to Fig. 20.6-6 shows that power capacity does not increase with conductor size above about 2,000 MCM. The power limit for HPOF cables is about 900 MVA at 550 kV.[1]

The critical length of a transmission line is defined as the distance over which the decrease in current equals the rated input capacity of the current. Clearly, transmission lines cannot be used over larger distances than the critical lengths without recharging. The critical length for a 500 kV HPOF cable is about 20 miles.[2]

The performance of HPOF cables, insofar as rating is concerned, may be improved by forced cooling. In this

---

[1]C. J. Baldwin and L. A. Kilar, "Progress and Prospects for Underground Transmission," paper presented at the 33rd Annual American Power Conference, Chicago, Ill., April 1971.

[2]Ref. [1] of Section 20.5.

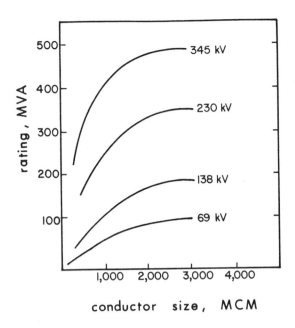

Fig. 20.6-6 Ratings in MVA of HPOF cables as a function
of conductor size in MCM for transmission voltages from 69 to 345 kV; reproduced from
Underground Power Transmission by Superconducting Cable, E. B. Forsyth, editor, Brookhaven National Laboratory, Report BNL 50325,
Upton, New York, 1972.

technique, a low-viscosity oil is pumped axially; oil-cooling

stations are required at distances of about one-half to one

mile.[2] The maximum capacity for cables of this type has

been estimated[1] to be 1,200 MVA.

By separating the three conductors required for a.c.

transmission and sheathing each conductor in non-magnetic

material, ratings of more than 2,500 MVA are achievable

with forced cooling.[1]

B. CGI Cables

An important improvement in cable performance is achieved by using rigid coaxial cylinders of aluminum, separated by spacers made of epoxy, and insulating this system with an electronegative gas such as SF_6 at a pressure of 2 atmospheres. A 600-ft length of compressed-gas-insulated (CGI) cable and rated for 2,000 MVA at 345 kV is in operation.[2] Designs calling for ratings up to 10,000 MVA have been proposed.[2]

C. Cryoresistive Cables

As the temperature is lowered significantly, the electrical resistivity decreases. This effect may be used in practice by constructing a refrigeration system to absorb heat while maintaining the cryoresistive cable at low temperatures (e.g., 78°K for Al; at 78°K, its resistivity is only one-tenth of the room-temperature value).[3] With a liquid nitrogen system, designs have been proposed with capacities of 2,000 to 5,000 MVA at 345 to 750 kV.[4]

---

[3] "Resistive Cryogenic Cable," EEI Project RP78-6, phase A, March 1969; phase B, March 1970; phase C, June 1971. Papers prepared for the Edison Electric Institute, New York, N.Y., by the General Electric Company, Schenectady, New York.

[4] S. H. Minnich and G. R. Fox, "Comparative Costs of Cryogenic Cables," paper No. 70 CF 169-PWR, presented at the IEEE Winter Power Meeting, New York, January 1970.

D. Superconducting Cables

Superconducting cables are under active development and will be discussed in Section 20.8. Here we note that the successful development of these devices will provide us with power-carrying capacities far greater than those achievable with other cables and that, hopefully, the ultimate costs of the underground cables will then be no higher than those of conventional aboveground cables. A composite performance map for cables is reproduced in Fig. 20.6-7.

20.7 Overhead Transmission Lines

Overhead transmission lines dot the American landscape and are likely to remain with us for many years to come. Conventional steel towers are being replaced by "esthetic poles," which are supposed to be less objectionable to the viewer. Because of the relatively high cost of copper ($\sim$\$0.65/lb in mid-1973 and more than \$1.00/lb by early 1974) compared with that of aluminum ($\sim$\$0.32/lb in mid-1973), overhead transmission lines are preferably constructed of current-carrying aluminum wires which encase a load-carrying steel core. Typical installation costs in mid-1973 were \$100,000/mile for a single large ($\geqslant$230 kV) overhead circuit, with a supplemental cost of \$25,000/mile for a second conductor.

Present generator output for a typical line is 12 kV d.c., which is transformed to $\sim$230 kV a.c. for long-distance

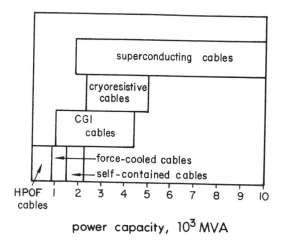

Fig. 20.6-7 Composite performance estimates for various
types of cables for underground transmission
of electricity; reproduced from Ref. [2].

transmission. The delivery lines to the consumers are provided with double- or triple-contingency provisions. A typical line segment is sketched in Fig. 20.7-1. Relays are used
to drop loads, as use decreases, in order to prevent cascad-
ing faults. The principal service failures are associated
with damage by lightning and contamination by moisture and
salts (which produce "flashover" between lines to carrying
poles and to the ground).

The flashover failure is controlled by using larger
sizes for the insulators and by water-wash-down of insulators. Fuses are used for line-protection against overheating.
Protection against lightning damage includes the use of open
circuits to allow reflection of lightning-induced surges, the
use of seven-wire, aluminum-clad steel grids with spikes

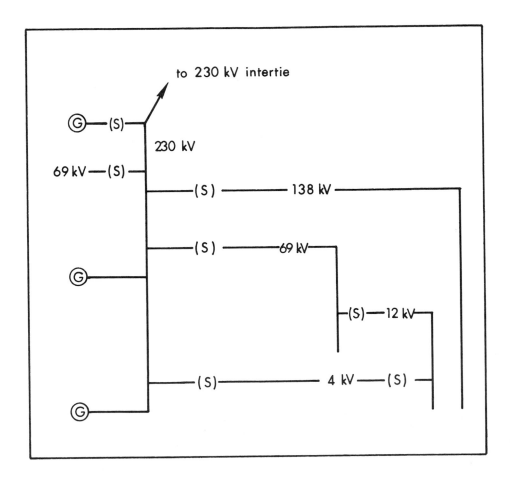

Fig. 20.7-1 An overhead transmission-line segment showing
             transformer (S) step-down to lower voltages,
             ground Ⓖ , and contingency interconnections.

for power dissipation, and the use of transformers with
lightning arrestors at substations; the transformers cost
(in 1973) about $100,000 for conversion of 238 kV to 10 to
12 kV.

Composite wire structures are employed to minimize
thermal breakage. Overhead transmission lines are designed

to carry expected ice and wind loads. Line specifications are
defined in the "Line Design Guide" issued by the Public
Utilities Commission. Examples of required performance
figures in the San Diego coastal and mountain regions, respectively, are the following: wind loading of 8 lb (corresponding to a wind speed of 57 mph) or 8 lb of wind loading
plus a specified number of inches of ice. As ice accumulates
below the carrying wire, a lentil-shaped structure that acts
like an airfoil may be built up. This structure undergoes lift
on exposure to winds and induces differential motion on line
segments, which may lead to failure.

20.8 Superconducting AC Power Lines[1]

H. Kamerlingh Onnes discovered superconductivity
in 1911 when he found that the electrical resistivity of mercury became immeasurably small below 4°K. Later studies
have shown that superconductivity can occur only below a
critical current I_c, temperature T_c, and magnetic field
strength H_c (see Fig. 20.8-1). Depending on the extent of
magnetization accomplished by an applied magnetic field, we
distinguish between type I superconductors (linear, revers-

---

[1] Ref. [1] in Section 20.5. Supplementary and more recent
information is contained in progress reports submitted on
the Brookhaven "Power Transmission Project" to the AEC.
See, also, R. A. Hein, "Superconductivity: Large-Scale
Applications--Bonanza or Bagatelle? Research in this
Decade Should Provide the Answer," Science 185, 211-222
(1974).

ible changes in magnetization are produced by an applied
magnetic field) and type II superconductors (initially linear
rises in magnetization are followed by decreasing magnetization as the applied magnetic field is increased and the system shows hysteresis when the applied magnetic field strength
is decreased after having been raised beyond the linear region). The characteristic saturation curves for these two
types of superconductors are shown schematically in Fig.
20.8-2. Of the commercially-available materials which become superconducting, most turn out to be type II superconductors. The operating region for superconducting power
lines using type II superconductors is expected to fall beyond
the linear region of the magnetization curve (at H_1 in Fig.
20.8-2b) but well below the levels where very high hysteresis
losses occur (see the line from H_1 to H_2 in Fig. 20.8-2b).

The magnetization curves are generally substantially
different for superconducting elements, alloys and compounds,
with the compounds possessing by far the largest critical
fields and critical temperatures (see Fig. 20.8-3 and Table
20.8-1). Representative superconductors and their properties are listed in Table 20.8-1.

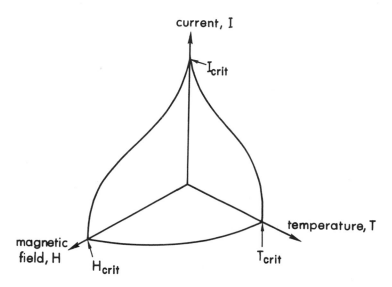

Fig. 20.8-1 Schematic diagram showing the boundaries of
             superconductivity in a three-dimensional space
             of current, field, and temperature. The sym-
             bols I_{crit}, T_{crit}, and H_{crit} denote the critical
             values above which superconductivity is not ob-
             served.

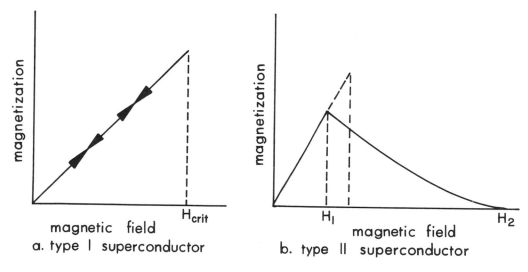

Fig. 20.8-2 Schematic diagrams showing the magnetization
             properties of type I and type II superconductors.
             Type I superconductors show no hysteresis up
             to H_{crit}; type II superconductors show hystere-
             sis between H_1 and H_2.

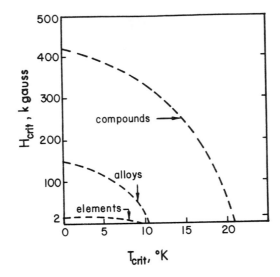

Fig. 20.8-3 Critical-temperature-field envelopes for three
            types of superconductors; reproduced from
            Ref. [1].

For elaboration of theoretical and experimental aspects of superconductivity, we refer to the literature.[2-6]
Over the years, B. T. Matthias of the University of California,

[2] K. Mendelssohn, The Quest for Absolute Zero, World University Library, Weidenfeld and Nicholson, London, 1966.

[3] E. A. Lyndon, Superconductivity, Methuen and Co., New
York, New York, 1969.

[4] P. G. de Gennes (translated by P. A. Pincus), Superconductivity of Metals and Alloys, W. A. Benjamin, Inc.,
New York, New York, 1966.

[5] D. Saint-James, E. J. Thomas, and G. Sarma, Type II
Superconductivity, Pergamon Press, Oxford, 1969.

[6] B. W. Roberts, Superconductive Materials and Some of
Their Properties, U. S. National Bureau of Standards,
Technical Note 482, Washington, D.C., 1969.

Table 20.8-1   Properties of selected superconductors;
reproduced from Ref. [1].

Material	T_{crit}, °K	H_{crit}, kOe[a]	Current density at 5 kOe, A/cm^2
elements			
Pb	7.2	0.8	0
Nb	9.3	2 to 20[b]	10^6
V	5.3	1	
alloys			
NbTi	10.0	120	10^6
NbZr	10.8	90	10^6
compounds			
$Pb_{1.0}Mo_{5.1}S_6$	14.4*	510 (at 4.2°K)*	
Nb_3Sn	18.3	230	10^7
V_3Ga	15 to 16	220	10^7
Nb_3Al	19.3	360	
V_3Si	17.2		
$Nb_3Al_xGe_y$	20.7	410 (at 4.2°K)	

[a] 1 kOe = 10^3 oersted = 10^3 gauss = 10^{-1} weber/m^2.
[b] The critical field value depends on the extent of cold-working.
* From S. Foner, E. J. McNiff, Jr., and E. J. Alexander, "600 kG Superconductors," Physics Letters 49A, 269-270 (1974).

San Diego, has been the preeminent discoverer of higher-temperature superconductors.

A summary of superconducting-cable development is given in Ref. [1]. The cables are either of the rigid, coaxial type or else flexible, multiply-interleaved wires. They are made of Nb-foil or of electroplated Nb. Maximum current-carrying capacities of the power lines, which were under development during 1972, fall between 2,080 and 10,700 A, while the maximum linear current densities vary from 100 to 580 amperes/cm. Installed costs were estimated[1] to vary from about \$610 to \$1,240/MVA-mile. The ultimate performance ratings for all types of cables have been summarized in Fig. 20.6-7. The preferred Brookhaven super-conducting design is an interleaved ribbon power cable.[1] A recent cost evaluation for these lines may be found in Ref. [7].

The performance limits of HPOF, CGI, cryoresistive, and superconducting cables are compared in Ref. [1]. The superconducting cable supports the highest power density and has the longest critical length.

A 1972 summary of estimated[1] specific costs for underground cables is reproduced in Fig. 20.8-4 and shows that the superconducting cables were believed to become the preferred transmission lines for sufficiently large powers transmitted. Capital investment-cost estimates[1] for super-conducting power lines as a function of transmitted power levels are shown in Fig. 20.8-5. More recent cost estimates may be found in Ref. [7].

We shall now list some of the critical development problems involved in the realization of superconducting pow-er lines.

---

[7]E. B. Forsyth, G. A. Mulligan, J. W. Beck, and J. A. Williams, "The Technical and Economic Feasibility of Superconducting Power Transmission: A Case Study," paper prepared for presentation at the 1974 IEEE Summer Meeting, Brookhaven National Laboratory Report 18602, February 8, 1974, Upton, New York.

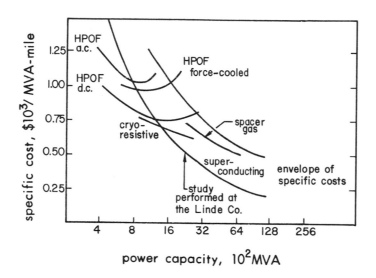

Fig. 20.8-4 Estimated (in 1972) specific cost of underground-
cable schemes; reproduced from Ref. [1].

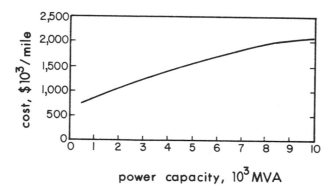

Fig. 20.8-5 Estimated (in 1972) capital investment for superconducting cable systems; reproduced from
Ref. [1].

(a) Cryogenic dielectrics with very low loss tangents must be developed. Here the loss tangent is the tangent of the phase-defect angle. Loss tangents vary from 10^{-3} for cellulose, to $\leq 2 \times 10^{-5}$ for teflon, to $\leq 10^{-6}$ for liquid He. Generally, values in the liquid-helium range are required for adequate performance.

(b) Dielectric breakdown may be a serious problem in view of the high electrical stresses that will develop with high-performance, superconducting power lines. The normal breakdown stress for liquid He at atmospheric pressure is 170 kV/cm for a 0.7 cm gap, but this value will be greatly reduced in case of bubble formation. The electrode areas for superconducting power lines are very much larger than for conventional power lines because superconducting currents are carried in very thin surface layers. The surface area may be increased by as much as a factor of 10^7. This fact magnifies problems associated with dielectric breakdown. Important new developments are required for cryogenic applications.

(c) Active development of higher-temperature superconductors should be pursued. Liquid He boils at 4.2°K, liquid H_2 at 20.3°K, and liquid N_2 at 77.3°K. The data in Table 20.8-1 show that only $Nb_3Al_xGe_y$ is (marginally, in view of the possible occurrence of temperature surges) compatible with cooling by liquid H_2. When a higher-temperature superconductor for use with liquid N_2 becomes commercially available, the economic evaluation of superconducting power lines will become far more favorable than it is now. Because

of surface-current conduction, niobium itself has operating
points such that it is readily driven out of the superconducting region by overload currents. On the other hand,
while the currents are carried in relatively thick layers of
Nb_3Sn, this material is brittle and must be supported on
metal foil or wires made of ductile material. It is also possible to use Nb on a ductile type II superconductor, which
will then carry loss currents, except that the required operating temperature is now again reduced to 4.4 to $5.0^{\circ}K$.

(d) There are special problems connected with the
details of the cable design. In the Brookhaven program, [1, 7]
a structure interleaved such that adjacent superconducting
ribbons carry currents in opposite directions has been constructed in order to minimize the strengths of residual magnetic fields at the conductor surfaces.

(e) Current cost estimates[1] of about $38/m^2 for
Nb_3Sn require verification on a large scale.

(f) Although U.S. helium reserves are ample if properly conserved, the long-term requirements are so large
that the termination in late 1973 of the U.S. helium conservation program[8] poses a serious long-term threat to requirements. Between 1967 and 1972, total He sales decreased
substantially (see Fig. 20.8-6), although U.S. capacity remained at 4.5×10^9 SCF/y (see Table 20.8-2). If we assume

---

[8]"Future Helium Supplies Rest with Court Case," Chemical
and Engineering News 51, 6-7, October 22, 1973.

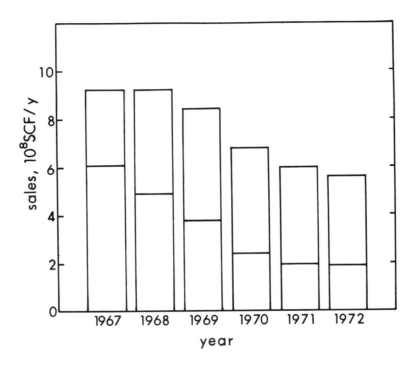

Fig. 20.8-6 Helium sales for the years 1967 to 1972. The
lower section of the bars refers to sales by the
U.S. Bureau of Mines, while the upper section
of the bars refers to sales by private industry.
Reproduced from Ref. [8]. Copyright © 1973
by the American Chemical Society.

a year 2100 U.S. capacity for electrical energy of 1.0×10^7
Mw$_e$ with 25,000 miles of underground transmission lines of
capacity $\geq 2,000$ MVA, the system will require $(1.25 \times 10^6$
SCF of He/mile of superconducting cable) $\times$ $(2.5 \times 10^4$ miles
of cable) $= 3.13 \times 10^{10}$ SCF of He which, although readily
available now, exceeds the 1972 conservation program of the
U.S. Bureau of Mines $(2.07 \times 10^{10}$ SCF). The long-term

Table 20.8-2 U.S. sources for He during 1972, in 10^9 SCF; reproduced from Ref. [8]. Copyright © 1973 by the American Chemical Society.

Source	Location	Capacity, 10^9 SCF
Bureau of Mines		
Excell	Masterson, TX	0.360
Keys	Keys, OK	0.420
subtotal		0.780
Private industry		
Kerr-McGee	Navajo, AZ	0.075
Kansas Refined Helium	Otis, KS	0.180
Alamo Chemical	Elkart, KS	0.140
Cities Service Cryogenics	Scott City, KS	0.200
subtotal		0.595
Conservation program companies		
Northern Helex	Bushton, KS	0.675
Philips Petroleum	Hansford County, TX / Dumas, TX	0.788
Cities Service Helex	Ulysses, KS	0.610
National Helium	Liberal, KS	1.052
subtotal		3.125
total		4.500

development of superconducting power lines requires maintenance of a long-term helium-conservation program unless superconductors operating at much higher temperatures are developed.

20.9 Conventional and Superconducting DC Power Lines

Conventional (i.e., non-superconducting) d.c. power lines possess both advantages and disadvantages, as compared with a.c. power lines. Their use is preferable when long distances ($\geqslant$400 miles) or shorter underground or underwater lengths ($\geqslant$20 miles) with large power requirements are involved. Direct-current transmission may be required for interconnection of asynchronous a.c. power systems (as between the U.K. and France). Conventional d.c. power lines are in existence in many parts of the world (the 850-mile Pacific Northwest to Pacific Southwest intertie operating at 800 kV and carrying up to 1,440 Mw_e initially; a 350-mile North-to-South-Island intertie in New Zealand operating at 500 kV, 600 Mw_e). The primary advantage of d.c. over a.c. power lines is associated with the absence of charging currents and, therefore, of essential (critical) length limitations. The impedance characteristics of d.c. power lines allow the power flow to be easily reversed. This property is particularly advantageous for intertie lines connecting regions which have peak power loads occurring at different times.

A d.c. cable has no charging current, dielectric hysteresis losses, or skin effect (most of the current flows near the boundary of a solid a.c. conductor because the inductance and reactance are higher near the center of the conductor). Thus, the current capacity of a d.c. cable is determined, almost entirely, by the resistive losses in the conductor. The insulating ability of a dielectric is substantially greater for d.c. than a.c. power transmission, which allows use of thinner insulation for d.c. cables. The cost[1] of a.c. to d.c. converter stations ($20 to $35 per kw_e in 1972) has tended to discourage the large-scale exploitation of these advantages.

The principal problems connected with the use of d.c. power lines involve the absence of suitable circuit breakers, filters, power-correction devices, and load taps. The technology necessary to overcome these problems may, however, be developed.

In general, a d.c. power line or cable will transmit more power for the same capital investment than the corresponding a.c. line or cable. The power transmitted by existing a.c. cables could be increased by at least a factor of two if these cables were converted to direct current.

The use of superconducting d.c. cables has been considered in Refs. [1] and [2] and, with great enthusiasm, by Garwin and Matisoo.[3] In addition to the advantages that conventional d.c. cables have over conventional a.c. cables, superconducting d.c. cables have no resistive losses and will

---

[1] Ref. [1] in Section 20.5.

[2] W. E. Keller and R. D. Taylor, USAEC-DAT DC Superconducting Power Transmission Line Project at LASL, Los Alamos Scientific Laboratory, Report LA-5468-PR, Los Alamos, New Mexico, 1973.

[3] R. L. Garwin and J. Matisoo, "Superconducting Lines for the Transmission of Large Amounts of Electrical Power Over Great Distances," Proceedings of the IEEE 55, 538-548 (1967).

operate at higher current densities than superconducting a.c.
cables. The refrigeration load of a d.c. cable is determined
solely by heat leaks, ripple, and load changes.

The construction and operation of a superconducting
d.c. cable appear to be technologically feasible.[2] The operation of superconducting d.c. cables will probably not be
identical with that of conventional d.c. lines. Power modulation of a conventional d.c. line is accomplished by controlling
the line current. Superconducting d.c. cables will be operated at high current levels and, therefore, voltage changes
will probably be used for power modulation.

Economic studies of three superconducting d.c. pow-
er-line designs[2] have led to the conclusion that the major
costs are associated with the cryogenic enclosure (33 to 54%)
and field installation excluding trenching (21 to 29%). The
costs attributed to the superconductor (2 to 11%) and refrigeration (3 to 16%) represent relatively small portions of the
total cost. A compilation[2] of estimates for the capital cost
of a 1×10^4 Mw$_e$ superconducting d.c. power line shows a
range from 0.66×10^6/mi to 2.7×10^6/mi, with an average
figure of 1.3×10^6/mi.

Superconducting d.c. power lines appear economically
competitive with overhead power-transmission modes for
transmitting very large power loads over long distances.
The estimated cost[2] for transmitting 1×10^4 Mw$_e$ over a
distance of 500 miles by a superconducting d.c. power line
is 1.5 to 3 times higher than the lower bound of the extrapolated cost of overhead a.c. transmission at 1,000 kV; the

d. c. line is competitive with multiple 345 kV or 500 kV over-head a. c. lines and costs (1/5) to (1/15) as much as the com-pressed-gas-insulated (CGI) d. c. cables using SF_6, which are presently the most economical underground d. c. cables.

A cost comparison[1] of superconducting a. c. and d. c. power lines leads to the following conclusions: the conductor cost for the d. c. line is reduced by a factor of 3 for a single cable (or 6 for a coaxial cable) per MVA; cryogenic systems costs are reduced by factors of 2 to 4 per MVA; reduced re-quirements for Dewar sizes may save 20% in d. c. operation; there are, however, costly converter requirements at the load ends with d. c. equipment. The economic break-even length for conversion from a. c. to d. c. is probably[1] at a minimum length of 250 miles.

20.10 Electric-Equipment Development Using Super-conductivity

Generally speaking, the development of heavy electri-cal equipment and other required components is proceeding in such a manner that these aspects of the electrical-equip-ment industry are not the pacing items in power delivery.

The introduction of superconductivity permits the construction of new devices such as cryogenic circuit break-ers. We refer to Ref. [1] for a discussion of current develop-

---

[1]"A Discussion on Recent Advances in Heavy Electrical Plant," Philosophical Transactions of the Royal Society of London 275, 33-253, August 1973.

ments in this field.

A rather conservative assessment of the early promise for application of superconductivity to rotating machinery, magnets used to support superfast trains, etc, has been given by Hein.[2] Hein[2] has expressed the view that a reasonable cost evaluation of the merit of superconducting power lines for a.c. and d.c. applications will be made by the end of the present decade.

---

[2]Ref. [1] in Section 20. 8.

PROBLEMS

Problems marked with a dagger (†) deal with the environmental impact of energy production, transportation, or use.

Problems marked with a single asterisk (*) require reading and literature search of original source material.

Problems for Chapter 9

1. The Colony plant for shale-oil recovery was designed to produce 50,000 bbl/d. The responsible industry consortium announced in late 1974 abandonment or deferral of development because of estimated capital-cost escalation from 460×10^6 to nearly 800×10^6 in current dollars. Estimate the effect of this inflationary price rise on product cost.

2. Describe briefly the essential features of each of the following technologies:
    (a) a pure in situ process for shale-oil recovery;
    (b) a mixed-mining-and-in-situ process for shale-oil recovery;
    (c) a strip-mining and aboveground retorting procedure for shale-oil recovery.

3. Describe briefly the essential features of each of the following fracturing procedures:
    (a) the drilling of channels followed by the use of chemical explosives;
    (b) leaching of the "leach zone" followed by fracturing with chemical explosives;
    (c) fracturing by electrolinking;
    (d) fracturing by underground nuclear explosions.
    Specify requirements for successful application of each of the fracturing techniques used.

4. Describe briefly the essential features of each of the

following procedures for _in situ_ shale-oil recovery:

(a) underground concurrent combustion-retorting with air;

(b) underground concurrent combustion-retorting with oxygen-enriched air;

(c) underground extraction with heated methane.

5. Describe a program of laboratory experiments for better definition of combustion parameters that are of interest in connection with underground retorting for _in situ_ recovery of shale oil.

6.[†] Give a likely scenario of environmental impacts for each of the following procedures if precautionary steps are not implemented for minimizing environmental impact:

(a) strip mining of shale oil and piling of spoil banks of spent shale after retorting by use of the TOSCO II process;

(b) nuclear fracturing followed by _in situ_ retorting with air.

7.[†] Discuss the problem of groundwater contamination if an aquifer is connected with an underground retort.

8.[*] Discuss the technology of shale-oil upgrading.

9.[*] Summarize our current knowledge about the chemical nature of kerogen.

10.[*] What practical experience developed in coal mining may be transcribed directly to shale-oil recovery?

Problems for Chapter 10

1.   Describe the design of a coal-slurry pipeline that is suitable for the delivery of 1×10^6 (bbl)$_e$ per day from Colorado to Los Angeles.

2.   Specify in detail examples of chemical processes involved in <u>in situ</u> coal gasification.

3.   What do you regard as the principal problems involved in doubling U.S. coal utilization during the ten-year period 1975-1985?

4.[†]   Discuss the potential environmental effects of <u>in situ</u> coal gasification.

5.[*]   Define research and development programs to support <u>in situ</u> gasification of coal.

6.[*]   Define research and development programs to support <u>in situ</u> production of liquid hydrocarbons from coal.

7.[*]   Specify in detail examples of chemical processes involved in the manufacture of liquid hydrocarbons from coal.

8.[*]   Prepare schematic process diagrams for each of the coal-gasification processes specified in Table 10.3-1.

9.[*]   Detail operating experience of the Lurgi reactor for coal gasification.

10.[*] Prepare a list of known and unknown reaction rates relating to coal gasification in the Lurgi reactor.

Problems for Chapter 11

1. What are the energy equivalents of 1 km^3 of NG and of H$_2$ at STP in Btu and in (bbl)$_e$ of petroleum?

2. What types of research, development, and field implementation should be initiated now in order to prepare us for smooth transition to a hydrogen economy by the year 2030?

3. What is the energy content of a large LNG delivery system in kt of TNT equivalent? Specify the carrying capacity assumed for delivery.

4. [†] Compare the nuclear-gasoline, nuclear-coal, and nuclear-hydrogen flow diagrams of Fig. 11.1-2 with special emphasis on the following aspects on these energy industries:

   (a) primary nuclear-energy requirement;
   (b) long-term availability of fuel;
   (c) environmental impact of large-scale use.

5. [†] Discuss the potentially advantageous environmental effects of a future transition to a hydrogen economy. Describe possible local, regional, and global impacts.

6. [*] Describe two thermal cycles for hydrogen production other than those listed in the text.

7. [*] Specify the chemical processes involved in each of the hydrogen applications listed in Table 11.1-1.

8. [*] Describe in your own words how an electrolytic process

with an overall efficiency exceeding 100% may be possible.

9. *   Review past experience of applications of H_2 for the following purposes:

(a) automotive use;

(b) use in dirigibles;

(c) use in high-speed transport aircraft.

10. *   Describe the experimental techniques that are used to measure the following basic combustion parameters: laminar flame speed, ignition energy, quenching distance, explosion limit.

11. *   What are your views on direct water photolysis for hydrogen production? What research should be done to develop an economically competitive procedure?

12. †,*   Specify the advantages and disadvantages of the following fuels for aircraft applications: jet fuel, methanol, hydrazine, liquid hydrogen.

Problems for Chapter 12

1.   What is your view on a reasonable schedule for developing flywheel technology as a major component of the energy-storage industries? What aspects of research and development should be emphasized over the near term?

2.   Prepare a detailed table of energy-storage costs in

$/wh$_e$ using data given in the text.   List separately the applicable values in wh$_e$/lb and in lb/wh$_e$.

3.   Discuss the development and likely costs of increasing the U.S. storage capability for NG and petroleum at a compound rate of 5% per year.

4.   Discuss the relative advantages of flywheel, compressed-air, and pumped-hydraulic energy-storage systems for application to peak-load demands of utility networks.

5.   Compare the system design and operating characteristics of flywheel/heat-engine hybrid and flywheel-only automobiles.

6.   Discuss the required coupling between energy-storage systems and wind-power and solar-energy systems.

7.[†,*]   Discuss environmental hazards associated with the following types of large-scale energy storage:

(a) a flywheel capable of delivering 1 Mwd;

(b) salt-dome storage of NG containing 10^8 (bbl)$_e$ of petroleum;

(c) a tank holding liquid hydrogen with the energy equivalent of 10^6 bbl of petroleum.

8.[*]   Specify the technological developments that must be accomplished to reduce the cost of flywheel-storage systems.

9.[*]   Specify possible future technological developments

that may reduce the costs of synthetic-fuel storage
to competitive levels with gasoline storage.

10.* Specify possible future technological developments
that may increase the energy-storage capacities of
electrical-energy storage systems.

Problems for Chapter 13

1. Summarize the essential physical effects that are
used in obtaining higher fossil-fuel utilization efficiency in systems using MHD power conversion.

2. Describe the fuel cells that are likely to be used
extensively in a hydrogen economy.

   (a) Specify a number of useful applications for these
   fuel cells.

   (b) What would be the capacity of an H_2-air fuel
   cell that is suitable for driving a small car over
   a distance of 50 miles?

   (c) How much would the fuel cell used in part (b)
   weigh?

   (d) What would it cost?

3. Evaluate the magnitude of the effective increase in
the fossil-fuel resource base resulting from widespread adoption of MHD power conversion.

4. Discuss the advantages of direct energy conversion
to electricity as compared to thermal-to-mechanical-
to-electrical energy conversion.

5. * Specify the technological developments that must be accomplished to reduce the cost of photovoltaic power conversion to competitive levels. What types of research and development must be done to facilitate large-scale implementation of photovoltaic devices?

6. †, * Discuss the environmental impacts of large-scale implementation of photovoltaic power generation. Consider both local and possible synoptic-scale effects.

7. * Discuss a possible large-scale application of thermo-electric power generation.

8. * Describe the development of the edge-defined crystal growth process. Comment on the estimated cost reductions achievable by this process.

9. * Discuss the past and future development of thermo-electric and thermionic power generation.

Problems for Chapter 14

1. What type of research and development program on solar-energy utilization do you consider to be appropriate to meet the goal of providing 10% of total U.S. energy needs by 1995?

2. At a conversion efficiency of 20%, what percentage of the continental U.S. land area will be required on the average to provide 10% of estimated total U.S.

energy needs? If 10^5 square miles of average land in the U.S. are used for electricity generation, what conversion efficiency is required to produce 3% of the estimated U.S. energy demands for the year 1985?

3.   If 10% of the estimated year 2000 world-wide energy demands are to be produced from solar energy, what land area will be required at an average conversion efficiency of 2%? Specify precisely the source of each of the required data inputs.

4.[†]   A desert region 100 miles by 100 miles in area has been designated for conversion to a solar farm for electricity production. The overall sunlight-to-electricity conversion efficiency is 10%. What is the average required change in the desert-surface albedo that must be made to accomplish the specified conversion and maintain desert temperatures unchanged? Discuss the possible local environmental impact.

5.   Summarize in your own words the essential physical features of an efficient solar-thermal collection unit. Describe important materials research that constitutes a feature of this application development.

6.   Calculate the Rankine-cycle efficiency for a secondary propane cycle operating under the conditions specified in Fig. 14.8-2.

7.[*]   Update the cost estimates summarized in Fig. 14.1-1 to 1975.

8.*   Obtain a firm capital-cost charge for installation of a solar water- and space-heating unit in your home. Assuming a 20-year life and repair or service charges amounting to 2% per year on the average, what is the yearly dollar cost of the proposed installation? How does this compare in cost with other heating units for your residence?

9.*   Discuss the biochemical aspects of hydrogen production from water on exposure to sunlight of an appropriate biosystem.

10.†,*   Design a metal hydride energy-storage system for your residence.

Problems for Chapter 15

1.   Verify each of the following statements:

    (a) the wind velocity is decreased by av_f ahead of a windmill rotor and av_f behind the windmill rotor, where $\underline{a}$ is the axial-interference factor;

    (b) the drag force exerted by the wind on the actuator disk is proportional to the product of the cross-sectional area of the disk and the pressure drop across the disk;

    (c) the power extracted from the wind is proportional to the cube of the free-steam velocity.

2.   Using the efficiency data in Table 15.3-1, what is the

likely upper limit of the power extracted in a 60-mph
wind with a rotor radius of 100 ft for

(a) a Savonius rotor?

(b) a wind turbine?

What are the corresponding values for a 20-mph wind?

3.   Discuss the importance of the specific output for a
wind-power system.

4.   When the wake-wind velocity is reduced to one-half of
the free-stream wind velocity, what percentage of the
maximum achievable wind-power utilization is actually reached?

5.   Verify that the power extracted from the wind assumes
a maximum value for an axial-interference factor $\underline{a}$
equal to 1/3.

6.* Obtain charts of average monthly wind speeds and directions for the region in which you reside.

7.* Describe the Savonius rotor and Darrieus vertical
windmills in detail. Why is the operation of these
devices independent of wind direction? Summarize
the current status of development work on one of
these designs.

8.* Update the cost estimates given in Table 15.4-1.

9.* Using reasonably expected performance estimates
(see Section 15.3), calculate the number of windmills

required for electric-power generation to satisfy
50% of the regional demands where you live.

10. [†,*]   Describe a wind-power utilization system for your
region, including considerations of preferred locations, environmental impact, prototype-development
costs, and aesthetic changes to the landscape.

Problems for Chapter 16

1.   Verify the entries given in Table 16.2-1 for the
potential annual electrical-energy production by
using the specified tidal ranges R and basin areas S.

2.   What type of tidal-power installation do you consider
to be appropriate for Passamaquoddy?

3.   Describe in your own words the operation of the
wave engine depicted in Fig. 16.8-2. Evaluate the
energy-utilization efficiency for this device.

4. [†,*]   Describe the environmental-impact history of the
Rance tidal-power development.

5.   Using only Newton's laws [e.g., Eq. (16.2-1)], show
that the tide-generating force produced by the sun
varies inversely as the cube of the mean distance
from the earth.

6.   Verify Eqs. (16.8-1) to (16.8-3) by starting from
Newton's laws.

7. [*]   Prepare a listing of existing tidal-power installations
with one of the following types of structures: one-

way, single-basin; linked-basin; low-head pumped
storage and tidal power.

8.[*]   What types of barrages are used at the Rance tidal-
power installation?

9.[*]   Prepare an economic evaluation of a tidal-power
utilization scheme.

10.[†,*]   Describe Salter's scheme (Ref. [5] in Section 16.8)
for conversion of the to and fro wave motion to useful energy. Show a schematic diagram of a proposed
design and estimate the achievable energy-conversion efficiency.

11.[*]   Outline the physical principles and analysis used in
Refs. [1] and [2] of Section 16.2 in order to estimate
the rate of tidal-energy dissipation on the earth.

Problems for Chapter 17

1.   If hydroelectric-plant outages average 3% per year
and the year 2000 hydroelectric generating capacity is
is 4×10^5 Mw$_e$, how many (bbl/d)$_e$ of energy will
be lost by the year 2000 because of hydroelectric-
plant outages?

2.   What is the hydroelectric-power production potential
for a reservoir with a mass-flow rate of 10^5 kg/sec
which is allowed to fall from an altitude of 5,500 ft
to a level of 1,350 ft?

3.   For a hydraulic efficiency of 80% and an energy head of 250 ft, what is the required water-flow rate for a 1,000-Mw$_e$ installation?

4.[*]   Give a current estimate of developed and undeveloped hydroelectric resources in Canada, Brazil, on the African Continent, and in the U.S.S.R.

5.[*]   Describe in detail the design, operation, cost, and achievable efficiency for a typical Pelton-type impulse turbine.

6.[*]   Compare the hydroelectric-power installations at the Grand Coulee and Hoover dams with respect to the following features: installed cost per kw$_e$ output, tons of cement used per kw$_e$, capital cost per service customer in 1970, installed cost for a flow rate of 10^5 kg/sec.

7.[†,*]   Construct a regional environmental-impact history of the Colorado River Basin associated with the construction of hydroelectric power plants and flood-control basins, as well as water diversion for agricultural use.

8.[†,*]   Review the development history and environmental impact of a major U.S. dam, with emphasis on flood-control and electric-power generation.

9.[*]   Present a detailed analysis of flow losses in an impulse turbine.

Problems for Chapter 18

1.   Some knowledgeable experts regard exploratory drill-
         ing as the only valid procedure available for hydro-
         thermal-resource assessment. What are your views
         on this assertion? Why?

2.   List the techniques that may be used for energy re-
         covery from hydrothermal wells. Describe repre-
         sentative utilization efficiencies that should be achiev-
         able for each of the following procedures:
         (a) the use of a secondary-fluid cycle;
         (b) a total impulse turbine for energy extraction;
         (c) a dry-steam system.
         How do the recovery efficiencies vary with the nature
         of the resource?

3.[*]   Compare electricity-production costs for two of the
         four following principal hydrothermal-resource re-
         covery programs: Wairakei, New Zealand; Cerro
         Prieto, Mexico; The Geysers, California; Lardarello,
         Italy.

4.[†,*] Describe a self-contained cycle in which a hydrother-
         mal resource is used for the production of potable
         water and the recovery of minerals. Obtain an esti-
         mate of the total potential recoverable water from
         one of the hydrothermal reservoirs for which you are
         able to find a resource assessment. Discuss potential

environmental impact associated with this type of resource exploitation.

Some people believe that energy recovery from hydrothermal sources will be less damaging to the environment than water recovery. Why do you agree or disagree with this assessment?

5.[†,*]   Give a review of the environmental changes experienced thus far for one of the following hydrothermal-resource developments: Wairakei, New Zealand; Cerro Prieto, Mexico; The Geysers, California; Lardarello, Italy.

6.[*]   Give a quantitative description of the following two indicators for down-hole temperature determinations:

(a) the SiO_2 measurement;

(b) the concentration ratio of sodium to potassium.

Specify the basic assumptions that are made in the use of these thermometers and discuss the existing experimental evidence relating to validation of the critical assumptions.

7.[*]   Describe important chemical reaction steps leading to scale formation in hydrothermal-recovery systems for brines from the Imperial Valley of California.

8.[*]   Discuss the physico-chemical differences between scale formation and corrosion.

Problems for Chapter 19

1.   (a) If you had property in Montana, on which a cylindri-
            cal hot volume (2 km in diameter, 5 km in height
            at a uniform temperature of 900°F) were discovered,
            how would you estimate its energy potential in bbl
            of petroleum equivalent?

        (b) If the current price for petroleum is $10/bbl, a
            utility offered you 90% of the energy-equivalent
            price of petroleum for dry steam, and your steam
            production costs were $0.25/$10^6$ Btu, how much
            would you expect the utility to pay for your proper-
            ty for either an outright purchase or for a long-
            term lease agreement?

2.   Enumerate the essential steps in the successful develop-
        ment of hot dry geothermal resources.

3.[†]   Discuss potentially adverse environmental impacts of
        exploitation of hot dry geothermal resources.

4.   Suggest some possible approaches to improved contain-
        ment of water in semi-porous rock strata.

5.[*]   Obtain cost comparisons for initiating energy recovery
        in a hot-granitic chamber using each of the following
        fracturing procedures:

        (a) drilling of access holes followed by introduction of
            chemical explosives such as nitroglycerine or TNT;

        (b) drilling of access holes followed by introduction of
            of a nuclear detonating device;

(c) drilling of access holes followed by hydraulic fracturing;

(d) fracturing by electrolinking.

6.[*] Compile an up-to-date listing of partially or completely dry, hot geothermal reservoirs, both in the U.S. and abroad.

7.[*] Estimate the total dollar value of each of the resources described in Problem 6 at a price of $1.00/10^6$ Btu for the recoverable portion of the energy reservoir.

8.[†,*] Define the critical technical problems that must be resolved in developing an economically-competitive source of dry steam from localized geothermal deposits.

Problems for Chapter 20

1. Using the data listed in Tables 20.2-1 or 20.2-3, calculate the $(bbl)_e$ of petroleum used for electricity generation in 1960 and 1970 and supplied from each of the following primary energy sources: hydroelectric energy, NG, coal, nuclear energy, oil.

2. Discuss the differences between the electricity-demand projections to the year 2000 given in Figs. 20.2-1 and 20.2-2.

3. How would you modify the electricity-pricing struc-

ture displayed in Fig. 20.4-1 in order to maximize the economic value of electrical-energy use? What type of pricing structure might be useful in smoothing out the time variations in power load shown in Fig. 20.4-2? What could be done to smooth out monthly variations in electricity use (see Fig. 20.4-3)?

4. Describe briefly the salient features of an electricity-distribution network, beginning with the generating system and ending with a 120-volt outlet in a residence. How would these systems differ for a utility-generating station located in a metropolitan area or in a remote desert location, each providing electrical energy for a population of one million people?

5.[†] Discuss the environmental impact of electrical-power transmission and distribution systems. Indicate the important differences between aboveground and underground systems. Comment on the relationship between potential environmental impact and system power-capacity.

6.[*] Summarize current developments on the production of higher temperature superconductors. What must be achieved to develop a commercial superconducting power line operating at the temperature of liquid N_2?

7. [*]   Update the 1972 specific-cost data given in Fig. 20.8-4 to 1975.

8. [*]   Describe recent or proposed applications of super-conductivity to electrical-generating facilities.

9. [†,*]   Obtain current cost estimates in your region for

(a) undergrounding of the electrical transmission and distribution network in new construction;

(b) undergrounding existing aboveground power lines. What plans exist for relocating aboveground lines of all types, including telephone lines and TV antennas, in your region? What percentage of the total charges collected by your local utility station are reserved for undergrounding? Do you believe this percentage should be increased? Why?

10. [*]   Describe the technological aspects of a.c. to d.c. power conversion and give applicable 1975 cost estimates.

INDEX

adiabatic flame temperature, 197, 198

Alberta (Canada), 1, 4

Allis-Chalmers Corporation, 147, 148, 150, 151, 525, 527, 530

American Electric Power Company, 647, 651, 652

American Gas Association, 131

American Petroleum Institute, 264

anaerobic fermentation, 374-376, 389

animal-waste utilization, 387, 388

Atlantic Richfield Company, 55, 56

band-gap energy, 315, 316

Battelle Pacific Northwest Laboratories, 261, 620, 626

batteries,
    costs, 251
    electric, 246
    lead-acid, 247, 248, 250, 251, 254, 280, 281
    nickel-cadmium, 248 250, 251, 254
    storage, 246-254

bipolar cell, 145-147

bitumen, 2, 5-8, 40

Bituminous Coal Research Institute, 106, 107

blackbody radiation, 378, 381 382, 384

capacitive-storage systems, 243, 244

Carnot cycle, 296, 417

Carnot efficiency, 155, 295, 296, 328, 347, 412, 416, 418, 419, 421, 422, 435, 600

coal,
    costs, 78, 80-82
    employment, 79
    exports, 73
    gasification, 72, 86-110
    gasification costs, 101, 109
    in situ recovery, 70, 86, 116-125
    liquefaction, 110-115
    production, 70-72, 75, 77
    resources, 73-76
    slurry pipelines, 82-85
    transportation, 81-85

Coal Mine Health and Safety Act of 1969, 71

compressed-air storage, 219, 259-262, 466

Consolidated Edison Company of New York, 647, 650, 652

Coriolis force, 484

corrosion, 500, 601, 602

cut-and-fill mining, 19

Debye length, 299

declining block rate, 653, 654

de Laval nozzle, 294

direct energy conversion, 283-335

discounted cash flow rate of return (DCF ROR), 9, 10, 30, 32-35, 47, 48, 53, 65-67, 125

dry steam,
    deposits, 553, 556
    utilization, 575-578

electrical-energy storage,
  218, 242-253
electricity,
    demands, 637-646, 654
    load fluctuations, 654-656
    production, 632-637
    rate design, 652-657
    transmission lines, 648-
    651, 658-660
Electric Power Research
  Institute, 374, 552
electric power transmission
  lines,
    characteristics, 660-665
    compressed-gas-insulated
    (CGI), 669, 671, 678
    cryoresistive, 669, 671,
    678
    high-pressure, oil-filled
    (HPOF), 666-668, 671,
    678
    overhead, 670-673
    superconducting, 670, 671,
    673-687
    underground, 660, 663
electrochemical cell, 160,
  161, 163
energy-conversion efficiency,
  7, 9, 72, 73, 102, 104, 106,
  121, 122, 135, 136, 140, 142,
  144, 155-158, 166, 240, 242,
  247, 255, 256, 259, 260, 292,
  295, 296, 301-304, 317, 320,
  328, 334, 348, 355, 356, 387,
  388, 390, 394, 395, 397, 401,
  461, 462, 485, 578, 600, 601
energy flow, 133, 136, 137

energy line, 517, 518
energy storage,
    costs, 181, 182, 184,
    216, 217, 240, 241, 251,
    257, 259, 261, 263, 264,
    266-282
    efficiency, 242, 255, 260,
    266, 272
equivalence ratio, 195, 199
exploratory drilling, 571-573

Faraday current, 290
Faraday effect, 285, 286
Fischer assay, 21, 25, 28,
  30, 41
flammability limits, 189-191,
  203-205
flywheel,
    costs, 240
    energy storage, 223-242
    heat-engine hybrid sys-
    tem, 231, 233, 237-239
    materials, 229
    peak-power storage, 241,
    242
    physical properties, 224-
    231
    shape factor, 225-228
    system technology, 231-
    236
fuel cells, 284, 295-310
fuel-production costs, 215
fuel-storage costs, 216

Garrett Research and De-
  velopment Company, 50
General Electric Company,
  148, 151, 155
geochemical exploration
  techniques, 567-569

geological exploration techniques, 564, 565

geophysical exploration techniques, 565-567

geopressured deposits, 553, 558, 560, 584, 587

geothermal energy,
  costs, 625, 626
  preliminary results, 626-631
  recovery, 620-624
  resources, 618-620

Great Canadian Oil Sands, Ltd. (GCOS), 1-3, 5-9

Hall current, 290, 291
heat of combustion, 186, 214
heat of fusion, 219, 221
heat of vaporization, 219
helium, 680-683
Hoover Dam, 538-541
hydraulic efficiency, 498, 519, 532, 533

hydraulic fracturing, 39, 119, 620, 621, 627, 629

hydraulic turbines,
  bulb-type, 496-498, 502, 529, 531
  fixed-blade, 527-529
  Francis, 524, 526, 527, 529, 532, 533
  Kaplan, 528-530, 532, 533
  Pelton, 523-525, 529, 532, 533
  straight-flow, 496-498
  tube-type, 496-498, 529, 532

hydroelectric power,
  economic considerations, 542-544
  environmental effects, 544-549

hydroelectric power (continued),
  generation, 514-548
  resources, 534-536
  technology, 520-533

hydrogen,
  applications, 127, 182, 186-202
  climatic impact, 210, 211
  consumption, 132, 186
  costs, 132, 133, 136-138, 149-151, 160, 170-174, 178, 181, 184, 185, 215, 216
  distribution, 127, 167, 176-179
  economy, 126-216
  pipelines, 167, 177-179
  pipeline technology, 173, 175, 176
  production, 127, 130, 138-167
  properties, 186-198, 203-210, 214
  requirements, 127-132
  safety, 127, 202-210
  storage, 127, 167, 176-179
  transmission, 167-174, 177-179

hydrogen-based fuels, 211-216

hydrogen-oxygen fuel cell, 297-299

hydrothermal energy,
  economic considerations, 603-608
  environmental effects, 609-617
  exploration, 561-575
  recovery efficiency, 600, 601

hydrothermal energy (continued),
    recovery technology, 591-601
    resources, 552-560
    utilization problems, 589-591
    utilization techniques, 575-591
Hygas Electrothermal Process, 95-100, 102, 103

ignition energy, 191, 192, 204
Imperial Valley (California), 17, 548, 558, 562, 572, 590, 614
inductive-storage systems, 244-246
Institute of Gas Technology, 95, 96, 170, 175, 348

kerogen, 10, 17, 21, 36, 39, 40, 50
Known Geothermal Resources Areas (KGRA), 574, 575

La Rance tidal-power installation, 476, 489, 496, 499, 501-503
Lardarello (Italy), 550, 556, 576, 594, 602, 610, 613
Larmor radius, 290
latent-heat storage, 219, 221, 222
Lawrence Livermore Laboratory, 43, 124, 583, 598
Leidenfrost effect, 208
liquified natural gas (LNG), 119, 181, 215, 216, 275-277
liquid hydrogen,
    costs, 178, 181, 184, 185, 215, 216, 280, 281

liquid hydrogen (continued),
    distribution, 177
    pipelines, 178
    safety, 206-210
    storage, 179-181, 184, 185, 216, 279, 281, 467
    transmission, 177-179
load factor, 135, 136, 261, 348, 603, 653, 655
Lockheed Aircraft Company, 237
Lockheed Missiles and Space Company, 231-232
Los Alamos Scientific Laboratory, 620, 626-628
low-temperature thermal cycles, 434, 435, 438
Ludington pumped-storage facility, 181, 257-259
Lurgi process, 102, 105, 106, 111

Marysville geothermal project, 630, 631
mechanical-energy storage, 218, 223-242
methanol, 187, 188, 190, 211-216, 278-282
MHD power conversion, 284-295
Mobil Oil Company, 51
Mollier diagram, 417, 422
molten-carbonate fuel cell, 307-310
moment of inertia, 224

National Academy of Sciences (NAS), 83
National Aeronautics and Space Administration (NASA), 175, 180, 303

National Petroleum Council, (NPC), 15, 61, 108, 113, 114, 641

natural gas,
costs, 133, 181, 215
demands, 130
pipelines, 168-174
properties, 186-190, 203-207, 214
storage, 181, 182, 184, 185, 216, 219, 271-277

net energy, 53, 55, 56, 58, 61-63

n-type semiconductor, 162, 311-316

nuclear cavity, 269-271, 625

nuclear fracturing, 20, 42, 44-48, 623, 624

nuclear stimulation, 586, 615, 616

ocean thermal energy conversion (OTEC),
cost estimates, 428-430
description, 405-428
environmental impact, 431-433

oil shale,
availability, 15
environmental impact, 15, 17
in situ recovery, 15, 18, 20, 21, 27, 35-37, 42, 43, 45, 47, 50, 125
mixed-mining-and-in-situ recovery, 20, 50, 51
oil recovery, 10, 13, 15, 20, 21, 23, 25, 38, 39, 51
resources, 16
retorting process, 20-22, 26, 31, 36, 40, 48, 49, 52, 54

open-pit mining, 19

Pacific Gas and Electric Company, 647, 651

Pacific Northwest-Southwest intertie, 648, 651, 684

Peltier effect, 330-332

petroleum storage, 219, 262-271

photovoltaic devices, 139, 284, 324-327, 402

photovoltaic power conversion, 310-327

Piceance Basin (Colorado), 13, 14

plant factor, 534, 543, 604, 606

Plowshare Program, 44, 615, 624

Pollution Probe, 5

p-type semiconductor, 311-316

pumped-hydraulic storage, 219, 253-259, 466, 493-496

pyrolysis, 21

quenching distance, 193, 195, 205

radioactivity, 44, 46, 616, 617

Rankine cycle, 407, 410, 412, 413, 415-419, 421-423, 426, 435, 436, 581, 582

room-and-pillar mining, 18, 19, 51, 60, 71

salt domes, 264-267, 271, 272

Salton Trough (California), 553, 554, 607

San Diego Region (California), 434-437
satellite solar-power stations (SSPS), 324, 325,
  399-406
scale formation, 601, 602
Scripps Institution of Oceanography, 511, 512
second law of thermodynamics,
  295, 296
Seebeck effect, 328, 329, 332
sensible-heat storage, 219, 220
shale oil,
    economics, 30-35
    environmental effects, 15,
      17, 27, 60
    in situ recovery, 15, 18,
      20, 21, 27, 35-53
    properties, 28, 29
    recovery, 10-25, 38-40,
      42, 44, 46, 47, 60, 62
    spent shale, 27, 30
    upgrading, 25-27, 32
Shell Oil Company, 3, 35, 48
Sinclair Oil Company, 36, 37,
  39
Smith-Putnam Wind-Turbine
  Experiment, 441, 462-465
solar cells, 310, 317-323, 403
solar energy
    availability, 353-365
    collectors, 366, 372, 374,
      377, 378, 380-383, 386
    cooling systems, 366, 368-
      371, 390-392
    costs, 337-340, 342-345
    distillation, 392, 393
    economics, 347, 393-396
    environmental impact,
      349-352
    farms, 355, 390

solar energy (continued),
    insolation, 353, 354
    lighting, 352
    ponds, 397, 398
    space heating, 337, 339,
      340, 342-345, 366-371
    systems integration,
      439, 440
    water heating, 342-345,
      366, 367, 369
solar-sea power plant (SSPP),
    current developments,
      427-430
    description, 405-428
    economic considerations,
      423-430
stoichiometric air-fuel
  ratio, 190, 197
stratigraphic column, 39,
  41
stripping ratio, 71, 72
superconducting power lines,
    alternating current
      (a.c.), 673-683
    costs, 678, 679
    direct current (d.c.),
      684-687
superconductivity, 246,
  673-677
superflywheels, 230, 234-
  236, 241
Syncrude of Canada, 3, 9
synthetic-fuel storage, 278-
  282, 466
synthetic natural gas (SNG),
  72, 107-110

tar sands,
    in situ recovery, 3, 5
    oil recovery, 2, 3, 5-9
    recovery economics,
      9-12

Teledyne Corporation, 147, 148

Tennessee Valley Authority (TVA), 543, 647, 649, 651

Texaco Corporation, 53

The Geysers (California), 550, 556, 562, 572, 575, 578, 591-599, 605-607, 610-613

The Oil Shale Corporation, (TOSCO), 19

thermal-energy storage, 218, 219, 222, 223

thermal exploration techniques, 569-571

thermionic power conversion, 284, 333-335

thermochemical hydrogen production, 152-160

thermoelectric power conversion, 284, 328-333

Thomson effect, 330-332

tidal energy, 475-507

tidal-energy dissipation, 484, 485, 508

tidal oscillations, 483, 484

tidal power,
    costs, 503-505
    environmental effects, 505-507
    resources, 484, 485, 487
    utilization techniques, 486, 488-496

tides,
    biweekly, 482
    description, 476-482
    diurnal, 480
    semidiurnal, 478

TOSCO II recovery process, 21, 23, 24, 30, 32, 50

Union Oil Company, 23, 30, 32

unipolar cell, 145-147

U.S. Atomic Energy Commission, 44, 333, 615

U.S. Bureau of Mines, 18, 21, 23, 25, 30, 106, 107, 119, 208, 264

U.S. Department of the Interior, 267, 589, 603

U.S. Federal Power Commission, 131, 537, 642, 643

U.S. Geological Survey, 534, 574, 630

Wairakei (New Zealand), 550, 558, 578, 579, 601, 613, 614

water,
    availability, 17, 83, 265, 609, 614
    electrolysis, 140-152, 299
    flow devices, 520-522
    photolysis, 160-167
    power use, 516-519

wave energy, 507-513

wet steam,
    deposits, 553, 557, 558
    utilization, 578-585

wind energy, 441-474

windmills,
    Darrieus, 449, 451
    Dutch plane-vane, 444, 445, 460
    early American, 446, 448, 460
    efficiency, 443, 449, 460
    horizontal, 444
    La Cour, 446, 447, 460

windmills (continued),
    Savonius rotor, 449, 450,
      460
    shrouded aerogenerator,
      472-474
    tip-to-wind speed ratio,
      459-461
    vertical, 444, 449

windmills (continued),
    wind turbine, 449-453,
      460
wind patterns, 442, 443
wind-power systems
    economics, 468-472
    large scale, 465-467
    specific output, 468-470